DATE DUE

SEP 1 4 2014	
SEP 2 5 2014	
OCT 0 9 2014	

DATE DUE

DEC 0 9 2009	
AUG 2 2 2011	
AUG 2 7 2012	

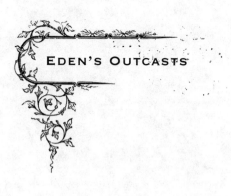

Eden's Outcasts

Record.

1834   Light on the Life.   117

Friday November 7 —

Conduct and Discipline.

I have been their less to-day than usual; Anna being confined to her chair and Louisa deeply interested in her amusements. I find that their presence is needful to inspire the depth and fervour of interest. If I see them but little; if I depend on the statements of their mother for the facts of the day, my record loses much of its freshness and force of delineation that are given from a personal survey of them through the day. It wants life, reality, naturalness: the spirit of fact is wanting, though the fact itself appears.

And thus it is with reference to all speculations on humanity — they must be had and perceived by the events and for —

IN A PAGE FROM BRONSON'S JOURNALS, OUTLINES OF HIS
AND LOUISA'S HANDS OVERLAP.
(COURTESY OF HOUGHTON LIBRARY, HARVARD UNIVERSITY)

EDEN'S OUTCASTS

THE STORY OF
LOUISA MAY ALCOTT
AND HER FATHER

JOHN MATTESON

W. W. NORTON & COMPANY

New York · London

For information about permission to reproduce selections from this book,
write to Permissions, W. W. Norton & Company, Inc.,
500 Fifth Avenue, New York, NY 10110

For information about special discounts for bulk purchases,
please contact W. W. Norton Special Sales at
specialsales@wwnorton.com or 800-233-4830.

Manufacturing by R.R. Donnelley Harrisonburg
Book design by Charlotte Staub
Production manager: Anna Oler

Library of Congress Cataloging-in-Publication Data

Matteson, John.
Eden's outcasts : the story of Louisa May Alcott and her father /
John Matteson. — 1st ed.
p. cm.
Includes bibliographical references and index.
ISBN-13: 978-0-393-05964-9 (hardcover) 1. Alcott, Louisa May,
1832–1888—Family. 2. Authors, American—Family relationships.
3. Fathers and daughters—United States—Biography. I. Title.
PS1018.M34 2007
818'.403—dc22

2007013707

W. W. Norton & Company, Inc.
500 Fifth Avenue, New York, N.Y. 10110
www.wwnorton.com

W. W. Norton & Company Ltd.
Castle House, 75/76 Wells Street, W1T 3QT

1 2 3 4 5 6 7 8 9 0

CONTENTS

ACKNOWLEDGMENTS

WRITING A BIOGRAPHY REQUIRES THE AUTHOR TO LIVE with his subjects. I am thankful to all the Alcotts and their friends for being such genial and buoyant company. A student of the Alcotts is also fortunate to be part of another family, consisting of those who have dedicated themselves to the study and preservation of the Alcott legacy. In the course of this project, I have been blessed by my associations with Madeleine B. Stern, Jan Turnquist, Sarah Elbert, Daniel Shealy, Joel Myerson, Katharine Houghton, and the late Leona Rostenberg. The staff of Orchard House, especially Jenny Gratz and Maria Powers, were always there with all the answers I needed. I would also like to thank everyone at Houghton Library for their impeccable assistance. Ann Shumard (my big sister) and Lizanne Garrett at the National Portrait Gallery moved with lightning speed to provide images and permissions. Mike Volmar at the Fruitlands Museum was always at the ready when needs arose. To all these extraordinary people, I am profoundly grateful.

Throughout the writing of this book, I have had the pleasure and privilege of teaching in the English department at John Jay College of Criminal Justice in the City University of New York. I have benefited in particular from the wise counsel and enthusiastic encouragement of three wonderful department chairs, Bob Crozier, Timothy Stevens, and Jon-Christian Suggs, who have always done everything possible to make my professional path a smooth and rewarding one. I would be less than what I am if it were not for the wise counsel and selfless support of Marc Dolan and Karen Kaplowitz. If kindness and humor help to make a job worth doing, then virtually every one of my colleagues deserves mention here, but to the following I am especially grateful: Ira Bloomgarden, Effie Cochran, Betsy Gitter, Richard Haw, Ann Huse, Livia Katz, Adam McKible, Marny Tabb, and Cristine Varholy. I also thank Jacob Marini for ably ferreting out grant money for this project during lean times. My thanks go as well to David Yaffe, whose friendship, humor, and encouragement are pearls beyond price.

I would like to thank Bill McPhaul for teaching me to write with precision and Victor Brombert for teaching me how to write with love. I shall be forever grateful to Dan Rodgers, Sacvan Bercovitch, and George Gopen, who embody in my eyes the very best of the teaching profession. I have been enriched beyond measure by the friendship and guidance of my mentors in the Columbia Ph.D. program: Andrew Delbanco, Ann Douglas, Karl Kroeber, Jonathan Levin, John Rosenberg, Priscilla Wald, and, primus inter pares, Robert A. Ferguson.

This book would not exist if it were not for the brilliant professionalism of my agent, Peter Steinberg. At W. W. Norton, I would have been lost without the superb, sensitive editing of Amy Cherry and the advice of Lydia Fitzpatrick. My copy editor, Elizabeth Pierson, was meticulous and supportive throughout the process.

With deep appreciation, I acknowledge a research grant from PSC-CUNY.

My wife, Michelle, never threatened to throw me out, even in my worst moments of authorial crankiness. I would have had far less inspiration to write this book if it were not for our daughter, Rebecca, who has probably done more than anyone else to help me understand Bronson and Louisa.

My mother, Rosemary Hamilton Matteson, always wanted to write a book. But life surprised her, and she raised a son who wrote one instead. This is her book.

EDEN'S OUTCASTS

DISGRACE

"The saints are popular alone in heaven,
not on earth; elect of God, they are spurned
by the world. They hate their age, its applause,
its awards, their own affections even."

—A. BRONSON ALCOTT, "Orphic
Sayings," *The Dial*, 1840

A T THE HOUGHTON LIBRARY OF HARVARD UNIVERSITY, there sits a massive collection of letters, news clippings, and other memorabilia compiled over the span of seven decades by Amos Bronson Alcott, a dedicated educator and reformer, a close friend of Emerson and Thoreau, and the father of the four sisters whom his second daughter, Louisa May Alcott, immortalized as Meg, Jo, Beth, and Amy in *Little Women*. Among these documents, neatly folded and carefully preserved, is a sales receipt from an auction that occurred when Louisa was only four years old and her father thirty-seven.[1] Bronson Alcott believed that every aspect of life had a lesson to impart, and he saved documents that reminded him not only of his successes but also of his most painful defeats. He kept this receipt long after any dispute might have been raised concerning it. He kept it, it seems, to help himself remember the cost of his pride, of his idealism, and of his all-too-ready faith in the capacity of ordinary people to embrace unfamiliar ideas.

The auction took place in Boston on April 13, 1837. The national economy was in the throes of a financial panic, and the prices asked for the merchandise were not high. Inspecting the lots before the sale began, a bargain hunter with scholarly leanings would have delighted in the richness of the sale: globes, school furniture of the highest quality, and busts of Socrates, Shakespeare, and Milton. And then there were the books—at least three hundred volumes, painstakingly assembled by their collector, too often with borrowed money. Many of them were literary classics. Some of them were English editions with the best leather bindings—a rare sight for American eyes, even in literary-minded Boston. Prospective buyers gazed upon the essays of John Locke and the poems of Byron and Shelley. Commentaries on the Bible sat side by side with books on elementary education. An appraising eyebrow or two were probably raised at a five-volume set of the dialogues of Plato. Without any particular ceremony, the sale commenced. A two-volume set of Coleridge's letters went for $2.25. A six-volume edition of Sir Walter Scott's novels changed hands for $1.50, and a book of family prayers went for thirty cents. Book by book, piece by piece, the library, the furniture, and everything else came under the hammer until all was gone. After the auctioneer deducted his commission and other expenses, the net proceeds of the sale came to $158.64. Alcott wrote in the aftermath of the sale, "their value in coin will, at this time, release me from pecuniary embarrassment."[2] Although the high-sounding phrase may have served for a moment to mask the starkness of his situation, Alcott well knew that he was losing far more than he was getting.

It is not recorded whether Alcott bothered to attend the auction. Although he had paid out "not a little of [his] small earnings" for the auctioned items, going perilously into debt to do so, he had bought only a portion of them for his personal use. Rather, the busts and desks, as well as fully half the books, had graced the interior of a small primary school, housed upstairs in the Masonic temple on Tremont Street. Founded by Alcott less than three years earlier, the Temple School had fallen on desperate times. Perhaps with the sale of the furniture and the library, it might somehow be kept afloat a while longer. Alcott tended to suffer most indignities in silence. He did not yet speak of the possibility that the school might soon have to close forever. At the moment, he seemed saddest to be losing the volumes of Plato, which, aside from his wife Abigail and his daughters, were possibly what he held dearest in the world. Nevertheless, Alcott, his hair already graying, tried to put on a brave face. The loss of the dialogues would have caused him much more grief, he said, if he had not already acquainted himself so thoroughly with their spirit.

An otherworldly perfectionism typified Alcott, a man who continually proclaimed the unimportance of the world of things. Like Plato himself, who posited a world of ideal forms of which our own world was only the shadowy, shattered image, Alcott prized ideas infinitely more than physical objects. The fact that he was forced to live a material existence seemed at best a misfortune and at worst a cosmic mistake. Before Alcott's marriage to Abigail May, the brother of his prospective bride had accurately observed Alcott's fundamental bent. He wrote to his sister, "Don't distress yourself about his poverty. His mind and heart are so much occupied with other things that poverty and riches do not seem to concern him."[3] Because he valued them so highly, understandings of the spirit tended to come into Alcott's grasp without effort. The material trappings of the world, however, he tended to ignore, and they in turn seemed almost willfully to keep their distance from him.

And yet, for all his allegiance to the invisible, Alcott was not indifferent to appearances, and the ones he liked best were those that reminded him of himself. One day, when leading a discussion on the subject of "Angelic and Demonic Man," Alcott entertained his listeners with his description of the kind of person who best reflected divine beauty and intelligence. The angelic man, as Alcott imagined him, had light-colored hair and clear blue eyes. He did not rely on logic, a faculty too easily contorted by evil, but on the gentler perceptions of the heart. The angelic man shunned the contentiousness of argument but delighted in the shared sympathies of genial conversation. When Alcott concluded, his description was answered with knowing smiles and probably a few rolled eyes. The speaker had just finished describing himself.[4]

Others who described Alcott tended to emphasize qualities that seemed not quite to belong to this world. They often discovered that they had said more about his character than his bodily presence. Alcott's dearest friend and benefactor, Ralph Waldo Emerson, called him "a God-made priest" and "a world builder."[5] Henry David Thoreau, a man renowned for the sharp lines of his descriptive prose, seemed stumped when it came to the gentle schoolmaster. After a day with Alcott, Thoreau told his journal, "He is broad & general but indefinite." Alcott was for him "a geometer—a visionary—The Laplace of ethics." When Thoreau called Alcott a "sky-blue" man, it was not clear whether he was referring to Alcott's eye color or his idealism.[6] In the first published version of his short story "The Hall of Fantasy," Nathaniel Hawthorne immortalized Alcott with the following tribute:

> There was no man . . . whose mere presence the language of whose look and manner, wrought such an impression as that of this great mystic innovator. So calm and gentle was he, so holy in aspect, so quiet in utterance of what his soul brooded upon, that one might readily conceive his Orphic Sayings to well upward from a fountain in his breast, which communicated with the infinite abyss of Thought.[7]

One should suppose that Emerson, Thoreau, and Hawthorne knew something about their subject, for Alcott's influence was interwoven not merely intellectually but personally into the lives of all three. Alcott was Emerson's most constant friend for more than forty-five years. When Alcott had conversations with his pupils at the Temple School recorded for posterity, Hawthorne's future wife, Sophia Peabody, acted as one of his scribes. In 1852, when Hawthorne was looking for a house in Concord, Massachusetts, it was Alcott's property that he wound up purchasing. When Thoreau was preparing to take up residence on the banks of Walden Pond, he discovered that he needed to borrow an ax to cut timber for his cabin. Apparently, he borrowed Alcott's. When Thoreau remembered the incident in *Walden*, however, he omitted the name of the lender. Instead he recorded, "The owner of the axe, as he released his hold on it, said that it was the apple of his eye, but I returned it sharper than I received it."[8]

This vignette might stand as an emblem of the kind of relationship Alcott tended to have with his better-remembered companions. Alcott cherished his theories and inspirations even more than his ax, but as with his ax, he was seldom able to hone his ideas into the form that would cut most efficiently. He shared his ideas almost as freely as he shared his tools, and it was in the hands of others that both acquired their gleaming sharpness. His contributions often received scant acknowledgment. Alcott was very likely the "Orphic poet" whom Emerson quotes at length toward the end of *Nature*, but his name is nowhere to be found. The spirit of Alcott pervades Hawthorne stories like "The Celestial Railroad" and the previously quoted "Hall of Fantasy," yet the paragraph in the latter that identifies him by name was stricken from all published versions of the tale save the first. Emerson, Thoreau, and Hawthorne all would have been great if they had never met Bronson Alcott. But none of them would have been precisely the same.

There was, of course, one renowned nineteenth-century American author who would never have existed at all without Bronson Alcott: his daughter, Louisa May. But even in his own daughter's work, Bronson is represented as a compromised figure, sometimes caricatured for the sake of comedy and sometimes wholly absent even when circumstances cry out for his presence. Most famously, when Louisa transformed herself and her sisters into Little Women, the March family's patriarch is almost absent from the narrative. Even when Mr. March at last makes his grand entrance in chapter 22 of the novel, almost the first words devoted to him are, "Mr. March became invisible . . . ."[9]

Indeed, to examine Alcott and his influence on those around him is sometimes to have a sense of dealing with an invisible man. This invisibility forms a key part of Bronson Alcott's curious destiny. The workings of his mind were misunderstood even by many of those who were closest to him, and the bulk of his writing was barely known to anyone, even in his own time. The one medium of communication of which he was an acknowledged master, the spoken word, vanished the moment he created it. The grand, ambitious projects by which he hoped to establish his name and unveil his ideas before the world tended to collapse into humiliation and futility. So long as Alcott could move within the sphere of the ethereal and evanescent, he moved with radiance and grace. As soon as he stepped into the world of things and actions or tried to project a durable image of himself, he began to lose his balance. When he attempted to astonish the world by performing a truly great task—and he found such tasks almost fatally irresistible—his ease, common sense, and good fortune deserted him entirely, and he fell to earth with a thud. The people who laid the best claim to understanding Alcott seem to have regarded him as a word made flesh, as a collection of ideas and principles that seemed only coincidentally to have lodged inside a body.

But this spirit did have a body. Bronson Alcott was slender and stood six feet tall. Anyone who, on meeting him, expected to shake the smooth, soft hand of a poet-philosopher would have been surprised by the muscular firmness of Alcott's grasp. The son of a Connecticut farmer, he believed that moral virtue could be strengthened by working the soil. In the bleakest periods of his life, he found comfort as well as income in tending his garden and chopping firewood for himself and his neighbors. It was through horticulture, more than through anything else except his family, that the philosophical Alcott maintained firm contact with the physical world.

His hands were rough. His manners were not. In his youth, when he was old enough to get off the farm, Alcott traveled five times through the South as a peddler of Yankee notions. The experience of meeting southern gentlemen and ladies and often sojourning in their homes made a profound impression. Alcott studied the grace and politeness that were shown him and acquired an almost courtly civility. One of his English friends, Thomas Cholmondeley, reported with some surprise that the American possessed the social polish of a British nobleman.[10] Surprisingly, however, for a man so dedicated to the world of the unseen, Alcott nursed a surprising weakness for fashion, although he usually lacked the means to indulge that interest very lavishly. After one of his youthful peddling excursions in the South, he squandered his earnings on a fancy suit of clothes. Around Boston, he was known for a somewhat outrageous taste in hats, and the cane he habitually carried was a concession more to style than to infirmity. Farm boy turned gentleman, peddler turned philosopher, Alcott defied attempts at categorization.

People disagreed as to whether Alcott's hair had been blond or reddish in his youth, and by the late 1830s it was already hard to settle the argument because his hair had whitened. It was growing thinner on the top of his head as well, although it extended long and carelessly down the back of his neck, as if by way of compensation. In his most appealing photographs, Alcott wears a calm but expectant expression, and a smile that seems both intelligent and profoundly trusting. Most acquaintances agreed that his most memorable features were his eyes—gentle, pale blue, and deeply set beneath a brow that in some photographs looks faintly Lincolnesque, although the face as a whole lacks Lincoln's gravity and shrewdness. Perhaps the most fascinating description of Alcott, however, came in verse form from the poet John Townsend Trowbridge, who, later in life, edited some of Louisa May Alcott's writings:

> Do you care to meet Alcott? His mind is a mirror
> Reflecting the unspoken thought of his hearer.

To the great, he is great; to the fool he's a fool—
In the world's dreary desert a crystalline pool
Where a lion looks in and a lion appears,
But an ass will see only his own ass's ears.[11]

But neither a wise man nor a fool would ever truly know Bronson Alcott without becoming acquainted with his family. At the time his library was sold, Alcott had been married almost seven years to Abigail May, a woman who, every bit as much as her husband, believed in the perfectibility of human beings. Abba, as her husband called her, believed that people had been given their weaknesses in order that they might triumph over them, and she stood perpetually ready to aid selflessly in the mighty causes of reform. Though she loved the world enough to change it, she was not always patient with it, and she frequently lost her composure when society refused to know what was good for it. For her husband and children, however, she had almost limitless tenderness and patience, and she had particular esteem for her husband's virtues. In her eyes, he was "an intelligent, philosophic, modest man."[12] She considered him "peculiarly sober [and] temperate," untainted by even "a single habit of personal indulgence."[13] In her letters, he was her "dear husband" and her "savior."[14] In truth, his refusals to compromise with the world sometimes exasperated her. Nevertheless, even when he did not earn enough to supply his family's wants— and such times were alarmingly frequent—she continued to find integrity in his willingness to "starve or freeze before he will sacrifice principle to comfort."[15] He returned her admiration. It was she, he wrote, "who first kindled me into that sweeter and holier birth—the gentler and fragrant life of Love."[16] When they had been married almost forty years, he wrote of his abundant reasons "to thank the Friend of families and Giver of good wives that I was led to her acquaintance and fellowship when life and a future opened before me."[17]

In April 1837, the couple had three daughters, ranging in age from six years to twenty-one months. As a supremely dedicated educator, fascinated by the undiscovered secrets of child development, Bronson had traced the progress of each of these girls literally from birth, compiling notes and commentaries that ran into the thousands of pages. It could justly be said that no father in America knew his children more thoroughly. Knowing them so well, he was keenly aware of how different they were. The eldest daughter, Anna, and the third daughter, Lizzie, had their father's even, placid temperament. Bronson had striven consciously to rear what he thought were perfect children, and Anna and Lizzie were living testaments to his theories of infant culture. But the middle daughter, now nearly four and a half years old, defied her father's attempts at understanding. Highly energetic, resistant to discipline, she had an innate turbulence that her father had tried without success to tame. She was, in Bronson's view, a creature of "impatience, querulousness, forwardness." From an early period, she had been "the undisciplined subject of her *instincts,* pursuing her purpose, by any means that will lead her to their attainment." Her father saw in her "signs of impending evil."[18]

Yet if this second daughter was fierce in her passions, she could be equally zealous in her loyalties. The critic Van Wyck Brooks told a story, more valuable perhaps for its mood than for its literal truth, of the day when, in preparation for the Temple School auction, the sheriff came to empty the premises of the fine books and furnishings that the schoolmaster had bought on credit and could no longer afford to keep. Brooks reports that the sheriff was going about his work when, suddenly, the teacher's daughter strode across the room toward him shouting, "Go away, bad man, you are making my father unhappy!" The anecdote ends with the schoolmaster, leading this daughter with one hand and her older sister Anna with the other, walking down the stairs "with mournful steps and slow."[19] The impatient, forward daughter who is said to have defended her father's classroom and his feelings with such ferocity was named Louisa May.

When he used the words "mournful steps and slow" to describe the Alcotts' exit from the temple that had so recently housed the father's wondrous school, Brooks intentionally echoed the closing lines of Milton's *Paradise Lost*, in which the disgraced but wiser Adam and Eve, "with wandering steps and slow," make their way out of the lost Garden of Eden.[20] Brooks chose aptly, for few Americans have ever tried so passionately to construct a latter-day Eden than Bronson Alcott, first in his attempts to create the ideal school for young children, and later in his efforts to establish a saintly community of scholars in which money would be unknown, where no creature would profit by the suffering of any other, and where every participant would be received and loved as a member of an enormous family. By the same token, however, few have paid so high a price for trying to find perfection in a fallen world.

Alcott's second daughter was too young to attend her father's ideal academy at the temple. Nevertheless, her relationship with her father, acted out within an unusually close and interdependent family, was to be made still closer by a series of astonishing coincidences. Bronson and Louisa May Alcott shared the same birthday, November 29. Although they were born thirty-three years apart, the books that made their literary reputations were published in the same month. And at the end of it all—well, perhaps that coincidence is best reserved for the final chapter. In any event, the similarities in their lives were more than a matter of timing.

For Louisa as well as for Bronson, life was a persistent but failed quest for perfection. First, she was to labor vainly to conquer her fierce temper and stubborn willfulness, trying to find the paradise that her father always swore lay within her. Then, she would struggle to bring happiness and comfort to a family continually besieged by want. Later, she would go to war, doing all in her power, if not to make America a paradise, then at least to make it a place where all people would be free. Still later, as a novelist, she would strive to produce in fiction what she could not bring about in the world: a vision of humanity enriched by personal sacrifice and enlightened by unselfish love. Both Bronson and Louisa May had ambitions of altering the world through literature. In ways that neither anticipated and in widely varying degrees, they succeeded. Yet it was in the lives they lived, rather than in the words they wrote or spoke, that they fought hardest for redemption: both to redeem themselves from their perceived failures and to redeem the world at large from the wickedness that both father and daughter sought earnestly to reform. They wanted perfection. In their search for it, they inevitably discovered flaws both in the world and within themselves. Pursuing paradise, they continually confirmed themselves as Eden's outcasts.

"Outcast" was a word Alcott used to describe himself in 1837, and he did not exaggerate. His fall was all the more devastating because it had been so sudden. In February, he had written of his lofty hopes of redeeming the world. His "present purpose" was "to restore to the perverted and debauched sense of man, some of the worthier conceptions of [the] divine relations, and of the instinct, from whence they take their rise. I would, first, attract the notice of man to the original nature of childhood, as the fit means of quickening the parental sentiment, which slumbers, or is overlaid, in the hearts of too many mothers." Almost daring fate, he had proclaimed, "the winds and waves of the terrestrial reach not the stable foundation of my faith; nor can they overthrow or efface [the] one purpose of my heart."[21]

Barely a month later, however, his journal reflected a terrible change. His patrons were withdrawing their support. The public, swayed by "vague and false accounts of my enterprise," had turned against him. Alcott could not find "a single individual who apprehends my great purpose, and is ready to step forward and aid me in this hour of need."[22] Alcott knew that, in the early months of 1837, something more precious than a library had been lost. The crisis at his school had arisen from a scandal of his own creation, a scandal touching on matters of sex and blasphemy. The newspapers and the pulpits were resounding with claims that he was depraving his students with impious and filthy ideas, casting scorn on the Bible, and schooling young children in the "naughtiness" by which babies were made. According to the press, he had, from a sheer love of notoriety, defied the sentiment of the wise and good and polluted the moral atmosphere.[23] Even many of Alcott's most loyal supporters, who had eagerly greeted the opening of the school and lauded its novel, progressive mission, were wondering privately whether their friend had lost his direction. His reputation was in ruins.

He had never laid an improper hand on any of his pupils, and no one insinuated that he had. His intentions toward the children had been only the best, and he had never, in his own view, breathed a corrupting word to them. It was with Alcott's words, however, that the people of Boston had taken issue, so violently that he could no longer cross the Common without overhearing whispers or having boys jeer at him. There had even been talk of mob action. Only a year before, his teaching methods, which had not changed, had made him one of the most admired men in the city. The sudden reversal of fortune was all but inconceivable. Alcott confided to his journal, "what my future movements shall be, time must decide. At present, I see not my way."[24] When present and future are equally in doubt, there is only one other vista upon which to gaze. One must begin, therefore, with a backward glance along the road that had led Bronson Alcott both to glory and dishonor.

CHAPTER ONE

BEGINNINGS

"His father had no patience with him,
called him a shiftless dreamer, and
threatened to burn the beloved books."
—LOUISA MAY ALCOTT, "Eli's Education,"
Spinning-Wheel Stories

I N A NUMBER OF SIGNIFICANT WAYS, LIFE DID NOT FULLY BEGIN
for Bronson Alcott until the year 1828, when three defining events
occurred within months of one another: he paid his first visit to the
city of Boston; he first heard the preaching of a young Unitarian minister
named Ralph Waldo Emerson; and he proposed marriage to a fascinating
woman named Abigail May. The city was to speak to his most celestial
dreams, only to reject him when he dreamed too boldly. The minister was
eventually to become his dearest, most understanding friend, and the
woman was to become his loving companion for nearly fifty years. During
the twenty-eight years that preceded this time of changed horizons, his life
had been gradually taking one form. The city, the friend, and the lover
altered that form profoundly, but the young man on whom they acted was
already unusual.

Born Amos Bronson Alcox, he entered the world before dawn on Spindle Hill in the town of Wolcott, Connecticut, in the rugged hill country
west of Hartford, on November 29, 1799, the eldest in a family that would
eventually boast of eight children. The town had been incorporated only
three years earlier, so recently that some people were still getting used to
calling it Wolcott, instead of the previous name of Farmingbury.[1] The new
baby's family, too, was still working out just what to call itself. His paternal great-grandfather, the first white man to settle in the area, had spelled

13

his name Alcock, after the fashion of his English ancestors, but by the time of Bronson's father's generation, the name had changed to Alcox. It continued in this form until the early 1820s, when Bronson and his cousin, Dr. William A. Alcox, agreed to change the name to Alcott. Around the same time he took the name Alcott, he ceased calling himself Amos and thereafter routinely signed his name A. Bronson Alcott. In the interest of clarity and at the risk of anachronism, the boy whom everyone called Amos will be referred to here by his adult name of Bronson.

If it took the Alcox family some time to work out the details of their name, there was little doubt in their minds as to who they were. While growing up, Bronson learned from his parents, Joseph and Anna, that he was directly descended from one of the men who had crossed the Atlantic on the *Arbella* in 1630 with Governor John Winthrop. It was on that voyage that Winthrop had given the sermon that first identified Puritan New England as "a city upon a hill." Winthrop had cautioned his shipmates that, as they set out to do the work of the Lord in a forbidding wilderness, the eyes of the world would be upon them. If the people of New England broke faith with God and fell away from a standard of moral perfection, he warned, "we shall be made a story and a by-word through the world [and] we shall shame the faces of many of God's worthy servants."[2] Those early New Englanders saw it as their mission to found a spiritual Eden that would enlighten and redeem the world. Reform and redemption, in a different sense, were also to be the missions of Bronson Alcott's life.

Bronson considered the natural surroundings of his youth surpassingly beautiful, and as a grown man he loved to recall "the light, blithe season of my boyhood and youth . . . breathing the air of my native hills . . . treading their summits at morning's dawn."[3] It is still an attractive place, where maple and cherry trees still rise lush and tall and ferns grow thick as grass. However, Alcott preferred not to recall that the soil was rocky and inhospitable to farming, and even he could not romanticize the relentless cold of the winter. The town was a still further cry from paradise. The year Bronson turned seventy-five, a history of Wolcott was published. The local pastor who wrote the introduction confessed "there is but little that is interesting in these remnants of a farm life which must, at its best, have been unusually prosaic and dreary."[4] Wolcott generally distrusted new ideas, and the notions of Deism and dissent that were making inroads in northeastern cities placed some of the residents literally in mortal fear. When Bronson was still a baby, one of the church deacons solemnly foretold that, if that dangerous infidel Thomas Jefferson were elected president, "the meeting houses would be burned to the ground, and Christians would be burned at the stake."[5] The city on a hill that Bronson romanticized was only a struggling town on a wind-beaten slope.

In 1806, Bronson's school day was interrupted by a total solar eclipse. Not knowing what else to do, Bronson and a group of boys gathered stones and threw them upward toward the bewildering phenomenon. In his excitement, Bronson stepped awkwardly and fell, dislocating his shoulder blade. More than sixty years later, Bronson reflected that this boyhood misfortune had been a prophecy of his life to come—"tilting at the sun and always catching the fall." Nevertheless, Bronson relished the memory of throwing the stones more than he rued the pain of the accident, and this too was true of his life. He wrote, "I suppose I am to toy with the sunbeams as long as I am dazzled by them."[6]

That same year, following the community's usual practice of wasting nothing and making do with whatever the Lord made handy, Bronson's father cobbled together two old buildings near the top of the hill to make a new house for the growing family. It was the first home that Bronson would remember. The widemouthed chimney kept the ground floor comfortably warm in wintertime, but upstairs, where Bronson slept, he gave thanks for the thick coverlets that his mother quilted. Well into old age, he was to recall the downstairs room for its deep-seated armchairs, its uncarpeted but scrupulously scoured floor, and the pipe and almanac that sat on the mantelpiece.[7] In an autobiographical poem, he remembered his home as a picture of domestic industry: his father weaving a basket, his mother spinning thread, and his sisters minding their sewing while his brothers peeled apples. Significantly, the only person in the scene not engaged in gainful work was Bronson himself. Instead, he sat to one side, finding "his Elysium" in his books.[8]

Bronson's seeming idleness was a puzzle to his father, Joseph Alcox. A grave, quiet man, Joseph was a skilled farmer whose frugality and preference for his own handiwork prompted him to make his own tools.[9] In bad weather, he could be found in his shop, crafting farm implements that he sold to neighboring farmers for extra money. During Bronson's boyhood, his father could lay claim to the best-tilled, best-fenced farm in the district. Of him, Bronson wrote, "He gave himself to life with the earnestness & simplicity of a child. He was the most diffident person I have ever known."[10] A man of few ambitions, either for himself or his family, Joseph took little part in public affairs and paid his bills. He was a man of virtues that, in later life, his eldest son found it easier to admire than imitate. Joseph could teach his son how to make farming implements and how to plow a straight furrow. But he was illiterate, and he could take no greater hand in his son's education.

It is tempting to look for parallels between the early life of Bronson Alcott and that of a boy born to another struggling family in rural isolation a little more than nine years later. Like Abraham Lincoln, Bronson grew up working the soil alongside a father who could barely read and write. The two boys were also similar in their innate thirsts for knowledge, in the shallowness of the intellectual springs from which they were first compelled to drink, and in the fact that whatever culture came to them was supplied by the maternal side of the family. Bronson learned his ABCs by copying letters with chalk on the floor of his mother's parlor. On winter days, if no chalk was available, he continued his practice by tracing letters with his finger in the snow. Anna Alcox, née Bronson, came from a family of some stature, and it was said that her arrival on Spindle Hill brought with it "a refinement of disposition and a grace of deportment" that had a good effect on the local minds and manners.[11] Her eldest son considered her "a woman of great good sense, sweetness of disposition, industry, and engaging manners."[12] The mild expression of her eyes always remained in Bronson's memory. She was a kindhearted, gentle mother who saw that her children never suffered from a lack of affection.

Looking backward, Bronson drew a picture of himself as "a comely child, his aspect sage, benign, / His carriage full of innocence and grace; / Complexion blond, blue eyes, locks brown and fine, / And frank expression in his rosy face."[13] He had not been perfect, he knew; he remembered himself as a willful boy, more interested in his idle fantasies than doing the work that the world and his parents foisted on him. Although he was permitted both in the morning and in the evening to write in his journal and devour his books, the time allotted never seemed enough for him.

Bronson never regretted having grown up on Spindle Hill. "It kept me pure," he wrote. "It soothed and refined my disposition. It was discipline and culture to me. I dwelt amidst the hills. I looked out upon rural images. I was enshrined in Nature. God spoke to me while I walked the fields." To his mother's gentle teachings, the hill added its own mute messages. "Nature was my parent," Bronson observed, "and from her, in the still communings of my solitudes, I learned divine wisdom, even when a child."[14]

Learning more conventional lessons, however, posed a problem. He was, he remembered, "confined to the narrow range of thought which . . . a small, isolated town could furnish . . . removed from the means of moral and intellectual improvement."[15] The available schooling was meager, and Bronson's progress was further impaired when he had to miss sessions to help with the planting, harvesting, and other exigencies of the Alcox farm. On those days when Bronson could attend, he received his lessons in a frame building that he later described as "disconsolate," unsheltered from the piercing sun in the summer and frozen by bleak winds in the winter. The children shivered through their lessons as they sat on stiff benches hacked from pine boards.[16] The schoolmaster was usually some favorite or relative of the district committee members, and the students were instructed in a mechanical fashion that called on no faculty other than memory. The parish library, the only ready source of printed material, contained fewer than a hundred volumes and was essentially defunct by the time Bronson was in his teens.

It was not long before the curious boy started looking for ways to distance himself intellectually from his environment. Using his father's tools, he made his own violin from a maple tree. In less active moods, he sat on the hillside, musing about the future. Apart from his mother, Bronson's only ally in this search for broader horizons was his cousin William, about sixteen months his senior. As teenagers, they exchanged stories and hand-delivered weekly letters to each other, discoursing as best they could on the books they read and their newfound ideas. They read each other's journals and discussed their dreams. They both thought that teaching might make a good profession, and they even aspired to authorship.[17] Bronson eventually sought leave from his father to cease working on Saturday afternoons, so that he might scour the area for more books. Families from miles around received visits from Bronson, inquiring whether they had any to lend him. Eventually, with the help of his cousin, Bronson began to accumulate a personal library from the castoffs of local parlors. A Bible was an early acquisition. Another find that influenced Bronson profoundly was James Burgh's *The Dignity of Human Nature*.[18] Also available on many a farmer's shelf was *The Pilgrim's Progress*, John Bunyan's venerable allegory of salvation, which had lost little of its popularity among the God-fearing since it first appeared in 1678. Unable to acquire his own copy, Bronson repeatedly borrowed the book from his cousin Riley, committing favorite portions to memory. He carried *The Pilgrim's Progress* into his father's fields, stealing moments while resting the family's oxen to thumb its pages.[19] After a long day's labor, he would sit in the chimney niche, with a candle in his hand, poring over the book's "enchanted pages" until late at night. When he was seventy-three, the very same copy of the book at last became his, placed in his hands by Ruth Frisbie Alcott, Riley's widow. Bronson seems never to have received a gift with heartier thanks.[20]

Far more than any other book, *The Pilgrim's Progress* captivated Bronson. He called it his "dear, delightful book" and later claimed that it was his most efficient teacher and the dictionary by which he learned the English tongue.[21] Looking back over a span of decades, he felt that it had done more than give a contour to his education and his thinking about spiritual matters:

> My early childhood was revived in my memory with a freshness and reality that no ordinary mind [*sic*] could have caused. This book is one of the few that gave me to myself. It is associated with reality. It unites me with my childhood, and seems to chronicle my Identity. How I was rapt in it![22]

If *The Pilgrim's Progress* teaches anything, it teaches one not to take the world's judgments at face value. It firmly proclaims the narrowness of the way that leads to salvation. One either serves the false gods of wealth and the good opinion of one's neighbors, or one serves the true God of Heaven. There is no third option. According to Bunyan, the person who lives in the service of temporal legality and civility has chosen a path to destruction; to heed the advice of the Worldly Wiseman, who praises earthly comforts and counsels only so much morality as would make one's way easiest in the current life, is to submit ultimately to spiritual bondage. Bunyan's stern warnings against temptation and self-gratification found an avid listener in young Bronson. *Paradise Lost,* it seemed to him, was a book to be read. *The Pilgrim's Progress* was a book to be lived. The allegorical trials of Bunyan's Christian seemed perpetually to reflect Bronson's own struggles toward a kind of earthly perfection.[23]

The Pilgrim's Progress not only held out to Bronson a way of living but, just as importantly, a way of reading every aspect of his experience. In *The Pilgrim's Progress*, a fact is never merely a fact. Every phenomenon is presented to the reader for its metaphorical relevance. Bunyan encourages the reader to regard the world as a divinely created symbol, to be observed for its spiritual, not its literal, significance. It seems beyond question that one of the shared traits that later attracted Emerson and Alcott to each other was their habit of thinking about the visible world, not as a sufficient truth in itself, but as pointing the way toward a greater, more satisfying truth that could be approached only through metaphor. Not long after their friendship began in earnest, during the period in which Alcott's influence on him was strongest, Emerson wrote, "Every natural fact is the symbol of some spiritual fact. Every appearance in nature corresponds to some state of mind."[24] Through the observation of metaphor in nature, Emerson reassured himself of the presence of divinity in the world.

But whereas the vision of the world as a physical bodying forth of a Platonic ideal was liberating for Emerson, this way of seeing was to become a disability for Bronson. Emerson had the flexibility to balance his understanding of the world between two seemingly contradictory models. He could accept a world in which every fact had two sides, one related to sensation and the other to morals. "Life," he wrote in *Representative Men*, "is a pitching of this penny,—heads or tails. We never tire of this game."[25] Bronson saw no attraction in the moral coin toss that Emerson found so fascinating. Solidity, he argued, "is an illusion of the senses. There is nothing solid. The nature of the Soul renders such a fact impossible."[26] Thanks in part to his reverence for *The Pilgrim's Progress*, Alcott's penny had only one side. He seems to have decided early on that it was only the spirit that truly mattered.

Curiously, however, although Bunyan's allegory was pivotally responsible for shaping Bronson's ideas of right conduct, it failed to impress on him the point that its author undoubtedly considered the most fundamental of all: the necessity of embracing the doctrines of Christianity. Bronson was essentially immune to the arguments of orthodoxy. He was confirmed in the Episcopal faith when he was sixteen, and he long remembered how worshippers filled the pews and galleries of the plain, two-storied meeting-house of his youth. He had enjoyed church, and he always felt that Sundays had been great days in those times.[27] Nevertheless, Alcott's experience of organized religion failed to bind him to its forms and dogmas. He never accepted the idea of Jesus as the Son of God. While he found himself "disposed to consider the author of the Christian system as a great and good and original man," Alcott could not convince himself to think of Jesus as anything other than a superb specimen of humanity.[28] He thought the writings of Confucius, the Bhagavad Gita, and other Eastern texts should be combined with the New Testament to create an ecumenical "Bible for Mankind."[29] He did not pray, and he taught his children to follow his example, explaining to them that their "thoughts, feelings, and resolutions" mattered more than private communication with God.[30]

One of the most enduring lessons that the boy appears to have absorbed on those long, pious Sundays was one he would have done well to unlearn. The preaching of those times generally reflects an infatuation with sonorous, convoluted, periodic sentences. In such discursive sentences, a point may be elegantly and elaborately made, but the reader bears the task of reducing the idea to its hard, crystalline form. Robert Richardson has observed that the well-padded, ornate sentence was a mainstay of Emerson's when he was trying to find his way as a minister.[31] Indeed, the transformation of Emerson the florid preacher into Emerson the compactly aphoristic, quotable essayist is one of the great marvels of American literature. It was a feat that Alcott found impossible to duplicate. Reading Alcott's journals, one frequently has the sense of a mind that worked through ideas with great deliberation and thoroughness. However, one searches in vain for the quick, decisive stroke. He writes as if assuming that his readers will have much time in which to enfold themselves in the densities of his prose.

Even an invisible, personal faith, however, must express itself in some physical, identifiable way. If Bronson Alcott could not comfortably find that expression through prayer or church membership, then he had to seek some other way. Like most people, he found it natural to evince belief by giving things up. Having no church to prescribe the forms of his self-denial, Alcott arrived at his own conclusions as to what earthly appetites were wrong and impious. He eventually came up with a very long list. He lived much of his life by the creed that one must prefer one's soul to one's body, and the needs of others to the wants of oneself. At its most rampant, his urge toward asceticism seemed to command him almost to relinquish life altogether.

Bronson's one chance at pursuing a formal education came when he was thirteen. His mother's brother, Dr. Tillotson Bronson, a tall, personable man of priestly cast, was then the head of the Episcopal Academy in Cheshire, Connecticut, a school that, as Alcott later recalled, "was a college in everything but the name."[32] Seeing promise in his nephew, Dr. Bronson offered to take the boy under his roof and enroll him in his school. The family agreed, and Bronson rode off with his uncle to see what might be made of him. Bronson's time at the Cheshire Academy was a turning point in his early life. Success at the academy might have meant an eventual matriculation at Yale and a future in the church. It would also have given him something less tangible but perhaps more important. To be a thinker in the truest sense requires being open to the enriching possibilities of a mental tug-of-war. Bronson Alcott did not have this flexibility when he arrived in Cheshire, and if he were ever to absorb it, this would have been an opportune time.

As it happened, his experiences at the academy seem to have had the contrary effect. Children grow up assuming that their own experiences are normal. The discovery of a larger world in which people speak differently and cleave to other assumptions can come as an overwhelming surprise. So it was with Bronson Alcott, abruptly placed in the midst of boys who did not say "nimshi" when they meant "fool" or "ollers" instead of "always." Cheshire made Bronson feel bumptious and strange. As an old man, he still remembered the sting of being called on to read in front of the other boys and promptly learning that his performance was not up to the mark. If Bronson's private studies had taught him some things his new classmates did not know, they were knowledgeable in matters never dreamed of in his philosophy. He could not fit in. His sojourn among the learned lasted only a month; he could not bear to stay any longer.

In the face of the suggestion that his instinctive methods of approaching knowledge might be inadequate, Bronson clenched himself still tighter against outward criticisms and clung ever more devotedly to his private god: a belief in his own genius, begotten within him by a wise and all-sustaining Nature. Throughout his life, his criterion for an idea was neither whether it was practical or provable, but whether it resonated with his spirit. Over time, the faith that he was both right and righteous became essential to Bronson; to renounce it would have been to lose all bearings in a bewildering world.

After his abortive attendance at the Cheshire Academy, Bronson's formal education was essentially at an end. He embarked on a series of small ventures, none of which led him anywhere in particular. He thought for a while that he might follow in his father's footsteps as a farmer. He worked awhile as a clockmaker and sold religious tracts from door to door. More than five years passed, and still he found nothing new to engage his soul.

He found out something important about that soul when he was sixteen. Hearing that there was to be a public hanging, he walked sixteen miles with William in order to see it. When the condemned man was thrown down and his neck snapped, Bronson fainted dead away. Another time, he was horrified to see a group of prisoners being marched up from their subterranean cells and driven to work at bayonet-point. He did not get over the effect of these sights for some time.[33] These experiences deepened his aversion to cruelty, which in later years became virtually absolute.

Such moments, however terrible, marked moments of excitement in a life of numbing routine. Eventually, the sameness of Bronson's surroundings and the idleness of his condition became unacceptable. His plan of escape was only half-baked when he put it into practice. He had, it seems, a vague understanding that schoolmasters from the northern states were wanted in the South. He had few qualifications, but, he must have reasoned, no fewer than his likely competitors. A month and a half shy of his nineteenth birthday, he traveled to New Haven and boarded the sloop *Three Sisters* for Norfolk, Virginia.

Upon arriving, he soon discovered that he had been misinformed; there was no teaching work available. He resorted to a fallback plan, becoming one of the throng of Yankee peddlers who wandered the country, selling all manner of small items to whoever would buy them. The Yankee peddler was a common sight from Cape Cod to Lake Erie, from Canada to Kentucky. It was common for young New England men to spend the winter traveling the upper South on trading expeditions, and return in the spring with the fruits of their industry and enterprise.[34] Literally thousands of these young men, most of them barely out of their teens, loaded wagons with combs, clocks, tinware, and other Yankee notions, selling them rapidly, and often at high profits.[35]

For his part, Bronson found the business instantly absorbing. He got off to a promising start by purchasing a stock of almanacs for three pennies each and promptly selling them for three times that amount. During the next five years, he made a total of five peddling trips to Virginia and the Carolinas, sometimes alone and sometimes in the company of various relatives. Laden with an assortment of soaps, jewelry, thimbles, scissors, playing cards, and almost every other thing imaginable, he walked along country roads and found shelter in friendly cottages and houses. Years later, he recalled how he had slogged through the Dismal Swamp at night in foul weather, picking his way through muddy pools and fallen cypresses, discerning his path with the help of lightning flashes.[36] In his haphazard wanderings, he got to know a fairly large piece of the country.

Bronson got to know himself as well. He took particular pleasure when his wanderings took him to the homes of the tidewater gentry, who sometimes repaid him in something more valuable than money: the opportunity to sample the graces and good manners of a class he had never known before. Near the age of eighty, he looked back on these times and averred that an observing peddler "cannot well fail of becoming more of a gentleman and make a fuller acquaintance of human nature by his calling. . . . A boy of genius disguised as a peddler has advantages denied to the courtier, even, of learning the laws of etiquette and civility."[37] When possible, he persuaded the people he visited to open not only their parlors to him but also their libraries. Indeed, it later seemed to him that he might have fared better in his business if he had not neglected it for "intellectual pleasures." By his own later admission, Bronson was too bashful and unlettered to take full advantage of the social opportunities that came his way through his contact with the worldly, cultivated families who welcomed him. Nevertheless, their influence enabled him to shed some of his awkwardness and to return home "a better behaved if not a wiser youth," imbued with the beginnings of a more gracious manner. For the first time, he was, he wrote, "disposed to meet people, [my] elders at least, respectfully."[38] Years later, an English acquaintance declared that Alcott possessed the courtly manners of "a very great peer."[39]

During this time, too, he made his first acquaintance with slavery, on very close terms. He sometimes slept in the cabins of slaves and awoke to find himself in the midst of their daily lives. In later years, he was destined to become a dedicated abolitionist—a proud friend of William Lloyd Garrison and a staunch admirer of John Brown. However, Alcott's experiences as a peddler did not immediately awaken him to the cause of freedom. Indeed, when he first heard Garrison speak, he found the latter's condemnations overly sweeping. No doubt mindful of his former hosts among the First Families of Virginia, whom he was prepared to forgive a great deal, Bronson criticized Garrison for his "want of discrimination . . . between the slave-holder who keeps his slaves from motives of expediency and the one whose principles are in favor of slavery."[40]

For a man of the spirit, Bronson was acquiring a taste for finer things, and in his first whiff of refinement he began to look on his beginnings with a mild hint of superiority and scorn. In January 1820, while on one of these adventures with his younger brother Chatfield, Bronson wrote his parents his earliest surviving letter, boasting of turning a thirty-three percent profit on his wares. Reading this letter, one is struck immediately by the artificiality of Bronson's tone. He writes of his pleasure in having learned that his parents are "in circumstances affluent enough to preclude the idea of complaining." He laces his first paragraph with words like "perusal," "dissimulation," and "felicitated," always seeking the elaborate word to do the work of a simpler one. It is not so much a letter as a performance. Bronson was either trying to win his parents' compliments or to lord his self-taught erudition over them. Likely enough, he was trying to do a little of both. He wanted to sound like anything but the son of a subsistence farmer.

Filled with the hubris of his initial successes, Bronson saw himself as the possible economic savior of his ill-financed family. He assured his mother and father that the reason he had left home had been "To make their cares, and burdens less, and try to help them some."[41] It was his chief delight, he told them, to earn them all he could, and he considered it almost a sure bet that his efforts would have them out of debt by his twenty-first birthday. His first two trips to the South went part of the way to fulfilling this promise, netting the family a respectable profit of $180.

Nevertheless, there was something about the peddling life that did not quite fit with Bronson's character. Despite his promise to his parents that he could make his business as respectable as any other, he was surely aware that the idea of a virtuous peddler would have struck most people as an oxymoron. Yale president Timothy Dwight worried that men engaged in peddlers' work would almost invariably fall into dishonesty. He reasoned that the commanding aim of such a tradesman would be to make a good bargain, and self-interest would lead him to think of every gainful bargain as a good one.[42] Moreover, the authority Alcott trusted more than any other, *The Pilgrim's Progress*, counseled that the marketplace was evil, perhaps inherently so. One of the most memorable scenes in Bunyan's work is the passage of Christian and his friend Faithful through the town of Vanity. The town maintains a Fair that is a paradise of venal merchants, where not only "Pleasures and Delights of all sorts" but also blood, bodies, and souls are for sale.[43] The patrons of the Fair denounce the pilgrims as fools and are unable to comprehend their language. The moral purity of the two visitors so fiercely clashes with the depravity of the inhabitants of Vanity that the latter take them prisoner and, after a hypocritical trial, burn Faithful at the stake. Viewing his career in the light of Bunyan's allegory must have caused Bronson to wonder whether he had forsaken the path of the pilgrim, simply to become a movable Vanity Fair. In March 1823, he wrote to his cousin William that, during his travels, he had overheard a troublesomely apt saying: "Peddling is a hard place to serve God, but a capital one to serve Mammon." Bronson now wished for the grace to amend his ways.[44]

The peddling life began to hold still less charm for him as his business fortunes turned for the worse. His third trip was the last one to turn a profit, and his earnings did not survive the trip home. Passing through New York on the way to Wolcott, Bronson came face-to-face with temptation. His seducer took the form of an immaculate black suit, a white cravat, and an amethystine pin. It wasn't a fair fight. Bronson returned home in sartorial glory but with his money squandered. He made two more sorties into the peddling trade, and they nearly ruined him. Although he apparently had some gifts as a salesman, he was less sagacious as a buyer. Joseph T. Allyn, the Norfolk trader from whom Bronson became accustomed to buying his stock, discovered that he could sell his goods to Alcott for considerably more than they were worth. By the time the naive young peddler realized that the shrewd fancy-goods dealer had made a "gudgeon" of him, he had become more deeply obliged to Allyn than he could manage. In 1822, Allyn took possession of Bronson's horse, wagon, and remaining merchandise in partial satisfaction of the young man's debt. Alcott's father, whom Bronson had grandly promised to free from debt "before . . . I am twenty-one," had to cover $270 of Bronson's debt to Allyn.[45] By 1823, the year of his last peddling excursion, Bronson owed his father $600. At twenty-three, he had had enough of the life of a salesman.

However, the next turn in his path showed him work for which he was much better suited. In the fall of 1823, he first took up the job of schoolmaster. He cannot have done so with a view to financial or social advancement, for schoolmasters in rural Connecticut generally enjoyed no more comfort or prestige than Washington Irving's Ichabod Crane. Almost immediately, however, Alcott found something in teaching that resonated deeply within him. He embraced and never abandoned the idea that educating the young was the greatest work that a person could undertake. Alcott argued that the work of teaching children was better even than preaching, since there was still time to imbue the youthful heart and mind with a reverence for goodness. "The minister has long preached," Alcott complained, "and what has he accomplished? Ask our penitentiaries . . . our almshouses. . . . Look into the individual life and behold the shifts of trade, of avarice, of petty prejudice, bickering, quarrels, spites." He was unwilling to waste his efforts on people whose habits were fixed. "Early education," he was sure, "was the enduring power."[46]

As he turned to teaching, he had more in his mind than reforming the characters of his pupils. At a certain point—no one seems to agree as to exactly when or to what extent—Bronson became familiar with the educational theories of Johann Heinrich Pestalozzi. A native of Zurich who derived deep inspiration from Jean-Jacques Rousseau, Pestalozzi believed in the innate intelligence of human beings. He contended that the best education sought to bring these latent powers to the surface, instead of cramming information into the student. Pestalozzi deplored the then-common assumption that harsh discipline achieved the best results in the classroom. Emphasizing that education must be social as well as intellectual, he maintained that the ideal classroom should replicate the nurturing atmosphere of a loving family.

Lacking the expertise in languages that would have made Pestalozzi's original work available to him, Alcott made extensive use of a series of English pamphlets based on Pestalozzi's doctrines, titled *Hints to Parents*. The anonymous *Hints* not only urged the very type of gentle, conversational method that Alcott adopted in his own teaching, but it also counseled the importance of making the educational environment as similar as possible to a tranquil, well-managed home. *Hints* emphasized from its very first pages "the invaluable opportunities afforded in the DOMESTIC CIRCLE for fostering the infant mind." It advocated "making schools more nearly resemble the paternal abode: thus rendering them more perfect representations of parental education, instruction, superintendence, and society." Although each of the *Hints to Parents* pamphlets focused on a particular area of education—arithmetic, language, geometric form, and so on—each began and ended with a stirring exhortation, urging parents to spare no effort in the pursuit of virtue, both in their children and in themselves. Like *The Pilgrim's Progress*, the pamphlets urged parents to deafen themselves to the judgments of a corrupt and vanity-ridden world. Of parents in general, *Hints* advised, "No consideration of earthly interest, no fear of human censure, no thirst for human applause, neither dread of singularity nor weak complaisance, must have power to slacken their zeal." Furthermore, it counseled that the pathway to the intellect led primarily through personal interaction and appeals to the feelings: "A child's mind must be awakened by its instructor's mind, not by its instructor's book—life must act upon life—the heart is the seat of life."[47]

Armed with such principles, Alcott ventured to find out whether Pestalozzian theory could be made to work in rural Connecticut. Establishing a school in the town of Cheshire, he pursued the hypothesis that children would be best served if their schoolmaster tried to make them happy and comfortable and encouraged them to reason independently. He decorated the dreary classrooms with flowers and pine boughs. He got rid of long tables with hard benches and replaced them with individual desks that he built with his own hands. He somehow scrounged the money to purchase a school library of over a hundred volumes at his own expense. He made up games for the children and sometimes joined in himself.[48] His classrooms became places of music and art. Rejecting the usages that had "rendered the school room . . . a place of suffering, confinement, and

*Hopeful and confident, Bronson Alcott posed
for this pencil sketch as a young man.*

hatred," Alcott made little use of corporal punishment. He governed his students not by threats but by conversation, appealing to their feelings and sense of justice. He established a classroom court, in which, under his supervision, the children reviewed each other's violations of the school's disciplinary code. The educational experience became both highly orderly and extremely inviting. Eager for more instruction, students often visited Alcott's home in the evenings to read and play with him. One day when Alcott was absent from the school, the students competently conducted business by themselves.[49]

To assist in the development of his own mind, he began to keep a journal of his thoughts and observations. The first entry was dated July 3, 1826, the day before John Adams and Thomas Jefferson died. Alcott continued his journals as long as he could use a pen. From its earliest entries, his journal conveyed his restless spirit and his utter impatience with orthodoxy. He privately lamented, "To dare to think, to think for oneself, is denominated pride and arrogance. And millions of minds are in this state of slavery and tyranny." He knew of only one escape from this bondage: "Rebel! . . . Let others grumble; dare to be singular. Let others direct; follow Reason."[50]

Distrustful of Alcott's singularity and his iconoclastic definition of reason, the parents of Cheshire were not long in starting to grumble. They neither understood nor trusted his methods. Although one visiting educator proclaimed Alcott's Cheshire school "the best common school in the state—probably in the United States," local opinion turned against him.[51] A local clergyman spoke out against Alcott's moral opinions, and the schoolmaster soon discovered that parents cared nothing for his educational theories. They wanted only practice, and his practices were beyond their willingness to comprehend. He closed his school and retreated to Spindle Hill.

Decisive moments in Bronson Alcott's life tended to come when, just as the promise of one venture began to fade as one constituent group lost confidence in him, his reputation suddenly reached the ears of another, more idealistic audience that was prepared to give him a new opportunity. Such was the case in May 1827, when his cousin William sent a report of his accomplishments in Cheshire to Samuel May, a graduate of Harvard Divinity School, now leading the Unitarian church in Brooklyn, Connecticut. May was a man of distinguished lineage in an era when lineage counted a great deal. The son of a prominent Boston merchant, Colonel Joseph May, Samuel was descended on his mother's side from the Sewalls and Quincys. His great-aunt Dorothy was the widow of John Hancock. To his great credit, Samuel May himself cared far less about a person's origins, his own included, than he cared about what one might do for humankind. If he benefited socially from his maternal connections, he appeared to draw strength of character from his father's side. Perhaps descended from Portuguese Jews who had fled the Inquisition, the Mays were known for their intelligence and fighting spirit, qualities that Samuel often turned to his advantage in support of worthy causes. Speaking of conditions that he had gratefully avoided in his own life, May once asserted, "No one shall be compelled by the poverty of his parents to live in darkness and sin."[52] He was dedicated to making that pronouncement a reality, working avidly not only for the reform of education but also for abolition, the improvement of prisons, and other forms of social welfare. Learning of Alcott's work in Cheshire, May wanted to meet the schoolmaster. As he later put it, "I at once felt assured the man must be a genius, and that I must know him more intimately."53 An invitation was promptly sent, and Bronson accepted.

The greatest surprise came immediately after Bronson came to the Mays' front door. Samuel was out of the house, and his wife was upstairs, recovering from a difficult childbirth. So it was that, when the door came open, it did not reveal the minister, but the dark-eyed, expressive face of his sister Abigail. She was a tall, dark-haired woman with abundant physical energy and a large frame, which her aristocratic family and her attendance at dancing school had taught her to carry with becoming grace. She never used her full name of Abigail, preferring the informality of Abby or Abba. At twenty-six, she had already passed the age at which most women of her time and station were married. Bronson eventually learned that there had once been a fiancé, a first cousin named Samuel May Frothingham, but he had suddenly died of a now-forgotten cause.

Perhaps more than ill fortune had helped to keep Abba single. Throughout her life, she had a forthrightness and a sharp tongue that might have discouraged a fainthearted suitor. In addition, as an infant she had been severely burned on her face and right hand. The extent of the lasting scars and physical impairment that resulted cannot be known. However, biographer Madelon Bedell has suggested that Abba's hand was permanently disfigured in some way that harmed appearance more than function.54 In any event, it is not fanciful to suppose that the loss of her fiancé, coupled with self-consciousness about her appearance—or a dearth of suitors because of her scars—had a deflating effect on her romantic expectations.

By her midtwenties, Abba May was thinking more about books than about men. By this time, her best friend, Lydia Maria Child, was already on her way to becoming one of the most respected women writers in the country. For her part, Abba had never been much attracted to formal study, but she read voraciously on her own, devouring biographies, philosophical works, and contemporary novels. She possessed both intellect and will, but, having no inspiring object to give focus to her determination, she believed that her intellectual stamina was not sufficient for concentrated work. She had written this critical self-assessment to her brother Charles:

I am a daily, nay, momentary sufferer for that mental discipline which can be acquired only in youth. . . . [W]hen I come to travel up the hill of science, or am obliged to contemplate the realities of life and condition, I find myself fatigued or weary without having gained by my toil. . . . I yield to despondency, rather than conquer by perseverance.[55]

But she felt no despondency the day Bronson Alcott first came to her brother's door. The stranger was tall, blond, and imperially gracious. She invited him in.

It is hard to say which of the May siblings was more immediately enraptured by Alcott, who spoke with such sparkle and sincerity about his theories of education. Samuel May found that his expectations were more than answered. He wrote, "I have never, but in one other instance, been so taken possession of by any man I ever met. He seemed to me like a born sage and saint." Bronson, May recognized, was a radical in the literal sense of the word, that is, his discernment went directly "to the root of all things, especially the subjects of education, mental, and moral culture."[56]

As he laid out his ideas and visions for the betterment of children's minds and spirits, Bronson was unconsciously making a strong impression in another direction as well. Abba May shared her brother's fervor for social causes. Decades later, her daughter Louisa wrote that Abba had "the blood of all the Mays and Sewalls 'a bilin' in her veins."[57] Without question, young Mr. Alcott's conversation caused that blood to rise a degree or two. However, not all of the heat came from political excitement. She was not so high-minded that she could ignore his more obvious charms: his upright carriage; his gracious, almost overly elaborate manners; the quick, playful uplift of his head; and his profound earnestness. Until Abba opened her brother's door that day, her life had lacked possibility and promise. Unexpectedly, she found herself sitting in the presence of an immeasurable fullness.

Bronson was a man of many internal rules and restraints who exerted great control over his displays of emotion. Abba was naturally more impulsive, but she knew more than enough of the manners of good society to make her immediate attraction to Bronson seem like polite interest. Her first acknowledgment of Bronson in her journal evinced cautious restraint. She wrote, "I found . . . an intelligent, philosophic modest man, whose reserved deportment authorized my showing many attentions."[58] It took Bronson almost a year to write down his initial impressions of Abba. By that time, he had seen her on many occasions, and his true first impressions had been reshaped by those subsequent interviews. Even so, as he recalled their first meeting, there was a stiff, fumbling quality to his prose that suggests a lingering discomfort with the feelings she had stirred in him. During this period, Alcott had affected the use of the royal "we" when writing about himself. Although he used this device in writing about all subjects, it is fun to suppose that, when he used it with respect to his courtship, he did so because he did not want to go it alone. He referred to her tentatively as:

> an interesting woman we had often portrayed in our imagination. In her we thought we saw its reality. . . . In refined and elevated conversation with a lady thus estimated by our reason and thus offering herself to our imagination, we could not but be pleased, interested, captivated.

At last, after all the circumlocutions and polysyllables, he permitted himself to come to the point: "How could we but be in love with [her]?"[59]

He wrote approvingly of Abba's lack of artifice and affectation. "All," he wrote, "was openness, simplicity, nature herself." He set down a series of her admirable qualities: "intelligence, sympathy, piety . . . tenderness of eye . . . beauty of moral countenance . . . joyousness of domestic performance."[60] He respected the fact that she thought for herself, and he was flattered to find that many of her conclusions were the same as his own. Moreover, she seemed genuinely interested in his driving passion: the instruction of the young. Bronson ended up staying with the Mays for about a week, during which time he became as attracted to the family as they were to him.

There was talk of Bronson's going to Boston to form a school under the aegis of a Scottish educator, William Russell, who was gaining recognition as the editor of the *American Journal of Education*. Abba, plucking up her courage, offered her services. Bronson, however, wanted to make one more attempt at establishing himself in his home state. Late in the autumn of 1827, he set up a school in Bristol, run on the same principles he had used in Cheshire. This time, however, the backlash against his progressivism was even swifter and more decisive. If he were to have any hope of continuing as an educator, he would have to pursue his dream in a city large-minded enough to have produced a family like the Mays. It was time to go to Boston.

On the way, he stopped at the Mays' house. This time, however, his

No image exists of Abba Alcott as a young woman.
When she sat for this photograph, long years of social activism
and challenging married life were behind her.
(Courtesy of the Louisa May Alcott Memorial Association)

interactions with Abba May were more strained. During the previous ten months they had been too much in each other's thoughts for them to repeat the naturalness of emotion with which they had first greeted each other, and both came away from this second encounter confused and troubled. Bronson reflexively took refuge in his formality and mannered correctness, leading Abba to curse the naïveté with which she had assumed warmer motives on his part. Expecting to greet a friend, she discovered "merely an acquaintance, whose reserve chilled me into silence."[61] It even occurred to her that he found her character disagreeable.

Once in Boston, Alcott wasted no time seeking out influences that he could incorporate into his understanding of the mind and its proper education. It was very nearly the last time in American history when society's intellectual leaders could be found primarily in the pulpit, and Alcott busily pursued enlightenment by hearing the leading ministers of the Unitarian church. Easily the greatest spokesperson of Unitarian belief was William

Ellery Channing, a man whose merits Alcott was quick to recognize. He observed, "Among the list of divines here of the liberal character, Dr. Channing ranks pre-eminent, both in originality of thought and felicity of expression."[62] A Rhode Island native, Dr. Channing had been the pastor of the Federal Street Church in Boston since 1803. He remained there until his death in 1842. Channing and his fellow Unitarians firmly rejected the doctrine, rooted in the minds of New Englanders since the seventeenth century, that humankind was born depraved and alienated by Adam's sins from the love and majesty of God. Channing and his followers refused to believe that a good God would produce a wicked creation and then punish it with everlasting misery for evils that He had allowed to exist in the first place. God, for the Unitarians, was infinitely good and kind, seeking always to encourage in his creation the highest development of virtue.

Channing routinely emphasized the paternal nature of God and implied that the world was a school for the spirit in which human beings were the pupils. In 1819, Channing had ascribed to God "a father's concerns for His creatures, a father's desire for their improvement, . . . a father's joy in their progress." Unitarians, he said, "look upon this world as a place of education, in which He is training men by prosperity and adversity, by aids and obstructions, by conflicts of reason and passion."[63] Channing saw God as both father and teacher, a view that dovetailed precisely with Alcott's ideas of education. The ideal teacher was to Alcott a type of spiritual father, who tried to bring, with both his words and his example, an image of divine goodness into the mind of the child. After arriving in Boston, Bronson strove whenever possible to employ a female assistant in his schools. With both a female and a male teacher in the room, he must have reasoned, the school would more closely approach the model of the family proposed by Pestalozzi. Eager to observe the results of Alcott's theories of spiritual education, Channing became a benefactor of the school that Alcott established on Common Street in the fall of 1828.[64]

On September 28, 1828, Alcott's diaries mention a first encounter with a man who, for the time being, was nothing more to him than an unusually gifted preacher. On that day, twenty-five-year-old Ralph Waldo Emerson read a sermon on the universality of the Deity to his congregation at the Second Church in Boston's North End. Alcott listened as Emerson decried the life of the average person, so intent on satisfying the monotonous wants of an unexceptional life that the omnipresent miracles of the universe are invisible to him.

> Let the sun go up the sky, and the moon shine, and innumerable stars move before him in orbits so vast that centuries will not fulfill them. . . . He does not care—he does not know—he is creeping in a little path of his own . . . following a few appetites . . . peering around for a little bread.[65]

Of this sort of rodentlike existence, Bronson was already a dedicated foe. It must have warmed him to hear these words that answered the intuitions of his own heart. In Emerson's words, too, he heard a cordial invitation to friendship and a sharing of spirit. In the knowledge of God, the young minister declared, "our hearts beat as one heart . . . we are touched with the same emotion; are struck with the same truth; and pray with one prayer."[66] Alcott and Emerson did not meet that Sunday. Still, there was a gravity of soul to this young minister that was well worth a closer look. Alcott wrote in his journal of Emerson and others like him, "To be favored with the acquaintance of such men as these is a privilege of which I am desirous to obtain and secure. . . . The same objects are before our view."[67]

Alcott was forming a useful connection with the educator William Russell, who had quickly come to respect him both as a teacher and as an expounder of educational theories. The lean-faced Russell visited Alcott's new school and left, as he put it, "With a clearer conception than I ever had before of the innate excellence of the human soul."[68] Russell's journal published a paper on Alcott's Cheshire school, as well as a paper by Alcott on Pestalozzian education. Before long, Russell was assisting with the instruction at Alcott's school. At the age of twenty-eight, Bronson was beginning to move among the intellectual circles of Boston.

At the same time, events of a more intimate nature were slowly and haltingly gathering momentum. The stiffness Alcott had exhibited during his last visit to Brooklyn had put Abba off only momentarily. No doubt realizing that an extra effort would be required to conquer his aloofness, she had embarked on a bold stratagem. She moved from Samuel's house to her father's home in Boston. From this nearer vantage point, she wrote to Alcott, offering herself not as a lover but as an assistant at the school he was soon to open.

In part, she was engaged in a romantic pursuit. In part, though, she was simply trying to recapture her self-esteem. She resolved, if not to capture his affections, then at least "that he should know me better and find I had some redeeming virtue."[69] Bronson, too, had obstacles to overcome. As much as the gentility of the Mays had delighted him, their attention also made him conscious of his countrified origins. Yes, his experiences in the South had taken the rough edges off his manners, but navigating an occasional drawing room or dance floor was not the same as forging a possibly permanent connection with an established family. He felt that he still evinced "so much of the rustic awkwardness and simplicity of natural life that I am often offending the more cultivated tastes" of more polite people.[70] Moreover, he was not in the habit of regarding himself as a romantic person. A devotee of principles, how could he succeed in something so unprincipled as a love affair? Also, as a practical matter, it seemed imprudent to accept Abba's offer of professional assistance. After all, Samuel May was to be his patron. It would hardly serve anyone's reputation if it were thought that May had extended his kindness on the basis of his sister's romantic affinities, nor was it wise to create the impression that Alcott had given Abba a job as a quid pro quo.

Samuel, too, fretted over the appearance of the thing. Fearing scandal, he cautioned Abba to be wary of "the remarks and opinions of the world," which a man might perhaps flout with impunity but which a woman could ignore only at the price of "incurring the greatest danger."[71] He fully expected "a censorious world to ascribe selfish views both to myself and you, if you were now to unite with him in his school."[72] Nevertheless, if Samuel May thought that a professional connection between his sister and the blue-eyed Connecticut dreamer would be impolitic, he felt quite differently about their social liaison. Though she needed no prompting, he encouraged Abba to look beyond the schoolmaster's social status:

> Don't distress yourself about his poverty. His mind and heart are so much occupied with other things that poverty and riches do not seem to concern him."[73]

In any event, Bronson did not hire Abba, and he continued to vacillate as to the more personal aspect of their relationship. He was afraid above all of making a premature advance. As he wrestled with the problem of making "a disclosure so important in the history of my happiness," speech failed him.[74] At last, he resorted to the only confidant and go-between whose ability to represent him he fully trusted: his journal. After some trepidation, he handed Abba the pages where he had written what he could not say.

He first gave her some relatively noncommittal extracts for her perusal, passages that expressed admiration for her character but steered clear of forthright declarations. At their next meeting, as the two went for a solitary walk, he tried again to verbalize his feelings, but he meandered off into high-flown abstractions. Bewildered, Abba complained, "The more he tried to explain, the more mysterious everything appeared to me." Finally, Bronson showed her the frankest portions of his journal, and they told Abba all she wished to know. An offer of marriage immediately followed, and Abba immediately accepted. Later that same day, she wrote to Samuel that she was "engaged to Mr. Alcott not in a school, but in the solemn—the momentous capacity of friend and wife."[75] She told Samuel, "I feel already an increase of moral energy—I have something to love—to live for—I have felt a loneliness in this world that was making a misanthrope of me in spite of everything I could do to overcome it." With the most ardent emotion, she swore that she would "live to promote the happiness of him with whom all my interests are blended."[76]

In the happiest moments, however, doubts can be especially troubling, perhaps because they stand out so starkly against the brightness of the scene. Abba confessed her awareness of both the differences of character that separated her from her fiancé and the scantness of his worldly means:

> He is moderate, I am impetuous—He is prudent and humble—I am
> forward and arbitrary. He is poor—but we are both industrious—why
> may we not be happy?[77]

Just how much a lack of money can press in on the most determined happiness, Abba was to discover. Just how accurate she was in listing humility and prudence among her new fiancé's virtues should be left for the wise to determine.

Bronson felt that their mutual disclosure of affection possessed "all the romance of poetry." Love had always been for him a diffuse, idealized emotion—something one felt generally for humankind or, somewhat more specifically, for a classroom of children. On his becoming engaged to Abigail May, love at last obtained a personal, physical form. Alcott wrote, "I then commenced *living*, not only for society, but for an *individual*. I identified a human soul with my own."[78]

The couple's delight in their engagement was marred three months later by the death of Abba's only surviving sister, Mrs. Samuel Greele, who left behind a five-year-old son and a two-year-old daughter. Abba, who had loved this sister deeply, was later to honor her memory by naming one of her own daughters after her. The maiden name of the departed sister was Louisa May.

CHAPTER TWO

A BIRTHDAY IN GERMANTOWN

> "[G]enius is the endowment of every spirit,
> and parents are its supervisors while on its
> terrestrial mission. May I fulfill my divine behest!"
>
> —A. BRONSON ALCOTT,
> *Journals,* January 4, 1835

> "'November is the most disagreeable
> month in the whole year,' said Margaret. . . .
> 'That's the reason I was born in it,' observed Jo."
>
> —LOUISA MAY ALCOTT,
> *Little Women,* chapter 15

AMOS BRONSON ALCOTT AND ABIGAIL MAY WERE MARRIED after an unhurried engagement on Sunday, May 23, 1830, at King's Chapel on Tremont Street. Bronson noted the day in his journal with ornate formality, revealing more about his taste for elaborate diction than disclosing the details of the event. He wrote, in full:

> Agreeably to preceding expectation, I was this day married by Rev. Mr. Greenwood, at King's Chapel. Passed the evening at Col. May's, and came to Mrs. Newell's, my place of board, with my friend, Miss May, after the civilities of the evening.[1]

It is hard to read these words without some disappointment. They give no hint of the music that was played, the adornments of the bride, the good wishes that were exchanged, or, most importantly, the sentiments of the couple themselves. Whatever deep significance Bronson may have attached to the word "friend," one expects a warmer word for a new bride. Bronson, however, was not deeply skilled as a reporter. The best descriptive passages in his journals are products of long reflection, written years, not hours, after the events in question. In addition, the distant quality of

Alcott's wedding-day journal entry confirms a general truth about the nature of his awareness. More often than not, Bronson Alcott tended to live more in his ideas than in his skin. At many of the moments when others are likely to feel most alive to the world of sense, Bronson seems to have been only contingently present, like an accidental, gossamer visitor to a ponderously material world.

The couple's financial prospects brightened two months after the wedding, when they received an anonymous gift of two thousand dollars, most likely from Abba's father, Colonel Joseph May. To his credit, Bronson immediately used more than a third of the money to settle, with interest, the debt that he had long owed his family at Spindle Hill. Indeed, he traveled there with Abba to have the pleasure of pressing the money into his mother's hand. Sadly, though, Alcott's father was not there to meet his daughter-in-law. The previous year, Joseph Alcox had died at the age of fifty-seven.

After the wedding, Alcott barely had time to resume his teaching in Boston before events started to lead him down a different road. During the same month that saw him married, he entered a contest. The *United States Gazette* of Philadelphia advertised a one-hundred-dollar prize for the best essay on education. Alcott responded with a twenty-seven-page opus, *Observations on the Principles and Methods of Infant Instruction*. *Observations* represents the most comprehensive statement on the subject of teaching that he ever committed to writing. Moreover, it reveals Alcott's state of mind near the time when his thinking about education was to be put to its most formidable test; only a month or so after their wedding, Abba became pregnant with the couple's first child. After this child was born, Alcott's roles as father and educator were never distinct. Thus, his *Observations* is as much a treatise on parenting as a theory of the classroom.

Alcott began by positing that a child possessed a collection of faculties that developed at different rates over time. He identified them, in ascending order of complexity, as "the animal nature, the affections, the conscience [and] the intellect." To accomplish its tasks, he argued, an education must address all these aspects of personality. "The whole being of the child," he insisted, "asks for expansion and guidance." Rather than being prematurely forced to concentrate only on the emergence of his intellect, the child should be encouraged to "associate pleasure with the action of all his faculties." Children naturally seek enjoyment. However, lacking judgment and experience, they either fail to find enjoyment or discover it in the wrong activities. Therefore, a teacher must seek and supply the means to guide the pupil to true and lasting sources of enjoyment.[2]

Since the first aspect of a child's character to emerge was its animal nature, his physical needs should initially be treated as paramount. It was essential to allow him unrestrained movement and ample opportunity for play, an activity that Alcott called "the appointed dispensation of childhood." Only when the exuberance of the body had been satisfied could the intellect be successfully addressed. The playroom, then, was the most effective preparation for the schoolroom. Always, Alcott declared, instruction should be invested "with an interest, a certainty, and a love, which future experience shall not diminish, nor maturer reason disapprove."[3]

Games and playtime were, of course, only the first steps. The instructor must also address the intellectual and moral constitution of the child, though never in a condescending or autocratic fashion. Rather, the chief avenue to the mind and soul of the child was through conversation, that is, through a system of Socratic dialogue that, while adjusted to the lesser intellect of the child, nevertheless treated the child as the moral peer of the instructor. "To train and elevate [the conscience] by frequent appeals to the unerring laws of reason, rectitude, and benevolence" was, for Alcott, "an all-important work." Socrates, however, was not the sole model, for Alcott also revered the teaching practices of Christ, especially his parables. Abstract reasoning should give way to "interesting incidents, familiar descriptions, approaching as nearly as possible to the circumstances and relations of life."[4]

Indeed, Alcott believed that the ideal teacher should be a modern Christ, entering the classroom not only with a solemn sense of moral duty but a surpassing love for his young charges. Perfecting of a growing spirit required the near perfection of the instructor:

> [T]he teacher should unite an amiableness of temper, a simplicity of manner, and a devotion to his work, which shall associate with it his happiness and duty. . . . He should possess the power of reaching the infant understanding in the simplest and happiest forms. . . . Free from

prejudices and particularities, he should impart instructions from the pure fountain of truth and love alone. Taking a benevolent view of the works of nature and the ways of Providence, his piety should diffuse itself through all his teachings.⁵

Not surprisingly, given his own haphazard, unfinished education, Alcott insisted that the teacher's formal training and store of academic knowledge were of relatively minor import. Alcott argued that the word "education" must be taken literally. It was a drawing out of what the child already possessed within, not a cramming in of facts and theories. As the child traveled the path to knowledge and spiritual unfoldment, the role of the teacher was neither to drive nor to lead the child; it was to accompany him.

Bronson did not win the contest. However, as with his cousin William's report on the Cheshire school, this document also opened a door. Alcott's *Observations* was printed by a Boston publishing house and caught the eye of a Pennsylvanian Quaker named Reuben Haines, a railroad entrepreneur and financier with a fancy for educational topics. In October 1830, on a visit to Boston, Haines sought Alcott out and made him an offer. Alcott and his wife were to move from Boston to Germantown, Pennsylvania, on the outskirts of Philadelphia, where Haines would provide them with a house free of rent and arrange for Bronson and his friend William Russell to open a school based on the principles of Bronson's *Observations*. Bronson responded to the proposal with enthusiasm. Abba could hardly have welcomed the news that she was to become a mother hundreds of miles away from the rest of the May family. Nevertheless, on December 14, 1830, now six months pregnant, Abba joined Bronson and the Russells on their difficult four-day journey over rutted roads and storm-tossed waters to Philadelphia.

When Alcott and Russell arrived in Germantown, they found the quiet farming community far below their expectations. Neither believed that the community was sufficiently forward-looking to appreciate their progressive approach to education. Therefore, instead of settling in Germantown, the Alcotts took rooms at a boardinghouse in Philadelphia. The two men kept Haines at bay for several weeks while they tried to locate patrons who might support them in establishing a school in Philadelphia. Finding no takers, they again agreed to Haines's original offer, which the philanthropist had kindly held open for them. Alcott instructed children from the ages of three to nine, while Russell worked with the older pupils.

Alcott's delay in committing himself to Haines meant that the house he had been promised was not immediately ready for occupancy. Thus, it was in a Germantown boardinghouse operated by a Mrs. Stuckart that Bronson prepared to open his school and Abba made ready for motherhood. The ensuing winter was a time of great excitement for Bronson but a season of loneliness for Abba. As her pregnancy neared its end, she became anxious and depressed. On March 15, 1831, she began thirty-six hours of labor.

The following evening, an hour before midnight, Abba delivered a daughter, whom the couple named Anna Bronson in honor of Bronson's mother. The baby was strong and healthy. Abba felt as if the child had opened "all the fountains of [her] better nature." The baby had "given love to life—and life to love." Abba doubted whether anyone else could comprehend "the sacred, pure emotions" that had "filled and at times overwhelmed" her.[6] Bronson was equally ecstatic. In his journal, he implicitly likened Anna's birth to the coming of the Christ child. One can almost hear the jubilant notes of Handel's *Messiah* in Alcott's words:

> "Unto us a child is given." Be it our ambition and delight, to train it up by the maxims of Him of whom the prophets of old spoke the same words. As agents of the Supreme Parent, may we guide it in the paths of truth, duty, and happiness.[7]

Bronson saw in Anna both a God-given duty and an experimental opportunity. In his current thinking, environment was all-important in the moral formation of a child. Even in the carefully constructed atmospheres of his primary schools, however, the children had always walked through the door as products of potentially contaminating influences. Never had Alcott had the chance to try out his educational theories on a pure subject, untainted by the petty prejudices of someone else's parenting.

In Anna, Bronson at last had the chance to supervise and observe the development of a child from its earliest moments, in an environment over which he could exert a high level of control. Alcott seized this opportunity with extraordinary zeal and ambition. Bronson was utterly confident of his innate genius. However, even though most of his childhood memories were fond, he bitterly regretted having been raised in an environment that had neither recognized nor fed his native brilliance. He resolved to give his child the spiritually indulgent upbringing he wished he had had. In this pursuit, Alcott accepted no half measures. He hoped to create an environment for his daughter that was not only better than what he had known but which, he believed, would come as close as possible to producing a perfect child.

Seeking from the first not to reprise the remoteness of his own father, Alcott could hardly be persuaded to leave the room where Abba and the infant lay. He was making good his determination to be a man, in Abba's words, "for domestic and parental excellence inferior to none." His presence "shed tranquility on the scene."[8] However, he did not stop there. From the day after Anna's birth, Alcott kept a separate journal regarding his daughter, titled "Observations on the Life of my First Child," in which he aspired to record literally every event in her mental and spiritual growth. He proposed to continue this journal religiously until Anna was old enough to continue it herself, not merely through the end of childhood but as near as possible to her death. He desired nothing less than "the history of one human mind, commenced in infancy and faithfully narrated . . . through all the vicissitudes of life to its close."[9] He hoped to create a document that would outstrip in value all that the world's philosophers had ever written about the human mind. The Alcott family nursery was to be more than a supreme locus of love and learning. It was also to be a laboratory for his children's minds and souls. Alcott undertook such journals not only for Anna but also for his next two daughters, Louisa and Elizabeth. He exposed them to stimuli and wrote down their reactions. He made minute observations of their movements, their facial expressions, their squeals of pleasure and fits of anger. Altogether, his writings on the early childhoods of his three eldest daughters eventually reached an astounding twenty-five hundred pages.

It is easy and, to some extent, justifiable to respond somewhat squeamishly to a man who would use his own children as the subjects of such an experiment. However, to read Alcott's painstakingly compiled notebooks is to realize that his motives, as well as his methods, were scrupulously kind. He was seeking to determine the nature of happiness and how to produce it, and harshness had no place in this search. In one of his experiments with Anna, Bronson affected a series of faces in order to note the baby's reactions. Curiosity prompted him to assume a deliberately frightening face. When Anna responded with panic, her father at once regretted his transgression. He wrote:

> This experiment must not be repeated. The influence of fear, even in its milder forms, upon the mind of infancy, must be unfavorable to its improvement and happiness. External objects should, as far as possible, excite only ideas of beauty, truth, and happiness.[10]

Moreover, Alcott was indulgent in his responses to Anna's inevitable assertions of frustration and anger. Indeed, he aspired to be a less controlling parent than the nature of his investigation would seem to suggest. When, at three months, Alcott noticed that Anna "indicated her opposition to whatever she thinks will diminish her happiness . . . uttering cries of uneasiness, dissatisfaction, etc.," he emphatically rejected the idea, which he knew many of his contemporaries would urge, that such displays of passion should be immediately checked and overcome. He wanted to train his child for independence, not servile obedience. "Liberty," Alcott maintained, "is a primary right of all created natures. . . . The child has his rights, as well as the adult. . . . The right of self-government, and the liberty to govern himself . . . are inherent principles of his nature."[11] Alcott's philosophy of the nursery reflected his philosophy of the state; he wanted not only to aid in the formation of a happy, intelligent child but to produce a republican citizen.

Anna Alcott enjoyed a pleasant, if highly scrutinized, babyhood. When she was almost two months old, the family moved into the house that Haines had promised them, a "little paradise," as Abba called it. There was a charming walkway lined with fruit trees, pines, and cedars. The furniture was new and of good quality. Busts of Newton and Locke, as well as flower vases, adorned the mantelpiece.[12] To make his experiment in child development as controlled as possible, Bronson took steps to minimize outside intrusions into the nursery. The family's serving girl was entrusted with maintaining the house, but the Alcotts reserved Anna's care for themselves. Bronson conducted his school at home, so that work would not call him away from wife and daughter. The Alcotts tried to insulate Anna not only against frightening faces, but also from sudden movements, loud voices, and "incessant prattle." They took pains to speak to her with "cheerful countenance . . . soft tones and deep interest."[13] Abba nursed her daughter frequently and on demand. She also confessed, "I am a great one to do what she indicates to have done." The idea was to anticipate Anna's wants and to address them quickly, in order to spare her from potentially damaging emotions. Reluctant to resort to discipline except when absolutely necessary, Bronson submitted to letting Anna pull his hair.[14] When Anna did raise a howl of protest over some imposition or other, Bronson reacted with a certain amount of approval: at least Anna was not fearful and passive like other children he had observed![15]

It was not that the Alcotts wanted to impose no restrictions on Anna's behavior, nor did they set out to spoil her. Their reluctance to introduce unpleasantness into Anna's world stemmed from their hypothesis that choices, even for an infant, should not be coerced, but should arise from an inner moral spirit. Alcott believed that the triumph of the child's higher nature must be voluntary and achieved through affection and reason, not fear of punishment. He desired a perfection of the will, not its subjugation. He was, therefore, thrown somewhat off balance when, around the age of six months, Anna began to behave in ways that seemed inconsistent with her supposed heavenly origins. She objected violently to having her mother even momentarily out of her sight. In general, she started displaying such imperious behavior that Bronson feared her will was surrendering to "passion," a word that, in this context, he equated with the worst aspects of animal nature.[16]

Thus troubled, Bronson resorted to discipline, only in accord with his theories. When Anna pulled his hair, he gently pulled hers. When she acted in an unloving manner, he withheld his own affection. By repaying her in kind, he meant for her to learn to do unto others as she would be done to. On the whole, this approach seemed to work better than unremitting indulgence. When Anna was twenty months old, Bronson boasted of her affectionate and intelligent nature. He felt that his daughter was manifesting her mother's heart and her father's mind—a combination he evidently considered optimal. Bronson also took pride in Anna's physical vigor, which he expected to serve her well as she confronted the trials of life.

One such trial was soon to arise. In October 1831, Reuben Haines unexpectedly died. The loss was catastrophic. Not only had Haines paid the rent for the Alcotts' home, but he had also underwritten the tuition of many of Bronson's pupils. Without these subsidies, the school's enrollment immediately declined. With determined effort, Alcott kept the school open for most of the following year, but the school was doomed. Abba called the philanthropist's death a "paralyzing blow" that "has prostrated all our hopes here."[17]

About the time they celebrated Anna's first birthday, the Alcotts learned that Abba was pregnant again. As he anticipated Anna's new sibling, Bronson was very much under the influence of his fellow pedagogue William Russell, who argued that children were beings of celestial origin and destination. Begotten by the stars, they were destined to return to them and to do so, one hoped, in a better, worthier condition than the one in which they had come. The role of the teacher was not only to prepare children for life in this world, which they entered as spiritual strangers, but to ready them for the celestial world, which was their eternal home. The prospect of welcoming another visitor from the heavens excited Bronson greatly.

It is fair to say that birth seemed more wonderful to Bronson than it did to Abba. As the due date neared, Abba again became depressed. This time, her feelings of dejection were so unusually severe that she never forgot them. Almost a decade later, struggling to manage the fitful temper of this second daughter, Abba wrote that her own dark frame of mind prior to delivery "accounts to me for many of her peculiarities and moods of mind, rather uncommon for a child of her age."[18] Bronson acknowledged that Abba had suffered a good deal during the summer months. Nevertheless, she seems to have done well at concealing the dimensions of her despondency from her husband. Bronson indeed believed that Abba had been "unusually cheerful amid the cares and anxieties of life, and of her situation."[19]

During these months, Alcott was less interested in Abba's condition than he was in a new piece of reading, which was raising him far beyond the immediate concerns of life. Two months before Louisa was born, he read for the first time *Aids to Reflection* by Samuel Taylor Coleridge, a book that soon rivaled *The Pilgrim's Progress* in its importance to him and, in his view, marked a new era in the life of his mind.[20] Though now chiefly remembered as a poet, Coleridge exerted a profound influence on American transcendentalism through his philosophical prose. He was the most eloquent English spokesman of an idealist movement that attempted to refute the conclusions of empiricist philosophers like John Locke. Locke had argued that human beings entered the world with their minds as empty slates and that the experience of the senses was the only source of human understanding. Locke's view might logically be taken to show that there was no relevant reality beyond the physical world. To understand themselves, human beings needed to look no farther than the data of their natural faculties.

Locke's thesis was understandably upsetting to those who believed that there was some deeper reality in the cosmos. His theory left no room for intuition or for the divine spark that, according to religious believers, animates and sanctifies the soul. Coleridge agreed with Locke that human beings were limited to their natural faculties. However, he argued, there existed a human faculty, reason, that was superior to mere physically based understanding. Reason emanated from the single, indivisible divine word of God, perfect and unchanging. Coleridge declared that this ability for perceiving divine truth was the highest capacity of human thought. Coleridge's concept of the reason resembled the Puritans' idea of grace; it was the regenerate portion of the person, the part that enabled a mystical communion with heaven. Despite Alcott's overall dedication to the life of the spirit, his thinking about child development had heretofore been basically Lockean. His emphasis on behavior and the senses is evident in the "Observations" he wrote regarding Anna. After reading Coleridge, though, Alcott never again supposed that empirical understanding the life of the senses and were paramount in human existence. Ironically, he was swept up by the tide of idealism at the very moment that his wife was about to give birth to the most intensely practical of his children.

On November 29, 1832, a half hour past midnight, Abba gave birth to a second daughter, whom Bronson described as "a very fine healthful child, much more so than Anna was at birth."[21] To his mother, he described the baby as "a very fine, fat, little creature . . . with a firm constitution for building up a fine character."[22] As Bronson had selected the name for his first daughter, it was Abba's turn to name the second. She chose Louisa May, in memory of her departed sister. To Abba, it was a name that, according to Bronson, connoted "every association connected with amiable benevolence and exalted worth." He hoped that its present possessor would rise to equal attainment.[23] Bronson, a man not indifferent to signs and portents, found it "a most interesting event" that Louisa May shared her father's birthday, entering the world on the day he turned thirty-three. When he wrote to his mother that Louisa had been born, Bronson underscored the words "on my own birth-day." Was there to be, perhaps, a supernatural bond between them that, from the first, transcended that of father and daughter?

If so, that bond was not to be one of physical similarity. In marked contrast to her blue-eyed, flaxen-haired father, Louisa had the dark features of her mother. She had something of an olive complexion and eyes that some called gray and others thought were black. The differences went deeper still. Even when Louisa was an infant, Bronson observed qualities in her that, in his own character, were all but absent. He noticed her "unusual vivacity and force of spirit" and the "wild exuberance" of her "powerful nature." In her father's eyes, she was a girl "fit for the scuffle of things."[24]

On the day Louisa was born, Bronson thought deeply about what family meant to him. It tied him to the physical world. Without a family, it seemed to him, his inner wants would have become morbid, and his affections would have been "dimmed and perverted." He concluded that few could find happiness if they were "shut out from the Nursery of the Soul."[25] However, the happiness of Louisa's birth almost crumbled into tragedy. Abba did not begin to lactate until Louisa was five days old, and the child's weight declined ominously. Making matters worse, the nurse hired by the family neglected to bathe the baby, so that the meconium was not washed from her body for several days. Nevertheless, even as a newborn, Louisa possessed unusual vitality, which neither hunger nor the threat of infection could fatally diminish. Soon she was thriving, a "sprightly merry little puss—quirking up her mouth and cooing at every sound."[26]

Bronson now commenced a second set of "Observations," dedicated to Louisa. New babies, of course, tend to draw attention away from their older siblings. Whereas he had filled more than 300 pages of observations on Anna during her first year, he wrote only about 120 pages on her in each of the two following years. His record of Louisa reached nearly 300 pages in the first twelve months, though it was palpably different from what he had written about Anna. His writings about Louisa are more the work of a philosopher than a behaviorist. Continually, his observations on Louisa go spiraling off into general reflections on the nature of the spirit. His recording of detail is far less meticulous.

The tone and focus of this set of "Observations" reflect the change that reading *Aids to Reflection* had wrought on Bronson's mind.[27] He was now more inclined to regard the visible human body as the mere outer clothing of the soul. During Louisa's infancy, Bronson was devouring idealist philosophy, particularly Coleridge and Plato. Although his lack of German prevented him from reading Kant, he did his best to absorb his thought through commentaries written in English. It would have been surprising if Bronson's writings about Louisa did not reflect this redoubled enthusiasm about unseen worlds, emphasizing the spirit over the body.

Anna did not take well to the new intruder, who seemed to have displaced her from the center of the family. The attentions once lavished on her were further eroded by the fact that, having lost the support of the late Mr. Haines, the family was compelled to take in boarders. Anna's behavior generally worsened, and she developed a habit of hitting her mother and of striking and scratching her sister. Believing that a twenty-month-old could be successfully reasoned with, Bronson responded by lecturing Anna, firmly but gently, on the impropriety of her conduct. After one such conversation, Bronson left the room. Anna promptly struck Louisa again and ran out after her father, entreating, "Father, punish! Father, punish!" Alcott saw the episode as evidence that Anna's conscience had awakened. It seems more likely that Anna, with a child's need for structure, was asking for a firmer boundary than her father had cared to set. Perhaps, too, she preferred negative attention to none at all. In any event, the scratching and hitting continued.[28]

Meanwhile, the Germantown school was breathing its last. Only eight pupils remained, far short of the twenty that, at a tuition of eighty dollars each, Bronson thought minimally necessary to support the family. William Russell had already decamped, returning to Boston. Alcott, for his part, decided to have one more go at Philadelphia. There, at least, he would have access to the excellent Loganian Library, and Abba might find more stimulating neighbors. Life in a boardinghouse would liberate Abba from the kitchen, enabling her to spend more time with her daughters. A wealthy Philadelphia acquaintance, Roberts Vaux, agreed to sponsor a small school in the city. On April 10, 1833, the Alcotts journeyed back to the City of Brotherly Love.

Unfortunately, Bronson's new school of fifteen pupils failed to inspire him. He had never had more than "limited faith in the moral intelligence of the Philadelphians as efficient patrons of early education." The above-average minds of the city seemed devoted to pecuniary gain. They were interested in "physiology and natural science," not psychology and ethics.[29] Unexpectedly, the move to Philadelphia had cast Alcott's career into the doldrums. It had also thrust his plan for raising the perfect family into chaos. His ideal of child culture required freedom of movement, and his cramped city apartment made such freedom impossible. Having no separate room for his study, a luxury he had enjoyed in Germantown, Alcott found that a "positive want of [his] being" had been taken from him.[30] The effect on Abba and the girls was just as bad. Bronson later recalled:

> [In Philadelphia] our arrangements were such that opportunity for free, uninterrupted thought was almost impossible. My companion suffered from the same cause. We were thrown in *each other's* way. The children were thrown in *our way.* The effect on all was depressing. . . . The space and freedom . . . we ought to have had, was denied us. Intellectual progress was retarded, and health prostrated thereby.[31]

Yet, the closer quarters meant that Anna now slept in her parents' room, and this arrangement improved her temper. However, she was still inclined to act more like a two-year-old than the avatar of divinity Bronson wanted her to become. At times, Bronson confessed, she was almost ungovernable. For her part, Louisa was more willful and wayward than Anna had been at the same age. Prone to fierce tantrums, she would throw herself on the floor and shriek when her desires were thwarted. Bronson's obsessive attention to parental behavior had also begun to undermine Abba's confidence in her motherly skills. "Mr. A. aids me in general principles," she told her brother Samuel, "but nobody can help me in the detail." Too often, Bronson's fastidious criticisms caused her to wonder, "Am I doing what is right? Am I doing too much?"[32] Committed in principle to her husband's theories of noncoercive parenting, she at last found that she could maintain order only by spanking. She even resorted to slapping Anna as a corrective measure. Observing Anna's new experience of what he gently called "power and pain," Bronson surmised that Abba's use of force was only making matters worse.[33]

With his domestic peace unraveling and his suppositions about child rearing being daily refuted, Bronson somehow found a way to press forward with his own education. As biographer Odell Shepard has observed, the Alcott who first made his way to Philadelphia in 1830 could make no claim to being a well-read man. By 1834, when he returned to Boston, he could hold his head up among the most studious people in the city. In addition to Coleridge and Plato, he was reading Pythagoras, Berkeley, Wordsworth, and Carlyle. However, it taxed him to keep up his reading while also running a school and helping to manage a chaotic household. Reluctantly, he finally did something that perhaps speaks better of his instinct for self-preservation than it does for his devotion to his family. For a brief period, he essentially ran away from home.

To be more precise, he split the family up, locating rooms for Abba and the girls back in Germantown while he took an attic room in the city. On weekends, he walked six miles each way to spend time with Abba and the girls. He was struggling to serve three masters at once: the necessity of earning a living; the care and nurture of his children; and the ceaselessly demanding appetite of his mind. Instead of intertwining, these three imperatives were tugging in opposite directions. Bronson had once complained that fathers were typically too remote from their families and "too often so much interested in personal matters that they give little time to the attention of their children."[34] Now he was learning why this was true.

Nevertheless, he was able to persuade himself that the separation was best for everyone. The girls had fresh air and room for exercise. As for Abba, he hoped that a separation would restore the "subtle ties of friendship which are worn away by constant familiarity." For his own part, Alcott greatly enjoyed his chamber in the city, whose window opened toward the rising sun and a stand of trees whose rich foliage trembled softly in the breeze.[35] Absorbing the peace and quiet of the scene, he made fine use of the time he spent alone. Branching into German Romanticism, he delved into Goethe, Schiller, and Herder and came to the conclusion that his ideas of teaching, while they had taken him in the right direction, had not gone far enough. In his 1830 essay on principles and methods, he had seen the juvenile mind as a succession of developing faculties, beginning with the animal nature and ending with the intellect. Coleridge and the great Germans showed him that he had stopped one step short of the end. The crowning achievement of education lay not in the culture of the understanding but in the perfection of the spiritual nature. Through symbolic stories and parables, he would henceforth lead his pupils to an awareness of their own divinity. He now needed only the proper venue to put his theory to the test.

It was now clear that this test would not be made in Philadelphia. Bronson had continued to try out unconventional teaching methods, including requiring his students to keep journals of their intellectual and spiritual progress. Mystified and, perhaps, faintly frightened by these kinds of assignments, parents began to withdraw their children from Alcott's tutelage.[36] By early May 1834, his school had lost forty percent of its enrollment, and further attrition was expected. In an attempt to rescue the venture, he called on all the parents who had disapproved of his methods. Decrying the evils of schools "where cunning . . . was made the usual motive of action" and kindness and forbearance were derided as signs of weakness, he asked them to reconsider. They refused, leaving Alcott to console himself with dire predictions concerning the children snatched from his protective arms. Of one boy removed by his parents, Alcott wrote ominously, "[H]e will doubtless fall a victim to misdirected measures. Temptations will come in his way and he will yield. The good convictions of his mind will die away."[37]

He had been convinced for some time that his best chance for success was in Boston.[38] To help facilitate a return, he appealed to William Ellery Channing, the eminent Unitarian minister who had helped to underwrite Alcott's Common Street School six years earlier. Alcott's desire to found a new school first came to Channing's attention by means of a letter from William Russell, who swore that Alcott would inaugurate a "new era" in education. Channing arranged to meet with Alcott at his summer home in Newport, Rhode Island. The minister's earlier favorable impressions were confirmed. Channing enthusiastically embraced Alcott's proposed return to Boston and promised his financial backing. He promptly set about finding supporters for Alcott's school and had soon assembled an impressive list of interested parties, including Massachusetts Chief Justice Lemuel Shaw and Boston's mayor, Josiah Quincy. Both men not only pledged economic support but also agreed to enroll children in the school. Channing also arranged to send his own daughter Mary. Thus, in September 1834, the Alcott family retraced its steps to Boston. Before the month was out,

Alcott had rented five rooms on the top floor of the Masonic temple on Tremont Street. With men like Channing, Shaw, and Quincy at his back, he could no longer call himself an obscure schoolmaster. Whether this School of Human Culture, known to all as the Temple School, brought its master renown or dishonor, it would do so under broad public scrutiny.

CHAPTER THREE

THE TEMPLE SCHOOL

"I say that the Christian world is anti-Christ."

—A. BRONSON ALCOTT,
Journals, November 1837

WINNING OVER THE LEADING CITIZENS OF BOSTON WAS
not the only brilliant stroke of fortune that attended the
founding of the Temple School. For his teaching assistant,
Alcott secured the services of Channing's former secretary, a young woman
who stood in the first rank of New England minds. Elizabeth Palmer
Peabody was the eldest of a trio of sisters who were to live at the very center of New England education and letters. The middle sister, Mary, became
the wife of the titan of American public education, Horace Mann. The
youngest, Sophia, married the great novelist Nathaniel Hawthorne. Elizabeth, by contrast, chose a grander object than a husband. She was intent
on "educating children morally and spiritually as well as intellectually from
the first." It was, she knew, "the vocation for which [she] had been educated from childhood."[1]

Peabody was barely five feet tall, but people often had the sense that
she was much taller. There was a largeness about her that expressed itself
in the penetrating quality of her thought and the size of her ambitions. At
the age of thirteen, she declared her desire to write her own translation of
the Bible. At seventeen, she opened her first school. She dressed unconven-
tionally and was typically too absorbed by her inner life and practical
objectives to pay careful attention to her appearance. Incurably disheveled,
forever on the move, Peabody was infuriated by those who maintained

that education should be parceled out according to gender. She herself was a potent argument for the capacity of women to excel in disciplines traditionally reserved for men. She eventually became proficient in ten languages, including Latin, Sanskrit, Hebrew, and Chinese.

Bronson thought Peabody blessed with "the most magnificent philosophic imagination" of anyone he knew.[2] Peabody more than returned the compliment. She had first met Bronson in August 1828 and, around that time, favorably reviewed his school in Russell's *American Journal of Education*. "From the first time I ever saw you with a child," she later told him, "I have felt and declared that you had more genius for education than I ever saw, or expected to see."[3] Her opinion of him rose still higher when Bronson showed her the journals of his Philadelphia pupils. She wrote to her sister Mary that she was "*amazed* beyond measure at the composition" and concluded that Alcott had more natural ability as a teacher than anyone else she had ever met. She proclaimed him to be an embodiment of intellectual light and predicted that he would "make an era in society."[4]

At the Temple School, Alcott's magnetic charm with children was indisputable, and his conversational method of teaching worked marvelously at drawing out creative thought. As one of his pupils there was later to remark, "I never knew I had a mind till I came to this school!"[5] Peabody provided much-needed ballast for Alcott's lighter-than-air visions. Unlike him, she had learned a degree of caution from her previous battles with conservatively minded parents and had acquired a fairly accurate idea of when not to press an issue. She also possessed expertise in areas where Alcott was thoroughly unqualified. Alcott had no command of Latin and a precarious grasp of mathematics. Using only his own talents, he could never have mounted a curriculum acceptable to high-ranking Boston families. By contrast, Peabody was a bona fide classical scholar and more than capable with numbers. By rights, if one were to consider only the raw abilities of the two, Alcott probably should have been Peabody's assistant, not the other way round.

However, there was a curious wrinkle in Peabody's personality that led her to prefer the second position. Despite her natural assertiveness, she had perhaps internalized some of her society's bias in favor of male leadership. Although never humble or reluctant to express an opinion, she took satisfaction from locating men of unusual genius and idealism and offering her

*In the spacious upstairs room of Boston's Masonic Temple, Bronson Alcott and
Elizabeth Palmer Peabody attempted to establish the ideal "School of Human Culture."*
(Courtesy of Houghton Library, Harvard University)

services as a faithful Sancho Panza. In attaching herself to Alcott, she not
only accepted a subordinate position beneath her full capacities, but she
volunteered to work for whatever wages Alcott might be capable of dis-
pensing. She thus virtually assured herself of never being paid.

In preparation for opening the school in September 1834, Alcott set
about creating the optimal environment for learning. Bronson had
recently written to Peabody that he found emblems—his word for what we
would call "symbols"—"extremely attractive and instructive to children."
The modern age, he thought, had done education a grave disservice by
stripping truth of its symbolic garments and making instruction "prosaic,
literal, worldly."[6] With these thoughts in mind, he created a schoolroom
rich in symbolic associations. The four-story Masonic Temple that housed
the school was something of a symbol in itself. Completed only two years
earlier, the temple hosted concerts, symposia, and other cultural events. In
the eyes of Bostonians, it represented their city's continuing place in the
vanguard of America's artistic and intellectual progress. The interior space
of the Temple School was cavernous by comparison with that of virtually
any other elementary school of its time. The main room was twenty yards

long, and the high ceiling supplied an apt visual emblem for Alcott's lofty ambitions. Sunlight streamed in through a large, ornate Gothic window, adding literal illumination to the figurative light that the teacher and his assistant daily cast on their young pupils.

As to furnishings and decorations, Alcott spared no expense. Carefully chosen busts of Plato, Socrates, Shakespeare, and Sir Walter Scott stood on pedestals in the four corners of the room. As the students worked at their lessons, a portrait of Dr. Channing looked benignly down on them. Paintings, maps, assorted statuary, and a copious library added still more splendor. Alcott himself sat at an elegant desk, ten feet in length. Knowing that conversation was to be the backbone of his instructional work, he had had the desk specially made in the shape of a crescent so that the children might be encouraged to sit in a semicircle in front of him, an arrangement favorable to verbal exchanges. Perched atop a tall bookshelf behind the instructor's chair was a larger-than-life bas-relief head of Jesus, positioned so that the instructor and the Savior were in the same line of sight. During a discussion of the Gospels, one of the young pupils told the schoolmaster, "I think you are a little like Jesus Christ."[7] Was it the teacher's kindhearted wisdom or the face looming above his head that prompted the comparison?

Alcott's classroom was far from permissive. Indeed, Elizabeth Peabody went so far as to call him "autocratic." However, Alcott was careful to give his authority the appearance of democratic sanction. The first day the school was in session, Alcott asked the children why they had come. "To learn," came the obvious response. Ah, but to learn what? the schoolmaster pursued. This question was a bit harder, so Alcott slowed down. After a series of inquiries, the children agreed that they had come "to learn to feel rightly, to think rightly, and to act rightly." They were there, Alcott implied, not so much to acquire facts as a reflective, useful state of mind. As the children came to this conclusion, Peabody wrote, "Every face was eager and interested."[8]

He also asked whether it might sometimes be necessary to punish them, and he did not proceed until the children admitted the reasonableness of this point. As a matter of both justice and personal honor, Alcott would not punish a child until the offender admitted the fairness of the punishment. During lessons, the children were strictly forbidden to talk among themselves. If this rule were breached by the slightest whisper, he would immediately stop the lesson and wait until order was restored. By pausing in this way, Alcott was, of course, taking time away from the good students as well, but he did this intentionally. He wanted to show everyone that moral transgression inevitably caused the good to suffer along with the bad, and meant for the well-behaved children to realize that one must sometimes bear the burden of another's wrongs, in order to bring them around to a sense of right.

Alcott did not do away with all corporal punishment. Indeed, one visitor to the school expressed regret that Alcott still occasionally resorted to the ruler. However, Alcott inflicted pain only as a regretted last resort, and he always led the offender out of view of the other children to do so, to spare humiliation. Alcott's most remarkable innovation, however, involved a startling reversal of normal practices. One day, when two boys had disobeyed in an especially offensive manner, Alcott reached for his ruler and called the two forward. However, instead of administering the expected blows on the hands, he announced his belief that it was far more terrible to inflict pain than to receive it. He extended his own hand and ordered the boys to strike *him*.

Peabody recorded that "a profound and deep stillness" then descended on the classroom. The two boys protested, but Alcott would not be moved. At last the boys obeyed, but they struck only very lightly. Not satisfied, Alcott demanded whether they thought they deserved no more punishment than that. The boys now struck harder, as Alcott stoically bore their blows. For the boys, however, the act was unbearable. As they brought the ruler down on Alcott's hand, they erupted into tears. A small moral revolution had occurred.9

Curious intellectuals came to the school in a steady stream. The comfortable sofa that Alcott reserved for guests played host to Channing, Emerson, and a formidable Englishwoman named Harriet Martineau, who had come to the United States to write a book, later titled *Society in America*. Invited by Peabody to observe the school, Martineau was one of the few visitors who left unimpressed. She wrote acidly of Alcott, "The master presupposes his little pupils possessed of all truth; and that his business is to bring it out into expression. . . . Large exposures might be made of the mischief this gentleman is doing to his pupils by relaxing their bodies, pampering their imaginations, over-stimulating the consciences of some, and hardening those of others."[10] Martineau's visit had two significant consequences. One was that Abba Alcott, perhaps sensing that Martineau would speak ill of her husband's school, fiercely confronted Peabody and berated her for inviting such a person. Abba's tirade, which was Peabody's first taste of Abba's infamous temper, marked the first rift in her association with the Alcotts. Secondly, Martineau brought back to England news of Alcott's work. The eventual consequences of this publicity were, for the Alcotts, both unexpected and enormously far-reaching.

Peabody, for her part, was elated by the students' progress in command of language and self-control. She secured Bronson's permission to keep a detailed journal of the school's proceedings, which she meant to publish as a testimony to his ideas and methods. Peabody confined her record principally to Alcott's lessons in language, in which the teacher transformed a spelling book into a treatise on practical ethics. "Look" gave rise to a discussion of inward reflections on the soul. "Veil" became a metaphor for the body's concealment of the spirit, and the world itself was presented as a veil for the mind of God. Pausing over the word "nook," Alcott asked his scholars if they had any hidden places in their minds. When some answered that they did, he expressed sorrow, stating that a perfect mind had no need of secret places.[11]

Leading them in this way, Alcott gave his students a rich understanding of the metaphoric power of language. On the subject of symbols and parables, he told Elizabeth Peabody, "I could not teach without [them]. My own mind would suffer, were it not fed upon ideas in this form, and spiritual instruction cannot be imparted so well by any other means."[12] His future friend Emerson was soon to offer similar ideas in his great book *Nature,* which asserts that "the use of the outer creation [is] to give us language for the beings and changes of the inward creation. Every word which is used to express a moral or intellectual fact . . . is found to be borrowed from some material appearance."[13] Not only did Alcott anticipate Emerson's doctrine by two years, but he made it comprehensible to young children.

During the early months of the Temple School's existence, in late October 1834, Bronson resumed his diaries on Anna and Louisa, now combining their experiences in a single record, "Observations on the Spiritual Nurture of My Children." Writing for only four weeks, he created a 260-page manuscript. After a monthlong hiatus, Bronson then added another

300 pages of observations, begun in January 1835, which he titled "Researches on Childhood." Bound together into a single volume, the two manuscripts combine factual impressions with speculations about the best ways to improve the children's behavior, supplemented as always by lengthy discourses on the nature of the human spirit. Never published, these observations are arguably Bronson's greatest achievement in documenting child development.

It has often been assumed that Bronson Alcott was an emotionally distant parent, more absorbed with philosophical abstraction than with the unglamorous work of raising children. A reading of Alcott's own records from these months, however, tells a different story. As much as his work at the Temple School would permit him, Alcott was wholly immersed in the spiritual growth of his daughters. It troubled him that he could not be with the children around the clock. When he was obliged to rely on Abba's reports of what Anna and Louisa had done in his absence, he felt that his records lost their freshness and "force of delineation."[14] He loved to walk with them, answering their questions and pointing out "objects calculated to excite pleasing and improving trains of thought."[15] Bronson also welcomed Anna and Louisa into his study. Sometimes he paused from his researches and meditations to trace the outlines of their hands or feet into his notebooks. Once, he helped them build an elaborate tower out of books, then carefully sketched it into his notes. He tucked them into bed at night, seldom leaving them without "something to make us laugh," as his daughters put it. It was rare, however, for him to tell them anything for the mere sake of being funny. "The humorous, or the ludicrous, merely" held little value for him unless it was connected with "something highly ideal."[16] Bronson Alcott never understood the value of humor, either as a buffer against the shocks of life or as a teaching tool.

Alcott could not express too strongly the importance of parental guidance in the awesome task of forming the juvenile mind. The influence of the parent must be supreme, and it was impossible to delegate. He was equally clear as to the one quality he thought necessary for doing this work well: "Love! Love! Includes both the art, and the results—the philosophy and the practice; and whosoever *loveth,* as becometh a parent, hath an art of Celestial Tuition."[17] If anything, Alcott's approach erred on the side of involvement, not that of aloofness, as when he postulated:

The world of the child should be the creation of the parents' theory—the offspring of an enlightened mind, and a feeling heart, and of this world the parent should be the sole director. . . . The parent, like the divinity, should exert a special oversight over all the relations of the sphere in which he moves: he should be the Providence that fills, sustains, and protects, every member of his domestic creation.[18]

In the care of Anna and Louisa, Bronson found pleasure and sacred duty hand in hand. Between the Temple School and his less visible work at home, he had found two occupations that filled him with interest and joy.

Nevertheless, there were frustrations in the Alcott nursery. One of the greatest came from Alcott's sense that, although his children were playing and learning directly under his eyes, the thing that he most wanted to see remained tantalizingly invisible. He wanted to observe his daughters with the eyes of both a parent and a scientist. He was convinced that there was a secret to the inner growth of children; and he had hoped that he might be the first to solve the riddle. He did not, of course, know precisely what he was looking for. He only knew, to his chronic disappointment, that he was not finding it. The soul remained inscrutable.

How little of the spirit's life *enacts* itself on the exterior scene, through the instrumentality and media of the sense! . . . I look on these *spirits* that daily ply their energies within these bodies of flesh—I behold the myriad changes of the *countenance,* through which the inner life *configurates* itself—I watch the ever-varying *pantomime* of the out-going will. . . . And how *little* do I learn from all this toil of the spirit!![19]

Alcott found himself playing a game of psychological hide-and-seek, as the elfin souls of his children darted and fluttered before his eyes and then, with an innocent giggle, vanished from view. He was convinced that all children, not merely his own, were metaphysical, but his vision stopped at the blank wall of the flesh.

With some regret, too, he had to concede that innate spiritual qualities and a carefully controlled home environment were not the sole ingredients in shaping character. Most significantly, he found he had underestimated the influence of his children's physical condition on their emotional development. Anna, he discovered, was not as robust as Louisa, who had grown rapidly and was now routinely prevailing in their nursery-room clashes.

Also, during the period of her father's "Observations," Anna was recovering from a severe foot sprain, and her injury had made her all the more passive. Bronson feared that Anna would fall into "the evils of indolence, imbecility of purpose, [and] extreme susceptibility of sentiment." He saw her good qualities as "the virtues . . . of a sickly growth," lacking "the sturdy, energetic, productive life that tells of maturity and perfection."[20] He noted in particular that Anna could not bear criticism. Fearful of discipline and desperate to maintain the good opinion of her parents, Anna would emphatically deny having done wrong even when her fault was obvious. In his records, Bronson had stern words for what he called Anna's "moral cowardice," but he ascribed this failing to her physical weakness and believed that punishing her would only weaken her further. Using the generic masculine pronoun, Bronson wrote out a spiritual prescription for such a child:

> He needs encouragement, rather than reproof—he should be raised from the dominion of his physical being, made strong by repeated trial, till fear of pain—mere animal pain, is removed; and hope, and faith, assume the rule of his spirit.[21]

While he did not refrain from pointing out Anna's shortcomings, Bronson was always careful not to crush her fragile feelings. He was soon pleased to report that, when properly addressed, Anna was perfectly docile and obedient.[22]

Louisa was a more difficult case. Bronson felt a natural resonance with Anna's nature. Being of a "more meditative cast" than her sister, Anna dwelt on sentiments, which she clothed "in imaginative drapings" and viewed "in the beautiful ideals of her own fancy."[23] Louisa, by contrast, cared more about things than concepts and ideals. Moreover, in vibrant contrast to Anna's physical and emotional passivity, Louisa possessed what Bronson called "a high and excessive flow of the animal nature," a quality that, he believed, made her liable to develop all the faults related to the will: "ferocity, ungovernable energy, [and] passionate obstinacy."[24]

Bronson saw Louisa as a younger version of her mother. Reflecting on Abba and Louisa, Bronson wrote, "They are more alike: the elements of their beings are similar: the *will* is the predominating power."[25] Before long, Bronson came to regard Anna and Louisa as opposites, and his observations of them became a sustained study in contrast. If, in Bronson's view, Anna's inclinations were epic, then Louisa's were fundamentally dramatic.

Whereas Anna shared her father's preference for vegetables, Louisa relished animal food—an appetite that Bronson saw as both a cause and effect of her "untameable spirit."[26] Anna inclined toward theorizing and creativity; Louisa, intent solely on practice, continually demolished Anna's fantasies— and belongings—with the rude force of a Hun. "One builds; the other demolishes," Bronson observed, "and between the struggle of contrary forces, their tranquility is disturbed."[27]

Bronson desperately wanted to cure Louisa's seemingly innate violence. In his records, he fretted endlessly over her fierce will and volcanic temper. He anxiously observed:

> There is a self-corroding nature—a spirit not yet conformed to the con-
> ditions of enjoyment. She follows her impulses, and these are often
> against the stream of her spirit's joy. Passion rages within; and *Strife*
> enacteth itself without. . . . The will has gathered around itself a breast-
> work of *Inclinations,* and bids defiance to every attack that ventures
> against its purpose. She retreats within the citadel of these, and braves
> every assault—yielding, if compelled, with sullen submission, or break-
> ing out in querulous complainings.[28]

Perhaps most damning in her father's eyes, though hardly unusual in a two-year-old child, was Louisa's utter immersion in her own wants and impulses. The very touchstone of Bronson Alcott's moral creed was self-surrender. It was therefore with grave disappointment that he wrote of Louisa, "Self-sacrifice is an act beyond her present apprehension; she must be led to it, by symbols in actual life—through *punishment* and *reward*."[29] Bronson valued self-denial to the point of self-injury. This kind of discipline, of course, was beyond his daughter's comprehension, and her instinctive pursuit of pleasure was to lead Bronson for many years to view Louisa as the most selfish of his children.

However, Bronson's native element was gentleness and reason, and the tools he thought of using against a stormy temper felt awkward in his hands. No matter how violently Louisa fought against him, Bronson refused to use the rod on her. And yet, when all else failed, he did resort to spanking, even though he knew that every blow he directed at her bottom was a ringing slap against his own theories of child rearing.[30] The spankings did not seem to work anyway. When possible, Bronson continued his practice of letting the punishment fit the crime. If, for example, Louisa threw away her food and treated Anna unkindly, he would send her to bed without supper and without the customary bedtime story and good-night kiss, explaining that children who misused their food or failed to love their sisters must be denied access to them. On one occasion, when Louisa had pinched Anna and pulled her hair, Bronson called Louisa to him and said, "Anna says that you took hold of her hair *so,*" and pulled her hair. He then continued, "And, that you pinched her cheek *so.*" After braving the pain for a moment, Louisa's fortitude gave way, and she admitted, "Father, I was naughty to hurt Anna so."[31] If Louisa could not comprehend the pain she gave to others, then she must experience it herself.

Much of Louisa's misbehavior probably stemmed from sibling rivalry, and when Anna's foot sprain made it harder for her to stand her ground, Louisa pressed her advantage. Bronson wrote, "Anna seems to fear her sister's approaches; and so alarming has she become to her, that some discipline will be necessary to reduce Louisa to tameness."[32] The best solution, he discovered, was to keep the sisters apart for a portion of the day. Bronson started taking Anna with him to the Temple School during the day and left Louisa at home with Abba. Yet this plan had a significant drawback, since each child now moved more exclusively under the influence of the parent to whom she was already closer. By taking Anna with him to school and leaving Louisa behind, Bronson purchased some domestic peace, but only at the cost of reaffirming that Anna was his child and Louisa was her mother's. With time, these attachments grew stronger. Once solidified, they never entirely changed.

Although he was most concerned with curbing Louisa's excesses of temper and will, Bronson was by no means indifferent to her admirable qualities. He felt that Louisa's understanding was more acute and her ability to imitate was better than her sister's.[33] He took early notice of the verve with which she acted out the dramas of the stories he read to her. He recorded with pride her "rapid progress in spoken language" and her extensive, choice vocabulary.[34] He also wrote of her "sturdiness of purpose," her "deep and affluent nature," and the exuberance of her powerful character.[35] He firmly believed that his dark daughter possessed "noble elements," and he only prayed that he might be able to tame and direct those elements to an equally noble purpose.[36]

What is most remarkable in all of this is the aptness of Bronson's perceptions. He saw in his infant daughter the salient character traits by which people came to know the adult Louisa May Alcott: a powerful will; a temper that she labored to control; an innate flair for the dramatic; and, of course, a superb command of language. Why did her father's early observations of her show such prophetic accuracy? It was certainly due in part to Bronson's gifts of perception and the earnestness with which he strove to see things in their right proportions. Yet one may perhaps argue that Bronson's prophecies were also self-fulfilling. Louisa was certainly made to know what her parents thought of her. Being continually told that she was willful, temperamental, and gifted in all things verbal, she probably became all the more so. In describing his daughter, Bronson also cast her more firmly in the mold in which she had begun.

Bronson seems never to have thought much about the possible effects of the exaggerated self-consciousness that he was instilling in his children. It seems impossible to deny, however, that, by ceaselessly calling on Louisa and her sisters to inspect their motives and to compare their conduct to a standard of saintly perfection, Bronson conferred on them a deeply mixed blessing. On the one hand, he shaped them into acutely thoughtful, generous beings whose lives were filled with acts of kindness and charity. On the other, he imposed a regimen of moral self-criticism that only a rare person, adult or child, could assume without flinching.

Although life under the Alcott roof was sometimes turbulent, Bronson remained more or less elated with fatherhood. In January 1835, while he was recording his "Researches," he told his own journal, "I am more interested in the domestic and parental relations than I have been at any former period. Life is fuller of serene joy and steady purpose. I am happier, have more of the faith that reposes on Providence and the love that binds me to human nature, more of the assurance of progression, than I have been wont to enjoy." He added that his children were "objects of great delight" and the charm of his domestic life, moving before him "in the majestic dignity of human nature." He was certain that, the more he shared his life with theirs, the more he saw that was worthy of reverence, the better he understood the words of the Gospel, "Of such is the Kingdom of Heaven."[37]

The summer of 1835 was extraordinary in every possible respect. A series of happy events began on June 24, when another daughter was born. In gratitude to his assistant, Alcott named the baby Elizabeth Peabody Alcott—the only one of his children not named after a blood relative. Elizabeth was fairer than her elder sisters and, apparently from the outset, was the model of serenity that Bronson had vainly hoped Anna and Louisa would be. Bronson immediately began a chronicle of Lizzie's life, this time with the clear ambition of publishing his findings. No longer content with mundane titles, he gave this work the poetic name of "Psyche, or, The Breath of Childhood." His goal this time was to give "some representation to the inner life as it is enacted in the spirit of childhood." Believing now that the spiritual kingdom of the soul could not be approached through mere external facts, he proposed to "enter within and find of what spiritual laws these phenomena are the exponents and signs."[38] With naive eagerness, he plunged into his impossible task.

Simultaneously, the Temple School continued to gain momentum. In July, only weeks after the birth of her namesake, Elizabeth Peabody published her *Record of a School*, to a radiant critical reception. Reviewers called the book "strikingly original" and "one of the most interesting books" that had passed beneath their notice. The *Portland Magazine* ventured to call Alcott "one of the best men that ever drew the breath of life." The *Eastern Magazine* averred "We are in love with this little volume," and the *Western Messenger* proclaimed "There is not a man or woman in our land, but may rise wiser and better" from having read Peabody's *Record*.[39] *Record of a School* was the fairest fruit of a brilliant partnership, reaching a popular audience while setting forth an original vision of education and the life of the spirit. Peabody even dared to hope that the book's sales might supply a financial cushion for herself and her sisters—a dream that sadly evaporated when a warehouse fire destroyed more than half the book's first printing. Nevertheless, without precisely meaning to, Bronson Alcott and Elizabeth Palmer Peabody had combined to produce the first classic of American transcendentalism.

Alcott was now a significant figure among Boston's intelligentsia. It was possible for him to meet almost whomever he wished, and he especially wanted to meet two men. The first was a stocky, gray-eyed Unitarian minister named Frederic Henry Hedge. A man of superior intellect, Hedge had graduated from Harvard after spending his adolescence at a German *Gymnasium*. Alcott admired Hedge's article on Coleridge in the *Christian*

Examiner, one of the first publications to herald the rise of transcendental philosophy. Likening its effect to that of inhaling "an exhilarating gas," Hedge offered the transcendental intoxicant to those with "minds that seek with faith and hope a solution of questions which [materialism] meddles not with, questions which relate to spirit and form. Substance and life, free will and fate."[40] In later years, Hedge remained one of the handful of persons whom Alcott honored with the title "Living Men . . . the free men and the brave, by whom great principles are to be honored among us."[41] Hedge, however, was cooler in his assessment of Alcott. The portly minister placed too much value on formal academic training and logical rigor to regard Bronson as anything more than an exceptionally gifted amateur.

By contrast, Bronson's meeting with the second man on his list was to be a pivotal moment in both his career and personal life. With Elizabeth Peabody's assistance, he secured an interview with a former Unitarian minister whose preaching he had once admired—a thin, six-foot-tall man whose blue eyes could either assure one of their possessor's infinite kindness or could call one to attention "like the reveille of a trumpet."[42] This second man was Ralph Waldo Emerson.

Recently turned thirty-two, Emerson had not yet published a word. Nevertheless, he had been preparing himself for an unusual career. He had been born in 1803 into a minister's family, which eventually counted eight children. Of these, a quintet of brothers lived to adulthood. Ralph, the second oldest of the five, preferred to be called Waldo. When he was not yet eight, his father died, leaving his widow scant means for raising the family. By carefully scrimping and taking in boarders, however, Ruth Emerson managed to send four of her sons to Harvard. Unlike his brothers William, Edward, and Charles Emerson, who all became lawyers, Waldo continued a long-standing family tradition by entering the ministry.[43] In 1829, the same year he became the junior pastor of Boston's Second Church, Emerson married his first wife, Ellen Tucker, with the knowledge that his bride had tuberculosis and was unlikely to live long. Eighteen months after they married, she was dead.

The following year, Emerson discovered that he no longer believed in the sacrament of Communion; if he were to find oneness with God, he would do so by seeking a higher, more spiritual relation to divinity. Having concluded that "Religion in the mind is not credulity and in the prac-

Ralph Waldo Emerson found Bronson Alcott
both "a God-made priest" and a "tedious archangel."
Their friendship lasted more than forty-five years.
(Courtesy of the Louisa May Alcott Memorial Association)

tice is not forms," Emerson resigned from the ministry in September 1832.[44] Three months later, seeking distance from death and professional disappointment, he sailed for Europe. His travels eventually led him to England, where he met Coleridge, Wordsworth, John Stuart Mill, and, most importantly for him, Thomas Carlyle, with whom he began a lifelong friendship. Emerson returned to Boston in October 1833, soon to be fired with a new confidence that, in the contemplation of nature, man could find a fit knowledge of himself and of God. "Nature is a language and every new fact one learns is a new world," he wrote. "I wish to learn this language."[45]

Thanks to the inheritance left him by his first wife, Emerson commanded a modest income of twelve hundred dollars a year, which he supplemented by lecturing. In the late summer 1835, he married Lidian Jackson and purchased the house in Concord where he was to live for the rest of his life. The preceding February, in the same building that held the Temple School, Alcott had heard Emerson lecture on "The Character of Michelangelo." "Few men among us," Alcott wrote afterward, "take nobler views of the mission, powers, and destinies of man than Mr. E."[46] However, he had to wait until July to make Emerson's acquaintance. He was not disappointed.

The meeting took place on a busy evening in the Alcott family's rented rooms at 3 Somerset Court. Alcott received a number of visitors that evening, including Abba's friend the famous novelist and reformer Lydia Maria Child. Emerson, for his part, brought along his favorite brother, Charles, and his aunt, Mary Moody Emerson, a woman of sharp wit and sprightly perceptions who exerted profound influence on her nephew's thinking. When Emerson departed, Alcott felt that he had been in the presence of a "revelation of the divine spirit."[47] Mary Moody Emerson was "dazzled" by Alcott's ideas, and her nephew Waldo promptly hailed him as "a wise man, simple, superior to display."[48]

In October, Emerson welcomed Alcott to Concord and showed him the white, L-shaped home into which he and Lidian had moved only five weeks earlier. The house boasted a spacious front room, looking out on the intersection of the two main roads that led eastward from Concord. Emerson made this room his study, and it was likely here that the two men passed a Saturday evening and the following Sunday discoursing on "various interesting topics of an intellectual and spiritual character." Although he thought that Emerson's fine literary taste sometimes interfered with his metaphysical consciousness, Alcott was delighted to find that, on most subjects, they shared a "striking conformity of taste and opinion." Emerson proudly showed Alcott his portrait of Carlyle, whom Emerson considered his ideal. Alcott also spoke again with Charles Emerson and marveled at the fact that both brothers were scholarly, "and yet the man is not lost in the scholar." Making Lidian Emerson's acquaintance crowned the weekend; Alcott thought the couple represented nothing less than "a new idea of life."[49] A powerful bond had been formed.

Emerson showed the full measure of his respect for his new friend when Harvard College celebrated its Phi Beta Kappa day. Emerson brought Alcott with him to mark the occasion. It was the latter's first visit to the campus. As the members of the Phi Beta Kappa society formed into lines for their procession into the college chapel, Alcott held back, thinking it best to enter only after the formally anointed scholars had found their seats. Guessing Alcott's sense of exclusion, Emerson took him by the arm.

"We will not mince matters," he told his guest lightly. "You are a member by right of genius." To Alcott's surprise and gratitude, Emerson guided him to a seat near the orator.[50]

Fortunately for Alcott, the thinkers who now surrounded him were, for Harvard men, unusually skeptical of the necessity of formal education. Many of them, Emerson included, had faint praise for the sterile formality of university life, holding that "Colleges and books only copy the language which the field and the work-yard made."[51] Revering the notion of a natural, intuitive genius, they received Alcott into their midst; he was the closest person to this ideal that they had ever seen. Still, the standard-bearers of the transcendentalist movement were not without their prejudices. When, in 1836, Hedge, Emerson, and a group of like thinkers were preparing to form the intellectual society eventually known as the Transcendental Club, a number of them, Hedge included, wanted to restrict membership to ministers and former ministers, a stipulation that would have excluded Alcott. For one of the first of many times, Emerson came to Alcott's aid, asserting, "You must admit Mr. Alcott over the professional limits, for he is a God-made priest."[52]

In truth, Alcott probably could have benefited from a circle of friends that demanded more in the way of broad influence and eclectic training. Even Alcott's staunchest defenders, like his early biographer Odell Shepard, confess that he read not to absorb new ideas but to be confirmed in what he already knew.[53] He had no ability whatever to set aside his own personality and enter into the lives and situations of others.[54] In the same letter in which he praised Alcott as a "God-made priest," Emerson admitted his friend's refusal to place himself anywhere other than the center of the universe. Alcott, Emerson observed, was "so resolute to force all thought & things to become rays from his centre, that, for the most part, they come."[55] Yet Emerson also realized that Alcott's confidence in his own authority was blinding him to a great deal of truth and beauty. For Shakespeare's plays and any other art that one could truly enjoy only by setting aside one's ego, Alcott had no use. All too enthusiastically, he embodied Emerson's maxim, "Trust thyself."

Around this time, Louisa was starting to show signs of overconfidence as well. One day, she came uncomfortably close to reducing the trio of Alcott sisters to a twosome. On a visit to the Frog Pond on Boston Common, Louisa rolled her hoop too near to the water's edge and fell in. Seized by panic as the waters closed over her, she felt a pair of hands grasp her. A young boy had seen her going under, and he reached her in time to pull her to safety. Remembering the event more than fifty years later, Louisa deemed only one feature of her rescuer worth recording: the boy was black. His deed left a lifelong impression. Louisa became, as she remembered, "a friend to the colored race then and there." In Abba's words, Louisa became "an abolitionist at the age of three."[56]

Not all of her earliest permanent memories concerned such dire moments. Despite her closeness to Abba, one of her first recollections was of building towers and bridges out of the great tomes in her father's library. Louisa also showed a precocious interest in looking *into* the books. She mulled over the pictures, pretended to read the pages, and scribbled in their margins. Her activities, she later observed, were an apt foreshadowing of her life to come: a life in which books were her most constant comfort; in which building castles—out of air, at least—never failed to entertain her; and in which scribbling became "a most profitable diversion."[57]

While Bronson and Abba admonished their girls to resist every selfish, worldly impulse, they encouraged them to indulge every creative and intellectual one. Even as she entered adulthood, their later-born daughter May, who showed artistic talent, would be allowed to draw on her bedroom walls. However, mere bodily appetites were rigorously checked. When Louisa was not yet three, Bronson decided to reenact the Fall of Man in the children's nursery. Humbly taking upon himself the role of God, he placed an apple atop his daughters' wardrobe and explained that the fruit belonged to him. After prompting them to agree that it was wrong for "little girls to take things [from] their fathers or mothers," he left the room. When he came back, he found that Anna and Louisa had acted perfectly their unsuspected roles as Adam and Eve. Only the core of the apple remained. Louisa, Anna reported, had gotten to the apple first. "I told her she must not," said Anna, "but she did, and then we eat some of it." Anna repented; Louisa seemed less sorry. The next day, Bronson left Louisa alone in the nursery with a second forbidden apple. Abba watched unseen as Louisa picked up the object of her desire and put it down several times, saying, "No. No, father's. Me not take father's apple. Naughty! Naughty!" Finally, she lost the struggle. Asked to explain the presence of another apple core, she explained, "Me could not help it! Me *must* have it!"[58]

At a birthday party, held jointly for her and her father at the Temple School, Louisa endured another lesson in self-denial. Bedecked with a crown of flowers, Louisa had been told to pass out cake to the other children. Discovering that there was one piece too few, Louisa held on tightly to the last plate. Having watched the tragedy unfold, Abba stepped forward. "It is always better to give away than to keep the nice things," she said. "I know my Louy will not let the little friend go without." Louisa handed over "the dear plummy cake" and received a kiss from her mother.[59] It was but one of the countless times in her childhood when the love of a family member was the only consolation for an unfilled stomach.

Her father, however, was finding consolations aplenty. Alcott gave Emerson his 1835 journal and his manuscript of "Psyche." Emerson sought out Alcott's opinions on his own work, a long essay called "Nature." They were mutually enthusiastic, and it seemed for a while as if, almost simultaneously, the two works might emerge as complementary pillars of the new New England philosophy, Emerson's work exploring the external world and Alcott's revealing the inner.

Alcott called Emerson's manuscript "a beautiful work," evincing a "high intellectual character." He delighted in Emerson's demonstration that the physical world is an emblem of the soul and that the mind "animates and fills the earth." He also saw his own influence in the book. He observed, "Mr. E. adverts, indirectly to my 'Psyche,' now in his hands, in the work."[60] In the last chapter of his essay, Emerson included a long passage that he claimed to have received from an anonymous "Orphic poet."[61] The fact that, a few years later, Alcott published a collection of "Orphic Sayings" in Emerson's magazine, *The Dial,* makes it still more likely that Alcott was Emerson's Orpheus.

Emerson's *Nature* remains the quintessential statement of transcendentalism. Alcott's "Psyche," however, has never been published. Emerson thought that the work contained some splendid passages and that his friend's work sometimes reflected "the rare power to awaken the highest faculties, to awaken the apprehension of the Absolute." However, he thought it was too long a book for one idea and that Alcott's style was labored and pedantic. Alcott had a regrettable fondness for verbs ending in "eth." He liked using vague, prophetic-sounding words like "mirror forth," "shape forth," and "image" just when a concrete phrasing was desperately needed.[62] When he wrote in his journals, Alcott's language was often graceful and cogent. He could also teach and speak with genius. Yet when he tried to write for an audience, his powers abruptly fled.

Emerson urged Alcott not to give up on "Psyche," counseling him instead not to "let it sleep or stop a day."[63] His school a brilliant success, and his manuscripts capturing the attention of some of America's best minds, there seemed no reason why Bronson Alcott should not proceed from triumph to triumph. Instead, the very confidence that had carried Alcott so high was about to induce errors of hubris that would soon lead to catastrophe.

Alcott's pride first became visible in the disdain he began to show toward the efforts of those who were helping to raise his children. The various maids hired to assist Abba never met with his approval, and his disparagements in his journals of parents who delegated the care of their children became frequent. Far more disturbing to the family, however, was the critical eye that Bronson turned toward the parenting skills of Abba. Apart from Bronson's strict and fastidious judgments, there is little evidence that Abba was anything less than a loving and able mother, as well as a firm supporter of her husband's theories. Over the coming decades, events would attest to her fierce devotion to her children. Yet Bronson's journals give her scant praise. When reflecting on what he called "the inadequacy of maternal culture" in his home, Bronson found particular fault with Abba's reluctance to discipline the girls.[64] Abba had, he felt, foresworn "positive discipline," leaving all matters of punishment to him. He was convinced that if he had supervised the children continually, no corporal punishment would ever have been necessary.[65] To stop the flood of animal nature, he wrote, "must be the work of great skill. . . . [T]heir strength and impetuosity must be guided and tamed by the hand of genius alone."[66] Although he occasionally admitted that Abba's influence was loving and beautiful, it was clear to him that only one parent under his roof possessed such genius.[67]

Alcott's stubborn sense of authority cost him much more dearly in his relationship with Elizabeth Peabody. Initially, all was well between them. Perhaps feeling awkward for having failed to pay her for her services, Alcott invited his assistant to move in with his family. Little dreaming that increased proximity could ever produce ill feeling between her and the employer she so greatly worshipped, Peabody accepted. She initially relished her comfortable room with its handsome fireplace and view of Dorchester Heights. As she took her meals at the Alcotts' table and played with her infant namesake, she gloried in the privileged position she enjoyed within this family that seemed to her the pinnacle of enlightenment.

Soon, however, her increased familiarity with her employer produced friction. She found that Bronson could barely tolerate dissent of any kind. A seemingly trivial dispute with him at dinner over the merits of Sylvester Graham, inventor of the graham cracker, led to a nasty quarrel. Peabody left the table wondering at Bronson's reflexive distaste for any mainstream position, and she started to suspect that Alcott's avowed love of reform was only a mask for envy and misanthropy. Alcott, for his part, was starting to find his friend "offensively assertive." Their partnership was beginning to fragment.[68]

But it was at the Temple School itself that Alcott's pride was setting the stage for his most poignant tragedy. Bronson had begun to carry the religious content of his instruction to a bold new level. In the spring term of 1836, Alcott added a weekly session of conversations with the schoolchildren, dealing with the biblical accounts of the life of Jesus. These discussions were limited to two hours every Wednesday morning, but Alcott soon came to regard them as the most noteworthy business of the school. As she had done in preparation for *Record of a School,* Elizabeth Peabody commenced a partial transcript of these conversations. Emboldened by the success of the previous book, Bronson thought that a volume of these conversations would be the ideal sequel, establishing him as a wise and original commentator on the life and teachings of Christ. In addition, the book would help to prove his dearly held postulate that divine truth was best approached through the thoughts and feelings of the very young.

The new project offered charming possibilities. Alcott had already shown his power to elicit moral gems from the mouths of babes. He would now have the chance to shine the light of infant wisdom on the highest mysteries that he knew. By calling forth the innocent voices of children, he might impart to the word of God a purer, sweeter expression than it had ever known. But there were problems almost from the beginning. Whereas in *Record of a School,* Bronson had trusted Elizabeth Peabody and the children to speak for themselves, he wanted this book to convey a precise, predetermined tone and message. Subverting the premise of his own project,

Bronson preferred for the children to express *his* formulations, rather than their own. Thus, as Peabody transcribed her notes, Bronson sometimes hovered nearby, ready to reword passages that did not suit his vision. Simultaneously, however, Bronson also desired the appearance of placing the children in the foreground. Breaking with Peabody's practice in *Record of a School,* where anonymity had been preserved, he wanted to publish the names of his pupils alongside their statements. Over her staunch objection, he had his way.

In the grace with which they mingled simplicity and profundity, in the gentle reverence with which he and his students shared their ideas of God and Christ, Bronson's *Conversations with Children on the Gospels* may well be his most exquisite written work. Inherent in all of them is Alcott's respect for the mental strivings of the children. Although his own views regarding the Gospels are clearly visible, the conversations seek as much as possible to question rather than assert, to draw an idea out instead of forcing one in. He told his class, "I have often been taught by what very small children have said; and astonished at their answers. . . . Has truth any age? . . . Is it not immortal? Truth is old . . . and Truth is young. . . . All wisdom is not in grown-up people."[69] Speaking about the story of the young Jesus in the temple, he made the following suggestion:

> Children are often about their father's business and parents are so much interested in their own, that they do not know it. . . . When fathers keep their children at work and give them no education, yet all the time they can obtain, the children devote to their own improvement—is not that "the Father's" business? Very often children are absorbed in what interests them, and their parents reprove them, and yet they may be about their "Father's business." And you should not roughly interrupt it.[70]

When morality demanded it, Bronson could be firm. For instance, when one child blamed the Jewish people for the death of Christ, Bronson immediately denounced the notion as "a wicked prejudice," to which the children added, evidently en masse, "There are no right prejudices."[71] In the main, he was open-minded and Socratic. On occasion, Bronson's tactics frustrated his pupils; they demanded an answer, and he offered only a question. In exasperation, one of the children burst out, "I cannot tell what you think; you sometimes talk on one side, and sometimes on the other. What do you think?" Alcott replied, "I prefer not to reply to such questions, because I do not wish to influence your opinions by mine. I teach what every pure person believes."[72] More than anything, he explained, he was teaching his pupils to know themselves, and this was the most important knowledge.

Nevertheless, Alcott's new manuscript made Peabody nervous. Not only did she feel that Alcott was fatally compromising the honesty of the book by revising her transcriptions, but she thought he was unfairly manipulating his pupils by proposing to identify them. It troubled her as well that she now sensed an air of smug superiority about her employer, which she feared the children might be absorbing as well. What Benjamin Franklin had once called a "foppery in morals," she now urged her partner to avoid.[73]

At the suggestion that he was straying into error, Alcott bristled. Peabody formed the distinct impression that the schoolmaster had no interest in any external influence, and like Emerson, she began to lament his arrogance. "It seems no part of his plan," she wrote, "to search the thoughts and views of other minds in any faith that they will help his own. . . . [H]e rather avoids than seeks any communication with persons who differ from himself."[74] In June 1836, when Peabody took a leave of absence to visit friends in Lowell, her younger sister Sophia moved in with the Alcotts and took over the transcription of the schoolroom conversations. Less circumspect than Elizabeth, Sophia rapturously recorded passages of dialogue that Elizabeth would surely have prudently excised. Thus Elizabeth's editorial touch was missing when it was needed most—when Bronson decided to use the story of the Virgin Mary as an opportunity to introduce his students to the mysteries of birth. When Elizabeth Peabody read the transcript of this conversation and furthermore discovered that one of the children had observed that babies are made out of "the naughtiness . . . of other people," she was aghast.

Alcott's intentions were pure. Although he did raise issues like conception and circumcision that a more prudent teacher would have left undisturbed, he referred to them only in a deeply respectful manner. When discussing birth with the children, he explained, "God draws a veil over these sacred events, and they ought never to be thought of except with reverence."[75] Declaring that every birth was as sacred as that of Jesus, Alcott began his discussion by asking whether any of the children had heard disagreeable or vulgar things about birth. He did not proceed before expressing the hope that none present would ever violate the sacredness of the subject.

Alcott's discussions of the scriptural passages were in strict keeping with his general philosophy of interpretation. Alcott regarded every aspect of the physical world as a spiritual symbol. If he were to be consistent in this view, then even (perhaps especially) the most intimate facts of life must have their metaphysical lessons to teach. When he conversed with the children about circumcision, he asked them not about the physical ritual but rather, "Was there any spiritual meaning in it?" He used the episode as an emblem of self-sacrifice and a means of illustrating "that pain is of no consequence, if it makes us better."[76]

Alcott's commentary on birth had a similar object. Indeed, the passage from the *Conversations* that lay at the heart of the ensuing scandal was an attempt, not to lead the children into contemplation of sexuality, but to unveil the spiritual truth that Alcott assumed to exist beneath every physical fact:

> The physiological facts, sometimes referred to, are only a sign of the spiritual birth. You have seen the rose opening from the seed with the assistance of the atmosphere; this is the birth of the rose. It typifies the bringing forth of the spirit, by pain, and labor, and patience. Edward B. [a boy in the class], it seems, has some profane notions of birth, connected with some physiological facts; but they are corrected here.[77]

Apart from this passage, most of the stir destined to arise from the *Conversations* resulted from the line that Elizabeth Peabody wanted to excise: the comment by one of Alcott's most insightful pupils, six-year-old Josiah Quincy, about the naughtiness of other people. Asked by Alcott to share his understanding of birth, Josiah had replied:

> It is to take up the body from the earth. The spirit comes from heaven, and takes up the naughtiness out of other people, which makes other people better. And these naughtinesses put together the body for the child; but the spirit is the best part of it.[78]

The hostile members of Alcott's readership were to seize on the phrase "naughtiness . . . of other people" as if they had found decisive evidence.

Surely, they supposed, if Alcott's pupils had fixed their minds on naughtiness, then the schoolmaster had put it there, and certainly naughtiness could mean nothing other than sex. Alcott, far more brazenly than Socrates in ancient times, was corrupting the youth of the American Athens.

Yet Josiah Quincy's remarks had nothing to do with sexual intercourse. Rather, he was striving to create some mythology to explain how an infant's spirit, which he had been led to think of as perfect, came to be housed in an imperfect, sinful body. His explanation, quite logical in view of the Christian teaching that Jesus took upon himself the sins of the world, was that each originally blameless infant spirit draws into itself at birth some of the "naughtiness" of the human race, thus partly cleansing the surrounding world of its evil. This evil, Josiah reasoned, must be the stuff from which bodies were formed. The proper minds of Boston, in their prurient reading of Josiah's speculations, showed a good deal more naughtiness than either the boy or his questioner had in mind.

Yet Peabody rightly divined that no one would pause to consider this fact. This was the Boston where, in 1834, citizens had stripped the clothes from the back of the abolitionist William Lloyd Garrison and led him through the streets with a rope around his neck. It was the Boston that, during that same year, had looked on as an anti-Catholic mob burned down a convent in neighboring Charlestown. It was the city where, a few years later, a freethinker named Abner Kneeland would be sent to jail for ridiculing the Immaculate Conception. It was also the city across the river from a still-conservative Harvard, which, in 1838, was to banish Emerson for daring to suggest that ordinary people might be as divine as Jesus. In short, it was a city that assumed that shared religious beliefs lay at the foundation of the social order and public morality. It tolerated free inquiry so long as the questioners did not appear to strike at the beliefs that, it was thought, gave structure to social and moral existence. However, once the line was crossed, Peabody realized, Boston's liberalism melted like April snow.

Peabody pleaded with Bronson to remove the potentially controversial passages. Bronson would compromise only by placing the questionable portions in a separate section in the back of the book. Almost at the same moment as this professional disagreement was unfolding, a personal quarrel brought a precipitous end to Peabody's association with the Temple

School. She came home to the Alcotts' apartments one day to find Bronson and Abba waiting for her and seething with anger. Straying into Peabody's room, Abba had uncovered letters from Elizabeth's sister Mary in which the latter had criticized Alcott's methods and had advised Elizabeth to free herself from any participation in her employer's "mistaken views." To the Alcotts, the letters were evidence of treason. To Elizabeth, the fact of their having read them was an inexcusable trespass. The desire for a break was mutual. In almost no time, Elizabeth had given notice and packed her bags. Almost as promptly, little Elizabeth Peabody Alcott was renamed Elizabeth Sewall Alcott. When the first volume of his *Conversations* was published in December 1836, Bronson had no one with whom to share either credit or blame.

The credit turned out to be scarce. The blame was thunderous. The *Boston Daily Advertiser* ran two full pages of editorial denunciations, calling the book's doctrines "radically false and mischievous."[79] The *Boston Courier*'s editor, Joseph Tinker Buckingham, had never seen "a more indecent and obscene book ([to] say nothing of its absurdity)." Pronouncing Alcott "insane or half-witted," he advised the schoolmaster's friends to "take care of him without delay."[80] Andrews Norton, a highly influential former professor of divinity at Harvard, echoed this view, calling the *Conversations* "one third absurd, one third blasphemous, and one third obscene."[81] When the editor of the more liberal *Christian Register* mildly called for sensible criticism of the generally excellent work of a "pure-minded, industrious, and well-meaning man," he was, by his own account, threatened with the Inquisition.[82]

Beneath this condemnation, the Temple School promptly withered. Only months after Alcott's *Conversations* were published, the once-thriving enrollment dwindled to ten pupils. Some of the families whose august social positions made them less vulnerable to criticism, like the Shaws and the Quincys, stayed longer than the first wave of defectors, but they, too, eventually found it not in their interest to continue. In April came the sad spectacle of the auction described in the prologue of this book. It had taken Bronson Alcott more than a decade to establish his reputation as a visionary educator. It took fewer than a half dozen pages of dialogue to destroy it.

Even so, he was not without friends. One of his most loyal defenders was Margaret Fuller. Only twenty-six when the Temple School scandal erupted, Fuller had not yet won fame as the editor of *The Dial* or as the author of her work on women's rights, *Woman in the Nineteenth Century.* Nevertheless, she was already highly respected among the leading transcendentalists and had acquired some personal interest in Alcott's reputation, having briefly taken over as his teaching assistant after Elizabeth Peabody resigned. Although she had once written privately of her "distrust" of her employer's mind, Fuller now championed Alcott as "a true and noble man . . . worthy of the palmy times of ancient Greece."[83] When she found out that Frederic Henry Hedge was planning to write an essay that would "cut up" Alcott, she wrote him a sharply worded letter. "There are plenty of fish in the net created solely for markets," she told him, "& no need to try your knife on a dolphin like him." She expressed her fervent wish that Hedge would not side with "the ugly, blinking owls who are now hooting . . . at this star of purest ray serene."[84] A few months later, Fuller further showed her appreciation of Alcott by taking a job at the Greene Street School in Providence, where the children frequently began the day with a "sacred" reading from *Conversations on the Gospels.*[85]

Peabody herself, despite strong reasons for no longer liking Alcott personally, stood up for his professional reputation. She wrote to the *Christian Register* in support of Alcott's *Conversations,* which she considered an important statement of resistance against "tyrannical custom, and an arbitrary imposition of the adult mind upon the young mind."[86] Emerson wrote a brief but spirited defense of Alcott and his book. He insisted that, if one were actually to read the *Conversations,* one would discover "a new theory of Christian instruction," emanating from "a strong mind and a pure heart." To Alcott himself, Emerson wrote, "I hate to have all the little dogs barking at you, for you have something better to do than to attend to them."[87]

But it was not only dogs that were barking. A host of creditors soon added their voices to the uproar. In his firm confidence in his school's continued success, coupled with his desire to make it an educator's paradise, Bronson had borrowed and spent with abandon. At a time when one could live comfortably on two thousand dollars a year, Bronson Alcott owed approximately six thousand. There seemed no way out.

It got worse. On Friday evenings at the temple, Alcott had been hosting a series of conversations for Sunday-school teachers. As the furor over his book reached its peak, word circulated that, on an appointed Friday, a mob would descend on the temple. It had not been in Alcott's nature to fight back directly against his detractors. He was convinced that, as a man of honor and dignity, he should preserve "unbroken silence" in the face of slander.[88] And yet, he was not a man to back down. As Emerson later wrote of him, "If there were a great courage, a great sacrifice, a self-immolation to be made, this & no other is the man for a crisis."[89] Alcott continued to hold his conversations, not knowing if the door might suddenly burst open or the windowpanes suddenly shatter. In the end, no attack took place, and Alcott observed with relief that "the minds of the disaffected" were at last "settling into quietude."[90]

Louisa may have been responding to tensions in the home or, perhaps, to the spirit of adventure that never entirely deserted her. Whatever the cause, around this time she developed a fondness for running away from home, a practice that she later called one of the delights of her childhood. She had, it seems, a preference for straying to the poorest neighborhoods, for her adult recollections were filled with images of great ash heaps where Irish beggar children shared their crusts, cold potatoes, and salt fish with their wayward visitor. At least once, she became lost. As the city streets darkened, the only ally that came to her side was a large curly-haired Newfoundland dog, which watched over her as she sobbed into its fur. At nine o'clock, the town crier found her fast asleep on a doorstep, snuggled comfortably against the still-vigilant animal.[91]

Episodes like this must have added some gray hairs to Abba's head, and they were assuredly the despair of Bronson. With the conviction that a carefully monitored environment was essential to the shaping of his children, he had tried to shield his daughters from the destructive influences of the city, a place that he described as "feculent" and infested with "seventy plagues."[92] He insisted that his girls were "suffering for the want of purer air" and that the corrupt urban landscape was making them "morbid in sensitivity." But whatever pollution or morbidity Louisa encountered on her flights from home, she evidently wanted more of it.

Louisa was at an age when girls tend to love their fathers desperately, when the mist of infallibility that encircles one's parents has not yet dissipated. Louisa lived with a father whose best friend called him an archangel and who did not bother to correct another man's child who compared him to Jesus Christ. Whether or not she knew these things, Louisa was given every encouragement to see Bronson as a godlike being. He was not a god who dispensed blessings freely. Whereas Bronson sought always to impose discipline on himself and his environment, Louisa seems to have sensed from the earliest age that her education lay partly in the rough and tumble precincts of the world. Her love of adventure struck her parents as curiously masculine. Within the family, she acquired the boyish-sounding nickname "Louy."

Louisa's unscheduled excursions were far from the greatest of Bronson's worries. Disgraced and penniless, he sank into a depression. Emerson tried to rally his friend, urging him to hone his writing skills and find his true vocation as an author. "Whatever you do at school or concerning your school," Emerson advised, "pray let not the pen halt, for that must be your last & longest lever to lift the world withal."93 Obligingly, Alcott turned his energies toward refining the ill-starred manuscript of "Psyche." He labored so furiously that Abba feared that, in giving life to "Psyche," he would cause the death of his own body. He expectantly handed the fruits of his labors to Emerson. Turning over the pages, Emerson sadly discovered that the work was not only filled with rhapsodic excess, but that Alcott's tone now reflected the bitterness of his recent experiences. The wounded self-righteousness of the following passage was all too typical:

> Reformer! thou findest thyself amidst thine age, yet alone. No living soul doth apprehend thy purpose. None sympathizes with thee. . . . Thou dost yearn for their good, but yet means are denied thee, by which thou canst realize thine ideal! Sad is the trial; yet needful! It will prove thy faith.94

What comes easily to us, we suppose must be effortless for all. Emerson wrote with relative ease. Having heard the fluency of Alcott's speech and having read the moody play of light and dark in the pages of his journals, he thought it no great task for Alcott to conquer the world in print. But the words that came at Alcott's bidding when he wrote for himself or spoke continued to elude him when he tried to write for others.

In the meantime, Alcott struggled on with the remnant of the Temple School. To reduce expenses, he first moved the school from its beautiful upstairs space to a darker, smaller room downstairs. Bronson himself was slipping into a darker, more introspective period. He was, he wrote, "an Idea without hands."95 When the downstairs school also proved too expensive, he closed it in June 1838. At the urging of a few loyal constituents, he tried teaching one more time, opening a school for the poor in his own parlor at 6 Beach Street, the less fashionable home to which the family had recently moved. This new school showed early promise, and the initial enrollment of fifteen rose encouragingly to twenty. However, the deathblow to this school was soon in coming.

As Bronson tried to face the collapse of his career with dignity and calm, his spirits were buoyed by the hope that, at last, he might have a son. As Abba's delivery time drew near, Bronson wrote to his mother that, despite all appearances, he found the future "bright and encouraging." He proclaimed himself "still the same Hoper that I have always been" and declared that he would continue to hope "through the tombs." He told his mother that, before he wrote again, another hoper would have joined the family. "I have the promise of a Boy," he added, and he predicted that the newborn's sisters would "jump for joy."[96] On April 6, 1839, Bronson and Abba had their boy. But the joy evaporated almost immediately. Though fully formed and outwardly perfect, the baby lived only a few hours. Bronson could barely bring himself to mention the loss. For years afterward, Abba observed April 6 as a personal day of mourning.[97]

History has little to say about the parents of Susan Robinson—little more than that, in the first half of 1839, they asked to enroll their daughter in Alcott's school and that they were black. Most teachers of Alcott's time would have dismissed the Robinsons out of hand. Alcott welcomed Susan. To his everlasting credit, he seems to have regarded her as neither more nor less deserving of special notice than any other new student. Indeed, no one would even remember the girl's first name if Anna Alcott had not mentioned it in her journal. However, the parents of Alcott's white students wasted no time in sending Bronson an ultimatum: if Susan remained, they would depart. Bronson's notation of the exchange was contemptuously brief: "My patrons, through Dr. John Flint, urge dismissal of the Robinson Child. I decline."[98] Overnight, Alcott's remaining support eroded. All of the parents except for the Robinsons and Bronson's longtime colleague William Russell withdrew their children. Of the five children available for him to teach, three were his own daughters.

It was over. By standing up for the humanity of Susan Robinson, Alcott had at last committed professional suicide. However, he at least had the satisfaction of knowing that the end had come, not under a cloud of disgrace, but in a small but significant blaze of courage. When he closed his books and dismissed his class on June 22, 1839, his career as a schoolteacher had come to an end.

Although he tried to maintain an outward stoicism in the face of his misfortunes, Bronson's private thoughts were resentful. Mentally, he took refuge in a fortress of self-righteousness, issuing scathing judgments against even the most mundane of worldly affairs. When Abba sent him to the butcher for a piece of meat and the tradesman sold him a more expensive cut than he requested, his condemnation was merciless. "What have I to do with butchers?" he snarled. "Death yawns at me as I walk up and down in this abode of skulls. Murder and blood are written on its stalls. . . . I tread amidst carcasses. I am in the presence of the slain."99 When Emerson wrote him a check for groceries, requiring him to venture into a bank to cash it, Alcott reacted as if he had been forced to enter a house of prostitution. Before his distracted eyes, the bank building transformed into "Mammon's Temple" where clusters of pagan devotees consulted "on appropriate rites whereby to honour their divinity."100 He rejected an invitation to dine with Emerson, Fuller, and the historian George Bancroft, scorning, as he saw it, to descend to "the tables of the fashionable, the voluptuous, the opulent."101 The simplest of kindnesses were now wicked temptations; the most moderate pleasures were damning indulgences. To carry his martyrdom to its apotheosis, Bronson had to be utterly in the right; the world had to be thoroughly wrong.

Bronson felt he could no longer live in a city, where, he claimed, Bacchus held court and the Prince of Devils ruled the mob.102 For some time, he had wanted to dwell among people of simpler values, who spoke with "greater purity than the artificial citizen or closeted bookworm." If there was to be a future for him, it must be close to the soil—and close to Emerson. In the first week of April 1840, with Abba expecting the couple's fourth child, the Alcotts gathered their modest belongings, loaded them onto the stage at Earl's Tavern on Hanover Street, and took the road that led to Concord.

CHAPTER FOUR

"ORPHEUS AT THE PLOUGH"

"The world's hope is in us."
—A. BRONSON ALCOTT,
"To Junius Alcott," June 30, 1842

THE CONCORD RIVER, WHICH FLOWS BY THE TOWN THAT bears its name, was known to the native tribes as Musketaquid, or Meadow River, because of the flat grasslands that lined its banks. In the summertime, it is from four to fifteen feet deep and from one hundred to three hundred feet wide. Around the time the Alcotts arrived, the winter ice on the river and the surrounding ponds broke up, cracking with a sound as loud as cannon fire. For some time after the ice had receded, the wind remained cold and bracing. In his book *A Week on the Concord and Merrimack Rivers*, Thoreau wrote of these winds and how they "heav[e] up the surface into dark billows or regular swells," so that the water looks like "a smaller Lake Huron, . . . very pleasant and exciting for a landsman to row or sail over."[1] In the more temperate months, wild grapes and cranberries grew thick there. Woodcocks, rails, and bitterns waded shyly through the marshy areas, and cardinals and titmice flitted through the air. A child wandering the banks, as Louisa often did, would sometimes surprise a muskrat or hear a splash as a startled terrapin plunged to safety. Her younger sister Lizzie, a few months short of her fifth birthday, took to her new pastoral surroundings with particular delight, and her father rejoiced that there were now "fields and woods, and brooks and flowers to please my little Queen."[2]

In the 1840s and for many decades thereafter, the lazy, peaceful river seemed to some visitors to have impressed its nature upon the inhabitants of the town. Even three decades after the Alcotts first set up housekeeping in the town, a visitor "could see no factory operatives going to work, dinner pails in hand,—no farmer driving his oxen afield—only two or three tranquil shopkeepers just taking down their shutters and one young lady having a 'constitutional' on horseback."[3] During the years that she lived there, Louisa May Alcott came to regard it as "one of the dullest little towns in Massachusetts."[4]

Yet with residents like Emerson, Thoreau, and, from time to time, Nathaniel Hawthorne, Concord deserved its reputation as the literary epicenter of pre–Civil War America. However, this reputation rested on fewer than a half dozen citizens. Take away Concord from the United States, and the United States seemed a relatively unlettered country. But take away a handful of persons from Concord, and Concord was no different from any other Massachusetts town. In *Walden*, Thoreau wondered aloud, "What does our Concord culture amount to? There is in this town, with a very few exceptions, no taste for the best or for very good books even in English literature, whose words all can read and spell. . . . Cannot students be boarded here and get a liberal education under the skies of Concord? . . . Alas! What with foddering the cattle and tending the store, we are kept from school too long, and our education is sadly neglected."[5]

Nevertheless, Bronson Alcott tended to see only possibilities in a new place, and his arrival in Concord signaled to him a rebirth of hope. In the days just after the family settled into Hosmer Cottage, the fresh spring weather gave him reason to believe in new beginnings. Eight days after Alcott first hung up his coat at the cottage, Emerson stood on the banks of Walden Pond as the south wind blew and warm light filled the woods. Emerson turned and said to a companion, "This world is so beautiful that I can hardly believe it exists."[6] Alcott was glad to be a part of this beauty, and he was also glad that the cottage met the approval of Abba and the girls. For the first time in years, Abba was going about the house singing.[7] Bronson wrote to Sam May with ebullient spirits. The neighbors, he told his brother-in-law, were courteous and kind, and he found his garden rich in promise. "I sow again in hope," he wrote, "and know full well that my harvest shall come in in due season, and there shall be bread and fullness in the land." The first harvest Bronson pulled from the soil of his new property was a metaphor. He suggested to May that his life thus far had been that of "an impatient husbandman, misauguring the signs of the spring time" and scattering his seed in the least hospitable of seasons, while the snow and frost still covered the fields. He swore that his late disappointments had taught him priceless lessons in faith, patience, and humility. Bronson claimed to have renounced all his pretenses as a moral and spiritual teacher. He wished no longer to set himself in opposition to "things as they are" and "the powers that be." He said that he sought only to achieve peaceful relations with the soil. "[I]n the bosom of nature, under the sky of God," he felt more certain of the fitness of his position than ever before.[8]

And yet, in the midst of optimism, his departure from Boston had some of the flavor of an exile, and he made no effort to shield his children from his sense of having been wronged. Nine-year-old Anna reported in her journal:

> Father told us how people had treated him, and why we came to live at Concord, and how we must give up a good many things that we like. I know it will be hard, but I mean to do it. I fear I shall complain sometimes about it.[9]

As far as education went, at least, the Alcott daughters had little cause to complain. Anna was enrolled at the Concord Academy, a school then under the management of Thoreau and his elder brother John. At the same time, Louisa and Lizzie took their lessons from a Miss Mary Russell, who taught at Emerson's house.

It is impossible to know the extent of the contact that took place between Louisa and Emerson. However, Louisa received some memorable lessons during this time from Anna's teacher Henry Thoreau. Since graduating from Harvard in 1837, Thoreau, now twenty-two years old, was taking the first steps in his career as a writer. The previous September, he and John had gone on the boating excursion that was to supply the basis for Thoreau's first book, *A Week on the Concord and Merrimack Rivers*. In addition to teaching at the academy, Thoreau was trying to become a poet and was exchanging manuscripts with Emerson. He was also at work on some pieces, both poetry and prose, that he hoped might be included in the first issue of a literary journal on which Emerson and Margaret Fuller were collaborating. Nevertheless, he found time to lead bands of local children through the woods and meadows near the town, pausing to point out the native birds and flora, which he knew like members of his family. When the season was right, Thoreau transformed his young followers into a crew of blackberry and huckleberry hunters, armed with empty baskets and a zeal for discovery.

Thoreau was not a handsome man. More than twenty years later, when she transformed Thoreau into the fictitious Mr. Warwick in her novel *Moods*, Louisa made note of his "massive head, covered with waves of ruddy brown hair, gray eyes that seemed to pierce through all disguises, [and] an eminent nose." But the ungainly features expressed a rare character; over the years, Louisa came to discern "power, intellect, and courage" stamped upon his face and figure.[10] Thoreau was not an inexhaustible talker like Louisa's father, but he put meanings into silences that others struggled to put into words. In the book about his river journey with his brother, Thoreau would later write, "The language of Friendship is not words, but meanings. It is an intelligence above language."[11] This intelligence, along with knowledge of nature, he shared with Louisa and her friends.

Unlike Emerson and Louisa's father, who appreciated nature principally as a collection of visible symbols of moral truth and the human spirit, Thoreau took a scientific and technical interest in nature. Still, he knew how to capture the imaginations of a young audience, and he fueled the fantasies of Concord's children by telling them that tanagers set the woods afire and by likening goldenrod to the banners of medieval crusaders. An anecdote much favored among Alcott enthusiasts tells of how Thoreau called young Louisa's attention to a cobweb and told her it was a handkerchief dropped by a fairy. He sometimes invited Louisa and the other children onto his boat and took them for cruises across the placid river. When the mood struck him, he played a flute, choosing a melody to harmonize with his feelings or the beauties of the landscape. During the first summer that the Alcotts spent in Concord, Thoreau wrote entries in his journal that might well have been apropos of his journeys with the children: "Any melodious sound apprises me of the infinite wealth of God." "Floating in still water, I too am a planet, and have my orbit, in space, and am no longer a satellite of the earth." On their excursions, Louisa likely felt in her heart what her mentor wrote one August day: "Surely joy is the condition of life."[12]

Never a model of feminine propriety, Louisa climbed elm trees, clambered over fences, and readily accepted dares from neighborhood boys to leap from the highest beam of a nearby barn. Her exuberant rambles contrasted with the discipline on which her father insisted at home, where a stimulating spirit of inquiry existed side by side with a solemn sense of duty. Always determined to make learning imaginative, Bronson contorted his body to represent letters of the alphabet for the edification of his daughters. With his silvery voice, he read aloud from the Bible and *The Pilgrim's Progress*. However, he promptly withheld enjoyment if the girls had not faithfully prepared their lessons. Still persuaded that the most effective punishment lay in knowing that one had caused another person to suffer, he would sometimes go without his own dinner if his daughters had not satisfied his expectations.

Louisa's life was already assuming the contours that were to characterize it for the next twenty-five years or more: an almost impossibly dissonant combination of superior intellectual opportunities and frightful worldly deprivation. A typical day for Louisa began with a trip to Emerson's house and might continue with a nature walk with Thoreau, only to end with a homeward trudge to a cottage where there was sometimes insufficient food, where the father wore the mantle of a social outcast, and where the mother tried to bear up under the weight of mounting debts and disappointments. Louisa's life was in one sense lavishly wealthy. In another, it was perilously poor.

Bronson had not ceased trying to check Louisa's discordant impulses, and he still did not fully accept the fact that she was fundamentally not like him. A poem that he wrote for her on her birthday in Concord encapsulates the struggle he perceived in her: "Two Passions strong divide our Life / Meek gentle Love, or boisterous strife."[13] It was all too clear which passion appeared to be winning. That same year, Emerson gave a lecture titled "Education," which offered some advice that Bronson might have profitably heeded in his relations with Louisa. Nature, Emerson said, had no love for repetitions. Nevertheless, he added, "a low self-love in the parent desires that his child should repeat his character . . . an expectation which the child, if justice is done him, will nobly disappoint." The father who insisted on re-creating himself through his offspring was unconsciously doing his utmost "to defeat [the child's] proper promise and produce the ordinary and mediocre."[14] Alcott may well have heard this lecture. Very likely, he supported its sentiments. But to agree philosophically is easier than to act accordingly.

As Louisa's awareness of both good and evil broadened and deepened, her father chopped wood and cut straight furrows through the uneven ground. When he was not working for himself, he hired himself out to neighbors. In good weather, he was always at work outdoors. On inclement days, he wrote or found some task in his modest woodshop. The children went to school in the village, while he and Abba did "all that farmers and farmers' wives find necessary." By the first day of summer, he boasted of a fine growing crop of vegetables, more than enough to supply the family. He felt that his labors were giving him a primeval dignity, and that God had been kind, not severe, when He had sent Adam "into the fields to earn his Bread in the sweat of his face."[15] But Alcott's hiatus from moral teaching was already over. He told his mother that he meant to go back to a classroom as soon as the public realized the good he could do them. In the meantime, a handful of young men and women found their way to his cottage for conversation and enlightenment.[16]

For now, though, the visual poetry of his new rustic life enchanted him. "My garden shall be my poem," he rhapsodized. "My spade and hoe the instruments of my wit and skill, my family and the Soul, my world of reality and faerie."[17] Self-consciously, Bronson was striving to epitomize the spirit that people were learning to call "transcendental": agrarian, antiurban, and individualistic to the point of indifference to the outside world. William Ellery Channing, from whom much of the new consciousness had first emanated, responded enthusiastically to Alcott's bucolic retreat, which realized one of the minister's most dearly held ideas: the union of labor and culture. In Channing's judgment, Alcott, "hiring himself out for day-labor and at the same time living in a region of high thought" was very likely the most interesting sight in Massachusetts. "Orpheus at the plough," Channing added, "is after my own heart."[18] Emerson also quietly applauded Alcott's agrarian impulse. He wrote in his journal, "I see with great pleasure this growing inclination in all persons who aim to speak the truth, for manual labor and the farm."[19] Curiously, moving to Concord and taking up the implements of a farmer were the most popular steps Bronson had taken in years.[20]

Ironically, one of Alcott's severest critics was the other man of his generation who, though a minor philosopher in his own right, was to be chiefly remembered for the writings of his famous offspring. It was around this time that Emerson introduced Alcott to Henry James Sr., who would father not only the renowned novelist but also the great psychologist William James and the incandescent diarist Alice James. The son of one of the wealthiest men in New York State, James possessed the financial independence that would have been required to render Alcott's disdain for commerce respectable. James was an amputee, having lost a leg in a tragic childhood accident. Whereas Alcott never fully accepted the existence of evil, James maintained that evil was endemic in the world and experiencing it essential to the formation of moral character. They may have differed most profoundly, however, as to the value of educating women. Alcott favored the strongest possible cultivation of the feminine mind. James, to the contrary, utterly dismissed the appropriateness of educating women. He once wrote, "The very virtue of woman . . . disqualifies her from all didactic dignity. Learning and wisdom do not become her."[21] Given the two men's philosophic differences, it is not surprising that their discussions were often volatile. In one of their early conversations, Alcott casually asserted that, like Jesus, he had never sinned. Astonished, James inquired whether Alcott had ever proclaimed, "I am the Resurrection and the Life." "Yes, often," came the calm reply. James fired back, "And has anyone ever believed you?"[22]

The credibility that Alcott most desired, however, was not as a saint but as a writer. During that first spring in Concord, Alcott, Emerson, Fuller, and fellow transcendentalist George Ripley were deeply absorbed in creating a magazine intended, as Fuller and Emerson were to say in its first issue, "to reprobate that rigor of our conventions of religion and education which is turning us to stone, which renounces hope, which looks only backward, which asks only such a future as the past."[23] The magazine was to stand for an unkempt but noble love of truth and a dedication to the beauties of the unseen. It would propose an antidote to narrowness.

Alcott's first contribution to the proposed journal was its name, *The Dial*. Just as a sundial marked the movement of the sun, Alcott thought, the soul was a dial reflecting the greater movements of the spirit.[24] This, too, was to be the work of the new magazine: to offer a visible index of the mightier and more mysterious motions of the heart and mind. Throughout the spring of 1840, Alcott toiled over his contribution to the maiden issue: fifty prophetic, aphoristic observations on topics ranging from prudence to Prometheus. He gave his work the grand title of "Orphic Sayings." Recognizing that some of his previous work had failed because of its verbosity, Alcott limited each of his observations to a single paragraph, sometimes even to a single sentence. By doing so, he evidently hoped to achieve the energetic concentration that distinguished Emerson's best prose.

Not long after he had settled in Concord, Alcott proudly handed the manuscript of his sayings to Emerson. At a few points, Emerson found incisive, well-crafted observations; at many more places, however, he cringed. With foreboding, he wrote to Fuller, "You will not like Alcott's papers; . . . I do not like them; . . . Mr. Ripley will not." As a whole Alcott's sayings were "open to the same fault as his former papers." Instead of boiling his thought down to its refined essence, Alcott had strayed into "cold vague generalities." In contrast to the other contributions to the first issue of *The Dial*, all of which appeared either anonymously or under initials, Emerson thought it essential for "Orphic Sayings" to be printed with the author's name. "Give them his name," Emerson suggested, "& those who know him will have his voice in their ear whilst they read, & the sayings will have a majestical sound." Despite his reservations, Emerson recommended publishing Alcott's aphorisms "pretty much as they stand."[25] Abba, at least, was confident. She wrote to her brother Samuel that Bronson had been writing a series of "Delphic letters" that, if people would only read them, would do "more for their souls than Paul or Pliny."[26]

Name and sound, however, were not enough to rescue "Orphic Sayings." At their best, they have a kindly, hortatory quality, encouraging readers to make themselves into better, spiritually larger beings. For instance, Alcott writes, "Engage in nothing that cripples or degrades you. Your first duty is self-culture, self-exaltation: you may not violate this high trust. Your self is sacred, profane it not. . . . Your influence on others is commensurate with the strength that you have found in yourself."[27] He is also memorable, when, in a saying he later added to the original fifty, he speaks of one of the things he knew best, the liberating nature of the ideal teacher: "The true teacher defends his pupils against his own personal influence. He inspires self-trust. He guides their eyes from himself to the spirit that quickens him.

He will have no disciples."[28] Read with patience, Alcott's "Orphic Sayings" speak confidently of the nobility of the soul, the ultimate unreality of death, and the vital, miraculous omnipresence of God.

However, far too many of Alcott's pronouncements are turgid and obscure, heavy and ponderous. His musings on "Aspiration" read like a vocabulary bee gone mad: "The insatiableness of her desires is an augury of the soul's eternity. . . . Intact, aspirant, she feels the appulses of both spiritual and material things; she would appropriate the realm she inherits by virtue of her incarnation: infinite appetencies direct all her members."[29] Still more baffling was his one-sentence statement on "Calculus":

> We need, what Genius is unconsciously seeking, and, by some daring generalization of the universe, shall assuredly discover, a spiritual calculus, a *novum organon,* whereby nature shall be divined in the soul, the soul in God, matter in spirit, polarity resolved into unity; and that power which pulsates in all life, animates and builds all organizations, shall manifest itself as one universal deific energy present alike at the outskirts and centre of the universe, whose centre and circumference are one; omniscient, omnipotent, self-subsisting, uncontained, yet containing all things in the unbroken synthesis of its being.[30]

The contemporary critics chose to bypass the uplifting message of "Orphic Sayings" and to concentrate on their pompous hilarities. The *Boston Transcript* published a parody titled "Gastric Sayings." The *Boston Post* printed a letter that likened Alcott's work to "a train of fifteen railroad cars with one passenger." Emerson's own brother William complained that the magazine had been marred by "Alcott's unintelligibles."[31] *The Dial* as a whole was off to a shaky beginning; Emerson wrote to Carlyle that the first issue, a "poor little thing," had been "honoured by attacks from almost every newspaper & magazine."[32] But Alcott suffered most of all. The inclusion of his full name, far from improving the reception given his "Sayings," made him the most identifiable target of ridicule. Undaunted, Alcott continued to turn out Orphic Sayings for inclusion in *The Dial*, and Emerson and Fuller bravely printed them. Numbering one hundred altogether, they stand as an incarnation of transcendentalism at its most ebullient and its most fatuous. They so severely damaged Alcott's reputation as a writer that no editor went near another important piece of his writing for a quarter century. In 1842, the publisher of *Conversations with Children on the Gospels* sold 750 copies of that book, at five cents a pound, for trunk lining.[33]

Despite such setbacks, Alcott had the comfort of knowing that country life was bringing health and happiness to his children. Fresh air and open space seemed to enliven the high-spirited Louisa more than ever. At the age of seven, she was, in her father's view, a "noisy little girl" who made "house and garden, barn and field, ring with her footsteps." Bronson sometimes had to ask Louisa to "step lightly, and speak soft, about the house" and to remind her that her "sober Father, and other grown people," cherished quiet. Still, he marveled at the way the little girl and her landscape appeared to harmonize. The "Garden, Flowers, Fields, Woods, and Brooks" all seemed able "to see and answer the voice and footsteps, the eye and hand" of the child who wandered past them. While she was in Boston visiting Abba's father, even the hens and chicks seemed to miss her. Bronson wrote, "[W]e find how much we love now we are separated."[34]

On July 26, the same month that the first *Dial* saw daylight, a fourth daughter joined the family. The "quiet little lady," whom her parents named Abigail May Alcott, was born at dawn on a Sunday morning. In her childhood, people called this youngest daughter Abby. When she was old enough to choose for herself, she preferred to be known by her middle name. Bronson may have felt a twinge of disappointment as he faced the likelihood that he was destined never to have a son. Nevertheless, he wrote to Sam May that he would "joyfully acquiesce" in the Providence that had given him "daughters of Love instead of sons of Light." Fully aware that responsibility for the fate of reform in America would fall on both genders, he welcomed the chance to "rear Women for the new order of things."[35] Despite this revolutionary sentiment, Bronson decided not to keep a journal chronicling the new baby's development. Unlike her three older sisters, Abby did not live her early childhood as the subject of an experiment. Louisa later called her "the flower of the family" and maintained that her youngest sister had been born under a lucky star.

Far more than his infant daughter, Bronson was in need of such a star. His efforts as a day laborer could not meet the needs of a family of six. Yet he was far from idle. Chopping wood for others and tending his own vegetables occupied him more than ten hours each day. Remarkably, he also managed a handful of speaking engagements. What stood between Bronson Alcott and solvency was not a want of effort but the utter strictness of his conscience. He was more firmly committed than ever to refusing any work that offended his moral principles. Abba observed her husband's rigidity with mounting concern. She wrote to her brother Samuel:

> No one will employ him in his way; he cannot work in theirs, if he thereby involve his conscience. He is so resolved in this matter that I believe he will starve and freeze before he will sacrifice principle to comfort. In this, I and my children are necessarily implicated.[36]

In February 1841, Abba's father passed away, leaving her a little more than two thousand dollars, which he had stipulated could not be used by Bronson or taken to satisfy his debts. Nevertheless, Bronson's creditors challenged the restriction, and the modest bequest was placed in escrow, beyond the family's reach for another four years.[37]

As it became apparent that Alcott could not meet his obligations, Emerson made a generous but rash proposal. He offered to dismiss his servants and take the Alcott family into his own house. Abba and Emerson's wife Lidian would manage the house together, and Bronson would work Emerson's land in lieu of rent. Abba, however, vetoed the proposal. She knew that such an arrangement would soon subordinate her family to the Emersons. She also knew how unsuited she was for getting along with another man's wife in such close quarters. Sounding rather ungrateful, she exclaimed, "I cannot gee and haw in another person's yoke, and I know that every body [*sic*] burns their fingers when they touch my fire."[38] Thoreau, not the Alcotts, moved in with the Emersons. Samuel May also offered lodging nearer him in a fine house, but Bronson, wishing to remain free, was not prepared to accept.

In 1841, on the first day of spring, Emerson published his towering *Essays, First Series*. He wrote and lectured brilliantly on "Self-Reliance," "The Method of Nature," and "The Poet." By contrast, it was a hard, slow year for the Alcotts. The previous summer, Bronson had talked with Emerson about a college that the two of them might found along with Fuller, George Ripley, Theodore Parker, and some of the other new thinkers of Massachusetts. For a while, Emerson had thought well of this "University which Mr. A. & I built out of straws," but nothing concrete issued from the scheme.[39] After such flights of dreamy creativity subsided, threadbare reality always rushed back in on Alcott. He was beginning to wear down both physically and mentally. In December, Abba's aunt Hannah Robie came from Boston to visit the cottage and was surprised to find the family living on nothing but "coarse brown sugar, bread, potatoes, apples, squash, and simple puddings."[40] Abba confided to her aunt that she was anxious about Bronson's health. She feared that the lack of sympathy and encouragement the world had shown her husband might finally depress him more than he could bear.[41]

January 1842 was a time of personal loss for the philosophers of Concord. On New Year's Day, Thoreau's brother John cut himself on a razor. He contracted tetanus. Racked with pain, he died ten days later in Henry's arms. On Monday the twenty-fourth, Emerson's beloved five-year-old son Waldo contracted scarlet fever. Three days later, he was dead. The next morning, Louisa innocently bounded up to Emerson's door to ask if her friend was feeling better. The gaunt man came out to meet her, so worn with watching and changed by sorrow that his appearance startled her. She could only stammer her query. "Child, he is dead," came the reply. Louisa remembered the moment always as her first glimpse of a great grief.[42] That same morning, Emerson announced the news to Margaret Fuller. "All his wonderful beauty could not save him," he lamented. The man who had published an essay called "Love" the year before now wondered whether he would ever dare to love anything again.[43] At Hosmer Cottage, there were no acute outward tragedies. However, Abba sensed a dark drama unfolding in her husband's mind. She wrote ominously to Samuel, "If his body dont fail his mind will—he experiences at times the most dreadful nervous excitation—his mind distorting every act however simple into the most complicated and adverse form—I am terror-stricken at this."[44] Yet even in this winter, with little food on his own table, Bronson chopped wood free of charge to fuel the fireplace of a woman with four children whose drunken husband had disappeared.[45]

Bronson always believed in a Providence that would rescue him. That Providence did not fail him now, though relief came from a most unlikely quarter. In 1837, when Harriet Martineau brought back to England her skeptical report of the Temple School, she had also brought with her a copy of Elizabeth Peabody's *Record of a School*, which found its way to a merchant-turned-educator, James Pierrepont Greaves. Greaves, who had lost his business during the Napoleonic Wars, had traveled to Switzerland in the 1820s to study under Pestalozzi, the same reformer whose writings inspired Alcott. After returning to England, he had established a school at Ham Common, Surrey, which he had unknowingly run on principles similar to Alcott's. Perusing Peabody's *Record*, he found a kindred spirit. Greaves sent Alcott a thirty-page letter raving about Alcott's method and requesting more copies of both the *Record* and *Conversations with Children on the Gospels*. Greaves pronounced the *Conversations* an "invaluable" text and circulated it among his own circle of admirers.

By 1840, the year the Alcotts made their exodus from Boston, Greaves's school had been christened "Alcott House." Perhaps in part because Greaves and his friends, unlike Alcott, had had considerable experience in business, Alcott House was a thriving success, boasting a full subscription of pupils and the enthusiastic endorsements of the English reform community. Greaves and the rest of his reform-minded cadre maintained a steady and worshipful correspondence with Alcott, to whom they had extended a standing invitation to come to England and observe their progress.

Alcott, of course, could never have paid for such a journey. There was one institution, however, where his credit was still strong, and that institution was Ralph Waldo Emerson. Emerson offered five hundred dollars to send his friend to Alcott House for the summer.[46] Emerson hoped that Alcott might not only find rejuvenation and support at the school that bore his name; perhaps, too, Alcott might find a kindred spirit in Thomas Carlyle. Emerson hoped that a rendezvous between Alcott and Carlyle, the two minds he respected above all others, might produce an astounding synergy. Yet Emerson also feared that the two might not find common ground, and he tried to find words to provide a lubricant for a meeting from which friction might well be expected.

Bronson had no trouble accepting Emerson's proposal. As Alcott readied himself for the voyage, Emerson labored over the letter of introduction he would send to Carlyle. Finding the task a hard one, he took up his journal and began jotting observations about his friend. The rambling, fitful entry reveals a divided mind, as if Emerson did not know whether to defend his friend to the death or disown him at the first opportunity. He called

Alcott "a man of ideas, a man of faith [who] speaks truth truly." When he had a loving, intelligent audience, Emerson continued, Alcott's "discourse soars to a wonderful height, so regular, so lucid, so playful . . . that the hearers seem no longer to have bodies or material gravity, but . . . they [almost] mount into the air at pleasure, or leap at one bound out of this poor solar system." But this rhapsody had barely subsided before Emerson noted less complimentary traits. He discerned a pair of damning flaws in Alcott's character that might come fully to the surface in a deeper crisis. The first was Alcott's utter insistence on his own character as the fundamental topic of all discourse. Emerson complained, "Unfortunately, his conversation never loses sight of his own personality. He never quotes; he never refers; his only illustration is his own biography. His topic yesterday is Alcott on the 17 October; today, Alcott on the 18 October; tomorrow, on the 19th." The other signature failing held potentially ominous consequences for Abba and her four daughters. Emerson observed, "He is quite ready at any moment to abandon his present residence & employment, his country, nay, his wife & children, on very short notice, to put any new dream into practice which has bubbled up in the effervescence of discourse." Near the end of his character study, Emerson washed his hands of it all: "This noble genius discredits genius to me. I do not want any more such persons to exist."[47]

Emerson ended up not using these notes. In the end, he asked only that Carlyle put out of his mind anything he had previously heard about Alcott and, more importantly, anything by him that he might have read. He counseled Carlyle, "Permit this stranger . . . to make a new & primary impression."[48] Carlyle might love or hate Alcott, Emerson admitted, but he should not let the American go until he had seen and understood him.

Alcott arranged for his brother Junius to move in with Abba and the children during his absence. He packed a quantity of apples and homemade bread, and took passage aboard the *Rosalind*, sailing from Boston on May 8. He carried not only Emerson's recommendation but also a letter from William Lloyd Garrison. With pride, he copied Garrison's words into a letter he sent home to Abba: "I am sure you will greatly admire the sweetness of his spirit the independence and originality of his mind, and the liberality of his soul."[49] After some initial queasiness, he had an easy voyage, passing the time with Wordsworth's *The Excursion* and Emerson's *Essays*. These books, as well as his fantasies, gave him better company than his fellow passengers. He lay awake at times, enraptured by sublime thoughts, "planting Edens—fabling worlds—building kingdoms and men—taking the hands of friends and lovers—of wives and babes."[50] It seemed more than likely to him that his long-sought path to paradise would lead past the gates of Alcott House.

Bronson had no idea what to make of London; from the moment he first saw it on June 5, its sheer vastness and energy awed and offended him in approximately equal measures. His ears and eyes were met by a city of din and smoke, in which the costly and magnificent collided improbably with the convenient and the plain. The only way to remain superior to his new surroundings was to judge them morally. In his letters to Abba, he denounced the city for its raw physicality. "All is for the body," he complained, "all seems body."[51] His senses had been stimulated to the point of pain, and the brusque, restless striving of the citizenry left him gasping. In their voices and manners, they betrayed a forceful, warlike temperament. Alcott expected neither repose nor tenderness, and he found none. "Every Englishman," he concluded, "is a fortification."[52] From this sweeping dismissal, however, he was more than ready to exempt the Alcott House reformers.

On June 7, Alcott called at the office of the *London Mercantile Price Current*, where he was cordially received by Charles Lane, one of Greaves's most ardent supporters. Lane, however, had some shocking news: Greaves had died of an unspecified cause shortly before Alcott had sailed for England. Nevertheless, Henry Gardiner Wright, who had taken charge of Alcott House, was waiting at the school to make Alcott's acquaintance. Lane proudly escorted Bronson there that same afternoon. Alcott, more intrigued by ideas than appearances, gave no more detailed description of the school than to call it a "charmed spot." Bronson immediately settled into a guestroom on the property. After a week in residence, he was in ecstasies. He felt as if he were again at the Temple School, but for his sense that "a wiser wisdom direct[ed], and a lovelier love preside[d]" over this English counterpart.[53]

Bronson was enthralled by Wright, whom he proclaimed "the first and only man whom I have found to see and know me even as I am seen and known by myself." It is wonderful to be understood. Little surprise, then, that Bronson, who had baffled almost all attempts to comprehend him,

*Thomas Carlyle. Emerson hoped
that the great English essayist would form a
friendship with Bronson. Instead, the two got on together
"almost as ill as it was possible for two honest men
kindly affected towards one another to do."*
(Courtesy of Houghton Library, Harvard University)

thought that he had discovered "a younger disciple of the same Eternal Verity which I have loved and served so long." Yet Alcott reserved even more elaborate praise for Lane, who, in his eyes, possessed an even greater wisdom and incarnate love. Casting aside such acquaintances as Emerson, Thoreau, Fuller, and Channing, Alcott called Lane "the deepest, sharpest intellect" he had ever met. Emerson, he thought, would feel as rich in the acquaintance of Lane as in the friendship of Carlyle.[54]

When he first compared Lane with Carlyle, Alcott had not yet met the latter, knowing him only from his writings and Emerson's praise. Alcott visited the great Scotsman numerous times during his trip, but each encounter confirmed more resoundingly than the last that the two had nothing in common, either in philosophy or manners. Carlyle approached philosophy through a strategy of fierce, relentless disputation. He saw truth as the synthesis of colliding opposites, and he wanted ideas that proved their worth in practice. Alcott expected truth to be unitary, unchanging and transcendent, and he did not mind if it were more beautiful than useful. He also thought that discussion should be polite and harmonious. The interviews between the two were thus fated for misunderstanding. Even Alcott's manners, with which he had disarmed more than one detractor, struck Carlyle as deficient. One day, when the tall American stayed for a meal, Carlyle was aghast to see Alcott take a helping of strawberries and mix them with his mashed potatoes. Carlyle soon concluded that he and Alcott got on together "almost as ill as it was possible for two honest men kindly affected towards one another to do."[55] Alcott, for his part, lumped Carlyle into his general assessment of Englishmen of letters, whom he saw as "all ridden by the hag Melancholy or the dragon Need, . . . wasting the costly gifts of genius in adorning the sepulchres of the dead."[56] Alcott was also put off by Carlyle's emphasis on grueling mental labor. He complained, "Work! work! is with him both motto and creed; but tis all toil of the brain . . . instead of devotion to living Humanity."[57]

Not wanting to wholly disappoint Emerson, Carlyle mustered some praise for the Connecticut Yankee. Alcott, he told Emerson, was "a genial, innocent, simple-hearted man, of much natural intelligence and goodness, with an air of rusticity, veracity and dignity withal, which in many ways appeals to me." In Carlyle's view, Alcott was "a kind of venerable Don Quixote, whom no one can even laugh at without loving." Carlyle was bemused, however, by Alcott's obsession with vegetarianism and his evident belief that humankind could be revolutionized by dietary reform. Alcott seemed "all bent on saving the world by return to acorns and the golden age." He saw in Alcott's endless theorizing only a "Potatoe-gospel, a mere imbecility which *cannot* be discussed in this busy world."[58]

The poet Robert Browning happened to call on Carlyle one day when Alcott was present, and he took the scene as a rare slice of comedy. He wrote, "a crazy or sound asleep—not dreaming—American was [there]—and talked! I have since heard, to my solace, that my outrageous laughters have made him ponder seriously the hopelessness of England."[59] Given a rough reception from London's best and brightest, Alcott found himself ever more closely attracted to his admirers at Alcott House. There, he was made to feel like a genius instead of a rustic, provincial crank. Wright and Lane were a wondrous support to a traveler in a strange land. The one other comfort that Alcott enjoyed was in his thoughts of home. He was as far from Abba as he was ever to be in his life, yet he felt closer to her than ever.

In Concord, without her husband, Abba was prey to a series of powerful emotions. In the days leading up to Bronson's departure, she had doubted whether she could manage the household without him. "Oh how great a task this is," she reflected. "It is with a trembling hand I take the rudder to guide this little bark alone." On her first morning without him, she awoke feeling sick and sad.[60] During her first few days on her own, she lost her appetite and wept uncontrollably. Walking alone through the fields near the cottage, she prayed aloud that her soul would be sustained by patience and her heart cheered by hope.[61] During Abba's marriage her children often gave her the strongest reason for resisting sadness, and for their sakes she now did her best to seem brave and happy.

After a while, however, she found that her appearance of contentment was not mere pretense. She began to feel that her husband's absence was not so terrible after all. Bronson's brother Junius proved to be a welcome assistant. Moreover, Bronson wrote often, and after twelve years of marriage, he had not forgotten how to write a love letter. From aboard the *Rosalind*, he wrote, "I have not left you; you have been my companion and company all the way, and have grown more and more precious to me, as the winds wafted us together across the seas." Nearing the end of his voyage, he wrote of the "mysterious sentiment, surpassingly humane and tender in this alliance of husband and wife. Now, my love mate, do I feel the sweetness of your regards, the preciousness of your love."[62] In London, it occurred to him that he had needed to put distance between himself and his wife and daughters to see them in all their actual beauty. He saw Anna looking with deepest meaning from her large eyes, Lizzie wearing her sweetest smile, Louisa running her swiftest to serve her mother and sisters. Interestingly, whereas he recalled the faces of Anna and Lizzie, he pictured Louisa in terms of her physical energy and her desire to win praise by helping others. Though she sometimes baffled him, he knew her basic character well. As his daughters became dear in his memory, invested, he said, "with a new and holier charm," words flowed from his pen to make them dearer in their mother's sight as well.[63]

Bronson wrote, too, of brighter days to come. He assured Abba, "Love and sacrifice like yours cannot baulk their possessor. Whatsoever the loving heart yields, it shall find again." Bronson felt as if his letters home were part of a second courtship. "Again, am I a youth," he wrote, and he added his belief that his and Abba's separation would help them rediscover "that intercourse which was ours in the prime and innocency of our espousals."[64]

Abba cherished these letters, delighting in what she called "his soul and heart in the full melody of his rich words." His loving phrases satisfied her "even more fully than . . . the grand diapason of his sweet voice and the rich deep harmony of serene looks."[65] Perhaps the best part of Bronson had always been his words, and these he was still able to give her. As time went by, she caught herself beginning to savor this fleeting time of independence. With some money released from her father's estate, she was able to pay off a dozen of the family's Concord creditors. When she was not sewing for money or minding the house, she had time to read magazines and novels. To encourage her daughters to write, she set up a family "post office" where the girls could leave notes for her and one another. She took simple human pleasure in observing "the lives and progress of our children—Anna, Louisa, Elizabeth and Abba, are so many epitomes of my life—I live, move, and have my being in them."[66] Two months after the *Rosalind* set sail, Mrs. Alcott may have surprised herself when she wrote in her journal, "I am enjoying this separation from my husband."[67] Her husband's trip was giving her time to be herself, as well as to reflect on their marriage and the person into whom it had shaped her.

Who, then, was Abigail May Alcott at the age of forty-two? She still felt strongly that she had made an excellent choice of husband. She considered him the best and dearest of men, and she remained confident that he was destined to live on "in the . . . eternal reverence of posterity." On their twelfth anniversary, two weeks after Bronson had left for England, Abba commented that the time since their wedding had been "great years for [her] soul" and that her life had become one of "wise discipline," bringing "great energies into action." Defeat, she felt, had made her strong.[68] She was thankful for her husband's misfortunes, for they had "nerved [her] up to do and bear."[69] When she thought of her husband, staunchly philosophical, willing to die for his principles, she realized that it was not the principles themselves, but his dedication to them, that made her love Bronson so. In her journal, she wrote as if she were addressing him directly: "It is your life [that] has been more to me than your doctrine or theories. I love your fidelity to the pursuit of truth, your careless notice of principalities and powers, and vigilant concern for those who, like yourself, have toiled for the light of truth." The day after Bronson sailed, Abba had resolved to "hope all things, believe all things."[70] Fidelity was a virtue that Abba could understand, and her resolutions tended to be uncommonly firm.

On Abby's second birthday, Uncle Junius took Abba and the girls for an excursion in his rowboat, the *Undine*. Abba wrote, "I seldom omit these occasions for showing my children the joy I feel in their birth and continuance with me on earth. I wish them to feel that we must live for each other. My life thus far has been devoted to them, and I know that they will find happiness hereafter in living for their mother."[71] On this day of pleasure, as sunlight danced on the water, Abba pondered the mysteries of nine-year-old Louisa, whose explosive nature continued to puzzle her. In her journal, she told of her sincere distress about her daughter's spirit, which seemed to promise so much but which also seemed beyond Abba's power to reach and soothe:

> United to great firmness of purpose and resolution, there is at times the greatest volatility and wretchedness of spirit—no hope, no heart for anything, sad, solemn, and desponding. Fine generous feelings, no selfishness, great good will to all, and strong attachment to a few.[72]

While his children back home decorated a miniature portrait of him with flowers and hoped for his safe return, Bronson pondered how the two shining aspects of his life, his family and Alcott House, might be brought together. He rejected the possibility of transplanting his wife and daughters to England, where he found nothing attractive apart from Alcott House. By far his preferred option was to take the essence of Alcott House back to Massachusetts with him. Finding that he was already bound to Wright and Lane "by ties which cannot be sundered," Alcott proposed to bring the two men with him to America. But he wanted them as more than neighbors. His plan was to establish, with their help, a "new plantation in America," a community of men and women consecrated to the ideals of education and culture that had underlain both the Temple School and its English counterpart. "It is not in Old, but in the New England," he grandly announced, "that God's Garden is to be planted, and the fruits matured for the sustenance of the swarming nations." Like his Puritan forebears, Bronson aspired to found a society in the New World that would be a city on a hill, a beacon of morality in a fallen world. This task seemed to him as good as accomplished, and he would not hear of its possible failure. He wrote, "I would not scatter so lavishly in hope as to reap mortification and defeat. . . . The heart's visions shall all be realized."73

The second Eden imagined by Wright, Lane, and Alcott would be agrarian. Taking Alcott's own daughters and Lane's son William as its first pupils, this great living school would be an ideal laboratory of moral education. Many of the three men's founding principles were decidedly radical. If their home were truly to be an earthly heaven, it must do nothing that made the rest of the world into more of a hell. Thus, all commodities that came from the labor of slaves were to be strictly excluded. In addition, the community would do away with money. On the principles that slaughtering animals was a form of murder and that consuming their milk, eggs, and labor was a species of theft, the Alcottian paradise was to shun the use of animal products and would rely as little as possible on animals for work.

The remaining major tenet of the community was the most extraordinary. Lane strongly believed that the most persistent enemy of human rights and social equality had always been the primitive preference that people felt toward their own families. He had written a detailed pamphlet in which he explained that the social evolution of humankind would not be complete until the human race arrived at a "third dispensation," whereby all people would cast aside their selfish devotion to their own spouses and children and would form, instead, a single, egalitarian human family. Lane persuaded Alcott that their community should be a model for this kind of "consociate" family, in which no member would have a higher claim than any other on the love and loyalty of his fellows.

For a brief period, Alcott hoped to bring a small army of followers from England to inaugurate the colony. He wrote to Abba that he was daily receiving letters from various parts of the kingdom expressing interest in the venture. As he composed lists of potential recruits, Alcott was already thinking about exclusion as well as inclusion. He wanted to populate his paradise with a moral elite for which, he expected, few would be suited. He wrote to Abba, "Almost every human being is disqualified now for such an enterprize [*sic*]—scarce one (of all our friends even) is emancipated from the bonds of self, and made free in the freedom of love." The scant number of spiritually eligible persons, however, did nothing to dim his enthusiasm. The more he pondered his dream, the more ecstatic his anticipation became.74

However, Bronson's hoped-for legion of approved acolytes failed to materialize. In the end, Wright was unable to persuade even his own wife, who feared that the ocean voyage would prove too perilous for their baby. Only the two most fervid English enthusiasts were game for the adventure. Lane resigned his post at the *Price Current*. Wright severed his connection with Alcott House, leaving the school in the hands of William Oldham, another of Greaves's disciples. Through the letters he received from Lane, Oldham was to follow, first eagerly and then anxiously, the progress of Alcott's search for an American Utopia. In mid-September, Lane, Wright, and Alcott, along with Lane's son William, boarded a ship for Boston.

Abba did not know what to think. She doubted her power to adapt to the kind of community her husband proposed, yet she had no heart to stand in the way of his achieving the "rich harvest of life and love" that he imagined.75 He had written to her that she was almost the only person in the world who believed in his dream; how could she bear to confess that she, too, doubted him?76 Moreover, she was certain that the purifying atmosphere of her husband's community would benefit her children. If her daughters were to fare well in the exchange, Abba decided, "surely then am I not injured, for they are the threads wrought into the texture of my life— the vesture with which I am covered."77 Even before Bronson's ship set sail for home, she began to travel about, trying on her own to find an acceptable property for the imagined community to call home. If her husband's grand project did fail, she would not be to blame.

After Alcott left England, Carlyle, having had more time to reflect on the nature of his American visitor, delivered a more critical verdict to Emerson than he had previously rendered. "I consider him entirely unlikely to accomplish anything considerable, except some kind of crabbed, semi-perverse, though still manful existence of his own." Although Carlyle admitted that living a manful existence was "no despicable thing," Alcott's choice of British associates horrified him. He had known Greaves, and he considered him a blockhead. Greaves's followers, in Carlyle's view, included some "bottomless imbeciles" and he admonished Emerson not to be seen in their company.[78]

Abba worked busily to prepare the cottage for her husband's return, determined that, even if the house was small, he would find it "swept and garnished." When Bronson and his allies arrived in Concord on October 21, she exulted, "Good news for Cottagers! Happy days these! Husband returned, accompanied by the dear Englishmen, the good and true. Welcome to these shores, [to] this home, to my bosom!" She wished, she wrote two days later, "to breathe out my soul in one long utterance of hope." Louisa was ecstatic too; she asked, "Mother, what makes me so happy?" Abba could not reply. She explained in her journal, "A big prayer had just then filled my breast and stifled utterance."[79]

As Alcott planned his commune, one might have wondered whether he was trying to march toward a shining future or to flee from a problematic past and present. Surely, he had reasons aplenty for wanting to escape Concord. As ever with him, living life within conventional society meant running up debts. By trying to create a self-sufficient community in the wilderness, one that would entirely renounce the use of currency, Bronson hoped at last to free himself from a world that seemed always to be demanding payment. Moreover, he was evidently tired of people, and he desperately craved greater solitude. For a while, Concord had seemed a sufficiently distant refuge from urban pressures and discontents, but it seemed to his sensitive perception that Concord, too, was falling victim to the encroachments of steam and steel. Alcott's proposed departure from Concord was, in part, an escape from mechanized modernity, a flight from both social and physical machinery.

But the escape could not be effected at once. An unforeseen obstacle quickly arose. In marked contrast with the militant celibacy of Charles Lane, Henry Wright seemed incapable of regulating his sexual life. His wife and child in England notwithstanding, Wright fell in love with a thirty-two-year-old radical feminist named Mary Gove, who had left her abusive and impecunious husband some time earlier. Both politically and physically passionate, she was impossible for Wright to resist. Weary of the severely spartan diet that Lane and Alcott had imposed at Dove Cottage and equally unwilling to abstain from other pleasures, Wright left his fellow reformers in the early winter of 1842–43 to seek his own version of the

*Charles Lane, whom Louisa
remembered as the "Dictator" of Fruitlands.*
(Courtesy of the Fruitlands Museum)

new Eden in Mrs. Gove's bedroom. Alcott was appalled at Wright's faithlessness. In a heated interview before the latter's departure, Alcott reproached him for his disorderly habits and unsteadiness of purpose. When the door of the cottage closed behind the exiting Henry Wright, Alcott also shut Wright out of his mind. From that day hence, there is not a single surviving scrap of paper on which Alcott so much as scribbled Wright's name. Even when Wright died of cancer in Mrs. Gove's arms just two years later, Bronson made no note of the event.

Charles Lane, on the other hand, settled comfortably with the Alcotts—comfortably, at least, for himself. Whatever physical energies he derived from the divine emanations of Concord, he appeared intent on conserving them. When Lane wrote to Alcott's brother Junius, describing his life at Hosmer Cottage, the latter could not have failed to notice the rather unequal division of labor that Lane described. While Lane gave the children lessons in French, geography, and other subjects, he evidently took no part in the manual labor of the household. Whereas he observed that "Mr. A. saws and chops, provides water, . . . prepares all the food, in which he tries new materials and mixtures, of a simple character," Lane himself passed his mornings in his room, enjoying "much God-like quiet."[80] He heartily approved of the simple breakfasts at the cottage, which consisted of bread, apples, and potatoes and were served, not on plates, but only with napkins. The only spice in evidence at these meals came from "conversation of a useful and interior kind."[81]

Initially, at least, Lane cut an interesting figure among the liberal New Englanders to whom Bronson introduced him. When not busily turning out articles for reform journals, he appeared alongside Bronson at intellectual gatherings and symposia. Evidently, they made an attractively balanced team; Bronson's mild tone and airy idealism were brilliantly complimented by the sharper accents of the Englishman, who spoke with a hard intellectual clarity. Emerson thought that the two could not open their mouths without proclaiming a new solar system.

The two also achieved a public relations coup when it was discovered that Alcott had refused to pay his annual dollar-and-a-half poll tax. On a winter's day, the town constable came to the door of Hosmer Cottage and presented Alcott with an arrest warrant. Alcott meekly consented to be removed to the jailhouse, and when informed that the jailer was not on the premises, quietly waited for two hours while the constable went to look for him. As Alcott stood by, warming to the idea of his small civic martyrdom, a local judge, Samuel Hoar, heard that his fellow Concordian was in danger of being incarcerated. Much to Alcott's disappointment, Judge Hoar paid the tax for him, and Alcott was told to go home. Nevertheless, Charles Lane seized on the incident to write an impassioned article for the *Liberator* on the subject of personal freedom, arguing that the payment of taxes should be voluntary and presenting Alcott as a brave resister of state slavery.

Yet Lane also had a talent for ruffling feathers. He strode through life with a firm conviction that he was morally superior to everyone he met, and he felt no great shyness about asserting this opinion. Ignoring Carlyle's caveat, Emerson had offered both Wright and Lane a room in his house when they first arrived in Concord. After briefly accepting this hospitality, Lane declared that Emerson lived all too comfortably and that his host's table was "*too good* for my simplicity."[82] Emerson could detect no trace of warmth in the Englishman, of whom he commented, "His nature and influence do not invite mine, but always freeze me."[83] As to the heft of his visitor's philosophical opinions, Emerson soon agreed with Carlyle. In his journal, he wrote that Lane and Wright were "two cockerels."[84]

Not only Emerson was put off by Lane's hauteur. During a philosophical discussion in which Emerson and Thoreau both took part, Lane surprised the company by accusing Thoreau, of all people, of ethical laxness and immoral self-indulgence. Lane averred that the love of nature that Thoreau championed was "the most subtle and dangerous of sins"—indeed, "a refined idolatry, much more to be dreaded than gross wickedness." When Thoreau suggested that Lane had no faculty for appreciating nature and therefore did not know what he was talking about, Alcott sided with Lane. Both he and his English friend, Bronson explained, had gone so far beyond material objects and were so filled with spiritual love and perception that their love of nature was incomprehensible to less enlightened natures. Lidian Emerson, who recorded the scene, found it "ineffably comic," although she noted that no one was laughing.[85] Small wonder, then, that when Emerson and Thoreau were asked to join Lane and Alcott's utopian venture, each discovered that he had better things to do.

No one was laughing at Hosmer Cottage either. Abba found it hard to abide Lane's cold insistence on discipline in all things and his hostility to innocent fun; on Bronson's and Louisa's joint birthday, she complained to her journal that she was being "frowned down into stiff quiet and peaceless order." To a woman accustomed to laughter and frolic, particularly one who had just finished enjoying five months of liberty, the change was especially irksome. By her own description, she was becoming morbidly sensitive to every detail of life, and she was starting to fear that her husband's experiment might "bereave [her] of [her] mind."[86] Seeing to the wants of Wright and Lane had also tired her out. The day before Christmas, in hopes that a short absence from home would help to put matters right, she left Concord to visit her Boston relatives. The fact that, of her four daughters, she took only Louisa with her, suggests that Louisa, too, was chafing under the influence of Charles Lane.

After her initial outburst of joyous enthusiasm when her father came home, Louisa seems to have returned to reality with a bump. After her carefree summer with her mother and sisters, the presence of two strange

Englishmen under the family roof required a tremendous readjustment. Moreover, she could hardly have been pleased to find that the more dominant of the two men was utterly without humor and wholly intolerant of frolicsome natures like hers. High-spirited children tend to regard sudden impositions of authority as challenges, and they tend to fight back. A contest of wills thus began to unfold at Hosmer Cottage, one whose intensity can be inferred from the somewhat pleading letter that Bronson wrote Louisa on her birthday, the same day that Abba lamented the climate of "restriction and form" that now pervaded her home.

Since coming back to Concord, Bronson wrote, he had been continually near Louisa, whom he called his "honest little girl," meeting her daily at the fireside and table, observing her in all her walks, studies, and amusements. Yet she had seemed to repel his attentions, valuing her distance more than his attempts to please and assist her. Bronson tried to explain his fatherly wishes: "I would have you feel my presence and be the happier, and better that I am here. I want, most of all things, to be a kindly influence on you, helping you to guide and govern your heart, keeping it in a state of sweet and loving peacefulness." It baffled him, then, to discover that she was determined to resist him, that she would rather form her own spirit than accept the spiritual shape that he imagined for her. He was utterly sure that what he offered her was best. She seemed equally certain that she did not want it. Her stubbornness must have tried his patience, but it was with patient, persuasive tones that he pursued his argument: "Will you not let me do you all the good that I would? And do you not know that I can do you little or none, unless you are disposed to let me; unless you give me your affections, incline your ears, and earnestly desire to become daily better and wiser, more kind, gentle, loving, diligent, heedful, serene." Then, as if knowing that his argument would fail, Bronson altered his tone. Without expressly accusing Louisa, he scribbled out a long litany of character flaws, including anger, impatience, evil appetites, greedy wants, ill-speaking, and rude behavior. These, he threatened, would drive the good spirit out of the poor, misguided soul, leaving it "to live in its own obstinate, perverse, proud discomfort; which is the very *Pain of Sin*, and is in the *Bible* called the worm that never dies."[87] In the space of a few lines, Bronson's gentle admonition had transformed into a Calvinist sermon in miniature.

One can only imagine how her father's letter made Louisa think or feel. Not surprisingly, though, it effected no miraculous transformation. She was not, of course, willingly any of the bad things that her father suggested. Rather, she was of an age when children, reminded of their faults, tend to cry, apologize, and vow to be better. But then they forget, and their parents wonder why. Bronson was an exceptional man. Louisa was to become an extraordinary woman. As a middle-aged father and a growing daughter, however, they shared most of their traits with the rest of the world—both earnestly willing the best, both wanting to communicate all that they had to tell each other, but each failing to receive the messages that the other was sending them. This is how fathers and daughters could be in the nineteenth century. The species has not changed.

Abba and Louisa came back to Concord after New Year's Day, ready for another try at domestic peace. Bronson, too, wanted nothing more than a serene and contented home. In his mind, his upcoming venture into communal living was largely motivated by his concern for his children and how best to teach them of celestial things in a fallen world. He had concluded his birthday letter to Louisa with the hope that the Alcotts would "become a family more closely united in loves that can never sunder us from each other." Two months later, he addressed to all four of his daughters a rhapsodic letter in which he promised to show them "what is . . . more lovely and more to be desired than every thing on which the eye can rest," the thing "for which the world and all its glories was [*sic*] made." He was referring to a kind and loving family and a house "from which sounds of content, and voices of confiding love alone ascend." Such a family was, he said, "the Jewel—the Pearl of priceless cost." He told his daughters that he wanted to prepare for them an "imperishable mansion"—a home as heaven. His dream seemed so near his grasp that he signed his letter, "Your Ascended Father."[88] The community he was readying himself to found would be the ultimate test of his ability to ascend.

As spring came to Concord in 1843, Alcott and Lane began to feel more urgently the need to find the land where they could build their paradise. The earlier in the growing season they could begin their work, the better the colony's chances for success. Emerson had by this time emphatically declined to take part in the enterprise, and he had spent the winter trying to talk Bronson out of the idea.[89] Two years earlier, Emerson had politely declined an invitation to join George Ripley's commune at Brook Farm. Now he made a similar refusal. He doubted that he would find improvement by retreating from the world of bustle and conflict; running away, he implied, was not instructive. Rather, he argued, "He will instruct & strengthen me, who . . . where he is . . . in the midst of poverty, toil, & traffic, extricates himself from the corruptions of the same."[90] The man who had once advised his readers "Build therefore your own world," wanted them to build on the spot where they already found themselves.

Alcott, who had gotten used to having Emerson underwrite his projects, was no doubt surprised when Emerson withheld not only his participation but also his financial backing from the utopian plan. Certainly Emerson was too well mannered to tell Bronson to his face what he had written about him in his journal: "For a founder of a family or institution, I would as soon exert myself to collect money for a madman."[91] The only money available for the venture was Lane's, and so he provided it: his life's savings of approximately $2,000, a portion of which went to free Alcott of his remaining debts in Concord, which amounted to $175. Lane also located a piece of land that might serve for the commune. Reluctant to settle on a place too close to Concord and, therefore, the interfering influence of Emerson, Lane declared his preference for a ninety-acre tract of fields, orchards, and woodlands near the hamlet of Harvard, Massachusetts, a town that shared only its name with the great university. Lane liked the remoteness of the spot. It was well to the west of Concord, and there was no road leading to the house. Lane and Alcott visited the property and inspected the weather-beaten farmhouse and barn, neither in the best condition but acceptable. "The capabilities are manifold," Lane wrote, "but the actualities humble."[92] He bargained down the owner, Maverick Wyman, to an affordable price: $1,800 for the land and rentfree use of the house for the first year. Without much ceremony, the deed was signed, and the land's legal ownership passed from one Maverick to two others. Alcott and Lane, however, refused to call themselves the owners of the property; rather, they had liberated the acreage from the bonds of commerce. Nevertheless, Lane congratulated himself on the handsomeness of the deal. To his friend William Oldham, back in England, Lane boasted, "this, I think you will admit . . . will entitle transcendentalism to some respect for its practicality."[93] The farm was given a new name: Fruitlands.

Bronson knew that Fruitlands would be the Rubicon of his life. In his view, the inspiration for the colony had been an expression of divine guidance, a holy directive that he must fulfill or lose all in the attempt. More realistically, it was the ultimate gambit of a man whose other choices had evaporated. Incalculable stakes lay in the balance. If the utopian farm succeeded, it would prove that human beings could thrive by adopting kinder, simpler relations with one another. Its example might light the way to a better way of living, and it would prove at last that Bronson Alcott was neither a failure nor a fool. But if the experiment did fail, it would be a byword of folly, a failure not only for Alcott but for all who dreamed of higher things. At the end of the road to Harvard, either ruin or redemption waited.

It took another week for the Alcotts to make ready for the move. Two of the converts whom Alcott and Lane had succeeded in winning for the cause, Wood Abram and Samuel Larned, went ahead of them along with Lane's son in order to prepare the farmhouse for occupation. Abba and her daughters packed up their belongings, contending with all the mixed emotions that arise when one leaves one home for another. Abba could not help looking back on all that had transpired during her three fleeting years in Concord. Her father had died, and her youngest daughter had been born. On the first of June, the day of the departure, nostalgia and hope crowded together in her mind. Early that morning, the family's belongings were loaded onto a large wagon. Abba and the girls said their farewells to Hosmer Cottage and took their places in the wagon. Lane settled in beside them. It remained only for Bronson to climb into the driver's seat, take the reins, and urge the horses forward.

CHAPTER FIVE

THE SOWING
OF THE SEEDS

"I know not why we may not live the true life."
—Journal of ABIGAIL MAY ALCOTT,
June 1, 1843

THE FARMHOUSE AT FRUITLANDS, WHICH STILL STANDS, does not offer a commanding view of the surrounding country. However, a short walk up the hillside is rewarded with a sweeping view of the Nashua Valley and the bluish slopes of Mount Monadnock in the far distance. Black-eyed Susans and Queen Anne's lace grow profusely in the meadow. Mockingbirds trill fantastic arias, damselflies ruffle the stillness of the air, and chipmunks dash boldly past the front door of the house. The look of the land today is far different from what it was when the Alcotts took possession. Most of the once-open, cultivated land has been overgrown by forest, so that even the rocky and rutted path that led to the house is visible only to those with a keen eye or an experienced guide. Where Lane and Alcott sowed their first and only crop, there now grow thick stands of ash, white pine, and wild cherry trees. They are not quite so thick, however, as the squadrons of mosquitoes and deer flies that rudely remind one that this, like any other place on earth, is not paradise.

Although Fruitlands was to be a highly literary commune, the best writer who lived there was only ten years old at the time. The closest Louisa May Alcott came to writing a memoir at Fruitlands was a short story called "Transcendental Wild Oats." The story has long tantalized those eager to know the truth about Fruitlands; it presents facts and fabrications side by side, offering no dependable guide as to which is which. In the story, Louisa recollects the day she first saw Fruitlands as being attended by "the pleasant accompaniments of wind, rain, and hail."[1] Charles Lane, however, wrote that the trip took place on a sharp, clear day, colder than normal for that time of year. In either case, it was not the best of days for traveling. But there was no time to waste. In Massachusetts, the first of June falls perilously late in the planting season. Spring wheat is in the ground by the end of April; potatoes should be planted no later than the last of May. Although the planting seasons for beans, barley, and sweet corn were not over by the time the Alcotts arrived at the Fruitlands farmhouse, these too would ideally have been planted earlier. Recalling his childhood, Bronson Alcott must surely have understood the prospects that await the farmer who spends the spring months discussing philosophy in fashionable people's parlors. Yet Lane had purhased the Fruitlands property only on May 25. Before they had even begun, Lane and Alcott had placed themselves in an almost unwinnable race against the calendar.

If Alcott and Lane had been patient, they could have used the summer and autumn of 1843 as a time of preparation, making the necessary repairs to the house and barn and raising the organic materials with which they might have fertilized the land during the following spring. But a cluster of worries had pressed Alcott and Lane to move forward without delay. First was the concern that their financial position would worsen in the next ten months. To Alcott, every month spent in Concord was likely to mean a deeper plunge into red ink. In America, Lane had no business contacts that might lead to employment. Moreover, there was the matter of principle to be addressed. Lane's journeys from London to Alcott House to Concord had followed a trajectory of renunciation, a path on which he was determined to continue. It would not do for the steps toward establishing Fruitlands to partake, any more than necessary, in the foul habits of getting and spending.

From Concord to Harvard, Massachusetts, is a distance of fourteen miles. For the seven travelers who made the journey, four of them children not yet in their teens, the trip took almost the entire day. In "Transcendental Wild Oats," Louisa recalled that the wagon borrowed for the journey was a large one, spacious enough to contain Bronson, who drove, Abba, their four daughters, and "a motley load" of possessions. Bronson's attention was perhaps more focused on his dreams and visions than his driving; in Louisa's narrative, the small horse that draws the wagon is left to follow the road "all his own way."² The mother holds an infant while another girl snuggles close to her father. The remaining two pass the early part of the journey chatting happily together and, as the afternoon extends toward evening, sing soft, murmuring lullabies to their dolls. "Timon Lion" the character in Louisa's story who stands for Charles Lane, strides alongside the wagon on foot; whether Lane's decision to walk was dictated by a lack of space or his stalwart disdain for luxury is unclear. Although Louisa also places a young, brown-faced boy in the scene, this detail is fictitious; the only boy who lived at Fruitlands, William Lane, was already at the homestead, awaiting his father's arrival.

Rolling slowly along the road, the family may have struck passersby as a picture of togetherness. On this togetherness, the success of Fruitlands was largely to depend. However, Louisa and her older sister, Anna, were becoming ever more capable of forming independent judgments about their parents. As a teacher, Bronson had always most loved working with younger children, in part, perhaps, because they were most willing to accept his ideas and authority uncritically. For Anna and Louisa, the time when their father could do no wrong was drawing to an end. This fact suggests an unspoken reason why Bronson became attracted to the idea of an insular community with himself at its head. Alcott was enchanted by fatherhood. He loved, as most men do, the adoring regard that prepubescent children lavish on their fathers. And like many fathers, he probably dreaded the almost inevitable withdrawal of affection that comes with adolescence. By removing his children from a world that judged him harshly, Alcott might have hoped to preserve his preeminent place in his daughters' hearts for a while longer. Indeed, had Fruitlands succeeded, Alcott would have remained perpetually a father in a symbolic sense, since the "consociate family," both young and old, would have owed him its filial love even after his daughters had moved on to more mature affections. It is unclear whether Alcott paused to consider that one often loses most quickly the thing one tries to maintain beyond its time. In June 1843, Anna and Louisa were very much "in the wagon" insofar as they still lived for their father's approval and believed that what he thought best must finally be right. For Louisa, at least, a change was coming.

Abba and the girls first saw the Fruitlands farmhouse in the late afternoon light. They could hardly have been in a mood to appreciate its rustic beauty.

Originally intended to serve only until "suitable and tasteful buildings in harmony with the natural scene" could be erected, the Fruitlands farmhouse was the home of the Alcotts throughout their experiment in communal living.
(Courtesy of the Fruitlands Museum)

The house is a two-story structure, painted so vividly red that its color was the only detail of living there that three-year-old May remembered as an adult. If, on approaching the house, Louisa or one of her sisters asked her father where she would be sleeping, Bronson would have gestured toward the low-pitched roof of the house. The only area in the house spacious enough to accommodate Anna, Louisa, and Lizzie was the attic.

In their desire to renounce the world, Alcott and Lane had been attracted to the Fruitlands property because the house was well removed from the main road. For this reason, and because the house lay at the end of an incline just steep enough to be treacherous, the last few hundred yards of the day's journey presented the greatest challenges to beast and traveler alike. No horse could have negotiated the rutted, uneven cart path without stumbling. Happily, though, catastrophe was avoided, and wearily triumphant, the Alcotts soon stepped over the threshold. Abba's first task in her new home was to assemble a hasty dinner of bread and potatoes. Tonight, however, was not the time to begin the task of putting the house in order. The travelers were so worn out by their journey that they lacked the will to set up the beds; they spent their first night at Fruitlands amid blankets and sheets spread on the floor.

At some point that day, Abba found time to scribble a paragraph into her journal. She did not write about the sights and sounds of the day, but rather of the high purpose of the commune and the sobering challenges that lay ahead. She wrote: "[T]here is much to strengthen our hearts and hands in the reflexion that our pursuits are innocent and true—that no selfish purpose actuates us—that we are living for the good of others." But Abba realized that the Alcotts and Lanes, acting alone, were too small a force to make the venture a success. Her tentative assessment was that, "if we can collect about us the true men and women; putting away the evil customs of society, I know not why we may not live the true life, putting away the evil customs of society and leading quiet exemplary lives." Yet Abba seemed already to be bracing herself for disappointment when she wrote, "tho we may fail it will be some consolation that we have ventured what none others have dared."[3]

The experiment had attracted a handful of recruits. They were not precisely "the true men and women" Abba had hoped for in her journal. In particular, "true women" seemed to be in short supply. Apart from Abba and her daughters, Fruitlands attracted only one woman during its entire existence, an Anna Page from Providence, Rhode Island, who did not arrive until August. In a concession to the world of commerce, Lane and Alcott hired a local farmhand, whom they paid by the week. As for the regular male adherents of the commune, they were a cast of characters well worthy of satirical fiction. Twenty-year-old Samuel Larned was a self-styled ascetic whose various programs of self-denial included once subsisting an entire year on nothing but crackers. Another, Abraham Everett, was later remembered by Anna Alcott as "the hermit," an interesting mark of distinction in a community that was not famously sociable. Everett, however, had a persuasive reason for feeling bitter about life within society and for renouncing the world of money and property; his relatives had once conspired to commit him to a madhouse as part of a scheme to cheat him out of an inheritance. In writing of him, Lane attested that Everett was quite sane, even if he was not "a spiritual being—at least not consciously and wishfully so."[4]

Surely the most visually arresting of the band of eccentrics was, to use Louisa's description, a "bland, bearded Englishman" by the name of Samuel Bower "who expected to be saved by eating uncooked food."[5] Mr.

Bower had another interesting proclivity. Whereas Alcott saw enemies in cotton and wool, Bower took the doctrine of abstention a step further and espoused naturism, claiming that clothes themselves were an obstacle to spiritual growth. Some uncertainty exists as to how freely Bower was permitted to indulge his disdain for clothing at Fruitlands. By some accounts, he bared all only during strolls after sundown; it has also been suggested that he was pressured into the compromise of draping himself in a sheet. In any event, the mental image of Bower, sheeted or sheetless, in daily contact with the real-life counterparts of Marmee and the March sisters, beggars the imagination.

Ironically, the most dependable assistance that was offered to the Lanes and Alcotts came from a man who never formally joined the community. He was Joseph Palmer, described by Anna Alcott as "the old farmer who plowed the sacred soil." Palmer, as if to add another lightly surreal touch to the community, hailed from a place called No Town, so named because it lay outside the limits of any municipality and was thus exempt from local taxation. Like Bower and Everett, Palmer was attracted to Fruitlands as a haven from the persecutions and judgments with which the world had pursued him. Palmer's offense against society had been wearing a beard. For the crime of being twenty years ahead of popular fashion, he had been jeered at, physically assaulted, and even refused Communion at church. Once, when he was set on by a group of men intent on holding him down and shaving him, Palmer had taken out a knife and stabbed one of them. For this act of self-defense, he was sent to jail, where he had to defend his beard again, this time against fellow inmates. Years after these events, when facial hair had become popular, Palmer met a preacher who had once denounced Palmer's beard from the pulpit. Palmer walked up to the man and stroked the latter's whiskers with his hand, murmuring, "Know ye that thy redeemer liveth?"[6] Palmer's experiences had led him to sympathize with others who were willing to suffer for principle. He brought the Alcotts furniture for the house and offered his labor for no pay. Whenever—and it was often—the Fruitlanders found that they lacked the right tools for a job, Palmer would drive to No Town and return with the required item.

Three days after arriving, once the rest of the furniture had come and she felt entitled to a few moments of leisure, Abba took a walk around the property, taking note of "woodland, vale, meadow, and pasture." She enthusiastically declared the view to be "one of the most expansive prospects in the country." All her worries vanished. Delight and confidence enfolded her. In the drawing rooms of Concord, perhaps, she had doubted Emerson when he proclaimed the sovereignty of Nature and smiled at her own husband's ecstatic immersion in the Over-soul. Here, on this hillside, however, all of it seemed undeniably real. While the impressions were still fresh, she hastened to her journal:

> One is transported from his littleness and the soul expands in such a region of sights and sounds. Between us and this vast expanse we may hold our hand and stand alone, an isolated being occupying but a foot of earth and living but for ourselves; or we may look again, and a feeling of diffusive illimitable benevolence possesses us as we take in this vast region of hill and plain.7

After her glorious experience of beauty on the hillside, it was soon time to descend again to house and kitchen. Later that same day, she was back in the realm of practicality, "gather[ing] an apron of chips while the children collected flowers." Abba mused briefly on the apt nature of the two kinds of collecting. "Like provident Mother Earth I gathered for use, they for beauty. Both gave pleasure. It was very characteristic in me, and most natural in them."8

Everyone agreed on the natural beauty of the farm. The improvements were another matter. Ironically for a settlement called Fruitlands, the property possessed only a scattering of fruit trees. When one of the community members, Isaac Hecker, resigned from the group, he cited the lack of fruit as one of his reasons; he considered himself a victim of false advertising. In a letter published in *The Dial*, written by Alcott and Lane with the general intention of promoting the project, the co-founders themselves felt bound to admit that the existing buildings were "ill-placed and unsightly as well as inconvenient." They meant to use them only until "suitable and tasteful buildings in harmony with the natural scene" could be erected.9 Containing only three bedrooms, one of which was initially set aside for guests or for "family" members other than the Alcotts and Lanes, the house was a cramped accommodation for the eight new occupants.

The complaints in *The Dial* piece notwithstanding, the house's simplicity was not devoid of charm. Walking through the front door, one entered a parlor where Lane and the Alcotts received both friends and curious visitors. To one's immediate left was the moderately sized room where Alcott at once established the commune's library and where his ever-present bust of Socrates glowered down on the well-stocked shelves and simple chairs. Whereas a spirit of Spartan self-denial reigned over the rest of Fruitlands, this small Temple of Minerva merited at least a partial exemption. It was said that the principal property of the community consisted in books. Louisa asserted in retrospect that the library was indeed "the best room in the house, and the few busts and pictures that still survived many flittings were added to beautify the sanctuary." It was here, she remembered, that the family met "for amusement, instruction, and worship."[10] In back of the two front rooms, with which it shared an enormous central fireplace, lay a single large room in which the consociates took their meals.

In the right rear, a narrow stairway led upstairs, where a wide landing gave access to the three bedrooms, the first two of which looked out from the front of the dwelling. The first of these Charles Lane shared with his son, although the word "shared" suggests a more generous arrangement than existed in fact, since the elder Lane actually claimed the entire room proper for himself. The luckless William was shunted off into an adjoining space no larger than a walk-in closet. The adjacent bedroom housed Alcott and his wife. Three-year-old May, judged too young to sleep on her own, shared her parents' quarters. A third bedroom, very small and located at the far end of the landing, accommodated other members of the commune or curious visitors, of whom there were many. Any visitor interested in seeing how a preadolescent girl lived in the new Eden would have been conducted, perhaps with some apologies, to the dark flight of stairs that communicated with the attic. It was not a cheery place. The only natural light entered through two small windows at either end, and the ceiling was so low that it is unlikely that either of the two older girls was able to stand upright. The space also trapped an unpleasant amount of heat. In her Fruitlands journal, in reference to the bracing predawn baths that were part of the daily routine, young Louisa wrote ecstatically, "I love cold water!"[11] Given the stifling repose from which she had just risen, it is easy to see why.

No record survives of the first day of work on the Fruitlands farm. However, the likely spirit of the moments before the first spade of earth was turned can perhaps be guessed from a later entry in the journal of Isaac Hecker. Although Hecker did not join the colony until July, he was on hand for another significant "first": the reaping of the first crops harvested by the community. He wrote, "When the first load of hay was driven into the barn and the first fork was about to be plunged into it, one of the family took off his hat and said, 'I take off my hat, not that I reverence the barn more than other places, but because this is the first fruit of our labor.' Then a few moments were given to silence, that holy thought might be awakened."[12] The scene on June 2 had probably been very much the same. Alcott, with his love of speech and ceremony, must have had more than a few well-chosen words to say. Heads were likely bared as the calm, even voice, imbued on this day with unique passion and purpose, wafted on the late spring breeze. The newly united family may have paused a few moments, wishing to experience in all its depth and expectation this moment when, they hoped, the history of humankind was to begin its transformation. Then it was time to begin.

More than two months after their arrival at Fruitlands, Alcott and Lane wrote a jointly composed letter to A. Brooke of Oakland, Ohio, who had been sufficiently intrigued by the experiment to ask them for a further description. The two founders admitted, "We have not yet drawn out any preordained plan of daily operations." They hastened to explain that this lack of rigor was not a sign of laxness, but rather a natural consequence of the community's philosophy, which held that the form of activity should derive from the inspirations of the soul, not some inflexible blueprint. "We are impressed," they asserted, "with the conviction that by a faithful reliance on the spirit which actuates us, we are sure of attaining to clear revelations of daily practical duties." They added, "Where the spirit of love and wisdom abounds, literal forms are needless, irksome, and hindrative; where the spirit is lacking, no preconceived rules can compensate."[13]

These pious sentiments were not entirely truthful; there were plenty of rules at Fruitlands, and enough structure to go with them for Lane and Alcott, in their letters to the outside world, to describe a daily routine. After the morning bath, the children assembled for music and singing lessons, conducted by Lane. Then came breakfast, after which the men went out to the fields, but not in the typical work clothing of the period. The basic principle of the farm—that the people who lived there would cause no avoidable harm to man or beast—had a profound influence on the acceptable wardrobe. Leather belts and shoes would be accepted only until a nonexploitative substitute could be discovered; the Fruitlands farmers experimented with wearing canvas on their feet, and there was talk of finding some kind of tree bark that could be made to serve. Wool clothing was an act of theft against sheep; cotton had been raised and picked by slaves. Therefore, both were excluded. Linen, however, raised no moral objections. Thus, when the Fruitlands men went to their work, they wore loose fitting, smocked linen tunics, designed by Alcott himself and bearing some resemblance to the bloomers that would later be sported by suffragettes.

Much of the work in the early days of Fruitlands involved planting the fields as rapidly as possible. Already ominously behind schedule, the men were further hindered by the strict principles they tried to impose on themselves. Their initial hope had been to use no animal labor whatsoever. However, it seems that Alcott had forgotten, and Lane had never known, how quickly middle-aged muscles can tire and blisters can emerge on hands that, to use Louisa's phrase, "had held nothing heavier than a pen for years."[14] After a few days of noble striving, it was reluctantly agreed that a yoke of cattle was needed to plow the land. In allowing themselves this luxury, Lane and Alcott pleaded strict necessity to the outside world. In their initial exertions, they wrote, "we have at the outset . . . encounter[ed] struggles and oppositions somewhat formidable. Until the land is restored to its pristine fertility . . . the human hand and simple implement cannot wholly supersede the employment of machinery and cattle."[15] However, they left no doubt that they would resume working exclusively with their own hands as soon as possible. To supply the oxen for the plow, the consociates turned to Palmer, who sagely used the opportunity to import a source of protein; instead of bringing two oxen, as promised, Palmer arrived with an ox and a cow, whose milk proved to be a handy supplement in later months. As Louisa remembered, the planting efforts were chaotic; three of the brethren, each acting independently, sowed the same field with a different grain; after consultation and a good deal of laughter, the commune decided to do nothing to correct the error, which could not be remedied in any event, and "see what would come of it."[16]

After the morning work, the family members gathered for what Lane liked to call, somewhat ornately, "the meridian meal," an occasion "when usually some interesting and deep-searching conversation gives rest to the body and development to the mind." The afternoons differed little from the mornings:

> Occupation, according to the season and the weather, engages us out of doors or within, until the evening meal,—when we again assemble in social communion, prolonged generally until sunset, when we resort to sweet repose for the next day's activity.[17]

If the meals at Fruitlands were served in modern prisons, they might support a complaint of cruel and unusual punishment. Not content to outlaw animal products, Lane and Alcott banned salt, cane sugar, spices, coffee, and tea as well. The most exotic flavoring permitted was maple sugar. The list of forbidden substances left virtually no room for creativity or variation. Louisa recalls, in "Transcendental Wild Oats," the numbing monotony of the menu: "Unleavened bread, porridge, and water for breakfast; bread, vegetables, and water for dinner; bread, fruit and water for supper." The Fruitlanders consumed hefty quantities of potatoes, dried fruit, peas, beans, and barley, all of which Abba struggled to make palatable. As Louisa recalled, no beast was sacrificed on the domestic altar, but "only a brave woman's taste, time, and temper."[18]

Despite the rough beginning, Alcott was able to report to his brother Junius on June 18 that he and his fellow pilgrims had finished the planting and pruning. Three acres of corn, he wrote, were almost ready for the hoe, in addition to two acres of potatoes and one of beans. An acre or two more were being prepared for barley, turnips, and carrots. In mid-June, Lane wrote that Alcott himself was "doing a thousand things." This description says much about Alcott's enthusiasm for the project. To make it work, it seems, Alcott needed to be in several places at once, and Alcott was indeed desperate to make it work. But Alcott's "doing a thousand things" may also suggest a seldom-discussed reason for the commune's eventual failure. For all his talk about the shared burdens and blessings of a consociate family, the Fruitlands farm remained for Alcott an intensely personal project. It appears that every endeavor that took place on the farm required his personal involvement; even where the work was shared, it needed to bear the stamp of his own individual effort. If Fruitlands was to be a Utopia, it was to be a Utopia as strictly defined by Messrs. Alcott and Lane.

At its high-water mark, the Fruitlands venture could claim no more than sixteen members. The smallness of the community, obviously, was a tremendous problem, but one wonders whether a community can be large enough to sustain itself and still call itself utopian. Emerson put the matter with a clearheaded succinctness and more than a touch of mockery:

> It takes 1680 men to make one Man, complete in all the faculties; that is, to be sure that you have got a good joiner, a good cook, a barber, a poet, a judge, an umbrella-maker, a mayor and aldermen, and so on. Your community should consist of 2000 persons, to prevent accidents of omission; and each community should take up 6000 acres of land. Now fancy the earth planted with fifties and hundreds of these phalanxes side by side,—what tillage, what architecture, what refectories, what dormitories, what reading rooms, what concerts, what lectures, what gardens, what baths![19]

Emerson realized that a social group of the size needed to sustain itself could not honestly call itself a "family": it was a small town. He also saw that a world filled with such earnest and inward-looking small towns, each isolated from the others by its own parochial ideology, would never achieve the economies of scale necessary to produce a paradise of culture. The new Eden, if it were ever to be built, would require diversity and size. Yet the community that Alcott had had in mind demanded both personal intimacy and almost perfect philosophical consensus. How, though, was it possible to have a community as large as the one Emerson thought necessary, in which all the members were intellectually in agreement? Charles Lane, it seemed, was hard-pressed to decide whether it was more important to have enough hands to do the work or to keep the commune ideologically pure. On the one hand, when he wrote to William Oldham at Alcott House, he urged him to "please advertise [the colony] to all youthful men and women, for such are much wanted here." On the other, he also asserted, "The value of our enterprise depends not upon numbers so much as upon the spirit from which we can live outwardly."[20]

The most impressive yield at Fruitlands was its luxuriant crop of words. When Alcott and Lane were not working to sustain the farm, they were writing. Alcott and Lane produced a variety of essays about the farm that were partly manifestos and partly solicitations. This was one of the paradoxes of Fruitlands: the community wished to be both removed from the corrupting world and yet highly visible to it. Isaac Hecker thought one of the farm's best points was its delightful solitude. But if it were to change the world, Fruitlands was also dependent on the public eye. In a gesture tending to reflect their singleness of purpose, Alcott and Lane acquired the practice of signing both their names to their essays, but it seems evident that they were primarily Lane's. Though Alcott still had great confidence in himself as a social theorist, Emerson's criticisms of his "Psyche" manuscript and the poor public reception of "Orphic Sayings" had punctured his self-assurance as a writer. He realized that Lane's terser style was preferable to his own rhapsodic digressions.

The spirit of restraint was evident not only in the tone of Lane's writing but also its content. Almost everything Lane wrote at Fruitlands is laden with a heavy spirit of negation and self-denial. He had a gift for making his Utopia sound sanctimoniously joyless, as in the following passage written in August:

> "Shall I sip tea or coffee?" the inquiry may be. No. Abstain from all ardent, as from alcoholic drinks. "Shall I consume pork, beef, or mutton?" Not if you value health and life. "Shall I stimulate with milk?" No. "Shall I warm my bathing water?" Not if cheerfulness is valuable. . . . "Shall I teach my children the dogmas inflicted on myself, under the pretense that I am transmitting truth?" Nay, if you love them, intrude not between them and the Spirit of all Truth.[21]

The pious litany of forbidden actions draws on still further. Shall the Fruitlands disciples become hirelings or hire others? Shall they subjugate cattle? Shall they trade? Shall they become parents? Shall they take an interest in politics? To all these questions, the Fruitlanders returned the same answer, a single word boldly printed in capital letters: "ABSTAIN." The core of reform, at least for Charles Lane, lay not in doing, but rather in refraining from doing. Americans as a people have always inclined toward action; our response to a problem is far more likely to be "What should we do?" instead of "What should we cease to do?" In advocating less rather than more, Lane and Alcott sounded a note that was seldom heard in public discourse in their own time, and which is even less audible today.

Two years later, near the banks of Walden Pond, Alcott's friend Thoreau had a conversation with an Irish laborer named John Field. It was an exchange of views that might easily have taken place at Fruitlands between Alcott and a neighboring farmer. Thoreau tried to impress Field with the beauty of a simple life and frugal diet. Thoreau explained to Field "that I did not use tea, nor coffee, nor milk, nor fresh meat, and so did not have to work to get them . . . but as he began with tea, and coffee, and butter, and milk, and beef, he had to work hard to pay for them." To Thoreau's surprise, Field was not persuaded. It seemed to him that the very point of coming to America was to live in a place where "you could get tea, and coffee, and meat every day." Thoreau made another sally, asserting that "the only true America was that country where you are at liberty to pursue such a mode of life as may enable you to do without these." Thoreau made no progress with Field, however, and their discussion ended with some unkindly mutterings about congenital Irish poverty.[22] Yet as the Fruitlands experiment had already shown, Field's was the majority opinion; one lived in America in order to get things, not to test one's character by doing without them.

There is a curious absence in the statements of purpose that issued from Fruitlands that summer—an absence that seems to signal that Lane's influence was more powerful than his partner's. The pieces written for *The Dial* and for various curious observers tended to say very little about the hoped-for influence of the community on its children. Lane's and Alcott's letter to the Ohioan Mr. Brooke says almost nothing about how life on the farm would especially improve the souls of children. Indeed, the letter to Brooke names becoming a parent among the acts a virtuous person should avoid— strange advice from two men who had sired five children between them.

Lane's and Alcott's omission of the concerns of the children seems at odds with the entire trajectory of Alcott's career to date. Throughout his life, Alcott saw himself first and foremost as an educator. He always believed that, to reform the world, one would have to break the cycle by which the hatreds and stupidities of parents were reborn in their children. He also recognized the frustrations of trying to teach one's children a better way to live, only to have one's messages contradicted by so much of what the children could see outside their front door. Now, however, that he had found the very place where he might shape his daughters' spirits with a minimum of interference, he appears to have taken less interest, not more, in the girls' development.

Surprisingly, it was Lane, not Alcott, who gave most of the lessons to the children at Fruitlands. One reason was that Lane possessed skill in areas, music, for instance, in which Alcott had neither talent nor training. The bulk of the teaching also fell to Lane because Alcott could not be in two places at once. The two principal tasks to be done at the commune were teaching and farming. Alcott, the son of a farmer and a longtime veteran of the classroom, was arguably Lane's superior at both. However, Lane, while at least competent as a teacher, was practically hopeless as a farmhand. Abba thought he was lazy. Years later, when Lane was again a houseguest of the Alcotts in Concord, his skills had not improved. As Louisa reported in a letter to a friend, "Our garden looks dreadful shabby, for Father has been gone to New York for a long time, and Mr. Lane does not understand gardening very well."[23] Thus, those who came to visit Fruitlands found Alcott ever more in the fields and Lane ever more with the children. Louisa, for one, resented this turn of events, since she never liked the Englishman to begin with. Once, in her Fruitlands diary, she notes that Lane was absent from the farm and could not resist adding, "and we were glad."[24] If the plan had been for the colony to bring Alcott and his daughters closer together, it was backfiring ominously.

Despite their father's diverted attention, however, if Fruitlands came close at any time to being a paradise for any of its participants, it was perhaps so for Alcott's daughters. Undeniably, they had their share of the housework, and the incessant moralizing of the adults must have been disagreeable at times, but the surviving documents also convey a spirit of delight that all the perfectionism that surrounded the children could not stifle. Louisa's first surviving efforts at journal writing date from the Fruitlands period. Though fragmentary and showing no more sophistication than one might expect from a precocious ten-year-old, her diary gives a charming account of the joys she experienced during her father's social experiment—an episode that, in her eyes, seemed at first no more serious than an extended picnic. One entry, much more complete than most, gives a breezy and endearing account of one day in a child's life at Fruitlands:

September 1st—I rose at five and had my bath. I love cold water! Then we had our singing lesson with Mr. Lane. After breakfast I washed dishes, and ran on the hill till nine, and had some thoughts—it was so beautiful up there. Did my lessons,—wrote and spelt and did sums; and Mr. Lane read a story, "The Judicious Father." I liked it very much, and I shall be kind to poor people.

Father asked us what was God's noblest work. Anna said *men*, but I said *babies*. Men are often bad; babies never are. We had a long talk, and I felt better after it and *cleared up*.

We had bread and fruit for dinner. I read and walked and played till suppertime. We sung [*sic*] in the evening. As I went to bed the moon came up very brightly and looked at me. . . . I get to sleep saying poetry—I know a great deal.[25]

Except for some morning dishwashing, Louisa's account of her day mentions nothing in the way of chores, in spite of the chronic shortage of hands on the farm. Looking back on the venture as an adult, Louisa complained about the amount of labor she had been required to do. Nevertheless, her diary reflects that by far the most important work a child could do at Fruitlands was to improve herself, both intellectually and morally. Most of the girls' reading at Fruitlands emphasized moral instruction. Alcott's discourse with Anna and Louisa on the nobility of God's creation shows that he was still elaborating the ethical themes and Socratic pedagogy he had employed at the Temple School almost a decade earlier. As he had done before, he was trying to draw out the authentic intuitions of the children, for he still regarded young minds as the most promising source of uncorrupted wisdom.

Nevertheless, some spontaneous utterances were apparently better than others. Since Louisa writes that her choice of babies as God's noblest creation required "clearing up," one may guess that Anna's response of "man" won greater favor with Bronson. Anna, always better attuned to her father's intuitions and more precisely aware of how to please him, was able to hit the mark without even giving the reason for her answer. Louisa, the more independent thinker and more candid observer of the world, gave both an answer and a plausible explanation, but her effort was singled out for correcting. Louisa looked to prove her assertion by reference to the world as she saw it; Anna was safer and more doctrinaire. Nevertheless, although Anna gave the desired response, it was Louisa's that triggered the "long talk." It is hard to say whether, at the age of ten, Louisa already grasped that the answer that inspires discussions is often a better answer than the "correct" one. In any event, by stating and defending her opinion, Louisa was already truer to the inquisitive, original spirit of Alcott's friend and protector Emerson than her father was prepared to recognize.

Lessons, however, were only one part of the Alcott girls' day. Alcott and Lane, for all their condemnation of physical self-indulgence, understood the importance of recreations that strengthened the body and sharpened the mind. Whereas meat and leather were not welcome at Fruitlands, music and, more surprisingly, card playing were. As is clear from Louisa's diary, play was a central part of her and her sisters' existence. Like all good transcendentalists, Lane and Alcott believed devoutly in the restorative power of the natural world, and Louisa shared their love of the outdoors. She responded to her natural surroundings with deep awareness and sympathetic energy.

Walking today on the hill that Louisa describes in her journal, one immediately understands its attraction to a youthful spirit. It has just the slope that is made for children. Not so steep as to present real danger, the hill is angled so that a child of ten does not run down it quite so much as she *flies*. For a girl of Louisa's imagination, to careen laughing and shouting down this hill at top speed was to share for a moment in the freedom and exaltation of the birds.

It is less easy to re-create the "thoughts" that Louisa had on the hillside: thoughts she deemed memorable enough to mention in her journal but not significant enough to describe. The omission is tantalizing. Louisa, of course, knew that her journals were not a wholly private matter. The Alcott family made a practice of reading one another's diaries and sharing comments on them. Especially given their father's propensity for close moral supervision, any thoughts that Louisa or her sisters wanted to keep to themselves were best left off the page. Louisa knew how fanatical an interest Bronson took in her mental workings. She knew it was important to tell her father that her mind was active, so she made sure to tell her journal that she had had *some* thoughts. As to *what* she was thinking, she justly saw that as no one's business but her own.

Perhaps no historical record is so rich or complete that it does not leave us hungry for a little more. Reading Louisa's journal, we want to know more about what she thought that day when she was young and the world seemed made of peace and beauty. How did the grass feel beneath her feet? What sights in the valley spread below her set her mind in motion? To no avail; the weary diarist sets aside her pen, puts out her light, and falls as silent as the moon that gazes in on her.

CHAPTER SIX

FIRST FRUITS

"I am lost in wonder."
—Diary of ISAAC HECKER,
Fruitlands, July 18, 1843

L OUISA, OF COURSE, WAS NOT THE ONLY JOURNAL-KEEPING
Alcott at Fruitlands. Throughout their time at the farm, Bronson, Abba, and elder sister Anna recorded their thoughts and
observations as well. Bronson, in particular, remained as assiduous a diarist
as ever. Whatever the outcome of his time in the wilderness, a Fruitlands
memoir based on his journals might possibly become the work that would
finally open the eyes of the world to his teachings. Even if this literary project, like too many of the ones that preceded it, failed to hit the mark,
Alcott could look forward to the day when his notes on Fruitlands, richly
bound like the other great, heavy volumes of his journals, would supply a
unique and durable memento of the greatest adventure of his life. Night
after night, tired out by the long day of work, Alcott made his way to the
farmhouse library to add more pages to his chronicle.

According to "Transcendental Wild Oats," Abba defied the ban on animal products by maintaining a lamp that burned whale oil. Nevertheless,
toward the end of the experiment she complained in her own diary about
the toll that poor light had exacted on her vision. In his ascetic purity, it is
unlikely that Bronson used her lamp, so his eyes probably bothered him all
the more. Then, too, there was the issue of physical pain. The summer's
toil had barely begun when Lane started to grumble about his sore, over-
worked hands. Bronson was not immune to blisters either. Nevertheless, as

long as he could hold a pen and keep his eyes open, Bronson would write. He was a creature of the word, and a life without writing and speaking would not have really counted as life. However, as he labored over his Fruitlands journal, he never suspected what would become of this work of his callused hand and teeming brain.

Unlike her father, twelve-year-old Anna had no grand ambitions as she kept her journal. Her handwriting was tiny but immaculate—the work of a young perfectionist. In her journal writing, as, it seemed, in all other aspects of life, Anna knew how to please her parents, and her journal is a record of sunshine and satisfaction. Louisa's diary, however, is peppered with barbs against people she disliked and candid observations of what she took to be their weak points. Louisa sometimes writes of being tired and cross; by contrast Anna tells us that her favorite word is "beautiful."[1] It is from Louisa's journal that we know that tears were shed at Fruitlands; it is due to Anna that we know the details of one of the happiest days in the history of the Consociate Family.

On the morning of Saturday, June 24, 1843, a clear, fresh day, Anna rose before five and made her way downstairs to the kitchen. At Fruitlands, as on any farm, early mornings were routine, but Anna had a special reason this morning to greet the dawn: her sister Elizabeth was to celebrate her eighth birthday. Alcott family celebrations were no more materially lavish than any other aspect of their lives. Presents were utilitarian and often homemade. While the family resided at Fruitlands, no special birthday exceptions were made to the usual vegetarian diet. Nevertheless, the simplicity of these occasions seems to have deepened, not diminished, their significance, operating as a stimulating challenge to creativity. Anna gave Lizzie a fan. Louisa had decided on a pincushion, and Lane's son William had selected a book, perhaps from his father's library. Abba, daring the community's censure by exploiting the products of worms, had fashioned Lizzie a little silk balloon. Even three-year-old Abby May was not left out; a small pitcher was to be given in her name. Anna led Louisa and William out to the grove behind the house, where they "fixed a little pine tree in the ground and hung all our presents on it."[2] Before being called in for breakfast, Anna had time to weave a wreath of oak leaves for each of the children.

Breakfast was followed by a merry procession to the wood. Except for

Wood Abram, who was at the plow, all the commune members joined in.[3] The morning air was still cool as Charles Lane took out his violin and opened the festivities by playing while the others sang. Next came a spiritual reading—a parable selected and read aloud by Bronson, who then added a quickly drafted five-stanza, ninety-nine-line ode of his own composition. The poem is as much about the community as it is about Elizabeth; Alcott does not get around to mentioning the birthday girl until the fourth stanza. Nevertheless, he expresses his tender feelings when he hails her as:

> The joyful advent of an angel soul
> That, twice four years ago
> Our mundane life to know
> Descended from the upper skies
> A presence to our very eyes . . .
> A rose in Fruitlands gentle dell,
> A child intent in doing well.[4]

Lane and Abba had also written poems, though theirs were much shorter. Lane's poem, titled "To Elizabeth," ended with the lines "May your whole life / Exempt from strife / Shine forth as calm and bright."[5] Abba's read in part, "Dear gentle Dove / So full of love, / My own dear child, / So good and mild."[6] If one were to use these birthday verses to describe a "Fruitlands School" of poetry, one would surely comment on their serenity of mood, to the point of blandness. Another noteworthy feature is the eccentric sense of meter. Alcott himself cared little about counting iambs; his lines contain five feet or three or four, depending on his whim. In the quoted passages from Abba and Lane, one observes a seeming reluctance to write a line of more than two metric feet. Although Lane ends with a line of trimeter, everything else is compressed into lines of only four syllables. Fruitlands was a place where even poetry tended to be devoid of luxury and self-indulgence.

The last gifts Lizzie received were imaginary. Bronson asked each of his family what flower she would give the birthday girl if she were able. Anna echoed Bronson's own choice, a rose. Louisa chose a lily of the valley for its connotations of innocence. Abby May, already attracted to dramatic displays of color, chose a tiger lily, which she called by its folk name of "wake-robin." Abba, focused as she often was on emotional ties, said she would give forget-me-nots for remembrance. Not to be left out, Lane added that he would give the girl "a piece of moss, or humility."[7] One hopes that Lane's announcement was greeted by knowing winks and a few eyes rolled heavenward. The quiet, unassuming Lizzie needed nothing less than another dose of humility; why couldn't the dour Englishman put aside his sackcloth and ashes—and his imaginary moss—long enough to enjoy a little girl's party?

In describing Elizabeth's party, Anna made no note of games or laughter. It was a warmly happy time, but also highly decorous and restrained. Decorum, too, presided at the lessons that Alcott and Lane continued to give the children in the farmhouse library. While most of these involved only the children and either Alcott or Lane, there were times when all the members of the two men's families were present. The children and Abba would arrange themselves in a semicircle around a chalkboard. On July 2, the session began not with discussion but with reading: two hours' worth from ten in the morning until noon. Then Mr. Alcott rose to deliver a talk that, perhaps because it was a Sunday, was as much a sermon as a lecture. As Abba wrote:

> Mr. Alcott most beautifully and forcibly illustrated on the black board the sacrifices and utter subjection of the body to the Soul, showing the [and here she drew a cross] on which the lusts of the flesh are to be sacrificed. Renunciation is the law; devotion to God's will the Gospel. The latter makes the former easy, sometimes delightful.[8]

Among the five children, his wife, and the celibate Lane, just whose "lusts of the flesh" did Bronson have in mind? Whose furtive urges did he mean to symbolically crucify? What further sacrifices did he propose to extract from his roomful of meatless, teetotal acolytes? Alcott's words showed no sense of moderation, and they reflected a refusal to differentiate among degrees of wrongdoing.

Besieged with exhortations to purge herself of desire, Louisa did her best to oblige. She had, it seems, two besetting faults that she could not master: her unruly temper and her desire for things she could not have. When her good intentions failed her and she lost her temper, her disappointment made her cry herself to sleep. She would then make noble resolutions once again and, for a while, feel "better in [her] heart." If only she kept all the moral promises she made, she observed, "I should be the best girl in the world. But I don't, and so am very bad." Louisa herself felt that she never achieved the goodness at which she aimed. Nearly forty years later, as she read over her Fruitlands diary, she added the notation, "Poor little sinner! *She says the same at fifty.*"9 As to her worldly yearnings, it was not always wealth that she coveted. After a visit to some of her mother's friends, who proudly showed Louisa their newborn son, she wrote, "I often wish I had a little brother but as I have not I shall try to be contented with what I have got (for Mother often says if we are not contented with what we have got it will be taken away from us) and I think it is very true."10 To help herself remember this lesson, she copied into the journal the words of a poem from her father's beloved *Pilgrim's Progress*:

> I am content with what I have,
> Little be it or much,
> And Lord! contentment still I crave
> Becaus[e] thou savest such.

At the age of thirty-five, Louisa would use the same lines to end the penultimate chapter of *Little Women*, part 1. But quoting Bunyan did not greatly ease her burden. As she remembered later, it was during these months that she started to feel "the family cares and peculiar trials." She had, as she later put it, taken up a cross for her family, and from that hour it began to grow.11

Bronson had conceived Fruitlands as an escape from the world's depravity. Louisa craved an escape from Fruitlands. In secret ways, she found it, but not by physically running away. Her retreats were less obvious than they had once been, though they were evidently more necessary than ever. One was physical exercise; few things lifted her spirits better than a "splendid run," and running remained a favorite recreation as long as her health allowed her to enjoy it.12 Her other preferred escapes gave her solace for the rest of her life. They were her imagination and her pen. In addition to her journal, Louisa kept an Imagination Book at Fruitlands. Now lost, it was, at the time, one of her most important possessions. One day after writing in it, she wrote in her journal, "Life is pleasanter than it used to be, and I don't care about dying any more." She also was writing poetry, "in a thin but copious stream," as she later recollected.[13] In her mind, in the word, and on the run, she was separate from the world and safe in a realm of light.

Meanwhile, Fruitlands was winding itself into paradox. The commune's retreat from the world of iniquity had seemingly made denunciations of sin all the more necessary. The Alcotts, the Lanes, and their tiny band of followers had fled into nature, immersing themselves in a life that left no distance between themselves and the land and sky. Nature, they had thought, would cure them and set them free. At the same time, however, Alcott and Lane felt compelled to guard against one of the most natural of all impulses: the urge toward selfish pleasure. The wilderness into which the Fruitlanders had escaped was supposed to restore their authentic spirits and bring them closer to communion with God. Nevertheless, it was still potentially a place of temptation. If they allowed the wilderness to speak to the wildness within themselves, then the entire enterprise would be threatened with moral collapse. Alcott and Lane hoped to discover a nature in which it was unnatural to want to procreate or to caress one's children. It is in no way surprising that they did not find it.

Around Independence Day, Emerson visited the farm. His first impressions were generally positive: "The sun & evening sky do not look calmer than Alcott & his family at Fruitlands. They seemed to have arrived at the fact, to have got rid of the show, & so to be serene."[14] Throughout his career, Emerson felt most comfortable with transcendentalism in his study and his parlor. He sincerely admired, but could never bring himself to imitate, men like Thoreau and Alcott who carried the doctrine into the field. For him, to see Alcott arrive at the fact was a thing of wonder. Nevertheless, Emerson seemed to know better than Alcott and Lane themselves the kinds of obstacles that lay ahead. For one thing, he already sensed that transcendentalism was a naturally introspective, solipsistic idea. One could practice it well enough as an individual, but converting it into a social philosophy was almost as great a miracle as changing water into wine. He added:

> I will not prejudge them successful: They look well in July; we will see them in December. I know they are better for themselves than as partners. One can easily see that they have yet to settle several things. Their saying that things are clear & they sane, does not make them so. If they

will in very deed be lovers & not selfish; if they will serve the town of Harvard, & make their neighbors feel them as benefactors, wherever they touch them; they are as safe as the sun.[15]

Emerson's statement about seeing the Fruitlanders in December proved prophetic, but his most discerning insight came in his prediction that the community would stand or fall according to its capacity to "in very deed be lovers & not selfish" and to benefit their neighbors in Harvard "wherever they touch them." Charles Lane stood staunchly for the idea that love, as people typically feel it toward spouses or children, was the epitome of selfishness. Moreover, the act of touching caused Lane profound discomfort. Alcott was imbibing similar notions. Emerson's observations that love requires selflessness and that, to benefit the world, one must touch it, would seem obvious everywhere but at Fruitlands. At Fruitlands, however, the ability to observe the obvious was strangely wanting.

Thoreau, who had moved temporarily to Staten Island, never visited Fruitlands. Others did, though, in unexpected numbers. Throughout the summer and into the fall, the farm welcomed a stream of travelers who came to indulge their curiosity or to pay their respects, but almost never to stay. Abba recorded an impressive list of the visitors: George Ripley, having lately established the idealistic community of Brook Farm, had come to compare notes on utopian living; the poet Ellery Channing, the nephew of the great Unitarian minister, had come from Concord. Abba's brother Samuel arrived with his whole family. William Russell, Bronson's old teaching partner, brought greetings from Andover. Theodore Parker, the radical minister, also paid his respects. The visitors came from New York, Philadelphia, Ohio, even North Carolina. Abba wrote in amazement, "I did not think so much curiosity could have existed among our friends to see our new home."[16]

But the attention was a mixed blessing. To be sure, it was flattering, and there was always the hope of recruiting some of the visitors. In reality, though, all the guests were draining the community's resources. Struggling to feed themselves, the Fruitlanders were frequently obliged to lay extra places at the kitchen table. Already burdened with all the sewing, cleaning, and mending, Abba was also expected to see to the casual wants of outsiders. Abba came to a sobering realization:

> The right people, with right motives, and holy purposes, do not come, and we are wearing ourselves out in the service of transient visitors, and ungrateful participants. This is a Hotel, where man and beast are entertained without pay, and at great expense.[17]

At Fruitlands, Alcott had dreamed of escaping the world. Ironically, however, the world had followed, and it had followed in the least useful manner—not with its hearts and minds, but only with its inquisitive eyes. Having sworn to use no work animals except when strictly necessary, Alcott now found himself feeding and watering the horses of strangers.

Meanwhile, it was on Abba's shoulders that the running of the "Hotel" principally fell. Alcott had a far stronger sense of gender equality than most of his countrymen. At least occasionally, he helped with the cooking, and as always, he devoted more of himself to his children than almost any other man of his generation. Nevertheless, there is no record in the annals of Fruitlands of a man washing a dish or mending a tunic. For the first two months of Fruitlands' existence, and for much of the time thereafter, poor, beleaguered Mrs. Alcott was the only adult female member of the community. Occasionally, she had assistance from her aunt Hannah Robie, whom Bronson deemed "a lady of great good sense and character" and who served Abba as "a loving and judicious counselor, a quiet, energetic friend."[18] However, Mrs. Robie had only so much time to donate. According to Louisa in "Transcendental Wild Oats," a visitor once asked Abba if the Fruitlands farm possessed any beasts of burden. The witty but rueful reply was, "Only one woman."[19]

Sometime in August, a modest amount of relief arrived from Providence, Rhode Island, in the buxom person of Miss Anna Page. Miss Page was brave enough to withstand the persiflage that no doubt followed a single woman who joined a wilderness community of freethinking men, even one that openly despised the pleasures of the flesh. No consistent portrait of her emerges. Louisa hated her, and she said so in her journal. In "Transcendental Wild Oats," only Charles Lane is subjected to more scathing treatment. In the story, Miss Page becomes Miss Jane Gage, a plump, egocentric character whose chief contribution to the community is to scribble an endless stack of inferior poems on lofty themes. Page attempted to teach the children their lessons, but since her method was different from Alcott's and Lane's, Louisa recalled that "the result was a chronic state of chaos in the minds of these much-afflicted innocents." In other respects as well, Louisa considered Page worse than useless: "Sleep, food, and poetic musings were the desires of dear Jane's life, and she shirked all duties as clogs upon her spiritual wings."[20] In Louisa's fictionalized account, Miss Gage also provides the focus of the ripest moment of pure comedy, when her clandestine weakness for animal protein is called to the attention of the rigidly inflexible Timon Lion:

> Unfortunately, the poor lady hankered after the flesh-pots, and endeavored to stay herself with private sips of milk, crackers, and cheese, and on one dire occasion she partook of fish at a neighbor's table. One of the children reported this sad lapse from virtue, and poor Jane was publicly reprimanded by Timon. "I took only a bit of the tail," sobbed the penitent poetess.

> "Yes, but the whole fish had to be tortured and slain that you might tempt your carnal appetite with that one taste of the tail. Know ye not, consumers of flesh meat, that ye are nursing the wolf and tiger in your bosoms?"[21]

Following this incident in Louisa's story, Miss Gage leaves the community in disgrace. The reasons for the real Anna Page's departure are less clear, and whether or not the battle of the fish tail actually occurred cannot be proven. Perhaps the story is a bit of wish fulfillment on the part of the adult Louisa, using her pen to gain some belated redress for the condescension and uninspiring lessons Miss Page had visited on her so long ago.

In Louisa's tale, Gage's carnivorous foibles are exposed by one of the children, who, according to the text, experienced "the naughty satisfaction of [a] young detective." It is worth supposing for a moment that the anecdote of the fish tail was at least partly founded on truth. It is easy to imagine the Alcott sisters, eager as always to please their father, appointing themselves the unofficial spies of the commune. It is entirely possible that Louisa, despising Miss Page as she did, played the role of detective in the episode, simultaneously advancing her father's aims and undermining a perceived antagonist. The chance to do Miss Page a nasty turn in the name of upholding the community's virtue may have been too tempting an opportunity to be missed, no matter how naughty Louisa knew she was being. At the age of ten, she seems to have known something about making foul seem fair.

A far different portrait of Anna Page, however, emerges from the journal of Abba, who was delighted to have her company and assistance. She described her new friend as "an amiable active woman whose kind word and gentle care-taking deed is [*sic*] very grateful to me."[22] Perhaps better than any other observer at the time, Page seems to have felt the difficulties of Abba's position. Whereas Alcott received praise from some quarters for the purity of his vision, it was Abba's unacknowledged toil that daily kept that vision from dissolving. Abba told her diary in late August:

> Miss Page made a good remark, and true as good, that a woman may live
> a whole life of sacrifice, and at her death meekly says, "I die a woman."
> A man passes a few years in experiments in self-denial and simple life,
> and he says, "Behold a God."[23]

Given the free access the Alcotts had to one another's journals, Abba's quotation of Anna Page can be seen as a calculatedly rebellious act; she might as well have written it on her husband's chalkboard. If Bronson had ever been a god in Abba's eyes, he was not now. She had had a fair idea of her husband's weaknesses before Fruitlands began, but she had hoped that, once the sordid world of the marketplace had been left behind, Bronson might flourish as he would never do so long as he was judged by worldly measures. Her hopes were not being rewarded.

Fish tail or no fish tail, Anna Page was gone from Fruitlands by late November. As summer turned to autumn, many of the other Fruitlanders were finding the rigors of consociate life harder to stomach, and not all the complaints concerned Charles Lane. For the first time in his life, Bronson Alcott was discovering what it was like to lead a group of adults in something more serious than a discussion, and he was bearing the responsibility uneasily. His task was complicated by the very philosophical ideals he was striving to uphold. At the heart of the transcendentalist impulse was the belief that one's own conscience was sovereign and that all should live according to the dictates of their own spirit. How, then, could Alcott and Lane legitimately object if the inner dictates of one of their followers called for a taste of meat or fish?

Like Rousseau in his *Social Contract*, Alcott and Lane would have insisted that humankind, at times, "must be forced to be free." They assumed that one could not develop one's mind and spirit properly without first learning to discipline the wants of the body. The problem, however, was that the pilgrims who had made the journey to Fruitlands had left society precisely because they had found its rules unacceptably confining. Samuel Bower with his penchant for naturism and Joseph Palmer with his law-flouting facial hair had already proclaimed their hostility toward forcing of any kind. Each Fruitlander had a particular view of truth and righteousness. Together, they formed a bedlam of good intentions. Emerson offered his diagnosis in the lecture "New England Reformers," which he delivered less than two months after the fall of Fruitlands.

> They defied each other, like a congress of kings, each of whom had a realm to rule. . . . One apostle thought all men should go to farming; and another, that no man should buy or sell: that the use of money was the cardinal evil; another, that the mischief was in our diet, that we eat and drink damnation. . . . Even the insect world was to be defended . . . and a society for the protection of ground-worms, slugs, and mosquitos was to be incorporated without delay.[24]

In these reform movements, Emerson quipped, "nothing was more remarkable than the discontent they begot in the movers."[25] It seemed that the phrase "transcendentalist community" was something of an oxymoron.

To prevent his own congress of kings from degenerating into utter chaos, Alcott could think of no other response than to pull tighter on the reins. Even Lane was astonished at Alcott's rigor. He confided to his friend Oldham, "Mr. Alcott makes such high requirements of all persons that few are likely to stay, even of his own family, unless he can become more tolerant of defect. He is an artist in human character requiring every painter to be a Michael Angelo."[26] Robert Carter, a friend and business partner of James Russell Lowell, wrote that Alcott had become "very strict, rather despotic in his rule of the Community," and that at least some of the members were able to stay the course only by defying his prohibitions in secret.[27]

Inevitably, Fruitlands witnessed rebellions against moral authority. At first, at least, they were small and furtive. Anna Alcott remembered that "when starving with the apple and bread diet, the disciples retired to drink milk in the barn." These milk parties doubtlessly took place clandestinely, without the knowledge of Alcott or Lane. When those two moral monitors were present, all remained piously vegetarian. But when their work took them out of sight, or perhaps while they slept, exhausted by the day's efforts, an odd, quiet procession made its way toward temptation. As time passed, though, the search for nourishment became less of a laughing matter. As the autumn drew on, clashes of wills became frequent, tearing at the community's former serenity, and Abba began to fear that her children might starve before the coming winter had run its course.[28]

The high hopes with which seekers of peace and beauty came to Fruitlands—and the disappointment with which they one by one departed— are both typified in the experiences of young Isaac Hecker, the only adult rank-and-file member of the group who left a written record of his stay at the farm. Hecker was unusual among the Fruitlanders in that he had known success in the larger world. Along with his brothers, he owned an extensive baking and milling enterprise. Even today, a brand of flour bears his family's name. Hecker pursued a deeper meaning in life by joining a succession of utopian projects. Before arriving at Fruitlands, Hecker had been at Brook Farm, where he would have enjoyed the company of Margaret Fuller and a genteel writer-turned-pig-farmer named Nathaniel Hawthorne. At Brook Farm, Hecker had been pleased to find "refining amusements and cultivated persons," and he had found himself growing deeply attached "to the company of those [he loved]" there.[29] But, "called with a stronger voice" that urged him toward sterner self-denial, Hecker decided to try Fruitlands. Hecker had another, more private reason for leaving Brook Farm. In the journal he wrote there, Hecker confessed an attraction to "one who is too much for me to speak of."[30] The pronoun Hecker used to describe this "one" was first written as "her," but then it was somewhat clumsily rewritten as "him." Whether the object of his crush was male or female, Hecker was unable to face up to his emotions; they did not agree with his self-image as an ascetic worshipper of the spirit.

Hecker stoically believed that "all our difficulties should be looked at in such a light as to improve and elevate our minds."[31] At first, Hecker thought that he had found elevation at Fruitlands, and his first diary entries from the farm speak enthusiastically of the "very fine things" that Lane and Alcott said to him. During those first few evenings, the men conversed long into the night about such topics as friendship, the role of clothing in society (the contributions of Samuel Bower would have been most intriguing), and the highest aim of earthly existence.[32] Hecker took an eager part in these discussions, and Lane, at least, looked on him as a member of bright promise.

Thereafter, however, doubts began to crowd swiftly in on all sides. Hecker's emotional bonds to his biological family were strong. He spoke so often of his life at home that Lane in particular began to wonder if he could truly devote himself to his new "family." Alcott, it seems, was more willing to reserve judgment. Hecker came from money—a feature that distinguished him from most of the other Fruitlands recruits. Already, Alcott was becoming dissatisfied with the land that Lane had purchased for the commune, and he had his eye on a more promising tract near Leominster. If only Hecker could persuade his brothers to supply some backing . . . well, the possibility cried out for exploration.

While there is no direct evidence that Alcott wanted to use Hecker for his fortune, Hecker himself was wary. The philosopher's "insinuating and persuasive way" made him uneasy, and he could not shake the suspicion that Alcott wanted him "because he thought I would bring money to the Community."[33] In a different way, Hecker also doubted himself, and only a week passed before he started to doubt his fitness for the enterprise. He did not feel that he could renounce the world as easily as Alcott and Lane evidently had. Moreover, Hecker's outlook was essentially Christian, and it bothered him that Alcott and Lane seemed to care only about creating an earthly paradise. As an old man, Hecker recollected that Alcott and Lane had no definite concept of the hereafter.[34] Though Hecker admitted that Alcott and Lane had "much, very much" to offer him, he quickly began to doubt that the Fruitlands philosophy was sufficient to his needs.[35]

On July 20, only nine days after Hecker's arrival, his two would-be mentors had decided to address his ambivalence head on. That night, they confronted him, demanding to know his "position with regard to my family, my duty, and my position here." Alcott asked what was keeping Hecker from committing himself wholeheartedly to the community. He was not prepared for the answer he received. Hecker had been saving up for this moment. He started with Alcott, whom he chided for his "want of frankness" and "his disposition to separateness rather than win cooperation with the aims of his own mind." Hecker also thought that Alcott was in a pretty poor position to criticize the familial attachments of others. The young man accused Alcott's own family of "tending to prevent his immediate plans of reformation." Furthermore, Hecker claimed that the two men had "too decided [a] tendency toward literature and writing for the prosperity and success of their enterprise."[36]

Three days later, Hecker went home, to "be true to the spirit with the help of God, and wait for further light and strength."[37] Alcott reacted with disgust. He went to Lane and said, "Well, Hecker has flunked out. He hadn't the courage to persevere. He's a coward." Feeling the unfairness of his friend's judgment, Lane replied, "No; you're mistaken. Hecker is right. He wanted more than we had to give him."[38] This exchange found its way to Hecker's ears. For the rest of his life, he never forgot either Alcott's curt dismissal or Lane's defense of him. Hecker later proved himself anything but a coward in matters of faith. Ordained as a Catholic priest in 1848, he went on to found the Paulist Fathers. At the end of his life, he pronounced Alcott, Thoreau, and even Emerson "three consecrated cranks."[39]

Louisa was still far from considering her father a crank. From the beginning, Fruitlands seems to have intensified her sense of the importance of family ties, though the concept of universal family being touted by Mr. Lane remained forever foreign to her. Critical as she was of Lane and openly hostile to Anna Page, she never wrote a single bitter word at Fruitlands about any member of her biological family except herself. One forms the impression that she thought of the non-Alcott members of the commune as intruders on her rightful sphere, sapping the attentions, energy, and patience of the people she loved. A Fruitlands of the Alcotts, by the Alcotts, and for the Alcotts would have been more to her liking. Louisa may have wanted to be good all the time to everyone, but the one day she awoke with the thought, "I must be *very* good" was her mother's birthday.[40]

At Fruitlands, Louisa absorbed different lessons from the ones her father had intended. She was discovering that the same word in different mouths could mean very different things and that the content of virtue itself might change, depending on the standpoint of the viewer. She also learned that the form of goodness that proclaimed itself most loudly might not be the most authentic or desirable. Mr. Lane preached kindness to all human beings alike; however, kindness divided so many ways seemed to leave a very thin slice for each. Louisa heard her own father arguing with serene confidence for the rights of all living beings. But when worm-eaten apples arrived at the dinner table or the autumn wind blew through her linen tunic, this generosity on all sides did not appear generous to *her*. Inevitably, she wondered whether earthly comforts were so terrible as her father made them out to be.

However, Louisa was also seeing quiet examples of kindness. She saw it in the patience with which her mother taught her how to sew and the pride with which her mother congratulated her on improving her handwriting. When, in mid-October, Abba and Lizzie planned a trip to Boston, Louisa was disconsolate, for she knew that, in their absence, "No one will be as good to me as Mother."[41] She saw kindness, too, in the taciturn figure of Joseph Palmer, who was always giving freely of his time and tools. Indeed, she sometimes saw this kindness in her father, at least as far as the rules of the society allowed. Aware of the unappealing nature of the simple bread he produced for his table, Alcott took to fashioning the loaves in the shapes of animals to make them more pleasing to the children. The example showed her that it was sometimes in the bending of the rules, not their strict enforcement, that a loving spirit could shine forth. Louisa dutifully copied into her diary the dreary maxims that made up the Fruitlands creed: "Vegetable diet and sweet repose—Animal food and nightmare"; "Pluck your body from the orchard—do not snatch it from the shamble."[42] But she knew that they contained less love than any one of her father's animal loaves.

On August 7, Emerson wrote to Margaret Fuller that he had had a visit from Alcott and Lane, who were on a trip to Boston together. Alcott was battling an unspecified illness, which became serious enough for Abba to pronounce him "'low indeed' and suffering from 'extreme debility'" on his return.[43] Bronson's mood, it seems, was no better than his health. Emerson told Fuller, "Mr. A. already anticipates the time when he shall be forsaken of all, & left alone, inasmuch as none will stand by him in the rigidness of his asceticism."[44]

Lane, too, was starting to have second thoughts. He mentioned to Emerson the presence of a colony of Shakers that lay across the Nashua River and within an easy distance of Fruitlands. Emerson deduced that the Englishman had become "very much engaged" with the Shaker settlement.

He also told Fuller that Lane meant to write something about the colony for *The Dial*. Lane even hinted that he might eventually join the Shakers and forsake Fruitlands altogether. The Shaker colony across the river from Fruitlands had been personally established by the religion's founder, and it had been thriving since 1781. The implicit comparison with Fruitlands, which was already struggling, was either embarrassing or intriguing. Why did the Shakers rise as the Fruitlanders fell into confusion? Lane thought he knew the answer, and his deductions would soon threaten to shatter the Alcott family forever.

CHAPTER SEVEN

LOST ILLUSIONS

"Then said *Charity* to *Christian, Have
you a family? are you a married man?
Chr.* I have a Wife and four small children.
Cha. *And why did you not bring them along
with you?*"

—JOHN BUNYAN,
The Pilgrim's Progress

O N AUGUST 4, 1843, BRONSON ALCOTT AND CHARLES LANE
set out from Fruitlands in the company of James Kay, a visitor
whose curiosity about things utopian had briefly lured him
from Philadelphia. They followed a rustic roadside sign that pointed
toward the Shaker community that lay two or three miles north of the
town of Harvard. Louisa, who stayed behind at the farm with her mother
and sisters, mentioned the men's excursion in her journal, adding that the
three did not come back until evening. Apparently, they had been expected
back earlier, but something about the Shaker settlement had caused them
to linger. The truth, not yet known to the other members of the Alcott
family, was that Lane and Bronson were in the early stages of a fascination
with the Shakers. On this August day, Lane was taking careful notes, which
he soon edited into an article for *The Dial*. True to form, his article spoke
critically of the aspects of the Shaker colony that had even a slight flavor of
worldliness. His sensitivities on the subject of animal rights were aroused
by the commune's stables, which he compared to a prison. He also took a
reproving tone as he noted that most of the members consumed "flesh-
meat," used milk in profusion, and liberally imbibed coffee and tea.[1] He
was equally displeased to find that the Shakers routinely traded with the
outside world. Doing a yearly volume of business worth about ten thousand dollars—a respectable sum in those times—the Shakers were too

prosperous for Lane to approve of them completely. On the whole, he argued, the Shakers engaged in "more extensive interchanges of money, and more frequent intercourse with the world, than seems compatible with a serene life."[2]

Overall, however, Lane's impressions were favorable. He saw in the community an agreeable appearance of order and prosperity. The fields and gardens, filled with cheerful, active laborers, and the vigor with which all kinds of improvements were daily being made, presented an all-too-clear contrast with Fruitlands. He also found his hosts to be open, hospitable people who spoke enthusiastically about life in their simple colony. Lane eagerly pressed his hosts to learn the secrets of their success. What he did not know already about the Shaker religion and social philosophy, the community elders were more than happy to fill in. The movement had been founded by a visionary Englishwoman named Ann Lee, whose memory her followers revered by referring to her always as "Mother." Like Lane, Ann Lee had been born in England and had been drawn to America by a spiritually inspired vision of reform; these similarities to Lane's own situation must surely have touched a place in his heart. Mother Ann had proclaimed that the true Christian God had both male and female attributes. The incarnation of the Holy Spirit in Jesus Christ had been only the first appearance of God in human form. The divine afflatus had now returned, and it had come to rest in Mother Ann's own person. Through her, God now commanded a new ordering of social life. Members of the Shaker religion were to regard themselves as belonging to the last generation of human mortals, committed to achieving spiritual perfection in this life, rather than passing the quest down to their children. Indeed, since perfection was the current aim of the Shakers, no children were necessary. Therefore, sexual relations, themselves a tawdry reminder of the Fall of Man, were no longer to be engaged in. To attain salvation, the Shakers not only retreated from the world, but also from procreation.

Although the Shaker communities comprised both sexes, a firm discipline prevented them from intermingling. Men and women in the community were prohibited from passing each other on a staircase, shaking hands, or exchanging gifts across the gender line. When it was necessary for a man and woman to speak to each other, they were permitted to do so only in the company of a chaperone. They walked, worked, and worshipped apart.3 If a family that already had children joined the Shakers, the children were taken from their parents and were permitted to see them only once a year, in a brief interview supervised by an elder.4 Lane listened engrossed. Their austere commitment, he wrote, "reigns so monarchically in their hearts that they have always a stirring topic whereon to speak, and an exalting object for which to act." He did not find the verbal arguments of the Shakers entirely persuasive; however, when he saw around him the real results of those arguments, their contentions "became almost irresistible."

Abba Alcott, however, regarded the Shakers with suspicion. Late in August, Bronson persuaded her to have a look for herself. Something was not quite right about them, she thought, and she tried to explain her misgivings in her journal:

> I gain but little from their domestic and internal arrangements. There is servitude somewhere, I have no doubt. There is a fat, sleek, comfortable look about the men, and among the women there is a stiff, awkward reserve that belongs to neither sublime resignation nor divine hope.5

Abba did not credit the Shakers or their principles with having worked any great miracles. She saw in the Shakers simply another social arrangement in which the men grew plump and the women grew solemn, and she was already familiar with conditions of that kind.

At the same time that Abba was setting down her suspicions regarding the Shakers, Lane was becoming ever more convinced that his own idea of paradise could never be realized as long as Abba remained on the scene. Although he wrote with approval that she had shed some of her aristocratic manner, passing, as he put it, "from the ladylike to the industrious order," he felt that she still had "much inward experience to realize." Most irritatingly, however, it seemed impossible to cure her of her particular fondness for her own children. Lane complained, "Her peculiar maternal love blinds her to all else—whom does it not so blind for a season?"6

But Abba's presumed blindness did not prevent her from grasping a truth that Lane refused to admit; she knew that hard work was more likely to save Fruitlands than a different social theory. As Abba continued her daily round of cooking and cleaning, she and the girls were finding out that life in Utopia was leaving them less time to spend with one another. The family post office that Abba had maintained from the time her daugh-

ters were first learning to write was still in service, but now the time for letter writing was scarce. Anna in particular missed these casual written
exchanges. In one of the few intrafamily notes that survives from Fruitlands, Anna wrote, "I do not write to you very often, dear mother, but I
love to dearly when I feel like it, and I love to have letters from you though
I do not expect them very often." Anna was also sorry to see how seldom
her mother was able to join the family for meals. "I enjoy my food much
better when you are at the table," Anna told her mother. With a common-
sense appeal to justice, she added, "If you prepare the food you ought to
eat it with us."[7]

Louisa tried as hard as she could to help the family through the bleak
autumn. She helped with the dishes and all the other chores she was old
enough to manage. Sometimes she and Anna gave their mother a rest by
cooking supper. At various times, Louisa helped with the ironing, the corn
husking, and the sewing. The evenings brought some rest, and one night
Louisa diverted herself by writing a poem about the sunset:

> Softly doth the sun descend
> To his couch behind the hill.
> Then, oh, then, I love to sit
> On mossy banks beside the rill.[8]

Anna praised the poem; Louisa herself thought it was poor. In any event,
it is telling that the simple act of sitting still and doing nothing was luxury
enough to move her to poetry. After sunset, her father and Mr. Lane droned
on with their wearisome metaphysics. Louisa's journal entry from November 2 may be taken as typical: "Anna and I did the work. In the evening Mr.
Lane asked us, 'What is man?' These were our answers: A human being; an
animal with a mind; a creature; a body; a soul and a mind. After a long talk
we went to bed very tired." Rereading this entry forty years later, Louisa
added in the margin, "No wonder [they were tired], after doing the work
and worrying their little wits with such lessons."[9]

In keeping with the objectives of the colony, Louisa was still doing her
best to gain mastery over her emotions, though the secret of their control
still escaped her. Her gladdest times came when she played pretend games
with Anna and Lizzie. On one of her more carefree days, she told her journal, "I ran in the wind and played be a horse [*sic*], and had a lovely time in

the woods with Anna and Lizzie. We were fairies, and made gowns and paper wings. I 'flied' the highest of all."[10]

As Bronson's daughters tried to fly, their impoverished circumstances seemed to pull them back down. Louisa felt the lack of things poignantly on her mother's birthday. She awoke that day with the thought that she must be especially good, and she ran to kiss her mother and to give her her best wishes. But she had little else to give—only a poem and a little cross that she had made out of moss. Mothers typically know how to transform even the smallest gifts from their children into priceless gems, but Louisa knew the difference. That evening, ironically after reading a story called "Contentment," Louisa wondered about what contentment might actually be. What she wrote in her diary was, by Fruitlands standards, a confession of heresy: "I wish I was rich, I wish I was good, and we were all a happy family this day."[11] At the wise age of ten, Louisa had accepted the idea that happiness was not complete and that goodness was not sufficient without some small amount of wealth. Here was the beginning of a long, resentful struggle against poverty. In founding a colony where commerce was to be abolished, Bronson had hoped to teach his children that money was meaningless and dispensable. However, the experience of want was ingraining the opposite lesson.

Meanwhile, the colony was falling apart. By midautumn, only the Alcotts and Lanes were left. Bronson and Lane faced two pressing tasks: to find replacements for the defectors and to make the farm ready for the coming winter. Lacking the resources to do both, they made a seemingly harebrained decision. With their crops still in the field and colder weather closing in, they elected to strike out across New England and New York, proceeding on foot whenever possible, in search of new recruits. Clad in their linen tunics, Alcott and Lane turned up in the drawing rooms of almost everyone they could think of who might join them. In New York alone, they paid visits to Emerson's older brother William, Horace Greeley, William Henry Channing, Margaret Fuller, and Lydia Maria Child.[12] When the last welcomed the two men, she politely asked what had brought them to New York. The befuddled Alcott replied, "I don't know. It seems a miracle we are here." On their strange, improbable journeys, Alcott and Lane saw much and spoke to many, but when they returned to Fruitlands, not a single convert came with them.

Still, at times, the two men had the capacity to spellbind. In later years, Louisa wrote of how, on one of their excursions, they took passage on a boat without any means of paying the fare. When pressed for payment, they offered the only thing they had of value: their eloquence. They rose before the assembled passengers and spoke brilliantly of things seen and unseen. When they had finished, the crowd took up a collection for the two travelers, which was handed over to the captain. Finding that the donations exceeded the price of the passage, the captain offered the remainder to Alcott and Lane. True to their principles, however, the reformers refused to accept even a penny. As if completing a mathematical proof, they remarked, "You see how well we get on without money" and went calmly on their way.[13]

Back at Fruitlands, however, there was no calm. The very day that Alcott and Lane set forth on a recruiting tour, Abba looked out the farmhouse window to see dark clouds gathering. In the fields lay the season's crop of barley, cut but not yet harvested. Joseph Palmer was away, tending to his cattle, and there was not a single man available to bring the grain into the granary. When the storm came, all would be ruined. As lightning darted across the sky, Abba called urgently to her three eldest daughters and to William Lane. Thrusting a basket into every hand, she hurried them into the fields, exhorting them to gather as if their lives depended on it. As the rains neared, they labored with a fury, dragging their loads to the granary and then dashing back to fill the hoppers again. At last the storm broke, and the little band ran for cover, but not before they had rescued enough barley to last for a few weeks.[14]

On the whole, the yield of all the consociates' plowing and planting was worse than disappointing, and when Lane and Alcott returned from the last of their autumn tours, it was clear that the colony's food stores would not last the winter. The sufficiency of the firewood, too, was seriously in doubt. The health of the tiny group was also becoming less robust. William Lane fell ill with a fever and required nursing for an entire month, too weak to raise his head. Eventually, his father also fell ill. Louisa, usually the most vigorous of children, was coughing heavily and complaining of pains in her side and head. As for Bronson, Abba reported to her brother Samuel that he was "low indeed." He was growing feeble and nervous. The tone of his voice was sepulchral, and his thoughts were turning morbid.

Thinking that some rest would help him, Abba suggested that he take a short, quiet journey in a chaise. Her husband replied darkly that, when he did journey, "it will be a long one and alone."[15] The prospects had become so bleak that they caused Bronson to question the very structure of his most personal relationships. One day in November, he privately accosted Lane, putting to him a question whose seed the Englishman had already planted in Bronson's mind: "Can a man act continually for the universal end, while he co-habits with a wife?"[16]

Bronson certainly would have known what answer to expect. Lane had long believed that Bronson's attachment to Abba and the girls was arresting his spiritual development and undermining the Fruitlands experiment. The example of the Shakers seemed to argue Lane's point. Although he sincerely respected Abba's capacity for hard work, he felt that her pride had not yet been eradicated and that her maternal love outweighed all other considerations. He wrote to his friend Oldham, "Mrs. Alcott has no spontaneous inclination towards a larger family than her own natural one, of spiritual ties she knows nothing."[17] When he visited Emerson in mid-December, Lane announced that he and Alcott now agreed that they had been wrong in lauding the maternal instinct and the family. They now both realized, he said, that such ideas were "the very mischief."[18]

And yet, when Bronson placed the matter bluntly before him, Lane wavered. He had no desire to play the role of "that devil [who] comes from Old England to separate husband and wife . . . though it might gratify New England to be able to say it."[19] Lane also knew that, without Abba, he and Alcott alone could not sustain a community. Although he now regarded some kind of separation as "inevitable," he refused to say the decisive word in the matter. If by the late autumn of 1843 Bronson's and Abba's marriage was teetering on the brink of collapse, Bronson was no less to blame than his meddlesome friend.

Circumstances were urging Bronson toward a crisis. Fruitlands had consumed virtually all his and Lane's earthly resources. If they went back to the life they had left behind, they would be destitute. Then there was the opinion of others to consider. If Fruitlands collapsed, who would again believe in the chance for a virtuous life on earth? In the late autumn of 1843, this question was causing Bronson Alcott to think very hard. In search of his soul, he had rejected much of the world. Perhaps what he required was one final, great renunciation.

Bronson's idea that he could save himself and his colony only by leaving his wife and daughters may have been partly inspired by the book that had dominated his formative years: *The Pilgrim's Progress*. At the beginning of Bunyan's allegory, the central figure, Christian, has a premonition that his city is soon to be destroyed by fire from heaven. Shaken by this intuition, he urges his wife and four children to join him in fleeing from the peril. However, his family cannot understand his strange preoccupation, and their hearts harden against him. Christian begins to run. When his wife and sons cry after him to come back, Christian "put his fingers in his Ears, and ran on crying, Life, Life, Eternal Life: so he looked not behind him, but fled towards the middle of the Plain."[20]

Bunyan's advice seems clear: no worldly attachment, not even the pleas of one's own astonished family, must stand between a person and salvation. Unlike Bunyan's pilgrim, Bronson had loved his wife and daughters enough to take them with him on his flight from a wicked world. Now, however, it seemed clear to him that the path of the soul must be individual. The person who was forced continually to pause and consider the wants and welfare of dependents would never have the focus and peace of mind that were the preconditions of enlightenment. Seeing no other way to preserve his ideal, Alcott decided that Lane must be right: if there were to be a Fruitlands at all, there must be one for men and another for women. To his distraught mind, dissolving the Alcott family seemed the only way to save it.

For Abba's part, she too was confronting the possibility that loyalty to her marriage might be the swiftest road to ruin. The shortage of fuel and foodstuffs, as well as the illnesses that were breaking out among the group, were daunting omens for the coming winter. Matters of moral salvation and family unity were yielding precedence to the starker question of mere survival. Abba had also begun to question the basic wholesomeness of the consociate ideal. Bronson and Lane had always been noticeably imprecise about the sexual arrangements that would prevail among the ideal universal family, and now Abba seems to have begun to worry about this unanswered question. She confided to her brother Samuel that she could see "no clean, healthy, safe course here in connexion with Mr. L."[21] To another brother, she wrote enigmatically, "I am not dead yet either to life or love, but the last few weeks have been filled with experiences of the deepest interest to me and my family."[22]

The precise meaning of these words cannot be deciphered. Perhaps Lane had decided that the spirit of community extended to the bedroom and was arguing for conjugal privileges. No less likely, given Lane's high regard for all forms of self-denial, he was urging Bronson and Abba to abstain from relations with each other.[23] Whether or not Bronson's chastity was at issue, Abba plainly feared for his sanity.[24] For her, the Fruitlands experiment was becoming too physically perilous and too emotionally strange to continue much longer. No matter how much she loved her husband—and no matter how bleak the prospects for a woman of her time who left her husband—Abba was perhaps almost as ready for a parting as Bronson.

The precise terms upon which Bronson contemplated dividing the family are unclear. Perhaps it was suggested that the Lanes and Alcotts would merge into the Shaker community. Perhaps Bronson meant for his wife and daughters to decamp entirely, leaving him and Lane to reconstruct Fruitlands as a sort of single-sex monastery. It is difficult, however, to see how either of these courses would have furthered Alcott's purposes. Absorption into the Shakers would have obliterated the conceptual foundations of his vision; it is inconceivable that Lane and Alcott might have converted the Shakers to vegetarianism or that the Shakers would have willingly cast aside Mother Ann in favor of Father Bronson. As for requiring Abba and the girls to depart, one wonders how Alcott and Lane would have lasted the winter, having sent their only remaining workforce into exile. There was, moreover, a peculiar irony in asking the women to leave for the supposed good of the community. When the other members of the commune had departed and Lane and Alcott had impulsively gone off on their pilgrimages, Abba and her daughters *had been* the Fruitlands community. This fact, however, was evidently not in Bronson's mind on November 20, the date when Louisa's journal first mentions the possibility of a separation.

November 20 was a busy day for Louisa. She awoke at five, washed the breakfast dishes, and then helped her mother with the rest of the work. In the afternoon, she looked after Abby May so that her mother could concentrate on her chores. Since Anna was visiting relatives in Boston, Louisa probably had more to do than usual, yet she still had time to make some things for her doll in the evening. She relates what happened next in matter-of-fact language. After a talk with Lane, Bronson consulted Abba and Louisa, asking if they saw any reason to separate. Louisa added, "Mother wanted to, she is so tired, I like it, but not the school part or Mr. L."[25]

The tensions in the farmhouse continued without resolution for three more weeks. During that time, on a snowy day, Louisa turned eleven and her father forty-four. Bronson's preoccupation with moral improvement did not take a holiday, however; in the evening, he quizzed the children as to the fault that troubled each of them most. Louisa named her bad temper, and no one seems to have disagreed. But even as Bronson emphasized self-restraint, Abba spoke up for the other pillar of Alcott girlhood: self-expression. Abba wrote a note to Louisa praising her diary, and Louisa proudly copied the little missive into her journal:

> I like to have you make observations about our conversations and your own thoughts. It helps you to express them and to understand your little self. Remember, dear girl, that a diary should be an epitome of your life. May it be a record of pure thought and good actions, then you will indeed be the precious child of your loving mother.[26]

All the pure thoughts and good actions Louisa could muster did not forestall the inevitable crisis. Even as the family celebrated the double birthday, Lane wrote to Oldham that Abba had seized control of the situation. She had informed him that, in response to the wishes of her friends, she had determined to "withdraw to a house which they will provide for herself and her four children." Moreover, she proposed to take the furniture with her, a gesture that would, as Lane put it, "leave me alone and naked in the new world."[27] Apparently Abba and Bronson kept the extent of their differences from the children for several weeks. The silence was finally broken barely two weeks before Christmas.

Charles Lane was not present; perhaps he had foreseen a tempest and thought it best not to be nearby. Nevertheless, he was having an unpleasant trip. In Concord, he was arrested for having refused to pay his taxes. When he declined to call on any friend to answer for him, the authorities had no choice but to put him in jail. There he languished for a short time until a local samaritan paid the arrearage. Coming home from a visit to Margaret Fuller in Boston, Emerson found Lane waiting for him, looking "sad & indisposed."[28]

On December 10, in the most anguished entry of her Fruitlands journal, Louisa wrote of a family meeting. In the evening, after another reading from *The Pilgrim's Progress*, Bronson assembled Abba and his two older daughters for a talk. Louisa did not record exactly what was said, but what she did write was telling enough: "I was very unhappy, and we all cried. Anna and I cried in bed, and I prayed to God to keep us all together."[29]

Neither Louisa the girl nor Louisa the grown woman made frequent mention of God in her journals. She did not often "pray in words," and she almost never divulged the content of her prayers.[30] Now, however, as her earthly father threatened to withdraw, she called desperately upon her Father in Heaven. Seven months earlier, she had been led to believe that family was everything. She had been asked to accept the notion that her own father was so exceptionally wise and loving that he could be not only her father but the sire of an entire community of work, devotion, and love. Now, that father who had seemed equal to any challenge seemed capable of any betrayal. Her mother, she knew, would still do all within her power, but on a December night in a lonely place, that power seemed small indeed. Louisa could not confidently look to her parents for security. She was only eleven years old.

The answer to Louisa's prayers lay with her father. Bronson Alcott had been driven to the most important decision he would ever make. He was being asked to choose, irrevocably, what he was going to live for. If he renounced his family and strove on alone, he might at last discover the god of his imaginings. But if he did so, he would always know that he had betrayed perhaps an even greater trust. He would be deserting the wife whom he had cherished and who had selflessly adopted his ideals as her own. Still worse, he would turn his back on the four little girls whom he had tried to acquaint with the beauty and perfection of their souls. He would never finish the work of teaching them how to love, share, and make brave choices, and the final example he would have set for them would be a lesson in human faithlessness and self-absorption. He could achieve the transcendence he sought only by committing a selfish sin, while the sinful world held forth the trust and love of others. Seven months earlier, when he brought his family to Fruitlands, Bronson had supposed that he could both separate himself from the world and take its dearest aspects with him. Now, that attempt to have the best of both had failed. He had to decide who he really was.

He did not decide immediately, and no surviving writing illuminates the process by which he chose. At Christmas, Abba sang and played with the children, trying to cheer them as the snows mounted outside the door. Bronson, however, was in Boston, attending a convention devoted to some obscure reform. During this trip, evidently, he reached his decision. The world and the family had won. On January 1, 1844, a day for new beginnings, Bronson returned from Boston. Though it is not clear precisely when or how he broached the news of his decision, it soon became understood that he would not be a consociate, but an Alcott. To ease their hardships, the family decided to accept an offer to move in with a local family, the Lovejoys, until spring. Abba wrote in her diary with obvious relief that "all connection with Fruitlands" had been dissolved.[31]

The response to Bronson's decision was predictably mixed. Lane, disappointed with what he saw as the triumph of his partner's weak, uxorious nature, packed his bags. On January 6, he and William left to live with the Shakers. Five days later, Abba exulted in a letter to her brother Samuel, "All Mr. Lane's efforts have been to disunite us. But Mr. Alcott's conjugal and paternal instincts were too strong for him."[32]

But the accumulated weight of the preceding months—the unrelenting toil, the continual moral self-examination, the gradual defection of his followers, and, finally, the near collapse of his family—had almost crushed Bronson. Not long after Lane's exodus, before his own journey to the Lovejoy home could take place, Bronson climbed the stairs of the Fruitlands farmhouse, lay down on his bed, and turned away from the door. There he lay, the prey of dark reflections. He did not stir. He refused to eat. It is generally assumed that he had decided to die.

Then, on the edge of despair, a change occurred. In her story "Transcendental Wild Oats," Louisa wrote nothing of the debate over whether her family would separate. However, she wrote long, poignant paragraphs about the days when her father lay silent, teetering between life and death, sanity and madness. These paragraphs are fiction, but they are the only account of those transformative hours by someone who observed them. For good reason, modern biographers of Bronson have rarely been able to resist quoting them at length:

> Then this dreamer, whose dream was the life of his life, resolved to carry out his idea to the bitter end. There seemed no place for him here,—no work, no friend. . . . Silently he lay down upon his bed, turned his face to the wall, and waited with pathetic patience for death to cut the knot which he could not untie. Days and nights went by, and neither food nor water passed his lips. Soul and body were dumbly struggling together, and no word of complaint betrayed what either suffered. . . .

> But the strong angels who sustain and teach perplexed and troubled souls came and went, leaving no trace without, but working miracles within. For, when all other sentiments had faded into dimness, all other hopes died utterly; when the bitterness of death was nearly over, when body was past any pang of hunger or thirst, and soul stood ready to depart, the love that outlives all else refused to die. Head had bowed to defeat . . . but heart could not grow cold who lived in its tender depths. . . .

> "My faithful wife, my little girls,—they have not forsaken me, they are mine by ties that none can break. What right have I to leave them alone? What right to escape from the burden and sorrow I have helped to bring? This duty remains to me, and I must do it manfully. For their sakes, the world will forgive me in time; for their sakes, God will sustain me now."

> Too feeble to rise, [he] groped for the food that always lay within his reach; and in the darkness and solitude of that memorable night ate and drank what was to him the bread and wine of a new communion, a new dedication of heart and life to the duties that were left him when the dreams fled.

> In the early dawn, when that sad wife crept fearfully to see what change had come to the patient face on the pillow, she found it smiling at her, saw a wasted hand outstretched to her, and heard a feeble voice cry bravely, "Hope!"[33]

Not long after the end of Fruitlands, Bronson wrote about the difference between success and failure. A man failed, he thought, "when [his] idea ruins him, when he is dwarfed and killed by it."[34] Success, on the other hand, meant using one's ideas as a means of growing. It also meant staying true to one's vision, regardless of the world's opinion. To succeed, therefore, was a matter of choice. Looking back on her father's recovery, Louisa wanted very much to observe it as a resurrection. She represented it as the death of her quixotic, communalist father and the birth of a new man, redeemed by family, cured of delusion, and tenderly consecrated to the welfare of the blood relations who had called him back from the abyss.

However, real lives rarely divide so neatly, and neither did Bronson's. When Alcott emerged from his sickroom, wan and harrowed by his ordeal, no one denied that he was a changed man. But what, precisely, was the nature of his transformation? If the experience left him more dedicated to his own family, this change required more time than the seven months at Fruitlands to complete itself. Indeed, nine months after the fall of his community, Bronson wrote to his brother Junius of his hopes to found another utopian society. Emerson, he said, had offered to give him a few acres and build him a house, and Samuel May had volunteered backing that would free him from the pressures of rents and landlords. Bronson meant to use the space to erect dwellings for several families, of which he imagined he would become the superpatriarch. He wrote, "I cannot consent to live solely for one family. I would stand in neighborly relations to several, and . . . institute a union and communion of families, instead of drawing aside within the precincts of one's own acres and kindred by blood."[35] Bronson's idealism had passed through his trials unaltered. What had changed was the measure of his ambition and energy. There was to be no second communion of families, not because Alcott could no longer dream, but because his will was spent and broken. Despite his protestations, he would eventually consent to live for one family, to till one garden, to strive for the reform and perfection of one spirit—his own. Though his desires remained qualitatively the same, he gradually adjusted their scope to the realm of the possible.

Tucked away among the Alcott family papers is a copy of a drawing of unstated origin, at the bottom of which can be read the handwritten caption "Removing from Fruitlands Jan. 1844." In the snow-covered scene, a team of oxen stands before a sled crowded almost to capacity with nine human figures. Either this is an exaggeration, since by the time of this last departure only the Alcott family remained on the premises, or the other figures are friends who have come to help the family vacate. In the back-

The Alcotts left Fruitlands in early January 1844, never to return.
Bronson saved this sketch depicting their departure for the rest of his life.
(Courtesy of Houghton Library, Harvard University)

ground, the farmhouse sits among a grove of bare trees. Curiously, there is still smoke rising from the chimney. In the middle ground, a bearded figure, evidently Joseph Palmer, applies a shovel to the cold earth, still determined to extract something of value from the ruined venture. Just being helped over the stile so she can board the wagon is a grown woman, presumably Abba. All the people in the sled appear drained of energy, but those who wear a visible expression at all appear to be smiling, perhaps with relief. Only two figures appear cross and discontented; the oxen are openly scowling, as if they somehow know that the experiment whose end they are witnessing has been for their benefit and will never be tried again. One would expect Bronson himself to figure prominently in the picture. Strange to say, it is difficult even to guess which of the figures he is meant to be.

Though the family had found a place for the winter, its future was no more certain than ever. As they made their slow and frigid way to the Lovejoys, the world that lay before them bore no clear features. They had survived a test to their unity. Now unity was all they had.

CHAPTER EIGHT

FATHER AND DAUGHTER

"Cultivate poverty like a garden herb."
—HENRY DAVID THOREAU, *Walden*

"Let not him that putteth his hand
to the plough look backwards!"
—HENRY WADSWORTH LONGFELLOW,
The Courtship of Miles Standish

AFTER FRUITLANDS, BRONSON REGAINED HIS PHYSICAL health sooner than he recovered his good humor. If Samuel Bower, the erstwhile Fruitlands nudist, was to be believed, Bronson claimed privately that he still saw his marriage as the great impediment to his achievement of perfection. According to Bower, Bronson had declared himself "a Shaker in principle" and had proclaimed that he "had long since been divorced from his wife by the high court of *his* work and that she was no longer anything to him." Bower told Elizabeth Palmer Peabody that only Alcott's consideration for his children had kept him from joining the Shakers.[1]

However, other facts suggest that Bronson was no longer quite so willing to leave Abba. In late January and early February, when Bronson had rallied sufficiently to pay visits to the utopian settlements at Northampton and Hopedale, he took Abba with him. Although he was still looking for an alternative to life within society, he was now interested only in situations that would accommodate his family as an undivided unit. The two returned from their trip disappointed. As Abba wrote, they were both persuaded "that there is nothing there for us, no sphere in which we could act without an unwarrantable alienation from our children."[2] Bronson felt that the reformist impulses of the communities he had seen were too mod-

est and that they were at best new phases of the spirit of traditional soci-
ety.3 Ironically, even if the Alcotts had been able to ride out the winter at
Fruitlands, they would not have been able to stave off the encroachment of
the machine age for very long; a scant six months after the community dissolved, the Massachusetts legislature authorized construction of a rail line
that bisected the Fruitlands property.4

Understandably, Bronson was frustrated after the loss of his colony,
and in a flash of anger, he might well have spoken bitterly of his family
obligations. In a more tranquil moment, though, Bronson wrote a poem
that gave a very different view of what his family had done for him. It reads,
in part:

> I drank the dregs of every cup
> All institutions I drank up,
> Athirst I quaffed Life's flowing bowls
> And smacked the liquor of all Souls
> One sparkling cup remained for me:
> The ever-brimming fount of family.5

When he was thinking carefully instead of railing impulsively at his discomforts, Bronson realized that family was the living water that had saved
him. Charles Lane, who had had a better chance than most to observe how
things really stood with the couple, did not report any estrangement. To
the contrary, he continued to maintain that "constancy to his wife and
inconstancy to the Spirit" had besmirched Alcott's life for all time.6

In the early months of 1844, Bronson still required saving in many
respects. The financial situation of the family had grown desperate. The
Fruitlands disaster had left Bronson with only thirty-two dollars to his
name.7 The Alcotts thanked heaven that the Lovejoys had taken them in,
but the means of regaining their independence were unclear. No plans
could be made until Bronson had regained his emotional balance, and he
was not yet his old self. Still unwilling to relinquish the dream that had
unraveled before his eyes, he continued to practice an austere regimen,
maintaining a spartan diet and wearing the linen leggings and tunics from
his experiment. To his credit, he no longer insisted that his family observe
the same strict purity; he allowed his daughters to put on the warmer
clothing that they received from friends and relatives. Eventually, he also

stopped insisting that the family abstain from meat and dairy products, although he himself continued as a vegetarian.

Bronson's later recollections of this period reveal a mind in distress, not firmly fixed within the boundaries of reality. His social thinking reached its most iconoclastic point; he seemed determined "to lay the axe at the root of every existing institution."[8] As soon as he was able, he flung himself into his manuscripts with almost self-destructive energy. His two projects of the moment were an account of Fruitlands and a more abstruse work he called "The Prometheus of Creation." He stayed indoors and worked from sunrise until midnight, sometimes laboring on toward dawn. Fed only on fruit, biscuits, water, and his unfathomable visions, he wrote with complete abandon. He also continued his dedication to cold baths, plunging himself into frigid water twice a day. This routine worked a strange effect on his enervated body and overburdened spirit. His delirious recounting of his sensations during one such bath reveals a state of hallucination, in which the perceptions of all five senses seemed engrossed:

> In the coldest mornings there was a crackling and lambent flash following the passage of my hand over the pile of the skin, and I shook flames from my finger ends, which seemed erect and blazing with the phosphoric light. The eyes, too, were lustrous, and shot sparkles whenever I closed them. On raising my head from the flood there was heard a melody in the ear, as of a sound of many waters; and rubbing the eyes gave out an iris of the primitive colors, beautiful to behold, but as evanescent as a twinkling. . . . I tasted mannas, and all the aromas of field and orchard scented the fountains, and the brain was haunted with many voiced melodies. I enjoyed this state for a couple months or more, but was left somewhat debilitated when spring came, and unfit for common concerns.[9]

By his own admission, it was difficult for him to write during such moods of elevation, yet he drove his pen forward, convinced that he had reached a lofty pinnacle of inspiration. It probably seemed more likely to the people around him that he was out of his mind.

Despite her husband's alarming behavior, Abba was more concerned by his continuing refusal to seek employment in the marketplace economy that he found so distasteful and bewildering. Although she still respected his faith in Divine Providence, she would have dearly loved to discover "a little more activity and industry" on his part—enough, at least, to put an end to their dependency on others.[10] Their friends still gave, but no longer without grumbling.

In his idleness, Bronson was infuriating. In his otherworldly visions, he was bizarre. Looking back on this period, he himself used the word "possessed" to describe his frame of mind.[11] It has been suggested, though never precisely proved, that in the aftermath of Fruitlands Bronson Alcott became temporarily insane. Yet such labels can obscure more than they elucidate. In "The Artist of the Beautiful," a story coincidentally published during the same year Bronson heard his many-voiced melodies, Hawthorne observed that madness is the easy method by which the world accounts for whatever lies beyond its most ordinary scope. But was there any other way to explain Bronson's strange elations and his desperate pursuit of ideal phantoms? Some lines from Hawthorne's story are appropriate to Bronson's mental state:

> Perhaps he was mad. The lack of sympathy—that contrast between himself and his neighbors, which took away the restraint of example—was enough to make him so. Or, possibly, he had caught just so much of ethereal radiance as served to bewilder him, in an earthly sense, by its intermixture with the common daylight.[12]

The world had no good yardstick for measuring Bronson Alcott. His inspirations seemed saintly to some and deluded to others. During that winter with the Lovejoys, there was probably not a person in the world who understood him. Only in the self-confirming workings of his own mind did his contemplations make sense, and it was within his own mind that Bronson did much of his living for the next decade or more.

Communal life had also had its effect on the Alcott daughters. Bronson privately conceded that, whereas he had hoped that Fruitlands would "provide the means of an improved culture in which my children might participate . . . to the extent of an enthusiast's dream," the results had been much to the contrary. When he looked back on his experiment in 1851, it seemed to him that his plans for the molding of his daughters' souls had been "frustrated, and at the greatest personal hazard and domestic cost." He reflected ruefully that years of toil and anxiety had been inadequate to repair the damage that his folly had inflicted. He took consolation, however, in the thought that his "dear intent [was] all the dearer for its hurts and delays" and in the hope that his dream might "ripen and fructify in some distant generation."[13]

Not everyone felt the same. The failure of Fruitlands seems to have prompted Hawthorne to revise his estimate of Alcott. A few months before the commune began, Hawthorne's story "The Hall of Fantasy" had hailed Bronson as "a prophet" and "a great mystic innovator . . . calm and gentle . . . holy in aspect."[14] These words of praise were intact when the story first appeared in the periodical *Pioneer* in February 1843. In 1846, however, when he revised the story for inclusion in *Mosses from an Old Manse*, Hawthorne deleted all references to Alcott. A few years later, in the sketch that introduces *The Scarlet Letter*, Hawthorne cast an additional slur in the direction of his mystical acquaintance. He wrote that even a corpulent eighty-year-old customs inspector with "no power of thought, no depth of feeling" was a welcome change of company "to a man who had known Alcott."[15]

Meanwhile, the catastrophe of Fruitlands had left its impression on the rest of the Concord literary community. Emerson sympathized deeply with this friend's distress. After Bronson paid him a visit soon after Fruitlands collapsed, Emerson wrote, "Very sad it was to see this half-god driven to the wall, reproaching men, & hesitating whether he should not reproach the gods."[16] Publicly, however, Emerson kept his distance. Less than two months after the end of Fruitlands, Emerson gave his lecture on "New England Reformers," the one in which he likened contemporary reformers to "a congress of kings." Kindly refraining from mentioning Fruitlands by name, he argued that society gained nothing "whilst a man, not himself renovated, attempts to renovate things around him: he has become tediously good in some particular, but negligent or narrow in the rest." Emerson feared that any community that retreated from the world would likely become "an asylum to those who have tried and failed, rather than a field to the strong."[17]

When in 1845 Thoreau set off for his famous sojourn at Walden Pond, he may have wanted to show that, Fruitlands notwithstanding, a world-shunning community could make itself viable and self-sufficient, even if it were just a community of one. *Walden* begins with a lengthy chapter titled "Economy," in which the author reckons the costs and profits of his experiment to the last half-penny. Anyone curious to know why Thoreau took such pains to

show the fiscal practicability of his paradise may find at least a partial explanation in Thoreau's desire to refute the evident lessons of Alcott's failure. In
the subtle pas de deux between idealism and practicality that gives *Walden*
much of its brilliance, the ghost of Fruitlands repeatedly figures.[18]

Despite his winter of furious scribbling, the Concord litterateur who
had the least to say in print about Fruitlands was Alcott himself. However,
his silence was due more to accident than intention. In July 1844, Alcott set
out with Anna on a trip to visit three visionary communities in upstate
New York, including John Humphrey Noyes's colony at Oneida. He
brought with him the journals he had compiled at Alcott House and Fruitlands, probably to have a record on hand as he compared notes with fellow
utopians. He also took along an assortment of letters and the "Prometheus
of Creation" manuscript. On their way home, Bronson and Anna spent a
night in Albany, New York. The next day, they loaded their luggage atop
the hotel's stagecoach and rode to the Hudson River to board a boat. Bronson left the coach for a few moments to help Anna board the vessel. When
he returned to get their trunk, he found to his horror that the stage had
driven away with it. Inside the trunk were Bronson's papers. Bronson sent
frantic, pleading letters to the hotel, and six years later, on a subsequent
trip to Albany, he was still looking for the lost trunk.[19] However, neither
the trunk nor its contents were ever recovered, and with his journals went
the possibility of his ever writing the history of the Consociate Family. At
the moment that the omnibus had pulled out of sight, the catastrophe of
Fruitlands was complete.

As critics picked over the wreckage of Fruitlands and Bronson mourned
the loss of his irreplaceable manuscripts, the Alcott family was regaining its
equilibrium. In the family's comfortable winter quarters with the Lovejoys,
Abba had recovered her strength. She sold a few small belongings to bring
in some extra cash, and her brother Samuel sent a few dollars. Later in the
year, to economize as much as possible, the family moved to another location in Still River, where they rented four rooms and a garden for twenty-
five dollars a year. Abba was buoyed by the hope that the worst of the
family's straits lay behind them. She did her best to keep her dissatisfac-
tions from her daughters. After all, she wrote, her children "are in no wise
participators of my anxiety, neither can they alleviate my suffering by their
sympathy."[20] That spring, the Alcotts celebrated their fourteenth wedding

anniversary. Abba marked the occasion by writing in her journal, "Whom confidence and love have wedded, let not doubt or distrust put asunder."[21]

Though Louisa never wrote about her father's emotional instability in the aftermath of Fruitlands, she must have been confused to find that Bronson, who had been so passionately involved in her early upbringing, now sometimes shrank from family contact and turned his gaze obsessively inward. At times, though, her father's behavior was worse than perplexing. It was simply scary. She had always known her father as everyone else had known him, as a man of diffidence, calm, and surpassing self-control. Now, with his sleepless nights and unearthly visions, he must have seemed like someone she hardly knew. The steady, thoughtful man who had seemed to understand so much was now himself a bit beyond understanding.

Bronson's distancing from his children may have been due only in part to his inner turmoil. It may also have arisen from the fact that his girls were growing up. Bronson's interest in children, even his own, was rooted primarily in his fascination with elementary education and preadolescent development. The older the child, and the more firmly fixed her character, the less intriguing he tended to find her. The changes Louisa was undergoing, as well as the transformation that he experienced, were making their separation more pronounced.

Fortunately for Louisa, she was becoming less dependent on her father for her daily happiness. Although life as an Alcott would always mean being held to certain standards, she had reached an age at which her self-esteem no longer depended solely on her parents' approval. In the months after Fruitlands, she began again to form attachments outside the family's circle. As spring returned to Massachusetts, Louisa and her sisters quickly found friends among the children of Still River. With a girl named Annie Clark, Anna, Louisa, and Lizzie tossed a ball, jumped rope, and rolled hoops with carefree abandon. Abba, as Annie Clark remembered, was like a guardian angel to the merry band of girls, often sitting among them and smiling at their pranks and pretendings.

That summer, Clark attended the birthday party of nine-year-old Lizzie, a somewhat more lavish and less stilted affair than it had been the previous year. The Lovejoys' kitchen was bedecked with evergreens, and the table was laden with tiny cakes and luscious cherries, all surrounding a huge cake at the center. The evening was marked by singing and by one of the first

Alcott family theatricals of which a description survives. Clark remembered
Louisa as the star of the evening. Her face and arms tinted brown in imitation of a Native American and dressed in a costume that seemed all made
of feathers, Louisa performed a song about an Indian girl, "bright Alfarata,"
and declaimed a poem that denounced the depredations of Europeans in
the New World. In character, she lamented the death of her people:

> I will weep for a season, on bitterness fed,
> For my kindred are gone to the hills of the dead;
> But they died not by hunger, or lingering decay;
> The steel of the white man hath swept them away.[22]

For the Alcott girls, and for Anna and Louisa in particular, playacting in
the home was to become a crucial form of self-expression. Not only did
acting supply an acceptable outlet for feelings that they could not freely
express otherwise, but it also was one of the first paths for Louisa's literary
imagination. It is noteworthy that, in this early performance, Louisa
assumed the character of an outcast from whom both land and family had
been brutally stolen: Louisa was capable of relating her own experiences of
deprivation to the sufferings of others.

That same month, Louisa also met Frederick Willis, a delicate boy of
fourteen who had come from Boston to spend the summer in the country.
When he wrote his reminiscences of her more than a half century later, he
remembered her clear, olive-brown complexion, set off by brown hair and
eyes. She had a life and a spirit to her that sometimes expressed itself in irri-
tability and nervousness. Along with her moods and impulsiveness, he
remembered above all her delight in motion. In his mind's eye, he saw her
running. She was like a gazelle, it seemed to him, the most beautiful girl
runner he ever knew. She leaped fences and climbed the tallest trees, never
giving the slightest thought to being ladylike or proper. Her second love
was nature. She was still passionately fond of fields and forests, and Fred
noticed the special harmony that she shared with animals, an affinity she
had, of course, learned from Thoreau.[23]

More surprisingly, Willis noticed in Louisa a great love of personal
beauty. Whereas in *Little Women* all the interest in outward appearance is
attributed to Meg and Amy, Louisa, too, had her childish vanities. Imagining that large eyes were a hallmark of beauty, she one day walked down

Washington Street in Boston with her eyes unnaturally wide. She was at first gratified when her expression attracted the attention of passersby. However, when she returned home and assumed the same look in the mirror, she was aghast to see that she had been affecting the deranged stare of a madwoman.[24]

Of Louisa's many passions, none distinguished her more than her delight in fantasy. Exploring the environs of Still River with Fred and Anna, Louisa discovered a rocky glen full of moss and ferns. There, the three devised a mystical realm known as Spiderland, where Fred reigned as king, Anna as queen, and Louisa as princess royal. Interestingly, Fred recollected the spot as a "nook," a telling word choice for those who know of Bronson's decree at the Temple School that there should be no "nooks" or secret places in the youthful mind. At the ages of twelve and thirteen, Louisa and Anna were actively inventing nooks, both physical and mental, where no overly inquisitive parent or teacher could enter.[25]

In the meantime, Bronson continued the battle to regain his peace of mind. Nevertheless, he could still be something of a morose presence. He accepted an invitation to speak at a Fourth of July church picnic but turned up his nose at the various delicacies that were served. When a plate of elaborately prepared cookies was passed his way, he was heard to mutter, well within the hearing of the pastor's wife who had baked them, "Vanity, and worse than vanity!"[26]

In October, the Alcotts came back to Concord, accepting the hospitality of Edmund Hosmer, who let them use half of his house while they searched for one of their own. Five months earlier, Abba had received word that her father's estate had at last been settled. Abba's legacy, some two thousand dollars, was more than enough to purchase a residence in or near the town. After all their seemingly endless wanderings, the family was to have a home. In addition to the six Alcotts, a seventh person was preparing to join the household, a young woman named Sophia Foord, who had consented to be the children's tutor. The Alcotts hired her with the understanding that, in due time, Bronson would set up a village school at Hillside, where he and Foord would share the teaching. Louisa, hoping to add a touch of grandeur, called Foord her governess.

It was Emerson who found the property they chose to buy: a 145-year-old structure that had recently belonged to a wheelwright named Horatio

Cogswell. No one seemed to know much about the history of the house, although Thoreau recollected a story that it had once been occupied by a man who believed he would never die. It was rumored that his ghost still lived in the house. Another previous owner had kept pigs in the front yard. Thankfully, however, the pigs had long since gone off to the butcher, and the ghost was never seen. He may have preferred someplace quieter. The house was not large, and once the half dozen Alcotts and Miss Foord had crowded in, it seems unlikely that a ghost could be comfortably fitted in besides.

Nevertheless, despite the lack of space, Bronson opened his home to others with a liberality that Louisa found irritating. In her 1845 journal she grumbled, "More people coming to live with us; I wish we could be together, and no one else. I don't see who is to clothe and feed us all, when we are so poor now."27 Though still intrigued by communal life, Bronson reluctantly accepted the task of caring only for his own family. "If a Holy Family is beyond us," he said, "we may at least exclude much that annoys and renders uncomely the Households on which we cast our eyes wheresoever we turn."28 By most measures other than financial, Bronson and Abba succeeded while at Hillside in doing just that.

Bronson christened their home the Hillside, in reference to the rather steep slope behind the structure. Seven years later, when Nathaniel Hawthorne bought the property, he changed its name to the Wayside, a name that he found "more morally suggestive." The "Way" near which the house was situated was the old road to Lexington, remembered as the route by which the British forces advanced toward and later retreated from the battle of Concord Bridge. Before the Alcotts' arrival, Hawthorne called the structure "a mean-looking affair [with] no suggestiveness about it." Although it had passed through countless haphazard renovations, it had never acquired the stately quality—the "venerableness," to use Hawthorne's term—that houses of such an age are expected to achieve.29

However, when the Alcotts moved into the house on April 1, 1845, Bronson was determined to look on the bright side. He loved the hosts of locust trees that covered the hillside and burst into fragrant bloom each summer. Among the locusts, young elms and white pines strove skyward, creating an ideal place for escaping the heat of the day. Almost always, a breeze was blowing, and the sunlight that sliced through the trembling leaves cast bright patterns on the ground. In such a bower, a dreaming man might quickly lose track of time, reflecting calmly on past errors and thinking hopefully of better days to come.

In Bronson's optimistic view, the house was not so small after all, and he invited his elderly mother and brother Junius to join them. Bronson's motives in extending this offer were not entirely unselfish. The property included some six to eight acres of fertile soil, purchased with a five-hundred-dollar gift from Emerson, and Alcott did not think himself equal to the task of planting it all by himself. Initially, Junius temporized. In the end, he declined. It was probably for the best. The presence of another family would have placed a strain on Bronson's resources, just when it seemed he might finally put his finances in order. A more ominous problem, however, lay with Junius himself, who it seemed was suffering from some form of mental imbalance that, as yet, no one was prepared to openly address.

Despite Junius's refusal, however, Bronson quickly undertook the imposing task of renovating the property. He had soon moved the barn to

*Bronson made extensive renovations to Hillside, giving the home
"a modest picturesqueness." The family's years here correspond
to the time described by Louisa in* Little Women.

(Courtesy of the Louisa May Alcott Memorial Association)

a more advantageous spot and was having it repaired with a view to storing the season's crops. As to the slope behind the house, he set about forming the lower portion into terraces, where he constructed arbors from the rough trunks and branches of trees "on a system of his own," as Hawthorne remarked.[30] He also had an ingenious plan for curing the lack of space in the house itself. With his carpenter friend Edmund Hosmer, Bronson cut an old wheelwright's shop on the property in two and grafted the two halves onto opposite sides of the house, creating a piazza on each side. He also added a porch to the front of the house and a peak to the center of the roof. Once Bronson added some coats of paint—a rusty olive tone was chosen to complement the tones of the landscape—even the grim-mouthed Hawthorne had to admit that Hillside now exuded "a modest picturesqueness."[31] It was a place that people noticed and remembered for a while after passing it.

At Hillside, Bronson and Abba welcomed a class of visitors who later remembered the house not because of its appearance but because it had offered them food and rest on the road to freedom. Dedicated to advancing the cause of African-Americans, the Alcotts offered Hillside as a station on the Underground Railroad. It is likely that the Alcotts sheltered more fugitives than there are records to prove; their work demanded secrecy. Bronson did, however, describe one fugitive who stayed a week with the family in 1847 before moving on toward Canada. The man was about thirty, "athletic, dextrous, sagacious, and self-relying." Bronson saw in him many of the qualities of a hero and pointed to him as "an impressive lesson to my children, bringing before them the wrongs of the black man and his tale of woes."[32] Louisa took an interest in one of the men whom her parents sheltered, and she started to teach him how to write. When she found that he was awkward with a pen and pencil, she continued the lessons with a lump of charcoal on the hearth. She remembered him as a "black George Washington."[33]

Hillside signified a new kind of liberty in Louisa's life as well, for it was here that, for the first time, both she and Anna acquired rooms of their own. Louisa had spent her preteen years with almost no experience of privacy. Understanding that some aspects of mind and character can be perfected only in solitude, Abba made Louisa's room as appealing an oasis as possible. She positioned Louisa's workbasket and desk by a window, and a steady perfume emanated from dried herbs kept in the closet. Perhaps best of all, the room had a door that opened directly onto the garden so that Louisa could slip off into the woods without being detected. "It does me good to be alone," Louisa wrote, and she began to thrive emotionally as she acquired a sense of a self, flourishing in the absence of parental surveillance.[34]

Hillside was a sanctuary for Bronson as well. He, too, found the refuge from critical observers that he desperately needed. The breakdown he had experienced after Fruitlands and the periods of delirium that followed had produced long-lasting effects on his spirit. In his journal soon after New Year's Day 1846, he wrote, "There is a martyrdom of the mind no less than of the body." Mentally, he was still on the cross. He asked himself who were the teachers of the age. After writing the names of Emerson, Garrison, and Carlyle, he at first wrote his own but then scratched it out, adding the notation, "no—for me the time is not quite ready."[35] Bronson thought it was time to wait, though just what he was waiting for, he himself could not have said.

Taking his unfitness for public life as proof of his integrity, Bronson turned away from activity outside his gateposts. The notes that he took on his typical daily routine reveal that he was far from idle, but they also show that he was principally absorbed in perfecting life within his domestic sphere. He rose at five, lit the fires, and helped the children with their ablutions. Breakfast was accompanied by conversation and the reading of a hymn. He devoted much of the early morning to reading and study but reserved the hours between ten and noon for instructing his daughters. Between the midday meal and three o'clock, he worked in the garden. He filled the remaining hours before supper by reading aloud with Abba and the girls. His garden and his children were his two emblems of hope and promise. Within two years, Bronson's almost single-handed labor transformed the neglected property into a place of rustic enchantment. He had planted a thriving orchard of two hundred apple and peach trees. The field that he cultivated on the other side of Lexington Road yielded abundant crops of beans, celery, cucumbers, spinach, potatoes, and other vegetables. A grapevine trailed near the piazza, and a fountain bubbled among well-tended flowerbeds. Hillside was, in a sense, a second Fruitlands without the complications of a consociate family. Although life at Hillside did not have the same experimental thrust of Fruitlands, life with Bronson Alcott was always something of an experiment.

Children, of course, require more managing than bean plants, and it takes far longer to judge the success of their cultivation. Here too, however, Bronson was reasonably content with the results. From time to time, his daughters joined him in the garden. Louisa helped with the weeds as her father expounded on the virtues, both practical and symbolic, of the herbs he had planted.[36] On the hill behind the house, the girls' play fantasies bore the marks of their father's reading; when the four clambered toward the summit, they consciously reenacted the journey of Bunyan's Pilgrim toward the Celestial City. Bronson's incessant need to instruct and enlighten continued at the dinner table. At mealtimes, Frederick Willis remembered, Bronson always simplified his language so that even the smallest listener would understand him. Holding an apple on his fork, Alcott might give a miniature lecture on its growth and development. Willis was fascinated by these performances and found Alcott's language charmingly poetic.[37] If nothing else, Bronson's dinner-table homilies made his daughters more ardent apostles of vegetarianism. Once, a visitor to the Alcotts' home arrived to discover the girls energetically shoveling coal into the cellar. They eagerly cried out to him, "See what vegetables will do? It's all vegetables!"[38]

By and large, the people of Concord smirked at Bronson's philosophizing; a popular joke held that Emerson was a seer and Alcott was a seersucker.[39] However, they could not deny that the quartet of girls he was raising were an asset to the community—"self-helpful, kindly, and bright" as Emerson's son Edward put it.[40] "I know not," Bronson wrote, "that I am not serving mankind as greatly in these humble services—in setting trees and teaching my children, these human shoots—as in the noisier and seemingly more widely useful sphere of public activity."[41]

Another humble service Bronson gladly continued to perform was to act as a companion to Emerson and Thoreau. As the latter made ready to take up residence at Walden Pond, Alcott followed his friend's preparations with interest. Alcott did not hesitate to lend his own efforts to Thoreau's experiment in ideal living. He was on hand at the beginning of May for the raising of Thoreau's house. Thoreau remarked that no man had ever been more honored by the character of his raisers than he was, and he trusted

*Henry David Thoreau. Louisa never forgot
his "power, intellect, and courage."*
(Courtesy of the National Portrait Gallery)

that they were destined to assist at the raising of loftier structures one day.[42] Alcott was a frequent visitor to Thoreau's hut on the pond, coming, as Thoreau put it, "through the village, through snow and rain and darkness, till he saw my lamp through the trees."[43] In *Walden*, Thoreau repaid Alcott's companionship with a heartfelt tribute, hailing his neighbor as the man of the most faith of any alive. It mattered little, Thoreau implied, that Alcott had no current occupation, for when his day finally came, "laws unsuspected by most will take effect, and masters of families and rulers will come to him for advice." Thoreau did not foresee that Alcott could ever die, for the simple reason that Nature could not spare him.[44]

Bronson's attempts to please his other great friend, Emerson, had more mixed results. Emerson's enthusiasm regarding Alcott had cooled somewhat. Certainly, he had been embarrassed on behalf of transcendentalism when Fruitlands fell apart. Much of Emerson's diffidence, however, resulted from the content of his character, rather than from any particular failing on Alcott's part. Something in Emerson's Yankee individualism made it both difficult and unnecessary for him to form warm personal attachments. His ability to find companions suffered because of his innate high-mindedness; he expected from friendship a more powerful unity of spirits than could be provided by mere mortals. "The higher the style we demand of friendship," he wrote, "of course the less easy to establish it with flesh and blood. . . . Friends such as we desire are dreams and fables."[45] Alcott was probably better able than anyone else at working his way around the defenses that Emerson erected against social intimacy. Even so, there were now fewer meetings between them than Alcott would have wished, causing him to value the time they shared all the more. He wrote fondly of days in May and June when the two strolled to Walden Pond, trading observations that Alcott thought would make a pretty volume, if only he had the genius for transcribing them.[46]

Bronson especially enjoyed entertaining Emerson in the rustic summer house he had built from willows on the grounds of Hillside. He considered himself the happiest of men to receive the poet under a canopy made by his own hands. His hospitality was to have a comic upshot. In the summer of 1847, Emerson made the mistake of admiring Bronson's summer cottage a bit too enthusiastically. Alcott was eager to do a favor for his friend, and Emerson understood the importance of giving Alcott a chance to feel useful. Bronson was promptly enlisted to construct a similar bower on Emerson's land. Alcott embraced the task with bold ambition, hoping both to reward his friend's many acts of kindness and to try out a fantastic theory of architecture that had been germinating in his brain. Alcott called his new style of building "the Sylvan," and through it he strove to free the structure from right angles and artificial forms. Rather, the building should look as if it had grown in autochthonous fashion from its natural surroundings.

Bronson enlisted the help of Thoreau, who had just ended his stay at Walden, and was soon laying the first timbers in the August heat.[47] He created nine arched entrances, to represent each of the ancient Muses. The roof dipped toward the center, but no one was sure whether this was an aspect of the design or a sign of imminent collapse. Day by day, the house took and changed shape, until it resembled the temple of some lost East Asian cult. Thoreau, who knew a few things about geometric relations and physical laws, began to be appalled. Generously, Emerson averred that a Palladio had been lost to the world when Alcott chose education and philosophy over architecture. Nevertheless, he confided to Margaret Fuller that he was becoming alarmed by the building's dimensions and apparent lack of stability. He began to refer to the structure as "Tumbledown Hall." His wife, Lidian, was terser. She called it "The Ruin."[48]

Inevitably, townspeople came by to gawk and snicker. Alcott comforted himself by recalling that people had also laughed at Michelangelo. In the end, Alcott's judgment was somewhat vindicated, since the derided "Ruin" stood for fifteen years. When Tumbledown Hall was finished, Bronson had given his friend both a unique gift and a wonderful story to tell.

However much Emerson meant to Bronson during this time, he meant still more to Louisa, who found in him both a literary idol and a sympathetic ear. Judging that the girl had some special merits, Emerson gave Louisa free access to his library. A brisk eight-minute walk separated Hillside from Emerson's home. Louisa, in her perpetual hurry, probably covered the distance in less time. On one of her visits, Emerson offered Louisa a little-known book, *Goethe's Correspondence with a Child*, consisting of a series of letters between the great German poet and a young woman named Bettine von Arnim. The idea of a young woman seeking wisdom from the elder sage appealed powerfully to Louisa. She wanted to be Emerson's Bettine, and she soon found ample excuses to spend more time under her hero's roof. Her attentions to him took on the form of an innocent, impossible courtship. She sang Mignon's Song "in very bad German" under his window and picked bouquets of wildflowers to leave at his door. She wrote him letters in which she laid bare her soul but, she later thanked heaven, was too shy and prudent to send them. Imagining him at her side, she went for meandering walks at night and gazed at the moon from the strong branches of a cherry tree until the cries of the owls scared her to bed.[49] Apparently, Emerson was either oblivious to the crush or politely ignored it. Louisa soon got over her passion, and she eventually burned the letters, but Emerson remained her "master," doing more for her, she was sure, than he ever knew. After his death, she recalled with warmest gratitude "the simple beauty of his life, the truth and wisdom of his books, [and] the example of a good, great man untempted and unspoiled by the world."[50]

Louisa also came along on some of her father's visits to Thoreau at the pond. In scholarly moods, Thoreau listened as the Alcott girls recited to him in French and German.⁵¹ A much better linguist than either Emerson or Alcott, Thoreau could have taught the Alcott sisters Latin and Greek, as well as some Native American languages, if he had been asked to. Instead, he gave them an easy, practical course on how to love the world.

Back at Hillside, Abba typically took charge of the evening's entertainment. Both Abba and Louisa were fond of whist, and they often invited neighborhood girls for an evening card party. As much as she enjoyed the game, it was sometimes nearly impossible to lure Louisa into the parlor if she had become engrossed in a good book. Other evenings, the Alcott girls would work at their sewing as one of them read aloud from Scott, Hawthorne, or Dickens. The last was a particular favorite, and the girls excelled in dramatizing scenes from his work. During her teen years, Louisa received essentially no formal schooling outside the home. However, reading Dickens with her family, poring over Goethe in Emerson's library, and scrambling through the woods with Thoreau comprised a unique education in themselves.

To Louisa's undoubted relief, another of her father's friends gradually withdrew from the Alcotts' lives during the Hillside years. Not long after Bronson purchased the home—almost inexplicably, considering the pain and chaos he had previously inflicted on them—Charles Lane briefly lived at Hillside, supervising part of the children's education. Lane tasked Louisa with writing out a list of her vices. Hoping to satisfy him, she produced a litany of nine, including those dreaded vipers of the soul "activity" and "love of cats." Lane told her to define gentleness and asked her who possessed it. "Father and Anna" was the reply. Who meant to have it? he then demanded. The desired admission followed: "Louisa, if she can."⁵² Louisa withstood Lane's assaults on her dignity, but she understandably hated him. Not only did his icy moralisms take the fun out of learning, but he also seemed to ruin everything he touched in her father's garden.⁵³ Louisa must have rejoiced when, in October 1845, Lane left, never again to trouble her with his strikingly imperfect notions of perfection.

Lane, however, was not the only source of discomfort in Louisa's educational life. The sisters' governess, Sophia Foord, was something of a mixed blessing. On the one hand, some of her teaching methods were pleasingly similar to Thoreau's. To teach botany, she took the girls into the woods. Louisa especially enjoyed a wading expedition to Flint's Pond, where she and her sisters "ma[de] the fishes run like mad" as they sloshed through the shallow water, and from which they returned "bawling and singing like crazy folks."[54] On the other hand, the craziness of the Alcott girls was too pronounced for Foord. In a frank conversation with Abba, she called the children "indolent" and laid the blame on the permissive practices of Abba and Bronson, whom she pronounced "faulty specimens of parental impotence."[55]

Foord had other reasons for feeling frustrated with her situation. Bronson's promised Hillside school and the money Foord expected to earn from it never materialized; Alcott's radicalism had frightened off the parents of potential pupils. He was even denied permission to speak at a statewide convention of the Teachers Institute; rejecting his request, the famous public-school reformer Horace Mann explained that Alcott's political opinions were unacceptably "hostile to the existence of the State."[56] Disappointed professionally, Foord was also unlucky in love. Infatuated with Thoreau, she wrote him a letter proposing marriage, and the naturalist replied with "as distinct a no as I have learned to pronounce."[57] Embarrassed, Foord left the Alcotts' employ. They did not replace her.

A happier influence on Louisa's life continued to be the outdoors. She wrote a series of "flower fables" to amuse Emerson's young daughter Ellen. In the fields, she played tag with her sisters and friends. In the orchards, she climbed apple trees, rattling her bones when she happened to fall. She wrote to a friend, "We are dreadfull [*sic*] wild people here in Concord, we do all the sinful things you can think of."[58] The sins were hardly serious, though some of them were amusing. On one of her rambles, Louisa encountered a crew of men who were chewing tobacco as they hoed potatoes. Ever curious, Louisa asked to try a quid. She chewed it so vigorously that its effects overpowered her, and she had to be carried home in a wheelbarrow.[59]

But it was an intoxicating experience of another kind that most profoundly transformed her. As the sun rose on a Thursday in the summer or autumn of 1845—she did not record the date—Louisa went for a run. The dew was not yet off the grass, and the moss was like velvet. Pausing in the silent woods to get her breath, she beheld the sun, slowly ascending above the wide meadows and looking as she had never seen it before. In the hush of that perfect morning, something changed inside her, and she felt a stirring for which she could find only one name: God. It came to her not through scripture, not through *The Pilgrim's Progress*, but through the power of the natural world. To Louisa, it was a "vital sense of His presence, tender and sustaining as a father's arms."[60] She had never felt this way before, and she prayed that she might keep the sense of His nearness forever. Almost forty years later, she wrote with satisfaction that she always had. Through all life's vicissitudes, she wrote, the feeling never changed, standing the test as she passed through "health & sickness, joy & sorrow, poverty & wealth."[61] Though she destroyed untold quantities of her early writings, Louisa always preserved the journal entry that told of this moment of conversion when reason and faith, in the guise of a morning sunbeam, shone into her heart.[62]

The Alcotts remained at Hillside until November 1848. These three and a half years were the longest period the Alcott children ever spent in one house. These Hillside years correspond to the adolescence celebrated and fictionalized in *Little Women*. They are the years when Louisa began writing in earnest, and they were the time when she acquired her adult character and her permanent sense of individuality. At the same time that she was coming to a clear sense of self, however, Louisa would have been hardpressed to define herself entirely apart from her sisters. Bronson, observing the strong, beautiful tie that united them, referred to his daughters collectively as "the golden band."[63]

As a group, the four could make a powerful impression, but not always the kind that their parents might have hoped. One afternoon, Louisa remembered, Bronson and Abba were entertaining Emerson and Margaret Fuller. As the four adults stood by the door, the conversation turned predictably to education. Apparently, Bronson lamented the lack of a school in which to pursue his theories. Fuller remarked, "Well, Mr. Alcott, you have been able to carry out your methods in your own family, and I should like to see your model children." In a few moments, she got her wish. The high-minded colloquy was interrupted by a chaotic uproar, and around the corner of the house came the heedless foursome. In a wheelbarrow, transformed by imagination into an ancient chariot, sat little Abby in the costume of a queen. Louisa, bitted, bridled, and harnessed to the royal car, was a horse, driven by Anna. Lizzie had taken the part of a dog, and she was barking as loudly as her gentle voice permitted. Louisa writes, "All were shouting and wild with fun, which, however, came to a sudden end as we espied the stately group before us." Louisa stumbled, and her three sisters all fell on top of her in a laughing heap. Abba gestured impressively toward the pile, saying, "Here are the model children, Miss Fuller."[64]

When Bronson thought of Anna, he imagined "her beauty-loving eyes and sweet visions of graceful motions and golden hues and all fair and mystic shows and shapes." She was the most even-tempered and amiable of the four. Her sense of humor was keen but without Louisa's tartness. While she partook enthusiastically in the games of her friends and sisters, her zest was tempered with a sense of dignity. She was more beautiful in her graceful bearing than in her physical features. Skilled in learning languages and a thoughtful writer, she perhaps exceeded all her sisters in terms of her pure intellectual gifts. Anna, too, wrote stories.[65] Unlike Louisa, however, she lacked the confidence to try to publish them. Her excellent mind was "shown more in the appreciation of others than in the expression of herself."[66] Years of experience with Louisa's temper had taught Anna that it was most prudent to let her younger sister have her way, and by the time the family settled at Hillside, she had fully accepted her role as Louisa's subordinate, an eager second but never a daring first. As a longtime friend remembered, "She loved to hide behind her gifted sister."[67]

Yet there was one ability that Anna did not hide. Almost everyone commented on her superior talents as an actress. In the family theatricals, it was she and Louisa who did almost all of the acting, each taking on five or six parts at once, sustaining the action amid a flurry of quick costume changes. As befitted their respective personalities, Anna played the sentimental roles, while Louisa inclined toward characters touched by the demonic or supernatural. Anna was, for a while, desirous of doing something in the world. Her grammar deserting her in the midst of her reverie, she once wrote, "I sometimes have strange feelings, a sort of longing after something I don't know what it is." She had "a foolish wish to do something great." In 1850, Louisa wrote, "Anna wants to be an actress, and so do I." However, Anna sensed that her dream of stardom would not come true. She felt in the back of her mind that she would likely "spend my life in a kitchen and die in the poor-house."[68] Acting professionally had just enough hint of scandal to cause a proper young woman like Anna to hesitate. Moreover, as years passed, Anna became prematurely hard of hearing, so that picking up stage cues at last grew difficult. Anna, always a true mother's helper, at last confirmed the expectations of those who had considered her "the most domestic" member of the family.[69]

Despite their differences, Anna and Louisa came to share a deep mutual regard. Anna's blend of talent and humility suited well their father's image of what a young woman should be. During the years at Hillside, she was sometimes Bronson's only bulwark against despair.[70] Although Bronson regarded his children as much more than subjects on which to test his theories of education, he may have thought of Anna as the experiment who turned out right.

When Bronson painted his third daughter, Elizabeth, with words, he chose pastel shades. He wrote of "her quiet-loving disposition and serene thought, her happy gentleness and deep contentment." Lizzie was the most enigmatic sister, a passive, quiet soul who generally felt much less creative passion than her sisters. Although friends often remarked on her love of the piano, which she played with skill and appreciation, one struggles to find instances in which Lizzie did anything bold or original. As Louisa writes of Lizzie's counterpart Beth in *Little Women*, "she seemed to live in a world of her own, only venturing out to meet the few whom she trusted and loved."[71] Yet even among these she was noticeably guarded. Whereas the rest of the family made it a common practice to read aloud from their journals at the dinner table or around the fireside, Lizzie steadfastly declined to do so.

In the family theatricals, Lizzie took modest parts. A page here, a messenger there, formed the core of her repertoire. Although Anna recalled that Lizzie enjoyed "constructing properties for stage adornment and transforming the frailest material into dazzling raiment," her preferred place during a performance was in the audience.[72] A number of spirited arguments with a young friend over the virtues of vegetarianism are virtually the only remembered instances in which she showed any heated emotion. While her parents entertained audacious schemes to save the world and her sisters began to conceive their private visions of wealth and success, little of their imaginative energy seems to have rubbed off on Lizzie. She seems never to have wanted more from life than a quiet, comfortable smallness. Yet Lizzie's meekness charmed her father. He referred to her as his "Little Tranquility," and it undoubtedly pleased him that her dreamy, quiet temperament was the very counterpart of his own. Like her father, as a playmate once observed, Lizzie was "all conscience."[73]

Abby May, with "her frolick joys and impetuous griefs . . . her fast falling footsteps, her sagacious eye and auburn locks," was a bright contrast to Lizzie.[74] The baby of the family, she was adroit at reaping the benefits that this status can entail. Born after the Temple School scandal, too young to have more than a dim recollection of Fruitlands, Abby escaped some of the greatest trials of being an Alcott daughter. She also had a quality that her forthright older sister Louisa often lacked: a subtle, prepossessing charm that made allies of people when she needed them most. When she reached adulthood, Abby decided that her first name was too babyish for her and started insisting that people call her May. Bronson lauded Abby May's talents and good disposition. He was aware that, because of her late arrival in the family, her prospects in life were somewhat fairer than those of her elder sisters, "who, with gifts no less promising, [had] yet been defrauded of deserved opportunities for study and culture" by the cloud of social disapproval that hung over the family since the closing of the Temple School. Of all his children, Bronson was most certain that his youngest daughter would make her way in the world.[75]

Louisa, however, continued to inspire more perplexity than confidence. In Bronson's mind, she conjured the image of a girl "with . . . quick and ready senses, . . . agile limbs, and boundless curiosity." He thought, too, of "her penetrating mind and tear-shedding heart, alive to all moving breathing things." Bronson admitted that she was a loving child, but her impulsiveness had continued to trouble him. He had always believed that if one approached a child with respect and openness, that child would eventually become a docile ally. However, Louisa's attempts to master herself still tended to meet with frustration and self-condemnation. When Louisa was thirteen, Bronson wrote in his journal of a day when he checked the diaries of his three eldest daughters to see how regularly they were being kept. Both Anna and Elizabeth passed the inspection. Louisa, who had been "unfaithful," was sent off to eat her dinner alone.[76] Bronson had once believed that all minds in childhood were fundamentally alike, and that education had the power to shape them toward a common purpose and a shared standard of moral excellence. Over time, however, he had revised his view. It now seemed to him that character was "more of a nature than of acquirement, and that the most you can do by culture is to adorn and give external polish to natural gifts."77 He believed that it was impossible to create or develop any spiritual qualities that were not inborn.

Worst of all, the rift within the family that had begun to widen when Bronson took Anna to the Temple School and left Louisa with her mother was greater than ever. Whereas Bronson counted Anna and Elizabeth as his own, Louisa turned to Abba as her source of courage and confidence. Now entering her teens, Louisa was well aware of the awkwardness with which she tended to impress people. "I am old for my age," she admitted, "and don't care much for girls' things. People think I'm wild and queer."78 Yet Abba made her gangly second daughter at home with her strangeness. She believed that her daughter's fitfulness was the sign of a spirit aspiring upward, of an energy that neither a sleepy Massachusetts town nor a teenaged body could easily contain. Abba slipped inspiring notes into Louisa's journal, and, always, she encouraged her daughter to write, not just as a means of moral examination, as her father would have it, but as a means of creative self-expression. The following excerpt is typical:

> I am sure your life has many fine passages well worth recording, and to me they are always precious. . . . Do write a little each day, dear, if but a line, to show me how bravely you begin the battle, how patiently you wait for the rewards sure to come when the victory is nobly won.79

Abba knew that, if Louisa had no way to express her "smothered sorrows" and smoldering emotions, they "might otherwise consume her young and tender heart."80 But also she sensed that Louisa, so eager to be good and so utterly unfitted for self-restraint, had something marvelous to give the world. On the late November day when Louisa turned fourteen, Abba acknowledged Louisa's adolescent loneliness, writing, "Your temperament is a peculiar one, and there are few who can really help you." But she also wrote, "Lift up your soul . . . to meet the highest for that alone can satisfy your great yearning nature. . . . [B]elieve me you are capable of ranking among the best." On that same birthday, Abba gave Louisa the first pen she could call her own, along with the hope that it might inspire her "when wrapt in pure poetic fire."81 Louisa must have felt that the tools of greatness were now at her command.

Unhappily, Bronson did not regard the bond between Abba and Louisa merely as one of love and loyalty; he saw in their alliance a threat to his authority and an implicit questioning of his principles. The same year he sent Louisa to eat alone for not seeing to her diary, Bronson wrote in his own journal, "Two devils, as yet, I am not quite divine enough to vanquish—the mother fiend and her daughter."[82]

Bronson rendered this judgment without identifying any specific quarrel or festering resentment that might have provoked him. No one disputes that Abba had a volatile temper. Even Louisa, ever her mother's staunchest defender, appears to concede as much in *Little Women*, in which Abba's counterpart Marmee asserts, "I am angry nearly every day of my life." Marmee admits that she has been trying to subdue her temper for forty years and has succeeded only in controlling it.[83] Yet if Abba was chronically angry, she had much to be angry about. In managing her frustrations as well as she did, she seems more saintly than demonic. It is sad to know that, despite all her loyalty and sacrifice, Bronson could still speak of her as a devil and a fiend. Bronson, certainly, was not always rational, and he was so convinced of his own moral excellence that he was prone to regard any criticism or resistance as a trial visited on him by some evil force. Thus, he was quick to exaggerate the evil of Abba's and Louisa's opposition.

Nevertheless, Bronson felt that he could benefit from Abba's and Louisa's resistance. Thinking perhaps of Socrates and Xanthippe, Bronson saw them as challenging him to reach new levels of tolerance and benignity. He wrote, "Count thyself divinely tasked if in thy self or thy family thou hast a devil or two to plague and try thy prowess and give thee occasion for celebrating thy victories by ringing all the bells of joy within thee."[84] At the same time, where moral certainty was concerned, as well as the stubbornness that can go with it, Abba was every bit a match for her husband. Weeks after moving into Hillside, she had written to her brother Samuel, "Nothing makes one so indifferent to the sins and mosquito-thrusts of life as the consciousness of being morally invulnerable."[85] Two ethically intransigent people in the same marriage are likely to fight some memorable battles. It seems that a strong marriage need not be perpetually harmonious.

One of the least appealing facets of Bronson Alcott's social thinking interacted with his understanding of his family. He was strangely taken with an unpleasant form of pseudoscience which held that the inner natures of human beings could be deduced from their physical coloring. In self-serving fashion, he decided that blond-haired, blue-eyed persons were the most spiritually developed of human beings and that darker pigments connoted darker natures that were nocturnal, earthy, and slumberous. He praised the "impregnable Saxondom" of both Old and New England and wrote, without flinching, "Blood is a destiny."[86] Bronson's racial categories alarmed even his most dedicated followers.[87] On one occasion, when Bronson was discoursing on the attributes of darker peoples, his friend Ednah Cheney objected that Emanuel Swedenborg, a philosopher whom Alcott deeply respected, had called blacks the most beloved of all races. Alcott dismissed the objection with the condescending words, "That is very nice of Mr. Swedenborg." In private conversation with Emerson, Alcott descended still lower, suggesting that male African Americans should be sterilized en masse.[88]

Studying America in the nineteenth century, one becomes sadly accustomed to encountering the unpleasant racial thinking of persons whom one naively wishes had had the power to see beyond the narrow conventions of their times. In Bronson Alcott's case, discovering this lack of understanding is especially disappointing since it seems so obviously to contradict the higher principles for which he daily sacrificed. Alcott despised slavery and, as has been seen, refused to use any product that slave labor had produced. He willingly bade farewell to the only career he ever loved because he would not dismiss a black child from his school. He risked prison by sheltering fugitive slaves in his house. As will be shown later, he exposed himself to being shot in a failed effort to win the release of another fugitive. Unlike some abolitionists who advocated the end of slavery but nothing more, Alcott advocated full political rights for freed slaves. At a time when the idea was far from popular, he supported the induction of black troops into the Union army. He was a sincere admirer of both John Brown and Frederick Douglass. How, then, could Alcott espouse a theory of race that consigned human beings, even his own family and friends, to categories of higher and lower? How could a man dedicated to the ideals of political equality and abolition find it so difficult to abolish his own enslavement to hierarchical thinking? Of all the contradictions that inhabited the mind of Bronson Alcott, not one is more baffling or disappointing than this, and it requires some explanation, however unsatisfying that explanation may be.

In his thinking about the organization of the universe, Alcott had conditioned himself to think about creation in vertical terms. He also thought that no aspect of the cosmos was morally neutral. He therefore found it almost impossible to observe differences of any kind without making moral judgments about them. He freely accepted the idea that some kinds of fruits and vegetables evinced greater moral excellence than others. Reasoning from flawed premises, he found moral and social significance in racial difference as well. Yet his theories did not blind him to cruelty of inequality and the horrors of slavery, nor did they hinder him from acting morally and honorably toward black people themselves.

A parallel issue is the influence that Bronson's racial theorizing had on his own home. It is easy to assume that Bronson used his theories of light and dark heredity to explain the rifts within his own family. Given his suppositions about angelic whiteness and devilish darkness, he could well have reasoned that, as a light-skinned Alcott, he would naturally be antagonized by his wife and second daughter, the hot-blooded products of the more Mediterranean May lineage. However, the facts will not entirely support a pigment-based explanation of Bronson's opinions of his family. A principal weakness in such an analysis is that it fails to account for Bronson's high regard for his eldest daughter, Anna. Daguerreotypes of Anna and Louisa reveal no great difference in their complexions or coloring. Lydia Hosmer Wood, a close friend of the Alcott family, wrote that Anna, not Louisa, was the darkest of the four Alcott children.[89] An examination of locks of Anna's and Louisa's hair now preserved at the Fruitlands Museum also confirms that Louisa's hair was a few shades lighter than Anna's. Just as Louisa's waywardness seemed to defy Bronson's theories on rearing the ideal child, so too did his amiable eldest daughter contradict Bronson's equation between darkness and deviltry.

A father is the pivot on which the developing self-awareness of growing girls frequently turns.[90] In striving to come to terms with the man who, above all others, influences one's evolving understanding of authority, maleness, and patriarchal power, children arrive at one of the most complex and emotionally perilous identifications that life requires one to make. For Louisa, neither understanding her father nor defining herself in relation to him came easily. She sincerely desired to be "good," as her father defined that word, and thus to win his approval. Yet to Bronson, goodness meant the repression of strong emotion and the extinction of selfish desire. If desires and emotions are essential parts of one's character, then Louisa could satisfy her father only by being something other than herself.

To Louisa's great disadvantage, Bronson also knew only one way of looking at genius, and his narrowness long prevented him from setting her talents at their proper value. For him, genius was the ability to see the world as a seamless, transcendent unity. Regarding the process of his own thought, he wrote, "I cannot sit and seize the warm life-thought as it runs through my vitals; but am one with my thought. . . . My genius is epic." He wished always to "hold inviolate the unity of my intuitions" and never "to dissolve the divine synthesis of my being."91 A person who fits Bronson Alcott's definition of genius might make a philosopher, but she will never make a novelist. To write compelling fiction, it is necessary to acknowledge desire and the obstacles to its fulfillment. From the earliest age, Louisa expressed passion. It was her form of genius to feel, to observe, and to understand emotional struggle. Her father believed that passion was not a pathway to knowledge but the most dangerous impediment to it. Bronson did not realize that the storm and stress he beheld in his daughter's spirit were part of her own intense search for truth.

With her volatile temper and fierce independence, Louisa was naturally disposed to rebel, but within the Alcott family the moral grounds for rebellion posed a problem. While there were abundant reasons for questioning Bronson's judgment, there were few who now questioned his dedication to moral purity. Emerson called him an archangel, even if he did add the word "tedious" to his description.92 Alcott himself tried to live his life in self-conscious imitation of Christ. To rebel against a household Christ, to take up arms against an archangel, is to define oneself de facto as the Devil. When Louisa's temper defied her efforts to soften it, when she felt frustration at the poverty that Bronson insisted was virtuous, or when he greeted her impulsiveness with cool disapproval or hapless incomprehension, she must have wondered whether she might not truly be a demon after all.

In a family of remarkably close relationships, in which high degrees of affection and loyalty were essential if the parents and children were to endure the threats of poverty and the judgments of a sneering and skeptical world, Louisa found one of the most important ties extremely difficult to establish and maintain. In myriad ways, she was a misfit: a fighter in a pacifist family; a coveter of wealth in a transcendental temple; a girl who yearned for all things boyish; a dark presence in the household of a man who praised and worshipped light. She knew that she had much to be proud of and that within her lay unsuspected gifts that, with luck and effort, she might one day share with a grateful world. For now, however, winning the understanding and support of the one man who mattered most was a daunting challenge.

A more formidable challenge for the family as a whole was economic. Abba tried to conceal the true extent of the family's poverty from her children, but at least where Louisa was concerned, the effort was in vain. Louisa wrote, "Money is never plentiful in a philosopher's house, and even the maternal pelican could not supply all our wants on the small income which was freely shared with every needy soul who asked for help."93 To ease the financial burden, Abba tried expedient measures like taking in a mentally retarded girl, Eliza Stearns, as a boarder. In the end, however, these efforts were in vain. The idyllic life of Hillside could not be sustained. In May 1848, in an attempt to trim back the debts, Abba accepted an offer to travel to Waterford, Maine, to take a job as the matron of a water-cure house. The original proposal had included Bronson; the house was to employ him as a preacher and teacher. Bronson, however, had declined the position, declaring with an exasperating calm that anticipated Melville's Bartleby, "I have [as] yet no clear call to any work beyond myself."94 Abba took Abby May along with her, and at first, she tackled the job of matron with enthusiasm. However, finding that the proprietors of the spa had not made adequate provisions for her daughter, she was soon forced to send Abby back home. Not long after, missing her family and feeling guilty of deserting the children in exchange for mere money, she resigned her post and returned to Concord. The job in Maine might have saved the house, but only at the price of undermining the family. Some other solution was needed.

On a gloomy November day, the Alcotts held a family council that was, in its way, every bit as devastating as the one at Fruitlands at which Bronson had proposed that he might leave the family. It appeared that the family could hope to make ends meet only if Abba and the girls found jobs, and the employment prospects in Concord were not promising. Therefore they decided to move back to Boston. Abba's friends could find her a good salary as a missionary for the poor. Anna, seventeen, and Louisa, nearly six-teen, were now old enough to try their hands at teaching. Anna, indeed, had already had some slight experience in this line, having taught a hand-ful of children during an extended visit to her cousin Lizzie Wells in Wal-pole, New Hampshire, the previous spring. As for Bronson, he felt that his three years of seclusion, introspection, and communion with nature had at last "restored him to hope and the service of mankind." Heaven, he felt, had won him health from sickness and hope from defeat, and he believed himself "a richer, a stronger, [and] a wiser man" for the lessons he had learned. In his Micawber-like way, he felt confident that he could establish a school or "a reading room, a journal, a press, a club."[95] Once in Boston, he intended to deliver conversations for a modest fee, distilling some dol-lars from his years of contemplation.

After the similarly wrenching meeting at Fruitlands, when she was only eleven, Louisa had cried and prayed. This time, she reacted differently. She took a brisk run over the hill and settled down for "a good think" in her favorite retreat, an old, abandoned cartwheel, lying half-hidden in the grass. Louisa had found it a good place to sit when struggling to work out her mathematics lessons, though she usually ended up scribbling poems and fairy tales instead of sums. The sky was a leaden gray, the trees bare, and the dry grass had surrendered to the frosty air. And yet, for all its gloom, the scene was not so different from the bare common, strewn with snow puddles, where her mentor Emerson experienced the moment of transcendence he had described in *Nature*. In such a place, one really could feel glad to the brink of fear. If the cold air touched her, it was only to stiffen her resolve:

> [T]he hopeful heart of fifteen beat warmly under the old red shawl, visions of success gave the gray clouds a silver lining, and I said defiantly, as I shook my fist at fate embodied in a crow cawing dismally on the fence near by,—
>
> "I *will* do something by-and-by. Don't care what, teach, sew, act, write, anything to help the family; and I'll be rich and famous and happy before I die, see if I won't!"[96]

As the old wheel creaked under Louisa's shifting weight, it seemed to her as though it had begun to turn, "stirred by the intense desire of an ambitious girl to work for those she loved and to find some reward when the duty was done."[97] Louisa strode back to Hillside cold but resolute. Almost forty years later, it seemed to her that this was the day when she ceased to be a child. She was still young, sentimental, and impulsive. Her nerves and feelings were not yet fully ready for the hard, patient slog that might one day yield success. Yet she was equipped with the loving support of a strong, united family and a will that could not easily be broken. She had also learned a lesson familiar to all persons of courage: that the only direction in which life moves is forward.

CHAPTER NINE

DESTITUTION

"Money is the root of all evil, and yet it is such
a useful root that we cannot get on without it
any more than we can without potatoes."

—LOUISA MAY ALCOTT,
Little Men, chapter 14

THE ALCOTTS DID NOT SELL THE HILLSIDE HOUSE. THEY could not find a buyer. Despite Bronson's substantial improvements to the house and grounds, the best offer came from a tenant who agreed to rent the property for one hundred fifty dollars a year. It was better than nothing. On November 17, 1848, the family moved back to Boston. Still not fully cognizant of their financial straits, the girls had dreamed of a fine home in the hub of New England. Instead, they found themselves in a basement apartment on Dedham Street. Even Bronson conceded that existence there was a "cramped and unvaried life."[1] Their new domain consisted of three rooms and a kitchen. There was a small backyard but not a tree in sight. The splendors of the city danced tantalizingly before Louisa's eyes, but she had no money with which to make any of them hers. Along with her sisters, she yearned for the country again. The bustle and dirt of Boston made it harder for Louisa to think. "Among my woods and hills I had fine free times alone," she remembered, "and though my thoughts were silly, I daresay, they helped to keep me happy and good."[2]

The move to Dedham Street ushered in the bleakest era in the Alcotts' lives. For the next several years, they would have no home of long duration. During the summer, when cholera and other diseases hung threateningly over the city, they were sometimes able to stay with wealthier relatives, who feared for the family's health. Otherwise, they were to inhabit a succession

*Anna Bronson Alcott, Bronson's eldest daughter, whom he
called a "peacemaker . . . beloved of all." During the lean
years in Boston, Anna's income as a teacher and
governess helped keep the family fed.*
(Courtesy of the Louisa May Alcott Memorial Association)

of dreary, cramped abodes in struggling, graceless neighborhoods. The
apartment on Dedham Street gave way to another on Groton Street, and
Groton Street was followed by even worse quarters on High Street, which
bordered on one of the most appalling slums in Boston.[3] Whatever their
address of the moment, they were to be, in Louisa's description, "Poor as
rats & apparently quite forgotten by every one but the Lord."[4]

Everyone in the family, except for Louisa, soon had a place to go. Having buried the hatchet with Elizabeth Palmer Peabody, Bronson leased an
additional room downtown, next door to the bookstore that his old colleague had established. In his rented space, Bronson offered daily conversations and lessons, bringing in a trickle of cash.[5] Peabody also provided

lessons to Lizzie and May, now thirteen and eight, respectively. Abba was offered a job as a missionary to the poor at a salary of thirty dollars a month. The position had been created for her through the agency of Hannah Robie, whose kindness during the Fruitlands episode was but one instance of her continuing interest in her niece Abba. Robie organized a cadre of philanthropic sponsors to guarantee Abba's salary, thus assuring that a wealth of good would be done both for the indigent of Boston and the nearly indigent Alcotts. Abba later opened an "intelligence office," the nineteenth-century equivalent of an employment agency, devoted principally to finding positions for the indigent. Economically speaking, there was little to separate her from her clients.

Anna, now old enough to work, took a situation as a governess. It fell to Louisa to keep the house in order. She felt "like a caged sea-gull as I washed dishes and cooked in the basement kitchen where my prospect was limited to succession of muddy boots."[6] Her work and surroundings supplied a metaphor for her inner life. She imagined that her mind was a room in confusion that she must put in order. No matter how she tried to sweep out the useless thoughts and foolish fancies, the mental cobwebs still got in. She judged herself to be a poor housekeeper of the soul, and she feared she would never get her room set right.[7]

For the first time in a few years, Louisa started keeping a journal. Bronson criticized her entries, observing that Anna's diary was principally about others, whereas Louisa wrote mostly about herself. It was an ironic critique, coming as it did from a man whose own journals were often indefatigably solipsistic.[8] While acknowledging that her father was right, Louisa defended her inward focus. Since she never *spoke* about herself, her journal was the one place where she could get a hold of the willful, moody girl she was forever trying to manage and see how she was progressing. Her journal was also a ready receptacle for the frustrations that heaped upon her when she considered "how poor we are, how much worry it is to live, and how many things I long to do and never can." With a flourish of drama but also with more than a hint of truth, she added, "Every day is a battle, and I'm so tired I don't want to live; only it's cowardly to die until you have done something."[9]

Her great solace came in the evenings, when her parents and sisters returned from their various labors with their vivid and varied tales of the city. Seen through the eyes of each, Boston presented a highly different aspect. Bronson, with the aid of Emerson, had succeeded in forming an intellectual society known as the Town and Country Club. The club graciously elected Alcott its corresponding secretary and librarian and, still more graciously, discussed paying the rent for his West Street rooms.[10] The club, whose membership was more or less handpicked by Alcott, included Thoreau, Samuel Gridley Howe, the abolitionist William Lloyd Garrison, the poet James Russell Lowell, and Thomas Wentworth Higginson, who was later both a key supporter of John Brown and a mentor of Emily Dickinson. The club, which hosted lectures by such luminaries as Emerson, Henry James Sr., and Theodore Parker, kept Bronson in steady contact with the best minds of liberal Massachusetts. The stories he brought home to Dedham Street spoke to Louisa of "the upper world, and the wise, good people who adorned it."[11] The sights and sounds that Abba related were of a darker, more somber tone. She had much to say about the poor who came to her for help each day. Sometimes she came home particularly disheveled, for there were days when her sympathy with the poor and helpless prompted her literally to give them the clothes off her back. Anna brought word from a middle realm, giving modest accounts of her success in the classroom, where her patience and gentle nature were proving to be valuable assets. To all this news, Lizzie and May added their joys and woes of the passing moment, and Louisa contributed her own tragicomic musings. One of the strongest adhesives holding the family together was narrative; the tales they shared of their daily lives formed a bridge of sympathy and shared effort. They were Louisa's only consolation amid the dirty pots and unmade beds.

Language offered another solace to Louisa during this period, for it was in the Dedham Street apartment and its successors that the girls' family theatricals enjoyed their greatest flowering. The sisters made every kind of prop imaginable, from a harp to a fairy's spangled wings, and they learned to recite pages of dialogue without error. Most often, the speeches came from Louisa's pen; she authored melodramas like "Norna, or the Witch's Curse," and "The Captive of Castile, or the Moorish Maiden's Vow." Later, Louisa's scripts gave way to scenes from Shakespeare, and she acted Hamlet with "a gloomy glare and a tragic stalk" that she thought superior to any professional performance she had ever seen.[12] It seemed for a time that acting might be the swiftest way out of poverty. Since the time of Fruitlands, Louisa had dreamed of becoming as famous as the soprano Jenny Lind, and now she thought her powers as a tragedian might make her another Sarah Siddon. Anna, too, had a full-blown case of stage fever, and the two would talk excitedly about the money they could make and the glittering lives they would lead. But Abba prudently cautioned the girls that they were too young for such adventures. "Wait," she told them, but "Wait" seemed to be the standing order regarding all ambitions and hopes for the future. "Waiting," Louisa wrote in her journal, "is so *hard*!"[13]

Abba was still her closest ally. However, looking back on it all later, Louisa acknowledged both parents when she wrote that she and her sisters "had the truest of guides and guards, and so learned the sweet uses of adversity, the value of honest work, . . . and the real significance of life."[14] The counsel and protection of both her parents mattered intensely during this period, though Abba and Bronson ministered to admittedly different needs. In this sense, Bronson served as the inspiration for Mr. March in *Little Women*:

> To outsiders, the five energetic women seemed to rule the house, and so they did in many things; but the quiet man sitting among his books was still the head of the family, the household conscience, anchor and comforter; for to him the busy, anxious women always turned in troublous times, finding him, in the truest sense of those sacred words, husband and father.[15]

Bronson Alcott's effectiveness as an anchor in matters other than ethical ones was more subject to question. Although fully capable of managing the affairs of the Town and Country Club, writing his journal, and giving conversations on a wide array of topics, he was in some ways still recovering from his post-Fruitlands breakdown. There was now a hidden emotional infirmity in the man that had not manifested itself in his younger days. Following the family's move to Boston, he again fell prey to strange, almost hallucinatory thoughts. In the summer of 1849, he worked feverishly on a manuscript that he called "Tablets," the most peculiar piece of writing he had yet attempted. Not to be confused with the rather successful book that Alcott was to publish in 1868, this "Tablets" was an attempt to synthesize an odd amalgam of readings that had captured his imagination. In addition to delving into the mystical philosophical work of Emanuel Swedenborg and Jakob Boehme and the writings of German naturalist Lorenz Oken, Alcott was also becoming fascinated with the theories of the renowned scientist Michael Faraday regarding the relation between magnetism and electricity. As he followed Faraday's work, it seemed to him that the Englishman was laying foundations not only for a new kind of scientific inquiry but also for a new understanding of spiritual life. Alcott began searching for a bridge between the worlds of physical matter and mental and emotional experience. As biographer Frederick Dahlstrand has put it, "His reading of Faraday led him to speculate that electricity, magnetism, and light were but three states of one substance; this substance was the mysterious nexus of spirit and matter, the immediate breath of life."[16] For a man of Alcott's utter lack of formal scientific training, some of the conclusions he drew from Faraday were remarkably astute. Whereas Faraday himself had worked out the essential identity between magnetism and electricity, many years were to elapse before science was to establish that light, too, consists of the same substance.

Not knowing what to do with his newfound insight, however, Alcott at once veered off in an occult direction. Influenced by another current interest, astrology, he began to construct a series of arcane tables—the "Tablets" from which his manuscript took its title—that purported to explain the various aspects of the human psyche. He began to illustrate his journals with charts and diagrams, all striving to work out a theory that would unify the brain, the body, magnetism, and the stars. He was, he wrote, in a "blaze of being."[17] The next year, he remembered the giddy, obsessed zeal with which he pursued his idea:

> [N]ow the mysterious meters and scales and planes are opened to us, and we view wonderingly the Crimson Tablets and report of them all day long. It is no longer Many but One with us; and all things and we live recluse, yet smoothly and sagely, as having made acquaintance suddenly as of some might and majestic friend, omniscient and benign, who . . . draws me toward him as by some secret force, some cerebral magnetism. . . . I am drawn on by enchantment.[18]

If Alcott's inspirations had come to a mystic of stronger literary gifts, for instance a William Blake or a Samuel Taylor Coleridge, they might have led to an outpouring of visionary poetry. In the less capable hands of Bronson Alcott, they dissolved into a blur of disconnected thoughts and overwrought imagery. As Alcott wrote "Tablets," his handwriting degenerated into a furious, almost illegible scrawl. He was writing at white heat, but for an incomprehensible purpose.

As he had done five years earlier during his stay in Still River, Bronson began to think of himself as a conduit for otherworldly energies. In "Tablets," he declared himself "a conductor of heavenly forces, and a wondrous instrument, a cerebral magnet, and electric battery, telegraph, glass, crucible, molten fluids traversing his frame—rising and bathing in his vessels." If the excerpts offered here create the impression of an author set somewhat off his hinges, there is good reason. At the same time that he was working on "Tablets," Bronson was experiencing mental states and visions that suggest a frighteningly disturbed mind. He found it impossible to "sleep without seeing goblins, or stumbling over the places of the dead." One day he turned up unannounced at the home of fellow transcendentalist Orestes Brownson and informed his astonished host that he, Bronson, was not merely God but, indeed, "greater than God." He experienced a vision of the universe as an immense spinal cord, symbolic of the means by which God's creatures progressed from lower to higher forms.[19] Immersed in his fantastic manuscript, he rose in search of starry wisdom and electric truths, magnetically drawn by a genius that looked more and more like madness.

As the calendar moved on toward autumn, his condition worsened. He was denying himself food and rest, acting more and more as he had done in Still River. He developed a persistent cough. There came, at last, a day when some internal threshold was breached. No one knows just what happened, but he wrote a poem about it later, encapsulating his fight to recover his sanity. Aptly, he called it "The Return," and it begins like this:

> As from himself he fled,
> Outcast, insane,
> Tormenting demons drove him from the gate.
> Away he sped,
> Casting his woes behind;
> His joys to find—
> His better mind.

Bronson centered the lines on the page, as if to emphasize the restored sense of balance that he came to feel after his inner storm subsided. But the poem begins with a moment of extreme imbalance, a psychic terror that seemed so real that the author had physically to run from it.[20] In Bronson Alcott's time, there was no neurologist or psychologist to explain his sometimes alarming states of mind. Nevertheless, it is reasonable to ask some indulgence from those who condemn Alcott's failure to earn a living for his family. If his episodes of hallucination and delusion in Still River in 1844 and in Boston in 1849 show us anything, it is that Alcott was suffering from a recurring disability, evidently exacerbated during periods of unusual stress. It seems that there really was a limit to the amount of mental strain that he could safely withstand. At times, he may truly have been incapable of regular employment. Alcott can be seen as suffering from a condition that he could not control, as a man who was, in fact, doing the best he could to meet the demands of life, but finding that he could only do pathetically little.

Alcott was not deaf to the gossip that denounced him for permitting Abba "to delve for the family" and accused him of "indifference to its welfare." He felt that the whisperings were unfair, but he did not know how to defend himself. "So it must seem to outsiders," he wrote, "nor will any words of mine put fairer face on things. No explanation can take the place of deeds in their eyes, and I must stand for the time as a thriftless if not a heartless and incapable fellow. So let it seem; but let it not be so."[21] The only justification he could give was that he "had one set of gifts and not the other, and fell so obliquely on my time that none caught my point of view to comprehend the person I was." He had left the body out of his equation for success. He now saw that this had been as disastrous an error as if he had omitted the soul.[22]

Bronson's ordeal left him an invalid, and he referred to his hoped-for recovery as a "restoration from the dead."[23] He sought sanctuary in Concord. In September, he traveled there twice, staying first with Emerson and later with the Hosmers, only a short walk from the cottage where he had lived in 1840. He took morning walks with Thoreau, pausing to loaf and discourse on the grassy hillsides. He swam with Emerson in Walden Pond and talked with him about the new book, *Representative Men*, that Emerson was making ready for press. Bronson found a precious tonic in the cool air, the peaceful mornings, and the invigorating sun. Being in Concord, it seemed to him, was like the touch of the earth to the mythical giant Antaeus, who lost his strength whenever his feet left the ground. Believing that Abba would be similarly rejuvenated by a visit to the town, he invited her to join him for at least "one clear day" before winter. He wanted her not only to visit Concord but also travel with him to Fruitlands, where, he reminded her, "*A man once lived.*"[24]

Between visits to Concord, he returned briefly to Boston. As during the aftermath of Fruitlands, family played a central role in his recovery. His poem "The Return," which begins with such torment, ends with a peaceful homecoming:

> Recovered,
> Himself again
> Over his threshold led
> Peace fills his breast,
> He finds his rest;
> Expecting angels his arrival wait.

After that strange, distracted summer of 1849, Bronson never again experienced a mental breakdown. Now, as he returned to Boston to face the world with renewed health, the question was no longer whether his family could save him, but whether he could return the favor.

During 1849, Bronson was not the only Alcott who toiled excitedly over a lengthy manuscript. Motivated in more or less equal parts by an urge to create, a desire for escapism, and the hope of earning some money for her family, sixteen-year-old Louisa set herself to work on her first novel, *The Inheritance*, which was never published in her lifetime. Louisa wanted nothing more fervently than to escape poverty. Not surprisingly, then, *The Inheritance* is a Cinderella story. The heroine, the impeccably virtuous Edith Adelon, is the penniless hired companion of a fabulously wealthy English family, the Hamiltons. Whereas the two children of the widowed Lady Hamilton behave generously toward Edith, her beauty and grace earn her the enmity of a Hamilton niece, Lady Ida Clare, who spends most of the novel plotting Edith's downfall. In the course of her ministrations to the poor, Edith encounters a stranger who, unbeknownst to all, harbors the secret of the heroine's birth. He sends her a packet containing a letter disclosing that her father was the long-lost heir to the Hamilton fortune. The packet also contains the father's will, naming Edith as the heiress to the very lands where she has been a servant. In a spectacular spirit of self-sacrifice, however, Edith contrives to destroy all evidence of her windfall, and her father's will is saved from burning only by the chance intervention of a servant boy. When, in the book's penultimate chapter, the Hamiltons confront Edith with the rescued document, she tears it to pieces, stating that she prefers her humble place among the loving Hamiltons to a place of rank and wealth. Providentially, a wealthy young lord is standing by to offer his own hand and fortune to her, but we are meant to understand that Edith did not expect his proposal when she gave up her fortune.

Observed in the light of the author's circumstances, *The Inheritance* is a fascinating piece of self-revelation. On the one hand, the story fiercely defends the virtue of loyalty and asserts a stout preference for family over fortune, very much in keeping with the Alcotts' system of values. By the same token, however, Edith rebels against her father by scorning his "will" both literally and figuratively, rejecting his intentions in favor of her own higher moral sense. *The Inheritance* ingeniously argues a point that the stormy, self-willed Louisa would gladly have explained to her father: that one can both be loyal to family and virtue *and* defy one's parents' wishes at the same time. Like much of her later fiction, *The Inheritance* is a covert plea for understanding the difficult process by which both characters and author must work out the ambiguities of personality and right behavior.

As Louisa made the first tentative steps toward her eventual career, her father, at fifty, faced the daunting task of resurrecting his own professional life. His name remained sufficiently notorious in Boston that he could not teach there. Therefore, he redoubled his efforts in the art he had first begun to craft in the 1830s. Beginning in December 1848, while still contending with his mental demons, he sought to earn a living by perfecting the art of public conversation.

Almost by design, an Alcott conversation was evanescent. Like an improvised musical solo, it was produced in order to fill the air with a momentary pulsation, imparting a flash of insight before moving on to the next equally ephemeral spark. In 1868, in an article titled "An Evening with Alcott," an anonymous news correspondent gave a description of the effect that Alcott created:

Do you remember what he says? Most likely not, or only certain isolated
but splendid phrases which shock you as especially out of the common
orbit of thought—or, in the strict, not conventional sense of the word,
eccentric. But you do not regret that no tangible opinions remain in
your memory, like a mellow autumn day, or, like a soft, tender melody,
you recall his conversation only as an ethereal and delicate influence.[25]

Alcott's conversations were intimate and personal. No one who ever saw
him converse had the impression of seeing a great orator. "Standing and
facing an audience," wrote the newspaperman just quoted, "he is as much
out of his place as an editor is out of his element in the pulpit." Seated in
an elegant parlor, however, among a circle of educated listeners, Alcott
transformed himself. He became an unrivaled philosophical and aesthetic
talker, "the sole and unique Master of the Arm-chair."

When Bronson spoke to an uninitiated audience, he explained to them
that, in his definition, conversation was an endeavor to find points on
which a company could sympathize in feeling. He thought it inappropri-
ate for anyone to present his own individual views for the sake of argument or debate. Such assertiveness had its place among larger companies,
but the leader of a conversation had a gentler task: to provide common
ground. He aspired to "touching those fine chords in every heart which
will inspire them to respond to one's own experience." When he did not
do so, he failed. "Conversation," Alcott insisted, "is not a comparison of
opinions. . . . Conversation should be magnetism."[26]

For Alcott, conversation also meant improvisation. The advance publicity for a conversation typically announced nothing more than the general theme of the discussion, such as a literary figure like Aeschylus or
Dante, or perhaps a virtue like civility. Alcott especially liked to explore an
idea through a famous person who exemplified it: he conversed on Order
as represented by Daniel Webster and Humanity as personified by
William Ellery Channing. Although he prepared carefully, he seems never
to have walked into the room with any prepared text. He had, it seems,
the unusual gift of being able to offer a steady flow of impromptu observations on complicated matters without losing either his train of thought
or a kind of dramatic tension. Of course, to preserve the conversational
quality of the evening, Alcott also needed to respond to queries and observations from the audience; his conversational art form was not only per-

formative but participatory, demanding flexibility as well as focus. In its aesthetic feel, an Alcott conversation might well be likened to the work of a jazz soloist.

Evidently, it was in their participatory aspect that Alcott's conversations were most likely to fall short of the mark. Few members of Alcott's typical audience were up to the twin challenges of adding thoughtfully to the conversation while also keeping their partisan opinions and personal egotisms in check. As early as 1837, following a conversation on self-sacrifice, Alcott lamented in his journal that he had almost given up the idea "of pursuing a subject in its direct and obvious bearing, with persons whose minds seem quite unfitted to the effort."[27] Thirty years later, he had apparently not solved the problem. The author of "An Evening with Alcott" observed that the conversation he witnessed was not a conversation in any ordinary sense, for no one had conversed. Rather, "the old man eloquent has all the evening all to himself—for the scattered spray of talk at the close of his discourse bears about the same relation to [conversation] that coppers do to the regular currency."[28]

Alcott regarded his conversations as a distinct genre of communication, which he hoped eventually to raise to an art form. He wrote in his journal in 1856, "Alcott is making the Conversation," just as he believed that Garrison had "made" the Convention, Greeley the Newspaper, and Emerson the Lecture. All these media, Alcott thought, were "purely American organs and institutions, which no country nor people besides ours can claim as we can." The reporter who wrote "An Evening with Alcott" considered the conversation "a feature of social life peculiar to Massachusetts," and was of the opinion that its flavor was "as essentially Yankee as . . . the Baldwin apple or the Concord grape." Curiously, however, as the writer was obliged to admit, the conversation lacked the traits that one instinctively associated with New England thinking. Alcott's conversations in particular were neither practical nor shrewd nor sharply definite in their opinions. They did not offer "common sense," but only "uncommon sense."[29]

As Alcott was well aware, however, his conversations were not a potent recipe for making money. In the years from 1848 to 1853, they earned a total of $750—a living wage for about six months.[30] In marked contrast to her father, Louisa became acutely conscious of the details of her personal finances. Beginning in 1850, at the age of eighteen, she kept a record in which she noted down to the dollar the amount of money that she took in every year. She was now keenly aware of the family's financial straits and eager to do what she could to alleviate them.

Alcott's life nearly came to an end in the summer of 1850, when he and the rest of the family contracted smallpox from, as Louisa put it, "some poor immigrants whom Mother took into our garden and fed one day."[31] The girls caught the disease only slightly. Abba's case was somewhat worse. Bronson became dangerously ill and, for several weeks, was too weakened to leave his bed. Thankfully, he recovered without suffering the facial scarring that often came with the disease. It was yet another instance, though hardly the last, of the price the family paid for its kindness to others.

Meanwhile, the women of the family struggled to keep bodies and souls together. Louisa now taught a school on Suffolk Street, which her father wistfully visited, wishing that he could have a school again. Louisa would gladly have given him hers. The vocation that he adored left her utterly cold. After teaching for two years, she reached the unabashed conclusion that she hated it. Although necessity drove her back to the classroom a number of times, she never changed her mind. At the same time, however, the professions that she found most appealing—acting and writing— seemed beyond her reach. But idleness was unacceptable, and not only as a matter of family economy. It was essential to Louisa's nature always to be doing or planning something. The question for her was not whether to be active, but how.

Louisa believed that the honest work one did willingly for pay was always noble at its core. This conviction, coupled with a feeling that she would explode if she did not soon find some hard but rewarding task, led her during the winter of early 1851 to accept a job in Dedham, ostensibly as a lady's companion. The position was offered by a ministerial-looking man who announced himself at Abba's intelligence office as the Hon. James Richardson. With ornate turns of phrase, he stated that his sister, a nervous invalid, required someone to give her company and to see to the minor household tasks that had become too burdensome for her. The work, he assured Abba, would be quite nominal, and the person selected for the position would be "one of the family in all respects."[32]

Perhaps it was the promise of being a family member that captured Louisa's fancy. When her mother asked whether she could suggest anyone for the job, Louisa responded "Only myself." She miscalculated terribly. In Louisa's mildly fictionalized telling of the story, Richardson's home sounds like an unholy union between Miss Havisham's estate and the House of Usher. The woman she was expected to befriend was a mousy, mentally feeble creature, who at the age of forty possessed the wits of a child. Mr. Richardson proved worst of all. He had conceived a paranoid delusion with regard to another servant, his elderly housekeeper, who he thought had attempted to poison him and whom he suspected of brewing further "nefarious plans."[33]

Yet Richardson's irrational loathing may have been preferable to the attraction he conceived toward Louisa. Before she arrived, he wrote long letters to the eighteen-year-old, expressing the hope that she would allow him "to minister to [her] young and cheerful nature." After she arrived, she soon discovered that her duties had more to do with Richardson himself than with his sister. Although her memoir of the episode contains no clear suggestion of sexual impropriety, her employer began to expect a kind of intimacy that was almost equally unsettling. One morning, he surreptitiously observed her as she prepared breakfast. When she discovered his presence, he begged her not to run away and remarked on the pleasure of seeing "something tasteful, young, and womanly" near him. At the end of each day, he compelled her to come to his study and listen as he read from crackbrained, abstruse texts. She became "a passive bucket, into which he was to pour all manner of philosophic, metaphysical, and sentimental rubbish." She was "to serve his needs, soothe his sufferings, and sympathize with all his sorrows—be a galley slave, in fact."[34] Before much time passed, she told Richardson flatly that she would rather scrub floors than listen to his reading.

Louisa's candor was promptly punished; she was burdened with the hardest tasks of the household and, as a crowning insult, was expected to black her master's boots. Seven weeks after her work in Dedham began, Louisa announced that she would be Richardson's drudge no more. Making her way back to Boston on a bleak March afternoon, she opened the pocketbook he had given her containing her wages and found that he had paid her only four dollars. In the story she based on her time with the Richardsons, Louisa writes that her family indignantly sent the pittance back. In her account book, however, she counted the four dollars as part of the year's income, suggesting that necessity may actually have triumphed over pride. Throughout her writing career, Louisa routinely transformed family tragedy into the stuff of comedy. Even twenty-three years after the fact, however, she was unable to perform such alchemy regarding her sojourn in Dedham; the tone of the piece she based on the episode is unmistakably bitter.

Fortunately, not all the influences she felt during this period were so degrading. She grew attracted to the preaching of the extraordinary minister Theodore Parker, who had been a visitor to Fruitlands and a sometime attendee at Alcott's conversations. His unorthodox opinions—he had been known to comment that Christianity would be better off without the Gospels—alienated many Bostonians, so much so that he was forced to preach at Boston's Music Hall instead of a regular church.[35] If Emerson represented the poetic aspect of transcendentalism and Alcott its educational side, then Theodore Parker was its political warrior. Parker's steel blue eyes would look intensely through his gold-rimmed spectacles as he urged his listeners to fight for social change and take up arms for abolition and equality. Parker's advocacy of women's rights resonated strongly with Louisa, and he soon joined Emerson and Thoreau among the leading transcendentalists to whom she felt a filial, almost romantic attachment. She was looking, it seems, for figures to fill the place in her life that her own father did not perfectly occupy, and yet, interestingly, she gravitated toward men whose opinions and characters were not vastly different from Bronson's. Instead of looking for an alternative to her father, she apparently craved a better version of him.

Soon after her return to Boston, Louisa's need to be up and doing was briefly enflamed, not by family concerns, but by a public controversy. On April 3, 1851, the escaped slave Thomas Sims was taken prisoner in Boston, giving the Supreme Judicial Court of Massachusetts the chance to decide the constitutionality of the new federal Fugitive Slave Law. Two months earlier, to the embarrassment of the local authorities, a crowd of free blacks had burst into the courtroom and forcibly liberated another fugitive, known as Shadrach, as his case was being argued. To avoid another incident of that kind, the courthouse where Sims was imprisoned was promptly surrounded by chains and an armed guard. When Chief Justice Lemuel Shaw was obliged to stoop beneath the chains in order to enter the courthouse, the symbolism of justice bowing down to power and oppression was too blatant to be ignored. Bronson, normally slow to anger, reacted with shame and indignation. He observed, "The question 'What has the North to do with slavery?' is visibly answered. . . . Such disgrace to the country, to the State, . . . to humanity . . . cannot be long borne with, nor silently." He promptly accepted a position on a vigilance committee, organized to protect other blacks from being arrested and, if possible, to rescue Sims. A few scenes like the spectacle in the courthouse square, he thought, would settle the nation's destiny.[36]

Louisa was as active on the slave's behalf as a young woman could be. Her sympathies must have been moved all the more by the knowledge that Sims was only seventeen, a year younger than herself. With her father, she attended a large gathering at the Tremont Temple, where Horace Mann, Wendell Phillips, and a host of others decried the hated law and pled eloquently for liberty. As the great reformers of New England heaped abuse on Daniel Webster, whose speech to the Senate the previous year had all but assured the law's passage, Louisa laid fanciful plans to liberate Sims from bondage. As a righteous sense of injustice mounted within her, she felt as if she were "ready to do anything,—fight or work, hoot or cry" to save the helpless young man she had never met.[37] Similarly, all of Bronson's waking moments were absorbed by the Sims crisis. When not attending meetings of his committee, he followed the forward press of events in person, first attending the court session where Sims's lawyer argued against the constitutionality of the law, then hearing Parker denounce the sins of the republic before a packed house at the Music Hall, and finally standing amid an anxious throng outside the courthouse, awaiting the judgment that would determine Sims's fate.

The news, when it came, could not have been worse. Judge Shaw upheld the law, and Sims was returned to Savannah, Georgia, where he received a public whipping that nearly killed him.[38] The trial of Sims, including the attendant security measures, had cost the city of Boston three thousand dollars. Bronson thought it would be a handsome piece of honor and justice if he and his antislavery compatriots would refuse to pay that amount in taxes and willingly go to prison for their noncompliance. His disillusion knew no bounds. Until April 1851, he had supposed that God had blessed him with a host of "beautiful properties": a city, a civilization, Christianity, and a country. He now doubted whether any of these birthrights was truly his.[39]

Bronson had long endured the knowledge that his country generally did not share his vision of reform. Yet the Sims affair had given him a renewed sense of the nation's perfidy. The country not only lacked interest in improving itself; it seemed determined to make itself worse. "The devil's claims are fairly admitted," he grumbled, "and his right to be here and take part in mundane affairs is unquestionable."[40] Though glad to play his part when the need arose, the ferment over Sims had reminded him of "the ultra-private person that I am, and how little in keeping with my habits is all that passes about me."[41] He could find no place that felt like his own.

Although Abba was more directly concerned with more localized injustice than with the national calamity of slavery, she too was out of patience with the world. She was working to exhaustion at her intelligence office, and her lonely struggles to aid the downtrodden were making her more combative. The same month that Thomas Sims went back to Georgia, Abba wrote to her brother Sam, "My life is one of daily protest against the oppressions and abuses of Society." The wage slavery that awaited the poor immigrants who flocked to Boston struck her as a "whole system of servitude" whose consequences were hardly better than southern slavery.[42] The men and women she had met whose relentless toil could not earn a living wage had filled her with pity and rage:

> Incompetent wages for labor performed, is the cruel tyranny of capitalist power over the laborers' necessities. The capitalist speculates on their bones and sinews. Will not this cause Poverty—Crime—Despair? . . . Is it not inhuman to tax a man's strength to the uttermost[?][43]

Louisa proudly realized that her mother "always did what came to her in the way of duty and charity, and let pride, taste, and comfort suffer for love's sake."[44] In her crusade, Abba collected sympathetic cases like stray kittens. Since she was running her service from the family's apartment, the line between work and home inevitably blurred, and as Louisa recollected, the family's meager rooms in High Street became "a shelter for lost girls, abused wives, friendless children, and weak or wicked men." She continued, "Father and Mother had no money to give, but gave them time, sympathy, help; and if blessings would make them rich, they would be millionaires. This is practical Christianity."[45]

In April 1852 a terrible reminder came of the Alcott family's emotional instability. On the twenty-fourth, Bronson's thirty-two-year-old brother Junius took his mother's hand and told her he was going to Boston. Instead, he went with his brother Ambrose to Couch and Alcotts, a nearby bolt and lathe factory that he and Ambrose had been managing.[46] Then, evidently before Ambrose could react, Junius did something unthinkable. In her journal, in plain, semiliterate phrasings, Bronson's mother described what happened next. Junius "went Streat into the wheel and was gon the nuse came that he was dead . . . but I bore it with reconcelation."[47] In his journal Bronson eulogized his favorite brother as a man of "tenderest sensibilities and . . . mystic mind."[48] He never wrote of him again. Louisa's surviving writings contain no mention at all of the death of the uncle for whom her father had felt such concern and had so often attempted to take under his own roof. One can hardly doubt, however, that the death cast a long shadow over the Alcotts.

Louisa's reactions can only be guessed. Her Uncle Junius, like her father, had experienced episodes of mystical awareness, coupled with behavior sufficiently erratic to raise worries among his extended family. The year of Junius's death, Louisa listed her favorite books in her journal. Among them was one that she prized especially highly, Charlotte Brontë's *Jane Eyre*. Both in her reading and in her lived experience, then, she was led to consider the plight of families cursed by hereditary insanity. Though no clear evidence exists to prove the point, it would be extraordinary if Louisa never reflected on the fate of her uncle, the trials of her father, and the latent propensities that might have been passed into her own blood. Her most significant writings for adults, the works into which she was to pour the greatest portion of her true self, were to return frequently to the specters of depression, inherited madness, and suicide.

Fortunately, not all the news that spring was so terrible. Shortly before Junius's death, there had come a much-needed modicum of financial relief. Nathaniel Hawthorne, having just completed a period of breathtaking productivity that had seen him produce *The Scarlet Letter*, *The House of the Seven Gables*, and *The Blithedale Romance* in only three years, had decided to return to Concord after a seven-year absence. His thoughts turned to the old Alcott home at Hillside, which the family still had not succeeded in selling. Despite Bronson's sporadic efforts to maintain it, the house had fallen into some disrepair, and withered vines now trailed where Bronson had once cultivated orderly and verdant bowers. However, Hawthorne knew a good acquisition when he saw one. He made an offer of fifteen hundred dollars.

Had he offered twice as much, Hawthorne would still have gotten a reasonable bargain. Nonetheless, fifteen hundred dollars was approximately what Bronson could expect to earn in ten years of conversing, so he accepted the novelist's terms: a $750 down payment, with the balance to be paid in a year's time. The monies were used to create a five-hundred-dollar trust for Bronson and a one-thousand-dollar trust for Abba. A newspaper called the *Semi-Weekly Eagle* caught wind of Hawthorne's purchase of the home. However, Alcott had lately been so removed from the public eye that the reporter thought he was probably dead. The *Eagle* was only able to speculate as follows: "If he is in heaven, he is certainly cutting up some shine or other there; and if in the antipodes of heaven, it is equally certain that he is giving a distinguished personage, supposed to have much to do with the affairs of the world, a vast deal of trouble."49

On the strength of this unexpected income, the Alcotts were at last able to secure better lodgings. They rented a four-story brick house at 20 Pinckney Street in Beacon Hill, then as now a stylish sector of the city. Despite the outward move upward, however, severing his tie with Concord exacted a cost from Bronson. Both psychologically and practically, the sale of Hillside divided him further from the place he called "classic land," the home of "the Americans *par excellence*." While living in Boston in 1850, he had written of Concord, " 'Tis at heart my own home. I must draw me closer to its bosom and my friends one day, for the cities cannot detain me long."50 Now it seemed as if his detention would last indefinitely.

Ensconced in a more congenial dwelling, Bronson experienced a renewed surge of ambition. During the winter of 1852–53, he mounted one of his busiest seasons of conversations, some of them sponsored by a group of Harvard Divinity School students, who asked him to lead a series of discussions on "Modern Life." The conversations were also attended by a tall undergraduate named Franklin Benjamin Sanborn, who was sufficiently taken with Alcott's performance that he sought and obtained an invitation to dine with the Alcott family. Sanborn quickly became one of Alcott's closest associates. He served at times as Alcott's unofficial secretary, conversing with him, recording his words, and helping him to compose and edit his writings.

In the fall of 1853, heeding a suggestion from Emerson, Alcott chose for the first time to take his conversations beyond the Northeast. He planned a tour that took him west through Syracuse, Rochester, Buffalo, Cincinnati, and Cleveland—what was then still considered the "West." Travel was a tonic for Bronson. The letters he wrote home from these western journeys, which became a habit with him in ensuing years, were the missives of a man who found himself "well, happy, and flourishing."[51] His audiences greeted him as an emissary of a distant culture, their personal link to the world of Emerson, Garrison, and Parker. Among dinner parties, teas, and of course conversations, his calendar was almost always full. Pleased to receive the attentions of "very select, sensible people," he suddenly felt important and admired, more so, it seems, than at any time since his trip to England.[52] "Nothing," he wrote to Abba, "can exceed the kindness and respect shown alike to the person and doctrines of your friend, here in this hospitable West."[53] The renewed sense of himself that he gained on this journey marked the beginning of his real recovery from his years of privation and ineffectuality. His confidence was in some measure rekindled. He returned to Boston a stronger man.

This initial tour of the West gave rise to one of the most endearing stories in Alcott family lore. Louisa told her journal that her father came home in February, a "half-frozen wanderer . . . hungry, tired, cold, and disappointed, but smiling gravely and as serene as ever." Abba and the girls fed and warmed him, not quite daring to ask whether he had earned any money. Alcott regaled the family with pleasant tales of his travels but skirted the subject of money until Abby May at last demanded, "Well, did people pay you?" The story goes that Alcott then took a single dollar bill from his pocketbook and said with a queer smile, "Only that! My overcoat was stolen, and I had to buy a shawl. Many promises were not kept, and travelling is costly, but I have opened the way, and another year shall do better." As the sisters fought back their tears, Abba kissed her husband, saying, "I call that doing *very well*. Since you are safely home, dear, we don't ask anything more." Louisa writes that she and Anna took the scene as "a little lesson in real love" that neither ever forgot.54 The story is often cited, not only as an instance of Abba's invincible patience and love, but also of Bronson's utter haplessness as a provider.

But the story, or much of it in any event, is only a story. Some of the details contradict the historic record. Bronson returned home in January, not February, and Anna was not waiting to greet him; rather, it appears that she met him in Syracuse, where she was teaching and living with Abba's brother Samuel, and she joined him for the last leg of his trip home. By far the most important discrepancy, however, has to do with the financial success of Bronson's tour. Far from having only a dollar to show for his three months' absence, Bronson had not only covered the expenses of the journey, but his letters reflect that he had sent home at least $180 from the road.55 In a letter that he sent Abba on his way home, he speculated that his earnings, along with sums from other sources, might be enough to "pay all debts." While he had wished to do still better, he found that his travels had not been "without hopeful significance."56 True, he was not paying all the bills, but he was paying more than Louisa indicated.

In May 1854, an African American named Anthony Burns absorbed the attention of the city. On May 24 Burns, a former slave, was taken captive on suspicion of being a fugitive from his former owner and was confined in the courthouse. It seemed a foregone conclusion that Edward Loring, the United States commissioner assigned to the case, would find in favor of Burns's alleged owner. If Burns were freed, it would have to be by extralegal means. To date, Thomas Sims had been the only fugitive slave returned from Boston under the 1850 law. Now, three years later, the city's antislavery Vigilance Committee, to which Bronson still belonged, was determined that Burns would not share Sims's fate. The day after Burns was taken, before leaving town to give a conversation in Worcester, Bronson attended a hastily convened meeting of the committee. When he boarded the westbound train, Bronson carried with him a letter from Samuel May to their mutual friend Thomas Wentworth Higginson, urging him to come to Boston and to notify as many other potential supporters as he could. That night, Alcott and Higginson stayed up long into the night to discuss Burns's rescue. Early the next morning, the twenty-sixth, they were on the train back to Boston, resolved to do what they could to restore Burns to freedom.

Their best opportunity came that evening. Higginson and another Burns ally, Martin Stowell, hastily concocted a plan to storm the court-house where Burns was being held and carry him to freedom. A mass rally was scheduled for that evening at Faneuil Hall, where Theodore Parker and the famous abolitionist Wendell Phillips were to deliver speeches. Higginson and Stowell arranged for a man to cry out from the gallery, announcing that a mob of blacks was already attacking the courthouse. In fact, there was no such mob; the plan was to incite the crowd at Faneuil Hall to rush en masse to the courthouse, where *they* might be exhorted to charge the building and rescue Burns.

There was no time, however, to properly orchestrate the plot. When approximately five hundred men, confused and leaderless, made their way from the meeting to the courthouse, there was no way to organize them into an effective force. Some fell on the building with uncontrolled fury, attacking with whatever makeshift weapons lay handy. Inside the court-house, Chief Justice Shaw was instructing a jury in a murder trial when suddenly the courtroom windows were shattered by a hail of bricks and cobblestones. Other members of the mob produced pistols and fired wildly into the building, fortunately hitting no one. Meanwhile, a small party that included Higginson had forced open the western door with an improvised battering ram, and they pressed forward into the anteroom. A detachment of officers armed with clubs awaited them. One of them struck Higginson in the face, splitting open his chin. A knife flashed. One of the courthouse defenders, an Irish-born truckman named James Batchelder, cried out, "I am stabbed!" and fell back on the carpet, fatally wounded. But the mob that Higginson expected to be at his back did not move. Driven back outside, he harangued them to no avail. At least two of his supporters, Stowell and a free black named Lewis Hayden, fired shots to cover Higginson's retreat. Moments later Higginson was across the street from the courthouse, tending his wound, when Bronson Alcott appeared at his side. Alcott had been at the Faneuil Hall meeting. Still, having strolled to the courthouse at a leisurely pace, he arrived just as word of the stabbing of Batchelder had begun to circulate. "Why are we not within?" he asked Higginson. "Because these people will not stand by us," came the reply. The police then appeared, and the two men were separated.

Then came an unforgettable moment of quiet courage. Twenty years later, recalling the scene outside the courthouse, Bronson remembered thinking that the wrong man on the wrong side had been killed. It was Burns's friends who most needed a martyr, not his captors. Bronson felt "an obscure instinct within me that to die was about the best use that could be made of a freeman at that crisis. . . . It seemed the moment for a sacrifice to be laid on the altar for the rights of freemen and the salvation of the Republic." He felt it would be a badge of shame for him to return to his house "erect and breathing . . . as I had left it."57 Carrying only his walking stick, Bronson calmly turned and walked alone toward the courthouse door. At any moment, an anxious guard inside the building might have shot him dead. Yet Alcott looked utterly serene as he climbed the courthouse steps. He walked to the entrance, paused to consider the discarded beam of timber that Higginson had used to breach the door, and nonchalantly strode inside. Higginson swore that, at that moment, he heard a shot fired inside the building, but Alcott was unperturbed. Standing on the very spot where Batchelder had fallen, he gazed for a moment up the staircase that led to Burns's cell. The stairs were lined with marshals, pistols and drawn swords at the ready. Having already given the defenders of the building ample cause to strike him down, Alcott decided that further provocation was pointless. Slowly, still betraying no sign of fear, he turned and left the building, never varying his measured pace. "Under the circumstances," Higginson wrote, "neither Plato nor Pythagoras could have done the thing better, and all minor criticisms of our minor sage appear trivial when one thinks of him as he appeared that night."58

The following day, a rumor circulated through Boston that a proslavery mob was preparing to sack Wendell Phillips's home after nightfall. After dark, Bronson, Samuel May, and three other committee members took up defensive positions in the house, ready to protect both the property and the terrified Mrs. Phillips.59 Like the other men, Bronson was armed with a pistol. In his hatred of slavery and cowardice, he was prepared to do to a rioter what he would have refused to do to a mosquito. Bronson Alcott, a quintessential man of peace, was never braver than when he was in the greatest peril.

The moment inside the courthouse might have served as an emblem of much of Bronson Alcott's career: admirably brave, thoroughly right-minded, and ultimately ineffectual in achieving his intentions. The Vigilance

Committee failed to rescue Burns. Tried without a jury and judged by a man who, by law, received an extra five dollars for ruling against him, Anthony Burns was found to be a fugitive and was sent to Virginia.[60] One week to the day after the botched storming of the courthouse, as many as fifty thousand onlookers lined the streets of Boston to watch as a heavily armed guard led Burns to the waiting ship. Windows along the route were festooned in black. Abba's uncle Samuel, still a fighting May at the age of seventy-eight, hung two American flags, upside down, from his windows. Bronson and Louisa watched as Burns was escorted to the wharf; they were so close to the captive that Louisa was able to discern the brand on his cheek.[61] She evidently remembered that mark years later when she created Robert Dane, the ex-slave with a disfigured face in her story "My Contraband."

Until that time, Bronson had declined even to vote in an election. The Burns affair changed his mind. He knew that more than voting was needed to change America. Nevertheless, from now on, he vowed, "I must see to it that my part is done hereafter to give us a Boston, a Mayor, a Governor, and a President—if indeed a single suffrage, or many, can mend matters essentially. So I shall vote."[62] Actually, however, he took his time in giving effect to his resolution. He found no state or presidential candidate worthy of his support until 1860, when he finally cast a ballot for another tall, enigmatic son of a poor farmer.

If the Burns trial was cause for despondency, the summer brought a reason to celebrate. On August 9, the day of its publication, Thoreau dined with Alcott and presented him with a copy of *Walden*. Alcott accepted the book gratefully and spent the next four days reading and rereading it. He also dusted off his copy of the book Thoreau had written while living by the pond, *A Week on the Concord and Merrimack Rivers*, convinced that, whether or not his friend's work was immediately popular, the passing years would "publish the author's surpassing merits."[63] It must have pleased Bronson to see *Walden* enjoy a modest success, selling more than seventeen hundred of its initial edition of two thousand copies by the end of 1854. He took pleasure not only in Thoreau's philosophy and prose, but also the latter's reminiscences of the days and evenings the two had spent together, trading thoughts, "revising mythology, rounding a fable here and there, and building castles in the air." Alcott, Thoreau said, had "enhanced the beauty of the landscape."[64]

In October, Bronson traveled to New York, where he compared philosophical notes with Henry James Sr., and called on the evangelist minister
Henry Ward Beecher. But the more important activity that fall belonged
to Louisa. Eager to earn money for the family, she set herself the task of
publishing her first book. Instead of trying her luck with *The Inheritance*,
she chose to revise the fanciful little stories she had extemporized seven
years earlier for the pleasure of Ellen Emerson. She shared her manuscript
with her father, who liked it enough to discuss it with a Boston publisher
named George Briggs. The conversation set forces in motion that must
have seemed marvelous to Louisa, for on December 4, *Flower Fables* was
released to the public. With great pride, she presented one of the first
copies to Miss Emerson. Only later, when the initial elation of being an
author had subsided, did Louisa stop to consider the economics of her triumph. Although the book was published in an edition of sixteen hundred
copies and, in Louisa's own opinion, "sold very well," she received only
somewhere between thirty-two and thirty-five dollars from the publisher.[65]
In her journal she railed at Briggs's dishonesty. More privately, she probably cursed herself for not having made a more favorable contract. Like her
father, she had sold her mental labor for much less than it was worth. She
might have seen herself as a fighting May, but at this early phase of her
publishing career she was looking like an impecunious Alcott through and
through.

Nevertheless, it was a thrill to be able to place a copy of *Flower Fables* in
her mother's Christmas stocking. In the note that she left along with the
gift, Louisa lavished thanks and credit on Abba. "Whatever beauty or
poetry is to be found in my little book," she wrote, "is owing to your interest in and encouragement of all my efforts from the first to the last."
Louisa knew, however, that *Flower Fables* was only a small beginning, significant more for what it might portend than for its own artistic value. She
also wrote to her mother, "I hope to pass in time from fairies and fables to
men and realities."[66] Instead of a book, Louisa gave Bronson a pair of slippers, along with a comic poem, inscribed to the family's "Attic philosopher." Her lyric tells of how Santa Claus, passing through Greece, caught
sight of Plato's sandals. Santa, she writes, first decided that this footwear
would make a wonderful gift for Alcott. On reflection, however, "feeling
the ancient sandals to be / Out of keeping with modern hose / He changed

them into these slippers you see, / More fitting a land of snows." Despite her jocular tone, Louisa could not resist a jibe or two at her father's lack of worldliness and his habitual neglect of the less visible portions of his wardrobe. The slippers, she adds, would serve not only "to shield the ten philosophical toes," but also "to hide from the eyes of the peeping old world / The holy Platonic blue socks." Louisa's poem concludes by wishing her father a long life "no matter how empty" his purse may be.[67]

The humor directed at Bronson, though of the gentlest kind, may suggest something important about Louisa's strategies for handling familial frustrations. Though still a strong-willed young woman, she was no longer the little girl with a violent temper she had once been. She had learned above all to address painful subjects with wit instead of fury. The mildly biting joke had become a standard means of responding to the aspects of her father's character that most exasperated her. In her teasing comparison of her father to Plato—indeed, "Plato" became a common nickname for Bronson in her journals—Louisa adopted a mock-reverential tone far preferable to outright confrontation.

The Christmas of *Flower Fables* and Platonic slippers was the last Christmas the family spent together in Boston. In the spring of 1855, Abba was driven to seek further ways to economize. A fine opportunity arose when Benjamin Willis, who had been married to Abba's now-deceased sister Elizabeth, offered the family the use of one of his houses in Walpole in southwestern New Hampshire, rent free, for two years. Everyone under the Alcott roof, according to Louisa, had had enough of Boston. They were in no position to decline Willis's proposal. In June, Louisa made the move a month ahead of the rest of her family. She initially thought Walpole "a lovely place, high among the hills." Helping in her cousin Louisa Willis's garden, she took delight in the smell of the fresh earth and the touch of green leaves. She liked to rise early and run up and down a nearby ravine, observing the woods as they woke up around her.[68] On July 16, the rest of the family came to join her. In the early days in Walpole, Louisa wrote happily of picnics, pleasant people, and good neighbors. Her greatest enjoyment, however, took the form of the amateur plays in which she and Anna took part, playing to audiences as large as one hundred and performing well enough to receive notices in the Boston papers.

For his part, Bronson returned to a life much like the one he had known when he first came to Concord in 1840. He worked in the fields, did odd jobs as a carpenter, and traded observations with townspeople. He took pleasure in the frankness and practicality of his new neighbors. He wrote, "There is profit in working with labouring men, and wholesomeness. Their wits are so handy and their senses so parallel to the world they work in and measure so well. . . . 'Tis refreshing to yoke one's idealism with this team of tug-along-the-rut of realism, and so get practical wisdom out of it, and sanity."69

Yet fall and winter told a different tale. The family soon was forced to recognize that both Anna and Louisa would have to earn a wage in order for ends to meet, and Walpole was hardly the place for a young woman to seek her fortune. In October, Anna went back to teaching in Syracuse, leaving her father "sad when so much goodness and grace leaves [*sic*] our house." The following month, on a rainy day, Louisa left for Boston with her small trunk of homemade clothes, hoping to sell her new manuscript, "Christmas Elves," which she thought superior to *Flower Fables*. Bronson was, however, for once the more practical of the two; although he helped Louisa prepare the work for submission, he feared that she was setting out too late in the season to succeed with a Christmas book. He was right. To her disappointment, Louisa peddled "Christmas Elves" in vain. Although she vowed to make a more timely effort on its behalf the following year, and although Bronson himself offered it to Phillips, Sampson of Boston, "Christmas Elves" was never published. Nevertheless, both Louisa's ambition and the unsatisfied wants of her family counseled the impossibility of turning back. If she was in Boston, then she would find a way to make Boston pay her. Taking a room that was offered her by her cousin Thomas Sewall and his family in their home on Chestnut Street, she took in sewing and began to turn out a steady stream of stories, which she sold for a pittance to the *Saturday Evening Gazette*.70 So long as she had "a head and a pair of hands," she would neither sit idle nor go home in defeat.71

Now that Walpole's summer vacationers were long gone, Bronson found it a duller, emptier place. The departures of Anna and Louisa made it all the more so. Separated from his cadre of Boston intellectuals, and with only Abba and his two younger daughters to cheer him, Bronson found it a challenge "to make the most of myself and them in this little river town and its quiet population."72 He discovered that the bonds of understanding that he thought he had forged with the working people of the town were not nearly as strong as he had hoped. Walpole was not Concord, and not even Bronson's optimism could make it so.

The day before she turned twenty-three, Louisa wrote a long, thoughtful letter to her father to mark their joint birthday. Her distance from home had prompted her to think deeply about the father with whom she shared a birth anniversary but, it often seemed, so little else. Their contrasts, she supposed, had existed from the hours of their respective births. She imagined her father in infancy as "a serene & placid baby" who had "descended from on high" instead of being born in the typical bloody, squawling fashion and who had almost immediately begun his "wise meditations . . . looking philosophically out of [his] cradle" at the great world beyond. The man who had grown from that serene infant seemed to her miraculously unaffected by the cares and sufferings that disfigure other mortals:

> Fifty six years have passed . . . & that peaceful baby's golden head is silver now, but the man looks as serenely . . . and meditates as wisely as he did in his cradle, & nothing but the lines on his face where troubles have been & four tall women at his side, show that years and trials have changed the wise child into a wiser old man.

Surely, Louisa thought, some good angel had dropped a charm into her father's cradle, enabling him "to walk thro[ugh] life in quiet sunshine while others groped [in] the dark," and she wished that she could learn its magic.

Louisa followed her fanciful account of her father's babyhood with a contrasting history of her own. Unlike her golden-haired sire, she had been "a crass crying brown baby, bawling at the disagreeable world where on a dismal November day" she found herself. Scrambling up to childhood, she had fallen "with a crash into girlhood." After countless falls "over fences, out of trees, up hill & down stairs" and being strengthened by such violent exercise, the "topsey turvey" girl now found herself an equally helter-skelter young woman, "big brown & brave, crying, not because she has come into the world but because she must go out of it before she has done half she wants to." She vowed that, "as the brown baby fought through its small trials so the brown woman will fight thro [*sic*] her big ones." If the fight did not end with her becoming queen of the world, at least she might end up knowing how to rule herself.[73]

Louisa had chosen her self-descriptive metaphors with care, knowing that they would resonate deeply in her father's mind. Her repeated emphasis on falling was, of course, a comic touch, but it was also likely meant to comment on her father's personal theory of genesis. Bronson had long been formulating the idea that the physical world had originated through a moral devolution of the divine spirit. Mankind, which had had its origins as a perfect, nonphysical entity, had become incarnate through having sinned. Nonhuman nature was the result of a further falling off from the spirit; it was nothing more than the excess and unnecessary matter that had been cast off by humanity. "Nature," Bronson was later to write, "is the waste man. The soul instinctively frees herself from all superfluous matter generated in building forth her own body, and, from this surplus-sage of substance, organizes in descending series the natural kingdoms."[74] In Alcott's cosmology, a physical person was a lapsed soul, a debased descendant of pure being.

Speaking of her father as having descended from on high, Louisa alluded to her father's own supposed descent from pure spirit. Writing of her own repeated physical falls, she called attention to her own fall from grace, and she insinuated that she had descended much farther than he from their perfect origins. Closer to nature than her father, she was also commensurately more distant from a divine origin. If one accepted Bronson's theory of the universe, Louisa seemed to be intentionally positioning herself as an inferior being. The letter feels as if it has been addressed to a seraph by a mere mortal. Nevertheless, Louisa took some earnest pride in the bold tenacity that she identified with her brownness. If, in some sense, she had been born for struggle and adversity, her trials had given her a spirit and a resiliency every bit as enviable as her father's golden-haired serenity.

Louisa still defined her success according to parental sanction and approval. She wrote, "the thought of what you all at home hoped & expected of me makes me careful of my words & actions that you may not be disappointed now as you have often been." The thought that she might disappoint her parents—more broadly, that her entire topsy-turvy nature might render her forever inadequate in their eyes—was for Louisa a real and continual source of worry. She cared enormously about redemption and vindication. She was determined to prove herself worthy, both to her family and to the world. As yet, she was not confident that she would succeed.

Some evidence of parental approval was on its way even as Louisa wrote her birthday missive. In writing his birthday letter to Louisa, Bronson reached for agricultural metaphors to express his appreciation for her. He told her, "as the sere stems regoice [*sic*] and pride themselves in the bloom and fragrence [*sic*] of the branches and flowers they still claim as theirs . . . so thy Childs' courage and spirit,—yours, and Anna's too—are daily prides and satisfactions to me." Extending his trope, he ventured to suggest that the deprivations of their upbringing might finally be to their advantage. After all, he noted, the fairest and best fruits tended to grow "not in the blandest climes, but in those attempered of sun and shower, of heat and cold." Similarly, thanks to the hard seasoning that they had had from their beginning, he hoped that these Alcott plants would turn out "all the more mellow and mature." To Bronson's mind, concerned as it was with growing things, his daughters were indeed the fruits of a garden, one that he had found harder to maintain than his literal ones. As his letter reveals, he was hardly oblivious to "the trials, moral and social," to which his eccentric way of life had subjected them.[75] What had been done, for good or ill, was irretrievable. He could only hope for the best.

Meanwhile, the environment of Walpole was continuing to display its limitations. Bronson was finding his country life "all too dull and prosy to be very interesting."[76] Louisa, with typical bluntness, supposed that a winter in Walpole could only be "a nice stupid winter," since lectures and meetings were lost arts there.[77] In March, she sent her father a photograph that she had had taken of herself. Presumably, it was the daguerreotype that is now invariably associated with the young Louisa. The image corresponds fairly closely with portions of the description she was to give to Sylvia Yule, the heroine of her first mature novel, *Moods*:

> The face was full of contradictions; youthful, maidenly, and intelligent, yet touched with the melancholy of a temperament too mixed to make life happy. . . . A most significant but not a beautiful face, because of its want of harmony, for the deep eyes among their fair surroundings disturbed the sight as a discord jars upon the ear; even when they smiled the shadow of black lashes seemed to fill them with a gloom never quite lost.[78]

Louisa May Alcott: a face "full of contradictions,
—youthful, maidenly, and intelligent, yet touched
with the unconscious melancholy that is
born of disappointment and desire"
(Courtesy of the Louisa May Alcott Memorial Association)

The intensity of his daughter's stare may have made Bronson fear that Louisa was pressing herself too hard, for he proposed that she soon return to Walpole. All the bills had been paid for the time being, he told her, and he intimated that the pleasure of her company and the knowledge that she was getting some rest from her writing mattered more to him than the dollars she could send home. It seemed to him that Louisa was "bent on making as long a stay from good bread and fine air and early hours as you can with any grace about you."[79] He missed her, and he wanted her back home again.

It was clear that Bronson thought of Walpole as a place of good health and wholesome living. Yet Walpole was to ruin the health of the gentlest Alcott. In June 1856, Abba, still dedicated to good works, found herself ministering to the needs of the Halls, one of the town's poorest families. The family inhabited a space above a cellar where swine had recently been kept. The landlord—a deacon of the church, as Louisa bitterly noted in her journal—had not troubled himself to have the cellar cleaned, and he did so only after Abba threatened legal action. Two small children in the flat had come down with scarlet fever, and Abba came to their aid. At her side stood two Alcott daughters still living at home, Lizzie and May. What followed was almost a reenactment of the Alcotts' exposure to smallpox in 1850, which had also resulted from contact with one of Abba's charity cases. This time, however, the consequences were more devastating. Both Lizzie and May caught the disease. May recovered quickly and completely. Lizzie, however, did not, and by the time Louisa was able to return home from Boston, her sister was seriously ill. For a time she lay near death. The fever did not kill Lizzie, but it left her perilously weak. Understating the case considerably, Louisa called the months that followed an "anxious time." She nursed Lizzie, took over her housework, and, amid the bustle and worry, managed to write a story a month during that careworn summer.

The Alcotts chose not to call in traditional doctors to treat Lizzie's illness. They were much taken at the time with the theories of Samuel Christian Hahnemann, the German physician credited with founding homeopathic medicine. Anticipating that Lizzie would soon throw off her illness, Bronson put much faith in the fact that she had never tasted animal food. By August 5, Lizzie's condition had improved enough that Bronson was able to write to his mother, "We are all well."[80] There remained little reason for the entire family to hover near Lizzie's bedside. With nothing to keep her in Walpole, Louisa laid plans for another winter in Boston. Bronson, now driven stir-crazy by the want of intellectual friendship in Walpole, planned a conversational tour of Boston, New Haven, New York, and Philadelphia.

Once on the road, he kept to a strict budget; eating only two meals a day and bravely resisting the temptations of the New York bookstores, he managed on a dollar a day.[81] Bronson avidly read his wife's letters for reports on Louisa's literary progress and confessed that her prospects gave him good hopes. He was developing confidence in her energy and creative powers. He declared, "I hope to be a Spectator of her triumphs fairly soon."[82] For her part, Louisa watched the newspapers for accounts of her father's conversations and took great pleasure in discovering that New York was receiving him well. On their birthday, she wrote to him that she loved "to see your name first among the lecturers, to hear it kindly spoken of in the papers and inquired about by good people here—to say nothing of the delight and pride I take in seeing you at last filling the place you are so fitted for." She thought it would be wise and creditable for the Gothamites to erect a statue to her modern Plato.[83]

The praise Louisa gave in one paragraph, however, she all but took back in the ensuing ones. Dryly writing about May's latest achievements in music, French, and drawing, she ventured to say that her youngest sister might become "what none of us can be, 'an accomplished Alcott.' " As to her own strivings, she claimed that her goal was to "prove that though an *Alcott* I can support myself."[84] Bronson's family history was a matter of deep pride to him. In 1852, he had spent months tracing the lines of his father's and mother's ancestry as far as the American records would allow him to go.[85] For Louisa to suggest that an Alcott was by definition a ne'er-do-well was to aim her joke at an especially sensitive spot.

Louisa's playful but piercing raillery notwithstanding, Bronson's reputation was beginning to revive. While in New York, he had the honor of being elected as a vice president of a women's rights convention, and the doors of illustrious men and women were open to him. Thoreau, visiting New York, joined with Alcott to seek out Horace Greeley and ride with the latter to his farm. The poet Alice Cary was also present for this visit, but Alcott was more interested in telling Thoreau about another poet he had met a month earlier: Walt Whitman.

Whitman had received Bronson while reclining on a couch, pillowing his head on a bended arm. He immediately impressed Alcott as an extraordinary person. No sooner had Alcott told his journal that Whitman was not easily described, than he launched into a vivid description: Whitman was "broad-shouldered, rouge-fleshed, Bacchus-browed, bearded like a satyr." Bronson marveled at the poet's brute power, genius, and audacity and noted Whitman's calico jacket, coarse overalls, and cowhide boots with an admiration approaching envy. Whitman's voice, too, was enchanting—deep, sharp, sometimes tender, and almost melting in its intonation. He was, Bronson thought, an Adamic figure, claiming never to have sinned and "quite innocent of repentance and man's fall."[86] Alcott could not wait for Thoreau to meet this singular man.

On November 9, the two Concordians heard Henry Ward Beecher

preach at Brooklyn's Plymouth Church. Alcott was entirely taken with Beecher's keen intelligence, broad humor, and lively human sympathies. Thoreau was less impressed, finding Beecher's performance "pagan."[87] They disagreed again the next day when Alcott introduced Thoreau to Whitman. The poet and the naturalist eyed each other, Alcott noted, "like two beasts, each wondering what the other would do, whether to snap or run; and it came to no more than cold compliments between them."[88] Whitman was surprised at Thoreau's indifference to current political events. Thoreau was taken aback by the sensuality of Whitman's conversation; he felt as if he were interviewing an animal.[89] Alcott reached the conclusion that both his friends were "hard to tame." He remained on excellent terms with both of them.

In February, on a return trip to New York, Bronson attended a production of Euripides' *Medea*, which affected him profoundly. The play tells of how Jason, the husband of Medea and the father of her children, forsakes her in order to marry a Corinthian princess. Jason deceives himself into believing that his new match will benefit all concerned; it will give his children a royal name, win a place in the palace for Medea, and in time, garner a crown for Jason himself. He persuades himself that his adulterous marriage is an act of duty. Jason ignores the chorus, who warn that he is betraying his wife, and he blames his domestic discord on the feminine—and therefore flawed—thinking of Medea. He declares, "The human race should produce children from some other source and a female sex should not exist. Then mankind would be free from every evil."[90] Medea responds in jealous fury. She not only poisons the princess and her father, but murders Jason's children with her own hands. In the final scene, Medea departs in a chariot pulled by dragons, carrying the children's corpses with her.

The play, "with all its appalling accompanyments [*sic*]," struck personally at Bronson's guilty memories, suggesting "events too vividly, perhaps, of home experiences, and the Courage of Principle." Euripides had taken Bronson back thirteen years, to a time when he, like Jason, had confused his selfish pursuits with altruism and when, along with Charles Lane, he had dreamed of building a little world made solely of men. Medea's chariot seemed to him like the ox-drawn sled moving slowly away from the ruin of his fond Utopia. He wrote to Abba, "I had 'Fruitlands' before me, and Ideas there celebrated and played oft to the applauding snows—the tragedy of ox-team and drifting Family wailing their woes to the wintry winds." Alluding to the period of madness that had followed, he added, "You shall imagine the Sequel, and the rest."[91] Alcott's personal farce had been replayed for him as Grand Guignol.

Coming home from New York, he stopped in New Haven to give a series of six conversations at Yale. He was pleased to find there a number of "bright boys . . . professing an unexpected interest."[92] One of these was William Torrey Harris, a Connecticut-born graduate of Andover who was so eager to make Alcott's acquaintance that he met him at the New Haven train station. Like Frank Sanborn, Harris almost instantaneously became Alcott's devotee. Later that year, Harris left the college without a degree, accepting a teaching position in St. Louis, where he dedicated himself to the study of Hegel and other German philosophers. In future years, when Alcott traveled west to St. Louis, he did so at Harris's standing invitation.

In the summer of 1857, the Alcotts reassembled in Walpole. Louisa and Anna had fine times together, and Lizzie, who had never fully regained her strength following the previous summer's fever, was cheered by all the activity and seemed to rally for a while. However, the long, cold winter had taken a toll, and her lingering frailty was now a cause of continual worry. To Louisa, it seemed that Lizzie's emotional attachment to the world was diffident and weak. "She never seemed to care for this world beyond home," Louisa wrote.[93] She was starting to wonder whether home was a sufficient reason for Lizzie to live.

That summer, Louisa came to understand and appreciate her father more than she had previously done. The change in her attitude was precipitated by the arrival of a welcome visitor. Bronson's mother, still hardy and sharp-minded at the age of eighty-four, made the journey to Walpole from her home in Oriskany Falls, New York, to spend time with her eldest son. She did not leave until November. For Louisa, who had spent little time with her grandmother, the visit was a minor revelation. It was not merely that she found the elder Mrs. Alcott "a sweet old lady . . . very smart, industrious and wise."[94] More importantly, both in her character and in the stories she told of the past, she helped Louisa to understand her father in the context of his youth.

Louisa had come to regard her father as a somewhat pitiable figure, a man who, though admirable for his ideals, was a hapless, fumbling personage, unable to boast of any concrete achievements. The presence of Bronson's mother changed all that. At last, Louisa could "see where Father got his nature."[95] She had observed her father through mature eyes only after his youthful enthusiasm had been spent and his most precious visions had been crushed by circumstance. She had, of course, not seen him as a bright and energetic youth, eager to recast the world in the contours of his dreams. But now her grandmother brought forth her recollections of the young Bronson, and Louisa was astonished to learn what an active and self-reliant person her father had formerly been. To her surprise, she learned that her father, like Louisa herself, had been formed by adversity, ambition, hard work, and struggle. She conceived the idea for a novel to be based on Bronson's life, with chapters based on his experiences on Spindle Hill, at the Temple School, Fruitlands, Concord, and Boston. She only hoped that she would live to write this great memoir of "the trials and triumphs of the Pathetic Family."[96]

In the fall of 1857, Abba took Lizzie to the seashore at Swampscott, hoping that a change of air and the influence of "the salutary Sea," as Bronson put it, might restore her health. Meanwhile, Bronson considered the possibility of moving back to Concord.[97] He decided to spend some time in the old town in September, exploring available properties and consulting with Emerson about the feasibility of his return. On the way there, he stopped at the seaside resort where Abba and Lizzie were staying. Although he generally thought Lizzie none the worse, she was slightly thinner and her features paler and more elongated than when he had last seen her three weeks earlier. The salt air had performed no miracle. The doctor whom the Alcotts had at last chosen to consult was hopeful, and Abba shared his view. However, Bronson thought the case "*a critical one*" and fretted that Lizzie had "neither flesh nor strength to spare, and the Eye falling upon her wasted form scarcely dares to hope for her continuance long." As always, however, Alcott tried to discern the soul as well as the body. Lizzie remained gentle, confiding, and pleasant, and her face seemed so full of hope that Bronson wondered why he should venture to fear or doubt.[98] And yet his doubts persisted.

On September 7, Bronson left Abba and Lizzie in Boston and traveled to Concord, where he began looking at the available real estate. He quickly fastened his attention on a house belonging to a John Moore, adjacent to the Alcotts' former home at Hillside. Shaded by elms and butternut trees, it was the first that one passed when walking westward from Hillside toward town. The property included an orchard of at least forty apple trees, ten acres of woodland, and an excellent well for drinking water. In an enthusiastic letter he sent to Anna, Louisa, and May, Bronson acknowledged that the house was old, but he added that nothing like it could be found near the center of town for a comparable price. He promised that as the family weighed the decision to buy the house, he would not press his position. However, his heart was obviously set on the property; he declared, " 'Tis the home for me." Like a child promising to be good in exchange for some much-desired treat, Bronson averred that he was "minded to take the reins a little more firmly in hand, and think you may rely on me for supports of labour and money in the years to come," adding that he could "do more for you, and for myself, from the Concord position, than any known to me."99 In the face of such eagerness, it would have been difficult to raise objections. On September 22, Bronson purchased Moore's estate, as surveyed by Henry David Thoreau, for $945.

Since the time of Louisa's birth, the Alcott family had changed residence on an average of more than once every two years. Bronson's two great yearnings, one for firmness of place and the other for ceaseless discovery, always contended inside him. In the late 1850s, the need for place at last prevailed. The Moore house on Lexington Road was to be his home for almost twenty years. Because of the apple trees on the property, he christened his newly acquired home "Orchard House." Taking an inspiration from Hawthorne, he sometimes referred to it as "the House of Seven Gables." Louisa, always ready to puncture a romantic soap bubble, called it "Apple Slump."

CHAPTER TEN

ORCHARD HOUSE

"My associations with the place are
of the happiest and holiest kind"

—A. BRONSON ALCOTT,
Journals, April 28, 1880

BRONSON FELT HE HAD A STROKE OF GREAT FORTUNE IN acquiring Orchard House, and he was flattered when friends told him it was one of the best-placed and most picturesque houses in Concord. The location was indeed opportune. From the front door, an easy stroll up the Lexington Road brought the traveler to Concord's handsome town square. The house was even a bit closer to Emerson's than Hillside had been.

In England, Hawthorne received word that the Alcotts were moving into Orchard House. Surprised that Bronson had been able to afford such a purchase, he reacted to the news with pleasure, though not for the kindly reasons one might suspect. Hawthorne knew how prone Alcott was to overextend himself, and he saw nothing wrong with being in a position to reap the advantages in case the philosopher stumbled once again. With cool opportunism, he wrote to his friend Howard Ticknor, "I understand that Mr. Alcott . . . has bought a piece of land adjacent to mine, and two old houses on it. . . . If he should swamp himself by his expenditures on this place, I should be very glad to take it off his hands. . . . You would oblige me by having an eye to this."[1]

In early October 1857, while Orchard House underwent extensive repairs, the Alcotts settled into a temporary home on Bedford Street in Concord. Believing that Lizzie's condition had stabilized, Bronson departed on

November 11 for a tour of the West. He stopped for more than a week in Buffalo, where a friend of Emerson's introduced him to former president Fillmore. The president and the philosopher spoke for two hours, trading opinions on slavery and the recent violence in Kansas. Alcott found Fillmore "candid, conservative, and fearful of consequences." In a letter to Abba, he paid Fillmore a left-handed compliment, pronouncing him "sincere in his timidities."[2]

In Bronson's absence Anna, Louisa, and Abby May amused themselves by acting in plays with young men from the town and the boys from Frank Sanborn's school. Anna soon attracted the attentions of a witty twenty-four-year-old named John Pratt, while Louisa took an interest in a blond, round-cheeked, motherless boy, Alf Whitman. No relation to the poet, Whitman boarded with the Pratts and often turned up alongside John when he came to visit Anna. Although the friendship of John and Anna soon blossomed into romance, there was no such possibility for Louisa and Alf. Alf, at fifteen, was ten years Louisa's junior. The attraction, though platonic, was nevertheless strong. They went to skating parties together, rowed on the Concord River, and acted opposite each other in a dramatization of Dickens's *The Haunted Man*. For years afterward they exchanged letters signed with their character names "Dolphus" and "Sophy." Alf thought of the Alcotts' home as an enchanted palace.[3] Louisa called Alf *"my* boy," and she thought that, if she were a goddess, he would be the kind of boy she would create.[4] It was not the only time when Louisa sought the close companionship of a much younger male. Always believing that she should have been born a boy, she loved to participate vicariously in the adventures and discoveries of boyhood. She also relished the role of surrogate mother or big sister. For the role of lover, however, she possessed neither map nor compass. Though Alf remained in Concord for less than a year, Louisa remembered him distinctly. When she wrote *Little Women*, Alf was one of the two models for the character of Laurie. But not everything was pleasant that winter. Along with the good times at the Alcott house, Alf remembered how Louisa would often excuse herself to climb the stairs and check on Lizzie.[5]

Although he had wanted to travel as far as St. Louis, Bronson had only reached Cincinnati when a letter from Concord alarmed him too greatly to continue his tour. Hastening home, he found Lizzie "wasted to the mere

Elizabeth Sewall Alcott,
the Alcotts' "dear child of grace."
When she died, Louisa and her mother
both thought they saw her spirit leave her body.
This is the only likeness of her known to exist.

(Courtesy of the Louisa May Alcott Memorial Association)

shadow of what she was."[6] Her spirits had dwindled too, and she spoke of how enticing she found the shades of Sleepy Hollow, a recently conse-crated cemetery that lay a short distance from Bedford Street. As her thoughts fixated on death, she commented strangely, "It will be something new in our family, and I can best be spared of the four."[7] Early in Febru-ary, she began to refuse her medicines. It seemed to Bronson that she had made her choice.

Around March 10, Lizzie put aside her sewing needle, saying that it was too heavy for her.[8] A painless serenity attends the last days of Beth March in *Little Women*. Lizzie was not so fortunate. On Friday the twelfth, in severe pain, she asked to lie in her father's arms and called the rest of the family to her side. Holding their hands and smiling, she seemed to Louisa and the others to be saying farewell. All the next day, the struggle continued. Lizzie begged for relief and stretched out her thin hands for the ether that had lost its power to soothe her. At midnight, a resolution finally came. With the family assembled around her bed, she said distinctly "Now I'm comfort-

able and so happy" and drifted into unconsciousness. Some time later, she
opened her eyes with a look that struck Louisa with its beauty.⁹

At three o'clock Sunday morning, on the cloudless night of March 14, it
was over. A few moments later, Louisa saw a shadow fall across the face of
her sister. Then, to her quiet astonishment, she watched as a light mist rose
from the body, floated upward, and vanished into the air. As she visually
followed the course of this phenomenon, Louisa noticed that her mother's
eyes were moving in the same direction. "What did you see?" Louisa asked.
Abba described the same mist. The attending physician, incredibly named
Dr. Christian Geist, confirmed what they had witnessed. It was, he said,
the life departing visibly.¹⁰ When she died, Lizzie looked to Louisa like a
woman of forty, her small frame worn down by the wasting illness and all
of her fine hair gone.¹¹

Wishing to be alone, the Alcotts sent no word to their friends and relatives in Boston until after the funeral. His daughter's passing moved Bronson to write with the lyric grace that too often evaded him: "This morning
is clear and calm, and so our Elizabeth ascends with transfigured features
to the heavenly airs she had sought so long."¹² Abba took Lizzie's passing
hardest. For days after her daughter's passing, she sat in the empty chamber, not yet believing that she would never again hear her daughter's voice
or see her face gazing up from the now-vacant pillow. Remembering all
that Lizzie had endured for two years, Louisa told herself and others that
Lizzie was "*well* at last," that she had found a place where rest, not suffering, made up the essential core of being.¹³ To Louisa, death seemed beautiful, a liberator for Lizzie and a teacher for those left behind.

The weather was beautiful on the fifteenth, and as Louisa wrote, "everything was simple and quiet as she would have liked it."¹⁴ Three of Bronson's
friends—Emerson, Thoreau, and Bronson's young disciple Sanborn—
carried Lizzie's coffin out of the house on Bedford Street and, later, to a
receiving tomb, where her body lay until her parents could purchase a plot
in Sleepy Hollow Cemetery. While noting that none of the three men had
come to visit since the Alcotts had returned to Concord, Louisa was
nonetheless grateful for the sympathy and respect they showed Bronson and
Lizzie that day.¹⁵ Emerson told the officiating minister, who did not know
the family well, that Lizzie was a good, unselfish, patient child, who made
friends even in death. Everyone seemed to forget that they were not bury-

ing a child but a woman of twenty-two. "So," Louisa wrote in her journal, "the first break comes."[16]

Both she and her father wrote poems to help them come to terms with the loss. Louisa wrote hers some days before Lizzie's death, and Bronson wrote his shortly after the end. He copied both of their lyrics into his journal. A decade later, Louisa rewrote her poem, with some revisions, into the text of *Little Women*. When she did so, however, she omitted the second stanza:

> Gentle pilgrim! First and fittest,
> Of our little household band;
> To journey trustfully before us
> Hence into the silent land.
> First, to teach us that love's charm
> Grows stronger being riven;
> Fittest, to become the Angel
> That shall beckon us to heaven.[17]

In this verse, Lizzie becomes what she never was in life: the leader of the family, the one who bravely goes ahead of the rest to prepare a place for all. Christ's promise that the last shall be first lies just beneath the surface of these words. As Louisa reflected on Lizzie's superior fitness to become an angel, she reflected as well on her own weaker qualifications. Thus, in the poem, Lizzie becomes not only a leader but a teacher, one whose remembered example will instill her older sister with the patience and courage that Louisa felt she so desperately lacked.

Bronson's poem was less sentimental and a good deal more frightening. Instead of focusing on the virtues of his lost daughter, he reflected guiltily on his inability, even in her last moments, to supply his child's most urgent needs:

> "Ether," she begged, "O Father give
> "With parting kiss my lips doth seal
> "Pure ether once, and let me live
> "Forgetful of this death I feel."
>
> We had it not. Away she turns,
> Denied the boon she dying asks,
> Her kindling eye with rapture churns,
> Immortal goblet takes and quaffs.[18]

Lizzie's dying plea to have her pain extinguished, as well as her final turning away from him, haunted Bronson. He was not merely the cloud-borne, insouciant dreamer that his detractors said he was, and all his philosophical detachment could not insulate him from this loss.

The day after the funeral was Anna's twenty-seventh birthday, a welcome reminder that life would go on. In the morning, the family shared a somber breakfast, and that evening they exchanged "pleasing memories of the dear one."[19] Anna was given Lizzie's desk as a present, a gesture that emphasized continuity instead of disjunction. The next day, a workman named McKee and his crew arrived to begin the renovation of Orchard House. At the beginning of April, in order to better supervise the construction, the family took up temporary residence next door in a wing of Hillside, which the Hawthornes, still in England, graciously provided for them.

With the passing of Lizzie, who had taken comfort during her last days in gathering the family around her and murmuring, "All here," a source of emotional cohesion was lost.[20] Whereas Lizzie's illness had brought the family closer together, her death temporarily had the opposite effect. May departed for Boston, and Anna went to stay with her friends the Pratts. Instinctively, they were seeking distance. Although Louisa averred that she did not miss Lizzie as much as she had expected, it was hard to deal with so many departures at once. Even her mother and father, though physically present, seemed distant, immersed as they were in other concerns—Abba in her memories and Bronson in the renovation. Whatever the many discomforts Louisa had known, loneliness had seldom been one of them. Now, it bore down on her with oppressive force.

During these months at Hillside, Bronson sometimes strayed into the upstairs study that had once been his, where he experienced deep feelings of nostalgia. He took down some books from Hawthorne's shelves and, to his surprise, discovered that their tastes barely overlapped. Everything in the room seemed both familiar and strange. Here, he had conversed with Fuller, Thoreau, and Emerson. Here, too, he had held sessions of discussion and discovery with his own children, in the only school the world could not deny him. The room also reminded him of Lizzie. "Then my dear departed child was here," he lamented, "around whom so much of my home delights are gathered."[21] If the renovations of Orchard House had not kept him so busy, Bronson's broodings about the past might have overwhelmed him. Already, he loved the house. "Standing quietly apart from the roadside," leaving space "for the overshadowing elms to lend their dignity and beauty to the scene," Orchard House delighted Bronson with its porches, gables, and chimney tops. It was more, he thought, than he deserved or would have dared to wish for.[22]

The family had a much-needed reason to celebrate on April 7, when Anna joyfully announced her engagement to John Pratt. Objectively, Bronson and Louisa had every reason to share the couple's delight. Pratt was, as Louisa freely confessed, "a model son and brother,—a true man,— full of fine possibilities."[23] But somehow the occasion was not entirely happy. The loss of Elizabeth was still fresh, and the shifting of emotional states could not occur without some internal friction. Bronson thought well of Pratt and did not question his fitness to marry his daughter. "Still," he wrote, "the thought is more than I am ready for at this moment."[24] Louisa, as always, was more dramatic. "Another sister is gone," she grieved in her journal.[25] Louisa remembered these emotions ten years later when she wrote the first part of *Little Women*. After learning that John Brooke has taken a romantic interest in Meg, Jo glowers darkly at the young man and wishes that she herself could somehow marry her sister in order to keep her in the family. The mere presence of Brooke's forgotten umbrella in the hallway is enough to elicit a shaken fist.[26] Louisa moaned in private over the engagement and swore she would never forgive Pratt taking Anna away from her.[27] No one seems to have regarded Louisa's agitation over Anna's engagement with any particular concern. However, she required more understanding than anyone realized.

When the Alcotts finally moved into Orchard House in July, Louisa felt out of place. Bronson was delighted with his many improvement projects, and Abba was grateful to be resting under a new roof. The future Mrs. Pratt was absorbed in her fiancé, and May was busy painting. Louisa, however, found herself at least momentarily thwarted. She had received an offer in June to act in Thomas Barry's theater in Boston, an opportunity that fanned her hopes of trying a new life. Unfortunately, Barry broke his leg and the plan was scrapped, but not before word of it leaked to the respectable relatives and caused a minor scandal.

Louisa was in a potentially suffocating position. At various times in the past, she had referred to both Anna and Lizzie as "the angel of the house."

In nineteenth-century New England, it was not uncommon for one daughter to be chosen, by design or circumstance, to mind the house and care for the parents as they passed into old age. The logical candidate for this role among the Alcotts had always been Elizabeth. Now, with Elizabeth gone and Anna on her way to the altar, it was starting to look more and more as if Louisa had drawn the short straw. She had, one suspects, long wished to be the closest of the Alcott sisters to her parents. The wish was coming true in an undesired way.

As the summer heat stretched over Concord, Louisa "simmered" plans for the future, as she put it, but sweeping, dusting, and dishpans took up much of her time.[28] The fact that she had seriously considered a career in the theater revealed her nagging doubts about her chances as an author. She remained outwardly confident that her creative nature would find its expression, but her path was not clear. She sold a story that summer titled "Only an Actress," which brought in enough money for some summer dresses and bonnets. She could sell tales with ease to the weekly magazines, but the work gave her only slight fulfillment. She was edging toward her personal Slough of Despond.

After her parents' new household was sufficiently settled, Louisa went to Boston to look for work. The family's finances remained precarious, and they still needed a breadwinner more than a housekeeper. The hunt for work went badly, and it seemed to her that, in the busy, anxious swirl of Boston, no one cared whether Miss Alcott from Concord found a position, or indeed, whether she lived at all. Her drive and determination abruptly deserted her. The family circle had lost two sisters. Perhaps it would be best for it to lose a third. She thought of jumping into the Charles River, and she could not banish the idea. Her feet led her to the Mill Dam, and she gazed hard into the water.

What happened next is not entirely clear. She never mentioned the incident in her journal, or if she did, she destroyed the entry. After the crisis was past, she wrote of it in a letter to the family, but there, too, she offered few details. However, a very similar trial is endured by one of her fictional creations, Christie Devon, the autobiographical heroine of *Work*. After a series of abortive careers, in which she fails not because of incompetence but because of ill luck and the weaknesses and cruelties of others, Christie is reduced to taking in sewing. Unable to pay her bills and falsely accused of dishonesty by her landlady, Christie makes one last attempt to find work. Echoing Louisa's loss of Anna to John Pratt, at the last house that Christie approaches before contemplating suicide, a wedding is underway. Reflecting on the new bride's happiness, Christie cries out, "Oh, it isn't fair, it isn't right, that she should have so much and I so little!"[29] Christie's steps lead her to a bridge:

> [S]he watched with curious interest the black water rolling sluggishly below. She knew it was no place for her, yet no one waited for her, no one would care if she staid for ever, and, yielding to the perilous fascination that drew her there, she lingered with a heavy throbbing in her temples, and a troop of wild fancies whirling through her brain. . . . With an ominous chill creeping through her blood, and a growing tumult in her mind, she thought, "I *must* go," but still stood motionless, leaning over the wide gulf. . . . Lower and lower she bent; looser and looser grew her hold on the pillar; faster and faster beat the pulses in her temples, and the rush of some blind impulse was swiftly coming on.[30]

In *Work*, an old friend who happens to be passing by saves Christie from suicide. In her own moment of crisis, Louisa was saved by her own strength. As she wrote to her family, "[I]t seemed so mean to turn & run away before the battle was over that I went home, set my teeth & vowed I'd *make* things work in spite of the world, the flesh & the devil." She resolved, she said, "to take Fate by the throat and shake a living out of her."[31]

Thus steeling herself, she launched herself on a new beginning by going to church. In the past, Theodore Parker had been a ready source of inspiration, and now she sought him out again. She was not disappointed. Though fighting his own grim battle with tuberculosis, Parker had not lost his galvanic powers as a preacher. Seeming to know just the words she needed to hear, Parker delivered a sermon on "Laborious Young Women," in which he advised, "Don't be too proud to ask, and accept the humblest work till you can find the task you want."[32] Louisa did not hesitate to take this advice. Although she did not feel that she knew Parker well, Louisa felt she must speak to him personally. When she presented herself at the Parkers' door, the minister was not at home. However, his wife was moved. She told Louisa that she was sure her husband and his friend Hannah Stevenson would find something for her to do.

The next day, Stevenson came with news of a less than inspiring posi-

A staunch enemy of slavery and a
friend of the downtrodden, Theodore Parker
helped to guide Louisa through her despair in 1858.
(Courtesy of the Louisa May Alcott Memorial Association)

tion. Louisa was to go to the Reform School in Winchester and work as a seamstress, sewing for ten hours a day. "May I depend on you, and do you like sewing?" Miss Stevenson asked her. Louisa did not care for falsehood. She replied that she would be dependable as long as her health held out. As for liking it, Louisa said bluntly that her preferences were beside the point. She would be grateful for anything. Stevenson seemed satisfied and withdrew. The next day, she came back and announced that she had offered the sewing job as a ruse, "a little test of your earnestness." In fact, she had found a place as a governess for only four hours a day. On hearing of her resolve to take the less attractive job, Theodore Parker exclaimed, "The girl has got true grit." Proud of herself for having stared down adversity, Louisa wrote her family to tell them all that had happened. She did not omit to say that she had thought of killing herself.[33]

How does one respond when a daughter announces that she has flirted with suicide? Beyond question, Louisa's declaration altered Bronson's thinking about her. He did not comment, either in his letters or his journal, about his precise reflections. However, he recognized that it was now vital to spend time with her. A month before Lizzie's death, Bronson had written in his journal, "Perhaps this precious fruit must be plucked away that I may divine the better those living symbols spreading around me still, remaining and spared to gladden my heart and homestead."[34] It may be that reading Louisa's letter made him realize that he had failed to learn this lesson well enough.

On October 11, he welcomed Louisa home from Boston, when she arrived for a brief visit. Two days later, as he sat shelling beans, he talked with her about her plans for the winter and her overall prospects.[35] Louisa returned to Boston on the fourteenth. Six days later, Bronson traveled to the city to be with her. He was at her side continually, escorting her to dinner, bringing her along to lectures as well as less formal philosophical discussions, and traveling together to Washington Street to look at a new bust of Emerson. He enjoyed this time with her; he wrote to Abba, "Louisa bore herself proudly and gave me great pleasure."[36] Near the end of the month, he looked around the city to find her a suitable apartment. On November 1, he wrote her a letter about a story she was writing. Although the letter has not been found, the evidence suggests that he was writing to encourage her to submit the manuscript to the prestigious *Atlantic Monthly*.[37] Later, Bronson personally delivered the manuscript to the magazine's editor, James Russell Lowell, with his own hands. Genuinely excited, Louisa wrote that, if her story was deemed good enough for *The Atlantic*, "I shall think I can do something."[38] Lowell eventually accepted the story, although it did not appear until March 1860.

In the aftermath of Louisa's darkest hour, her father tried to lead her back toward the light. The month after his visit, Louisa felt braver and more cheerful.[39] Although she was abundantly aware of Bronson's faults, she sympathized with him. According to Anna, she spoke of her father's visit with great pleasure and said, "The Lord is on his side, & if his white head and meek old face don't move people's hearts, they haven't got any."[40] If Louisa ever again came so close to despair, she never wrote about the experience.

In December, Louisa had one more reason not to feel isolated. Her younger sister May, now eighteen and eager to start trying her luck in the world, came to Boston to study drawing at the School of Design. The sisters roomed together at a boardinghouse on Chestnut Street. Bronson was pleased to learn that May was aggressively pursuing her ambition to become an artist, and he was still more delighted to discover that May's teacher was Salisbury Tuckerman, who had been one of Bronson's pupils at the Temple School.[41]

Louisa was highly conscious of the changes she was undergoing, and as she told her journal, she could see that Lizzie's death and Anna's betrothal had "taken a deep hold, and changed or developed me." She believed that the soul of her dead sister was powerfully with her and was giving her the strength she had asked for in her memorial poem. "Lizzie helps me spiritually," she wrote, "and a little success makes me more self-reliant." Her recent trials had also brought her instinctively nearer to God. "When feeling most alone," she declared, "I find refuge in the Almighty Friend. If this is experiencing religion I have done it."[42] Nevertheless, as was more than once the case, she was slow to acknowledge the human help that had benefited her. Shortly after Bronson returned to Concord, she wrote, "Now that Mother is too tired to be wearied with my moods, I have to manage them alone, and am learning that work of head and hand is my salvation when disappointment or weariness burden and darken my soul."[43] It is mildly ironic that Louisa was to become an author who uniquely celebrated the sustaining and strengthening power of family. While it is almost impossible to consider her apart from her family, she often found it important to represent her personal triumphs as solitary achievements, whose critical motivation came from within. Undeniably, there was to be much truth in her self-perception as the family savior. Yet it is remarkable to observe the extent to which she preferred to give support than to receive it.

Louisa's story for *The Atlantic*, "Love and Self-Love," can be read as veiled autobiography.[44] Though narrated from the viewpoint of a man, Basil Ventnor, it is just as much the story of an orphaned sixteen-year-old named Effie Home. Rejected by a wealthy grandfather who did not approve of her parents' marriage, Effie touches the charitable nature of Ventnor, a man twice her age. Persuaded that they are too close in age for him to adopt her without exciting scandal, Ventnor fulfills the last request of Effie's dying guardian and marries the teenager. Effie falls in love with Ventnor. However, he is unable to return her love on an equal basis, partly because he sees his relationship to her as a matter of self-abnegating duty and partly because his heart belongs to a former lover, Agnes, who has thrown him over for another man. Moreover, Ventnor egotistically imagines that, because he has given Effie his name and protection, he owes her nothing more. The relationship becomes progressively unequal.

Unexpectedly, Agnes returns, now widowed and seeking to rekindle her former romance. The intimacy of Ventnor and Agnes soon becomes too much for Effie to bear. One moonlit evening, as the three glide downstream in a rowboat and the two older lovers relive their romantic past, Effie impulsively plunges into the water. His conscience suddenly awakened, Ventnor plunges in and rescues her. Effie hovers near death for weeks. When she returns to health, Ventnor finds her nature fundamentally changed. As Alcott tells it, "The *child* Effie lay dead beneath the ripples of the river, but the *woman* rose up from that bed of suffering like one consecrated to life's high duties by the bitter baptism of that dark hour."[45] She becomes a perfectly dutiful, if emotionally remote, spouse. Unable to love the girl, Ventnor gradually discovers that he reveres and admires the woman. Determined to give Effie her freedom, he sends her back to her grandfather and secretly prepares to dissolve their marriage. Before he can do so, however, he loses his fortune. Hearing of his distress, Effie comes back to him, and the two proclaim their mutual affection; each is now capable of both duty and passion. Effie reveals that her grandfather has died, leaving her his entire estate, and all ends blissfully.

By ambiguously presenting Ventnor as potentially either a father or a lover, "Love and Self-Love" implies a perilous choice regarding the categories of affection. It suggests that two people who fail initially to achieve a deep connection can nevertheless find satisfaction if they start again on a less volatile basis of respect and duty. "Love and Self-Love" speaks as eloquently of the maturing relationship between Bronson and Louisa as anything she ever wrote, and great significance lies in the fact that she wrote the story as her relationship with her family was emerging from crisis and near the time when she briefly considered suicide. "Love and Self-Love," of course, also describes a suicide attempt, but that attempt is not really about physical death. Rather, it concerns the death of an immature spiritual self, which departs only to be replaced by a wiser, more resilient soul.

The resurrected, wiser Effie finds that deep feelings need not seek exuberant expression. She eventually achieves the acceptance she craves, but only after she has mastered the art of self-control. Louisa's moment at the Mill Dam seems to have marked a similar crossroads in the development of her emotional nature. Like Effie with regard to Ventnor, she had previously sought to elicit from her father an effusive response that he was not capable of giving. Indeed, it can be argued that Louisa's youthful romanticism placed her in an analogous relation with the world at large. She wanted to embrace life, and she wanted life to receive her and her talents with passionate enthusiasm. She did not realize at once that the world is, at bottom, phlegmatic, and that, for most of us, impressing it takes much more patience and effort than she had thus far dedicated to that purpose.

Had Bronson read between the lines of "Love and Self-Love," he would perhaps have detected some insights into his own psychology. Although Louisa portrays Ventnor as a man of fine charitable instincts, she represents his apparent unselfishness as a symptom of a deeper narcissism. Shunning the world, engrossing himself in his books, Ventnor appears to be a man of modest appetites. However, Ventnor deems himself superior to others precisely because of his ability to resist pleasure. Through her portrayal of Ventnor, Louisa makes the incisive point that self-discipline, pursued so obsessively that it harms and alienates others, is its own species of sinful self-absorption. No one had taught Louisa this lesson more effectively than her father.

As she passed her twenty-sixth birthday, Louisa was far from deciding that life was sweet and wonderful merely because her fortunes had taken a momentarily upward turn. She was prepared to treat life as an absurd joke and to proceed on that basis, accepting irony as a means of greeting adversity on its own bitter terms. She voiced her satirical outlook in a letter to Anna in which she suggested that the allegedly all-wise Creator might do well to begin again from scratch:

> As the poet remarks, "Life is a strife, 'tis a struggle, 'tis a dream," and if he goes on to say it were also "a bubble," I should feel gratified and sincerely hope some sportive young angel should smash said bubble in his

infantine glee and the Almighty bubble-blowing company would start another with rather more of the soothing properties of soap & a little less salt water, one less empty and shiny and one one [*sic*] which there wasn't such a tendency to slip and pitch, to say nothing of falling off into space & being seen no more.[46]

Anna thought the passage funny and copied it into a letter to Bronson. There is no sure way of telling whether he saw through the humorous gloss and into the cynical nihilism beneath. In any event, it must have pleased him to know that his stormiest child was making people laugh again.

Bronson received this letter on the road, during another tour of the West. Louisa remarked that he had set out full of hope. "Dear man!" she observed. "How happy he will be if people will only listen to and *pay* for his wisdom."[47] Western excursions were becoming something of a habit with him, and if they still did not bring the profits he imagined, he always seemed to locate high-minded persons generous enough to house him and cover his expenses. He outfitted himself simply and carried his own bags.[48] In the homes of his hosts, he found warm fires to sit by and babies to play with. To Anna, as well as to others, her father's ability to inspire kindness and receive blessings seemed a sort of ongoing miracle. She asked, "Doesn't it sometimes seem as though Providence took trusting spirits like your own into his especial keeping, and smoothed the rough places, or is it that people who 'live in the clouds' don't so much mind the little troubles that beset us of the earthly mould?"[49] Anna knew no better way to account for her father. He was a lily of the field, one of the rarest species of holy fool. Those who loved him learned to emphasize the adjective instead of the noun.

By mid-December, Bronson was in Chicago. On this trip, he admitted, his expectations were moderate. Everyone seemed pinched for money, and he hoped only to "glean something as we go." He sent home an unspecified amount of money for the holidays, apologizing that its meagerness was "in keeping with our humble fortunes." In a wan, philosophic tone, he added, "Blessed be *something* to those who have so long waited for *nothing*."[50] He felt the sadness of knowing that the first Christmas at Orchard House would pass without him. He wrote to Louisa in Boston and urged her to make up for his own absence, "to run up and warm the House of Seven Gables and as many fireplaces." He took pride, he said, in her enterprise and courage, and he advised her to make her Christmas visit to Concord as long as possible, and make "the house joyous to its inmates all."[51]

Louisa honored her father's wish, though her mother and Anna disagreed in their description of her visit. Abba wrote to Bronson, "Louisa is with us and we are having cosy times. She is not very well and is enjoying the freedom of her home and the joys of rest, rest."[52] Anna's account described a much more vivacious visitor. She related that Louisa had come "bringing news, gossip, & fun, enough to keep us laughing the whole time, & doing us heaps of good into the bargain."[53] Louisa surprised everyone by saying that she did not want to go back to Boston and was quite willing to stay longer if only her obligations did not call her away. Abba and Anna reluctantly let her go.[54]

"The past year," Bronson wrote in early 1859, "has changed the aspects of life to us all."[55] With Lizzie's death and Anna's betrothal, it had seemed to Louisa at various times in 1858 that the family would dissolve. To the contrary, it had reformed itself on a different basis, and as the year ended, all were appreciative of one another's strengths and confident of one another's love. But if, as 1859 began, the Alcotts seemed able to withstand all challenges, the greater Union of the United States inspired far less confidence. Before the year had run its course, the mounting disquietude over slavery would erupt into violence, and the repercussions would be felt within the Alcotts' closest circle.

It was a hard winter for Abba, who became seriously ill in January. Anna took over the housekeeping but wished her sisters, both in Boston, could be with her to take the gloom out of the dismal days.[56] Louisa responded, coming home for a week to ease Anna's burdens and take care of their mother. She began to wonder whether nursing might be her true calling. Bronson wrote that necessity alone prevented him from hastening to Abba's side. He called it "good and true" of Louisa to have come so quickly when needed.[57] He was at a loss to explain the urge that sent him forth on his tours when he suspected that his usefulness and welcome would always be greatest at home. He was, perhaps, as perplexed as anyone by his life of "wandering thus far from one's fireside and chambers, to sit solitary often and strange in strangers' houses and companies to which one feels drawn by sympathies he is sometimes ashamed to own, and yet is fated to admit."[58] He perhaps sensed that, to continue thinking independently, he had to keep moving independently as well. In choosing the road over his hearth and study, he continually chose the harder path, as if deep armchair comfort were a kind of death to the spirit.

Abba was evidently better by the time her husband came back from his journey in early March.[59] Bronson was very much of two minds about the inland regions of the country. On the one hand, he found everywhere "in this wide West . . . earnest men and women, seeking faith if they have lost it, or [e]stablishing themselves as they may in the little they have chanced to keep."[60] And yet the turgid streams, the sparse cornfields, and the dreary monotony of the prairie depressed him. The flatness of the land seemed mirrored in the flat speech of its inhabitants. Was there not a flatness of the mind at work as well? Travel for a month in that wild country, he claimed, "and you shall come round home, whatever you were at starting, the Cynic confirmed, the Skeptic and the Sloven, in spite of yourself."[61] On coming home, he observed, "I perceive that I am neither a planter of the backwoods, pioneer, nor settler there, but an inhabitant of the Mind, and given to friendship and ideas. The ancient society, the Old England of New England, Massachusetts for me."[62]

The trip had tired him out. He spent the early spring reading over old books and putting his garden back in order, always a task of some magnitude after a New England winter. Meanwhile, Louisa was taking pleasure in the praise she was receiving for a new story, "Mark Field's Mistake," published in the *Saturday Evening Gazette.* She was busy with teaching, writing, sewing, and gathering all the available benefits of lectures, books, and good people. She wrote that life was her college. She hoped to graduate well and earn some honors.[63] In April, she finished her teaching for the spring, with the hope that she would never again have to stand before a classroom. The qualities that had made her father a remarkable teacher—his patience, his love of trying new methods, and his fascination with the slow, mysterious progress of children—were ones she had not inherited.

At almost the same time that Louisa was grumbling to her journal about the miseries of teaching, Bronson received news that heralded his improbable return to the profession after an absence of twenty years. On April 7, Franklin Sanborn came to Orchard House to announce that the town's school board, under Sanborn's leadership, had decided to offer Alcott the position of superintendent of the Concord schools. The job would require him to pay periodic visits to the town's schools and report to the board at its monthly meetings. The salary was a paltry one hundred dollars a year. Nevertheless, it was the first regular employment that Alcott had had since the closing of his last school in 1839. Bronson said he would accept only if the board were willing to allow him the freedom of action to make the job truly his own, and if they accepted that he would discharge his duties in a manner consistent with his own ideas on education. The committee, certainly at Sanborn's insistence, assented, and Bronson became a paid employee of the town that had never known quite what to do with him.

In May, Sanborn played host to an extraordinary guest. Sanborn's friend immediately struck Bronson with his simplicity and sense. He seemed to impress everyone with his courage and religious earnestness. He had a sharply angled jaw and a curious wildness in his blue-gray eyes. He let people know that he and his younger traveling companion, Jeremiah Anderson, were armed and would defend themselves if necessary. On May 8 the visitor spoke at the town hall, and the next morning Concord murmured and speculated about the ideas and intentions of Captain John Brown. Brown had also spoken in Concord two years earlier, in March 1857. At that time, however, Alcott was in New Haven. Thus, when he went to hear Brown, Bronson knew the speaker only by reputation. It was a reputation for mingling the highest of motives with the most horrible of means.

Like Bronson, Brown was a native of Connecticut. He had lived much of his life in Ohio and had failed in a variety of business ventures. Following the murder of an antislavery newspaper editor in Alton, Illinois, in 1837, Brown had stood up at a prayer meeting in Ohio and consecrated his life to the destruction of slavery. Not until he moved to Kansas in the mid-1850s, however, could Brown begin to carry out his vow. When he arrived, the territory was already plunged into violence over the question of whether it would enter the Union as a free or slave state. David Rice Atchison, a proslavery senator from Missouri, thought it would be a good idea "to kill every God-damned abolitionist in the territory."[64] The territory's proslavery legislature, seated by a corrupt election, had passed laws making it a crime to express opinions against slavery. Long before their father came to join them, John Brown's sons, all staunch abolitionists, had considered it wise to carry weapons on all occasions.[65] On May 21, 1856, a mob of about eight hundred proslavery Missourians attacked the free-soil stronghold of

The earliest known photograph of Captain John Brown,
whom Louisa called "St. John the Just."
(Courtesy of the National Portrait Gallery)

Lawrence, looting shops and homes, burning the hotel, and destroying the two newspaper offices. Enraged by this attack and further goaded by news of Preston Brooks's infamous caning of Charles Sumner on the floor of the United States Senate, Brown and his sons swore vengeance. During the night of May 24–25, with the help of three other men, they abducted five proslavery men from their homes near Pottawatomie Creek. Under Brown's direction, his band then executed their captives with broadswords. Two years later, Brown and his followers gunned down a slaveholder, liberated eleven blacks, and escorted them to Canada.

At the time of Fruitlands, while Bronson Alcott refused to wear wool for fear of committing an offense against the sheep, John Brown had made his living as a wool trader and had also dabbled in the cattle business. One can only imagine the righteous invectives that Alcott would have spewed forth on hearing of such a man. And yet, when Brown stood before him at Concord Town Hall not as a defrauder of sheep but as a killer of men, Alcott lauded him as a hero. He pasted a large portrait of Brown into his journal and lionized him as "a disciple of the right, an idealist in thought and affairs of state." Alcott called him "about the manliest man I have ever seen." If Alcott was at all troubled by Brown's criminal past, he suppressed his scruples. Such a magnificent child of nature, Alcott concluded, was "superior to legal traditions."[66]

Alcott's transcendental brethren also worshipped Brown. In the words of Walt Whitman, Emerson came out for Brown "with the power, the overwhelmingness, of an avalanche."[67] Thoreau claimed Brown as a fellow transcendentalist and called his activities in Kansas "the public practice of Humanity." In Brown's determination to obey only the law of freedom, Emerson and Thoreau saw their theoretical principles translated into sublime activism. But it was more than this. For long, frustrating years, most opponents of slavery in America had worked within the bounds of the law and followed the meek, forgiving doctrines of Christ. They had always hoped that patience and compromise on their parts would inspire commensurate concessions from the South. Instead, they had seen African Americans yanked from their midst and sent south to be enslaved without having a chance to defend themselves. They had seen a senator beaten senseless in the Capitol. They had watched as a slaveholding chief justice proclaimed that a Negro had no rights that a white man was bound to respect. By 1859, countless despisers of slavery, Emerson, Thoreau, and Alcott included, had had enough of turning the other cheek. In Brown, they had an advocate whose religion told him not to forgive, but to strike back in holy vengeance. Where the first wrong was the enslavement of four million Americans, they were prepared to test whether a second wrong could make a right.

At the town hall, Bronson was proud to shake Brown's hand. A month later, when Alcott heard rumors that his friend Frank Sanborn was supplying aid to Brown, he noted the fact with approval in his journal. He was not yet aware that Sanborn, Theodore Parker, and Thomas Higginson were all members of the "Secret Six," the half dozen men who were Brown's strongest backers.

Later, in the autumn, Louisa too was eager for a fight. In September, as part of an event called the Great State Encampment, young men in uniform performed military maneuvers and drills near Concord. As she watched them, Louisa grumbled about the limitations of gender that denied her the kind of action she most desired. "I like a camp, and long for a war, to see how it all seems," she wrote. "I can't fight, but I can nurse."[68] She did not know that Captain Brown was about to bring her wish perilously close to coming true.

At the head of his journal entry for October 23, 1859, Bronson wrote the words "Capt. John Brown" in red ink.[69] It was his first reference to the raid on Harpers Ferry, Virginia, carried out by Brown and a company of twenty-one men on October 16. Brown had planned to seize the town's arsenal, liberate its slave population, and then lead an ever-increasing force of freed blacks and antislavery sympathizers through the Virginia mountains, cutting a swath of liberty through the southern states. He thought that a sustained campaign of abolitionist violence could break the will of the slaveholding society and bring an end to the hated institution. He miscalculated tragically. When Brown chose Harpers Ferry as the starting point for his revolution, he failed to realize what a series of Civil War generals later discovered: that the town, while easily captured, was virtually impossible to defend. Once federal forces had been summoned to the area—under the command of Colonel Robert E. Lee—the fate of the insurrection was sealed. Less than two days after the raid began, it was crushed, and the man whom Bronson had called "the type and synonym of the Just" was a prisoner.[70] As soon as he received the news, Alcott grasped "the impossibility of any justice being done" to Brown."[71]

Brown's capture touched off a whirlwind of activity in Concord. Louisa wrote to Alf Whitman, now living in Kansas, "We are boiling over with excitement here for many of our people . . . are concerned in it."[72] Each night there was a meeting to express indignation at the wickedness of the country and the frailty of human courage. Abba was perhaps the most agitated of the family; Louisa was afraid she would "die of spontaneous combustion" if things were not set right soon.[73] But setting things right was impossible. Alcott, Thoreau, and Sanborn racked their brains to determine what, if anything, could be done for the captive. Thoreau wrote an eloquent speech, which he called "A Plea for Captain John Brown." Alcott initially favored a dramatic covert operation. He calculated that there was enough courage and intrepidity among Massachusetts men that one could muster a band "to steal South, since they cannot march openly there, and rescue him from the slaveholders, the states and the United States Courts, and save him from the impending crisis."[74] After reflection, however, he changed his mind. Not only would it be virtually impossible to penetrate the armory where Brown was being held, but it was by no means sure that Brown, who had long ago accepted the possibility of martyrdom, would consent to being liberated. Furthermore, Alcott reasoned, "the spectacle of a martyrdom such as his must needs be . . . of greater service to the country, and to the coming in of a righteous rule, than years and tens of years of agitation by the press."[75]

Thoreau and Sanborn both advised diplomacy. They talked of sending an emissary to Virginia to seek an interview with Governor Wise. Sanborn in particular thought Bronson possessed "some advantages" that made him the man for this work.[76] Presumably, Sanborn was thinking of the mildness of Alcott's demeanor, which might mitigate the impression created by Brown's fiery words and countenance. In addition, Alcott's experience in the ways of southern gentility might help to sway the governor. Sanborn even entertained the outlandish idea that, while dealing with Wise, Alcott might simultaneously contact Brown and hatch an escape plot. There was much talking and planning. There was no action. All they were finally able to agree on was an impressive memorial service on December 2, the day of Brown's execution. Sanborn read a dirge that he had written, Thoreau read poetry, Alcott read from the Bible and from Plato, and Emerson read from Brown's own writings. Never at a loss for words, they seemed at a loss for anything else.

From the career and martyrdom of John Brown, Bronson took important lessons, both political and personal. They reminded him that one might more effectively change the world by acting in it instead of writing, talking, or withdrawing into a position of ascetic refusal. They also proved that, despite their contradictions, a righteous spirit and a violent nature might exist within the same person. The warrior spirit had always struck Bronson as a primitive trait, needing to be mastered as one strove upward from humanness to a more angelic form. He found it hard to believe that the most important struggle in a life might be against an outward enemy rather than an inner one. Nevertheless, Brown showed him that the fighter, just as much as the self-denying saint, could deserve respect and love.

Bronson's feelings toward a fighter in his own family can be seen in a journal entry he wrote later that winter. On February 17, he brought home the March issue of *The Atlantic Monthly*, which included "Love and Self-Love." He gave it to Louisa, he said, "to encourage and lead her to some appreciation of the fair destiny that awaits her if she will be true to her gifts as she has begun." His delight, of course, was shared by Abba. Bronson seemed to sense that, somehow, the character and struggles of his wife would figure largely in Louisa's prose. In the same entry, he wrote that Abba was "a heroine in her ways, and with a deep experience, all tested and awaiting her daughter's pen." Before closing up his diary for the night, he added, thinking of Louisa, "I am pleased, and proud of thee."[77]

Five months after Brown's execution, Brown's widow came to Concord, and the Alcotts held a reception for her at Orchard House. She arrived with her daughter-in-law, whose husband Watson Brown had been killed while fighting alongside his father at Harpers Ferry. The younger woman also brought her infant son, Frederick Watson Brown, who Louisa thought was "a fair, heroic-looking baby" as befitted his lineage. Louisa kissed the child as she would have greeted a little saint, and she felt honored when he sucked her fingers. In the face of Watson Brown's widow, Louisa saw all the heartbreak of bitter sacrifice.

The homespun dignity of the guests of honor clashed absurdly with the unexpected chaos of the event. Word of the visit had leaked to the community, and the house was soon crammed with twice the number of the invited guests. As the polite supper transformed into a "tea fight," Louisa bravely marshaled the cake and tea, making sure that the regular antislavery stalwarts were served first. She would have gladly done much more to honor the memory of the man she called St. John the Just.

Only a few days before the reception for Mrs. Brown, the parlor of Orchard House had been the scene of a more sedate and far happier occasion. On May 23, thirty years to the day after her father and mother were wed, Anna had married John Pratt. Bronson was pleased to record that the day was "all grace and becomingness," and he took both the sunshine and the luxuriant blossoms in his apple orchard as strong omens for the couple's happiness.[78] Orchard House was filled with "flowers, friends and happiness," as Louisa put it.[79] Elizabeth Palmer Peabody, her quarrels with Bronson now a distant memory, was in attendance. Sanborn, Thoreau, and the Emersons were all present to hear Uncle Samuel May offer a prayer and join the couple in matrimony. Louisa recalled that he performed the rites "with no fuss, but much love, and we all stood round her."[80] Anna wore a silver-gray silk dress, and her bodice and hair were adorned with lilies of the valley, her new husband's favorite flower. Louisa, also in gray and bedecked with roses, humorously likened her costume to sackcloth and ashes; she still could not think of the day as entirely joyous. "I mourn the loss of my Nan," she wrote, "and am not comforted."[81] The wedding party enjoyed a feast sent by Hope Shaw, the wife of the chief justice. Then, on the front lawn, beneath the ancient elms, the assembled relatives and heroes of transcendentalism danced in a circle around the newlyweds. Louisa called it a pretty picture to remember. As Anna and John were preparing to leave, Emerson begged permission to kiss the bride. To Louisa, it seemed that a kiss from such a man, who remained the god of her idolatry, would make even matrimony worthwhile.[82] Bronson also felt profoundly the alteration of his family circle. In his mind, joy and sorrow, hope and fear for his good child mingled in a befuddling fashion. "I cannot yet write about it," he told his journal. All the conflicting emotions that he wanted to put onto paper came out only as, "Ah! Anna."[83] The couple set up housekeeping in Chelsea, north of Boston, though Anna was never away from Concord for very long.

The next month was marked by a farewell. On June 17, Louisa attended a memorial service in Boston for Theodore Parker, who had lost his battle with tuberculosis in Florence, Italy, a few weeks earlier. There was no man apart from Emerson and Thoreau whom Louisa admired more, and she was grateful that he had called her his friend. Bronson, too, felt the loss, for he knew of no one who could take up the minister's work and carry it forward. June was also the time of a return. On the twenty-eighth, the Hawthornes came back to Concord, and the Alcotts soon had to accustom themselves to the strange habits of the author whose compulsive interest in observing human behavior verged on the voyeuristic. To Louisa, Hawthorne seemed as queer as ever. It was certainly unnerving to catch glimpses of him darting through the hills or skimming by as if he expected the House of Alcott to reach out and clutch him. For his part, the novelist was too shy and introspective to share Bronson's inexhaustible love of conversation. He also could not have felt entirely at ease in the radical political atmosphere of Lexington Road. Since his college days at Bowdoin, Hawthorne had been a bosom friend of Franklin Pierce, who had occupied the White House for four years as a proslavery Democrat. Like Pierce, whose friendship certainly colored his own political views, Hawthorne felt it was wrong to jeopardize the Union over the question of emancipation, which he viewed as a local issue. As for John Brown, Hawthorne thought no man had ever been more justly hanged. It is likely that, in his conversations with the other literary lions of the town, he acquired some practice in biting his tongue.

He was less guarded as to his opinions within his own family. Once, at the behest of his children, Hawthorne poked fun at his neighbor in a poem aping the style of Edward Lear:

> There lived a Sage at Appleslump
> Whose dinner never made him plump;
> Give him carrots, potatoes, squash, turnips and peas,
> And a handful of crackers without any cheese,
> And a cup of cold water to wash down all these,
> And he'd prate of the Spirit as long as you please,
> This airy Sage of Appleslump.[84]

Hawthorne's wife, the former Sophia Peabody, made periodic social overtures to Abba and always seemed to be on the scene when the Alcotts most needed a helpful neighbor. However, she could hardly have forgotten that she was dealing with the man and woman who had pried into her sister Elizabeth's private correspondence, and she was less than fond of Abba's notorious temper. The Hawthorne children were a mixed lot in Louisa's eyes. She had little good to say about sixteen-year-old Una, whose only talent seemed to be horseback riding. She regarded Rose, the baby of the family, as an attractive child with an artistic look. Since she always liked boys best, it is not surprising that Louisa saved her warmest regards for Julian, "a worthy boy full of pictures, fishing rods and fun."[85] As she was forming her opinions of the Hawthorne children, they were looking back at her, and not without discernment.

More than sixty years later, Julian Hawthorne wrote a pair of short memoirs of the days when his family and the Alcotts were neighbors. Somewhat distorted by a fading memory and still more by an inclination to fictionalize, Julian's recollections are only intermittently reliable. However, his mental image of Louisa remained clear. When he first met her, she was "a black-haired, red-cheeked, long-legged hobbledehoy of 28," though she seemed much younger to him. He observed "power in her jaw and control in her black eyes," and he considered her a natural leader. He recalled her honesty, her common sense, and her inherent grasp of comedy and humor. Like her sisters, she was jolly and wholly un-Platonic. How she had come from a father like Bronson, he could not imagine.[86] Especially dear to Julian's memory was the mildly racy practice of coed swimming in Walden Pond, in which he and his sisters indulged with Louisa, Abby May, and the Emerson children. These encounters stirred his romantic interest in Abby, and some rather restricted Victorian lovemaking reportedly ensued. The young Hawthorne felt no romantic yearnings for Louisa, who was four-teen years his senior, though it puzzled him that, to his knowledge, she had never had a love affair. The only explanation he could give was that her self-control was even greater than her capacity for passion, and that she could set aside personal happiness "for what she deemed just cause."[87]

More and more often, the cause for which Louisa put aside more care-free amusements was her writing, an activity that now sometimes absorbed her to an almost alarming degree. Louisa had a name for the kind of cre-ative fit that enabled her to produce prodigious amounts of writing in com-pressed periods of time. Such a mood, she said, was a "vortex," a revealing term for the state into which she periodically descended. Louisa's most detailed description of this descent came in an intensely autobiographical chapter in *Little Women*. In the passage below, Louisa's fictitious counter-part Jo March flings herself into her first novel with single-minded fury:

> Every few weeks she would shut herself up in her room, put on her scribbling suit, and "fall into a vortex," as she expressed it, writing away at her novel with all her heart and soul, for till that was finished she could find no peace. . . . When the writing fit came on, she gave herself up to it with entire abandon, and led a blissful life, unconscious of want, care, or bad weather, while she sat safe and happy in an imaginary world, full of friends almost as real and dear to her as any in the flesh. Sleep for-sook her eyes, meals stood untasted, day and night were all too short to enjoy the happiness which blessed her only at such times. . . . The divine afflatus usually lasted a week or two, and then she emerged from her "vortex" hungry, sleepy, cross, or despondent.[88]

To describe her creative process, Louisa used the imagery of a whirlpool, with its connotations of downward spiral and chaos. Time and again in the western literary tradition, wandering seekers after truth and love—Orpheus, Odysseus, Aeneas, Dante—must descend into Hell before their quests can be fulfilled. For Louisa, the search for artistic excellence also involved a chaotic descent. In her downward plunges, however, she did not experience feelings of anguish or torment. Falling into the vortex was, for her, a lone but exhilarating mental journey into the heart of wonder.

Louisa's headlong rushes into creativity, followed by periods of irritable despondency, seem to have been the pattern of activity that she found most conducive to her art. However, they also signified a turbulence that would express itself again and again through the course of her career. She found it impossible to do anything by half measures. At this early moment in her creative life, when she was young and strong, she could manage these vortices without ill consequences. She would not always be able to make such demands on herself without paying the price.

In December 1860, May's zeal for independence led her to look beyond Massachusetts. Like Anna before her, she went to Syracuse to live with her Uncle Samuel and, like a good Alcott, take her turn as a schoolmistress. Louisa escorted her to Boston on the first leg of her journey. The lonesome feeling of watching this youngest bird leave the nest was relieved somewhat when Emerson invited Louisa to hear him speak on the subject of Genius—a clear indication that he regarded her as a respectable intellect. Nevertheless, a palpable dreariness descended over Orchard House. In May's absence, Louisa and her parents passed a quiet Christmas, having only flowers and apples to exchange as gifts. There was no merrymaking, with Anna and May both elsewhere and Lizzie resting under the snow. Ironically, her parents had finally found a permanent family home, just in time to watch that family disperse. Louisa's own irony was still sharper. The sister with the deepest talents and the fiercest ambition, she was finding it hardest to claim an independent life in the world.

As Louisa closed her journal for the year 1860 and wondered whether greater chances would come her way, Bronson wrote to his mother about her, observing, "She is not wanting in Talent and Character. I see nothing to prevent her becoming a favorite with the public, as she becomes generally known. Her mother hopes good things of her,—in which hope her father certainly joins." And he wrote that her book was nearly ready.[89]

CHAPTER ELEVEN

WAR

"Action and blood now get the game.
Disdain treads on the peaceful name."
—A. BRONSON ALCOTT, *Journals*, 1863

THE YEAR 1861, WHICH WAS TO MARK A CATACLYSM IN American history, began quietly at Orchard House. Upstairs, Louisa busied herself with the manuscript of a full-length novel that she had provisionally called "Success," a title she no doubt hoped would prove prophetic. After sending Anna and her husband a book on marriage titled *Faithful Forever*, Bronson sampled his home-brewed hard cider and brought bottles around to the neighbors. The Hawthornes marked the new year by giving Bronson and Abba a wooden bread dish, which Bronson described as "ornamented with wheat ears and very pretty."[1] Louisa herself received thirteen New Year's gifts, including a pen, a mince pie, and a bonnet. She was moved to remark on the "most uncommon fit of generosity [that has] seemed to seize people on my behalf."[2] Emerson, too, continued in his generous ways. Whenever the family seemed more pinched than usual, a small sum would magically appear from under a book or behind a candlestick. Although Emerson tried to keep his contributions to the Alcotts' fortunes anonymous, Louisa was not fooled for a second. Of the thirty dollars that Bronson earned that January from a series of conversations at Emerson's house, she guessed that twenty had been slipped into the till by Emerson himself. Louisa was grateful for Emerson's "sweet way of bestowing gifts," and she wrote admiringly, "A true friend is this tender and illustrious man."[3]

Louisa had to break off her work on "Success" when her mother became briefly but seriously ill. When she got back to writing in February, it was not "Success" but the manuscript of another embryonic novel, *Moods*, that absorbed her attention. Nothing else that Louisa ever wrote seized her imagination and energies as much as *Moods*. When writing the first draft of the novel the previous August, she confessed to being "quite possessed by my work." She descended into her "vortex" on February 2 and remained there twenty-three days, during which time she found sleep almost impossible. Except for a daily run on the country roads at dusk, Louisa barely rose from her writing desk. Abba, initially stirred by Louisa's excitement, made her daughter an actual thinking cap out of green silk and red ribbon. Later, however, Abba came to view her daughter's single-mindedness with anxious concern. Thirty years of marriage to a compulsive writer had not prepared her for a daughter who almost forgot to eat when her muse was in view. Abba tried to be helpful, making sure, for instance, that a steady supply of tea made its way upstairs, but her requests that Louisa join the family for meals were seldom granted. Midway between admiration and sarcasm, May observed from a distance that her sister was "living for immortality."[4]

Bronson was captivated by Louisa's creative intensity. He pronounced his daughter's dedication "fine," and he brought up "his reddest apples and hardest cider for [Louisa's] Pegasus to feed upon." Her headlong, single-minded passion appealed strongly to him, just as her refusals of food and sleep resonated with his ascetic temperament. On those rare occasions when she did come down to supper, he was delighted by the "dashes of wit and amusement" with which she stirred up "us chimney corner-ancients."[5] Louisa wrote that all kinds of fun was going on in Orchard House and that, for all she cared, the world might dissolve into chaos as long as she and her inkstand alit in the same place. Down in his study, Bronson too was writing with purpose. He had begun to conceive a book on the philosophical dimensions of horticulture, in which the garden would serve as an extended metaphor for the fertile and well-cultivated mind. He was in marvelous spirits, for it seemed he had finally found a subject that might satisfy both his philosophical interest and a reading public. Happily, he wrote to May that he was getting something good to show for his season's work.[6]

At the end of her vortex, Louisa was exhausted. She "found that [her] mind was too rampant for [her] body . . . [her] head was dizzy, legs shaky."7 There can be no doubt that she saw dramatic similarities between herself and the heroine of her story, Sylvia Yule, an impetuous young woman who seemed incapable of controlling the fits of strong emotion that periodically seized control of her, and whose efforts to fit in were continually thwarted by her rebellious impulses. When Louisa looked over what she had written, she was aware that the manuscript was still not in the shape she wanted and that much more revision was in store. But whereas one vortex was sufficient for many of her books, not even two could do the trick for *Moods*. Louisa continued to write and rewrite *Moods* even after its publication in 1864. She was not to publish the last, definitive version of the novel until 1882. It was a project she could neither perfect nor abandon.

Although the book never completely pleased her—none of her work ever did—Louisa nevertheless felt a sense of achievement when she put down her pen on February 25, 1861. The fact that she had produced a complete manuscript was ample reason to feel satisfied, but her greatest triumph of the winter came when she plucked up her courage and read the manuscript aloud to her family. The reaction was better than she dared hope. The responses of both her mother and Anna were predictably sympathetic; the former pronounced the writing wonderful, and the latter laughed and wept, "as she always does," Louisa noted. To Louisa's delight, Bronson's verdict was the most emphatic of the three. He declared, "Emerson must see this. Where did you get your metaphysics?" Never mind the fact that to live almost thirty years under Bronson Alcott's roof without acquiring any metaphysics would have required fierce determination. What mattered was that she had spoken a language that had kindled a flame in her father's mind. Flush with the evening's success, she told her journal, "I had a good time, even if it never comes to anything, for it was worth something to have my three dearest sit up till midnight listening with wide-open eyes to Lu's first novel."8 For the time being, though, she was content to let *Moods* be a private victory. Although Emerson asked to read it, she was afraid to show it to him. She was still less prepared to look for a publisher.

Despite the Alcotts' happiness, the rest of the country was beset with brooding expectation. In late December 1860, South Carolina had seceded from the Union. In the ensuing months, ten more states would follow suit. As war appeared ever more likely, even a seemingly apolitical event like the annual Concord School Exhibition, held in March, could generate controversy. A few days after President Lincoln was inaugurated, Louisa dashed off a set of patriotic lyrics to be sung to the tune of "All the Blue Bonnets Are over the Border." She included the lines: "Here are our future men, / Here our John Browns again; / Here are young Philipses [*sic*] eyeing our blunders." Emerson pronounced the lyrics "very excellent." Much influenced by his eminent friend's opinion, Bronson hailed Louisa's effort as "the pride of his life" and arranged for it to be sung at the exhibition.

The mention of John Brown was enough to cause a flutter among the "old fogies," as Louisa called them, and an attempt was made to prevent the offending stanza from being sung. The attempted censorship stunned Bronson, especially because it was leveled at the daughter whose worth he was coming more and more to appreciate. Abba angrily denounced the entire town. Louisa was defiant; if the attendees would not sing the entire song, she would not let them sing any of it. Fortunately, Emerson rescued the situation. When Bronson suggested that it might be prudent to give in, he declared, "No, no, that [stanza] is the best. It must be sung, & not only sung but read. *I* will read it." And so he did, to the astonishment of the crowd and to Louisa's great surprise and pride.[9]

The festival was a grand success. Thoreau thought that the speeches and recitations of the young scholars reflected such credit on their superintendent that "Alcott is at present perhaps the most successful man in the town."[10] The gathering ended with a touching scene, orchestrated without the superintendent's knowledge. Frank Sanborn asked the crowd to stay for a moment while Bronson was invited to the stage. There, he was met by a tall, handsome boy who made a brief speech about the love, respect, and gratitude that the children felt for him. He then presented Bronson with fine new editions of George Herbert's poems and, inevitably, *The Pilgrim's Progress*. Bronson blushed, and his eyes filled with tears. He hugged the beautiful books tightly to his chest and managed a few words of thanks before the children rose to shout and applaud him. In Louisa's eyes, her father deserved all the adulation and more. She sent Anna a glowing account of the day, at first reporting that the festival had "stirred up the stupid town immensely." Then, realizing that this was the wrong occasion for pettiness, she crossed out the adjective.[11]

Secession brought troubled thoughts to the minds of Bronson's transcendental brethren. Normally the most peaceful of souls, they now confronted a moral problem whose only apparent solution demanded violence. As the crisis over Fort Sumter neared its decisive moment, Thoreau, who had been so galvanized by the raid on Harpers Ferry, now seemed to wish only that the bad news would go away. He wrote to his abolitionist friend Parker Pillsbury, "I hope [my prospective reader] *ignores* Fort Sumpter [*sic*], & Old Abe, & all that. . . . What business have you, if you are 'an angel of light' to be pondering over the deeds of darkness?"[12]

Four days after the first shot was fired, Emerson called the war "the most wanton piece of mischief that bad boys ever devised."[13] However, he soon took a more sympathetic view of the war fever. He started keeping a separate journal of his thoughts about the conflict, and in it he wrote, "I do not wish to abdicate so extensive a privilege as the use of the sword or the bullet. For the peace of the man who has forsworn the use of the bullet seems to me not quite peace." There were invisible scriptures, he said, that could be read only "by the light of war fires."[14]

When the war finally came in April with the firing on Fort Sumter, Bronson recorded the event in his journal with red ink. He believed that the cannonade over Charleston Harbor had done more for abolition in one day than Garrison and Phillips had accomplished in thirty years. Just as the battle at Concord Bridge in 1775 began a war that led to independence, Bronson was confident that Fort Sumter was the first engagement in a fight that "is to give us nationality."[15] Greatly simplifying the actual state of affairs, Bronson commented that the North's resolve was unanimous, and he pronounced this perceived unity of purpose "a victory in itself."[16] Lest any fool should doubt the Alcotts' sympathies in the conflict, the family took in John Brown's daughters as boarders.[17]

All at once, the Concord town common was thick with blue-coated recruits, fumbling to obey the orders of sergeants still trying to master the tones of command. Louisa, observing the strange goings-on, was amused by the amateurism of the newly enlisted soldiers. She wrote that the hapless recruits "poke each other's eyes out, bang their heads & blow themselves up with gunpowder most valiantly."[18] Although she derided their skill, however, Louisa admired their spirit. She was stirred by emotions both martial and maternal. She longed "to fly at some body & free my mind on several points," but in a softer moment she wrote: "[I]n a little town like this we all seem like one family in times like these."[19] Almost before anyone knew it, Concord's young men began to disappear, bound for what many imagined would be a brief summer of adventure and glory.

The families of the New England literati were by no means exempt from the call of battle. Emerson's son Edward formed a detachment of soldiers called the Concord Cadets. Garth Wilkinson James, a younger brother of William and Henry James and son of the older Henry, with whom Bronson still traded philosophical ripostes, also enlisted. The Alcott women, too, took up the cause; for the better part of a month after the outbreak of the war, Abba and Louisa could be found at Concord Town Hall, helping out with the sewing of some five hundred "patriotic blue shirts" for the soldiers. Louisa wrote to Alf Whitman that, after having done her share, she was more than happy to put down her needle and take up her pen, since the former tool was her abomination and the latter her delight.[20]

During these weeks, Louisa was struggling with a sense of personal insignificance, which her exclusion from the grand events of the war had heightened and which no amount of sewing could diminish. She told her journal, "I long to be a man; but as I can't fight, I will content myself with working for those who can." Yearning to do something to help defeat the "saucy southerners," she started spending her spare time curled up with a medical treatise on gunshot wounds. When she was able, she meant to take a turn at nursing in the Union army hospitals. Such appointments were not freely given and would require appealing to some social connections. Nevertheless, by the time the army had gotten itself into "a comfortably smashed condition," Louisa hoped she could answer the call.[21]

Meanwhile, the days dragged on. During the first winter of the war, still too pinched to refuse work, she took one last stab at teaching, this time at a kindergarten in the Warren Street Chapel in Boston. James T. Fields, publisher of *The Atlantic Monthly*, graciously lent Louisa forty dollars to outfit her classroom and convinced her to board with his family. Bronson wished her well, but he was privately skeptical. So long as she cared most about her books and studies, he did not see how she could succeed in teaching, "an art that demands the freedom of every gift for attaining its ends."[22] As he feared, the job proved both unpleasant and unprofitable, and Louisa was unable to pay back the cost of her board, let alone Fields's loan. To trim expenses, she tried moving back home and commuting from Concord. However, the daily round trip of forty miles quickly wore on her, and she was grateful when May agreed to fill in for the last month of the school term. Abba complained that the venture had been a swindle of Louisa's time and money, and Louisa dubbed it a "wasted winter."[23]

Despite this failure, and despite the fact that he had published "Love and Self-Love," Mr. Fields affronted Louisa's pride with a statement she never forgot. "Stick to your teaching," he bluntly advised her. "You can't write." He could hardly have hit on a surer way to stoke her determination. She replied hotly, "I won't teach, I can write, and I'll prove it."[24] She also quietly resolved to pay back his loan one day, if she had to sell her hair to do it. The one bright spot in the winter of 1861–62 was the circle of acquaintances Louisa made while residing with the Fields family. As a literary salon, James Fields's home rivaled the parlors of Concord, and his guests during Louisa's tenancy included Longfellow, Fanny Kemble, Oliver Wendell Holmes Sr., and Harriet Beecher Stowe. These were not threadbare, self-denying intellectuals like her father or Thoreau, but popular writers of high quality who had found ways to spin their art into gold. If Fields's suggestion that she stick to teaching had not confirmed her will to succeed as a writer, the experience of "living in style in a very smart house with very clever people" would probably have served the same end.[25]

Bronson found little to do to support the war effort directly. Although he never questioned the need for military force, violence was too foreign to his nature for him to find a place in explosive events of the moment. He found himself an aging pacifist whose theories of life suddenly seemed irrelevant. One morning, he overheard some neighborhood boys marching down Lexington Road like soldiers and declaring that they wished they had a chance to shoot the enemy. He asked them to wait a few minutes and returned with an armload of pumpkins. He invited the boys to gratify their warlike zeal by attacking the pumpkins. When they had worn themselves out with this play, he lectured them on the wickedness of their blood-thirsty passions.[26] When a neighborhood woman stitched together an American flag spangled not with stars but with hearts, Alcott assisted at its raising, delivering a little speech on the occasion.[27] Having no part to play in the hostilities, Bronson turned to the place where he continued to exert complete control: his garden. During the first winter of the war, he wrote voluminously in his journal on the subject of apple trees and, citing Confucius, argued that one who diligently sows the ground wins more merit than by reciting a thousand prayers.[28] It was the work of a man eager to consider himself useful.

Bronson closely followed the reports of battles, perusing the newspapers "with an avidity unknown before."[29] He agonized with each Union defeat and rejoiced with the victories that, at first, seemed all too few. Through the winter of 1861–62, he was a frequent visitor to Thoreau's house. Thoreau had gotten over his initial indifference to the war, and the two friends fulminated at what Thoreau called "the temporizing policy of our rulers." Frustrated by the failure to win a quick victory, Thoreau blamed the people "for their indifference to the true issues of national honor and justice."[30] After these discussions, however, Bronson's most deeply felt concern was not for the fate of the country but for the health of his comrade. Thoreau was dying.

His health troubles had begun in December 1860, when he contracted a bad cold that he may well have caught from Bronson. The cold had led to bronchitis. During the first half of 1861, in an attempt to regain his health, he had traveled west to Minnesota but had returned with symptoms of tuberculosis and an acceptance of the likelihood that he would die young. In recent months, the pace of the disease had quickened. Thoreau had last been able to visit Walden Pond in September. He had stopped writing in his journal in November. Now, in the new year, hope had faded entirely. Bronson spent the evening of New Year's Day 1862 with Thoreau and was "sad to find him failing and feeble."[31] Through the rest of the winter and into the spring, Bronson reported his friend's condition in his journal. The news was never good. On May 4, Alcott and the poet Ellery Channing, who had traveled with Thoreau on his excursions to Cape Cod and the Maine woods, paid one last visit to the bed from which their friend could no longer stir. Two afternoons later, Channing came to Orchard House with the word that the struggle was over. Soon after, Emerson also came to the Alcott home to commiserate. Bronson went as soon as he could to see Thoreau's mother, who told him about her son's last moments.

Thoreau's sister Sophia then took Alcott to his friend's chamber, where they gazed on the face of the dead man. But for its pallor, the face still looked alive.[32]

Emerson scandalized the portion of the town that regarded Henry as an infidel by arranging a church funeral for him. Thoreau had never been a churchgoer, and he himself would very likely have disapproved of Emerson's decision. Nevertheless, Emerson said his sorrow was so great that he wanted all the world to mourn with him. The day of the ceremony, May 9, was calm and clear, and as the mourners entered the churchyard, they were welcomed by the songs of birds and the sight of early violets blooming in the grass. Bronson, Louisa, and Anna all attended, and Bronson read aloud from Thoreau's works. Louisa was proud that her father was chosen to give the readings, and she found the church farewell fitting. She told her longtime friend Sophia Foord, "If ever a man was a real Christian it was Henry, & I think his own wise & pious thoughts read by one who loved him & whose own life was a beautiful example of religious faith, convinced many."[33]

Neither Bronson nor Louisa found it comfortable or proper to express their loss with extravagant displays. Although his journal mentions Channing's sadness, Bronson did not record his own reaction to Thoreau's death. After the funeral, Louisa kept busy with her stories—a handy reason, perhaps, for avoiding conversation. She asserted that she could never mourn for men like Thoreau "because they never seem lost to me but nearer & dearer for the solemn change."[34] She predicted that his life would blossom and bear fruit long after it was gone. Nevertheless, the void that Thoreau left behind was palpable, and it gave Louisa one less reason for remaining in Concord. Through the summer months, she turned out more of her vivid dramatic tales, which she considered silly but which found an eager reception from magazines like *The Monitor* and *Frank Leslie's Illustrated Newspaper*. For the latter, she submitted a tale called "Pauline's Passion and Punishment" in hopes of winning a one-hundred-dollar prize.

As the war entered its second summer, whatever anguish Bronson initially felt about its violence was giving way to his irresistible need to idealize. It was a tendency that people who had seen the war firsthand were likely to find absurd. Fresh from her brilliant literary debut, *Life in the Iron-Mills*, Rebecca Harding Davis came to Concord to meet Hawthorne.

At the Wayside she attended a dinner party with Alcott and Emerson that dimmed her view of transcendentalism in general and Alcott in particular. Before dinner, Alcott stood in front of the fireplace in Hawthorne's small parlor, proclaiming the war "an armed angel . . . awakening the nation to a lofty life unknown before." Waving his hands like the conductor of a one-man orchestra, he chanted his praise of the rifle and the sword, raised in a righteous cause. Davis, who came from Wheeling, Virginia, and was no great enemy of slavery, quietly took offense at Alcott's words and their "strained, high note of exaltation." She later wrote:

> I had just come up from the border where I had seen the actual war; the filthy spewings of it; the political jobbery . . . the malignant personal hatreds wearing patriotic masks, and glutted by burning homes and outraged women. . . . War may be an armed angel with a mission, but she has the personal habits of the slums.

*During the Civil War, novelist Nathaniel Hawthorne was
the Alcotts' remote and skittish next-door neighbor.
Bronson found "something of strangeness even
in his cherished intimacies."*
(Courtesy of the Louisa May Alcott Memorial Association)

Hawthorne, according to Davis, wore a look of mockery as he sat backward astride a chair, listening to Alcott's monologue. At last, he said gravely, "We cannot see this thing at so long a range," and he quietly conducted the party into the dining room.

Earlier in the day, Hawthorne had warned Davis about Alcott's obsession with vegetarianism. "You may begin at Plato or the day's news," Hawthorne told his guest, "and he will come around to pears. He is now convinced . . . that pears exercise a more direct and ennobling influence on us than any other vegetable or fruit." By the end of the meal, Alcott did indeed announce the spiritual influence of pears, and Hawthorne laughed aloud to see his prediction come true."[35] Yet although Davis thought him ridiculous, Alcott remained more sensitive to the sufferings of war than she knew. When he read the accounts of Antietam in September, the old feelings of helplessness and pity came back. He wrote, "What can one do but read the news and weep at our victories even?"[36]

For Louisa, a supreme test of confidence was drawing near. It was hastened, perhaps, by the news that Anna and John were expecting their first child, another sign that time was passing. "At twenty-five," Louisa would later write in *Little Women*, "girls begin to talk about being old maids, but secretly resolve that they never will; at thirty, they say nothing about it, but quietly accept the fact."[37] Louisa was to turn thirty on November 29, 1862. She had no interest in quietly accepting the fact. The notation in her journal for that month, "Thirty years old. Decide to go to Washington as a nurse if I could find a place," illustrates that the birthday and her redoubled desire to break out of old patterns were no coincidence. Uninterested in enlisting dewy-eyed young women heeding the call of romance instead of duty, Dorothea Dix, the head of the Union's nursing corps, had publicly announced that she would consider no applicants under thirty. Louisa had heard good reports of the facilities at the Armory Square Hospital in Washington. She hoped to rely on Hannah Stevenson, who had found Louisa a job in the aftermath of the latter's brush with suicide and who wielded some influence with the necessary authorities. Louisa sent in her name and, as she awaited a reply, made ready for a great change.

Louisa received her orders on the morning of December 11. She had not been assigned to the Armory Square but to a less desirable institution in Georgetown known as the Union Hotel Hospital, a place Louisa learned to refer to in jest as "The Hurly-Burly House." Louisa was to report for duty as soon as possible, and the rest of that Thursday was spent in a whirl of activity. Abba, Anna, and May, back from Syracuse, all helped to stuff Louisa's traveling bag with all there was of home that such a bag could carry. Sophia Hawthorne looked in to see whether she could help. There were too many hands for the necessary tasks. Someone remembered to make tea but, in the confusion, put in salt instead of sugar.[38] Bronson was away that day making school visits; for all the documents show, he and Louisa may not even have had a chance to say good-bye. Proud as he was of his daughter's decision, he also knew that she was going to a dangerous post; he told someone that he was sending his only son to war.[39] Louisa was equally aware that she might never see the family again. She maintained a brave face until the very last, but when it was time to go, she began to cry. Everyone broke down. Already knowing the answer, she asked her mother as she held her close, "Shall I stay?" "No, go! and the Lord be with you," was the reply.[40] As Louisa turned to catch a last glimpse of Orchard House, she saw her mother waving a handkerchief. May, along with Julian Hawthorne, escorted Louisa to the Concord train station.[41] Louisa rode to Boston, where she spent one last civilian night with her cousin Lizzie Wells.

Friday was, if possible, more frantic than Thursday had been. Always eager to economize, Louisa scoured Boston to obtain the free rail pass to which her military appointment entitled her. Each official referred her to another, usually in some building on the side of town from which she had just come. She crossed and recrossed the city, clashing with languid and indifferent bureaucrats seemingly intent on denying her the essential documents.[42] She got the last of her papers in order, just in time to join Anna and her husband for a hasty farewell dinner. The couple accompanied Louisa to the station so that theirs might be the last in a series of numbing good-byes.

The sun in that dark season had already faded as Louisa sank into her seat on the train. Abruptly, after two days of furious bustle, hours of empty time lay ahead of her—time to check over her tickets, put them in a safe place, then lose and rediscover them again; time to count the small fund some family friends had given her to buy necessities for herself and modest gifts for her patients. She had time to gaze out onto the darkening landscape as city gave way to open fields. Feeling lonely, she let her seatmate draw her into a long conversation about "the war, the weather, music, Carlyle, skating, genius, hoops, and the immortality of the soul."[43] Any topic was fine as long as it kept away the blues.

The train did not take Louisa directly to Washington. In New London, Connecticut, she transferred to a steamship, which carried her through the night to New Jersey. A rank novice at seafaring, she spent a wide-eyed night imagining that the boat was about to sink and wondering how she would save herself if it did. When, to her mild astonishment, the boat landed safely in Jersey City, she made her way to the train for Washington. Although the places through which she passed were unknown to her, they evoked clear emotions. As the train puffed its way through Philadelphia, Louisa regretted that she did not have time to stop and seek out her birthplace in Germantown. In Baltimore, her train passed not far from the spot where, two springs before, a mob of southern sympathizers had attacked the Sixth Massachusetts Regiment on its way to Washington. As she remembered the riot, Louisa's temper rose as if the assault had just happened, and she felt "as if I should enjoy throwing a stone at somebody, hard."[44]

Louisa's journey ended as it had begun, in early evening. As her hired carriage drew her through the streets toward Georgetown, she caught her first glimpse of the unfinished Capitol dome and gazed in wonder at the White House. On her arrival at the Union Hotel Hospital, she received the welcome of Mrs. Hannah Ropes, the hospital matron. The kindly woman noted Louisa's arrival in her journal that night: "We are cheered by the arrival of Miss Alcott from Concord—the prospect of a really good nurse, a gentlewoman who can do more than merely keep the patients from falling out of bed."[45]

All through the time of Louisa's journey, quite unknown to her, events had been unfolding in a fatefully simultaneous fashion. The new commander of Lincoln's Army of the Potomac, Ambrose Burnside, had decided to attempt a strike against Lee's Army of Northern Virginia before the coming winter would bring a pause to significant maneuvers. On December 11, the very day that Louisa received her orders, Burnside's engineers were hastily laying pontoon bridges across the Rappahannock River, and the Army of the Potomac prepared to cross into the evacuated town of Fredericksburg. The next day, as Louisa scoured Boston in search of an official to authorize her train pass, Union soldiers vandalized the Virginia town, smashing china and wrecking furniture. That night, as Louisa's train plunged into the night south of Boston, blue-coated amateur musicians played raucous versions of patriotic tunes on pianos that had been dragged into the streets of Fredericksburg, and officers gazed anxiously up at the strongly fortified Confederate positions above the town, wondering if Burnside's battle plan would lead to victory.[46]

Their worst doubts were confirmed the next day. On the damp, leaden Saturday afternoon of December 13, 1862, while Louisa's train was steaming through Pennsylvania and Maryland, Burnside sent fourteen separate brigades up the sloping hillside known as Marye's Heights. Near the top was a stone wall. Behind it, an entire corps of Lee's army lay waiting. When the rebels opened fire, their fusillade was as thick and rapid as machine-gun fire. Of the thousands who answered the order to charge, not a single Union soldier came within thirty yards of the wall. Using a strangely placid simile, Union corps commander Darius Couch later described watching the brigades "melt like snow coming down on warm ground."[47] After nightfall, in Georgetown, Louisa first turned down the blankets in her upstairs room at the Union Hotel Hospital. Forty miles to the southwest, on the sloping ground above Fredericksburg, the bitterly cold air was filled with the despairing cries of literally thousands of wounded men. Louisa had completed her journey to the Union Hotel Hospital. For many of the Fredericksburg wounded, a journey to the same destination was about to begin.

Louisa wrote a mildly fictionalized version of her time as an army nurse: a short book called *Hospital Sketches* that she published within months of returning from service. Shying away from overt autobiography, Louisa dispensed with her real name in *Hospital Sketches*, adopting the alias of Tribulation Periwinkle. Despite the superficial camouflage, however, *Hospital Sketches* is a virtually true account. Not only did Louisa assemble the manuscript while her recollections were fresh, but her principal source material was unimpeachable; according to Clara Gowing, an Alcott family friend, all but a few of the narrative's passages were taken directly from the letters, now lost, that Louisa had sent home to her parents.[48]

One particular in which *Hospital Sketches* varies from the truth is in its narrator's denial of any deeply felt motivation to join the cause. Miss Periwinkle decides to take up nursing only because she wants "something to do," and going off to tend to wounded soldiers is only one of the possibilities suggested by her well-meaning relations. Louisa, to the contrary, ached to have a part in the war from its outset, and military nursing appealed both to her maternal instinct and her love of a good fight. In a dispatch written for the *New York Times*, Walt Whitman observed that "a benevolent person, with the right qualities and tact, cannot, perhaps, make a better investment of himself at present anywhere upon the varied surface of this whole big world than in these military hospitals."[49]

Coincidentally, Whitman's first personal encounter with war also came on the heels of Fredericksburg. What he saw nauseated him. "Here in the hospitals," he wrote, "I am present at the most appalling things. . . . [Hours] afterward . . . I feel sick and actually tremble when I recall the thing and have it in my mind again."[50] Although Louisa reported for duty at her hospital on the day of the battle, four days went by before the first of the wounded began to arrive. During that brief period of grace, Louisa settled in and began to acquaint herself with her new tasks. Even before the flood of wounded arrived from Fredericksburg, she had a great deal of work to do. In between major engagements, the hospitals were kept busy administering to soldiers who had been felled by disease. Louisa reported that she was surrounded by "pneumonia on one side, diphtheria on the other, [and] five typhoids on the opposite."[51] Moreover, only three months had gone by since the battle of Antietam, the bloodiest one-day battle of the war, and a number of casualties from that battle were yet to be discharged. During Louisa's first morning, a soldier died before her eyes. Not much later, she learned that one of the nurses in charge of a ward of patients had departed without leave. Despite her inexperience, Louisa was immediately entrusted with the supervision of forty beds, incongruously located in an erstwhile ballroom. She washed faces, dispensed medicines, and tried to look as professional and competent as possible as she and the other nurses awaited the wounded from the recent battle.

One of Louisa's first patients was, in her description, "a boy with pneumonia." She sat with him all day and, in a gesture both kind and symbolic, placed her mother's shawl around the young man as he sat up, fighting for breath. When he smiled at her and said, "You are real motherly, ma'am," she felt for the first time as if she were getting on. She hoped that she looked motherly to all the men in the ward, for, she wrote, "my thirty years made me feel old, and the suffering round me made me long to comfort everyone."[52]

Louisa's work began in earnest on the morning of December 17, when an African American boy, in an excited tone that might have been mistaken for joy, cried out, "They's comin' in, I tell yer, heaps on 'em!"[53] The rest of the day was a baffling swirl of sensations—unspeakable odors, the sight of men without arms and legs, the sound of heavy feet, and the urgent shouts of doctors, nurses, and orderlies. Louisa noticed, however, that one sound was surprisingly absent from the general uproar. Scarcely a cry of pain went up from the men, no matter how grotesquely they had been wounded. Louisa often longed to groan for them "when pride kept their white lips shut, while great drops stood on their foreheads, and the bed shook with the irrepressible tremor of their tortured bodies."[54]

Her first weapons in her war to save the Union were a sponge, a basin, and a bar of brown soap; removing the dirt from the endless stream of wounded consumed the first part of the day. When the scrubbing and rinsing were done, Louisa and the other nurses dispensed bread, soup, meat, and coffee to all who were well enough to eat. One man, his right arm too shattered to save, struggled to write a letter to a girlfriend with his left. Another, shot through the stomach, asked for water. By the time Louisa was able to find a cup for him, he was dead. There was little time, however, to reflect on any individual tragedy. Until eleven that night, Louisa did whatever she could do to comfort her charges—mopping feverish faces, smoothing rumpled beds, and even singing lullabies.

The days that followed arranged themselves into a routine constant enough that Louisa was able to describe a typical day in her journal. It began at six, when she rose and dressed by gaslight. She then risked the fury of the men in her ward by throwing open the windows to admit the frigid winter air. Much as she understood their objections to the chill, she was convinced that the alternative was worse. When the windows were closed, the room received almost no ventilation, and Louisa was terrified that the absence of fresh air would turn the room into a more lethal pestilence-box than it already was. Despite her best efforts, it remained a dirty, damp place where the odors of wounds, stables, kitchens, and washrooms perniciously mingled. As a futile defense against them, she carried a bottle of lavender water, whose contents she liberally scattered. She poked up the fires, laid blankets where they were needed, and lightened the atmosphere as best she could with joking and conversation.[55]

Her breakfast would have sent a devoted Fruitlander into spasms. It was an unchanging menu of fried beef, bread with salted butter, and coffee that she described as "washy."[56] The discussions around the table added no seasoning to the heavy, unappetizing fare; Louisa found most of her colleagues either bland or pompously opinionated, and it was all she could do to keep from laughing aloud at their ill-tutored arrogance. After breakfast, she could be found doing any of a dozen things, often almost simultaneously. She gave out rations and washed faces. She dusted tables and chased after supplies. She sewed bandages, dispensed medicine, and changed dressings. She was perpetually nettled by the incompetence of the attendants she supervised, who even needed to be shown how to sweep a floor and make a bed. Her daily battle with "disorder, discomfort, [and] bad management" eased a bit after the midday meal, when she took time to write letters for the soldiers who could not write for themselves.[57] The duty she found hardest was answering letters that had come for men who had not lived to receive them. Newspapers, gossip, and the evening medicinal doses occupied her colleagues during the relatively unhurried hours after supper. When time permitted, Louisa read to the soldiers from the Dickens novels that she had brought with her for that purpose. The day typically ended at nine, when a bell sounded the call for lights-out.

The evenings, however, were not all the same, thanks to Dr. John Winslow, the recently appointed surgeon on Louisa's ward. Dr. John, as he permitted Louisa to call him, quoted freely from Browning and often came to her room to share a few selections from his portable library. He went for walks with her when time allowed and took her to the Capitol to hear the House chaplain read a somewhat flowery sermon, followed by dinner at a German restaurant. Dr. Winslow seems to have had more than friendship on his mind, and Louisa observed with a tingling awareness that her companion "is given to confidences in the twilight, & altogether is amiably amusing, & exceeding *young*."[58] The emphasis on the last word was Louisa's. What might have happened, either for good or ill, if she had been more receptive to the young doctor's attentions is a matter of entertaining speculation. However, restraint and propriety won out; the good doctor invited Louisa to his room, and she did not go.

The fortunes of another John possessed a more powerful, though decidedly unromantic, hold on Louisa's heart. His full name was John Suhre, a blacksmith from Virginia who had come to the hospital gravely wounded. Unmarried and twenty-eight years old when the war began, Suhre had remained loyal to the Union when his state had seceded. However, he had not been able to join the army as soon as he would have liked, for he was responsible for the welfare of his widowed mother and younger siblings. Their needs had kept him from marrying, but enlisting posed a harder question. Enlisting, he had reasoned, meant helping his neighbor, whereas marriage would have meant only pleasing himself. For a long time, he had weighed his obligations to family against his duty to country, until the day when his mother decided the issue by pressing a keepsake ring into his hand and saying, "Go." Fredericksburg had been his first battle. A rebel bullet had pierced his left lung and broken a rib, so that every breath stabbed him like a knife.

Although he did not know it, he was beyond saving. Louisa was sent to tell him so because the surgeon in charge of his case did not have the heart to deliver the message himself. John impressed her with his quiet courage and simple morality. She later wrote, "The army needed men like John, earnest, brave, and faithful; fighting for liberty and justice with both heart and hand, true soldiers of the Lord."[59] For all his pain, John gave almost no outward sign of distress, and Louisa was surprised when the surgeon told her that, of all the patients in the ward, he suffered the most. Even the blacksmith had a limit, though. Her news still undelivered, Louisa noticed that great silent tears were rolling from his eyes. Louisa described what followed:

> [S]traightway my fear vanished, my heart opened wide and took him in, as, gathering the bent head in my arms, as freely as if he had been a little child, I said, "Let me help you bear it, John."
>
> Never, on any human countenance, have I seen so swift and beautiful a look of gratitude, surprise and comfort, as that which answered me more eloquently then the whispered—
>
> "Thank you, ma'am, this is right good! this is what I wanted!"[60]

Of all the moments that influenced Louisa's thinking about human relationships, none was more important than this. It exemplified what she came to see as the greatest good in life: the sweetness of sharing another's adversity. In much of her best fiction, emotional climaxes occur when central female characters offer to share the burdens of those they love. Alcott heroines tend to interpret times of challenge as opportunities to transcend selfishness. These opportunities are almost always accepted.

John Suhre died only two days after Louisa offered to share his suffering. To the end, he remained a model of quiet fortitude, crying out only once in bitter agony, "For God's sake, give me air." Louisa held his hand as the end came. He grasped her hand so tightly that his fingers left four white marks on the back of it.[61] As when she had lost her sister Lizzie, Louisa reflected on the idea of death as a welcome friend and healer. In *Hospital Sketches*, she was to write of death as the "diviner brother" of sleep and as "a better nurse than [I, who] healed . . . with a touch."[62] Observing Suhre's peaceful expression, Louisa imagined that his half-hour's acquaintance with death had made friends of the two. Many sentimental writers of Louisa's time sought to ease the pain of loss by making death sound sweet and good. In Louisa's hands, however, this device never sounds false or maudlin. She had, it seems, a strength of mind and an inner stoicism that truly shielded her from a fear of dying. To her, the idea of death as a holy healer was entirely plausible.

In this atmosphere of suffering and death, Louisa's reflections turned to the memory of another lost hero, the recently departed Thoreau. In Concord, at the actual time of his passing, she had borne the event more or less silently. Now, with the benefit of a little time and distance, she found a voice for her feelings. One night, as she kept watch over a dying soldier, Louisa reached for a piece of paper. By the end of her watch, she had finished her best-remembered poem, "Thoreau's Flute." The poem begins with a somber lament of her mentor's death, but the mood changes as, miraculously, the wind blows through the dead man's flute, playing a song of hope:

> Then from the flute, untouched by hands,
>   There came a low, harmonious breath:
>   "For such as he there is no death;—
> His life the eternal life commands;
> Above man's aims his nature rose.
>   The wisdom of a just content
>   Made one small spot a continent,
> And turned to poetry life's prose.[63]

Louisa spun her lyric around the interweaving of two spirits: the soul of her departed friend and the wind that wafted through the flute he had left behind. The flute becomes a humble medium between this world and the next, translating the wind with which Thoreau's soul has now merged into the words that glorify his memory. Once a voice on behalf of nature, Thoreau's voice is now one with nature; the breath that no longer fills his consumptive lungs still carries its message of peace to those sensitive enough to hear. Hardly thinking she had written the finest poem she would ever write, Louisa put it away and did not remember it until months later. More urgent matters now filled her mind.

Subjected to overwork, rewarded with an inadequate diet, and constantly exposed to life-threatening disease, a nurse in a Civil War hospital could wear out quickly. With some exaggeration, Louisa claimed never to have had a sick day in her life before starting her nursing career. Nevertheless, she began coughing as soon as she arrived at the hospital, a symptom that the matron initially dismissed as a sympathetic reaction to the maladies of her patients.[64] However, Louisa was in danger of becoming one of those nurses who, to use her own description, "sometimes, in their sympathy, forget that they are mortal, and run the risk of being made immortal, sooner than is agreeable to their partial friends."[65] Less than three weeks after her arrival, Louisa was already beginning to lose her strength. Perhaps irritated by her perceived weakness, she refused to slacken her pace. She persisted in starting each day with a brisk run. Her colleagues warned that she was driving herself too hard and predicted that she would soon develop pneumonia. She ignored them.

On New Year's Eve, Louisa's spirits received a welcome boost, for at midnight the Emancipation Proclamation went into effect. She lay awake in her plain, drafty room until midnight, when church bells throughout the city rang in the New Year, as well as the other more portentous beginning. Much to the annoyance of her more politically detached roommate, she "danced" from her bed and threw open the window. With a voice already weakened by disease, she cheered feebly and waved her handkerchief at a group of black men who were celebrating in the street below. Throughout the night, Louisa recalled, the black population of Georgetown "tooted and tramped, fired crackers, sang 'Glory Hallelujah,' and took comfort, poor souls! in their own way."[66] During her brief stint at the hospital, nothing gave Louisa more satisfaction than the sights and sounds of that night of freedom.

On the home front, Bronson, too, celebrated Lincoln's proclamation. He pasted a copy of the document in his journal, and on New Year's Day he attended an emancipation meeting at the Tremont Temple in Boston, where, he observed, "the black men have the eloquence, and carry the meeting as they ought."[67] A week later, the Alcotts received a letter from Louisa giving lively descriptions of her work at the hospital. Bronson's reaction to her words mingled pride with concern. He wrote, "She seems active [and] interested, and, if her strength is adequate to the task, could not better serve herself or the country. But I fear this will end in her breaking down presently."[68]

Not realizing how accurately he had judged the case, Bronson agreed to give a series of four conversations, arranged by Emerson and Dudley Bradford, to commence at Temperance Hall on January 19. The titles dealt in broad generalities: Nature, Politics, Letters, and Religion. However, the brief parenthetical descriptions he added in his journal suggest an interesting approach to the material. Beside each of the first three subjects, Bronson listed a series of names. "Nature" was to be typified by Thoreau, Agassiz, and Goethe; "Politics" would be a discussion of William Lloyd Garrison, Wendell Phillips, and John Brown; and "Letters" would treat Emerson and Hawthorne. Alcott had borrowed the idea of using particular men to personify concepts from Carlyle and Emerson. What was significant, however, was that, with the sole exception of Goethe, Bronson was confining himself to people he had personally known. At the age of sixty-two, Bronson was becoming more connected with lived experience, coming to see that personality and biography might not only embody larger ideas, but might matter as much as the ideas themselves. Just as importantly, he was starting to understand how greatly his life had been shaped by his friendships. This realization would yield finer fruit as the years passed.

The breakdown that Bronson feared for Louisa was not long in coming. There was a sudden lapse in the steady stream of letters she sent home. Disturbed by the silence, Julian Hawthorne began stopping by Orchard House regularly in hopes of news. Pale and sad, Abba could only shake her head.[69] Louisa herself had been the last to admit that she was on the verge of collapse, and she had struggled on as long as she could. On January 9, the hospital matron wrote that both she and Louisa were ill and suffering terribly but that, despite their condition, they had worked together on three dying men and saved all of them. She called Louisa "a splendid young woman."[70] But she was not invincible. One morning, Louisa's head felt like a cannonball, and her feet seemed glued to the floor.[71] Half-aware of the anxious voices and expressions around her, she staggered upstairs to bed. For some days afterward, she was still able to walk downstairs to take meals. Eventually, even this exertion became too much for her.

Louisa's fellow nurses, too busy for politeness and pleasantries, had previously struck her as remote and unfriendly. Now that she was ill, however, she found herself surrounded by care and kindness; a healthy colleague was taken for granted, but an ailing one received all the respect and attention that was due a stricken comrade-in-arms. The attendants from Louisa's ward regularly climbed the stairs to fill her woodbox and to bring progress reports and hand-fashioned presents from her patients below. Dr. Winslow now came to her room not as a potential beau but as a worried physician. He haunted her room, she said, bringing the things she needed and acting in general "like a motherly little man as he is."[72] Several of the nurses visited each evening with food and conversation. Louisa found herself "so beteaed and betoasted, petted and served, that [she] was quite 'in the lap of luxury.' "[73] However, she still preferred doing to having things done for her, and even after she was confined to her room, she continued to do sewing for the men. She still had two months to go before her orders expired, and she was determined not only to serve the time but to fill it with as much usefulness as her condition would allow.

But that condition was worsening each day. The doctors now had a firm diagnosis: typhoid pneumonia. Her cough became more persistent, and her body no longer seemed to belong to her. Her perceptions became jumbled, and fact and hallucination began to mingle. Louisa remembered, "Hours began to get confused, people looked odd; queer faces haunted the room, and the nights were one long fight with weariness and pain."[74] On the morning of January 14, the Alcotts received a wire from the hospital matron. Mrs. Ropes, her own health failing as fast as Louisa's, wrote that Louisa's service as a nurse could no longer continue. Someone must come for her, and come quickly.

Bronson wasted no time. He cancelled his conversation engagement and caught the noon train, traveling on the same tracks that Louisa had ridden only six weeks before. The passage to Jersey City was slowed by fog, and he spent helpless hours waiting for the weather to clear. From Jersey City, he took the evening train and rode all night to reach Georgetown. On the morning of the sixteenth, when he was led to Louisa's room, his eyes fell on a shocking tableau. The wind whistled in through five broken windowpanes that no one in the hospital had had time to repair. Rats could be heard scuttling in the walls. A virtually opaque mirror, a blue pitcher, a tin basin, and a pair of yellow mugs comprised the toilet accessories. There, on a thin mattress laid on a stark iron bed, lay Louisa. She was able to recognize the "grey-headed gentleman [who] rose like a ghost" above her, but she was barely recognizable herself. She was thin and weak. The normally robust color of her cheeks had given way to a wraithlike pallor. Bronson's ability to suppress his emotions had often annoyed and frustrated people, Louisa included, but now it was for the best. Whatever anguish he felt, he tried not to show. All that Louisa recalled his saying at that moment was, "Come home."75

Louisa had resisted every other voice that had told her to quit. But now, the simple summons of her father signaled to her that the fight was over. "At the sight of him," she wrote, "my resolution melted away, [and] my heart turned traitor to my boys. . . . I answered, 'Yes, father.' "76 With his two simple words, Bronson released Louisa from much more than her obligations to the hospital. All her life, she had hoped to please her father. Sometimes she had clearly disappointed him. On other occasions, he had given approval, but seldom as she had hoped he would. Almost always, it had seemed, more was expected. Now, however, she finally knew that it was all right. She had done enough.

Five days passed before Louisa could be taken home. Her doctors believed that she was too weak to be moved.77 Although he did not see how his daughter could grow stronger by staying where she was, Bronson reluctantly agreed to wait. Having already heard about some of Louisa's patients in her letters, he satisfied his curiosity by walking around the ward and seeing them. The experience left him with few words. "Horrid war," he wrote. "And one sees its horrors in hospitals if anywhere."78

As a matter of hospital policy, parents of the sick and wounded were discouraged from spending too much time with their children, so despite his concern, Bronson was not permitted to stay with Louisa. Leaving her to the care of her fellow nurses, Bronson took a few hours to have a look around Washington. Like his daughter a few weeks earlier, he went to the Senate chamber where, by a wonderful coincidence, President Lincoln was in attendance. Alcott sat near him. In recording his brief encounter with the chief executive, Alcott remarked on his honest bearings and strong face, "more comely than the papers and portraits have shown him." He added tersely that Lincoln's "behavior was good." In those days, personal access even to the highest elected officials was freer than one can easily imagine today; it was by no means out of the question for Bronson to obtain a meeting with the great man. Bronson mused for a while on this chance of a lifetime, but he wisely rejected it. He wrote, "I wished to have had an interview but am too anxious about Louisa and without time to seek it."[79]

Any disagreements about whether Louisa should be promptly taken home were settled in tragic fashion on January 20, when the matron, Mrs. Ropes, died. The doctors consented at once to Louisa's departure, but heavy rains prevented any movement until the following day. Dorothea Dix herself appeared at the train station to see Louisa off and present her with gifts. Bronson, who had more pressing matters on his mind, vaguely described them as "good things for Louisa's comfort."[80]

They traveled all day and through the night. On the evening of January 22 they arrived in Boston too late to catch the train for Concord. They spent the night with relatives of Abba. By the time they reached Orchard House the next day, Louisa was not in her right mind. She had the impression that the house had lost its roof and that no one there wanted to see her. The exhaustion and illness of the previous six weeks had changed her so profoundly that Sophia Hawthorne said she would not have recognized her. For his part, Nathaniel Hawthorne wrote to his publisher that the fever looked very threatening and that he feared she would not pull through. Lying in her great mahogany sleigh bed, barely conscious of the anxious stir around her, Louisa spent the next two days adrift between sleep and delirium.

In a journal entry describing her journey to Georgetown, Louisa had called the moment "a solemn time, but I'm glad to live in it; and am sure it will do me good whether I come out alive or dead."[81] She very nearly had come out dead, but she also had lived more intensely and with more visible purpose than she ever had before. But as Dr. Bartlett made his daily visits and her family hoped for the best, it was not clear that she would live to turn her experiences and her purpose to account.

CHAPTER TWELVE

SHADOWS AND SUNLIGHT

"All my dreams [are] getting
fulfilled in a most amazing way."

—LOUISA MAY ALCOTT,
Journals, October 1863

THREE WEEKS PASSED BEFORE LOUISA CAME FULLY OUT OF her delirium. Well into February she struggled through "the crisis of typhoid," as Abba described it to her brother Samuel. She added, "Poor Louy . . . left us a brave handsome woman . . . and is returned to us almost a wreck of body and mind."[1] Abba also shared her worst fears with Sophia Hawthorne. Sophia wrote that, during those anxious weeks, her only activity was finding ways to help Louisa and the other Alcotts through the ordeal.[2] Emerson, as always, lent support, this time by placing in Abba's kitchen "a nice strong woman" to do the housework. However, Abba wrote, "While I am able to move I will not have a nurse. It would not relieve my anxiety, and might hinder my own action."[3] As Abba observed, Louisa's condition demanded great care and judgment. Whatever aid the neighbors might give, there was much that the family dared not entrust to outsiders.

Bronson, Abba, and May looked after Louisa in shifts around the clock, trying to soothe her distracted mind and searching her discolored face for any promising change. Only Anna, living some twenty miles away in Chelsea and now in the advanced stages of her pregnancy, did not take part in looking after Louisa. From a distance, however, Anna, too, followed the patient's progress; during the first week of Louisa's convalescence, Bronson sent Anna continual updates on Louisa's condition. His letters relayed the facts in a direct manner, but they also emphasized the optimistic reports of the doctors and the hope of a speedy recovery. It is reasonable to suppose that he wished to avoid disturbing his pregnant daughter's tranquility by painting too grim a picture. Even so, Bronson admitted that the trip home had been almost all Louisa could withstand. She had, he told Anna, "required all her strength and courage to come through." She would still need all her patience to recover from her illness and fatigue.4 Bronson's journal entries, so frequently full of metaphysical musings, were now terse and factual: "Wait on L."; "Watch and wait on our patient"; "Sit with Louisa into the night, reading from Gospels and Herder." A week went by before he mentioned getting any rest.5

The vigil was exhausting and occasionally terrifying. Abba told Samuel, "Her mind wanders and she lies whole hours muttering incoherent things, then going off into long slumbers, or [arising] in a panic of terror, flying off the bed in terrible confusion."6 When Louisa tossed about on her bed, Abba would try to calm her by saying, "Lie still, my dear." On hearing this, however, Louisa would look at her with frightened, unrecognizing eyes. Once, Louisa rose from her bed and made an impassioned speech that sounded strangely like Latin. Only later was she able to explain that, in her delusional state, she had decided that her mother was "a stout, handsome Spaniard, dressed in black velvet with very soft hands," whom Louisa believed she had married. From the lips of this dreaded spouse, the gentle command to lie still was far from comforting. He seemed always to be coming at her through windows and out of closets. When she had made her pseudo-Latin plea, she thought she was making an appeal before the Pope.7

Louisa's other fever dreams were no less vivid. She imagined she was in Baltimore and a mob was breaking down a door to get her. In other fancies she was "being hung for a witch, burned, stoned, and otherwise mal-treated." Two of the nurses and a doctor from the Union Hotel Hospital tempted her to join them in worshipping the Devil. One night, hearing a crash coming from Louisa's room, May rushed in to find her sister on the floor. Louisa sharply upbraided May, asking her how she could have left her alone with so many men. Louisa thought she was still at the hospital, surrounded by wounded soldiers who refused either to die or get better.8 It is something of a relief to realize that Louisa herself did not regard her visions seriously and recorded them only because she found them enter-taining. Having never been gravely ill before, she found the experience "all new & very interesting."[9] Although Bronson wrote that Louisa dreaded the return of the fever fits that came upon her "twice in the twenty four hours," she herself wrote later that she had enjoyed her fever "very much, at least the crazy part."[10] Undoubtedly she was the only one who found her hallucinations amusing.

Abba, all but exhausted from watching and worrying, could not contain her rage in response to the misfortunes that continued to beset her family. Their sufferings, it seemed to her, defied any earthly understanding of pro-portion or justice. Although Dr. Bartlett assured her that the signs were favorable, Abba no longer had any faith in medicine, and she seemed about to lose a profounder faith as well. Haunted by her experience with Lizzie, she confessed, "I hate Drs. and all their nonsense." However, she added, "the efficacy of good nursing I do know and appreciate and believe if she is to be saved from violent death or the stern ravages of chronic ail-ments, it will be by faithful vigilant care." This, Abba vowed, her beloved Louisa would have "if all the rest of the world goes to the dogs." Indeed, she had had enough of the world and the way it had repaid her efforts, as well as those of her husband and children, to be charitable, generous, and kind. On the subject of the thankless earth, she wrote:

> [W]e have been cruelly dealt by, in it, and owe it no more sacrifices of flesh and blood. If we have sinned greatly against the Lord and these are the compensations he takes, he is welcome and I am sure will be satis-fied if the amount of personal suffering and misery caused is the true test of the penalty.[11]

But the sacrifice of Louisa was not demanded. The changes were imper-ceptible at first, but gradually, as Julian Hawthorne put it, Louisa was climb-ing painfully out of the grave toward life.[12] On February 2, Anna's father-in-law came to take Bronson's place by the sickbed so that the latter could give a series of conversations in Boston. Two days later, Bronson returned to discover that the fever had finally broken. Louisa was now sleep-ing more soundly and, when awake, impatiently asked for food. Two weeks after Louisa's return, the worst was apparently over. As snow fell on Con-cord, Bronson sat with her parts of the night, reading and conversing. By the middle of the month, Louisa was holding up her end of these conversations. She remembered very little of her ordeal. The face she saw in the mirror was so large-eyed and emaciated that she did not recognize herself. Her first attempts at walking brought only frustration; she cried because her legs "wouldn't go."[13] Though she was improving, the nights seemed horribly long, and the days were idle and fretful. For such a naturally active woman, the waiting for strength to return was almost intolerable.

She felt a great indignity, too, on discovering that her doctors had shaved her head. She lamented the loss of her fine hair, a yard and a half in length and, in her view, her "one beauty." Five years later, in *Little Women*, Louisa was to use another illness during wartime as the reason for a similar sacrifice. As Mr. March lies dangerously ill in a Washington hospital, Jo raises twenty-five dollars to contribute toward his comfort and safe return by selling her hair. Echoing Louisa's journal, Jo's sacrificed hair is mourned as her only beautifying feature. Nevertheless, as Louisa conceded in her journal, "a wig outside is better than a loss of wits inside."[14]

With Louisa on the mend, Bronson was able to resume his conversations with a clear conscience. His first efforts were unsteady, owing to his lingering exhaustion from his long vigils at his daughter's bedside. Louisa observed, "He was tired out with taking care of me, poor old gentleman, & typhus was not inspiring."[15] However, his conversational tactic of linking general concepts and qualities to individuals was starting to work well. His talks on Hawthorne the Novelist, Thoreau the Naturalist, and Emerson the Rhapsodist received favorable notices in the papers. One observer wrote, "Mr. Alcott is one of a class of thinkers who have done more for our literature and politics and religion than any that America has yet seen."[16] Although listeners sometimes complained that his characterizations lacked sufficient variety and that some shades of personality completely escaped him, they were still intrigued by his personal reminiscences, which were genially related and never marred by "the sting of gossip."[17] Bronson himself had concluded that a signal failing of the transcendentalist movement had been its insistence on cosmic universality and its refusal to take adequate account of the person. In a conversation he gave in Boston on March 23, he reflected, "Impersonality—Law, Right, Justice, Truth—these were the central ideas; but where the Power was in which they inhered, how they were related to one another, what was to give them vitality—these questions were quite neglected, and left out of sight."[18] Bronson quietly resolved never again to ignore the individual. Although his prose would never lose its tendency to stray into the ether, his new appreciation of the personal signaled a welcome change in his writing habits.

Louisa's recovery and the critical success of her father's conversations were only the first of the great joys that came to Orchard House that season. On March 28, only six days after Louisa was well enough to leave her room for the first time, she joined her mother and May in looking out on a snow-covered landscape, waiting for Bronson to bring some eagerly anticipated news. Late that night, Bronson, "all wet and white" from the storm, burst through the front door. Waving his bag aloft, he cried out his great tidings: Anna had given birth to a healthy boy. In unison, the three women opened their mouths and, by Louisa's account, screamed for about two minutes. Then Abba began to cry, Louisa to laugh, and May to pepper her father with questions about the baby's weight, length, and coloring that he, in his own distracted excitement, could not answer. Red-faced and damp, Bronson could do little more than smile and repeat in a besotted voice, "Anna's boy, yes, yes, Anna's boy."[19]

Two days later, Bronson was still in ecstasies when he wrote to congratulate his firstborn daughter. His letter contained a hint of condolence; Anna had been convinced that she was carrying a girl, whom she had decided to name Louisa Catherine. She had given no thought at all to boys' names, and some days passed before her son acquired the name of Frederick Alcott Pratt. Bronson reassured Anna, saying, "Boys are blessings too." The rest of his condolences, however, were less congenially phrased. He confessed that he had wished for a boy years ago, when Anna herself was born. Moreover, he added, he would have found it "a hard joke" if someone had told him that no boys were to join the family until thirty-three years after his "first disappointment."[20] Well intentioned as Bronson's remarks undoubtedly were, one can only sympathize with Anna. Bringing forth her first child only to be called a "disappointment" by the man whose approval she most coveted, she may well have thought that the harder joke was on her.

March ended with both Anna and baby in fine condition and Louisa evidently on the road to health. Unfortunately, Louisa's convalescence was not all that it appeared. During her recovery, Louisa complained to Bronson of a perpetually sore throat. She also found herself "longing to eat, [but with] no mouth to do it with, mine being so sore and full of all manner of queer sensations it was nothing but a plague."[21] Abba had also noted to her brother Samuel, "Her throat and teeth and tongue are in the most tender and sensitive state."[22] Louisa's sore throat and strange oral sensations were the results not of her disease but of the treatment she had received from the Union Hotel Hospital physicians. Her doctors, following what they considered sound practice in cases of typhoid, had given Louisa heavy, repeated doses of mercurous chloride, a compound more commonly known as calomel. In so doing, they had permanently poisoned her.

For the next seven years, Louisa had no idea what was wrong with her. Unaware of the toxins that had lodged permanently in her system, she had no accurate explanation for her searing headaches, her chronic weariness, and the intermittent pain in her legs. She had no good name for the condition that had stolen her youthful vigor and was later to disable her for months at a time. She attributed her symptoms to neuralgia or—not implausibly in view of her writing habits—to overwork. It was not until 1870 that, while traveling through France, she happened on an English physician who finally explained that she was suffering the effects of her erstwhile "cure." Louisa was, in effect, a lingering casualty of the Civil War, and the last twenty-five years of her life were the history of a glacially slow mortal illness.[23] Except for the fledgling drafts of *Moods*, all of the work for which she is now remembered was written after the causes of her death had been set in motion.

Until the spring of 1863, Louisa had never had a reason to doubt her physical strength. As a tomboy, she had run and played tirelessly. As a robust young woman, she had always relied on her seemingly inexhaustible stamina. While she had lain in the throes of fever and mercury poisoning, that stamina had saved her life. However, the struggle had weakened her permanently. Julian Hawthorne was aghast at the change. He could barely reconcile the "hollow-eyed, almost fleshless wreck [with] the Louisa we had known and loved."[24] It seemed that the alteration had gone far beyond the merely physical. Emotionally, it was as if a veil now separated her from the world. Occasionally, it would slip aside, and "a flash of humor or a shaft of wit would come out of the shadow."[25] At other times, however, it seemed that her illness and the haunting memories of the hospital had marked her with an indelible air of gravity and melancholy. Louisa's six-week errand of mercy had exacted a staggering cost.

Yet, strangely, the experience that made a ruin of Louisa's body also bestowed a host of blessings. The first of these was philosophical. In April, when the fever had left her and before the lasting effects of the calomel treatment became evident, Louisa experienced a rebirth of joy and enthusiasm for life. Now strong enough to go for rides and walks around Concord, Louisa greeted the spring feeling "as if born again[;] everything was so beautiful and new." She hoped that she too had become a new person, and she speculated that the Washington experience might do her lasting good.[26]

Louisa's ordeal also raised her in her father's estimation. To Bronson and Abba, their daughter's recovery was a kind of miracle. Louisa, it seemed, had walked through the same valley as Lizzie, but Louisa had returned. Because of her vitality, Louisa had been easy to take for granted. As much as Bronson might have fretted over the soul of his dark daughter, he had certainly never lost sleep worrying about the soundness of her body. But now Bronson saw her with new eyes. Louisa's life was transformed from a subject of criticism to a cause for thanksgiving. When Louisa was an infant, Bronson had seen her as a personification of God's glory. During long years, this perception had at times faded. Now, with this second birth, enacted through illness and recovery, that glory again emerged.

There was another reason for Bronson to see Louisa from a new perspective. In late March, when Louisa was out of danger, Bronson wrote a letter to his mother, now in her nineties but still mentally alert. In it, he told of Louisa's service to the army, her resulting illness, and the anxious weeks of her recovery. He wrote, "That was our contribution to the war and one we should not have made willingly had we known the danger and the sacrifices."[27] It is a significant statement. Ever since he had first met Charles Lane, Bronson had valued no human activity more highly than self-sacrifice. Certainly, Louisa had sacrificed before this time, accepting menial jobs and churning out potboiler fiction in an attempt to pay down the family debt. However, these gestures of self-sacrifice had been made for money, and any enterprise connected with cash had a lesser value in Bronson's eyes. Now Louisa had sacrificed nobly and grandly. Bronson had finally come to recognize that some sacrifices are too great to expect from anyone. Louisa's willingness to die for liberty and union, coupled with her very nearly having done so, was heroic in his eyes. At a devastating price, she had earned a place in her father's admiration that she was never to forfeit.

Louisa's nursing experience also transformed her as a writer. Before she had gone off to war, her tales had an aspect of grotesque fantasy that betrayed a lack of experience in the world. Now, her fertile imagination was tempered by a sad but strong knowledge of the way things were. As Julian Hawthorne observed, "Her experiences influenced her writing, manifestly mellowed and deepened it; she could not have touched a million hearts except from the depth of her own."[28] Her time at the hospital also gave her a sudden wealth of writing material. She now had an authentic story to tell, and she did not guess how eager people would be to hear it. At the beginning of May, the Army of the Potomac, now under the inept command of Joseph Hooker, suffered a demoralizing defeat at Chancellorsville, and the fortunes of the Union in the eastern theater declined to their lowest point. Northern readers were ready for patriotic inspiration. Earlier that spring, someone, almost certainly Bronson, had shared Louisa's letters from Georgetown with Frank Sanborn and his friend Moncure Conway, who had joined forces to edit an antislavery journal called the *Boston Commonwealth*. The two men were quite taken with Louisa's descriptions, which they found witty and full of sincere feeling. Partly teasing, but in truth very much in earnest, Sanborn asked Louisa in April if she would like to revise her letters into a collection of short literary sketches, to be serialized in the magazine.

Louisa thought Sanborn and Conway rated her work too highly, but as always, she needed money. Perhaps just as importantly, her long, unavoidable hiatus from writing may have been starting to wear on her. Drafting the sketches probably seemed like a good way to convince herself that life was returning to normal. And if she required any more incentive to start writing again, that same April brought an envelope from Frank Leslie, containing a check for one hundred dollars. Her anonymous thriller, "Pauline's Passion and Punishment," had won the contest she had entered the previous autumn. Louisa speedily finished reworking her hospital letters and recollections, and on May 22 the first of four "Hospital Sketches" graced the pages of the *Boston Commonwealth*. The date marked a watershed in her literary career. The sketches were popular beyond Louisa's highest expectations, and by her own account, people bought the issues of the *Commonwealth* faster than the printer could supply them. In the 1860s, the word "hit" was already being used to connote a popular success. To Louisa's bemused wonder, she had one on her hands. "I find," she wrote, "I've done a good thing without knowing it."[29]

Henry James Sr., wrote to applaud her "charming pictures of hospital service."[30] To reward her efforts, he sent along a copy of his own book, *Shadow and Substance*. Far more wonderfully, however, not one but two publishers approached her with offers to release her sketches in book form. The two competitors for her work were the firm of Roberts Brothers and a fiery Scottish abolitionist named James Redpath. A raw novice in the domain of book publishing in the summer of 1863, Louisa had little sense of the comparative practical merits of the two printers. She eventually leaned toward the Scotsman. Redpath, a friend of Sanborn's, had had at least some connection with Bronson for several years. Shortly after Lincoln's election, Redpath had written to Bronson, asking him to attend an antislavery convention that Redpath had organized.[31] Now, as he angled for the rights to *Hospital Sketches*, Redpath courted not only Louisa's favor but Bronson's as well, sending the latter a complimentary copy of his company's edition of the abolitionist Wendell Phillips's speeches, lectures, and letters. Bronson praised the book, as well as Redpath's personal service to the cause of freedom in publishing such a "solid and superb" volume.[32] There can be little doubt that Bronson wanted Redpath as Louisa's publisher. For her part, Louisa liked Redpath's politics, and her Alcott sensibilities may also have been swayed by the Scotsman's promise to donate at least five cents from each copy sold to orphans made homeless or fatherless by the war. Louisa had gone into nursing to advance the cause of union and freedom; she thought it only right that her book should also promote that cause.

Bronson was undoubtedly pleased when Louisa signed her contract with Redpath, though Louisa herself came to regret the decision. Despite Redpath's honorable convictions, Louisa gradually recognized that he was unskilled as a publisher and was more interested in allocating her profits virtuously than in maximizing them. When Redpath became more insistent and sanctimonious as to the percentage to be donated to orphans, Louisa reminded him that her family, too, knew what it was to receive alms, and that so long as the Alcott fortunes remained precarious, her charity must begin at home. She wrote to him, "I . . . am sure that 'he who giveth to the poor lendeth to the Lord' & on that principle devote time and earnings to the care of my father and mother. . . . On this account I often have to deny myself the little I could do for other charities, & seem ungenerous that I may be just."[33] Like her parents, Louisa was deeply generous. Unlike them, she was learning to temper her giving impulse with prudence.

In later years, Louisa always claimed that a more astute publisher could have made more money with *Hospital Sketches*. She was probably correct. Nevertheless, she acknowledged, writing the book "showed me *my style*, & taking the hint I went where glory waited me."[34] Moreover, it was thrilling for her to go around Concord toward the end of summer and see her neighbors laughing and crying over the book. She could not quite contain her mirth upon learning that one rash youth had bought eight copies at once. From Venice the American consul—the future literary lion William Dean Howells—sent his compliments to Nurse Periwinkle.

Perhaps the crowning tribute to *Hospital Sketches* came that September. A company of Concord soldiers, recently under fire at Gettysburg, came home to a town bedecked with flags and patriotic wreathes. Louisa wrote of seeing Welcome Home banners stuck "in every stickable place."[35] The town drum corps, consisting of eight little boys trying to cope with eight large drums, strove doggedly to stay in rhythm. Julian Hawthorne, recently accepted to Harvard College, helped to produce enough lemonade "to flavor Walden Pond." A score of Concord's fairest young ladies, May Alcott among them, donned white frocks to serve the refreshments. Louisa brought out her nurse's uniform for the occasion and supervised preparations, unaware that a small ceremony was being planned for her as well. The company of sixty young veterans marched up to Orchard House. There, the captain called the column to a halt, the company wheeled to face the home, and the men raised their caps in salute to Louisa. After briefly mingling with the crowd that had come to watch the parade, the men fell back into ranks, gave a hearty cheer for the proud ex-nurse, and marched on.[36]

Louisa could claim another noteworthy product of her weeks at Union Hotel Hospital: her poem "Thoreau's Flute," which Sophia Hawthorne admired enough to send to James T. Fields at *The Atlantic*. Louisa was highly gratified to have the poem appear there, but her response was tinged with a worldly consciousness that was now sadly characteristic. She wrote, "being a mercenary creature I liked the $10 [received for the poem] nearly as well as the honor of being . . . 'a literary celebrity.' "[37]

In January, Louisa had been near death. Only seven months later, she was one of the most celebrated women in Massachusetts. In his journal, Bronson noted the favorable reviews of her book and expressed his own judgment that it was "handsomely printed, and likely to be popular," especially among army personnel. He wrote, "I see nothing in the way of a good appreciation of Louisa's merits as a woman and a writer. Nothing could be more surprising to her or agreeable to us."[38]

Bronson was continuing to garner praise for his supervision of the schools, even if Concord's real political power resided in more conservative hands than he would have liked. Like many grandparents, he was evidently more at ease with his grandchild than he had been with his own offspring. When, in his journal, he noted Freddy's infantile accomplishments, it was no longer with the clinical eye of an eager pseudoscientist but with the simple pleasure of a proud patriarch. In October, Bronson looked forward to the day, not far off, when little Freddy would be able to take solid food. He promised Anna that when the baby was ready for fruit, he would have all he wanted from Grandpa's garden.

It seems that Anna's success as a new mother, as well as Louisa's emerging stature as an author, was inspiring Bronson to imagine what he himself might now achieve. He sent a copy of "The Rhapsodist," his essay on Emerson, to James Fields, who commented on it favorably. Bronson was working on an idea for a book of characters, in which he would sketch the personalities and ideas of the many luminaries he had known, including Emerson, Thoreau, Hawthorne, Carlyle, the elder Henry James, and Margaret Fuller. His sketch of Thoreau, called "The Forester," had already been published in *The Atlantic Monthly* in April 1862. If he had failed to keep pace with the great minds around him, there still might be a place for him as their biographer.

In the autumn of 1863, as Bronson worked on his sketches of famous friends, Louisa was writing at high speed, trying to keep up with the suddenly enthusiastic demand for her work. Redpath wanted another book. James T. Fields, the same editor who had once told Louisa to stick to teaching, also inquired about a book. For the time being, Louisa satisfied him with a story for *The Atlantic*—a tale of race and revenge that she titled "My Contraband." Narrated by Miss Dane, a Civil War nurse, the story tells of Robert, a freed slave who works as an orderly in Dane's hospital. Among the critically wounded patients, Robert discovers a Confederate captain, Ned Fairfax, the son of Robert's deceased former master, who, by way of an illicit union with a slave woman, was also Robert's father. Robert prepares to murder the captain, for, as he further reveals to Miss Dane, the younger Fairfax had once sold Robert to another plantation so that he might force himself on Robert's young wife, Lucy. Nurse Dane talks Robert out of killing the captain, persuading him to go to Massachusetts and start life as a free man while Dane searches for Lucy. In gratitude, Robert takes the nurse's last name as his own. On learning that Lucy committed suicide after being disgraced by the captain, Robert joins the Fifty-fourth Massachusetts Infantry, the famous African-American regiment led in real life by Robert Gould Shaw. Coincidence again intervenes. Robert and Captain Fairfax, fully recovered, meet in battle. After mortally wounding Robert, Fairfax is killed. Before he dies, Robert finds himself under the care of Nurse Dane, who looks on as he leaves "the shadow of the life that was [for] the sunshine of the life to be."[39]

"My Contraband" treats its title character with measured respect, and the story overtly challenges the image of the passive, long-suffering slave on which Harriet Beecher Stowe had relied in *Uncle Tom's Cabin*. Nurse Dane insists on calling her orderly "Robert" instead of the more condescending "Bob," and Alcott emphasizes that her hero is "no saintly 'Uncle Tom.' "[40] Unfortunately, Alcott's resistance to this stereotype is somewhat blunted by the fact that Robert is of mixed race. Whereas Stowe had argued that people of pure-blooded African descent were naturally disposed toward saintly Christianity, she had also suggested that slaves with some Caucasian blood were innately rebellious and resentful of servitude. If Alcott intentionally distinguished Robert from Uncle Tom, she also made him predictably similar to Stowe's mixed-blood rebel George Harris. She substituted one racial commonplace for another.

"My Contraband" is more successful in its examination of the ties that unite human beings and in illustrating that love, not money, creates the more durable claims. Although the story concerns slavery, the possessive pronoun in its title refers to the bond of affection between Nurse Dane and Robert, not to a condition of ownership. Elsewhere in the story, Alcott reiterates the idea that possessive pronouns should only connect human beings if love exists between them; Robert pointedly declines to use the word "our" when referring to his and Fairfax's father because he is ashamed to use language that would link the three of them together. Lucy's suicide also shows the limits of ownership, serving notice that Fairfax can never possess her. "My Contraband" suggests that we can call our own only those whom we hold in our hearts.

Success was all very astonishing to Louisa. So many of her dreams were now being fulfilled that she felt as if the world were coming to an end. On being offered another teaching job, she took ever so slightly smug pleasure in replying, "[M]y time is fully occupied with my pen & I find story writing not only pleasanter than teaching but far more profitable."[41] Louisa viewed the change in her fortunes as a Cinderella story, except that she refused to acknowledge any fairy godmother. She wrote that she had experienced "a sudden hoist for a meek and lowly scribbler who . . . never had a literary friend to lend her a helping hand!"[42]

Coming from a young woman who lived next door to Hawthorne, who had rowed across Walden Pond with Thoreau, who had been granted free access to Emerson's library, and whose father's home had welcomed countless other literati, this claim of literary isolation comes as a surprise. To be sure, Louisa had lacked financial comfort, but in terms of the variety and depth of her literary acquaintances, was there a young woman in America who could claim to be her superior? Whatever the merits of Louisa's characterization, what may matter most is her motivation for stating it. She remained slow to accept or acknowledge help from others. She had absorbed both the radically communitarian ethic that had underlain Fruitlands and the spirit of Yankee independence expressed in Emerson's "Self-Reliance." From these contradictory influences, she had taken equally contradictory lessons. It was heavenly for Louisa to be able to give; it was awkward at best for her to admit to receiving. The monetary debts that her family had accrued, she was in haste to repay. The invisible, nondischargeable debts of influence and encouragement that she owed to Emerson, Thoreau, and indeed her own father, she found strangely hard to confess. At the same time that she wrote her stories, Louisa was constructing a personal narrative in which she needed to be either the lonely victim or the unaided hero.

If anything, Louisa may have had too many literary advisors when, in October, she finished another draft of *Moods*, at the request of James Redpath. Alcott later described the process of revising *Moods*, in somewhat fictionalized form, in the "Literary Lessons" chapter of *Little Women*. Every member of the March family has a clear idea of how to turn Jo's novel into a masterpiece, but each suggestion leads her further from her original conception. Perplexed by their earnest but skewed advice, Jo revises her novel into a hodgepodge that, in its attempts to please all, pleases no one. It seems that the Alcott family's reactions to the *Moods* manuscript were less critical. In a letter to Redpath, Louisa claimed that her parents and sisters considered the story "fine." Moreover, although Louisa noted with pleasure that her manuscript made her family laugh and cry, she also wrote, "they are no judges," suggesting that she was not likely to be easily swayed by their suggestions.43 However, potent pressure to revise came from prospective publishers, whose specifications forced Louisa to reshape her story in ways she instinctively disapproved and soon came to heartily regret.

The chief problem with the manuscript was its length. By Louisa's own admission, it was so vast as to be appalling. Still, she hoped that only "one or two things" would need to be omitted. She was not prepared for the shock she received when Redpath summoned her to the printing house and explained that, to make the book salable, she would have to cut it down by half. Louisa refused outright; she felt she had already edited the book almost as much as either she or it could bear. She withdrew the manuscript from Redpath's consideration and never dealt with him professionally again. Bronson suggested that she send the book to Hawthorne's publisher, Howard Ticknor, but he responded with a polite refusal. The manuscript went back on a shelf, its future uncertain.

Next door to the Alcotts, another story was drawing to a close. Bronson spent the last Sunday evening of February 1864 with Hawthorne. After more than twenty years of acquaintance, the novelist remained distant and aloof, much to Bronson's regret. Still willing to overlook the novelist's eccentricities, Alcott continued to desire a closer relationship and wrote, "[I] see him seldomer than I would were he more disposed to seek his neighbors."44 Alcott also noted that Hawthorne had stopped writing but seemed not to have guessed the cause: Hawthorne was gravely ill. By the beginning of May, he was no longer concealing his frailty. He planned a trip to New Hampshire with his old friend former president Pierce in hopes of recovering his strength. Shortly before Hawthorne's departure, Alcott was with his grandson when he caught sight of Hawthorne at the gate of Wayside. They spoke briefly, with Hawthorne only asking Alcott if he was well. Exchanging a few pleasantries seemed to be all that Hawthorne could manage, and Alcott wondered how a man in such poor condition could withstand a journey. A few days later, news arrived from Plymouth that Hawthorne had died. The next day, Louisa sent Sophia a bouquet of violets, picked on the hill where Hawthorne had been fond of walking. Although Sophia sent Louisa a note of thanks, Louisa felt a discomfort that kind words and a handful of violets could do little to dispel. She wrote, "We did all we could to heal the breach between the families but they held off, so we let things rest."45 On the twenty-third, a day "serene and suitable for a poet's sleep," Louisa helped arrange the flowers for Hawthorne's funeral.46 Although Bronson listed many of the famous attendees in his journal, including Pierce, Emerson, and Longfellow, he did not mention whether Abba and May were there. Sophia Hawthorne described her husband's funeral as a festival of life. The occasion moved Bronson to reflect not so much on the deceased in particular but more generally as to the passage of time. "Fair figures one by one are fading from sight," he wrote.47

Louisa still vacillated over what to do with *Moods*. While financial interest argued for a speedy publication, Louisa's artistic sense told her not to compromise on the book's contents. The dilemma might have lasted longer had it not been for the intervention of Caroline Dall. A long-time acquaintance of the Alcotts, Dall had gotten to know Louisa's mother well through their shared interest in charitable causes.48 While visiting the Alcotts in September, Dall read over some of Louisa's stories. Favorably impressed, she asked whether she might take the manuscript of *Moods* home with her. Dall adored *Moods*. She declared that no other American author possessed Louisa's promise and that, despite some unevenness in execution, the book was "often magnifecent [*sic*]."49 She forwarded it to her friend the publisher A. K. Loring. Loring also took an extreme liking to the story, but his view echoed Redpath's: the book must be cut down. His other advice was both commercially sensible and staunchly middle-brow. He liked "a story that touches and moves me . . . a story of constant action, bustle and motion."⁵⁰ His instincts told him that readers were likely to skip conversations and descriptive scenes in their haste to find out what the characters were going to *do*. For Loring, activity should culminate in a forcibly told lesson in life, leaving the reader not only enchanted but morally improved. In short, Loring wanted a best-seller, not a thoughtful disquisition on the human heart and mind.

Disappointed, Louisa was at first unable to accept Loring's commentary. She flung her manuscript into a spidery cupboard and vowed never to touch it again. Of course, it would have been easier for her to give up breathing than to honor this pledge. The next month, a vortex came upon her and she fell to work again on *Moods*, "as if mind and body had nothing to do with one another." For two weeks, like "a thinking machine in full operation," Louisa barely ate or slept.⁵¹ Then the fit subsided, leaving her dismal, tired, and complaining of blue devils. *Moods*, however, had been transformed. Ten chapters had been excised, and the work was now, in Louisa's judgment, simple, strong, and short. She fired off the rewritten text to Loring, who praised it lavishly. He proposed to publish it without delay.

Louisa's excitement in learning that her novel was to be published dissipated abruptly when Loring began to send her proofs of the chapters. In print, the chapters seemed small and stupid and no longer her own. It occurred to her that the entire project might be a mistake, but there was no turning back. She corrected the proofs, sent them back, and hoped for the best. *Moods* was published on December 25, and Louisa received her personal copies in time to give one of them to her mother for Christmas. In the note she penned to go along with the gift, Louisa thanked her mother for the sympathy, help, and love that had meant so much to her during many hard years. Louisa then added, "I hope Success will sweeten me and make me what I long to become more than a great writer—a good daughter."⁵²

But even as she expressed pride in her accomplishment, Louisa knew that *Moods* was not all she had hoped it would be. It had been too aggressively poked, prodded, redacted, and rewritten to retain the freshness of its original conception. A subplot was cut back so severely that a once-central character now appeared only in the first chapter, and the relation between her story and the remainder of the novel was rendered vexingly unclear.

The Alcott family with Orchard House in the background, around 1865.
Louisa is seated on ground at left. Abba is next. Anna Alcott Pratt stands by her son
Frederick Alcott Pratt, seated in the baby carriage. Bronson Alcott is at the far right.
This is the only known photograph in which Bronson and Louisa appear together.

(Courtesy of the Louisa May Alcott Memorial Association)

Louisa had begun the novel as a psychological study of her heroine. By the time the editing was finished, the story no longer read like a nuanced meditation on an unbalanced mind, but like a tangled romance. A work of high ambition and extreme candor, *Moods* fell victim to the inexperience of its author and to the overly commercial sensibilities of its editor.

It is a pity that *Moods* ended up as such a compromise, for no book Louisa wrote ever mattered to her more intensely than this one. Louisa had worked on *Moods* off and on for more than four years. Even after the book was published, Louisa could not bring herself to leave it alone; she republished the book, heavily revised, in 1882. Even then, it did not satisfy her. Rereading her journals a few years before her death, Louisa wrote commentaries to herself in the margins. All the marginalia dealing with *Moods* express regret and disappointment, mingled with a certain sad affection for the book she wanted to make great but, after more than twenty years and countless rewrites, was able only to make good.[53]

Whereas Louisa most often wrote in response to financial pressure, *Moods* came from an authentic impulse to express and explain herself. She told her journal, "It has always seemed as if 'Moods' grew in spite of me, & that I had little to do with it except to put into words the thoughts that would not let me rest until I had."[54] That expression begins with the quotation from Emerson that serves as the epigraph to the 1864 edition of *Moods*: "Life is a train of moods like a string of beads; and as we pass through them they prove to be many colored lenses, which paint the world their own hue, and each shows us only what lies in its own focus."[55] *Moods* is indeed Alcott's attempt to rewrite into fiction Emerson's reflections on the life of the emotions. The epigraph comes, not from one of her mentor's confident early works like *Nature* or "Self-Reliance," but from the more skeptical later essay "Experience," written after grief had taught Emerson to regard life as a maze of contingencies, in which we must continually ask, "Where do we find ourselves?" *Moods* is concerned less with the glories of the individual spirit than with its sometimes self-defeating contradictions and illogic.

The book offers a compelling character in the person of Sylvia Yule, whose efforts to triumph over her impulsive nature and to discover inner tranquility closely resemble Alcott's own. Like Alcott, Sylvia has absorbed "pride, intellect, and will" from her father, while inheriting from her mother "passion, imagination, and the fateful melancholy of a woman defrauded of her dearest hope."[56] Sylvia thus feels within her spirit two warring principles that she lacks the power to reconcile. She sees her own character as an unanswerable riddle, and she finds herself forever at the mercy of violently opposing impulses, or as the book's title would have it, "moods."

As she was later to do in *Little Women*, Louisa chose not to assign equal prominence to each of her heroine's parents. In *Moods*, however, it is the maternal figure who is thrust into the shadows. Sylvia's mother has died in childbirth, and it is the Bronson-like father who, after years of emotional remoteness, becomes uniquely dear to his daughter. As Alcott describes it, "No one was so much to her as he; no one so fully entered her thoughts and feelings. . . . As man and woman they talked, as father and daughter they loved; and the beautiful relation became their truest solace and support."[57]

Initially, however, the more significant man in Sylvia's life is Adam Warwick, a figure modeled on Thoreau. A "violently virtuous" man who "always takes the shortest way, no matter how rough it is," Warwick sympathizes with Sylvia from the outset.[58] His formidable integrity appears at first to offer Sylvia the balance she requires. However, his dedication to principle proves every bit as extreme as Sylvia's emotional nature, and the mind preoccupied by ideas stands revealed as no more satisfactory than the heart absorbed by feeling.

Eventually, Sylvia must choose between Warwick, who speaks compellingly to her romantic soul, and a representative of sober practicality. This safer choice is Geoffrey Moor. Moor appeals to Sylvia precisely because he inspires no passion. He has also just spent five years caring for a dying sister, a service that appears to qualify him to help Sylvia conquer her mental instability. She reaches out to him as a platonic friend, little imagining the difficulties of preventing their attachment from edging toward marriage, with all its daunting implications of sex and permanence. Incapable of understanding her intentions, Moor proposes. Sylvia at first rebuffs him, but in the mistaken belief that Warwick has left never to return, she consents. Warwick resurfaces soon after the two are married, and all three characters ruminate on the injustice of an institution that presumes to confer lifelong exclusive rights to another's love and loyalty. Warwick argues that unhappy marriages will remain "the tragedies of our day . . . till we learn that there are truer laws to be obeyed than those custom sanctions."[59]

Although speeches like these prompted some to accuse Alcott of advocating free love, *Moods* retreats from the tantalizing possibilities of following such "truer laws." Moor and Warwick sportingly consent to travel together to Europe for a yearlong sabbatical while Sylvia decides whether she can love her husband. While away, the two reconcile through literature, coauthoring a book to which Moor contributes poems and Warwick supplies essays. On the return voyage, their boat sinks, and Warwick heroically and conveniently drowns. In the 1864 text, Sylvia dies of consumption. However, in the 1882 version, inspired by the advice that "in making the joy of others we often find our own," Sylvia gives up morbid self-contemplation in order to serve others. She dedicates herself first to her father and, after his death, to Moor.

Sylvia, like the young Louisa, struggles to be good, but her mercurial temperament prevents her from keeping her repeated resolutions to be better. Her self-descriptions express frustration and plead for understanding: "I don't try to be odd; I long to be quiet and satisfied, but I cannot; and when I do . . . wild things, it is not because I am thoughtless or idle, but because I am trying to be good and happy. . . . [S]ometimes I think I am a born disappointment."[60] Although the narrator suggests that many of Sylvia's failings would be cured by the presence of "a wise and tender mother," Sylvia herself makes no attempt to blame her volatile nature on external forces, insisting that her problems are her own: "I know I'm whimsical, and hard to please, and have no doubt the fault was in myself."[61] She understands that to deny responsibility for her condition would also be to forfeit her claim to autonomy.

But Sylvia's troubles cannot be cured by mere understanding. Sylvia confesses that she is "always in extremes," and her brother observes despairingly that Sylvia is "either overflowing with unnatural spirits or melancholy enough to break one's heart."[62] In one chapter, Sylvia is depicted lying abjectly in bed, "tired of everybody and everything." A few chapters later, she impulsively rushes off in the direction of a wildfire and is nearly burned alive. In a later chapter, Sylvia thanks God that she has not had a child, to whom she might have passed on her "mental ills."[63] Sylvia's abrupt oscillations between depression and euphoria, her seeking of pleasure through irresponsible behavior, and her intimation that her imbalance may be hereditary add up to a now-recognizable psychological profile. Although medical science had not yet found the modern terminology for Sylvia's symptoms, Alcott created a persuasive portrait of a manic-depressive heroine.

Louisa's exposition of Sylvia's personality is highly convincing, so much so that one has cause to consider whether the author's knowledge of manic-depressive states came solely from observing others. The question demands to be posed: if Louisa May Alcott were alive today, might she herself have been diagnosed with some form of manic-depressive illness? Louisa's evident interest in mood disorders, her own mercurial character, and her seemingly obsessive work habits all argue that the query should be raised. Certainly, modern research has supported the argument that writers and artists are substantially more prone to this illness than the general population; indeed, many lines of evidence indicate a strong relation between mood disorders and creative achievement.[64]

Moreover, many of the diagnostic clues that can indicate a manic-depressive condition were present in Louisa's life. Manic-depressive illness is hereditary. Louisa's Uncle Junius engaged in erratic behavior that inflicted years of worry on the family until his death by suicide in 1852. More than once, Bronson's own behavior raised questions about his mental stability. After Fruitlands dissolved, he nearly starved himself to death. Fourteen years later, Louisa had her own flirtation with suicide. Additionally, both she and Bronson experienced mental states consistent with mania. Mania is known to manifest itself in periods of high, indefatigable energy, racing thoughts, markedly decreased need for sleep, and sharp spikes in level of productivity, followed by sustained moods of lassitude and dejection, coupled with an inability to exercise one's will. In this connection, one thinks not only of Bronson's periods of visionary euphoria but also of Louisa's "vortices." No definitive interpretation of Louisa's emotional condition has emerged. The brilliant Alcott biographer Madeleine Stern maintains that Louisa's vortices were simply part of her writing method and do not reflect any mental abnormality.[65] However, Kay Redfield Jamison, a highly respected expert on manic-depressive illness, believes that the evidence, taken as a whole, "does not irrefutably show, but is consistent with, the strong likelihood that Louisa May Alcott suffered from a form of manic-depressive illness."[66]

In our own time, most educated persons understand the basic concepts of mental abnormality, and many accept as commonplace the likelihood of a connection between literary creativity and the symptoms of manic-depressive illness. If Louisa May Alcott, like many other writers, experienced such symptoms, perhaps few readers will find the news earth-shattering. What may be of greater interest is not Louisa's mental condition itself, but her extraordinary experience of coping with it while living in the social and intellectual culture that defined her world, as well as in her particular family. Despite its insistence on the uniqueness of the individual, transcendentalism proceeded from the premise that the mental workings of all people were fundamentally similar. Emerson began his great *Essays, First*

Series by asserting, "There is one mind common to all individual men. . . . Who hath access to this universal mind is a party to all that is or can be done, for this is the only and sovereign agent."[67] In *Moods*, Louisa confronted the possibility that the mind was anything but universal—that one's thoughts and feelings can be so frustrated and touched by unseen agents that even the attempt to communicate them can become a source of anguish. Emerson famously wrote, "To believe your own thought, to believe that what is true for you in your private heart is true for all men,— that is genius."[68] But to know that one's thought and truth are not those of others and yet to manage to live a functioning life among them requires a kind of genius also.

Louisa's struggles with emotional control were a frequent source of profound distress to herself and her family during her years of growing up. Bronson's response to all emotional discontents was to urge self-mastery and self-denial. He maintained that reason could always quell the passions and that anyone who really desired it could achieve a Christlike equanimity. There was no obvious place in Bronson's theory of the mind for mental states that the individual could *not* control—no room for the idea that the roots of an unbalanced temperament might be medical instead of moral. Urged by her family to triumph over her recurrent bouts of temper and periods of dejection, and continually reassured that it was within her power to do so, Louisa felt troubled when even her best efforts fell short of success. On one level, the awareness that neither she nor anyone around her could fully understand her emotional volatility must have been horrible. Yet the clash between her personality and her family's prescriptions of self-control may also have produced some positive effects. For one thing, Louisa seems to have discovered early on that one means of getting the family to accept her moods was to give them an artistic expression. Had her vortices produced nothing creative, her parents would likely have regarded them as episodes of pointless self-indulgence. Instead, because Louisa could channel her flights into literary art, they won for her a degree of latitude and acceptance. When genius burned on the second story of Orchard House, her family learned both to admire the impulse and to leave it alone.

Louisa's parents' exhortations toward self-control may have helped her to withstand the emotional difficulties that she experienced. The grace and

determination with which her parents bore their poverty, their long practice of self-denial, the forbearance that they displayed toward each other's
difficult personalities—all these argued the value of never giving in to hard-
ship. Louisa may never have fully conquered her temper or her tempestu-
ous mood swings, but Abba and Bronson always gave her reasons to keep
trying. It has been suggested that the unyielding asceticism of Louisa's parents was a harmful force in her personal development. However, it may be
argued with equal good faith that the staunchness with which they encouraged her to confront her inner failings was precisely what kept her sane.

Abba Alcott read her gift copy of *Moods* almost from cover to cover
before going to bed on Christmas night. Bronson, too, devoured the book
at once. Some time later, he was initially befuddled and then pleased when
Henry James Sr., forgetting the name of Louisa's novel, told him, "They
are reading *Dumps* at home with great interest."[69] If, in fact, the novel was
meant as a plea for understanding with regard to Louisa's emotions, Bronson did not respond to this aspect of the work in writing. However, he did
receive it as a highly promising work of art and social commentary. He
wrote, "She has succeeded better in her treatment of the social problem [of
marriage] than did Goethe or George Sand." He felt that she had written
a greater book than she realized, one that might open the way "to a career
of wide usefulness, if not of permanent fame as a novelist and a woman."[70]

That same Christmas of 1864, General William Tecumseh Sherman
offered a gift to President Lincoln: the city of Savannah, Georgia. As the
Alcotts rang in the year 1865, the end of the war was finally in sight. In February, Louisa worked awhile on "Success," but finding that thrillers were
half the work and paid better than serious fiction, she "soon dropped it &
fell back on rubbishy tales." Two months later, on Sunday, April 2, Grant's
army marched into Richmond. The night before, Louisa had been in
Boston, watching Edwin Booth in a production of *Hamlet*. She called his
performance the finest she had ever seen him give. In a Maryland rooming
house, Edwin's younger brother John was plotting a different spectacle.

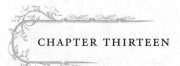

CHAPTER THIRTEEN

JOURNEYS EAST AND WEST

"I am more desirous of seeing than of saying."
—A. BRONSON ALCOTT, *Journals,* February 9, 1866

"Let's be merry while we may.
And lay up a bit for a rainy day."

—LOUISA MAY ALCOTT,
"To Abigail May Alcott," January 1, 1868

L IKE MANY AMERICANS, BRONSON ALCOTT APPRECIATED Abraham Lincoln much more deeply after Booth's bullet had been fired and Secretary of War Stanton had solemnly pronounced that his former chief "belong[ed] to the ages." Although he had broken from his habitual abstention from the polls to vote for Lincoln in 1860, and again in 1864, Bronson had felt more enthusiasm for union and abolition than for the candidate who represented them. However, on April 15, 1865, when word came of the horror at Ford's Theatre, Alcott's estimate of Lincoln instantly transformed. He called the fallen president "a martyr to justice and republicanism" and a "cherished idol," whose death had plunged the country into a woe in which "all men" took part. With reflexive optimism, however, Bronson predicted that Lincoln's murder would "knit us in closer and more religious bonds to God and the right, and redound to the preservation of our national honor and glory."[1]

Like her father, Louisa was initially horrified to hear of the assassination, but her later reflections were complex. Although she had reveled in the fall of Richmond, she now wrote, "I am glad to have seen such a strange & sudden change in a nation's feelings."[2] She did not explain just where this gladness came from. Perhaps her experience of life had made her more at home with bittersweet emotions than with pure jubilation. In much of Louisa's writing, the emotional keynote is not unreflective joy, but the darker but more durable happiness that comes from hardships bravely shared. In the days of late April 1865, the nation collectively experienced feelings that were continually present in Louisa's heart. For once, the world appeared to feel as she did. On the day of mourning, only one sight struck her as significant enough to record in her journal: the novel spectacle of a black man and a white man walking arm in arm. She "exulted thereat."[3] For the moment, there seemed to be every reason to suppose that a republic of freedom and equality was at hand.

For Louisa and her family in general, there was less cause for sorrow than for celebration. Despite Louisa's own misgivings about the book, *Moods* had already gone into a third printing.[4] Her magazine potboilers, published under the name of A. M. Barnard, were selling briskly. On June 24, the day that would have marked Lizzie's thirtieth birthday, Anna gave birth to her second son, John Sewall Pratt. The prospects seemed as glorious outdoors as in. Bronson told his journal that he had never known "such a series of bright, benign days . . . as if Nature, partaking of the temper of the country, had also begun her cycle of reconstruction to intimate her sympathy and delight in the brilliant prospects and peaceful reign of our new republic."[5] On Independence Day, he wrote, "the republic now begins to look sweet and beautiful, as if honest, patriotic citizens might walk upright without shame or apologies."[6] Before the war, Alcott had always known that his ideal republic was unattainable because of slavery. It now seemed to him that the country was free to enter an era of enlightenment and justice.

Bronson hoped that the war would be only the first episode in a surging national movement toward deeper social reforms. He was mistaken. The reserves of American idealism were deep, but they had been drained low by four years of unspeakable violence. Relatively few Americans now took any interest in further moral crusades. It now seemed not only prudent but natural for people to start putting their own interests first. As the massive productive energies that had been mobilized to fight a war were converted to peaceful ends, per capita wealth and the availability of consumer goods soon reached unprecedented levels. No longer finding its heroes on the battlefields of Tennessee and Virginia, the nation took to measuring people by their audacious acquisition and lavish expenditure of money. Far from the golden age that Alcott anticipated, the nation instead entered a gilded one, soon to be derided by Mark Twain and Charles Dudley Warner in their famous satire. America had learned, as Walt Whitman was to put it, "the lessons of the concrete."[7]

As far as the philosophical mood of the nation was concerned, Bronson Alcott's moment seemed to have passed. Despite his highly capable performance, even his position as superintendent of the Concord schools was taken from him. The day before Lincoln's assassination, Alcott learned that he was to be removed from office, evidently as a result of an obscure political deal.[8] It was to people like his daughter Louisa, who was rapidly learning how to write for a commercial audience and who still carefully noted every dollar earned in her journals, that the postbellum age appeared to belong.

In mid-July, Louisa received an attractive offer. William Fletcher Weld, a fabulously wealthy Boston shipping merchant, had an infirm daughter, Anna, whose health and character he thought might benefit from travel. Having learned of Louisa's medical experience and of her unsatisfied wanderlust, he suggested that Louisa accompany Anna and her half brother George to Europe as a nurse and travel companion. Weld envisioned a grand tour for his offspring, including visits to London, the Rhine Valley, Italy, Switzerland, and France. The entire excursion might last as long as a year. Although Louisa had long dreamed of such an opportunity, she at first hesitated to accept. It would be risky to take an extended break from her writing routine just as she was gaining such firm recognition, and she was not sure how her family would manage without her. Despite her concerns, the family verdict was unanimous in favor of her going. Louisa's 1873 novel *Work* contains a chapter called "Companion," tangentially based on Louisa's tenure with Miss Weld. In the novel, while debating whether to become an invalid's companion, the heroine, Christie Devon, reflects, "My own experience of illness has taught me how to sympathize with others and love to lighten pain."[9] Louisa possessed the same qualifications, and she had no objection to using them. Thus, after "a week of work & worry," Louisa packed her trunk.[10]

On July 17, the night before she left Concord, the Alcotts entertained William Torrey Harris, on a visit from St. Louis. Harris urged Bronson to get over his inertia and to try to publish his manuscripts; it seemed to him that Bronson's recent work would find favor with readers of all classes.

Harris's visit also reawakened Bronson's interest in the Midwest. Alcott reflected that, whereas the transcendentalist era in New England was at an end, a receptive audience for his philosophy might still await him amid the plains and prairies.

On the morning of the twentieth, as the Cunard steamer *China* made its way out of Boston harbor, its most illustrious passenger stood not at the bow of the boat gazing forward, but at the stern looking back. Bronson was sorry to see Louisa go. He wrote that, for the moment, the family felt "disposed to blame the good fortune that takes her from us, almost the fair winds that waft her over the waves."[11] He also knew, however, that his daughter needed a restorative trip almost as much as Miss Weld. He saw that she was "a good deal worn with literary labor and deserving some diversion to recruit her paling spirits and fancy," and he hoped that, when she returned, "we may find her . . . refreshed, enriched, and polished for the future literary victories which I am sure she is to win."[12]

Louisa found her voyage anything but refreshing. Ocean travel was uncomfortable. It was also soon evident that she and Anna Weld were to be companions only in a nominal sense. Anna played a fine game of backgammon, but this skill seems to have been her chief attribute. She was a peevish young woman with no literary inclinations that Louisa could observe. Indeed, months later, when they stopped in Frankfurt, Anna and George could not fathom Louisa's interest in seeing Goethe's home. "Who," they obtusely demanded, "was Goethe to fuss about?"[13]

It was not merely that Anna Weld was a philistine. The commercial nature of their relationship also divided the two women. Although she did not put it into writing, Louisa surely felt the strangeness of the position of one who becomes a friend for hire. To receive money in exchange for smiling at dull conversation, for treating another's trivial whims and disappointments as weighty matters, for exchanging the contacts and pleasantries one typically reserves for earnest friendships—how could a forthright, honest person like Louisa carry out such duties without a moral twinge? In *Work*, Christie Devon soothes the invalid entrusted to her by singing, reading aloud, and gently massaging the young woman's temples with cool water. Louisa likely gave similar attentions to Miss Weld, and it pleased her whenever the latter appeared to improve. Nevertheless, Louisa's service remained unambiguously a job. Finding no promise of friendship among her fellow passengers either, she kept mostly to her books and did her best to pass the time until Saturday, July 29, when Liverpool finally came into view.

A grimy, functional city, Liverpool impressed Louisa primarily with the number and desperate appearance of its beggars. She was glad the following Monday to board a train for London, the city of Dickens, Thackeray, and Carlyle that had lived in her imagination since childhood. As the train passed through the countryside, Louisa described what she saw as "unyan-kee." Each field seemed newly weeded and every garden looked as if it had just been put in order. What impressed her most profoundly, however, was the lack of urgency that she saw in all directions. "Nothing was abrupt," she wrote home to her father, "nobody in a hurry, and nowhere did you see the desperately go ahead style of life that we have. The very cows in America look fast . . . but here the plump cattle stood . . . with a reposeful air that is very soothing."[14] In this placid climate, Louisa realized by contrast the extent to which not only her nation, but she herself, was propelled by restless desire. It is no accident that she addressed to her father in particular her reflections on the headlong speed of American life. Bronson had long been infuriatingly deliberate, taking it almost as a point of honor to reject the prevailing sharp-elbowed bustle of his country. Now, Louisa was discovering a place that seemed in sympathy with her father's principles.

The four days that the two women spent in London were dull and drizzly, and matters were made worse by Miss Weld's complaints of poor health. Two days after their arrival, Louisa was able to persuade her fussy companion to come with her to Westminster Abbey. Although Miss Weld was soon fatigued, Louisa managed to perform a pilgrimage of sorts, paying homage at the tombs of Spenser, Milton, and Ben Jonson. On the whole, she felt as if she had fallen into a novel.[15]

Once her parents got over the strangeness of having an empty place at the dinner table, Louisa's departure caused relatively few changes in the daily routine at Orchard House, except that, under Bronson's indifferent management, the bills again stopped getting paid on time. If falling back slightly into debt did not faze him, Bronson did find himself ruffled by a piercing critique of *Moods* in the *North American Review*. On the brighter side, the notice praised the second half of the novel for its beauty and vigor, and the reviewer kindly stated that only two or three Americans were currently capable of writing a better novel. In its harsher passages, however, the review was scathing. It complained that the book was "innocent of any doctrine whatever" and commented particularly on the author's ignorance of human nature and her confidence in spite of her ignorance.[16] Bronson hotly denounced the review as being "of a popular cast, flippant, and undeserving."[17] What may have hurt Bronson most deeply was that the piece was written by the son and namesake of his old friend and philosophical sparring partner, Henry James Sr. Although Bronson was doubtlessly aware that the younger Henry had some literary inclination of his own, many years were still to pass before the world would hear about *The Portrait of a Lady*, *The Ambassadors*, and *The Golden Bowl*. As it was, Bronson must have wondered what this young, unproven upstart knew about writing a novel, anyway.

As the leaves turned and fell, Bronson busied himself by building a new front fence, fashioning the gates with his own hands and working the posts and stretchers into designs that he proudly pronounced "grotesque." Given the modern understanding of the word, it hardly sounds as if Bronson was paying himself a compliment. To Bronson, however, grotesqueness signaled a love of natural objects for their own sake, as well as a conscious rejection of fixed artistic laws. Bronson continued to admire John Ruskin, who had argued for a positive kind of grotesque, resulting from the play of a serious mind and giving pleasure to the viewer according to the delight the worker had taken in making the artifact.[18] Bronson built his fences like a true Ruskinian disciple, disdaining the straight lines of his neighbors' pickets and refusing to paint his work "with some tint that nature and art alike disown."[19] In his midsixties, Bronson was taking as much joy as ever in the work of his hands. As always, the only toil that struck him as real came directly from his own brain, limbs, and tools. The power of capital—things created for their exchange value or the ability of money to create well-being and advantages—remained either too abstract or too demeaning for him to accept.

By contrast, in Europe, Louisa had never stopped thinking about how to turn almost everything she saw into a salable product. Her journey up the Rhine, her stay in a French pension, and a day's wanderings through London in search of the places she had known only through reading Dickens: all would eventually be converted into short articles for *The Indepen-*

dent, a New York journal with an interest in travel pieces.[20] Louisa was now very little different from the woman who, three years later, was to write the book that made her famous. Her attachment to family, her fierce and countervailing need to proclaim her independence, and her profound regard for self-sacrifice and shared struggle were all firmly established parts of her character and were ready to emerge as components of her literary vision. There remained but one more indispensable formative experience before the defining phase of her career might begin. It was waiting for her in Vevey, Switzerland, at a pension nestled behind five tall poplar trees on the shore of Lake Geneva.

It was the end of September 1865 when Louisa and the Welds arrived at this place of unique beauty, one where, as the younger Henry James observed a few years later, grandeur and charm were constantly interfused and harmonized. Through the sloping land above the lake, visitors followed grass-grown footpaths through fertile orchards. Quaint villages nestled so deeply in the greenery that an observer looking upward from the lake hardly knew they were there. The particular shimmer of the lake also impressed itself on people's imaginations and memories. To James, the water seemed to fling up its blue reflection into his approving eyes.[21] The blueness of the water also struck Louisa as she and the Welds arrived under sail from Lausanne. She was equally enchanted by Pension Victoria, where George Weld told his half sister and Louisa good-bye and departed for Paris. The pension, which the two ladies called home until December 6, lay at the base of a hillside adorned by a vineyard and a rose garden. Looking up from behind the house toward the summit, one could see a venerable chapel and a stately chateau. On the opposite side, a terrace wall rose directly out of the lake and was continuously washed by its waters. The terrace looked out across the lake, dominated by the white Alps of Savoy, which greeted Louisa's eyes "shining in the sun like some celestial country seen in dreams."[22]

The pension played host to an assortment of guests whose diversity Louisa found both amusing and eye-opening. Across the residence's dinner table, her frank American gaze met the stare of a Russian baron, whose manner Louisa considered turbulent and barbaric. She chuckled inwardly at an overfed Frenchman who imagined that he resembled the emperor and was continually striking Napoleonic poses. Two elderly sisters from

Scotland engaged Louisa's literary interest by prattling about Sir Walter Scott, whom they claimed to have known personally in their youth. An Irish dowager, morbidly immersed in recollections of death, sat heavily bedecked in crepe and would not remove her black gloves even at meals.

Nearby sat a handsome, courtly English colonel of "gigantic powers" who had accepted the task of filling his six pale little daughters with knowledge and excruciatingly correct breeding, although he seemed to have denied them the luxury of personalities.[23] His half dozen captive pupils seemed to be all the same age, and their father and mother dressed them identically. They spoke four languages and were walking storehouses of geological and astronomical data. Nevertheless, Louisa felt sorry for the sextet of scholars, whom she dreaded to approach lest they respond with a torrent of historic dates or algebraic equations. Anyone who knew her history would have understood Louisa's pity as she heard the colonel lecture his children on "the Spanish inquisition, the population of Switzerland, the politics of Russia, and other lively topics, equally well suited to infant minds."[24] The barrage of information against innocent brains surely reminded her of the methods of Dr. Blimber in Dickens's *Dombey and Son*, and more personally and painfully, the imperious assaults of Charles Lane. Her father's strange but gentle methods seemed obviously preferable to the teachings of all the colonels in England.

Louisa reserved her harshest judgments, however, for another guest of military rank: Colonel Polk, a former Confederate who had brought his wife and daughter to Europe to distance himself from the memory of the war that had cost him virtually all his property, including five hundred slaves. Throughout their uneasy time under a shared roof, Colonel Polk routinely raised Louisa's blood pressure with tales of Yankee treachery and his fervent assertions that his loving slaves had been forced away by the northern armies and were yearning yet to come back to their master. A different story was recounted by the Polks' black servant Betty, who privately told Louisa and one of the English ladies that the family's more able-bodied slaves had run off as soon as the Union soldiers had come near. Those too old to fend for themselves had lingered in the hope that, having extracted a lifetime of labor from them, Colonel Polk might now repay his debt by taking care of them. Instead, Betty said, "He runned away hissef, and lef 'em to starve."[25] When the Englishwoman circulated this account among the other guests of the pension, the Polks, who had thus far enjoyed the sympathy of most of the guests, saw their popularity fade appreciably, much to Louisa's delight. However, the colonel was still not deterred from singing the praises of Jefferson Davis and gleefully recollecting how a rebel surgeon had intentionally amputated the healthy limb of a wounded northern soldier. Hearing such anecdotes, Louisa must have reflected that, while the war may have ended, the peace had not begun.

But all else that Louisa heard and saw at the Pension Victoria paled in comparison with a single radiant acquaintance: a young Polish man who cut a striking figure in his blue-and-white university suit and cap and whose name gave her New England tongue no end of difficulty. In *The Independent*, she gave his first name as Stanislas and abandoned her effort at his surname after the initial W., advising her readers that "two hiccoughs and a sneeze will give the last name better than letters."[26] In truth, Louisa knew the name of Ladislas Wisniewski as well as her own. Ladislas's brief but unforgettable passage through the life of Louisa May Alcott began with a cough. Sitting by the fire at the pension on a blustery autumn day, Louisa heard someone in the adjoining passageway trying to clear his lungs as the wind rushed in through an open door. She soon beheld a tall, thin young man of about twenty with an intelligent face and the prepossessing manners of a foreigner. With nothing more than courtesy in her mind, she moved over slightly to make a space for him before the fire.

Ladislas's delayed reaction, however, betokened more than courtesy. That evening at dinner, finding that he was seated too far from her to initiate much conversation, he surprised Louisa by rising and bowing toward her. Raising his glass to his casual benefactress, he announced in French, "I drink good health to the Mademoiselle."[27] Louisa, wondering perhaps whether she was observing the correct form, returned his wish, but the shadow that instantly crossed his face informed her that her reply had not satisfied him. It dawned on her that he had intended something more heartfelt than a compliment. She was not conscious of any feelings toward Wisniewski until the following day when, during a friendly conversation, he disclosed a pair of facts that she found almost irresistible. He was, he said, a veteran of a recent nationalist revolt against the occupying forces of Tsar Alexander. In broken English—the prettiest Louisa had ever heard—he told of being thrown into prison after taking part in a student uprising.

Reminded of the "brave boys in blue" she had tended in Georgetown, Louisa was already in a fair way to being captivated.[28] Her sympathies became fully engaged, however, when she discovered the reason for young Ladislas's cough. As a result of his struggles against the tsar, the young Pole's health had been broken. During his imprisonment, he had contracted tuberculosis. Ladislas tried to make light of his disease and did not care to mention it. Nevertheless, Louisa believed that this boy in blue, like John Suhre and so many of the others she had met in Georgetown, was dying.

However, it was impossible in Ladislas's company to think only of the foreboding future. Despite his weakened state, the young man was a whirligig of a fellow. The topics of conversation into which they drew each other seemed unending, even though Louisa's bad French and Ladislas's limited exposure to English presented some barriers. Louisa decided on a less cumbersome nickname for Ladislas, "Laddie," and appointed herself his English tutor. Laddie responded by helping Louisa, never a quick study at languages, with her French. Louisa found his progress more impressive than hers, although she wrote that he would occasionally slap his forehead and exclaim, "I am imbecile! I never can will shall to have learn this beast of English!"[29] Laddie was also an accomplished musician. With a Russian woman who was also staying at the Victoria, he put on impromptu piano recitals. Louisa had long enjoyed the writings of George Sand. Only a few days before arriving at the pension, she had taken time in Frankfurt to buy some pictures of her bohemian idol. Now, as she listened to her own minor Chopin, it must have seemed to her that, in a modest way, she had stepped into George Sand's world. In a stylish cravat and collar, Laddie seemed to grow more deeply inspired the longer he played. Louisa wrote that, as he and the Russian came together in their artistic furor, the piano vibrated, the stools creaked, and the candles danced in their sockets. The guests at the pension sat rapt as the four hands flew over the keys, and it seemed faintly possible that both the musicians and the instrument might vanish into a musical whirlwind.

Laddie's willingness to share a keyboard with a Russian at first surprised Louisa and eventually won her admiration. Laddie had spoken to her not only of his own mistreatment during the rebellion, but also of how tsarist troops had massacred a crowd numbering in the hundreds for singing the Polish national hymn. Touched by the story, Louisa asked him to play the song at the piano. Laddie demurred; he did not wish to offend the Russian guests at the pension, especially the irritable baron. "Then play it," she urged him. "He dare not forbid it here, and I should rather enjoy that little insult to your bitter enemy." Laddie, however, was good-natured but firm as he gave Louisa a lesson in manners: "Ah, Mademoiselle, it is true we are enemies, but we are also gentlemen."[30]

Laddie shared confidences with Louisa and slipped little notes under her door, which he referred to as chapters in the great history that they would write together. Their dictionaries and grammar books became serviceable go-betweens, supplying a prim and respectable reason for meeting but easy enough to cast aside when the mood called for games and dancing instead of conjugations. As she and Laddie wandered the shore of the lake, they made splendid plans for the future. It is hard to imagine, though, what plans they could realistically have entertained. For the fiery American woman, well into her thirties and her fortunes still unmade, any candid look into the future must have included much hard work with uncertain prospects of reward. For the gentle, infirm Pole, the word "future" could never have been spoken without a hint of hollowness. It was the present that these two must look to. There would not always be time, but there was time now for walks in the chateau garden, for taking a sailboat out onto the lake, and for wondering why time must always go on.

November 29, Louisa's birthday, was wild and windswept, "very like me," she observed, "in its fitful changes of sunshine and shade."[31] Thousands of miles away, her father was turning sixty-six, precisely twice her own age. She thought of him and felt a trifle empty at having to miss the modest ceremony that they always had on that day. Anna Weld brightened the day by giving her a painting of the nearby castle of Chillon. Laddie, with nothing tangible to give, played her a concert and wished her "All good and happiness on earth and a high place in heaven." Louisa admitted to herself that, despite the pleasant times with her father, she usually felt sad on her birthday. Today, however, was an exception; she was happy and hopeful and enjoyed everything with unusual relish. It was true that she felt rather old for thirty-three, but as she gratefully acknowledged, there was much in her life to keep her young.[32]

The romance lasted into December. Louisa and Miss Weld had intended to move on to Nice earlier, but an outbreak of cholera in that city had combined with their current sense of comfort to dampen their enthusiasm for the trip. When they at last decided to press on, the farewell festival that the pension organized in their honor was not sufficient to dispel the melancholy. Laddie traveled with them as far as Lausanne and then, kissing their hands, he bade them a disconsolate farewell. For Louisa and Miss Weld, the journey to the Mediterranean was a sullen passage, its discomforts perhaps sharpened by the fact, now apparent, that Miss Weld, too, had been attracted to Laddie and considered him *her* particular favorite. At some point, Louisa went back to the page of her journal in which she had initially commented on her "little romance" with Laddie and scratched out what she had written with such vigor that she destroyed the paper. It is the only place in her surviving journals where she canceled an entry with such violence. Next to the remaining portion of the entry, she wrote, "Couldn't be."[33] However, it was easier to efface Laddie from her journal than from her memory. She wrote about him in *The Independent* and years later in a story titled "My Boys" in a collection of sketches she called *Aunt Jo's Scrap-Bag*. In these factual reminiscences of him, Louisa noticeably avoided the word "love." Yet there is no better word for what she felt.

Throughout most of her stay in Nice, which lasted until May 1866, Louisa's state of mind was at a pronounced variance with the splendor of her surroundings. Having come this far, Miss Weld no longer desired to travel, and her time with Laddie had taught her little about bearing illness with good grace. Louisa could not fail to appreciate the beauty of the promenade that curved gently along the bay and played host each day to an array of handsome carriages and fashionable people. However, the well-stocked shops, the picturesque buildings, and the profusion of roses, orange trees, and palms failed to lift her spirits. She was homesick, and even if the days brought perfect weather, they brought no activity that Louisa found either pleasant or interesting. Making matters worse, Laddie sent them letters that expressed a despairing state of mind, and his laments struck Miss Weld as deeply unsettling. Louisa wrote in her journal, somewhat enigmatically, "I could not advise them to be happy as they desired, so everything went wrong & both worried."[34] Although Louisa was occasionally able to escape for a walk among the vineyards and olive trees, the overall situation was oppressive and untenable. Recollecting her Christmas in Nice, she later wrote, "With friends, health, & a little money, how jolly one might be in this perpetual summer."[35] But these three ingredients were wanting. By February, she could no longer bear the prospect of catering indefinitely to Miss Weld's whims and frailties. She gave notice that she would quit her post as the latter's companion at the beginning of May. Leaving Anna in the care of a maid and a substitute companion, Louisa climbed aboard the Paris-bound train on May 1 feeling she had performed an act of self-emancipation, long overdue. For the rest of her life, she never again accepted nonliterary employment.

When she disembarked in Paris, she was not prepared for the surprise that greeted her. There, in the crowd, waving his familiar blue-and-white cap, was Laddie. He had come to Paris to reunite with some of his old student compatriots and to teach music until conditions were ripe for a return to Poland. By some stratagem, he had found out the names of the people with whom Louisa was going to stay in Paris and had learned from them the details of her itinerary. The sight of Laddie was thoroughly agreeable to her; it was evident to her now that his romantic gestures meant nothing more to him than a jolly amusement, fun and flattering perhaps, but in no sense serious. His amorous triflings were a sign of immaturity, but this very immaturity had been largely responsible for her feelings toward him from the start. In at least one measure of adulthood, however, he may have been her superior. He, perhaps more than she, had always grasped the impossibility of their situation and had been the first to realize that, where a deeper attachment was out of the question, flirtation and frivolity might be pleasing ends in themselves. Louisa had only sixteen days to spend in Paris before pushing on to London. The time was long enough, though, for her to say later, "We had a happy life together."[36] Their days were filled with sightseeing, long walks in the Bois de Boulogne, and listening to afternoon music in the Tuileries Gardens. One form of enjoyment was shunned, however. Laddie was unable to go to evening dances or concert halls, for fear that the close and stuffy atmosphere would harm his lungs.

To Louisa's thinking, the difference in their ages allayed improper suspicions rather than inciting them. She told readers of her *Scrap-Bag*, "My twelve years' seniority made our adventures quite proper."[37] While admitting that Wisniewski was "captivating and romantic," she emphasized the respectable distance between them by classifying him as a "boy."[38] The nickname she gave him, "Laddie," also underscored his boyishness. A second nickname was Ladislas's own suggestion. Back home, his mother had tenderly called him "Varjo." He asked that Louisa use this name too. During their time in Paris, he grew more playfully daring, encouraging her to call him not only Varjo but "ma drogha," which, he explained without a hint of mischief, meant "my friend" in Polish. Louisa innocently consented. Only after the phrase excited chuckles and knowing glances from Laddie's Polish friends did he reveal that she had been calling him "my darling" in the most tender fashion. Evidently, Louisa's "boy" took great amusement from the ambiguities of their connection.

The significant emotional attractions in Louisa's life had always in them some spirit of charity, which both enabled her to justify her passion and to maintain a protective sense of hierarchy in the relationship. Alf Whitman had lost his mother. The soldiers at the Union Hotel Hospital were wounded and dependent. Laddie was an expatriate freedom fighter who appeared to be mortally ill. To describe all of them, Louisa resorted to the phrase "my boys." In her journal, she called her time with Laddie "a little romance."[39] Yet it was also clear that she could not allow her feelings toward him to be merely pleasurable or self-indulgent. Laddie's brave sacrifice of his health and his subsequent need for help and care gave Louisa an opportunity to sympathize and to give, and this fact mattered to her every bit as much as his physical beauty and well-mannered charm. These sympathies were genuine, but they were also a way to keep the little romance little.

Carolyn Heilbrun rightly warns that to read Louisa May Alcott with a consciousness of Freud is to enter at once into problematic territory.[40] Sentiments like those Alcott expresses regarding Laddie come to us as from an Eden of the psyche; they are messages that we, with our own cultural understandings of human urges and emotions, are both too clever and too clumsy to reliably decode. In being attracted to a young man with an evidently fatal disease and who undeniably reminded her of her wounded Civil War soldiers, was Louisa unconsciously eroticizing death? What motivated her to infuse her feelings of romance with such maternal overtones? A twenty-first-century reader feels remiss in leaving such questions unasked. However, one who respects the guileless wish of a kind woman to give solace to the dying and a mother's protection to a charming but luckless youth feels like a scoundrel in asking them. One conclusion, however, seems inescapable. When Louisa experienced feelings of tender attachment, she had an almost reflexive wish to raise that attachment to a level of sanctity. All her life, she had been taught that love should be pure and disinterested, and her model for such affections had always been the family. Hardly surprising, then, that the greatest gift she thought she could give Laddie was to receive him as a figurative son.

On May 17 they saw each other for the last time. At the train station, as she held the bottle of cologne he had given her as a remembrance, Louisa must have felt that the only sin at such a moment was dishonesty. The twelve years that divided them vanished. The silly conceit that he was merely her boy fell away. Years later, the young readers of *Aunt Jo's Scrap-Bag* read about a moment a bit beyond their comprehension: "I drew down his tall head and kissed him tenderly, feeling that in this world there were no more meetings for us. Then I ran away and buried myself in an empty railway carriage, hugging the little cologne bottle he had given me." She still kept with her a dried December rose from Vevey, a rose that preserved for her the memory of Laddie, "the last and dearest of [her] boys."

Louisa's description of her parting from Laddie as a self-interment and her choice of a faded rose as the emblem of their relationship speak poignantly of her sense of loss and lament. In one sense, the descriptions were apt: Laddie was her last significant romance, perhaps the only real one. However, that loss was not quite so permanent as she feared. To her grateful surprise, Laddie did not die soon after their parting. Indeed, he lived to return to Poland, maintained a correspondence with Louisa for several years, and before finally disappearing from the surviving documents, was able to tell Louisa of having married and become the father of two daughters. His life in fiction proved even longer. As Louisa freely admitted, Laddie, along with her old Concord friend Alf Whitman, jointly supplied the inspiration for Laurie, the effervescent boy next door in *Little Women*.[41]

Louisa spent seven weeks in London, taking in all that the city had to offer. She was perhaps most grateful for the chance to indulge her ongoing fascination with Dickens. She spent a day eagerly crisscrossing the city in search of real-life locations that had surfaced in the pages of *Martin Chuzzlewit*, *Dombey and Son*, and *David Copperfield*. She even managed to secure admission to a reading by the author himself and doubtlessly looked forward to the event with expectations that could only be disappointed.

And disappointed they were, from the very moment that the great man appeared on stage, bedecked with gaudy rings and sporting foppish curls. Repelled by the sight of his false teeth and the sound of his voice, which was that of "a worn-out actor," Louisa now had a clear image of the kind of literary celebrity she did not want to become.[42]

As Louisa explored an old world to the east, Bronson embarked on another excursion to the Midwest. Since the death of Lincoln, Bronson had begun to reconsider his ideas of inherent eastern superiority, as well as his sense of what qualities were most authentically American. From the banks of the Mississippi, he wrote to Abba that he had not found anywhere "a more profound treatment in the true American spirit, than these men exhibit." In St. Louis, he observed, philosophers like William Harris were "powers and influences." The educated men he found here, he thought, had a unique practicality. Their thought was quick and forceful, and they looked at life through a perspective of clear logic to which Bronson was unaccustomed. He proclaimed that the waters of the Mississippi bathed the shore of a "New New England," and he felt that eastern men, so slow to believe in things that originated elsewhere, might benefit from performing the same pilgrimage that he had made. Euphorically, he averred that the possibilities of the wondrous West were infinite.[43]

Certainly Bronson's personal prospects in this rising city were encouraging. On February 26, he wrote to Abba that he had had an engagement every evening.[44] His conversations were winning favor, and the attendance was strong both in numbers and in quality of participation. He was glad to report that he and his audiences had been working smoothly together, and his friends were encouraging him to prepare a new lecture on New England from the standpoint of its relations to the West.

Despite his optimistic letters home, however, he was impressing people more as a personality than as a thinker. When, at Harris's invitation, he addressed the St. Louis Philosophical Society, his audience grew restive. Alcott had chosen to set forth his theory of genesis, which held that human beings were originally bodiless souls, engendered by a force of "pure being." The material world had come to exist because these souls had sinned and, in their falling away from perfection, had created a descending series of natural kingdoms.[45] The theory made great sense to Alcott but not to the Philosophical Society. Schooled in Hegelian dialectic, they expected reason, not divination. Harris's respected associate Henry Brockmeyer, who later dubbed Alcott's speculations on the birth of the cosmos a collection of "infantile asininities," openly heckled the speaker. Under pressure to artic-ulate his ideas as a logically derived system, Alcott could only bluster. Another audience member provoked a laugh by suggesting that only an Alcott could rightly interpret an Alcott. Visibly upset by the lack of cour-tesy, Bronson meekly bore the jibes and submitted to "the gantlet of their fierce logic" as best he could. Though unimpressed by his lack of rigor, the society members could at least recognize a good sport. They rewarded Alcott's perseverance by electing him an auxiliary member.[46]

Alcott's social encounters more than made up for his awkward moments at the podium. While in St. Louis, he took tea with General John Pope, who had led the Union army at Second Manassas. Passing homeward through Cincinnati, he stayed at the home of Judge Alphonso Taft. Alcott had pre-viously passed within the orbit of three presidents. In addition to discussing abolition with Fillmore and observing Lincoln in the Senate chamber, he had likely been introduced to Franklin Pierce by their mutual friend Hawthorne. Now he came unknowingly into the presence of a fourth, when he was introduced to the judge's eight-year-old son, William Howard.

On March 17, Bronson was back home. Comfortably reinstated at Orchard House, he thought of Louisa, still overseas. He waited only a day after his return to send her a letter. Though he was anxious to see her again, he also advised her to "get all you can before setting your face homewards." Calling her his "noble daughter," he suggested that she might come with him on some future western tour. He closed with an exhortation and a state-ment of deepest pride: "The doors are opened wide for the freest exercise of your good Gifts, fame, if you must have it, and a world wide influence. Permit me to claim you in my name, and for your sex and country."[47]

Louisa came home on July 20 to a joyful reception. Bronson met her at the station. At the rustic gate of Orchard House, Louisa first caught sight of Anna and the boys. May was the least able to contain her excitement; Louisa described her as "flying wildly around the lawn."[48] But perhaps the most wonderful sight was Abba standing at the front door, her face wet with tears. Louisa fell into her mother's arms and, at that moment, knew that she was truly home. A stream of friends came by to wish her well and to see how her travels had affected her. They all agreed that she was changed for the better, a judgment Louisa was happy to accept, for as she said, she would always have room for improvement.

As for the family, some had fared better than others in her absence. Her father and May, she felt, were essentially unchanged. Anna's boys were sturdy and affectionate, though chasing them around seemed to have worn their mother down somewhat. However, Louisa was concerned about her mother, who looked old, sick, and tired. Abba had always boasted about the invincibility of the May constitution. Indeed, between the two of them, it is hard to say whether it was Mr. or Mrs. Alcott who presumed more heavily on a sense of genetic invincibility. Now, however, it seemed that Abba had drawn a bit too hard on her reserves. As it happened, she still had more than a decade of life ahead of her, but Louisa could no longer trick herself into believing that her beloved mother would live forever. "I never expect to see the strong, energetic 'Marmee' of old times," Louisa wrote a few months later, "but, thank the Lord, she is still here."[49] Abba had lived a hard life, bravely expending herself for all who asked. Now, Louisa believed, it was time for others to live for her.

Louisa allowed herself a few days to rest and to play the role of the returning heroine, but it was not possible to remain idle for very long. She was not surprised to find the family accounts once again in arrears. Among the debts to be repaid was a sum of four hundred dollars, which Abba had borrowed to extend Louisa's stay in London. It had seemed only right to her that Louisa should enjoy a little ease after nine months of "hard work and solitary confinement."[50] By August, Louisa was churning out copy for the many papers and magazines that wanted something of hers to grace their pages. Two long tales for *Frank Leslie's Illustrated* brought in two hundred dollars. Her travel sketches for *The Independent* netted her another seventy-five dollars. All in all, she sent twelve stories to press in less than three months. The work was comfortingly steady but not glamorous. The éclat of *Hospital Sketches* and the promising reception that had greeted *Moods* were now distant memories. Even if Louisa's work was now to be purely literary, the ceaseless dashing off of stories to satisfy creditors instead of serving an inner muse must have felt like grubbing all the same.

In November, Bronson received melancholy tidings from an old acquaintance. William Oldham, who had kept Alcott House afloat when Charles Lane and Henry Wright had gone with Bronson to America, wrote to say that Bronson's namesake school was no more. Oldham wrote that, after finally returning to England, Charles Lane had reestablished himself at Alcott House but had then embroiled himself in some kind of scandal. Oldham was too delicate to offer details. He confided only that the matter involved Lane's "moral character" and had reflected fatally on the entire school. Oldham, "no longer able to endure the consciousness of evil," had dissolved the school, and all its constituents had "scattered to the winds."[51] Lane had slunk back to London to finish as he had begun, as the editor of a financial newspaper. His career as a tyrannizing moralist was over.

The winter of 1866–67 brought bad weather and ill health to Orchard House. The family plunged into a period of doldrums and did not emerge for six months. In the late autumn, Bronson had set off with high hopes for another visit to his philosopher friends in St. Louis, giving conversations as he went. His absence meant that Louisa had to assume the primary role in dealing with her mother's ill health, all the while trying to write as much as possible to keep up with the family's obligations. During December, she was frequently ill and constantly worried by a stack of bills whose end she never expected to see. Far away in Missouri, sampling Rhine wines and attending concerts of Beethoven and Mendelssohn, Bronson did not guess the strain Louisa was undergoing. It is true that the respect he felt for her was now enormous, and that she was constantly in his thoughts. When he wrote home to Abba, he was certain to send his love to the Author and Artist, namely, Louisa and May. However, his admiration for Louisa's abilities had its unfortunate side; he thought she could do almost anything. "Louisa is an arsenal of powers," he counseled Abba, "if you will but call them forth to your assistance. I hope the blaze of her Genius is kindled with that of her chamber-fire."[52]

As was often the case, a yawning gap stood between Bronson's ability to observe general truths and his capacity for realizing how those very truths affected the people closest to him. He wrote to Abba that one of the topics on which he had been offering a conversation was "Woman," a subject about which, he thought, "the philosophers here along with the common men, I suspect, as every where [sic], need enlightening." It seemed to him that, in the West, as elsewhere, the women paid the dearest price for "all good that is going."[53] His observation aptly described what went on under his own roof, yet he took no discernible steps to correct the imbalance.

Bronson's tour met with unaccustomed financial success, bringing in two hundred dollars. Nevertheless, when he returned home just five days before Christmas, grateful for a cup of his homemade cider and Abba's sympathetic embrace, he was hungry, dirty, and exhausted. Sadly, Bronson's homecoming did little to cheer a house where everyone was tired and ill, including Louisa. Complaining of heavy colds and neuralgia, she blamed her year of milder weather in Europe for having weakened her resistance. Her distress continued long into the new year.

Thoroughly spent from her frenzied burst of story writing, she spent January doing little more than sitting in a dark room and aching, her head and eyes "full of neuralgia."[54] Her condition was basically unchanged in February, and when she tried to get back to work in March, the effort was too much for her and she retreated again to her bed, worse than ever. On February 23, Frank Sanborn had written to a friend that Louisa had been alarmingly ill. Though no one had feared for her life, Sanborn had worried about the effect on her "writing organs."[55] It was not until mid-April that Bronson was able to write that Louisa was recovering her strength and spirits.[56] At the same time, Abba suffered a rheumatic fever, and her eyes continued to trouble her. Bronson, too, battled ill health in the new year and was able to do essentially nothing during a month's confinement.[57] Nevertheless, he remained optimistic. In April, following the death of a mutual acquaintance, one of Bronson's friends observed, "Death is the one universal fact." "Except life," Bronson replied, and his listener promptly agreed.[58]

Louisa was not fully back to work until the late spring. She prepared a triptych of travel sketches for *The Independent* and accepted a proposal from Horace B. Fuller, a Boston publisher, to write a collection of children's stories, which he hoped to have ready for the Christmas season. Louisa's efforts on the project, which she called "Morning-Glories," experienced a thankful interruption when her uncle Samuel May sent her and May fifty dollars each for a summer trip. In August, after dutifully handing over half her sum to her mother to settle still more bills, Louisa departed with May to Clark's Island near Plymouth for what she called "a harem scarem fortnight." When she returned, however, she plunged back into the dozen stories required for Fuller's book. She confided to her journal: "I dread debt more than the devil!"[59]

In September 1867, two offers came, though neither initially held much interest for her. Horace Fuller, evidently pleased with *Morning-Glories and Other Stories*, asked her to become the editor of a children's illustrated magazine known as *Merry's Museum*. At virtually the same time, another suggestion arrived from Thomas Niles, a partner in the publishing firm of Roberts Brothers, whose offer for *Hospital Sketches* Louisa had rejected four years earlier. Niles, seeking to fill gaps in the public demand for books, had been intrigued by the general absence of good books for girls, and it seemed to him that Louisa might be the right person to write one. Although Louisa had made a few experiments in writing for children, most notably in her early collection *Flower Fables*, she had never thought of herself as a writer of juvenile books. Still, the *Merry's Museum* post offered a salary of five hundred dollars a year, and a few dollars might also be gathered from Niles's inspiration. Thus, Louisa told both Fuller and Niles that she would try. She soon found that she did not care for either task.[60] Even though she obediently started a manuscript for Niles, she referred to the project as a "job" and, not liking it, soon put it aside. Perhaps because it is harder to abandon an ongoing commitment, and because of the firm prospect of five hundred dollars a year, she was less ready to turn her back on *Merry's Museum*. Fuller assured her that the work would be fairly light, requiring only that she read manuscripts and write a short tale and an editorial every month.

The compensation was generous enough that she could afford to move out of Orchard House and live on her own. Louisa settled into a room at 6 Hayward Place in Boston, an address that she jauntily nicknamed "Gamp's Garret" in honor of a favorite character from Dickens's *Martin Chuzzlewit*. She relished the convenience of her new confines. The Garret, for which she proudly purchased her own furniture, was not far from Fuller's offices. More importantly, she was well removed from Concord, which she now associated with ill health and having to satisfy the unceasing needs of her parents.

Louisa rang in 1868 with eager expectations and cheerful confidence. Her burdens were eased by the fact that May was earning an income by teaching drawing classes and Anna's husband John was more than capable of providing for his wife and two sons. Warm and secure in Gamp's Garret, Louisa finally had quiet, freedom, sufficient work, and, for the moment, the strength to do it. Despite the illness that had prostrated her for the first four months of the previous year, she had managed to write twenty-five stories since the previous January. If her health remained good, there seemed no limit to what she might now accomplish.

Nevertheless, she still thought it wisest to do a host of moderately compensated smaller jobs, instead of trying for one major success. On New Year's Day, she carefully counted up her likely resources for the coming year. In addition to the five hundred dollars from *Merry's Museum*, she could expect twenty dollars a month for the stories she intended to write for *The Youth's Companion*. *Frank Leslie's Illustrated Newspaper* would never be interested in high art, but it was willing to pay fifty to one hundred dollars for all the thrillers she could churn out.[61] Above all, she wanted independence for herself and solvency for the family. If she could reach these goals by a steady stream of piecework, then so be it. On the same day that she worked out her financial prospects for the year, her indoor hyacinth bloomed. In the new flower, she allowed herself to detect an omen—a little flag of truce, she imagined, "from all the enemies with whom we have been fighting all these years."[62]

Louisa did not confuse her newfound freedom, which she treasured, with isolation, which she dreaded. Even in the midst of an ambitious writing schedule, she pursued projects that kept her closely connected with her family. She made a bonnet for May and cut a flannel wrap for her mother to shield her from the Concord snows.[63] Clearly, her choice to live apart from the family implied no rejection of them. Rather, the need for separateness came from her starting to accept what had once been inconceivable to her: the fact that her energies were finite. At the same time, the demand for her stories was making her time more valuable than ever. She could now accomplish more good by writing than by seeing to the daily management of Orchard House.

The concept of family was very much on Louisa's mind during these days. While accepting that married life was not the best vocation for her, she nevertheless considered a successful marriage "a woman's tenderest ties."[64] Comparing her life with her sister Anna's during January 1868, she wrote, "She is a happy woman! I sell *my* children, and though they feed me, they don't love me as hers do."[65] In February, Louisa had a chance to enter the public debate on the Woman Question. She arrived home on a snowy Valentine's Day to discover an agent from the *New York Ledger* wait-

ing for her. Proffering a hundred-dollar bill, he invited her to write an article of advice for young women. Louisa wrote that a hundred dollars in cash
was enough incentive for her to tackle writing a Greek oration.[66] She
accepted the advance and promptly wrote a column calculated to show, as
she put it, that "liberty is a better husband than love to many of us."[67]
Titling her article "Happy Women," Louisa claimed a broad range of
meanings for her adjective. She told her young readers that, too often, the
loss of happiness and self-respect that comes with an ill-considered marriage "is poorly repaid by the barren honor of being called 'Mrs.' instead of
'Miss.' "[68] She called their attention to a class of "superior women" who,
for diverse reasons, had elected to remain single and to devote themselves
to whatever higher calling their tastes and talents had decreed for them.
The bulk of the column was devoted to sketches of four women who had
found their highest purpose in exercising their talents outside the home.
The first three were a doctor, a music teacher, and a home missionary, a
woman "ordinary in all things but one—a cheerful, helpful spirit, that
loves its neighbor better than itself."[69] Although each had pursued vocation instead of romance or domesticity, none had lived a loveless existence.
Each, in her own way, had found an affection as enduring and sincere as
any husband could bestow.

The last of the quartet of happy women, identified only by the initial
"A," was a self-portrait. Louisa introduced "A" as "a woman of strongly
individual type, who in the course of an unusually varied experience has
seen so much of . . . 'the tragedy of modern married life' that she is afraid
to try it." She called herself "one of a peculiar nature" who, realizing that
an experiment in matrimony would be "doubly hazardous" for her, had
instinctively chosen to remain unmarried.[70] As in her journal entry about
Anna, Louisa spoke of her writings as a metaphorical family. Perhaps, she
suggested, the offspring of her devoted union with literature might be
unlovely in the eyes of others. Nevertheless, they had been a profitable
source of satisfaction to her own maternal heart. Love and labor, she said,
accompanied her like two good angels and her divine Friend had filled her
world with strength and beauty. Thanks to these kind influences, she pronounced herself "not unhappy."[71]

Much meaning can be intuited from double negatives, though in this
case the inferences are far from clear. Earlier in the column, Louisa had not

hesitated to confer the label of "happy" on her three figurative sisters in celibacy. Her self-assessment was more ambivalent and guarded. Was her self-deprecation merely a modest observance of authorial etiquette, or did she really doubt her contentment more than that of the other independent women she knew? It was very much in character for Louisa to understate her sense of good fortune. In any event, it would have been more comforting if Louisa had advanced more positive reasons for not marrying. Her argument would have been more appealing if she had refrained from calling her own situation "peculiar" and from confessing her own dread of matrimony. Nevertheless, she sounded an inspiring note when she urged her young readers to choose their paths without fear of loneliness or ridicule, to cherish their talents, and to use them, if they chose, for higher, greater purposes than convention decreed. The world was full of work, she wrote, and never had there been a greater opportunity for women to do it.

In the first two months of 1868, Louisa behaved as if she wanted to do all of the world's work by herself. She was finding, to her annoyance, that *Merry's Museum* was demanding much more of her time than had been promised. Relations with the magazine's management were so unpleasant that, nine years later, she still described them as "very disagreeable . . . throughout."[72] She wrote eight long stories and ten short ones, read and edited stacks of manuscripts for *Merry's Museum*, and found time to act in a dozen stage performances for charity. On February 17, she had been buoyed by a visit from her father, who was eager to share his plans about his own book, which was finally near enough to completion that he was ready to show the manuscript to prospective editors. This book, *Tablets*, was the philosophical volume about gardening and domesticity that Bronson had first conceived near the start of the Civil War; it had been a protracted labor of love for him ever since.

Bronson escorted Louisa to a meeting of the Radical Club. One assumes that Louisa bore the evening's entertainment graciously. Afterward, however, she told her journal that she had been regaled by "a curious jumble of fools and philosophers."[73] After passing the night in Gamp's Garret, Bronson called on Roberts Brothers. To his great delight, Roberts responded warmly to *Tablets* and agreed to publish it. Always ready to put in a word on Louisa's behalf, Bronson also mentioned the book for girls that the firm had proposed to Louisa the preceding fall. Although Louisa had evidently given up on the project, Roberts Brothers was still under the impression that the book was going forward and was expecting at least two hundred pages by September at the latest—the same month they meant to publish *Tablets*. The literary partner of the firm spoke highly of Louisa's abilities and prospects; obviously they were expecting great things from her.

Bronson was still unfamiliar with the names at Roberts Brothers when he told Louisa the news. At first, he wrote that the partner who had spoken so warmly of his daughter was Mr. Nash. Before sending the letter, Bronson scratched out his mistake and wrote in the name that Louisa already knew: Thomas Niles. Bronson's usually horrendous business sense was, for once, leading in the right direction. He saw correctly that Niles had sensed enticing possibilities in handling both his work and Louisa's simultaneously. Bronson wrote to Louisa that his visit to the firm had turned "a brighter page" for both himself and Louisa, both "personally and pecuniarily."[74] He urged her to come home and get to work on the story.

Louisa was reluctant to make any change. However, for reasons that are not precisely clear, she concluded that, once again, she was needed at home. Thus, on February 28, she packed up her belongings, spent one last evening acting for charity, and rode back to Orchard House the next day. Contrary to her father's wishes, Louisa did not begin at once on her girls book. The steady income from her other tales and from *Merry's Museum* was serving to provide her mother with a host of comforts. The sight of the aging woman, nestled in her sunny room and free from the anxiety of debt, meant more to Louisa than any personal success. Months passed, and still Louisa procrastinated. In May, Bronson was again in touch with Niles. Since Louisa had made no progress on the book for girls, he asked whether she might satisfy Roberts Brothers by writing a fairy book instead. Niles, however, remained firm. Louisa still balked at the idea. "I don't enjoy this sort of thing," she wrote. "Never liked girls or knew many, except my sisters."[75] Perhaps a good story might be fashioned out of the Alcott girls' lives, but Louisa thought it unlikely. She consulted her mother, Anna, and May and found that they all approved, and she might go ahead with the idea.

"Plod away" was Louisa's own phrase for it.[76] Ever since *Moods* had failed to win the critical adulation she had wanted, she had found it hard to think of her writing as an aesthetic pursuit. Increasingly, it was her professional discipline, not her creative spirit, that fueled her vortices and kept her at her task for hours at a time. Nevertheless she acknowledged that Niles was right in principle: there were too few simple, lively books for girls. With no particular enthusiasm for her task, in a mood not much better than that of the character she was about to create, she picked up her pen and began to write: " 'Christmas won't be Christmas without any presents,' grumbled Jo, lying on the rug."

CHAPTER FOURTEEN

MIRACLES

"Genius is infinite patience."

—LOUISA MAY ALCOTT,
quoting Michelangelo in a letter to
John Preston True, October 24, 1878

I T WAS NEVER LOUISA'S PREFERENCE TO SIT STILL, NOT EVEN when she was engrossed in a writing vortex. Whereas Bronson was most comfortable in his study, surrounded by his books and journals and seated at his large mahogany table, his daughter often moved about restlessly, too stirred by her ideas to remain wholly stationary. On those occasions when she took up a position on the parlor sofa, the family approached at their own risk. It was not a pleasant experience to pose an innocent question to Louisa just when her mind was working through a delicate thought or a complex sentence. At some point, though, a system was developed. Next to her, Louisa would keep a bolster pillow, which acted like a tollgate for conversation. If the pillow stood on its end, the family was free to disturb her. If the pillow lay on its side, however, they should tread lightly and keep their interjections to themselves.

For the most part, though, Louisa wrote in her bedroom at the desk that Bronson built for her. A wooden semicircle, painted white and attached to the southern wall, it is no more than two and a half feet wide. Apart from the graceful curving of the three supporting pieces underneath it, it is utterly plain. What matters about the desk is simply that it is there and that Bronson took the trouble to make it. It was then uncommon for women to be supplied with desks of their own. The desk was a gesture of Bronson's confidence in Louisa and a mute assertion that he saw the value

Thomas Niles, Louisa's editor at Roberts Brothers,
found the first dozen chapters of Little Women *"dull."*
Then he showed them to his niece.
(Courtesy of the Louisa May Alcott Memorial Association)

of what she was doing. The desk is situated between two windows that look out on Lexington Road, but one must turn in one's chair to look out of these windows. Staring straight ahead, Louisa would have seen only the bare wall in front of her: the blank canvas of inspiration.

For this book, however, inspiration was a thorny issue. If Louisa took pleasure in writing *Little Women*, she never said so. Giddy excitement and an innocent faith in her own genius had motivated *Moods*. The righteous cause of freedom had gotten her through *Hospital Sketches*. Now she began working as hastily as ever, but more with a view to filling Niles's order than with any high ambition. Indeed, she later recalled intending to prove to him that she could not write a successful girls book.[1] She partly hoped that Niles would see for himself that *Little Women* was an uninteresting hash and would leave her to her potboilers and *Merry's Museum*. She came close to convincing him. In June, she sent him the first dozen chapters. He thought they were dull, and Louisa agreed, but she pressed onward.[2]

As she worked, a word of encouragement came. Niles told her that he had shown the early chapters to his niece, Lillie Almy, who had laughed over them until she cried.[3] Niles revised his earlier judgment; he had been reading with the eye of a literary editor, not the sensibilities of an adolescent girl. Seen by a reader whose viewpoint really mattered, the early chapters of *Little Women* had attractions he had failed to recognize. Louisa now pursued the project so single-mindedly that, from the day in June when she complained about the flatness of her first twelve chapters, she did not take time out to write a single entry in her journal until July 15, when she announced that the book, or more accurately, the portion now known as part 1, was complete. In two and a half months, she had written 402 manuscript pages.[4]

The work, reluctantly begun, had eventually absorbed her. At the end of it, she had briefly broken down. Years later, she remembered her effort as "too much work for one young woman."[5] Considering the depth and duration of the creative vortex from which she now emerged, it is not surprising that Louisa was thoroughly exhausted, her head feeling like a great mass of pain.[6] Her vortices had always been a combination of lavish creative self-indulgence and harsh physical self-denial. Now that Louisa was in her midthirties and prematurely frail, the experience of the vortex was more harrowing than gratifying. Nevertheless, Louisa knew only one way to write a novel. An iron will, rather than a poetic muse, seemed her strongest creative ally.

She hoped, but could not be sure, that there would be a part 2. Niles, for his part, was now convinced that the book would "hit." He showed the twenty-two-chapter manuscript to the daughters of some other families, who pronounced the story "splendid!" Hearing of their approval, Louisa wrote, "It is for them, they are the best critics, so I should be satisfied."[7] Niles had but one request; he wanted Louisa to add a twenty-third chapter with some teasing allusions that would open the way for a sequel. Louisa promptly obliged, concluding with this overt appeal:

> So grouped the curtain falls upon Meg, Jo, Beth and Amy. Whether it ever rises again, depends upon the reception given to the first act of the domestic drama, called "LITTLE WOMEN."[8]

On August 26, when the proofs of the book arrived, Louisa was pleased to find that *Little Women*, in her still-cautious judgment, was "better than I expected."[9]

With pleasure, Louisa observed that her story was "not a bit sensational, but simple and true, for we really lived most of it." If the book did become popular, she thought, its success would be due to these qualities.[10] Yet there was also a complexity to what she had written, deriving from the fact that her concept of the book evolved considerably between the writing of the first dozen "dull" chapters and those that followed. Her idea of the book was to change yet again as she worked her way through part 2. Starting as a mere job that lacked a clear plan of development, *Little Women* metamorphosed into a carefully conceived whole, satisfying its readers even as it deliberately defied their wishes and expectations.

Properly seen, *Little Women* is not one book but three, each with its peculiar strengths and curiosities. The first phase of the book's development concerns the first dozen chapters that, on first reading, Alcott and Niles found lacking in interest. In retrospect, it seems odd that they thought so, since many of the most indelible moments of the novel occur in those first twelve chapters. To a reader who has smiled at the March sisters cheerfully surrendering their Christmas breakfast to a more needy family; who has shared Meg's injured pride as she compares her shabby wardrobe to the finery of Annie Moffat; who has felt outrage when Amy burns Jo's treasured manuscript, only to have that feeling yield to dismay when Jo's retaliatory neglect causes Amy to fall through the ice—to such a reader, Louisa's harsh preliminary judgment of these chapters can come only as a surprise. Not only are the anecdotes of these chapters rich and memorable, but the four girls are never more vivacious and entertaining. The very fact that they begin the novel so deeply flawed and prone to mishaps makes them in some ways more interesting than in the later portions of the novel, when they have gained more self-control.

Nevertheless, Louisa's judgment had some merit. In these early chapters, she was developing characters and spinning out a series of vignettes of family life, but she was not yet writing a novel. Each of the early chapters could almost stand as a short story in itself. The stronger thematic links needed to construct a larger framework have yet to appear. A certain flatness to her plot also derives from the fact that the March sisters' motivations are all fundamentally similar. Each one has to overcome a particular defining vice: Meg struggles with her vanity; Jo with her temper; Beth her debilitating shyness; and Amy her selfishness. The inward battles of the four are sympathetically rendered, and they are realistic enough to have given encouragement and comfort to countless young readers trying to master similar faults. Yet the theme of moral struggle presented a problem for the development of the larger work: if each character were defined by a single flaw, what was to keep them from collapsing into sameness once those flaws were under control? Alcott had not fully worked out the answer to this question as she wrote these early chapters. Indeed, the unifying element at this stage of her work was not her concept of plot, but rather the sustained analogy that she constructed between her emerging text and another book that she and much of her readership already found familiar.

The text that underlies the first half of *Little Women* is *The Pilgrim's Progress*, the book that had directed Bronson's ethics from childhood and which he had passed on as a moral talisman to his daughters. Louisa's reliance on Bunyan's allegory is deliberately transparent, as reflected in several of the early chapter titles: "Beth Finds the Palace Beautiful"; "Amy's Valley of Humiliation"; "Jo Meets Apollyon." Alcott also acknowledges her debt to Bunyan by prefacing her novel with an adaptation of the poem that precedes part 2 of *The Pilgrim's Progress*. In the original verse, Bunyan addresses his book as follows:

> Go then, my little Book and shew to all
> That entertain, and bid thee welcome shall,
> What thou shalt keep close, shut up from the rest,
> And wish what thou shalt shew them may be blest.[11]

In her story itself, however, Alcott does not passively imitate Bunyan. She is continually revising her model in order to state her own ideas about the nature of morality and a well-written book. Alcott reiterates the quoted lines in her preface but alters the third to read, "What thou dost keep close shut up *in thy breast* [italics added]."[12] Her emendation figuratively transforms her book into a living being, offering not merely moral prescriptions but the feelings that give them their practical truth. Alcott's substituted words infuse her text with greater intimacy and a more feminine sensibility. Bunyan describes a recollected dream; Alcott speaks from the previously locked precincts of her heart.

Although the specific references in *Little Women* tend overwhelmingly to concern part 1 of *The Pilgrim's Progress*, the larger thematics of Alcott's novel are more closely related to the lesser-known second part of Bunyan's allegory. In Bunyan's part 1, Christian sets forth alone to seek salvation while his wife, Christiana, timidly remains behind with the couple's children. It is only in part 2 that Christiana, who previously doubted her husband's sanity, realizes that Christian was offering her the only path away from destruction and that she and her children must now follow in his footsteps to the Celestial City. She tells her children:

> I formerly foolishly imagin'd [that] the Troubles of your Father . . . proceeded of a foolish fancy that he had, or for that he was over run with Melancholy Humours; yet now 'twill not out of my mind, but that they sprang from another cause, to wit, for that the Light of Light was given him.[13]

Bronson Alcott, of course, had also passed through his "foolish fancies" and "melancholy humors" before finding the light that had saved him. The dominant question in part 1 of *Little Women* is the same that animates part 2 of *The Pilgrim's Progress*: will the family of a sanctified but now absent father be able to follow him to salvation?

While intentional, Louisa's invocations of *The Pilgrim's Progress* are also ingeniously ironic. Alcott resists mimicking the trajectory of the earlier work and wryly questions its moral conclusions. Whereas in Bunyan's allegory the spirit saves itself only by moving outward and away from the familiar and the domestic, the movement advocated in *Little Women* is circular. Although Jo, Amy, and Mr. March all leave home to find a place in the larger world, their redemption requires each of them to come home. Alcott also illustrates, Bunyan's allegory notwithstanding, that the process of moral transformation need not require any physical journey at all. In *Little Women*, the principal school of ethics, especially in those chapters most strongly influenced by Bunyan, remains the home.

In recasting Bunyan's moral drama in a realistic, female-dominated setting, Alcott makes a claim on behalf of the domestic sphere, arguing that the character formation that takes place in kitchens and parlors is every bit as important as the soul-making that takes place during Christian's masculine odyssey. *Little Women* expands and improves on Bunyan's allegory by reminding us that, contrary to what *The Pilgrim's Progress* may suggest, moral improvement is seldom an individual pursuit. Although each of the March sisters wrestles separately with a signature weakness, they are present to assist in one another's struggles, and it is as members of a community that they reap the benefits of their heightened virtue. In Bunyan's expression of Christian ethics, there is a core of selfishness: one is to save one's own soul even if it means leaving others to perish. For the March family, however, salvation is unthinkable in the absence of good works, and we are meant to agree with Jo when she exclaims, "I do think that families are the most beautiful things in all the world!"[14] Home is the Celestial City toward which the March sisters always unconsciously strive.

There is no evidence that Louisa revised her first dozen chapters in response to Thomas Niles's initially negative judgment. Indeed, Niles observed that he thought he had never supervised a book that had required so little alteration or correction.[15] Following the first twelve chapters, however, the structure of Alcott's narrative promptly becomes more sustained, and her plot acquires a longer view. The change begins in chapter 13, "Castles in the Air." Nestled on a hillside on a September afternoon, the March sisters and their friend Laurie exchange visions of what they want to achieve in life. Meg seeks material comfort; Jo and Amy covet success, respectively, in literature and art; Beth wants only to stay at home and care for the family. From this moment, Alcott's story forms itself around a different question; we are prompted to examine how well the March sisters measure up to their own expectations. Prior to this moment, self-mastery has been presented as paramount. Henceforth, however, the novel's moral universe becomes more complicated, for the March family's ethics of self-denial and family unity may eventually run counter to the fulfillment of personal ambition and individual dreams. The remainder of *Little Women* continually wrestles with the possibility—an uncomfortable one for a veteran of Fruitlands, Abba Alcott's intelligence office, and the Union Hotel Hospital—that living for the realization of one's self-gratifying dreams might actually be a good thing.

Early in part 1, Alcott distributes her attention fairly evenly among the four sisters. Thereafter, the novel becomes ever more focused on Louisa's alter ego, Jo. As Jo receives more attention, the same concerns that troubled Louisa as an adolescent move to the foreground. In earlier chapters, the process of growing into adulthood has been taken for granted. Gradually, however, one discovers that *Little Women* is not just about growing up. It is also about the dread of growing up. Eager to lead her siblings into almost every other kind of adventure, Jo not only resists her own coming of age, but also resents the comparative ease with which her sisters appear to be making the transition. In chapter 14, Jo anxiously pleads, "Don't try to make me grow up before my time . . . ; let me be a little girl as long as I can."[16] Soon after, she wishes that wearing a flatiron on her head would keep her from getting older.[17] At first Jo would rather be a boy than a girl. Later, Alcott shows that Jo would rather remain a girl than become a woman.

Jo's desire for an artificially prolonged childhood arises in part from Louisa's contradictory experiences in growing up as an Alcott. On the one hand, the Alcott girls had been expected early in life to begin working and bringing in the money that Bronson was unwilling or unable to earn. The inclinations of their parents toward philosophy and reform had also led the girls to ponder questions usually reserved for older heads. Simultaneously, however, Abba and Bronson had shielded their children from other aspects of worldly sophistication. At an age when many of her contemporaries were already married, Louisa was still very much under her parents' protection, writing fairy tales when her peers were reading them to their own infants. Time played strange tricks in the Alcott family, where children were both enfolded in innocence and expected to be mature beyond their years.

Moreover, while they lavished intellectual and moral stimuli on their daughters, Bronson and Abba were not clear as to what ought to become of all that knowledge and training when its recipients reached womanhood. The two daughters Bronson loved best, Anna and Lizzie, never achieved a life outside the domestic sphere. In *Little Women*, even the meek and accommodating Beth admits in despair that her choice of a domestic life has resulted more from a failure of talent and imagination than a vision of fulfillment: "I'm not like the rest of you; I never made any plans about what I'd do when I grew up. . . . I couldn't seem to imagine myself anything but stupid little Beth, trotting about at home, of no use anywhere but there."[18] The Alcott family emphasis on juvenile self-culture would seem to have been largely futile, even absurd, if it necessarily gave way to mature self-sacrifice. If childhood were all about self-discovery and adulthood were all about self-denial, who indeed would want to grow up?

The struggles of the first dozen chapters of *Little Women*, as well as Jo's ongoing battle not to grow up, are principally internal. However, the second half of part 1 shows the March sisters dealing primarily with external challenges, most notably Beth's illness and Mr. March's brush with death in a Union army hospital in Washington. Significantly, whereas one may associate *Little Women* with Louisa's years at Hillside, the real-life correlatives of these two challenges—Lizzie's initial bout with scarlet fever and Louisa's nursing service—happened much later. Because the chronology of her story forced Louisa to keep her women "little," it is the family's father, not a daughter, who goes away to war.

When Mr. March returns from the front, it is as if his daughters, having studied their moral lessons, must submit to examinations. All four pass with honors; March commends each girl in turn for the substantial conquest of her particular fault. Interestingly, when he praises Jo, he takes special notice of his daughter's face, which he says is "thin and pale."[19] It is the face of Louisa after *her* return from Union Hotel Hospital. As the author who created her had done, Jo wins her father's acceptance after an experience of war has aged her and demanded that she sacrifice. Mr. March admits that he will miss the wild girl that Jo once was, though he is pleased to see the "strong, helpful, tender-hearted woman" who stands in her place.[20]

The reunion is a moment not only of judgment but also of unveiling. After twenty-one chapters of anticipation, the reader finally prepares to meet the father of the little women. In introducing the reader to Mr. March, however, Alcott is less than obliging. Like a resurrected messiah, Mr. March returns to judge and to bless. Curiously, however, these are almost his only functions. When he first appears, Alcott declines to describe him other than to say that he is "tall." No sooner does she bring him into the scene than she obscures him again. Only two sentences after entering his home, he becomes "invisible in the embrace of four pairs of loving arms."[21] Louisa uses the love of the March family to hide Jo's father and shelter him from scrutiny.

For the rest of the novel, Mr. March is present in the household, but he never receives more than sparse attention. Unlike Bronson, he is a man of few words, remaining virtually barricaded in his study for the duration of the novel. There are a host of practical reasons why *Little Women* belongs to Marmee and the March sisters, instead of yielding much of the spotlight to a Bronson-like patriarch. When Louisa wrote *Little Women*, she was still planning to write a book with Bronson as its focus. "The Cost of an Idea," her projected tale of her father's upbringing and quixotic struggles, had been on her list of projects for more than a decade, and her journal reflects her intention to write it as late as 1872.[22] It would have been unwise if, in *Little Women*, she had drawn heavily on the material she expected to use in this other work.

Moreover, Louisa had expressly promised Thomas Niles a girls book, and since she had recently finished her essay "Happy Women," the theme of feminine autonomy was very much on her mind. To have injected a father too forcefully into *Little Women* would have interfered with the story she wanted to tell about the virtues and difficulties of womanhood. Paradoxically, if Bronson was too masculine to fit Louisa's vision of a female household, he may not have been manly enough to find a place in an ideal fictional family. His gentle nature, his fascination with child rearing, and his rejection of the masculine world of commerce made him more of a second mother to his children than a traditional father. For this reason, Alcott biographer Madeleine Stern has stated that a fuller representation of Bronson in *Little Women* might have been "redundant" of Louisa's characterization of Marmee.[23]

Furthermore, Alcott knew something about the public for which she was writing. Just three years earlier, the nation had concluded a war that had torn approximately three million men away from their hearthsides and killed more than six hundred thousand of them.[24] The number of Megs, Jos, Beths, and Amys they left behind can never be precisely ascertained. It seems clear that Alcott wanted to write a book in sympathy with these children's losses and to offer her young readers an example of how one might carry on when one's family was no longer whole. For all of these reasons, Louisa acted judiciously when she chose to keep Mr. March primarily in the shadows.

And yet Bronson Alcott is firmly present in *Little Women* through the Bunyanesque subtext of the novel. The elder Alcott identified his moral outlook so deeply with Bunyan's that, whenever Louisa alludes to *The Pilgrim's Progress* in *Little Women*, she suffuses the scene with her father's ethical ideas. Like Christian, Mr. March in *Little Women* is not physically present during the pivotal portions of his family's journey toward redemption. However, he does not need to be. In imitation of Bunyan's hero, he has already blazed a spiritual trail, making it easier for his family to complete the same journey. If Bronson, in the form of Mr. March, is barely present in the overt action of *Little Women*, he is spiritually omnipresent.

The public response to part 1 of *Little Women* was astounding. Julian Hawthorne, with what degree of exaggeration and invention is anyone's guess, related in his memoirs the story Louisa told of the day she learned she had written a best-seller. Having had no news of her manuscript for months, she resolved to visit the publisher and demand an explanation. When she arrived, she saw a small brigade of truckmen loading packing crates onto drays and a busy detachment of clerks hurrying in and out of the building. Suspecting that the establishment had been seized for debts, she mounted the stairs to the office of the publisher, who was signing a check. Without looking up, he waved his hand dismissively. "Go away," he grumbled, "I've given orders—most important. How did you get in here?"

Louisa's resolve stiffened. "I want my manuscript!" she exclaimed.

"I told you to get out—" the man began. Looking up for the first time, though, he froze as if petrified by a gorgon. An instant later, the story goes, he vaulted over his desk toward her and grasped her by the elbows with the aspect of a madman. As she feared for her safety, Louisa suddenly understood what he was trying to tell her: "My dear—dearest Miss Alcott! At such a juncture! You got my letter? No? No matter! Nothing parallel to it has occurred in my experience! All else put aside—street blocked—country aroused—overwhelmed—paralyzed! *Uncle Tom's Cabin* backed off the stage! Two thousand more copies ordered this very day from Chicago alone! But that's a fleabite—tens of thousands—why, dearest girl, it's the triumph of the century!" The check on the publisher's desk had her name on it, and the packing crates were filled with copies of *Little Women*.[25]

Very little, if any, of this anecdote truly happened as Hawthorne describes it. The quoted sales figures are vastly overstated, and Hawthorne himself admits "the amusing exaggeration" of Louisa's "spirited account." Yet the underlying import of the story is true enough. The first printing of two thousand copies sold out within days of the book's release, and another forty-five hundred were in print by the end of the year.[26] Before she could even begin the second half of her story, part 1 of *Little Women* had made Louisa May Alcott famous and very nearly rich.[27]

Fan mail poured in. Niles told her that an edition was being prepared for publication in England. There was no question now that a second part would be wanted. "A little success is so inspiring," Louisa told her journal, and she plunged back into a creative vortex on November 1, vowing to write a chapter a day.[28] She worked "like a steam engine," taking a daily run as her only recreation and barely stopping to eat or sleep.[29] Falling behind the ambitious schedule she had set for herself, she spent her birthday alone, "writing hard."[30]

Only three months separated the publication of part 1 at the end of September 1868 and Louisa's delivery of part 2 to Roberts Brothers on New Year's Day 1869, but in the interval, much more than Louisa's level of enthusiasm had changed. Whereas she had based her work thus far on events from her family's past and had felt some obligation to stay reasonably close to fact, she would now be able to "launch into the future"; thus her "fancy" would have "more play."[31] Had she been able to indulge this fancy without restraint, Louisa would have used part 2 to craft Jo into a grown woman very much resembling the veiled self-portrait she had drawn in "Happy Women." Having created her main character in her own image, Louisa knew precisely the life that, from Jo's point of view, would constitute a happy ending: the professionally satisfying career of "a literary spinster."[32] More broadly, she wanted part 2 to be a searching inquiry into the moral ambiguities of adulthood from which her main characters' youth had thus far kept them exempt. As long as the highest goods in the March sisters' world are their mutual support and the approving judgments of their parents, there is little or no conflict between moral action and the kind of gratification they have been taught to prize most highly. However, Alcott causes tension to erupt forcefully in part 2 when other objectives—wealth, professional achievement, or an independent sense of one's value—become more important than pleasing Marmee. Part 1 is about the formation of character. Part 2 is about young women who, having achieved a sense of self, must struggle against worldly forces—for example, mortality and male-dominated social conventions—that threaten to diminish or destroy those selves. This theme makes the second half of *Little Women* a deeper, more thoughtful work than the first.

Yet Louisa's freedom to write part 2 as she chose was circumscribed in another, unexpected fashion. As her fans clamored for a sequel, they expressed a virtually unanimous opinion: they demanded that Jo should marry Laurie, the boy based on Alf Whitman and Ladislas Wisniewski and given the character name of Theodore Laurence, or "Laurie." Louisa, who had wanted her book to show what girls could accomplish for themselves, read with deepening disappointment the letters sent by "girls [who] ask who the little women [will] marry. As if that was the only end and aim of a woman's life."33 To her annoyance, Thomas Niles sided with public opinion, and she complained acidly about "publishers [who] wont [*sic*] let authors finish up as they like but insist . . . on having people married off in a wholesale manner."34 She felt that Roberts Brothers had compelled her to finish her novel "in a very stupid style."35 The profusion of romantic pairings-off that Niles demanded led one of her friends to quip that the sequel might as well be called "Wedding Marches."36 As happened more than once in her career, Louisa found herself torn between popular taste and artistic integrity.

Not quite daring to defy both public and publisher, she offered a compromise. While remaining firm in her determination not to "marry Jo to Laurie to please anyone," she contrived a "funny match" for her with the kindly, philosophical Professor Bhaer.37 Laurie, too, finds wedded bliss in the sequel, but in the seemingly unlikely arms of the youngest March daughter, Amy. Even as Louisa adopted this middle course, she feared that it would please no one.

As it happened, however, Louisa's decision neither to write a safe, predictable denouement nor to give Jo the ending she thought her heroine deserved is largely responsible for the artistic triumph of *Little Women*, part 2. Part 1 had concluded with resolute cheerfulness, with Beth evidently recovering from her bout with scarlet fever, Mr. March safely home, and Meg engaged to her true love. What gives part 2 its enduring power is that not one of the March sisters gets what she had once believed would make her happy and that none of the visions of the future expressed in the "Castles in the Air" chapter are realized. Materialistic Meg, though happily married to the virtuous John Brooke, has fallen far short of her dreams of luxury. Jo and Amy have deferred their artistic ambitions and settled down with their respective husbands. Even Beth, who modestly wished only "to stay safe at home with mother and father," has been denied her wish by death.[38] Marriage is the quintessential happy ending to a children's tale. Yet subversively, Alcott disposes of Jo's and Amy's weddings in the most anticlimactic fashion possible. Amy and Laurie cheat the reader by marrying offstage. Whereas Alcott has earlier devoted an elaborate description to Meg's wedding, she treats Jo's marriage in a solitary, perplexing sentence. As a single woman, Jo has been forthright and energetic. Her wedding, to the contrary, finds her dazed and passive: "Almost before she knew where she was, Jo found herself married and settled at Plumfield."[39] By spurning Laurie and marrying the professor, Jo has avoided being stifled by conventional romanticism. Her marriage to Bhaer will eventually lead, in some sense, to fulfillment and freedom. Nevertheless, those who feel shortchanged when Jo's bold opposition to matrimony crumbles have a right to their reaction. The defeat of opportunities for women seems complete when it is revealed that Plumfield, the school that Jo and her husband establish, admits only boys. Both Jo and Amy still hope to find a place in their lives for artistic achievement, and Jo reflects, rather unconvincingly, that the life of literary glory she once imagined for herself seems "selfish, lonely and cold to me now."[40] Nevertheless, *Little Women* appears to end as a story, not of dreams come true, but of dreams at best compromised and at worst thwarted.

The wisdom of part 2 asserts that happiness can be both serendipitous and self-denying. Meg, Jo, and Amy do not find selfish gratification; rather, they find contentment by renouncing their immediate individual ambitions and returning to the interdependence of family. It is an ending that Bronson Alcott must certainly have appreciated. Indeed, one can see in Professor Bhaer some of Bronson's outlines: they are both threadbare, philosophical men with an altruistic love of children and a contempt for the kind of cleverness whose chief virtue is its profitability. Alcott describes Bhaer and Mr. March as sharing a "kindred spirit."[41] In marrying Jo to Bhaer, Louisa endorsed her father's ideals. She also repeated a pattern in her love plots that began with *Moods* and was to resurface in her other full-length adult novel, *Work*. In all three novels, the heroine faces a choice between a man who stirs her passion and one who speaks eloquently to her sense of moral duty. The latter figure invariably prevails.

Modern readers, conditioned to equate happiness with personal achievement and, perhaps, less inclined than Alcott's original audience to regard duty and domestic bliss as sufficient objectives in life, are likely to view the last chapters of *Little Women* as a defeat for the March sisters, whose brave, happy beginnings seem to have led only to conventionality and subservience. For many of us, Jo's and Amy's settling into matrimony seems a betrayal of their earlier promise and courage. Jo, however, seems not to think so. She believes that her dreams have not been lost, but rather transmuted into a more charitable form. If, as Alcott evidently intended, we regard Jo's matronly life at Plumfield as a triumph, we can understand a key tenet of Alcott's feminist ideal. Women's rights, for Alcott, was never an end in itself. Rather, expanding opportunities for women was the great and necessary means by which previously neglected talents and energies might be made available to benefit a societal family, such as Alcott embodies in Plumfield. Jo learns that abilities used to benefit only oneself are thrown away. Used to advance only one's biological family, they remain largely wasted. Only when one gives freely to all do talent and effort attain their highest value.

Although this altruism lies at the root of Alcott's feminism, it is also the reason modern readers sometimes misconceive her as antifeminist. It can be argued that women historically accepted a subservient position precisely because of their willingness to sacrifice for the perceived greater good of the family. If Alcott was proposing a social order in which women were educated to feel a sense of family obligation to the entire community, might not her vision deepen, rather than diminish, the problem of sexual inequality? Perhaps the best answer is that Alcott expected the self-sacrifice of good men as well as good women. Her ideal of equality touched principally on opportunities to serve rather than any presumed right to seek one's individual happiness.

Apart from its confrontation of gender issues, another ethical ambiguity haunts the pages of *Little Women*. Earnestly intent on inculcating spiritual and moral lessons, the novel nevertheless steers away from conventional theism and toward the more material concerns that began to obsess America after the Civil War. It has been aptly observed that, even though their father is a clergyman, the March sisters never set foot in a church. Moreover, Jo's famous opening grumble, "Christmas won't be Christmas without any presents," is the lament of a child who needs no persuading that the true spirit of her culture is commercial, not ecclesiastic.[42] Of course, Alcott's father and his transcendental brethren had striven to retain a reverential view of the world while discarding outward forms and unbending dogmas, and Louisa was bound to inherit the philosophical problem that their heresies had raised: how, in the absence of a sturdily organized faith, does one preserve both the feel of a religious life and the ideal of an ethical existence? Lacking a system of either rituals or sacraments through which to practice their piety, the March sisters are pressed repeatedly in the direction of good works. Indeed, few books narrate more acts of unselfish generosity than *Little Women*. However, it is this impulse toward charity that exposes Beth to scarlet fever, and the power of the Marches to do good is generally restricted by their limited means. Although one feels deep admiration when the girls give up their Christmas breakfasts to a more abject family, the greatest acts of philanthropy in the novel, for instance the founding of Plumfield, are made possible only by the accumulated capital of wealthy people like Grandfather Laurence and Aunt March. To cynical eyes, *Little Women* may be a novel of the Gilded Age after all.[43]

Part 2 of *Little Women* was every bit as successful as its predecessor. It is a matter of some irony that *Little Women*, Alcott's hymn to genteel poverty, put a permanent end to the real Alcott family's days of chronic want. Flush with royalty checks, Louisa paid all the family's debts and, to her astonished delight, had money left over to invest. As Roberts Brothers readied part 2 of *Little Women* for release, she had dared to tell her journal, "My dream is beginning to come true."[44] As a turning point in the fortunes of the Alcott family, the publication of *Little Women* cannot be overestimated. Yet at virtually the same moment that *Little Women* was making Louisa the most renowned female author in America, Bronson was enjoying a success that was, in its way, also extraordinary. More than thirty years had passed since the publication of *Conversations with Children on the Gospels*. In those years, the public careers of his great literary contemporaries—Emerson, Hawthorne, Thoreau, Melville—had risen to their highest glory and subsided. Few would have expected the elder Alcott, now aged sixty-eight, finally to present the world with a completed book. Yet in the marvelous year of 1868, there were suddenly two bestselling authors residing under the roof of Orchard House. Both *Little Women* and *Tablets* were published in September 1868. Born thirty-three

Bronson Alcott in his sixties.
After decades of obscurity, he won respect as
a writer, speaker, and "the Father of Little Women.*"*
(Courtesy of the Louisa May Alcott Memorial Association)

years apart, father and daughter achieved their most significant literary breakthroughs in the same month.

Tablets had nothing in common with the hallucinatory manuscript of the same name on which Bronson had labored during his period of precarious mental health in 1849. In that abandoned work, Alcott had striven to unlock cosmic secrets. Now, his greatest desire was to offer his readers peace. In the headlong scramble that society had rapidly become, Alcott's calm, measured tones and his virtually complete refusal to acknowledge the world of toil and trouble were refreshing and welcome. The *Boston Daily Advertiser* caught the spirit of the book accurately when it observed, "[Mr. Alcott's] *Tablets* are like windows through which the busy worker, pausing for a minute in the rush and distraction of his thousand little cares and duties, may look out into great spaces and draw a deep, full breath, may look far into the past, far forward into the future, and far up into the heavens."[45] Bronson himself took great satisfaction in the book; he felt that its diction came nearer to his ideal of good writing than anything else he had ever produced.[46]

Tablets is organized into two large sections, each designated by the author as a "book," although both were contained in the same volume. Anyone who knew Bronson would have been surprised to see that the first of the two books was titled "Practical." Surely one might have supposed that the author would find himself more at home in book 2, titled "Speculative." Even if Alcott's ideas of practicality differed from those of his neighbors, however, there is a wisdom in book 1 which, if not strictly pragmatic, gives the reader a sense of steadiness and comfort that few writers can easily achieve. Instead of embracing just one theme, Bronson set forth his thoughts on a series of subjects that, to him, comprised the core of earthly contentment: The Garden; Recreation, Fellowship, Friendship; Culture; Books. Among his "practical" observations, he also presented his ideas on women, family, and children. Significantly, however, he chose to classify all of these under the broader chapter called "Friendship." Bronson was now well past thinking about the family as an object for utopian experimentation, and he no longer saw children through the eyes of a behavioral psychologist. In *Tablets*, he reflected not on what adults might consciously do for children, but rather on what children unconsciously do for us. Without them, he wrote, "The world were a solitude, homes desolate, hearts homeless. . . . Children save us."[47] He gently reproved adults who, in seeking to initiate children into the world grown-ups think best, pull them down into a lower, sadder state. Better, perhaps, for the child to lead the parent, than the reverse. In Bronson's mind, the voice of a child whispered reverently:

> Is not your paradise an Inferno? Please never name it. . . . Would you destroy my paradise, too? Come with me, come, and I will show you Elysium; I know all about it, I am not deceived. I feel it to be solid, safe. It makes good its pledges always. I have a home of all delights, . . . while you seem [a vagabond] . . . bereft of friends. . . . Am I to quit my present satisfactions for your promised joys? Unkind! this taking me from my paradise, unless you conduct me to a happier?[48]

Bronson had once thought he had known better than anyone else the true nature of a worldly Elysium. He now quietly conceded that, in a child's play garden, there were greater worlds than had been dreamt of in his and Charles Lane's philosophy.

Like the work of fiction that was simultaneously absorbing the efforts of his daughter, *Tablets* pays homage to domestic life and celebrates the home as the wellspring of virtue. But whereas *Little Women* is about the change from childhood to maturity and takes the individual life as its measuring unit, *Tablets* emphasizes the aspects of human existence that remain essentially unchanged across generations. Bronson's metaphorical means for transcending time was the idea of the garden, a place that connected him not only with the earth but also with distant ages. In his discourse on the garden, which takes up more than one fourth of the total length of *Tablets*, Alcott makes the obvious association between the modern garden and Eden, but he also cites Homer, Xenophon, Virgil, Columella, and the Bhagavad Gita. If the literary associations are grand, Alcott's applications of them emphasize humility. A garden, he writes, "may be the smallest conceivable, a flower bed only, yet it is prized none the less for that. It is loved all the more for its smallness, and the better cared for."[49] Even the physical appearance of Bronson's book, which Louisa called "very simple outside, wise and beautiful within," reinforced his message of simplicity.[50]

To grow and eat one's own food was, for Bronson, to commune with an otherwise lost Arcadian past. In his efforts to raise the garden to a revered condition of nobility, Bronson occasionally stumbled into historic triviality and Orphic silliness, as when he reported that "the Emperor Tiberius held parsnips in high repute," and when he proclaimed, "Lettuce has always been loyal."[51] Nevertheless, Bronson's tribute to the garden is a convincing document. In *Tablets*, the soil becomes an aid to virtue, a spur to reflection, and a passport to serenity. "A people's freshest literature," he wrote, "springs from free soil, tilled by free men. Every man owes primary duty to the soil, and shall be held incapable by coming generations, if he neglect planting an orchard at least, if not a family, or book for their benefit."[52] Like Voltaire's Candide, Alcott finds refuge and redemption in work; his garden is not an Edenic place of ease, but a place where elemental tasks, earnestly undertaken, "promote us from things to persons."[53] Removing the worker from the realms of anxiety and caprice, work, as Alcott ideally perceives it, "revenges on fortune, and so keeps us by THE ONE amidst the multitude of our perplexities—against reverses, and above want."[54]

Perhaps Alcott's most effusive words are reserved for women, in whom he observes a keenness of insight denied to men: "Entering the school of sensibility with life, she seizes personal qualities by a subtlety of logic over-leaping all deductions of the slower reason; her divinations touching the quick of things as if herself were personally part of the chemistry of life itself."[55] To men seeking advice regarding womankind, Alcott urges that they should offer two things that women were too often denied: respectful treatment and the ballot box. No republic could call itself great, he insisted, while it excluded women from public life. He cautioned, "Certainly liberty is in danger of running into license while woman is excluded from exercising political as well as social restraint upon its excesses. Nor is the state planted securely till she possess equal privileges with men in form-ing its laws and taking . . . part in their administration."[56]

One of the first great works of transcendentalism, Emerson's *Nature*, begins with the complaint "Our age is retrospective."[57] The second half of *Tablets*, one of the last great transcendental texts, begins with the rallying cry "Our time is revolutionary."[58] In Alcott's estimation, the American Age was to be an age of glory.

While its commercial success did not approach that of *Little Women*, *Tablets* promptly went into a second edition.[59] It also garnered enthusiastic reviews. Of these, none was sweeter than the assessment of the *Chicago Tribune*: "Mr. Emerson has been to Mr. Alcott as Plato to Socrates. He has elaborated where the elder thinker did little but meditate and converse. He has written for the world what his senior contemporary has wrought out in his closet. Alcott was an Emersonian Transcendentalist before Emerson."[60] Bronson himself would never have claimed a superior relation to Emerson, who, he admitted, "has no peer with his pen."[61] Nevertheless, the percep-tion that the two were in the same class must have gratified him greatly.

Although *Tablets* discourses broadly and abstractly on the nature of women, family, and friends, it contains no anecdotes or personalities. *Lit-tle Women* is also a search for truth and love and the meaning of life, but it follows the path not of philosophy but of memory. Not seeking a high, smooth road to perfection, it began with the idea that goodness was not a status but a struggle. It did not take its freshness from the soil but from the struggles of people who try, fail, and forgive. Now, more than a century later, *Little Women* remains available everywhere; *Tablets*, by contrast, is out of print and long forgotten. To those with access to the latter volume, however, it is a rare treat to read the two works side by side, as two complementary glimpses into the past, and into the heart of the Alcott family.

CHAPTER FIFTEEN

"THE WISE AND BEAUTIFUL TRUTHS OF THE FATHER"

> "Under every privation, every wrong, and
> with the keen sense of injustice present,
> the dear family were sustained."
>
> —A. BRONSON ALCOTT,
> *Journals,* June 10–14, 1878

I N HIS JOURNAL, BRONSON KEPT CLOSER TRACK OF LOUISA'S SALES figures than his own.[1] He spent part of an early September day in 1869 reading over the notices of *Little Women.* He had a fine collection of them, assembled from all over the country and from every major city. The general verdict placed his daughter in the first rank of writers of fiction. Bronson received this judgment with happy disbelief. He felt even deeper pride, however, in Louisa's modest reaction to it all. She received her accolades as if there had been some strange mistake that was sure to be corrected soon. Louisa judged herself unworthy. The public emphatically disagreed, and for once, Bronson was more than happy to side against his daughter.

Bronson paused to consider how Louisa's success fitted into his own life, a life filled with fitful seeking after grand achievements and equally full of disappointments. No child who had sat in his classroom or at his table had ever acted in a public fashion to carry on the work of conscience and creativity Bronson had begun. None, that is, until Louisa, the one who had once seemed least of all to embody or even to understand his spirit and principles. So often the victim of ironic circumstance, Bronson could justifiably glory in this turn of fate. He had long ago surmised that the family was the best of all models for a school. Now, he observed with satisfaction that his family had yielded his truest scholars:

I, indeed, have great reason to rejoice in my children, finding in them so many of their mother's excellencies, and have especially to thank the Friend of families and Giver of good wives that I was led to her acquaintance and fellowship when life and a future opened before me.[2]

Bronson then wrote the most accurate assessment of his and Abba's lives that he ever committed to paper: "Our children are our best works—if indeed we may claim them as ours, save in the nurture we bestowed on them."[3]

For those hungry for a happy ending, the story of Bronson and Louisa May Alcott might comfortably end here. The goals that had danced so enticingly but inaccessibly before Louisa's eyes when she was a growing girl—fame, wealth, and the admiration of her father—were all securely hers. Bronson, having finally written a successful book and having acquired the enduring sobriquet "the Father of Little Women," had earned the assurance of an eager and interested audience. Almost simultaneously, and with each other's assistance, father and daughter had arrived at an apex in their lives.

Yet Louisa could not thoroughly enjoy her hard-won happiness. Since childhood she had heard in her mind the voice of incessant want. Just as her father had become used to finding contentment in what he had, Louisa had become habituated to desire. If happiness means the fulfillment of all one's wishes, then Louisa was fated never to know happiness, for she never ran out of wishes. She was by no means a greedy or selfish person; indeed, her wishes for others far outnumbered and routinely took precedence over her own quiet longings. Nevertheless, her characteristic state of mind had in it a sense of constant insufficiency that she seemed powerless to eradicate.

Then, too, there was the continuing problem of her health. Finishing *Little Women* had exhausted her. Once accustomed to working fourteen hours a day, she now had days when she could not write at all. Even in April, more than three months after sending the second half of *Little Women* to Roberts Brothers, she still felt "quite used up."[4] Still not suspecting that her ill health stemmed from a less treatable cause than overwork, she wanted only to rest and recover, but her suddenly adoring public clamored for her. Louisa was initially charmed by the letters she received from admiring children.5 Before long, however, she became astonished by the forwardness with which fans and journalists alike presumed upon her time and patience. She wrote in her journal, "People begin to come and stare at the Alcotts. Reporters haunt the place to look at the authoress, who dodges into the woods *à la* Hawthorne, and won't be even a very small lion."6

People were coming to Concord in droves, and not just to peer at Louisa and her family. A great many Americans were feeling an urge to recover some portion of the tranquility that the Civil War and its aftermath had stolen from them. To some of them, the town of Concord, with its gentle, tree-lined roads and its reputation for detached contemplation, spoke irresistibly. In its own day, transcendentalism may have struck these visitors as strange and quixotic. Now that its apostles were gray or departed, the revelations of the Over-soul seemed no longer a threatening disruption to the status quo but a welcome refuge from it. As a result, Louisa complained, "No spot is safe, no hour sacred, and fame is beginning to be considered an expensive luxury by the Concordians."7 For much of the year, Louisa was able to evade the questing throngs by removing to Boston. Sharing quarters with her sister May, she spent the winter of 1868–69 in the city, first in a new hotel on Beacon Street and later at a boardinghouse at 53 Chauncy Street. But when spring and Louisa both returned to Orchard House, she was again annoyed by the intrusions of the philosophy-struck and the curious who had mistaken her for an exhibit.

In early May, resurrecting her alter ego of Tribulation Periwinkle from *Hospital Sketches*, she sent a letter of withering satire to the *Springfield Republican*, in which she deftly lampooned the modern-day pilgrims. She reported in jest that a new hotel called "The Sphinx's Head" was soon to welcome the transcendental tourists, who would be served "Walden water, aesthetic tea, and wine that never grew within the belly of the grape." After dining on wild apples and Orphic acorns and warming themselves by the sacred fires, fed from the Emersonian woodpile, devotees would be issued telescopes with which to view "the soarings of the Oversoul." She also imagined a daily program of events for the entertainment of the faithful, for instance: "Emerson will walk at 4 p.m. . . . Channing may be seen with the naked eye at sunset. The new Hermit will grind his meal at noon, precisely." Among the rest, Louisa could not resist a jibe at her inexhaustibly

Louisa May Alcott at the height of her popularity.
(Courtesy of the Louisa May Alcott Memorial Association)

garrulous father. Her bulletin also advertised: "Alcott will converse from 8 a.m. till 11 p.m."[8] Louisa imagined what fun it would be to repel inquisitive strangers with a garden hose. It was ever clearer to her that she needed to escape.

Her initial retreats from the Boston area were relatively modest. She passed a quiet midsummer month with her cousins the Frothinghams at their house in Quebec. Mount Desert Island, off the coast of Maine, also became a refuge, and she spent August there with May. Meanwhile, the stream of revenue from *Little Women* flowed on. She entrusted the money that remained after paying the family's debts to her financially savvy cousin Samuel Sewall. Upon sending him the first two hundred dollars, she had exulted, "What richness to have a little not needed!"[9] Her growing nest egg was, she admitted, enabling her to bear her neuralgia more cheerfully.

Bronson could not help crowing over Louisa's financial success. He boasted to Frank Sanborn at the beginning of September that twenty-three thousand copies of *Little Women* had been printed and added that *Hospital Sketches*, now reissued with eight other stories under the title *Hospital Sketches and Camp and Fireside Stories*, was also enjoying a revival. He was eager for her to begin the novel about his life that she had first conceived a dozen years earlier, "The Cost of an Idea." Bronson felt that this book would be "a taking piece of family biography, as attractive as any fiction and having the merit of being purely American."[10] The Americanness of Louisa's work mattered greatly to Bronson. Not only did he maintain that she was among the first to draw her work from the life, scenes, and character of New England, but she had absorbed less foreign sentiment than any other writer he knew. If in other ways Bronson fretted over Louisa's lack of formal education, he felt her writing style was one aspect in which the absence of too much academic influence had served her well. It was, he thought, her "freedom from the trammels of school and sects" that gave her work its irresistible frankness and truth.[11]

At the end of August, Louisa returned from Maine, improved in spirits though not in physical vigor. Bronson hoped that she might begin writing "The Cost of an Idea" immediately. He proposed taking her to Spindle Hill, which she had not seen since childhood, so that she might begin her research. However, Louisa's health required a series of postponements. In mid-October, Bronson observed that she was still far from well.[12] Louisa was also eager for a return trip to Europe, but this too would have to wait. In the meantime, Louisa found it more prudent to work on a book that would require no field research, but would draw instead on the readier resources of her own experience and imagination. She may also have sensed that her readers might prefer a story of another virtuous young heroine to the quixotic flounderings of a misunderstood philosopher. In October, she took another room in Boston with May. Paying little heed to her chronic pain, she descended into another writing vortex. Her imagination was captured by the image of an innocent but morally sturdy young girl who stands firm against the materialistic frivolities that seduce her more worldly and citified friends. She called the new book *An Old-Fashioned Girl*.

Like Dickens, Stowe, and others before her, Louisa had learned the trick of selling the same story twice: first as a magazine serial and then as a hardbound book. Initially serialized in monthly installments in *Merry's Museum*

throughout the second half of 1869, *An Old-Fashioned Girl* did not appear
in book form until April 1870. Although the response from both readers
and critics was generally enthusiastic, the reviewer for *The Atlantic
Monthly* was not alone in complaining that the book contained some bad
grammar and even some poor writing. In response to such criticism,
Louisa told her family, "If people knew how O.F.G. was written, in what a
hurry and pain and woe, they would wonder that there was any grammar
at all."[13]

Louisa tended to discuss her work in disparaging terms, and her ready
dismissal of *An Old-Fashioned Girl* therefore comes as no surprise. Nevertheless, the book ranks among the best of Alcott's children's fiction. Unlike
many of her novels for juveniles, which are really little more than a series
of sketches and vignettes, *An Old-Fashioned Girl* is confidently plotted and
steadily develops its central theme: the shallowness of fashionable living
and its particularly destructive effect on young women, whom it renders
physically weak, emotionally vacant, and morally aimless. Alcott's caution-
ary tale trains much of its focus on the Shaw family, who, but for the
beneficent influence of an ethically upright outsider, would doubtless have
tumbled into ruin. Mrs. Shaw, an otherwise inoffensive woman, is a model
citizen of Alcott's modern-day Vanity Fair. Her three children, also essentially good-natured but lacking any useful guidance, seek lives of ease, popularity, and pleasure. Fourteen-year-old Tom is forming the neglectful
habits that will later plunge him into debt and expel him from college. His
sister Fanny divides her time between reading cheap novels and buying
costly hats. Even six-year-old Maud proves a quick study of her elders' vanities; she is already adroit at aping the fashionable nerves and sick
headaches of her mother. The only moral ballast within the household is
supplied by Mr. Shaw and his seventy-year-old mother. However, the latter is too old to have her counsels regarded, and the former has become too
enmeshed in the pursuit of wealth to assert any real authority.

Salvation arrives in the person of Fanny's friend Polly Milton. Coming
from the countryside to pay a lengthy visit to the Shaws, Polly is initially
scandalized by their worldly manners. Fortunately, she refrains from
openly rebuking her hosts, and over time and despite innumerable setbacks, the Shaw children learn from her the merits of selflessness and the
evils of vanity. Mrs. Shaw proves something of a lost cause. When, how-

ever, Mr. Shaw's business fails, all three of his children rally around him, having finally understood Polly's example of sincere caring and faithful industry.

The more interesting problem for Alcott the author is not how Polly is to reform the Shaws, but how to tell so didactic a story without having it dissolve into a cloying, condescending sermon. *An Old-Fashioned Girl* escapes this fate in large part because Polly avoids the unctuousness that might be expected of her. Her goodness is neither self-righteous nor self-congratulating; it flows from an unaffected nature and a simple belief that kindness creates more happiness than self-indulgence. The real strength of Alcott's tale, however, derives from the book's firm advocacy of women's rights, supported by its conviction that sexual equality is not the cause of a political faction but a tenet of common sense. In demonstrating Polly's superiority over the Fanny Shaws of the world, Alcott protests a social system that fosters a commercialized sense of human value, a system particularly degrading to women. Allowed to participate in the marketplace only as purchasers, Fanny and her friends are themselves reduced to ornamental commodities. By resisting to define herself in objectifying economic terms, Polly tacitly insists that to live is not to have, but to think, to feel, and to do.

Although this credo appears obvious to Polly, it brings her into such conflict with her materialistic surroundings that she becomes something of a radical in spite of herself. Between the seventh and eighth chapters of the novel, six years pass, and Fanny, Tom, and Polly reenter the scene as young adults. Asked to guess what new occupation Polly has adopted—she has become a music teacher—Tom supposes that she is going to deliver lectures on women's rights. Utterly accustomed to his sister's passive conformity, Tom can only interpret Polly's simple desire to be active and useful as an overtly political stance. But Polly does not lecture. She does not vocally urge the values of independent work and compassionate charity so much as she embodies them. This fact is indeed the reason why *An Old-Fashioned Girl,* although it is a women's rights novel, seldom feels like one. The radical new women in the story do not contort themselves to fit any particular social manifesto. They simply have the self-confidence to do what they feel natural doing. They embody Alcott's essential concept of a free woman: one who claims the power and opportunity to explore and follow her own nature. Alcott was no doubt aware of the irony of her novel's title. Her old-fashioned girl is the most forward-looking character on the scene, and her supposedly outworn virtues—simplicity of taste, self-reliance, and forthright expression—are precisely the values her new world needs.

In the late nineteenth and early twentieth centuries, American writers turned continually to the subject of divided families—families ironically broken apart not by want but by prosperity. Time and again, one encounters characters like Hurstwood in Dreiser's *Sister Carrie*, Abner Spragg in Wharton's *The Custom of the Country*, and the host of faceless, nameless toilers in Howells' *A Traveler from Altruria*. They are men whose wives and daughters have no other purpose in life than to spend and be seen. To keep up with the ceaseless demands of fashion, these characters devote themselves to the making of money, so that at last their relationships with their homes and the people who live there become almost solely economic.

Alcott should, perhaps, receive more credit for creating a character who, by more than twenty years, anticipates the better-known exemplars of his type. In some respects, Mr. Shaw is yet another of the shadowy fathers of Alcott's fiction: aloof, quiet, and more or less excluded from the main action of the story. He provides an abundant life for his family. Nevertheless, he figures as an image of the depressing consequences that can ensue when a father behaves entirely differently from Bronson Alcott. Although Louisa sees some honor in the way Mr. Shaw goes to his office "with the regularity of a machine," she also leaves the reader to infer that Shaw's offspring would need less reforming if he had given them more of his time and less of an allowance.[14] Louisa goes so far as to suggest that a well-provided childhood is a hindrance to happiness and achievement. With her modest appetites, Polly fits easily into a way of life in which talent, energy, and character matter most. Genius blossoms best, Alcott writes, "when poverty [is] head gardener."[15]

As the last installments of *An Old-Fashioned Girl* were appearing in *Merry's Museum*, Bronson was making ready for another western tour, which would take him through fourteen cities, culminating in a sojourn in St. Louis, a city for which he was acquiring a deepening fondness. He was also developing a deep appreciation for the man who had first invited him to St. Louis, William Torrey Harris. In 1867, Harris had founded the *Jour-*

nal of Speculative Philosophy, the first American philosophical journal that did not espouse a particular theological agenda. Bronson thought very highly of Harris's *journal*, and he also felt that Harris's review of *Tablets* had been the only one that had "penetrated to the core of its thought."[16] Opportunities to interact with Harris and the heartland in general, "so friendly to free and formidable thinking," were almost impossible for Bronson to resist.[17]

The welcomes that awaited Bronson along his way west in 1869 were unlike anything he had ever seen. The drawing rooms where he gave his conversations were crowded to capacity, and when the trip was over his appearances had earned him more than seven hundred dollars. Perhaps the publication of *Tablets* helped somewhat to swell the audience for his stately, poetic discourses on Health, Social Life, and Culture. Undeniably, however, it was *Little Women* that made by far the greatest difference. His most popular lectures now were his observations on New England authors. He was accustomed to sharing stories of his personal encounters with Emerson, Thoreau, Hawthorne, Fuller, and Ellery Channing. Though he knew quite a bit less about them, he was also pleased to give his opinions regarding Holmes, Lowell, Whittier, and Longfellow.[18] But it was his closeness to Louisa that had made him so popular. To his credit, Bronson never advertised a lecture on the subject of her life, and he told her story only when the audience asked him to do so. However, such requests were routine. He was now also a popular guest among school audiences, as most of the students were familiar with the book and were eager to know about the real Jo March and to see the face of her proud father.

Bronson seems to have been happy to give the people what they wanted. True, his conversations now took on a far more personal, less philosophical tenor, but he had both the inventiveness and the good grace to regard the new kind of colloquy simply as a new genre, which he christened "the popular conversation." In such a talk, he observed, "one does not venture deeply into metaphysical discriminations, but treats of living traits and personal anecdote chiefly."[19] Within the realm of personal observations, he found himself drawn to speak chiefly of Emerson, and he sometimes wondered whether his dilations upon his dearest friend tended to crowd out his other subjects to an excessive degree. As to Louisa, he also had a dramatic story to tell, and he knew how to tell it. With irrepressible

*Louisa's sister May and Alice Bartlett share a comic
moment on their tour of Europe.*
(Courtesy of the Louisa May Alcott Memorial Association)

pleasure, he wrote, "I am introduced as the father of Little Women, and I
am riding in the Chariot of Glory wherever I go."[20]

After sending *An Old-Fashioned Girl* to press, Louisa was able to turn her thoughts to a more leisurely prospect. She had long wanted to go with May to Europe, so that her sister might find artistic guidance and inspiration and so Louisa herself might finally recover her health. In the spring of 1870, an irresistible opportunity arose. Alice Bartlett, a friend of May's, requested her company on a trip to France, Switzerland, and Italy. May insisted that Louisa be included. On April 1, the same day that marked the publication of *An Old-Fashioned Girl*, Anna's husband John escorted the sisters by train to New York, to join Alice Bartlett. The next day, the trio of travelers boarded the French steamer *Lafayette* on its way to Brest, France.

The first months of her travels with May were among the happiest times in Louisa's life. Although there was to be no Laddie to add romance to her travels, this excursion to Europe was otherwise far more pleasant than the previous one. One key difference was Alice's charm. Also, Louisa was now free from an urgent need to turn everything she saw into a travel article. Of course, she would not have been herself if she completely ceased to observe the world with an author's eye, and after the trip was over she did describe some of the incidents of her travels in a second volume of *Aunt Jo's Scrap-Bag*. Nevertheless, for once, no necessity tugged urgently at her sleeve.

Unfortunately, she did not recover her health as quickly as she had hoped. Also, her ingrained habit of penny-pinching made her anxious about the money she was spending. She maintained that if the trip made her well and gave May a good time, it was well worth the expense.[21] But her condition showed no signs of improvement. To the contrary, Louisa developed a persistent ache in one of her legs, and as she and May made their way through Brittany, she was in a desperate state over the pain. Her fortunes turned, however, when she consulted William Kane, a handsome, gray-haired English doctor who at last made the connection between her chronic ill health and the massive doses of calomel she had been given seven years earlier. Kane, while serving as an army surgeon in India, had fallen ill and had been treated with calomel. He had never gotten the mercury out of his body. He discussed with her the reasons why her pain came and went, and why it did not stay in the same places. The mercury, as Louisa paraphrased his explanation, "lies round in a body and don't do much harm till a weak spot appears when it goes there and makes trouble." Dr. Kane advised Louisa to take iodine of potash, which had given him relief from mercury deposits in his arms. She followed his suggestion.[22] For a while, it seemed to work. A few weeks after beginning the treatment, she wrote to Abba, "I'm getting better so fast and enjoying so much."[23] Her good humor continued as the traveling party left France and settled for the summer in Switzerland. For the first time since she was a running, laughing girl at Hillside, Louisa had to hunt for reasons not to enjoy herself.

Nevertheless, she did find a few. To begin with, she was not so carefree as to forget her finances, and her letters home were peppered with investment advice. A more personal concern caused her deeper unrest: she was not sufficiently confident of her mother's health to feel entirely at ease. Louisa quietly dreaded the possibility that death might come to Orchard House in her absence. The relief of not having to look after her parents for a year was all but negated by her worries about how they would survive without her.

If, in this sense, she was too far from home, she found that in another she was still too close. To her bemused chagrin, she learned that she had not gone far enough to escape the adulation that pursued the author of *Little Women*. She was most gratified, it seemed, when praise came to her by accident, as when a boy on the train to New York had placed a new copy of *An Old-Fashioned Girl* in her lap with the recommendation, "Bully book, Ma'am! Sell a lot, better have it." When the boy discovered that his would-be customer had written the book herself, his shocked exclamation of "No!" was more delicious still.[24] In general, however, the attentions of her public continued to irritate her. Undoubtedly meaning well, Abba sent Louisa a parcel of fan mail—perhaps, indeed, more than one. With emphasis, Louisa begged her mother not to send "any more letters from *so cracked girls*."[25] She explained that she had no time to answer them and that she had to pay for every one that was forwarded to her. She demanded, "the rampant infants must wait."[26]

The public wanted more stories, and Thomas Niles dutifully conveyed requests from papers and magazines for new material. She sent Niles her gratitude, but having come abroad for rest she was determined to stay off the literary treadmill until her year's holiday was at an end. Perceiving that the requests would not cease on their own, Louisa finally dashed off a sop to her readers: a comic poem titled "The Lay of a Golden Goose," in which she transformed the story of her own success into a barnyard allegory. It is a simple verse, full of observations about youthful yearnings for fortune and glory, and how absurd such aspirations seem to all but those who feel them from within. The poem tells of the dismissive mockery of those wedded to convention. Yet, as in these stanzas, it also tells of the indomitable self-confidence that enables both geese and brave young women to withstand it all:

> She could not sing, she could not fly,
> Nor even walk with grace,
> And all the farm-yard had declared
> A puddle was her place.
>
> But something stronger than herself
> Would cry, "Go on, go on!
> Remember, though an humble fowl
> You're cousin to a swan."27

Barnyard opinion, of course, changes dramatically when it is discovered that the goose has been laying golden eggs. Derision promptly gives way to an incessant demand for more eggs. More realistically than most ugly-duckling fables, Alcott's poem ends not with the feathered heroine enshrined in fame and comfort but, rather, paddling for her life across the Atlantic to escape her idolaters.

The poem relates that, safe in the Alps, the goose regained "the health she had so nearly lost."28 Though she was still not entirely well, Louisa was now feeling rejuvenated by her travels. Shortly before leaving Bex for Vevey, the scene of her innocent dalliance with Laddie, she wrote to Niles that she was rising from her ashes in a phoenixlike manner.29 It was a good thing, Louisa thought, that the books already in print were doing so well, since she could not bring herself to write anything beyond a few odds and ends, more in the way of notes than an actual manuscript. She now caught herself "dawdl[ing] round without an idea in [her] head."30 Having been told by her friend Alice that no one did anything in Italy, where she planned to spend the ensuing six months, Louisa looked forward to another half year of idleness before finally getting back to work. European living was agreeing with her so much that, in September, she talked of extending her holiday still further. Although it seemed obvious to her that someone should go home in the spring to look after family business, she saw no reason why May, instead of her, should not be the one to return.

In October, the sisters left Switzerland for Italy, passing through Florence, Milan, Parma, and Pisa on their way to Rome. Whereas the beauty and romance of the ancient city enchanted May, Louisa saw her surroundings, as she put it, "through blue glasses."[31] Not only was poor health dampening her spirits, but some of the anti-Catholic feeling she had imbibed during her teenage years in Boston made her critical of what she saw. She felt continually oppressed by "a sense of sin, dirt, and general decay of all things."[32]

In December came devastating news. John Pratt, Anna's devoted husband of ten years, had died suddenly. Louisa had long since put aside the

G. P. A. Healy, whose canvas of Lincoln hangs in the White House, painted this portrait of Louisa on her trip to Rome.

(Courtesy of the Louisa May Alcott Memorial Association)

jealousy and resentment she had felt when John had first entered the family, and she grieved at his passing. She lamented, "No born brother was ever dearer, & each year I loved & respected & admired him more and more."[33] The letters from America indicated that Anna was bearing the situation bravely. Louisa wrote to Anna that the ten happy years the couple had shared could never be taken away. Although she considered cutting her travels short in order to be by her sister's side, Louisa found that there was no need for her presence since a favorite cousin, Lizzie Wells, had rushed to Concord to attend to the dying man. At Louisa's behest, Wells now remained there to fill the place Louisa had left empty. Louisa was still not well, and she thought it prudent to remain where she was and to gather strength in order to be the more useful when she did return. For the time being, she had one way to help her sister and nephews.

Despite her plan to take a break from writing while in Europe, Louisa seems to have begun her next novel before word of Pratt's death reached her.[34] After she heard the news, however, her writing took on a new purpose: both the spirit and the proceeds from this novel must belong to the two "little men" who had been left without a father. She threw herself determinedly into her manuscript, vowing that Anna and "the dear little boys" would not be left in want. She resorted to the most commercially appealing characters she was ever to devise: the March family.

While *Little Men* is ostensibly a sequel to *Little Women*, it greatly differs in spirit and tone from its predecessor. The once irrepressible Jo has been overtaken by both time and responsibility. Although barely two years of real time had elapsed between the release of part 2 of *Little Women* and the appearance of *Little Men*, Jo is now a "thin old woman"—the image of how Louisa viewed herself in the aftermath of war and disease.[35] The focal location of the novel is not the March family home but the boys' academy at Plumfield, which Jo and Professor Bhaer had founded in the last chapter of *Little Women*. Whereas the March home had been a school for life only in a metaphorical sense, the scene of *Little Men* openly proclaims the book's intention to instruct.

Whereas *Little Women*, after its episodic beginnings, acquires both cohesiveness and direction, *Little Men* remains principally a series of anecdotes and sketches. Its lack of thematic unity is easily explained. If the principal building blocks of *Little Women* were Louisa's concrete recollections of Hillside, then *Little Men* emerged primarily from her idealizing imagination. The reviewer from the *Ladies' Repository* of Boston made an apt point in observing, "[T]he first story is real and the second made; and the unmistakable charm of being told straight out of real life, which was the spirit and soul of the earlier work, is wanting in this."[36]

As *Little Men* ventured into the airy realm of idealism, Louisa's inspiration inevitably drifted toward reflections on her father. The novel does not address Bronson's biography any more than *Little Women* had done; Mr. March again remains politely on the story's periphery. Nevertheless, *Little Men* owes its educational spirit and agenda almost entirely to Bronson. When, in 1871, the Alcotts' publisher decided to capitalize on *Little Men's* success by reissuing Elizabeth Peabody's *Record of a School*, Louisa wrote the following lines for inclusion in Peabody's preface: "As many people . . . inquire if there ever was or could be a school like Plumfield, I am glad to reply by giving them a record of the real school which suggested some of the scenes described in *Little Men*. . . . Not only is it a duty and a pleasure, but there is a certain fitness in making the childish fiction of the daughter play the grateful part of herald to the wise and beautiful truths of the father." The "thanks and commendations" for Plumfield, she graciously conceded, all belonged to Bronson.[37]

Yet Louisa's statements need some refining. In truth, the genealogy of Plumfield is more complicated, as might be expected from the fact that the Temple School exerted little direct influence on Louisa's own education. She never attended the Temple School. Its last remnant closed when she was five, and her memories of it were few. Indeed, in its vision of school as a kind of extended family, Plumfield more closely resembles another experiment that Louisa remembered more clearly. Rather than simply replicating the Temple School, Plumfield combines the discipline and introspection of that institution with the pastoralism and consociate family structure of Fruitlands. In contrast to Alcott's classroom-centered teaching at the Temple School, Plumfield resembles Fruitlands in that the process of learning is an around-the-clock experience, deriving as much from the work and play of the community as from the formal lessons of the instructor. It was Fruitlands that opened Louisa's youthful eyes to the possibility of forming intimate spiritual attachments on a basis other than blood or romance. From Fruitlands to Plumfield, she transposed the concept that the word "family" might describe adults and children united by a spiritual vision and a moral project.

The curious fact is that Fruitlands was such a miserable failure while *Little Men* was such a resounding success, selling in six figures in its first year. The difference rests on a charming irony. In establishing Fruitlands as an actual place, Bronson Alcott, perhaps for the only time of his life, was too much of a realist. The flesh-and-blood utopianism of Fruitlands attracted few followers. Refined into fiction, however, the idea of such a community found favor even among those who claimed that it could never really be. Whereas Fruitlands was experienced only by a handful of impractical dreamers, Plumfield has left its mark on the imaginations of generations of children, sowing seeds of idealism to sprout where they may.

Louisa had left America the day after the release of *An Old-Fashioned Girl*. She returned on the same day that *Little Men* appeared in American bookstores. The twelve-day voyage from England aboard the steamer *Malta* was anxious and uncomfortable. Not only had Louisa's fourteen months overseas failed to put an end to her chronic pain, but a number of the passengers on the ship were stricken by smallpox. Unaware that her bout with the disease twenty years earlier had immunized her against a second infection, Louisa moved nervously among the sufferers.[38]

When the interminable journey finally ended and she disembarked in Boston, she was greeted by the welcome sight of her father and Thomas Niles, who had come to meet her with a great red placard advertising *Little Men* pinned up in their carriage. She was delighted to learn that the book had sold fifty thousand advance copies. On arriving at Orchard House, she found matters in better shape than she might have expected. Her upstairs room had been "refurnished and much adorned by Father's earnings."[39] Although Anna still mourned the loss of her husband "like a tender turtle-dove," she was physically well and met her sister's solicitous gaze with a look of serenity.[40] The nephews were now tall, bright lads who pleased Louisa not only with their cleverness but also with their devotion to their grandmother. Marmee herself, however, looked weak and aged, and Louisa resolved never to travel far from her again. Friends of both Bronson and Louisa descended on the house in droves, and the general excitement moved Bronson to write that no season in his recent memory had been so crowded with surprises.[41]

Amid all the bustle, Louisa took time to repay one last debt. In 1862, James T. Fields, the editor of *The Atlantic* who had told her to stick to teaching, had lent her forty dollars to help her furnish a kindergarten. He had told her, perhaps with a note of derision, that she could repay him when she had made "a pot of gold." Louisa had forgotten neither the loan nor the words that had gone with it. She now sent the money back with many thanks and with perhaps the slightest hint of revenge.[42]

The joy of Louisa's reunion with the family gave way to darker reflections in July when news came from Syracuse that Abba's brother Samuel had died. Slighting Emerson for the moment, she called her uncle "our best friend for years." She added, "Peace to his ashes."[43]

Coming home temporarily did for Louisa what her time overseas had failed to accomplish. For a month after her return, she felt better than she had felt for two years. She was too accustomed to the frailties of her body to expect good health to last, but she enjoyed it heartily until, in July, the inevitable slide into discomfort began again. She did have the strength to go on writing, or failing that, to revise scores of pages of odds and ends for publication as a sequence of bagatelles known collectively as the *Aunt Jo's Scrap-Bag* series. The first volume in the sequence appeared in 1872 and was eventually followed by five others, the last appearing in 1882. Although of relatively slight importance to understanding Alcott as a writer, the *Scrap-Bag* series says much about the acumen of Louisa and her publishers as businesspeople. The books were small and easily portable—just the thing, as Roberts Brothers surely anticipated, to purchase as an amusement for a child going on a holiday or to stuff into a stocking at Christmas. Their anecdotes are short, simple, and well suited to the casual reader. The series emerged from a desire to find yet another niche in the reading market that Alcott's writing might address, and Louisa was more than fit for the task of filling it.

As the title of the *Aunt Jo's Scrap-Bag* series reflects, Louisa found some value in blurring the distinction between her real self and her fictitious alter ego, Jo March. Just as her imagined character had taken on many of the features of her creator, so too did Louisa find fun in partially becoming Jo, attaching stories to her name and using Jo's persona to narrate events that had happened to the real woman. Sometimes she referred to her real family as "the Marches."[44] When she wrote to one fan, she took the identification still further, averring that her father was, like Mr. March, a minister.[45] It is possible that Louisa elided the distinction between herself and Jo because she sensed that the character she had created—genial, happily married, and above all, healthy—was a more appealing persona for the public than the real woman she had become. In her depictions of Jo, as well as in the more literally autobiographical pieces in the *Scrap-Bag* series and elsewhere, Louisa did not hesitate to romanticize both the situations she described and the characters of heroines. Louisa plainly understood the commercial appeal of sketches and stories that played gently on the reader's sentiments, and she lavishly obliged her public with images of self-reliant young women braving daunting odds with the encouragement of loyal and loving friends. At the same time that Louisa was satisfying her reading public, she was adroitly managing the public's perception of her real-life personality. The Louisa May Alcott who appears in her autobiographical sketches is as brilliantly crafted a heroine as Jo March ever was.

Nevertheless, there was no way for Louisa to remain faithful to the image she had created for herself. In the first place, the image of Jo with which she identified herself was internally inconsistent, owing simply to the realities of time. There are two Jo Marches: the athletic teenager of *Little Women* and the matronly Aunt Jo of *Little Men* and, much later, *Jo's Boys.* With the typical greediness of human beings, Louisa's readers wanted to imagine that she was both Jos at once. This in itself was a feat that no illusionist could perform, but her devotees demanded still more. They wanted to imagine Jo/Louisa as a petite, perky young woman with unlimited stores of laughter and goodwill. Louisa secretly prayed for a pox to descend on them. She complained, "Why people will think Jo small when she is described as tall I don't see, & why insist that she must be young when she is said to be 30 at the end of the book?"[46] It must have been peculiar and even painful for her to reflect on the ever increasing distance that separated the older Jo March, still sprightly and energetic, from the real-life original, a self-confessed "tired out old lady . . . with nothing left of her youth but a yard or more of chestnut hair that *won't* turn grey though it is time it did."[47] Louisa wrote this description of herself when she was still not forty-two.

In contrast, her father was acting like anything but a tired old man.

Between 1869 and 1875, years that saw him age from seventy to seventy-six, he took four tours of the Midwest, where he now regularly found eager audiences for his conversations. He hoped to make annual western excursions thereafter and was deterred from doing so only because he could not bring himself to leave Abba, whose health was growing considerably weaker. He was in regular contact with his St. Louis friend William Torrey Harris, and in Illinois he had found a loyal friend in Dr. Hiram K. Jones, a devotee of the ancient Greeks who led an active and intellectually vibrant Plato Club in Jacksonville.

It was now not unusual for Alcott to return to Concord after several months of speaking with eight hundred dollars in his pocket. He spoke against religious orthodoxy and in favor of a "New Church" in which worship would be free, individual, and spontaneous. He inveighed against the writings of Darwin, which he lacked the scientific knowledge to fully appreciate but in which he perceived a threat to free will and a challenge to the spiritual nature of humankind. "Any faith declaring a divorce from the supernatural, and seeking to prop itself upon *Nature* alone," he averred, "falls short of satisfying the deepest needs of humanity."[48] To his great pleasure, Bronson had many opportunities to address school audiences, to whom he expounded his theories of education and moral culture. As was now habitual with him, he also regaled his audiences with verbal sketches of his great transcendental brethren, tending to save for last a discourse on Louisa. He liked to tell of how, as a girl, she came home from school one day and said the master could not spell, and it was no use for her to attend his school any longer. Alcott told his listeners that, thereafter, she said she was merely visiting the school as an observer. With a touch of humor, he added that she had never stopped observing. Explaining his own current popularity, Alcott conjectured that people were treating him well for his daughter's sake.[49]

On the night of July 23, 1872, Emerson's house caught fire. Neighbors rushed to the family's aid and, in a desperate attempt to save the philosopher's library, began pitching books by the armload out the windows. Louisa stood guard over the scorched, sodden pile.[50] Though some were damaged, none of the precious volumes was lost. The structure was saved, but the Emersons were forced to relocate while extensive repairs were undertaken. Emerson suffered deeply from the shock of the blaze, and

Bronson was also stunned. He lamented, "We shall never sit again *in the same rooms!*"[51]

The same year, between western journeys, Bronson also published a second successful book. *Concord Days* purports to be six months of entries from Alcott's 1869 journal. The work is divided into a half dozen sections, each named for a month, moving sequentially from April to September. Dated as if to represent a chronological record, it treats topics as diverse as Goethe, The Ideal Church, and Berries. Yet the organizing principle of *Concord Days* is much looser than it first appears. Far from an authentic six-month window into Alcott's life, the book offers material written over a span of more than thirty years. It is an eclectic scrapbook of Alcottiana, including excerpts not only from journals of various years but also transcripts of conversations with adult audiences; biographical sketches of Hawthorne, Emerson, Margaret Fuller, and others; and even a long extract from the once-pilloried *Conversations with Children on the Gospels.* Shedding the egotism of his youth, he also quotes extensively from the work of others, including poetry from Ellery Channing and journal entries from Thoreau. In the background of the work, the seasons change. Apple blossoms appear, Independence Day comes and passes, and near the end, autumn breathes coolly on Walden Pond. Although its noteworthy qualities are many, *Concord Days* may be most significant as a book of friends. As compared to earlier times, his ideal life was no longer so much one of celestial reveries. It was centered, instead, among the people he admired and loved.

The structure of *Concord Days* both reflects and denies the passing of time; although the selections appear to proceed sequentially, Alcott leaps blithely from year to year, even decade to decade with barely an acknowledgement. In sections on Plato and Plotinus, even ancient days are revisited and revived. Alcott begins *Concord Days* on a melancholy note, gazing around his study at the massive volumes of his journals, "showy seen from without, with far too little of life transcribed within."[52] His lament is twofold. He complains both that his life has been too empty of achievement and that, even when a moment was worth recording, he lacked the artist's skill to render it adequately in print. "[C]ould I succeed in sketching to the life a single day's doings," he writes, "[I] should esteem myself as having accomplished the chiefest feat in literature."[53] As a whole, however,

Concord Days puts the lie to Alcott's laments, both as to the insignificance of his life and his failure to preserve it in a vibrant form. *Concord Days* may be thought of as a kind of prose *Leaves of Grass*, lacking Whitman's genius but partaking of his desire to transmute the whole of his experience into a living book. Alcott was attempting, as Whitman described his own project, "to put *a Person,* a human being . . . in the latter half of the Nineteenth Century, in America, freely, fully and truly on record."[54] Alcott invites the reader for "a turn about his grounds, a sally into the woods, climbing the hill-top, sauntering by brook-sides."[55] We pass through his garden, are asked to observe the rustic fences and gates made by his own hands, and are offered a place by his open fire. We meet his friends, peer into his books, and perhaps fidget a bit as he drones on a trifle too long on his theories of Genesis and the foibles of the current age. What Whitman wrote of his leaves can also be said of *Concord Days*: "Camerado, this is no book, / Who touches this touches a man."[56]

To a lesser, though still important, extent, *Concord Days* also touches on a family. May Alcott, sketchbook in hand, walks with her father as he visits the site of Thoreau's hut. Bronson's grandsons sail toy boats on the brook and amuse him with "their playful panorama." Without naming her, he praises Abba, wondering what he would have left undone, or have done badly, "without her counsels to temper [my] adventurous idealism." The family as a whole, Bronson adds, "is the sensitive plant of civility, the measure of culture. . . . Sown in the family, the seeds of holiness are here to be cherished and ripened for immortality." Louisa's presence is seldom felt, unless perhaps in Alcott's advice to aspiring writers: "You may read selections [from your manuscript] to sensible women,—if young the better; and if it stand these trials, you may offer it to a publisher."[57] Does this allusion mean that Alcott had solicited the literary advice of Louisa, surely the most sensible younger woman in his acquaintance? Unfortunately, there is scant evidence to suggest that Bronson either did or did not share manuscripts and suggestions with her. Hints like this one, however, give grounds for speculation.

Although *Concord Days* begins with melancholy, it ends with cheerful exhortation. In the closing subchapter, "Ideals," Alcott urges his readers to realize the best that is in them and to seek out tasks that demand more than a lifetime can give them. "Step by step," he writes, "one climbs the pinnacles of excellence; life itself is but the stretch for that mountain of holiness. . . . Who ceases to aspire, dies. Our pursuits our prayers; our ideals our gods."[58]

Louisa, like her father, had not ceased to aspire. She still dreamed of winning a reputation as an author of serious novels for adults. In November 1872, two months after Bronson published *Concord Days*, came an opportunity to do just that. Henry Ward Beecher's magazine, the *Christian Union*, offered Louisa three thousand dollars for a serial to run in weekly installments for six months. She accepted the thousand-dollar advance and proceeded to resurrect an unfinished manuscript she had begun even before she had written the first draft of *Moods*. She had called the project "Success" when she had first conceived it in her midtwenties. Now, she supplanted that optimistic noun with one that she had learned to see as the more fundamental truth of existence: *Work*.

She found it almost impossible to write at an easy, measured pace. As with *Moods* and *Little Women*, she "fired up the engine." "The thing possesses me," she told her journal, "and I must obey till it's done."[59] If the sense of creative abandon was still the same, however, it was no longer accompanied by the romantic sense of sacrificing herself for art. She now likened herself to a galley slave, chained to her oar by Beecher's thousand dollars. She drove herself beyond reason, and when she put aside her novel, it was to write eight shorter tales she had promised another publisher for thirty-five dollars each. Shortly after *Work* was completed, she accepted another offer to write another ten tales at fifty dollars each. Once the fastest running girl in all of Concord, Louisa was turning into a literary Atalanta, pausing too often to snatch up a few more golden apples while the prize she most desired, a truly brilliant novel for a mature audience, slipped away from her.

Objectively speaking, there was now no real need for her to press herself so mercilessly. Despite the abundance that surrounded her, however, and despite the fact that her work brought her less and less pleasure, Louisa could not stop writing. To some who have experienced poverty early in life, no subsequent amount of money or security seems entirely sufficient, for one lives forever in the fear that a time of need will come again. Concerned that one day her talent, or more likely her popularity, might desert her, she told the editor of the *Boston Globe*, "I find that I must make my hay while my sun shines, & so wish to earn all I can before Fortune's wheel takes a turn & carries me down again."[60] She kept writing, too, because, on an emotional level, she could not help herself. There was a compulsive quality to her experiences of the vortex, and she seemed unable to resist the allure of the poetic maelstrom even when she knew that such prolonged fits of creativity were bad for her health. Then, too, she may have worked herself to exhaustion because she saw no further benefit in rest. A year of relaxation in Europe had not restored her health, and after speaking with Dr. Kane, she had good reason to believe that wellness would never truly come again. If she were to be ill whether she worked or not, the decision could only have been obvious.

Because she needed to produce three copies of *Work*—one for Beecher and one each for her English and American book publishers—Louisa wrote three pages at once, one on top of another, using impression paper. The uncomfortable steel pens that she used, coupled with the added pressure needed to make a triple impression, resulted in permanent partial paralysis to her thumb. She then taught herself to write with her left hand. Her constitution was less and less able to withstand the punishment she inflicted on it, and at last she slowed her pace for fear of a breakdown. In November a terrible fire in Boston disrupted her writing. In February, she was again forced to stop work when a telegram from Bronson urged her to return to Concord because it was thought that Anna was dying of pneumonia. Thankfully, the fire spared Louisa's apartment, Anna survived her illness, and the manuscript of *Work* went on. In March 1873, it was done.

The story of the frequently ill-starred attempts of a plucky young woman, Christie Devon, to find employment that can sustain both her body and soul, *Work* takes up a theme that Alcott introduced in *An Old-Fashioned Girl*, in which Fanny Shaw wonders if the time would ever come "when women could earn a little money and success, without paying such a heavy price for them." The heaviest possible price is almost exacted from Christie, whose failed attempts to find a secure place in the working world bring her within moments of suicide. Two of Alcott's philosophical heroes, Emerson and Thomas Carlyle, had urged that labor is the process by which a person achieves full humanity. While Alcott agreed that work could be ennobling, she had also learned firsthand that undercompensated, unappreciated work could wear down and diminish the laborer. As Christie discovers, performing the very tasks that strengthen her competence and character leads a leisure-loving society to regard her as an inferior. Almost throughout *Work*, Alcott's female characters either possess practical knowledge and strength of character but lack the worldly means to make a difference in society, or vice versa.

During her picaresque wanderings in the first third of the novel, Christie performs with reasonable skill the tasks of maidservant, actress, governess, hired companion, and seamstress. She is driven from each occupation in turn by the impossibility of remaining under employers who have infected the employment relation with their own character flaws. Far from denouncing the impersonal nature of the marketplace, Christie's history indicates that, in the occupations available to women other than factory work, employment relations were often too personal and that the need for cash too frequently meant exposure to the whims and cruelties of careless or obdurate employers. Economic relations in the book are unsatisfactory so long as they involve either the mere exchange of money for service or the flaunted superiority of one class over another. Alcott writes, "There are many Christies, willing to work, yet unable to bear the contact with coarser natures which makes labor seem degrading, or to endure the hard struggle for the bare necessities of life when life has lost all that makes it beautiful."[61] Hepsey Johnson, a black domestic who becomes Christie's first friend in the novel, puts the matter simply: "Folks don't seem to 'member dat we've got feelin's."[62]

And yet, where the relationship is graced by mutual respect and sympathy, no task is truly distasteful. As Christie's benefactor, Mrs. Wilkins, puts it, "There warn't never a hard job that ever I'd hated but what grew easy when I remembered who it was done for."[63] Mrs. Wilkins is a laundress, but she is almost always shown working in her kitchen; Hepsey is employed as a cook. Both of them are nurturing characters, and their shared association with food illustrates that work must not only produce wealth. It must nourish both body and soul. In *Work*, Alcott explores the possible connection between love and money in both its highest and lowest forms. When Christie gives a hundred hard-earned dollars to Hepsey to help her guide slaves to freedom, Alcott invokes the language of the marketplace to highlight the act of charity. She calls the gift an "investment" and observes that "shares in the Underground Railroad pay splendid divi-

dends that never fail."[64] The other side of the love-cash nexus is personified in Rachel, a former prostitute whom Christie befriends while the two
are working as seamstresses, and whose experience illustrates the tragedies
that result when physical intimacy becomes commodified. Christie's kindness to Rachel is more than repaid when the latter appears just in time to
save Christie from throwing herself in the river.

Soon after Christie's brush with death, the story veers into a love trian-
gle somewhat stalely reminiscent of *Moods*. Again, one of the candidates
for Christie's affections, a florist named David Sterling, is modeled on
Thoreau. Christie rejects a wealthy suitor and accepts Sterling, and the
story teeters on the brink of predictability until the outbreak of the Civil
War inspires both Sterling and Christie to enlist, he in the army, she in the
nursing corps. At their hastily planned wedding, both are in uniform.
David is killed in action, leaving Christie to raise their baby daughter and
to wonder whether she will ever find the work for which her life of struggle and trial has prepared her. The question is answered when, near the eve
of her fortieth birthday, Christie attends a women's rights meeting. It soon
becomes apparent that the wealthy women in attendance and their working comrades have no idea how to communicate with each other. Standing
at the lowest step of the speakers' platform, symbolically bridging the space
between high and low, Christie gives an eloquent, impromptu address
whose spirit unites and inspires the crowd. Her sufferings have shaped her
unawares into a potent women's rights activist.

The closing tableau of *Work* reunites many of the women whom
Christie has met on her journey, including Hepsey, Mrs. Wilkins, and
Rachel, who, it has been revealed, is actually Sterling's sister, long presumed dead. Gathered together in the name of creating a better place for
women in American life, Christie's friends join hands as "a loving league of
sisters, old and young, black and white, rich and poor."[65] Again, Alcott
redefines family according to shared mission rather than bloodlines. However, Christie's alliance is different in that it excludes any masculine presence. The war has made casualties of both of Christie's lovers, making
room for the higher love of sisterhood. At age eleven, Louisa had cried
when her father suggested dividing their family along gender lines. Now,
only a few years younger than her father had been at Fruitlands, Alcott saw
intriguing possibilities in single-sex community. The ending of the novel

reconstructs not only the idea of family but also the meaning of the book's title. Whereas "work" had once signified to Christie the grubbing, lonely life of a menial laborer, the word is ultimately made synonymous with the holy labors of reform.

Despite its reassuring ending, *Work* is Alcott's most harrowing book. Her account of Christie's near suicide shocked many readers, some of whom sent her personal letters demanding to know why she had included it. "*I* did not like the suicide in 'Work,'" she replied to one such letter, "but as much of that chapter was true I let it stand as a warning to several people who need it to my knowledge, & to many whom I do not know."[66] Although Louisa's thoughts of killing herself had long since passed, the memory of her suicidal depression had refused to lie quietly. Louisa had confessed it, one supposes, not merely as a service to others but as an unburdening of her own soul.

But does Louisa's allusion to "the suicide in 'Work'" refer to Christie's brush with drowning? Notably, Louisa's letter does not refer to the *attempted* suicide in the novel, but to *the* suicide. If we take her literally, she is alluding to another moment in the novel that, though less obviously so, may be equally confessional. Earlier in the novel, Christie finds work as a companion to an invalid named Helen Carrol. After the two women have forged a friendship, Helen confesses the family's secret: they suffer from hereditary mental illness: "We are all mad or shall be," she relates, "and for years we have gone recklessly on bequeathing this awful inheritance to our descendants. It should end with us . . . none of us should marry."[67] Of this illness, Helen further relates, "When one generation goes free it falls more heavily upon the rest."[68] Helen eventually ends her own torment by completing the only successful suicide in *Work*.

Louisa certainly knew of her Uncle Junius's long struggle for mental health, which had ended with his suicide. She had witnessed firsthand her father's episodes of strange behavior following the demise of Fruitlands. In addition, she was more than conscious of her own potentially self-destructive moods and consuming creative "vortices." As befits the taut drama of her novel, the inherited derangement of the fictitious Carrol family is infinitely more devastating than any instabilities that haunted the Alcotts. However, it is not unreasonable to ask whether Louisa was daunted by the possibility of inherited mental imbalance in her own family, and whether this same anxiety played an unspoken role in Louisa's own decision not to marry. As is more than once the case with Alcott, the fiction teasingly invites speculations that the surviving facts can neither confirm nor dispel.

Louisa herself was dissatisfied with *Work*, which, like *Moods*, she had begun with great ambition, only to create a finished product that was good, not great. When her health permitted her, she could produce a flow of words virtually at will. However, it seemed that when she tried to write the books whose artistic success mattered most to her, inspiration did not come at her bidding. The truth was hard to avoid: she was a seasoned, disciplined writer whose voice resonated with young readers as no American's ever had before. However, the highest levels of adult writing seemed stubbornly closed to her. She had, she felt, been forced to endure too many interruptions. She would have liked to write one book in peace and see whether then, at last, she could produce something to her liking. Perhaps, in time, she would get the chance.

The four years that followed *Work* were ones of sustained financial comfort and productivity, as both Bronson and Louisa continued to reap the rewards that *Little Women, Tablets,* and their successors showered on Orchard House. As might be expected of a man in his seventies and his grown daughter in her forties, they were less involved in each other's daily lives than they had previously been. Unable to settle in a single place, Louisa oscillated between Orchard House and various rented rooms in the city, always missing her family while in Boston and always yearning for urbane excitements while in Concord. Abba's health was now much broken, and Louisa spent most of her time in Concord either caring for her mother or searching for someone else to do it. Moreover, her own health problems gave her little rest. Sometimes the pain from the ineradicable mercury made it impossible for her to write. Nights came when she could find no sleep without the help of morphine. In January 1874, she told her journal, "When I had youth I had no money; now that I have the money I have no time; and when I get the time, if I ever do, I shall have no health to enjoy life."[69]

Louisa had grown no more comfortable with her celebrity status, and she continued to view it as part of the unwelcome price she paid for making a comfortable living. Over a hundred people a month sometimes descended on Orchard House to spend a moment with their beloved Little Woman. "I asked for bread," she quipped, "and got a stone,—in the shape of a pedestal."[70] At one public appearance, an energetic matron worked her arm like a pump handle and exclaimed, "If you ever come to Oshkosh, your feet will not be allowed to touch the ground: you will be borne in the arms of the people." Louisa vowed never to visit Oshkosh.[71] Despite it all, she added two more juvenile novels to her list of accomplishments, *Eight Cousins* in 1875 and a sequel, *Rose in Bloom*, in 1876. She also became increasingly involved in charitable concerns, visiting New York in 1875 and finding herself moved by the plights of indigent newsboys and the inmates of mental institutions. Closer to home, she loaned three thousand dollars to Dr. Rhoda Lawrence of Roxbury, Massachusetts, to establish a nursing home, remarking at the time that it was "just the place many of us used up people need to go for repairs."[72]

In contrast, Bronson hungered for more recognition rather than less. Although his popularity had never been greater, he found that a man in his midseventies, whatever his recent achievements, was seldom the first to receive an invitation to social or intellectual functions. Louisa noticed that at times he seemed "rather sad, to be left out of so much that he would enjoy and should be asked to help and adorn."[73] She felt that, if she had a little more money, she would like to bring all the best people "to see and entertain *him*."[74] Bronson's lack of a college education remained a source of regret to him. He wrote that he now felt at home strolling academic grounds, feeling, as he put it, "a certain inborn title to their honors and advantages."[75] Nevertheless, as he stood inside the Harvard College Library one day in 1874, he felt "overmastered" and could not help wondering whether access to such a place sixty years earlier might have made him a wiser man.[76] His need for inclusion was intensely gratified when, the following year, Harvard's Phi Beta Kappa Society offered him an honorary membership. He responded so excitedly that his letter of acceptance contained two uncharacteristic misspellings.[77]

It was perhaps hard for everyone to realize that May Alcott, the petted baby of Hosmer Cottage and the little girl of Hillside, was now a woman in her mid-thirties. Like Louisa, she had struggled to satisfy her artistic impulses while fulfilling her domestic obligations to the family. As shown by the somewhat amateurish illustrations that she contributed to part 1 of

Little Women, May's skills were initially slow to mature, yet more recently she had been making impressive strides. After returning from Europe alongside Louisa in 1871, she had sailed east again in April 1873, "brave and happy and hopeful," for a year's study in London.[78] This journey would have been impossible if not for Louisa, who cheerfully gave her sister a thousand dollars and a like number of blessings. During her stay, May became adept at copying the Turner canvases that hung in the National Gallery. Her copies caught the eye of Ruskin, the greatest authority on the artist's works, who proclaimed that she had "caught Turner's spirit wonderfully."[79]

After she returned home the following March, however, May was forced to put aside her artistic ambitions as she became immersed in the daily work of Orchard House, taking up the hard, monotonous tasks that her mother was now too weak to perform. In between periods of housework, May was able to teach some classes and offer inspiration to other local artists. Among them was the young Daniel Chester French, who later sculpted the great statue of Lincoln housed in the Lincoln Memorial.[80] However, May herself soon found that she needed more time for creativity, as well as more professional instruction and aesthetic stimulus than Massachusetts could give her. On September 9, 1876, she embarked again for Europe aboard the steamship *China*.

Bronson and Louisa escorted her as far as the dock. Prey to all the throat-constricting feelings that come with parting, they stood and watched as their blue-clad "dear girl" waved her handkerchief and the ship receded toward the horizon. "God be with her!" Louisa told her journal. Reflecting on all that May had lately done to sustain and support their parents, she added, "She has done her distasteful work faithfully, and deserved a reward."[81] Without May's blithe and energetic presence, Orchard House at once felt older and quieter. Anna took over May's role as housekeeper, while Louisa soldiered on as "nurse, chambermaid & money maker" and complained in her journal of "dull times."[82]

In Louisa's estimation, 1877 began well.[83] Anna's son Fred rang in the year by playing "America" on the piano. Bronson, having recently written a series of short pieces called "Philosophemes" for Harris's *Journal of Speculative Philosophy*, was putting the final touches on another book, *Table Talk*, a volume similar in both tone and topics to *Tablets* and *Concord Days*. Abba, though by no means energetic, was "cosey with her sewing, letters . . . and the success of her 'girls.'"[84] She especially enjoyed having Louisa nearby during the dreary winter days. Her daughter's presence created "a new atmosphere in the house—and we all feel more protected when she is about us."[85] Louisa gave herself a much-needed break from juvenile literature, accepting an offer to write a novella for a Roberts Brothers project called the No Name series. The premise of this series was to solicit manuscripts from well-known authors and then publish them anonymously, inviting the readers to guess the author of each work. Louisa contributed *A Modern Mephistopheles*, a thrilling tale reminiscent of her early anonymous potboilers. Everything under the Alcott roof seemed the picture of industry and stability. Yet this year would be the Alcotts' last at Orchard House.

It is ironic that the Alcott family's years at Orchard House—a place that, during their years of occupancy, brimmed with the joy, vitality, pain, and passion that make up the very core of living—should have been framed by a pair of lingering deaths. In 1858, the Alcotts moved into the house before there had even been time to transport Lizzie's remains to a permanent resting place. Now, almost two decades later, the failing health of Abba dominated their thoughts as they prepared to leave the home that they had known longer than any other. The decision to leave the house was Abba's. She made her wishes known after Louisa helped to buy Anna and her boys the house on Main Street that had belonged to the Thoreau family. As her illness worsened, Abba wanted as much of her family to be with her as possible. It was decided that she and Bronson would move along with Anna and the boys. Louisa would live there when she was in town. Anna and her sons moved into the Thoreau house in July, but it was impossible for the rest of the family to follow immediately, for Abba was now extremely feeble. In early September her condition declined dramatically. The doctor's diagnosis was "water on the chest," and he told the family that the beginning of the end had come. Although Abba protested that Louisa's cares were already too many, Louisa forgot her own needs "in taking care of poor Marmee, who suffered much and longed to go."[86]

In September, making one of the obtusely insensitive gestures of which he was sometimes guilty, Bronson left his ailing wife and traveled to Connecticut to spend time in the region of his birth. He returned at the beginning of October, hoping that his stories of Abba's old friends in Brooklyn,

Connecticut, would rally her spirits. To his surprise, she was too exhausted even to listen to him. She desired only sleep. The next day, she was still too tired and feeble to listen long to her husband's stories. Outside, the autumnal weather was beautiful, and Bronson set about gathering his abundant harvest of grapes. Within the walls of the old house, however, the talk was of medicines and worry. A nurse was brought in to look after Abba, and Anna came to be on hand in case her mother worsened. The family received a stream of anxious visitors. Lidian Emerson, Frank Sanborn's wife, and untold others all brought presents of fruit or flowers, as well as their good wishes. What mattered most to Abba, however, was having her family nearby. She used her daughter's childhood nickname when she said, "Stay by, Louy, and help me if I suffer too much."[87]

October 8 was Abba's seventy-seventh birthday, and the family marked the day with what Louisa called "a sad little celebration."[88] The bright morning sun shone in on a profusion of flowers. In addition to the gifts that Anna, Louisa, and he offered her, Bronson presented his wife with a letter. He turned his thoughts to the past. "May we not say, happy hours, if not years, have been ours, and blessed in our children, our children's children. Our cup has been full, sometimes overflowing with gladness, and may we not thank the giver of life for our fullness of blessings." With surprising frankness, he wished his wife "a happy transit into the new existence."[89] Abba herself thought the day had been beautifully celebrated, but a shadow hung over the day. Everyone knew that Abba would not have another birthday. Louisa hired a nurse in hopes of giving herself a bit of rest. Nevertheless, she still pushed herself beyond her endurance and also fell ill. For a week, it appeared that both mother and daughter might pass away. However, as she put it, Louisa pulled through and got up slowly to help her mother die.[90]

Their patient's health had forced Bronson and Louisa to delay the move to Main Street countless times. At last, however, on November 14, they transported Abba from Orchard House to Anna's home. As her family carried her upstairs in an armchair, Abba softly joked, "This is the beginning of my ascension."[91] Both she and Bronson liked the new house. Bronson called it "a picture," and even if the study was smaller than the one he had left behind, he thought it an honor to sit in the same room where Thoreau had written. Nestled in a room filled with sunshine, flowers, and old-fashioned furniture, Abba was, at least, comfortable. After a week in her new surroundings, however, she ceased to care for anything. Bronson and Louisa both advised May, still in Europe, not to come home now; she would not be assured of finding her mother alive even if she sailed at once. On Sunday, November 25, Abba spoke her last words to Bronson: "You are laying a very soft pillow for me to rest upon." Louisa found the words emblematic. "In truth," she wrote, "his love has always been that to her energetic spirit through this long companionship of nearly fifty years."[92] As the sun set and a steady rain fell outside, Abba Alcott fell asleep in Louisa's arms. Although Orchard House remained in his name, Bronson decided that he would never live there again. It would not be the same house without Abba. Orchard House stood tenantless until June 1880, when Alcott's friend Harris came from St. Louis and rented it.

For a while, both Bronson and Louisa needed to look for reasons to keep on living. Louisa reported that her father seemed "restless, with his anchor gone."[93] The following June, as Louisa planned to write a memoir of her mother, she and Bronson went through Abba's papers, copying over some of her letters and journals. It was especially melancholy work for Bronson, who found that his late wife's papers gave him an admittance to her inmost soul that not even nearly a half century of marriage had done. Much of what he found made him sad and even ashamed. "My heart bleeds," he wrote, "with the memories of those days, and even long years, of cheerless anxiety and hopeless dependence." With bitter self-accusation, he rued "my seeming incompetency, my utter inability to relieve the burdens laid upon her and my children during these years of helplessness." His error, as it now seemed to him, had been an excess of faith; he had "trusted too confidingly to that justice and generosity which Christian professions imply."[94]

And yet, even now, it seemed to him that he had not been precisely wrong. He had lived for the best of purposes, and if he had anticipated too much generosity from the world, he had expected no more than he had been prepared to give. He still could not quite concede the terrible possibility that, in a sinful world, a spirit filled with too much faith, hope, and charity might itself be guilty of a fault. He was grateful, at least, that Abba had found her compensation through her daughters. He reproached himself with the thought that she had not gotten enough of it from him. In turn, Louisa found that she could not write the memoir of her mother; her emotions were too powerful. Instead of weaving her mother's writings into a published work, she chose to commit the great majority of them to the flames. Her decision has cost historians priceless insights into the mind of an extraordinary woman.

In earlier times, Bronson might have found solace in conversation with Emerson. Now, however, somewhat embarrassed by his increasingly common lapses of memory, Alcott's oldest friend was seeking solitude, and his friends were reluctant to disturb him. For want of individuals who could satisfy his yearnings for intellectual friendship, Bronson sought to take part in meetings and conferences. However, some of these forays proved unfortunate. At a meeting of the Moral Education Association in Boston in May 1878, he held forth on a subject on which he would have been well advised to keep silent: the importance of pure heredity. As Alcott was speaking, a child happened to wander toward the platform. Bronson gestured toward the boy as a handy personification of ideal Christian heredity. It was then pointed out to him that the child in question was the offspring of a Mr. and Mrs. Hazard, who were prominent in the scandalous Free Love movement.[95] Sometimes, the results of his appearances were more sad than comic. When Bronson rose to speak at a conference of Unitarian ministers, a Reverend Ware brusquely told him that he was in no sense a minister and had no right to address the body. To Alcott's mortification, not a single person present said a word in his defense. He bitterly told his journal, "I am, I perceive, left to the conviction of being still deemed an outcast, an Ishmaelite."[96]

Louisa also suffered in the aftermath of Abba's death. A great warmth had gone out of her life, and she could find no motive to go on. Her only comfort was that she had realized her ambition of making her mother's final years easy. It can be argued that, ever since she was a child, Louisa's two dominating raisons d'être had been to earn her father's approval and to assure her mother's comfort. The first goal had long been accomplished; the second no longer existed. Louisa told her journal, "My duty is done, and now I shall be glad to follow her."[97] Feeling empty and futile, she settled in for a winter of idleness, ill health, and wistful reminiscence.

No good news came until spring, and then it came from far away. On March 22, May Alcott, now thirty-seven, was married in London to Ernest

Nieriker, a handsome Swiss businessman some fifteen years her junior. May's letters describing Nieriker and their happiness together were ebullient. At a great distance Louisa shared their happiness. She sent them a wedding present of a thousand dollars and tried without success to figure out how to visit the couple. Despite her obvious pleasure, a grain of the old sibling jealousy crept into the journal entry in which Louisa meditated on her sister's good fortune. "How different our lives are just now!—I so lonely, sad, and sick; she so happy, well and blest. She always had the cream of things." But then the generous side of Louisa's spirit won out. She continued, ". . . And deserved it. My time is yet to come somewhere else, when I am ready for it."[98]

Unlike Louisa, Bronson seems not to have felt like waiting for his time to come to him. On the contrary, Abba's passing seems to have persuaded him that now, more than ever, he must hasten to realize the dreams that he had not yet fulfilled. He intended to live his remaining years of good health with a cheerful determination to do all that his aging mind and body would allow him to accomplish. He knew that there was no better way to remember Abba than to continue "cherishing her generous counsels and following in the path of her unselfish example."[99] Improbable as it seemed, there were still a handful of triumphs left for Bronson Alcott.

The first and most important of these was finally to give substance to an air castle that he and Emerson had built together almost forty years earlier, while they and Margaret Fuller were collaborating on *The Dial*: a philosophical college to be established in Concord. The stimulus to revive the idea returned in the summer of 1878 when a group of midwestern thinkers, led by Hiram Jones, the Illinois Platonist, came to Concord for two weeks of philosophical discussions. Alcott had a delightful time trading insights with his visitors, and he started to have thoughts about what might be done the following year. A year-round college was out of the question, being beyond both Alcott's financial means to establish and beyond his physical stamina to administer. Instead, Alcott envisioned a monthlong summer course of lectures, to be held, for want of a better venue, in the parlor of Orchard House. Tuition would be affordable—only fifteen dollars for the entire session—and students of all ages and either sex would be received on equal footing. In composing his ideal faculty, Alcott drew on a lifetime of friends and acquaintances. He could count on Frank Sanborn,

*Both William Torrey Harris and Elizabeth Palmer Peabody addressed
the attendees at the Concord School of Philosophy. They are shown
here beneath a large tree a few yards from the Hillside Chapel.*

(Courtesy of the Louisa May Alcott Memorial Association)

and he hoped to entice William Torrey Harris, who had not yet moved east
from St. Louis. His longtime friend Ednah Cheney would certainly be
there, and he also wanted to include his great teaching colleague from the
1830s, Elizabeth Palmer Peabody. And, of course, the venture would be
unthinkable without the presence of Emerson, even though that worthiest
of worthies had now lost much of his former mental vigor.

With great excitement, Alcott pitched his idea to anyone who would listen and solicited participants for his symposium. On January 19, 1879, he and Sanborn composed a prospectus to be sent to interested parties across the country. Despite his failing faculties, Emerson promised to take part. So, too, did William Torrey Harris, Dr. Jones, Peabody, Bronson's erstwhile partner in abolitionism Thomas Wentworth Higginson, and a small cadre of Harvard professors. Letters in response to the prospectus poured in from as far away as Kansas. Uncharacteristically for an Alcott project, plans for the gathering came together with astonishing ease. Alcott christened his brainchild the Concord School of Philosophy.

The school convened on July 15, 1879, with Bronson as its dean and Orchard House as its lecture hall. As a practical matter, the number of pupils in the school was limited to fifty since no more than that could be squeezed into the available space.[100] As it was, they filled both the study and the adjoining room. All the area within hearing distance was spoken for. Those lucky enough to find a spot in the main room filed in past walls decorated with portraits of Whitman, Pascal, Shakespeare, Emerson, and Alcott himself. A reproduction of Raphael's *The School of Athens* also looked down on the scene.[101] The faculty typically occupied a sofa that extended halfway across one end of the lecture room. The lecturer sat in the central seat, with Alcott on his right and Sanborn on his left.[102] According to the press reports, although Harris was perhaps the most erudite member of the faculty, Alcott was the most striking personage. At least one observer considered him "in feeling and spirit, the youngest man of the faculty."[103] While the lectures were being delivered, he was silent, attentive, apparently wrapped up in thought. When the speaker finished, however, it was usually Alcott who began the responsive conversation. Soon six or seven students were taking part. On occasion, the hour reserved for discussion expanded to two. A correspondent wrote of the silver-haired dean, "He has never said better things than he is saying now. . . . He never seemed happier. His face glows with enthusiasm, and is radiant with joy."[104]

On August 2, Emerson gave his sole address of the session, a lecture titled "Memory." In one sense, his choice of topic was a bit awkward, since his own memory was now thoroughly unreliable. On the day when he spoke to the Concord School, he appeared with his daughter Ellen at his side, who patiently helped with his phrasings when words escaped him and guided his eyes when he lost his place in his manuscript. In another way,

however, Emerson's decision to speak about memory could not have been
more apt, for there was no fitter time or place for memory than Alcott's
parlor in the summer of 1879. For some of its attendees, the great marvel
of Alcott's school was its power to make the past seem present. The students were gathered in the room adjoining the one where Anna Alcott was
married. Intentionally or not, the faculty represented most of the salient
events in Alcott's life. The Temple School was there in the person of Elizabeth Palmer Peabody. The flower of transcendentalism, now sere and
faded, still glowed in the serene face of Emerson. The struggles for abolition were remembered in the persons of Sanborn and Higginson, and the
western prairies where Alcott had won a loyal following had sent their
ambassadors in Harris and Hiram Jones. Thoreau, too, was present in an
indirect sense. One evening, the attendees of the school gathered at a
nearby church to hear H. G. O. Blake, the editor of Thoreau's published
works, read excerpts from the sage's journal. One of Blake's selections
seemed especially to fit the mood of the occasion: "There is no remedy for
love but to love more."[105]

Up from Boston to help manage the event, Louisa found that the drift
of the school's discussions lay outside the range of her intellectual interest.
Indeed, the sight of so many gifted minds immersed in what she regarded
as idle disputation struck her as somewhat scandalous. She confessed that
if the Concord philosophers had more philanthropy in their blood, she
would have found the proceedings enjoyable. However, she decided, "speculation seems a waste of time when there is so much real work crying to be
done. Why discuss the Unknowable till our poor are fed & the wicked
saved?" She also groaned a bit beneath the burden of keeping up with the
needs of the multitude of visitors who descended on the family. Louisa
counted sixteen callers in one day as she and Anna did their best to "keep
the hotel going."[106]

Despite the impracticality and annoyance of it all, however, she looked
on the Concord School with both pride and amusement. It delighted her
to see that her father had had his dream realized at last. He was, she wrote,
"in glory, with plenty of talk to swim in." She also enjoyed observing the
blow that was being dealt to Concord's redoubtable provincialism. As the
budding philosophers from across America swarmed about the town,
roosting on the Alcotts' steps "like hens waiting for corn," it was hard for

the locals to continue to maintain that all the culture of the nation was native to Concord.[107]

The success of the Concord School's inaugural season instilled Bronson with renewed vigor and ambition. Even the absence of Abba was less painful now. At seventy-nine, he scorned the notion that "at three-score and ten, or at four score even," one should equate age with infirmity and give one's consent to oblivion.[108] That fall, he undertook another tour of the Midwest, this time only as far as Ohio, remarking that he actually found the excursion easier than in younger days. At every stop on his itinerary, he knew that friends would greet him with a warm bed, an ample table, and of course the conversations that were his greatest delight. Now that Abba was gone and Orchard House was no longer home, he sometimes must have felt more at home on the road than at his own hearthside.

Nevertheless, Bronson tore himself from the hospitalities of his western friends to return to Concord in time to celebrate a milestone: his eightieth birthday on November 29. Louisa came up from Boston so that, as she turned forty-seven, she and her father could be together. Although Louisa's health made merrymaking feel like hard work, she did her best to put on a festive mood. Bronson, however, had no trouble feeling happy; his return had been brightened by the news that he found waiting for him. On November 8, in Paris, May had given birth to a daughter, named Louisa May Nieriker in honor of the baby's illustrious aunt. "Surely," Bronson told his journal, "a generous Providence bestows blessings profusely upon us." He felt confident that Abba was smiling down from heaven upon May and her baby, and he was equally sure that, when life was done, the entire Alcott family would share a reunion "in holier bonds of affection."[109] It could not be otherwise, he reasoned, in a universe where "Love never perishes."[110]

Louisa also exulted. "Too much happiness for me" was the phrase she wrote in her journal.[111] Her choice of words was telling, however, for there was something unnamable about this happiness that she did not trust. Although the first reports from France gave no cause for alarm, she could not free herself from forebodings. She felt strangely as if the atmosphere of bliss could endure only for a moment, as liable to vanish as the last golden leaves of autumn. Her premonitions were soon confirmed. News came that May had suffered complications after the delivery. She was too ill to nurse her child, and the tone of the communiqués from Paris grew anxious. Louisa yearned to be with her sister. However, she herself was not well enough to attempt an ocean journey, and she could not possibly reach Paris in time to be of any service. Her helplessness struck her as a penance for her sins, which seemed greater to her than to anyone around her. On Christmas Eve, a local man drowned in the Concord River. Louisa took the accident as an omen. All she could do was wait.

On the morning of December 31, Bronson was at the Concord post office, hoping to receive more news. Louisa, who had again left her rooms in Boston and was staying with her father, came downstairs to find Emerson, holding a telegram and gazing, red-eyed, at May's portrait. Ernest Nieriker had cabled Emerson instead of wiring the Alcotts directly. He trusted that the aging philosopher would know how to soften the blow. Nieriker's thoughtfulness was futile, for Emerson was overcome himself. Choked, perhaps trembling, he could only say, "My child, I wish I could prepare you; but alas, alas!" He handed her the telegram. Weeks of worry had already done for Louisa what Emerson could not. "I *am* prepared," she said as she took the message from him.[112] She read the stark words without surprise. Later that morning, she told the news to her father and her now sole surviving sister. Two days earlier, May had died.

No other event was ever so hard for Louisa to bear. The birth of her niece had taken her to the heights of happiness, and the sudden fall was almost impossible to accept. May had also had premonitions about the outcome of her pregnancy. She had written Louisa, "If I die when baby comes, don't mourn, for I have had as much happiness in this short time as many in twenty years."[113] Yet these recollected words gave only bittersweet comfort. By an odd coincidence, the news of May's death arrived on the final day of a decade that had seen much in the way of triumph for both Louisa and her father. Now, those victories meant no more than a handful of ashes. Louisa's old observation that everything seemed to go by contraries with her was never more achingly true. Now every single branch of her family had been touched by death, and a strange, scarred remnant was all that was left of the Alcotts in their prime.

Bronson and Louisa both sought solace in writing. Bronson wrote a sketch of May in his journal, in which he praised her lively fancy, her positive, independent manner, and her fine sense of honor and decorum. He recalled with pride that "failure was unknown in her vocabulary of effort." He retained a clear image of the last time he glimpsed her, standing on the deck of the eastbound steamer and waving her handkerchief until she was lost in the distance.[114] Louisa tried to block out the pain by plunging into a vortex. She was at work on another children's novel, *Jack and Jill*, and the project seemed to offer a shelter from memory. The stratagem failed. The tide of sorrow swept over her, and she put aside her work in tears. She felt that there had been a mistake. It was wrong that May should have been taken when her life was at its richest, while she, Louisa, had done her work and would have gone without regret.

As they had done when Lizzie died, Louisa and her father also tried to console themselves with poetry. In an eight-stanza elegy written less than a week after the news arrived, Bronson achieved a poignant simplicity of language that had too often eluded him. In the lines "Ah! gentle May, / Couldst thou not stay? / Why hurriedst thou so swift away?" there is perhaps no poetic genius, but the spareness conveys perfectly the helpless incomprehension of grief. One stanza in particular shows plainly a father's anguish:

> I wake in tears and sorrow:
> Wearily I say,
> "Come, come, fair morrow,
> And chase my grief away!"
> Night-long I say,
> "Haste, haste, fair morrow,
> And bear my grief away!"
> All night long.
> My sad, sad song.[115]

Louisa's poem is a summation of her sister's life, according a stanza to each of the parts that existence had called on her to play. It is a biography told through quickly rising and subsiding images, flashing forth and disappearing as rapidly as May's life had passed away. Syntactically, each stanza is a sentence fragment, emphasizing the incompleteness of the subject's foreshortened life. Louisa's words, inadequate though they were, were her only way of preserving a trace of her "maiden, full of lofty dreams, /

Slender and fair and tall," who never ceased "seeking everywhere / Ideal beauty, grace and strength."[116]

Apart from the many messages of condolence that came from France, England, and America, the lone consolation was May's baby, who, by all the reports they received from Ernst Nieriker, was healthy and thriving. They soon learned, to their great excitement, that the baby would soon be with them. It had been May's dying wish that her daughter would be sent to America for Louisa to raise. Treating his wife's desires as a sacred trust, Nieriker arranged for his daughter to be sent to America during the autumn of her first year. By a means that she would never have anticipated or asked for, Louisa was at last to be a mother. Months before the girl was to arrive, Louisa had given her a nickname, "Lulu," and she spent much of the summer cleaning and fussing about in anticipation of her adopted daughter's arrival.

Not all her interest, however, was concentrated on the private sphere. Twenty-seven years earlier, Louisa's mother had organized a petition to the Massachusetts constitutional convention, demanding the extension of all civil rights to women.[117] In 1873, she had boldly declared, "I am seventy-three, but I mean to go to the polls before I die, even if my daughters have to carry me."[118] However, Abba Alcott had died without ever having fulfilled this dream. Louisa's own chance came in March 1880, when a change in the law permitted the tax-paying women of Concord to vote for the school committee. Wasting no time, Louisa became the first Concord woman ever to register to vote. On the appointed day, she appeared with nineteen other women at the town meeting where the balloting was to occur. Bronson was also there, and "with a fatherly desire to make the new step as easy as possible," he proposed that the ladies should be allowed to vote first. The motion carried, and the twenty women filed forward to deposit their ballots. No sooner had the last female vote been cast than Judge Ebenezer Hoar shocked the assembly by moving that the polls be closed. Before any objection could be mounted, this motion also carried. Not only had the women voted, but they had cast the only ballots to be tallied. Louisa noticed that some of the men looked disturbed at having been denied their rights. However, after more than two centuries of exclusively male suffrage, many agreed that, for one day at least, turnabout was fair play.[119]

That spring, as Louisa voted, read, walked, rested, and tried to forget the loss of her sister, Bronson forged ahead with an architectural project that greatly absorbed his attentions. Anxious lest his school should pass a second summer without a permanent home, he had the foundations laid in March for a building that he called "the Hillside Chapel." It was built only twenty-five paces or so up the hill from the side door of Orchard House. The structure strongly represents the values of the man who conceived it. Unpainted and somewhat rough in its appearance, wrought from solid New England timbers, the chapel invites the visitor to enter through a sharply peaked doorway, reminiscent of Gothic forms. One immediately walks up a wooden flight of stairs into the building's single room: a lecture hall with a high ceiling and a slightly elevated stage across the far side to accommodate speakers. Large enough for oratory, it is intimate enough for Bronson's favored medium, a conversation. Like the summer house that Alcott had built for Emerson a generation earlier, it savors of the untutored but earnest beauty of a premodern era.

As the second annual sessions of Bronson's school unfolded at the newly finished chapel, Louisa made preparations for Lulu. In early September, she put the last touches on the nursery and said a prayer over the white crib where the baby was to sleep. On September 19, Bronson chose red ink instead of black to write the first two words of his journal entry: "She Comes!" Louisa went to the pier in Boston that day for the long-anticipated meeting. As one baby after another came into view, she wondered whether each in turn might be hers. At last, the ship's captain emerged from the crowd, holding a little child dressed in white and sporting a crown of wispy yellow hair. There was a moment of recognition. Louisa held out her arms and said the baby's name. Lulu gazed at the strange woman for an instant and then said quizzically, "Marmar?" Seconds later, she was nestled close against her aunt "as if she had found her own people and home at last." For many nights afterward, Louisa would creep into the nursery to assure herself that it was not all a dream and that Lulu was really there.[120] Bronson called the child "a new trust and study . . . for us all" and added, "Childhood and age are the complements of life and human culture."[121]

On October 12, 1880, Bronson departed on what was to be his final western tour. In many respects, it was the grandest of all, lasting until May 14 of the following year and covering thirty-seven cities and towns. Heedless of the usual effects of age—he turned eighty-one during the course of his journey—he traveled five thousand miles and sometimes spoke three times a day. Although he charged nothing for more than half his appearances, he earned between a thousand and twelve hundred dollars, at a time when a new house sold for less than four thousand dollars and a night in a New York hotel cost a dollar. No longer needful of life's necessities, Bronson used some of the money from his tour to add a new wing to the Thoreau house. It seems that he did not feel fully alive unless he was altering his landscape in some fashion.

Otherwise, 1881 was a less productive year than most for the Alcotts. Louisa was so busy with Lulu that she wrote only one line in her journal from January to September. Lulu was a delight to Bronson's eyes as well. Borne back to the past by nostalgia and the presence of a toddler, he gave his friends copies of a long autobiographical poem, *New Connecticut*, which recounted his youth and adolescence on Spindle Hill. His only annoyances of the moment were Lulu's doctors, who recommended the addition of meat to her diet. Bronson railed against these men who "would demonize the little saint" and swore to guard against such assaults on the sweetness of her soul.[122]

In September, Bronson and Louisa went together to have tea at Frank Sanborn's house and to converse with Sanborn's houseguest, Walt Whitman. Whitman was somewhat intimidated by the company, which also included Emerson, and he seemed to be choosing his words with some delicacy. Now in his sixties, he stooped a bit and leaned on a staff for support, but Bronson still detected "a certain youthfulness . . . speaking forth from his ruff of beard and open-bosom collar."[123] Whitman approached Bronson as the living historian of transcendentalism, and he peppered the older Alcott with questions about Fuller and Thoreau. He asked, too, about Emerson, who, though physically present in the room, was now too mentally enfeebled to make extensive responses. Bronson tried to persuade Whitman to accept his theory of the fall of Adam and Eve, but he found the younger man impervious to the idea that human beings were creatures of sin. To the contrary, Whitman declared that existing civilization was an improvement on all that had gone before, and he looked confidently to America as the eventual birthplace of a new, still better type of man.[124] Bronson must have been both surprised and gratified to find a prophet even more optimistic than himself.

In December, Louisa received a letter from a poor woman in the Midwest who had no money to buy Christmas presents for her children. The children had suggested that she write to Santa Claus. Instead, she wrote to Miss Alcott. More amused than offended by the presumption, Louisa put together a box of gifts. Lulu, much interested in the proceedings, generously offered to add some of her own favorite toys. Louisa graciously declined. After sending the package, Louisa did what she almost always did on the heels of a funny occurrence. She wrote a story about it, which she sold for one hundred dollars.[125] The incident was marvelously typical of the two sides of Louisa. When the call for charity came, she answered it readily. However, she was almost reflexive in her ability to turn the situation into art, and then into profit. A time was fast coming, however, in which even her resourceful spirit would be tested to the full.

CHAPTER SIXTEEN

"COME UP WITH ME"

"Hope, and keep busy; and, whatever happens,
remember that you can never be fatherless."

—LOUISA MAY ALCOTT,
Little Women, chapter 16

THE YEAR 1882 BEGAN WITH GOOD NEWS. IN JANUARY, Roberts Brothers published Louisa's revised edition of *Moods*— the author's last word on the book that had bedeviled her for more than twenty years. In her preface to the revised edition, Louisa thought it wise to explain the original purpose of the novel. She wrote that, despite the public's perception, she had never meant to write a book about the institution of marriage. Rather, she had intended to explore "the mistakes of a moody nature, guided by impulse, not principle."[1] Louisa believed that the fundamental idea of the book was still sound. Indeed, she had found that her mature observation and experience had confirmed much of what her younger mind had grasped by intuition and imagination. It was time, then, to give her first novel "a place among its more successful sisters; for into it went the love, labor, and enthusiasm that no later book can possess."[2]

The 1882 edition of *Moods* is more than a revision. "Restoration" is a more aptly descriptive word. All traces of the novel's subplot have been expunged, and through its excision, the novel gains substantially in clarity. The story is now Sylvia's, and her inner conflicts are clearly the problems most in need of resolution. Instead of presenting only one instance of Sylvia's self-destructive impulses—her rash investigation of the brushfire— the revised text draws her twice more into danger. Early in the novel, she

400

makes her way to a rock on a stormy seacoast and sings forth her delight in the windswept scene while, unobserved, the rising tide comes in and all but inundates her path to safety. As the water rushes in, the mercurial Sylvia, still unconscious of her peril, feels her spirits plummet as she thinks of her dead mother and reflects that it might be pleasant to join her. Only Warwick's arrival at the critical moment saves her from drowning. The episode, initially joyous, ends with the emotional feel—and very nearly the effect—of a suicide attempt. Later, on a boating expedition with Warwick, Moor, and her brother, Sylvia heedlessly rejoices when a violent thunderstorm disrupts the outing. As her boatmates row for their lives, Sylvia laughs and strains to experience every impression of the storm, even as lightning strikes nearby. Almost fifty years earlier, when Louisa was two, Bronson had written about her, "On the impetuous stream of instinct, she has set sail, and, regardless, alike, of the quicksands and rocks of the careering . . . countercurrents that oppose her course, she looks only toward the objects of her desire and steers proudly, adventurously. . . . The stronger the opposing gale, the more sullenly and obstinately does she ply her energies."[3] Given the Alcotts' practice of sharing journals, Louisa may well have known about Bronson's early description of the bold sailing of her reckless spirit. If her father's journal entry was not the direct inspiration for Sylvia's stormy boat ride, the echoes are nevertheless strong.

The scenes restored to *Moods* in 1882 make explicit what the 1864 edition left obscure: that Sylvia Yule is a heroine determined to *feel*, even if her forays into sensation and emotion threaten to annihilate her. Implicit in the 1882 edition of *Moods* is a critique of the romantic notions of the transcendentalist movement, particularly its faith in nature as a benevolent and restorative influence. Louisa believed that nature is a fitful, savage force and that sympathetic conformity with its energies can physically and psychologically shatter a human being.

The 1882 *Moods* is also more candid as to the precarious nature of Sylvia's mental health, making clear that her excesses of emotion raise continual threats to her well-being. The revised text also comments more frankly on her mercurial personality, calling her "a changeful thing," haunted by "the melancholy of a temperament too mixed to make life happy."[4] With a directness of voice only partially developed in the earlier edition, Sylvia is now free to say, "I know that I need something to lean upon, believe in, and love; for I am not steadfast, and every wind blows me about. . . . I ask all whom I dare to help me, yet I am not helped. . . . So I stumble to and fro, longing, hoping, looking for the way to go, yet never finding it."5

Along with the broader elaboration of Sylvia's condition come new reflections on how her suffering might be eased. In another restored passage, Sylvia entertains Warwick, Moor, and her brother by acting a series of scenes from Shakespeare. Warwick intuits that performance and imagination are therapeutic tools for Sylvia, noting that "pent-up emotions can find a safer vent in this way than in melancholy dreams or daring action." He also adds that less restraint, not more, is likelier to change Sylvia for the better: "Let her alone, give her plenty of liberty, and I think time and experience will make a noble woman of her."6 He turns out to be only partly right. Sylvia needs not only freedom but a good talking to.

This she receives when, as in the original version, she seeks advice from her cousin Faith after telling Moor of her love for Warwick. Faith's basic prescription does not change; she still believes that Sylvia should give her love to neither of the two men who have sought it. In the revised text, however, she adds a stirring injunction; Sylvia can, and must, achieve a fundamental change in character: "You have been the victim of moods, now live by principle, and hold fast by the duty you see and acknowledge."7 The 1882 Sylvia heeds this advice with a will that the 1864 Sylvia could not have mustered. Moor returns, not to watch his beloved but erring wife slip tragically into the grave, but to discover that she has, indeed, learned to become a good and devoted wife. Now no longer marred by the moods that nearly wrecked her youth, Sylvia prepares for a future in which love and duty will go hand in hand. Despite this happy ending, it is easy to regret the reform of the younger, more impulsive Sylvia, who, for all her mental disturbance, was a good deal more fun.

In the 1864 *Moods*, Sylvia dies, the judgment of her doctor being that she "had lived too fast, wasted health ignorantly, and was past help." Sylvia converts this diagnosis into a cosmic judgment, claiming, "It is I, who, by wasting life, have lost the right to live."8 By 1882, Louisa had revised not only her novel but also her thoughts about one's ability to overcome emotional distress. The 1882 text reflects peace of mind and a firm confidence in the power of self-control. In the first published text of

Moods, the reconciliation between Mr. Yule and his daughter, while indicative of a moral rebirth on Sylvia's part, is not sufficient to save the latter from death, and Sylvia's father blames himself for his daughter's downfall. In the later text, however, when Sylvia rescues her relationship with her father, she also saves herself. In the 1882 text, the sentimentalized death in the family at the end of the novel is Mr. Yule's, not Sylvia's. Instead of an edifying sermon, Mr. Yule's last gift to Sylvia is a kiss, and his last words to her are a simple blessing. They have learned to communicate, not with lectures, but with love.

Bronson also began 1882 with an impressive flourish of literary creativity. Finished now with transcendental prose, he had turned his efforts to poetry. That winter, he authored forty sonnets that Louisa regarded as "remarkable."[9] In April they were published under the title *Sonnets and Canzonets*. As Frank Sanborn conceded in the essay that introduces the volume, Bronson had made little effort to keep up with the changing poetic styles and conventions of his time, and the verses generally reflect a certain quaintness of expression. Taken as a group, however, the poems are a fitting retrospective of Alcott's life, and they illustrate the extent to which Bronson, in old age, had exchanged the transcendental for the personal. Virtually all of the poems are versified reminiscences, including a charming series of lyrics that tell the story of Bronson's courtship of Abba—some from his perspective, and others from hers. In later poems, Bronson recollects many of his famous friends, including Hawthorne, "Romancer, far more coy than that coy sex"; Thoreau, "Masterful of genius . . . and unique"; and Margaret Fuller, "Sibyl rapt, whose sympathetic soul / Infused the myst'ries [her] tongue failed to tell."[10] Bronson also wrote at least one poem for each of his four daughters. Elizabeth receives honor as a "dear child of grace, so patient and so strong."[11] The grief is still fresh in "Love's Morrow," a poem for the recently departed May that contains the poignant couplet, "Ah! gentle May / couldst thou not stay?"[12]

The collection also contains a sonnet inspired by Louisa. The aspects of his famous daughter that Bronson chose to emphasize reveal much about his sense of her value as a person. The poem deals with Louisa's nursing service, the act of self-sacrifice by which she finally secured her father's respect. He has relatively little to say about her career as an author or about her popular success. The poem, which bears similarities to Milton's sonnet

on his blindness, is expressed in a single sentence, a sentence barely sufficient to contain the deep emotions it exudes:

> When I remember with what buoyant heart,
> Midst war's alarms and woes of civil strife,
> In youthful eagerness, thou didst depart,
> At peril of thy safety, peace, and life,
> To nurse the wounded soldier, swathe the dead—
> How piercèd soon by fever's poisoned dart,
> And brought unconscious home, with wildered head—
> Thou, ever since, mid languor and dull pain,
> To conquer fortune, cherish kindred dear,
> Hast with grave studies vexed a sprightly brain,
> In myriad households kindled love and cheer;
> Ne'er from thyself by Fame's loud trump beguiled,
> Sounding in this and the farther hemisphere:—
> I press thee to my heart, as Duty's faithful child.[13]

Louisa worried that, between his writing and his work at the Concord
School of Philosophy, her father was driving himself too hard. She sometimes
had to remind him that he was eighty-two. Whether or not Bronson appreciated Louisa's fretting, he shrugged it off. In the proem to *Sonnets and Canzonets*, Bronson boasted that he had been "long left unwounded by the grisly
foe / Who sometime pierces all with fatal shaft."[14] He continued to believe
that, in his vegetarian diet and other moderate habits, he had discovered a
fountain of youth. As early as 1870, he had written hopefully of living to see
one hundred.[15] Six years later, he took an informal inventory of his hereditary ills and was delighted to report that they were few. Given his long practice of temperance, he still saw no reason why he might not "possibly reach
my hundredth birthday, and retire with the century, (1899)."[16]

Emerson, however, was almost gone. Some said that he had never recovered from the shock of a fire in his house in 1872. Modern retrospection
has raised the likelihood of Alzheimer's disease. Louisa and Bronson both
found his decline pathetic to witness. The previous fall, a week before
Bronson's and Louisa's birthday, a young man named Edward Bok called
on Louisa in hopes that she might gain him an audience with Emerson.
Although she cautioned him against expecting too much, Bok insisted that
he would rather meet the great man in his weakened state than not at all.

When he and Louisa were ushered into Emerson's study, the initial impression was by no means disappointing. Wearing a long black coat, Emerson rose from behind his desk and decorously took the younger man's hand. However, he said nothing. Without explanation, he turned away from his guests and walked toward the window. There he stood, gazing outside as if no one were in the room with him. At length, still without a word, he walked back to his desk, bowed to Mr. Bok, and took his seat. To break the oppressive silence, Louisa asked her old friend if he had read a new book by John Ruskin. With calm surprise, Emerson turned his eyes upon her, trying to recall something. Finally, he spoke: "Did you speak to me, madam?" Louisa replied with tears.[17]

Even though Emerson was no longer the man they had known, neither Louisa nor Bronson abandoned him. Bronson kept up his frequent visits until the end. Despite Emerson's illness, his parlor remained a gathering place for the intellectuals of Concord. Emerson still presided over these social functions, although he was mostly silent now.[18]

Early in the spring of 1882, Bronson presented his old companion with a copy of *Sonnets and Canzonets*, several of whose verses honored a friendship that had now endured for more than forty-five years. Recalling the literary liaison in which he had been the lesser but in some ways more devoted partner, he looked back on the times when Emerson had patiently striven, without great success, to translate Alcott's flights of inspiration into readable form:

> If I from Poesy could not all abstain,
> He my poor verses oft did quite undress,
> New wrapt in words my thought's veiled nakedness
> Or kindly clipt my steed's luxuriant mane.[19]

Editing is not often so sensual.

Another sonnet devoted to Emerson warmly evokes memories of mornings when he and Alcott "did toss / From lip to lip, in lively colloquy, / Plato, Plotinus, or some schoolman's gloss."[20] It also recalls leisurely swims in Walden Pond where the two men raised "deeper ripples" and concludes by imagining Emerson gazing fondly at the stars before pressing his head on his pillow. Bronson's lines reveal the depth of the two men's friendship, stated in words that, in another context, might even be taken as erotic. In his friendship and intellectual engagement with Emerson, Alcott found a pleasure that was both intense and entirely chaste—a pleasure that, while not sexual, could be expressed only in the language of Eros.

It seemed to Bronson that his old friend was pleased with *Sonnets and Canzonets*. Although he sometimes failed to recognize old friends, Emerson was still responsive to poetry, and he pleased Bronson by reading several of the sonnets aloud with emphasis and evident delight.[21] Emerson himself had written nothing of consequence since his eulogy for Thoreau, some twenty springs before. At that time, Bronson had yet to taste a single publishing success, and Louisa had been grubbing along, a story here and a poem there. Now both enjoyed reputations fit to be considered alongside Emerson's own. Emerson had always maintained that each life had its unique value. The difference in circumstance between one destiny and another was, in his view, merely costume. "Heaven," he had written, "is large, and affords space for all modes of love and fortitude."[22] Before his own powers fell into deep decline, Emerson had had the satisfaction of knowing that Bronson and Louisa had found their places too.

One day in mid-April, Emerson forgot his overcoat and caught a chill. On the twenty-first, he closed up his study and walked upstairs to bed. He did not come down the next day. Five days later, on a cloudless Wednesday morning, Bronson came to Emerson's door. Ellen conducted him upstairs to the sickroom, where he went to the bedside and took the hand of his friend. Emerson ventured to ask, "You are quite well?"[23] Bronson replied that he was but that it was strange to find Emerson in bed. Emerson tried to say more, but his words were broken and indistinct. After an interval, Bronson thought he should go. Before he could leave, however, the dying man indicated that he had something more to say. Bronson told Louisa what happened next, and she wrote it in her journal:

> E. held [my father's] hand, looking up at the tall, rosy old man, & saying with that smile of love that has been father's sunshine for so many years, "*You* are very well. Keep so, keep so." After Father left he called him back & grasped his hand again as if he knew it was for the last time, & the kind eyes said, "Good by [*sic*], my friend."[24]

Bronson felt shaken as he made his way home. When Lulu met him at the door, overflowing with childish babble and joy, he felt a wave of gratitude.[25]

The next day, April 27, 1882, Emerson passed away. Louisa, who had once complained of having been entirely isolated in her strivings for literary glory, now freely admitted that she had not been alone. Not only had Emerson been the best friend that her father had ever had; he was also "the man who has helped me most by his life, his books, his society. I can never tell all he has been to me."[26] In a piece for *The Youth's Companion*, with an openness that she had never expressed in print when Emerson was alive, Louisa now recollected how, at fifteen, she had ventured into his library and bravely asked for recommendations. Her father's friend had patiently led her around the book-lined room, introducing her to Shakespeare, Dante, and Goethe. When she expressed interest in books well beyond her comprehension, he had smiled indulgently and advised her to wait. For many of these books, Louisa confessed, she was still waiting, "because in his own I have found the truest delight, the best inspiration of my life."[27]

On Sunday the thirtieth of April, Emerson was laid to rest. Louisa fashioned a golden lyre out of jonquils, which she placed in the church for the funeral. The private ceremony at Emerson's house was followed by an impressive public service, attended by a large crowd. Bronson read the sonnet in which he had proclaimed his affection for the deceased. Then he and Louisa again made the now familiar journey to the remote corner of Sleepy Hollow. The hilltop under the pines was filling up with heroes, family members, and friends, and their world was becoming correspondingly emptied.

Yet paradoxically, with each new departure, Bronson's stature seemed to increase. He was essentially the last man of the generation that had made Concord a center of the American intellect. He was a living link between minds and moments now past and new listeners eager to ask "What was it like?" By the same token, he had outlasted his critics. He had won followers among those who were too young to remember him either as a troublesome outcast or a ridiculed pariah, but knew him only as a kindly sage. Strangely, although he had devoted so much of his life to cultivating his inward existence, he had arguably succeeded much more notably as a friend than as a philosopher.

That summer, Bronson opened the Concord School of Philosophy for its fourth year. By Louisa's count, he gave fifty lectures during the session, an astonishing total for a man of his years.[28] Louisa arranged flowers and oak branches to adorn the school but made herself scarce when the reporters came. A highlight of the program was Emerson Day on July 22, which Louisa called "a regular scrabble."[29] Bronson's school was now firmly established, not only having won credibility among metaphysicians, but also having gained respect from the many Concord townspeople who respected dollars more than dogmas. As Louisa wrote in her journal, "The School is pronounced a success because it brings money to the town. Even philosophers can't do without food, beds, & washing, so all rejoice & the new craze flourishes."[30] Bronson would surely have tried to meet everyone who came if Anna had not cooled his ardor by showing him a list of some four hundred callers. Bronson Alcott, aged eighty-two, had become a profitable tourist attraction.

The acclaim had its drawbacks. Bronson, who had long hoped for public attention, was not always at ease now that it had finally come. He was besieged by reporters, who, it seemed to him, were determined to miss the true flavor of his remarks. Whenever a newspaperman came to report on one of his discourses at the school, Bronson felt himself being exposed to "misconception and frequent mortification." Although his conversational style might have been expected to find favor with lay listeners, Bronson found it hard to win over the gentlemen of the press, who seemed to come prepared for something more elaborate and imposing. It seemed that his "finest and subtle transitions" never made their way into the reporters' notebooks. The full sense of his observations was invariably lost, and the resulting transcriptions were "hardly more than a medley of incoherent thoughts, a jumble of sentences." The good news, of course, was that people were no longer calling him crazy, and the misunderstandings he now had to endure, while frustrating, had no undertones of malice. Also, he was now wise enough to know that misinformed publicity was publicity all the same. "Let it pass," he told himself.[31]

When he was not busy giving conversations and chatting with the school's attendees, Bronson had time to take a step back and look at the loveliness he had helped to create. The rustic chapel and the foliage entwined about its door were beautiful to his eyes. Someone was thoughtful enough to photograph Bronson sitting on those steps. He holds a cane, looking as if he had just arrived after walking a long distance, and his smile

A delight of Bronson's old age was his Concord School of Philosophy. Here he sits proudly at the entrance to the Hillside Chapel.

(Courtesy of the Louisa May Alcott Memorial Association)

is one of a satisfaction beyond price. The distance he had come to sit on these steps was indeed incredible. One rarely sees an image of a man more precisely in his proper place.

On September 30, 1882, Bronson and his one surviving sister made a pilgrimage to the old family farm at Spindle Hill. The two passed the day walking down the roads and wood-paths that had once defined their world. The fields no longer yielded any harvest. The fences had vanished, as had the simple farmhouse where Bronson had been born. Sweet fern now grew in wild abundance where he had once labored to sow the seeds of his father's crops. The trees in the orchard had become leggy and unproductive and then had mostly died away. Bronson struggled to call up recollections of the old neighbors, their descendants now scattered. Most of the houses were abandoned. At the others, unknown faces appeared in answer to a hopeful knock. As Bronson wrote, "all [was] gone to ruin."[32]

Still, Bronson himself felt like anything but a ruin. His appetite for life was as insatiable as ever. He had lately written a pair of sonnets on immortality. As the autumn rains fell outside his window, he wrote not of his nostalgia but of his "thoughts of the future." Although he admitted some curiosity about "the geography and way of life" he would encounter after death, he still thought Thoreau had spoken wisely when he advised people to live in "one world at a time."[33] Nearing eighty-three, he was eager to know what services he had yet to perform on this side of the grave. The great charms of this life, he still believed, were to have work and to enjoy doing it.

In October, in Boston, Louisa finally felt well enough to begin work on *Jo's Boys*, the last of the *Little Women* trilogy. On the twenty-second, John Brown's widow paid a visit to Bronson, whose kindness to her family she had never forgotten. She spoke in monosyllables and was not interested in answering Bronson's questions about her. Bronson may have read her the sonnet he had written on her late husband for *Sonnets and Canzonets*, which eulogized Brown as a prophet of God and the messiah of the slaves. That evening, Bronson took tea with William Torrey Harris at Orchard House, where the two men and a caller named Ames disputed long into the night regarding the significance of the fall of Adam. Alcott tried to explain his theory of the first disobedience and of man's rehabilitation, but

Harris and his friend were unconvinced. Bronson recorded in his journal his failure to persuade them. He had written his last sentence.[34]

On the twenty-fourth, barely started on her new manuscript, Louisa received a telegram. Her father had suffered a massive paralytic stroke.[35] She rushed to Concord, but there was nothing she could do. Although Bronson appeared to recognize Louisa, he could not speak, nor could he move his right side. Louisa found the transformation from a vigorous man to a helpless invalid almost unbearable to look on. It seemed to her that, all at once, her father was tired of living, though, as she put it, "his active mind beats against the prison bars."[36] The doctors offered little hope, and Louisa and Anna spent anxious days both fearing and, for Bronson's sake, half hoping that the end would come soon.

Bronson was a strong man, however, and the stroke could not wholly destroy what it had tragically disabled. If his face seemed vacant to Louisa now, it also seemed oddly contented as he sat in his invalid's chair and gazed out on the world. Although he remained speechless for several weeks, it was evident that he was trying hard to recover. He could not read, but he liked holding books and looking over their pages. Fifty years ago, he had taught children how to write. Now he faced the task of teaching the same lessons to his left hand, the only one that he could now control. By November 4, he was able to make letters on a sheet of paper. Occasionally a word was produced, although the letters most often came out in a random order. Friends sent good wishes, but Louisa thought he was not yet able to comprehend them.[37] As November passed, he slept most of the time. Even as his doctor warned that death was imminent, some of Bronson's faculties gradually started to return. At the beginning of the month, he was able to consume only milk and wine jelly. By the eighteenth, he was able to take spoon food and to speak in a halting, broken voice, sometimes putting words together in a way only he understood. His first intelligible word was "up," an utterance that Louisa thought "very characteristic of this beautiful, aspiring soul almost on the wing for Heaven."[38] In general, however, Louisa was troubled all the more by what she regarded as "this pathetic fumbling after the lost intelligence & vigor."[39] Bronson, for his part, seemed focused on positive thinking. When his words could be deciphered, they played down the seriousness of his condition and reaffirmed the strength he felt in God. Even when he was asleep, Louisa overheard him say, "I am taking a predicament," "True Godliness and the Ideal," and "The Devil is never real, only Truth."[40] While Louisa prayed for a speedy end, it seemed that Bronson's heart was set on a speedy recovery.

On November 29, the two were together for their birthday. Bronson enjoyed the fruit and flowers he received from well-wishers, but he was quite positive that he was turning twenty-three instead of eighty-three. Louisa, he insisted, was a girl of fifteen.[41] At Christmastime, Sanborn and Harris came to call. They were to become frequent visitors at Bronson's bedside, although Louisa continually feared that their high spirits would excite her father more than was prudent. From time to time, she even turned the two friends away, believing that her father required rest more than stimulation. On this occasion, though, the influence seemed all to the good. As his two disciples rallied him with pleasantries about the School of Philosophy, Bronson sat up among his pillows and laughed at their jokes. Louisa had decorated the window with a green wreath. Noticing it, Bronson touched it over and over again, saying, "Christmas. I remember."[42]

Although Bronson was, on most days, a gentle invalid, he sometimes became angry. One day, Louisa found him in a worried and petulant mood, having clashed with his nurse. She reproved him softly, saying, "You are a philosopher and must not be upset by small trials." The hint was sufficient. The old man gave his daughter a bright look and said, "Yes, I am. I will do it." When the nurse returned, Bronson held out his hand and said, with an air of gentlemanly contrition, "I was cross, I confess. Forgive me; I am so old."[43] This glimpse of Bronson's courtly and gentle nature, emerging from the confusion of his weakened brain, reminded Louisa of Shakespeare's Lear. However, there was no Regan or Goneril in this version of the drama, only a steadfast Cordelia. Once disfavored for her forthrightness and independence, Louisa was now her father's loyal daughter.

In *Sonnets and Canzonets*, Bronson had offered tribute to Louisa as "Duty's faithful child." During his long, nearly silent illness, it was Louisa's turn to express in verse what her father now meant to her. On his eighty-sixth birthday, she presented him with a poem that conjoined his life with the adventures of the fictional hero to whom, in Bronson's eyes, there had never been an equal: Bunyan's stalwart Christian.

> Dear pilgrim, waiting patiently,
> The long, long journey nearly done . . .
> From youth to age, through weal and woe,
> Climbing forever nearer God. . . .
>
> Neglect is changed to honor now;
> The heavy cross may be laid down;
> The white head wins and wears at length
> The prophet's, not the martyr's crown. . . .
>
> The staff set by, the sandals off,
> Still pondering the precious scroll,
> Serene and strong, he waits the call
> That frees and wings a happy soul.
>
> Then, beautiful as when it lured
> The boy's aspiring eyes,
> Before the pilgrim's longing sight
> Shall the Celestial City rise.[44]

As much sympathy as Louisa felt for her father, she also felt fear on her own account. She had no doubt that Bronson's stroke had been induced by overwork. Now, she could not help imagining herself in her father's place, for she felt she had been following the same path herself. "I did not practise [*sic*] what I preached," she confided to a friend. "And indeed I have great cause for fear that I may be some day stricken down as he is."[45] But there was no question of her breaking down now. Lulu needed a surrogate mother, and so did her father.

Louisa was too busy now to keep the same kind of detailed journal that she had generally maintained since her late teens. She had to content herself with pausing to "jot down a fact now and then." She did the best she could to keep up with the needs of her two dependents, but she found she lacked the nerves and strength to take full responsibility for Lulu, let alone for an infirm parent as well. The preferred solution, she was well aware, would be to hire a nanny for the one and a nurse for the other, but she cared so deeply about both of them that her standards were hard to satisfy. When she did have time to open her diary, her entries offered a litany of nurses hired and quickly discharged. As a group, she found these women "incapable, lazy, or nervous with too much tea." The most promising of the lot, immortalized in Louisa's journal only as "Mrs. F.," harmonized well with Bronson despite his fretful and unreasonable moments, but one day she turned up tipsy and was asked to leave.[46]

Of course, where Lulu was concerned, no governess could be good enough, and, accordingly, none of them was. This one was too lofty. Another had no idea of government. The women who tried the job were incapable and proud. The girls were rough and vulgar. Louisa felt that the New England girls had brains and conscience enough for the job, but they lacked stamina. The Irish girls, to whom Louisa condescendingly referred as "Pats," were strong but had no principle.[47] Lulu's own nature did not make things any easier. Louisa considered her "a fine specimen of a hearty, happy, natural child," but what she leniently viewed as heartiness seemed to strike more objective observers as an intractable will.[48] Lulu had inherited her mother's determination to have things her own way, and her stubbornness was the frustration of a series of caregivers. Louisa regretted the rapid succession of Lulu's nurses. She knew that this lack of continuity was hardly the best tonic for her niece's fitful nature. By the fall of 1883, when Lulu turned four, Louisa had more or less resigned herself to the impossibility of finding adequate care outside the family. Her journals contained no more talk of searching for governesses. So far as Louisa's health permitted her, she was to be Lulu's mother.

Devoting herself equally to her father's care, however, was an almost impossible challenge. If she meant to continue with her writing and attend to Lulu, she was in a poor position to see to the wants of a man who was now as dependent as a child. In October 1883, she was trying valiantly to minister to the needs of both her beloveds, but she was finding that Bronson required more care with each successive month. Between her "two babies, both looking for me at once," Louisa felt "like a nursin' ma with twins."[49] Indeed, the two contended for Louisa's attention like a pair of infants. Once the doting grandfather, Bronson was now jealous of Lulu and told Louisa to keep the child away. Lulu, for her part, took offense if Louisa kissed Bronson first, not her. The infighting amused Louisa, but it tired her too. Indeed, fatigue was becoming an almost constant fact of her daily life.

Some changes in living arrangements became necessary. Anna and Louisa decided that winters in Concord were too hard for Bronson, and that a regular place of retreat in the summers would benefit everyone. In a

*Following the death of her sister May, Louisa became the
adoptive mother of Louisa May ("Lulu") Nieriker, who
outlived Louisa by eighty-seven years.*

(Courtesy of the Louisa May Alcott Memorial Association)

transaction that was sensible but unquestionably laden with emotion, Orchard House was sold to William Torrey Harris, who had been renting the home for four years. Louisa used the proceeds to buy a summer cottage in Nonquitt, Massachusetts, a resort town south of New Bedford. For winter quarters, the family rented a handsome townhouse in Louisburg Square, Boston. Although Anna retained ownership of the Thoreau house, the family's ties to Concord had not been this tenuous since the 1850s.

Louisa was determined to return to a piece of unfinished business. Niles was eager for a new novel, and Louisa, who had published nothing but short pieces since her revision of *Moods*, missed working on a large project. In December 1884, she tried to finish *Jo's Boys*. For three straight days, she wrote for two hours. In the old days, such an effort would have seemed a trifle. Now, it was too much for her. Overcome by a violent attack of vertigo, she had no choice but to stop. She was ill for a week. Reluctantly, she put her papers aside and resigned herself, for the moment "to dawdl[ing] and go[ing] about as other people do."⁵⁰ For a woman who had always been anything but ordinary, acting like other people was the least normal of behaviors. Thankfully, Christmas remained enjoyable, due in large part to the strong ties that held the patchwork family together. Bronson especially seemed to take delight in having Anna, Louisa, and Lulu under the same roof. As Louisa observed, he lived in a narrow world now, but it seemed sufficient to make him happy.

Throughout much of 1885, Louisa continued to seek a cure that would allow her to get back to work. From January to March, she paid for a series of sessions with a practitioner of mind cure. At first, the effect was agreeable; she imagined that her head was filled with blue clouds and sunshine, and she felt herself floating away. The benefits of the treatments were only temporary, however, and Louisa soon lost patience. "God and Nature," she concluded, "can't be hustled about every ten minutes to cure a dozen different ails."⁵¹ Traditional doctors, however, were not much help either, and it was not until the late spring of 1886 that Louisa felt well enough to complete *Jo's Boys*. Making the most of a rare stretch of good health and spirits, she fell upon her work with a vengeance, churning out fifteen chapters in June, adding the final necessary touches in July, and then triumphantly corking her inkstand. A period of peace seemed at hand. Shortly before completing *Jo's Boys*, Louisa soothed herself by addressing a poem to her brain, as she gazed back on the mental labors of a lifetime and looked forward to the time of tranquility that she hoped awaited her:

> Rest, weary brain, thy task is done.
> The burden of the day is past;
> Thy wage is earned & freely paid.
> Thy holiday begins at last.
>
> There is no need for thee to seethe
> With romance, poem, play or plot,
> As when stern Duty was the spur
> That kept poor Pegasus atrot. . . .
>
> Rest, & rejoice in thy one gift,
> For sure it is a happy art

To conquer fate, win friends and live
Enshrined in many a childish heart.[52]

In her correspondence from this period, Louisa maintained that her career was far from over. For too long, she believed, necessity and her unexpected success in the genre had confined her to children's literature. She hoped that she might now at last have the chance to write a few of the adult novels that she had simmering in her mind.[53] Nevertheless, "To My Brain" conveys acutely her weariness and resignation.

Louisa's inability to work steadily on her final chronicle of the March family left its mark on the novel's form. Whereas both *Little Women* and *Little Men* also had an episodic nature, changing focus chapter by chapter from one character to another, this quality is even more pronounced in *Jo's Boys*. Although Plumfield remains nominally the center of the work, that center has lost much of its gravitational force as the younger generation has approached adulthood and begun to seek independence. Scenes shift with dizzying rapidity in the middle third of the book, where, in successive chapters, one of Plumfield's alumni endures a fiery shipwreck, followed by a desperate struggle for survival aboard a lifeboat; another is imprisoned for manslaughter; and a third nearly falls victim to debauchery in the fashionable drawing rooms of Leipzig. Such events make *Jo's Boys* by far the most exciting of the *Little Women* trilogy, as well as the closest in spirit to Louisa's blood-and-thunder inclinations. However, they do little to promote a sense of cohesive plot development, and much of the book is an elaborate tying up of loose ends.

Louisa regarded *Jo's Boys* with dissatisfaction. She introduced it with a preface that sounds like an apology, pleading that, "Having been written at long intervals during the past seven years," the book was "far more faulty than any of its very imperfect predecessors."[54] Nevertheless, she gave her readers to understand that she had felt a duty to complete the March saga and that her sense of duty had, in the end, outweighed her aesthetic scruples. She also explained that, because the real-life models for Marmee and Amy were now dead, *Jo's Boys* had little to say about them. Indeed, Louisa included the death of her mother in the story itself. Interestingly, however, May's fictional alter ego is permitted to live on, although her role in the action is minimal. Louisa did not want to burden her young readers with the death of a second little woman, nor could she bring herself to reenact in fiction the loss that had been so hard to bear in reality. Similarly, Louisa chose not to visit any collapse of health on Mr. March. In full possession of his faculties until the last, the elderly chaplain of Plumfield continues to preside over the souls of its pupils, superintending their progress with serene pleasure and occasionally turning up to discuss Greek comedy and Platonic theory.

In this, her last treatment of her father in fiction, Louisa's attitude is reverential. She describes Mr. March as "ever-young" and speaks admiringly of the "prophetic eye" of "the wise old man [who] was universally beloved" and whom many of his flock thanked all their lives for the help he had given to their hearts and souls. However, as always with Mr. March, the record is conspicuously barren of specifics. In the entire book, the chaplain dispenses only one significant piece of advice, and even that suggestion is played for laughs; he counsels Dan, the roughest, most mercurial, and least literary of all his daughter's little men, to settle near Jacksonville, Illinois, because it has a Plato Club and "a most ardent thirst for philosophy."⁵⁵ None of the shipwrecks, homicides, or mine explosions that dot the narrative touch Mr. March even remotely, and those who truly crave the answers to life's varied dilemmas know that it is Aunt Jo, not her stately, smiling father, to whom they must turn. As her own father stared out his window and quietly turned the pages of his journals, Louisa found that, as a writer, she could approach him in a spirit of love, but not a spirit of analysis. Mr. March remained the same enigma he had been since *Little Women*, deeply respected but never deeply known.

Jo's Boys is noteworthy, however, for its elaboration of Louisa's ideas on women's rights, and the book serves to correct the reversals of feminine ambition that Roberts Brothers and her conservative readership had initially argued her into adding at the close of *Little Women*. In *Jo's Boys*, despite the mutterings of some prematurely crusty young alumni, Plumfield has become fully coeducational. It has also added a college, committed to the right of all sexes, colors, creeds, and classes to the best possible education. Most significantly, Nan, the girl student who first crosses the gender barrier at Plumfield and who acts as Jo's spiritual successor in *Little Men* and *Jo's Boys*, deftly fends off the inept romantic advances of Tommy Bangs and remains happily unmarried. Having escaped the snares of matrimony, she is able to preserve her independence and achieve her dream of becoming a doctor. Jo's earlier concessions to the social status quo eventually result in happier, more enlightened lives for all, both female and male.

Although Meg's daughter Josie anticipates Billie Jean King by matching the boys stroke for stroke on the tennis court, the juxtaposing of young male and female scholars is in no other instance competitive. Alcott's educational ideal does not focus on the winning of personal honor. Rather, it calls for each person, male and female, to cultivate his or her talents without regard to sex, so that each may optimally serve the community. At Plumfield, stigma attaches neither to the young woman who studies ancient Greek nor to the one who is happiest in the college's sewing circle. To be useful is to be blessed; all other considerations are beside the point. In her holding that all honest, useful work is equally valid, Louisa remained true to the ideals of her mentor Emerson, who, as William James observed, believed that "no position is insignificant, if the life that fills it out be only genuine."[56] Louisa was hostile to any limitation on women's opportunities. Nevertheless, she would have been mystified by any feminist credo that implicitly valued traditionally masculine pursuits above the conventionally feminine. In her view, it was idiotic to force a born physician to stay home and bake pies, yet it was equally foolish to disparage the person who loved to bake pies, and baked them well. Louisa does not hesitate to enlist the opinion of Bronson's alter ego in support of her egalitarian views. Mr. March rejects the idea that women must always submit to men as "the old-fashioned belief." While admitting that changing old attitudes can take time, Mr. March states his own impression that "the woman's hour has struck; and . . . the boys must do their best, for the girls are abreast now, and may reach the goal first."[57]

The changes are manifest in Jo herself, who has not only been a successful mother to her own children and countless others, but has also won accolades as an author. Like *Little Women*, Jo's breakthrough opus is a hastily scribbled family story, written with no great hope of success. To Jo's astonishment, the book "sailed with a fair wind . . . straight into public favor, and came home heavily laden with an unexpected cargo of gold and glory."[58] Jo's triumphs in both domestic and professional life appear to repudiate the apparent message of *Little Women* that one must choose among one's satisfactions. In her last appearance, Jo March, who had once bravely martyred herself for the greater good, is resurrected as a woman who has been able to have it all.

While writing *Jo's Boys*, Louisa had worried that her young audience, after fifteen years, might have outgrown its interest in the March family. To the contrary, she discovered that her first generation of readers was now raising children of its own, equally ready to be captivated. Louisa, however, had had her fill of the March family and their protégés. As the manuscript approached completion, she sounded faintly murderous when she wrote to tell Thomas Niles of her desire to "finish off these dreadful boys." She closed the same letter saying "Sha'n't we be glad when it is done?"59

To vent her frustration, Louisa used odd moments in *Jo's Boys* to take satirical vengeance on her admiring audience. In "Jo's Last Scrape," a chapter that is both the comic highlight of the book and the author's earnest plea for privacy, entire boarding schools descend on Jo's home in search of mementos. A literary charlatan asks her to affix her name to his manuscript, and another eccentric acolyte demands both a pair of Jo's stockings to weave into a rug and the opportunity to catch a grasshopper in the author's garden. When a critic suggested that the chapter was too personal and should have been omitted, Louisa replied that there was no other way in which the rising generation of autograph fiends could be reached so well and pleasantly. With "a little good-natured ridicule," she hoped to teach them "not to harass the authors whom they hold in thier [*sic*] regard."60 Despite the lighthearted tone of "Jo's Last Scrape," Louisa was only partly able to conceal the annoyance she felt toward the army of juvenile readers who have reduced Mrs. Bhaer, as they had reduced Louisa herself, to "only a literary nurse maid who provides moral pap for the young." The phrase sounds more like W. C. Fields than Louisa May Alcott. It is a bitter self-description.

When she reached the last page of *Jo's Boys*, Louisa confessed her strong temptation to polish her manuscript off "with an earthquake which should engulf Plumfield and its environs so deeply in the bowels of the earth that no youthful Schliemann could ever find a vestige of it."61 She dated her preface to the book July 4, 1886, declaring once and for all her independence from the March family and the task of writing juvenile novels. Orders for *Jo's Boys* were immediately brisk, and Roberts Brothers printed thirty thousand copies in the first two months of its publication. Louisa could count on the lordly sum of twenty thousand dollars in publishing income for the year. Having sent Lulu with Anna to the seaside for the summer, Louisa had plenty of quiet now. Despite medical warnings that the effort of finishing *Jo's Boys* might dangerously tax her strength, she found herself surprisingly invigorated. She hoped that, at last, she would be free to write serious books for mature readers.

Her hopes proved premature. The ideas, it seems, crowded in too fast to be sorted out, and even with Lulu absent, the demands of keeping the house in order kept her too busy. Most disappointingly, however, the improvements in Louisa's health and emotional outlook proved transitory. By mid-September, all her apparent gains in strength and enthusiasm had evaporated, brought to a sudden end by a round of headaches and dizzy spells. She was "much discouraged," she wrote, and life again seemed "a burden with constant pain & weariness."[62] Her journal entries, ever more fragmentary, noted some days of comfort but told more often of coughs, a pounding head, and a rebellious stomach. The doctors firmly advised against another full-length book, and Louisa could choose only to submit.

Her steadfast hope now came from God, as she explained in a letter she wrote that autumn to Florence Phillips, a young woman whom she had met on one of her excursions to Nonquitt. Some, Louisa acknowledged, might know God through an epiphany of joy, but the God who mattered to her now had been revealed to her through poverty and pain. The last veil that had separated her from divine love had been pushed aside by sorrow, when her mother had died. When she cried for Abba, she knew that God was very near. Of her firm faith, she wrote, "It needs no logic, no preaching to make me *sure* of it. The instinct is there & following it as fast as one can brings the fact home at last in a way that cannot be doubted."[63] Her God was very much like the characters who had played the part of ministering angels in her novels: quietly present, sharing burdens, not banishing pain but making it sweeter and easier to withstand. If not restoring health, He at least might provide patience and peace.

There was, however, a kind of repose that the Lord could not provide and that Louisa needed to seek for herself. It was time for her to give up caring for Bronson and Lulu. Dr. Rhoda Lawrence, who had used Louisa's money eleven years earlier to found a nursing home in Roxbury and who now came to give her benefactor therapeutic massages, invited Louisa to sample the fruits of her own charity. Louisa May Alcott, now fifty-four, began the year 1887 as a patient in Dr. Lawrence's convalescent home on Dunreath Place, Roxbury.

Bronson remained with Anna at 10 Louisburg Square, a very fashionable address in Boston. He was comfortable and alert but still incapable of meaningful work. He had clear memories of all his old friends, and he took pleasure in being paid social visits and being in the company of his family. However, his right side had never regained normal function. Just how much progress he made in learning how to write with his left hand is unclear, but the issue was rendered moot by his mental state. Although he could carry on simple conversations, he was unable to express complex ideas. Once a week, attendants carried him to a waiting carriage for a drive around town. His greatest joy remained his books, including, Louisa noted, the ones that he had written himself. He kept these near him constantly and loved to boast that he had written four of them after the age of seventy.[64] The greatest comforts of all, however, may have been the books that only Bronson himself could fully appreciate: the sixty-odd volumes of journals that, but for the tomes from the early forties lost in Albany, gave such a complete record of an eventful and contemplative life. Indeed, Bronson had more than his journals to remind him of old times. He also had kept a collection of books that he called his "autobiographical collections." These were scrapbooks of memorabilia collected over the course of decades: newspaper clippings, advertisements for his conversations, almost every scrap of paper imaginable pertaining to himself and his family. Although his waking hours were bright with memories, Bronson slept much of the day now. One day, he looked up from a newspaper and remarked, "Beecher has gone now; all go but me." He was now one of the last living representatives of a generation that had given a new conscience to America. Once Louisa took up residence in Dr. Lawrence's rest home, she seldom saw her father. During 1887, under doctor's orders mandating complete rest, Louisa spent weeks at a time without leaving the home, relying on the ever-faithful Anna for news of the outside world. When she did go to visit her father, it was with the constant awareness that *this* might be the last meeting before he slipped away.

As to Louisa's own prognosis, the doctors were more optimistic, though one may reasonably question the absoluteness of their candor. One of the many physicians who took his turn at trying to cure her was Dr. Milbrey Green, who based his therapy on plant remedies. Louisa was as much attracted to his common sense and positive attitude as to these botanical concoctions. In a letter to Anna, she transcribed the following conversation with Green:

> Dr. G. . . . [said] all was doing well and [gave] me a fourth kind of tonic.
> . . . I said, "Well, now the oyster will go into her shell again." The conversation continued: "You mustn't call yourself that when you are doing so nicely. Why, some of my patients have to lie in bed in dark rooms for months before I can get them where you are. We are going to have some more fine books in a year or two." "Do you *honestly* think so?" "Certainly, why not?" & he looked as much surprised as if I'd denied that I had a nose on my face. "Oh, I never expect to be well again, only patched up for a while. At 55 one doesn't hope for much."[65]

Louisa both hoped and did not hope. Like her father after his stroke, she was bent on recovery. She was willing to try any regimen of baths, exotic herbs, or rest cure that might give her the years of health that the doctors promised her. Dr. Green had said that one or two years of patient conformity with his instructions would bring twenty years of productive life. The plain appearance of things, however, contradicted the bold predictions. In September 1887, she noted her weight as 136 pounds, already low for a woman of her large frame. By February 27, 1888, the figure was down to 113. She jauntily observed, "Now we will see how much I gain in the next 6 [months]," but it was getting harder to deny what was happening to her.[66] Her life had become a ceaseless round of reporting symptoms, absorbing medications, and experiencing pain.

On March 1, Louisa went to visit Bronson and Anna at Louisburg Square. She brought flowers, and her father smelled them gratefully. Smiling up from his pillow, Bronson looked sweet and feeble. As Louisa knelt at his bedside, the dying philosopher made an eerie request. Noticing his benign countenance, Louisa said, "Father, here is your Louy. What are you thinking of as you lie here so happily?" He took her hand in his and, with a gesture toward the ceiling, replied, "I am going *up. Come with me.*" Instead of being aghast at the suggestion, Louisa replied gently, "I wish I could."[67] Her father kissed her. "Come soon," he said. When they parted company,

Louisa had much to occupy her mind—enough, apparently, to make her forget to put on her wrap as she stepped out into the late winter air.

Three days later, around eleven in the morning, Amos Bronson Alcott died. As he slipped away, Louisa was across town at her nursing home on Dunreath Place, unaware that her father's end had come. She wrote a letter to her friend Maria Porter, who had sent her a photograph of May. Knowing that Bronson was near death, Mrs. Porter had expressed her hope that Louisa would find the same strength to bear her father's passing that had been hers when Abba had died. Louisa replied that sorrow had no place in such circumstances and that death was never terrible when it came, "as now, in the likeness of a friend." She would be glad, she said, "when the dear old man falls asleep after this long & innocent life."[68] Over long decades, the father and daughter had judged each other often, and not always in the most lenient terms. However, the last adjective Louisa ever wrote with reference to her father was "innocent." If ever he had wronged her, those wrongs were now forgotten. In a postscript to Mrs. Porter, Louisa wrote that she expected to spend another year at "Saint's Rest," the name she had given to Dr. Lawrence's house. Thereafter, she added, "I am promised twenty years of health. I don't want so many, & have no idea I shall see them. But as I don't live for myself I hold on for others, and shall find time to die some day, I hope."[69]

That same morning, Louisa wrote a brief note to Anna. She complained of a dull pain and the sensation of a weight of iron pressing down on her head. As she wrote these two letters, Louisa began to feel feverish. She sent for Dr. Green, who expressed concern but offered no specific diagnosis. It occurred to her that some rest might do her good. She settled into her bed and closed her eyes. She opened them once more, just long enough to recognize the worried faces of Dr. Lawrence and her nephew John. Before news of Bronson's death could reach her, Louisa's sleep had deepened into a coma. Anna joined the bedside vigil, but there was nothing to do but wait. Before sunrise on March 6, barely forty hours after Bronson's death, Louisa, too, was dead. When the story of their last conversation circulated and people became aware of Bronson's request that his daughter might come up with him, it was hard not to entertain the macabre idea that Louisa had accepted her father's invitation.

Among her papers, Louisa had left an unpublished poem, simply titled

"Free." Written with the suspicion that her death was not far off, it may have given some comfort to those who found it, reassuring them that Louisa had greeted death as a blessed liberation. It reads in part:

> Sing, happy soul! And singing soar.
> No weary flesh now fetters thee.
> Thy wings have burst the narrow cell
> And heaven's boundless blue is free.
> Yet cast one grateful, backward glance
> Toward the life forever done,
> For even when a poor, blind worm,
> Thou hadst thy share of shade and sun.[70]

Bronson was buried on the morning of Louisa's death. The cemetery where he is interred, Sleepy Hollow, was itself an offspring of transcendental thinking. A reaction against the somber aesthetics of the barren churchyard, it was intended as a place that would enfold the dead and the bereaved in the redemptive beauty of nature. At Sleepy Hollow's dedication in 1855, Emerson had told those gathered, "The being that can share a thought and a feeling so sublime as confidence in truth is no mushroom. Our dissatisfaction with any other solution is the blazing evidence of immortality."[71] No one had believed more confidently in truth than Bronson Alcott. In what he deemed to be its earnest service, he had endured ridicule and poverty. With the innocent faith of a child, he had placed all his trust in a voice that had always summoned him upward. On a cheerless March day, the earth of Sleepy Hollow received his body. He had always been certain that a finer part of him would be welcomed elsewhere.

The mound above Bronson's coffin was still fresh when, on March 8, his daughter joined him. The funeral was held in the family's home at 10 Louisburg Square in Boston, the same place where Bronson's had been conducted two days before. The same mourners were there, and the same minister, Cyrus Bartol, delivered Louisa's eulogy. Then it was time for Louisa's remains to follow those of Bronson to Sleepy Hollow. It is impossible to know the thoughts of Anna, the oldest and now the last of the little women, as she stood on this hill whose soil contained not only so much of the literary life of America, but of her own life as well.

Lulu Nieriker, now eight, had lost a second mother. Her father came to visit her after Louisa's death and, the following year, sent a relative to bring the girl back to Europe. Anna went with them to assure herself of the fitness of her niece's new home. She left Lulu there, satisfied that Ernest Nieriker was "a good man," whom she respected "more and more every day." Before her death, Louisa had legally adopted Anna's younger son John, a stratagem that enabled him to inherit her copyrights. These he held as a trustee, dividing the income with Lulu, his brother Fred, and his mother. Anna Alcott Pratt outlived her father and sister by only five years. Her two sons remained in Concord. Fred Pratt died in 1910. John passed away in 1923. Raised in Zurich, Louisa May Nieriker married an Austrian, Emil Rasim. Sheltered by Switzerland's neutrality from the ravages of two world wars, she raised a daughter of her own, was widowed early, and lived to the age of ninety-six.[72]

On Spindle Hill, near a sloping crossroads where the traffic goes too fast, a heavy stone marker indicates the spot near which Bronson Alcott was born. It is easy to drive by without seeing it, and not everyone who lives in the neighborhood knows it is there. In Concord, tourists now come to snap pictures and lay flowers in a corner of Sleepy Hollow Cemetery known as Author's Ridge. Apart from Westminster Abbey and Père Lachaise, one doubts that there are many places on earth richer in literary remains. Barely a dozen paces separate Bronson's grave from Henry Thoreau's, and Hawthorne's is nearer still. Emerson lies a short distance away. His monument, a large, white, rough-hewn monolith, is the only one on Author's Ridge that is in any sense imposing. Although more ornate markers were later erected to commemorate both the Thoreau and Alcott families, the original headstones are startling in their simplicity. Thoreau's bears the name "Henry," and nothing more. The grave of Hawthorne carries only the last name, and there is nothing but the small floral tributes of admirers to distinguish his place from those of various other members of the family. The Alcotts lie in an orderly row along an asphalt-covered path beneath sheltering oaks and pines. The stones are engraved only with dates and initials. "A.B.A.," the good but enigmatic patriarch, is on the far right. Next to him is "A.M.A.," the sometimes angry but always loyal wife and mother. Then come three daughters, in the order in which they left the world, "E.S.A.," "M.A.N.," and lastly "L.M.A." Anna, buried as a Pratt, not an Alcott, is a few strides back from the path, alongside her beloved John. The earth beneath one of the stones contains nothing; although Louisa had hoped to one day bring May's remains back to Concord, she never succeeded. Bronson's and Abba's youngest girl, perhaps the boldest adventurer of all, never came home. With this exception, the family is still close together. Of the five who are represented in this neat little row, only Louisa has any additional personal memorial: a narrow marble rectangle that says "Louisa M. Alcott" and a bronze-colored medallion identifying her as a veteran of the United States Army. No reference is made to any other accomplishment of this astonishing family.

To know what this family did accomplish, one must descend the hill and walk along Lexington Road to Orchard House. The Hillside Chapel, home of the Concord School of Philosophy, still stands on the property, and each summer it still welcomes scholars who gather to discuss the Alcott legacy. But something deeper can be learned from looking at the children who never stop coming to Bronson's and Louisa's house. They are eager, hushed, and wide-eyed. They come to see something they cannot describe but most certainly feel, something that comes neither precisely from the Marches nor the Alcotts, but is perhaps an idea of how life and families ought to be. Louisa once wrote to an admirer, "To all of us comes [a] desire for something to hold by, look up to, and believe in."[73] In the eyes of the children who come to Orchard House, it is possible to see not only this desire, but also its partial satisfaction. Louisa May Alcott, who poured her life's experience into works of fiction, never wrote the great book for adults of which she thought she was capable. Her youngest sister left a number of attractive canvases and some whimsical drawings on her bedroom wall. Few people know the other two sisters as anything more than characters in a book. Bronson Alcott spent his life chasing a nameless, evanescent ideal and filling up massive journals that only scholars care to read. Were it not for the pen of her gifted daughter, Abba Alcott, though better known than most of the nineteenth-century women who toiled ceaselessly for their families, would have left a principally invisible legacy. However, through some strange spiritual alchemy, the novelist, her sisters, and the parents who raised them created something extraordinary. Louisa May Nieriker summarized it best in an interview she gave in the last year of her life. She said, "The Alcotts were *large*."[74] The largeness endures.

Bronson Alcott expected the world to be miraculous. Talk with anyone who has read and loved *Little Women*, and you may conclude that he was right after all.

To the extent that a written page permits knowledge of a different time and departed souls, this book has tried to reveal them. However, as Bronson Alcott learned to his bemusement, the life written is never the same as the life lived. Journals and letters tell much. Biographers can sift the sands as they think wisest. But the bonds that two persons share consist also of encouraging words, a reassuring hand on a tired shoulder, fleeting smiles, and soon-forgotten quarrels. These contacts, so indispensable to existence, leave no durable trace. As writers, as reformers, and as inspirations, Bronson and Louisa still exist for us. Yet this existence, on whatever terms we may experience it, is no more than a shadow when measured against the way they existed for each other.

NOTES

PROLOGUE: DISGRACE

1. Sales at Auction by J. L. Cunningham, 13 April 1837, MS Am 1130.9(2), Houghton Library, Harvard University.
2. A. B. Alcott, Journal for 1837, Week XIV, MS Am 1130.12(10), p. 244, Houghton Library, Harvard University.
3. Shepard, *Pedlar's Progress*, 130.
4. Ibid., 240.
5. Ralph Waldo Emerson to Frederic Henry Hedge, Concord, 20 July 1836, in *Letters*, II, 29.
6. Thoreau, *Journal, 1842–1848*, 223; *Journal, 1853*, 101.
7. N. Hawthorne, "The Hall of Fantasy," in *Tales and Sketches*, 1491–92.
8. Thoreau, *Walden*, 39.
9. L. M. Alcott, *Little Women, Little Men, Jo's Boys*, 229.
10. Sanborn, *Recollections*, II, 476.
11. Shepard, *Pedlar's Progress*, 242.
12. Abigail May Alcott, Journal, 5 August 1828, in Bedell, *Alcotts*, 3.
13. Abigail May Alcott to Samuel J. May, 6 October 1834, in Barton, *Transcendental Wife*, 43.
14. Barton, *Transcendental Wife*, 56.
15. Abigail May Alcott to Samuel J. May, November 1840, in Barton, *Transcendental Wife*, 71.
16. A. B. Alcott to Abigail May Alcott, Ham Common, England, 2 July 1842, in *Letters*, 80.
17. A. B. Alcott, 4 September 1869, *Journals*, 400.
18. A. B. Alcott, "Observations on the Spiritual Nurture," 152, 161, 151.
19. Brooks, *Flowering of New England*, 231–32.
20. Milton, *Paradise Lost*, XII, l. 648, in *Complete Poems*, 469.

21. A. B. Alcott, Journal for 1837, Week VII, 98–100.

22. A. B. Alcott, Journal for 1837, Week XIII, 209.

23. Unidentified clipping, A. B. Alcott, Journal for 1837, 218.

24. A. B. Alcott, April 1837, Week XV, *Journals*, 88.

CHAPTER ONE: BEGINNINGS

1. Orcutt, *History of Wolcott*, 177–78.

2. Winthrop, "A Modell of Christian Charity," in Warner, ed., *American Sermons*, 42.

3. A. B. Alcott, 13 March 1839, *Journals*, 117.

4. Orcutt, *History of Wolcott*, xii.

5. Ibid., 281.

6. A. B. Alcott, 7 August 1869, *Journals*, 398.

7. A. B. Alcott, *New Connecticut*, 15.

8. Ibid., 20.

9. Ibid., 13.

10. A. B. Alcott, Journal for 1850, 1 July, MS Am 1130.12(20), pp. 87–88, Houghton Library, Harvard University.

11. Orcutt, *History of Wolcott*, 239.

12. A. B. Alcott to E. Bronson Cooke, Concord, 30 August 1863, in *Letters*, 348.

13. A. B. Alcott, *New Connecticut*, 20.

14. A. B. Alcott, 24 July 1839, *Journals*, 133–34.

15. A. B. Alcott, 4 December 1828, *Journals*, 16.

16. A. B. Alcott, *New Connecticut*, 23.

17. Ibid., 152.

18. A. B. Alcott, 16 June 1875, *Journals*, 459.

19. A. B. Alcott, 17 October 1869, *Journals*, 401.

20. A. B. Alcott, 13 June 1873, *Journals*, 435.

21. A. B. Alcott, 8 January 1839, *Journals*, 111; *New Connecticut*, 49.

22. A. B. Alcott, 8 January 1839, *Journals*, 111.

23. A. B. Alcott, 8 January 1876, *Journals*, 464.

24. Emerson, *Nature*, in *Essays and Lectures*, 20.

25. Emerson, *Representative Men*, in *Essays and Lectures*, 690.

26. A. B. Alcott, 17 April 1839, *Journals*, 124.

27. A. B. Alcott, 15 June 1873, *Journals*, 436–37.

28. A. B. Alcott, 16 June 1828, *Journals*, 10.

29. A. B. Alcott, 10 May 1846, *Journals*, 180; Dahlstrand, *Amos Bronson Alcott,* 213.

30. Bedell, *Alcotts*, 110–11.

31. Richardson, *Emerson*, 80.

32. A. B. Alcott to Anna Bronson Alcott, Concord, 23 September 1861, in *Letters*, 323.

33. A. B. Alcott, *Conversations*, 251.

34. Douglas, *Autobiography*, 25.

35. Rainer, "The 'Sharper' Image," 31.

36. A. B. Alcott, March 1846, *Journals*, 173.

37. A. B. Alcott, 19 February 1879, *Journals*, 495.

38. Ibid.

39. Orcutt, *History of Wolcott*, 244.

40. A. B. Alcott, 16 October 1830, *Journals*, 25.

41. A. B. Alcott to Mr. and Mrs. Joseph Chatfield Alcox, Norfolk, Va., 24 January 1820, in *Letters*, 2.

42. Dwight, *Travels*, I, 223.

43. Bunyan, *Pilgrim's Progress*, 86.

44. A. B. Alcott to William Andrus Alcott, March 1823, in *New Connecticut*, 226–27.

45. Rainer, "The 'Sharper' Image," 33.

46. A. B. Alcott, 31 July 1831, *Journals*, 29–30.

47. Anonymous, *Hints to Parents*, I, 3; V, 105–6; V, 3; I, 32.

48. Shepard, *Pedlar's Progress*, 77; Bedell, *Alcotts*, 17.

49. Dahlstrand, *Amos Bronson Alcott*, 37–39.

50. A. B. Alcott, 6 December 1826, *Journals*, 7.

51. Shepard, *Pedlar's Progress*, 97.

52. Elbert, *Hunger for Home*, 11.

53. Bedell, *Alcotts*, 4.

54. Ibid., 27.

55. Abigail May Alcott to Charles May, 20 October 1827, in Bedell, *Alcotts*, 31.

56. Saxton, *Louisa May*, 29.

57. Louisa May Alcott to Mrs. Bowles, Concord, 5 May (n.y.), in *Selected Letters*, 338.

58. Bedell, *Alcotts*, 3.

59. A. B. Alcott, 2 August 1828, *Journals*, 12.

60. Ibid.

61. Barton, *Transcendental Wife*, 12.

62. A. B. Alcott, 15 February 1829, *Journals*, 19.

63. William Ellery Channing, "Unitarian Christianity," in Hochfield, ed., *Selected Writings*, 40.

64. Dahlstrand, *Amos Bronson Alcott*, 63.

65. Emerson, *Complete Sermons*, I, 203.

66. Ibid., 205.

67. A. B. Alcott, 15 February 1829, *Journals*, 19.

68. Shepard, *Pedlar's Progress*, 124.

69. Bedell, *Alcotts*, 40.

70. A. B. Alcott, 13 April 1830, *Journals*, 24.

71. Samuel J. May to Abigail May, 21 July 1828, in Saxton, *Louisa May*, 39.

72. Ibid.

73. Shepard, *Pedlar's Progress*, 130.

74. A. B. Alcott, 29 November 1828, *Journals*, 16.

75. Abigail May Alcott to Samuel J. May, Boston, August 1828, MS Am 1130.9, Houghton Library, Harvard University.

76. Ibid.

77. Ibid.

78. Bedell, *Alcotts*, 44.

CHAPTER TWO: A BIRTHDAY IN GERMANTOWN

1. A. B. Alcott, 23 May 1830, *Journals*, 400.

2. A. B. Alcott, *Observations on the Principles*, 4–6.

3. Ibid., 5.

4. Ibid., 9–10.

5. Ibid., 8.

6. Abigail May Alcott to Samuel and Lucretia May, Germantown, Pa., 27 March 1831, MS Am 1130.9, Houghton Library, Harvard University.

7. A. B. Alcott, 16 March 1831, *Journals*, 28.

8. Bedell, *Alcotts*, 56–57.

9. A. B. Alcott, 18 (?) June 1831, *Journals*, 28.

10. A. B. Alcott, "Observations on the Life," 17.

11. Ibid., 45–46.

12. Bedell, *Alcotts*, 60–61.

13. A. B. Alcott, "Observations on the Life," 26.

14. Strickland, "Transcendentalist Father," 23.

15. Ibid., 21–22.

16. Ibid., 24.

17. Dahlstrand, *Amos Bronson Alcott*, 92; Bedell, *Alcotts*, 63.

18. Abigail May Alcott, Journal Entry for 26 July 1842, in A. B. Alcott, *Journals,* 145.

19. A. B. Alcott to Anna Alcott (Mrs. Joseph Alcox), Germantown, Pa., 29 November 1832, in *Letters*, 18.

20. A. B. Alcott, Journals for 1832–33, MS Am 1130.12(6), p. 41, Houghton Library, Harvard University.

21. A. B. Alcott to Colonel Joseph May, Germantown, Pa., 29 November 1832, in *Letters*, 19.

22. A. B. Alcott to Anna Alcott (Mrs. Joseph Alcox), Germantown, Pa., 29 November 1832, in *Letters*, 18.

23. A. B. Alcott to Colonel Joseph May, 29 November 1832, in *Letters*, 20.

24. Bedell, *Alcotts*, 66.

25. A. B. Alcott, 29 November 1832, *Journals*, 33.

26. Abigail May Alcott to Samuel J. and Lucretia May ("Sam and Lu"), Germantown, Pa., 20 February 1833, MS Am 1130.9.

27. Biographers of the family have seen this shift in emphasis in ways that tend to suggest that Bronson loved Louisa less than Anna. They take his more speculative focus as evidence of a "retreat within himself," revealing a lack of interest in this second baby or a failure to see her as anything other than an abstraction. Saxton, *Louisa May*, 76. Surely the most bizarre interpretation is offered by the usually perspicacious Madelon Bedell, who insinuates that Bronson's downplaying of Louisa's physical aspects arose from his attempt to repress a sexual attraction to the infant. Bedell, *Alcotts*, 65–66. The fact that Alcott's reading had assumed a more metaphysical character at the time of Louisa's birth seems to offer a simpler and less accusatory explanation.

28. Strickland, "Transcendentalist Father," 32, 34.

29. A. B. Alcott, February 1833, *Journals*, 36.

30. A. B. Alcott, Journal, 23 April 1834, in Strickland, "Transcendentalist Father," 39.

31. Ibid.

32. Abigail May Alcott to Samuel and Lucretia May, Philadelphia, 22 June 1833, MS Am 1130.9.

33. Strickland, "Transcendentalist Father," 38.

34. A. B. Alcott, "Observations on the Life," 10 July 1831.

35. A. B. Alcott, 12 June 1834, *Journals*, 44.

36. Dahlstrand, *Amos Bronson Alcott*, 103.

37. A. B. Alcott, 28 April 1834, *Journals*, 42.

38. A. B. Alcott, June 1832, *Journals*, 31.

CHAPTER THREE: THE TEMPLE SCHOOL

1. Marshall, *Peabody Sisters*, 107.

2. Ibid., 295.

3. McCuskey, *Bronson Alcott*, 51.

4. Marshall, *Peabody Sisters*, 295.

5. Peabody, *Record of a School*, 70.

6. A. B. Alcott to Elizabeth Palmer Peabody, Boston, n.d., in *Letters*, 21.

7. A. B. Alcott, *Conversations*, 200.

8. Peabody, *Record of a School*, 2.

9. Ibid., 145.

10. Martineau, *Society*, III, 175.

11. Peabody, *Record of a School*, 35.

12. Ibid., 9.

13. Emerson, *Nature*, in *Essays and Lectures*, 20.

14. A. B. Alcott, "Observations on the Spiritual Nurture," 121.

15. Ibid., 84.

16. Ibid., 124

17. A. B. Alcott, "Researches on Childhood," 23.

18. A. B. Alcott, "Observations on the Spiritual Nurture," 69.

19. Ibid., 235–36.

20. Ibid., 80.

21. Ibid., 59.

22. Ibid., 239.

23. Ibid., 23.

24. A. B. Alcott, "Researches on Childhood," 79–80.

25. Ibid., 105.

26. A. B. Alcott, "Observations on the Spiritual Nurture," 23, 25.

27. Ibid., 37.

28. Ibid., 239.

29. Ibid., 240.

30. One instance of spanking is recounted in detail in "Observations on the Spiritual Nurture," 109–10.

31. A. B. Alcott, "Researches on Childhood," 123.

32. A. B. Alcott, "Observations on the Spiritual Nurture," 161.

33. Ibid., 107.

34. Ibid., 170, 164.

35. A. B. Alcott, "Researches on Childhood," 27, 84.

36. A. B. Alcott, "Observations on the Spiritual Nurture," 136.

37. A. B. Alcott, 21 January 1835, *Journals*, 55.

38. A. B. Alcott, 24 June 1835, *Journals*, 57.

39. "Critical Notices," *New-England Magazine*, September 1835; *Portland Magazine*, 1 September 1835; *Eastern Magazine*, October 1835; *The Western Messenger*, November 1835.

40. Frederic Henry Hedge, "Coleridge's Literary Character—German Metaphysics," *The Christian Examiner* 14 (March 1833), in Hochfield, ed., *Selected Writings*, 124.

41. A. B. Alcott, October, Week XLII, *Journals*, 105.

42. Julian Hawthorne, quoted in Richardson, *Emerson*, 195.

43. Emerson, *Journals and Miscellaneous Notebooks*, II, 239.

44. Richardson, *Emerson*, 126.

45. Emerson, *Early Lectures*, I, 26.

46. A. B. Alcott, 5 February 1835, *Journals*, 56.

47. Dahlstrand, *Amos Bronson Alcott*, 131.

48. Richardson, *Emerson*, 214.

49. A. B. Alcott, 20 October 1835, *Journals*, 69.

50. A. B. Alcott, 10 April 1875, *Journals*, 456–57.

51. Emerson, "The American Scholar," in *Essays and Lectures*, 62.

52. Ralph Waldo Emerson to Frederic Henry Hedge, Concord, 20 July 1836, in *Letters*, II, 29.

53. Shepard, *Pedlar's Progress*, 152.

54. Richardson, *Emerson*, 212.

55. Ralph Waldo Emerson to Frederic Henry Hedge, Concord, 20 July 1836, in *Letters*, II, 30.

56. L. M. Alcott, "Recollections of My Childhood," in Shealy, ed., *Alcott*, 33.

57. Ibid.

58. Bedell, *Alcotts*, 81–82.

59. Cheney, ed., *Louisa May Alcott*, 18.

60. A. B. Alcott, 2 August 1836 and 11 September 1836, *Journals*, 78.

61. Because the lines of the "poet" are not taken from any identified manuscript, some have disputed whether Alcott was the bard to whom Emerson was indebted. However, the ideas expressed are, as Odell Shepard notes, "Alcottian throughout." In A. B. Alcott, *Journals*, 78n.

62. Ralph Waldo Emerson to Amos Bronson Alcott, Concord, 27 February 1836, in *Letters*, II, 4–5.

63. Ibid., 5.

64. A. B. Alcott, "Researches on Childhood," 105.

65. A. B. Alcott, "Observations on the Spiritual Nurture," 112.

66. Ibid., 38–39.

67. When he used the word "genius," Alcott typically intended something other than an "exceptionally gifted person." He sometimes meant the unique motivating force within a given human being or, as here, a meaning derived from classical Latin, that of a "guardian spirit." Thus, this journal entry was not quite the expression of egotism that it appears, though there was certainly arrogance aplenty in Bronson's opinion of himself as a parent.

68. Marshall, *Peabody Sisters*, 320–22.

69. A. B. Alcott, *Conversations*, 254–55.

70. Ibid., 255.

71. Ibid., 66.

72. Ibid., 185.

73. Franklin, *Autobiography*, 101; Marshall, *Peabody Sisters*, 318–19.

74. Bedell, *Alcotts*, 122.

75. A. B. Alcott, *Conversations*, 63.

76. Ibid., 91, 242.

77. Ibid.,63n, 228n.

78. Ibid., 68n.

79. A. B. Alcott, Autobiographical Collections, 1834–39, MS Am 1130.11(3), p. 123, Houghton Library, Harvard University.

80. Ibid., 131.

81. Ibid., 134.

82. Dahlstrand, *Amos Bronson Alcott*, 141.

83. Capper, *Margaret Fuller*, 198; Bedell, *Alcotts*, 131.

84. Margaret Fuller to Frederic Henry Hedge, 6 April 1837, in *Letters*, I, 265.

85. Capper, *Margaret Fuller*, 209.

86. (Elizabeth Palmer Peabody), "Mr. Alcott's Book and School," *Christian Register and Boston Observer,* 29 April 1837, quoted in Marshall, *Peabody Sisters,* 326.

87. Ralph Waldo Emerson to Amos Bronson Alcott, Concord, 24 March 1837, in *Letters,* II, 61.

88. A. B. Alcott, April 1837, Week XV, *Journals,* 88.

89. Emerson, *Journals and Miscellaneous Notebooks,* VIII, 212.

90. A. B. Alcott, April 1837, Week XV, *Journals,* 88.

91. Louisa May Alcott, "Recollections of My Childhood," 33.

92. Dahlstrand, *Amos Bronson Alcott,* 146.

93. Ralph Waldo Emerson to Amos Bronson Alcott, Concord, 24 March 1837, in *Letters,* II, 62.

94. A. B. Alcott, "Psyche," 260.

95. A. B. Alcott, November 1837, Week XLV, *Journals,* 94.

96. A. B. Alcott to Anna Alcox, 18 March 1839, in *Letters,* 42.

97. Bedell, *Alcotts,* 147.

98. Ibid., 149.

99. A. B. Alcott, 5 February 1839, *Journals,* 115.

100. Dahlstrand, *Amos Bronson Alcott,* 156.

101. A. B. Alcott, 5 December 1839, *Journals,* 137.

102. Dahlstrand, *Amos Bronson Alcott,* 180; A. B. Alcott, 18 October 1839, *Journals,* 136.

CHAPTER FOUR: "ORPHEUS AT THE PLOUGH"

1. Thoreau, *A Week on the Concord,* 8.

2. A. B. Alcott to Elizabeth Sewall Alcott, Concord, 24 June 1840, in *Letters,* 50.

3. Anonymous, "Rambles in Concord, Part I," in A. B. Alcott, Autobiographical Collections, 1868–71, MS Am 1130.11(7), Houghton Library, Harvard University.

4. L. M. Alcott to the *Springfield Republican,* Concord, 4 May 1869, in *Selected Letters,* 127.

5. Thoreau, *Walden,* 103, 106.

6. Emerson, *Journals of Ralph Waldo Emerson,* V, 382.

7. Ralph Waldo Emerson to Margaret Fuller, Concord, 15 April 1840, in *Letters,* II, 281.

8. A. B. Alcott to Samuel May, Concord, 6 April 1840, in *Letters,* 47.

9. Anna Alcott, Diary, in Dahlstrand, *Amos Bronson Alcott,* 181.

10. L. M. Alcott, *Moods,* 36.

11. Thoreau, *A Week on the Concord,* 222.

12. Thoreau, *Journal, 1837–1844,* 164, 172, 171, 168.

13. A. B. Alcott to Louisa May Alcott, Concord, 29 November 1840, in *Letters,* 54.

14. Emerson, "Education," in *Early Lectures,* III, 295–96.

15. A. B. Alcott to Samuel May, Concord, 29 July 1840, in *Letters,* 51.

16. A. B. Alcott to Mrs. Anna Alcott, Concord, 21 June 1840, in *Letters,* 48.

17. Bedell, *Alcotts*, 150.

18. Shepard, *Pedlar's Progress*, 294.

19. Emerson, *Journals of Ralph Waldo Emerson*, V, 380.

20. Ralph Waldo Emerson to Margaret Fuller, Concord, 15 April 1840, in *Letters*, II, 281.

21. Henry James Sr., "Women and the 'Woman's Movement,' " quoted in Strouse, *Alice James*, 45.

22. Strouse, *Alice James*, 13.

23. (R. W. Emerson and Margaret Fuller), "The Editors to the Reader," *The Dial* I (1840), 1.

24. Dahlstrand, *Amos Bronson Alcott*, 182.

25. Ralph Waldo Emerson to Margaret Fuller, Concord, 8 May 1840, in *Letters*, II, 294.

26. Abigail May Alcott to Samuel J. May, Concord, 24 January 1841, MS Am 1130.9(25), Houghton Library, Harvard University.

27. A. B. Alcott, "Orphic Sayings," *The Dial* I (1840), 86.

28. A. B. Alcott, "Orphic Sayings," *The Dial* I (1841), 357.

29. A. B. Alcott, "Orphic Sayings," *The Dial* I (1840), 87.

30. Ibid., 93.

31. William Emerson to Ralph Waldo Emerson (?), 28 August 1840, in R. W. Emerson, *Letters,* II, 312n.

32. Ralph Waldo Emerson to Thomas Carlyle, Concord, 30 August 1840, in *Selected Letters*, 224.

33. Emerson, *Journals and Miscellaneous Notebooks*, VIII, 181.

34. A. B. Alcott to Louisa May Alcott, Concord, 21 June 1840, in *Letters*, 49.

35. A. B. Alcott to Samuel J. May, Concord, 29 July 1840, in *Letters*, 51.

36. Abigail May Alcott to Samuel May, November 1840, in Barton, *Transcendental Wife*, 71.

37. Bedell, *Alcotts*, 162, 234.

38. Abigail May Alcott to Samuel J. May, Concord, 24 January 1841, MS Am 1130.9(25).

39. Ralph Waldo Emerson to Margaret Fuller, Concord, 16 August 1840, in *Letters*, II, 323.

40. Sanborn, *Bronson Alcott*, 12.

41. Ibid., 11.

42. Richardson, *Emerson*, 359.

43. Ralph Waldo Emerson to Margaret Fuller, Concord, 28 January 1842, in *Selected Letters*, 263.

44. Abigail May Alcott to Samuel J. May, Concord, 18 January 1842, in Elbert, *Hunger for Home*, 45.

45. Dahlstrand, *Amos Bronson Alcott*, 187.

46. Richardson, *Emerson*, 363.

47. Emerson, *Journals and Miscellaneous Notebooks*, VIII, 210–15.

48. Ralph Waldo Emerson to Thomas Carlyle, Concord, 31 March 1842, in Emerson and Carlyle, *Correspondence*, 320.

49. A. B. Alcott to Mrs. A. Bronson Alcott, Ship Rosalind, English Channel, 31 May 1842, in *Letters*, 65–66.

50. Ibid., 67.

51. A. B. Alcott to Mrs. A. Bronson Alcott, Ham Common, 12 June 1842, in *Letters*, 69.

52. A. B. Alcott to Mrs. A. Bronson Alcott, London, 17 June 1842, in *Letters*, 72.

53. A. B. Alcott to Mrs. A. Bronson Alcott, Ham Common, 12 June 1842, in *Letters*, 69.

54. Ibid., 69–71.

55. Thomas Carlyle to Ralph Waldo Emerson, London, 29 August 1842, in Emerson and Carlyle, *Correspondence*, 329.

56. A. B. Alcott to Ralph Waldo Emerson, Ham Common, 2 July 1842, in *Letters*, 81.

57. A. B. Alcott to Mrs. A. Bronson Alcott, Ham Common, 16 July 1842, in *Letters*, 85.

58. Thomas Carlyle to Ralph Waldo Emerson, London, 19 July 1842, in Emerson and Carlyle, *Correspondence*, 326.

59. Robert Browning to Alfred Donnett, 30 September 1842, in Emerson and Carlyle, *Correspondence*, 329n.

60. Abigail May Alcott, Journal Entry for 7 May 1842, in A. B. Alcott, *Journals*, 142.

61. Bedell, *Alcotts*, 190–91.

62. A. B. Alcott to Mrs. A. Bronson Alcott, 31 May 1842, in *Letters*, 65, 67.

63. A. B. Alcott to Mrs. A. Bronson Alcott, 17 June and 31 May 1842, in *Letters*, 73, 67.

64. A. B. Alcott to Mrs. A. Bronson Alcott, 31 May 1842, in *Letters*, 67.

65. Abigail May Alcott, Journal Entry for 8 July 1842, in A. B. Alcott, *Journals*, 143.

66. Bedell, *Alcotts*, 193.

67. Abigail May Alcott, Journal Entry for 8 July 1842, in A. B. Alcott, *Journals*, 143.

68. Abigail May Alcott, Journal Entry for 22 May 1842, in A. B. Alcott, *Journals*, 142–43.

69. Abigail May Alcott, Journal Entry for 21 July 1842, in A. B. Alcott, *Journals*, 144.

70. Abigail May Alcott, Journal Entry for 9 May 1842, in A. B. Alcott, *Journals*, 142.

71. Abigail May Alcott, Journal Entry for 26 July 1842, in A. B. Alcott, *Journals*, 145.

72. Ibid.

73. A. B. Alcott to Junius S. Alcott, Ham Common, 30 June 1842, in *Letters*, 74.

74. A. B. Alcott to Mrs. A. Bronson Alcott, Ham Common, 16 August 1842, in *Letters*, 89–90.

75. Abigail May Alcott, Journal Entry for 4 September 1842, in A. B. Alcott, *Journals*, 146–47.

76. A. B. Alcott, to Mrs. A. Bronson Alcott, Ham Common, 16 August 1842, in *Letters*, 90.

77. Abigail May Alcott, Journal Entry for 16 September 1842, in A. B. Alcott, *Journals*, 147.

78. Thomas Carlyle to Ralph Waldo Emerson, London, 11 March 1843, in Emerson and Carlyle, *Correspondence*, 338.

79. Abigail May Alcott, Journal Entry for 21 and 23 October 1842, in A. B. Alcott, *Journals*, 148.

80. Sanborn, *Bronson Alcott*, 26.

81. Ibid.

82. Charles Lane to William Oldham, 30 November 1842, in Bedell, *Alcotts*, 195.

83. Emerson, *Journals and Miscellaneous Notebooks*, VIII, 404.

84. Ibid., 367.

85. Sanborn, *Bronson Alcott,* 43–44.

86. Abigail May Alcott, Journal Entry for 29 November 1842, in A. B. Alcott, *Journals*, 148–49.

87. A. B. Alcott to Louisa May Alcott, Concord, 29 November 1842, in *Letters*, 93.

88. A. B. Alcott to Anna, Louisa, Elizabeth, and May Alcott, Concord, 1 February 1843, in *Letters*, 96–97.

89. Bedell, *Alcotts,* 202.

90. Emerson, *Journals and Miscellaneous Notebooks*, VIII, 310.

91. Ibid., 301.

92. Charles Lane to William Oldham, Concord, 31 May 1843, in Sears, comp., *Bronson Alcott's Fruitlands*, 14.

93. Ibid., 15.

CHAPTER FIVE: THE SOWING OF THE SEEDS

1. L. M. Alcott, "Transcendental Wild Oats," in Sears, comp., *Bronson Alcott's Fruitlands*, 147.

2. Ibid.

3. Abigail May Alcott, Journal Entry for 1 June 1843, in A. B. Alcott, *Journals*, 152–53.

4. Charles Lane to William Oldham, Fruitlands, 28 June 1843, in Sears, comp., *Bronson Alcott's Fruitlands*, 26.

5. L. M. Alcott, "Transcendental Wild Oats," 152.

6. Sears, comp., *Bronson Alcott's Fruitlands*, 59.

7. Abigail May Alcott, Journal Entry for 1 June 1843, in A. B. Alcott, *Journals*, 153.

8. Ibid.

9. A. B. Alcott and Charles Lane, "Intelligence," *The Dial* 4 (1843), 135.

10. L. M. Alcott, "Transcendental Wild Oats," 156.

11. L. M. Alcott, 1 September 1843, *Journals*, 45.

12. Sears, comp., *Bronson Alcott's Fruitlands*, 76.

13. Ibid., 43.

14. L. M. Alcott, "Transcendental Wild Oats," 154.

15. Sears, comp., *Bronson Alcott's Fruitlands*, 47–48.

16. L. M. Alcott, "Transcendental Wild Oats," 158–59.

17. Charles Lane and A. B. Alcott to A. Brooke, Fruitlands, n.d., in Sears, comp., *Bronson Alcott's Fruitlands*, 50.

18. L. M. Alcott, "Transcendental Wild Oats," 157.

19. Ralph Waldo Emerson, "Fourierism and the Socialists," *The Dial* 3 (1842), 87.

20. Charles Lane to William Oldham, 30 July 1843, in Sears, comp., *Bronson Alcott's Fruitlands*, 31–32.

21. Charles Lane and A. B. Alcott to A. Brooke, in Sears, comp., *Bronson Alcott's Fruit-lands*, 51.

22. Thoreau, *Walden*, 197–201.

23. L. M. Alcott to Sophia Gardner, Concord, 23 September 1845, in *Selected Letters*, 4.

24. L. M. Alcott, 10 December 1843, *Journals*, 47.

25. L. M. Alcott, 1 September 1843, *Journals*, 45.

CHAPTER SIX: FIRST FRUITS

1. This judgment as to Anna's pervading optimism is based on the surviving record. Her journal entries from the fall and winter, like some of Louisa's, were removed and destroyed by Bronson.

2. Anna Alcott, Journal, 24 June 1843, in Sears, comp., *Bronson Alcott's Fruitlands*, 93.

3. A. B. Alcott to Elizabeth Sewall Alcott, Fruitlands, 24 June 1843, in *Letters*, 105.

4. Ibid., 105–06.

5. Charles Lane, "To Elizabeth," in Sears, comp., *Bronson Alcott's Fruitlands*, 94.

6. Abigail May Alcott, Diary, 25 June 1843, in Bedell, *Alcotts*, 215.

7. Sears, comp., *Bronson Alcott's Fruitlands*, 94.

8. Abigail May Alcott, Journal Entry for 2 July 1843, in A. B. Alcott, *Journals*, 153.

9. L. M. Alcott, 24 September 1843, *Journals*, 45.

10. L. M. Alcott, 23 December 1843, *Journals*, 48.

11. L. M. Alcott, 25 December 1843, *Journals*, 50. Louisa was somewhat inconsistent in pinpointing the time when she first became aware of life's difficulty. She wrote else-where that "the trials of life" did not begin for her until the family moved to Hillside. L. M. Alcott, "Recollections of My Childhood," in Shealy, ed., *Alcott*, 36.

12. L. M. Alcott, n.d. 1843, *Journals*, 51. Remarkably, although her health had radically declined, Louisa continued to go for runs until the summer before her death. *Jour-nals*, 17 and 18 July 1887, 307.

13. L. M. Alcott, n.d. 1843, *Journals*, 51.

14. Emerson, *Journals and Miscellaneous Notebooks*, VIII, 433.

15. Ibid.

16. Abigail May Alcott, Journal Entry for 24 July 1843, in A. B. Alcott, *Journals*, 153.

17. Abigail May Alcott to Charles May, 6 November 1843, MS Am 1130.9(25), Houghton Library, Harvard University.

18. Abigail May Alcott to Samuel J. May, 4 November 1843, MS Am 1130.9(25).

19. L. M. Alcott, "Transcendental Wild Oats," in Sears, comp., *Bronson Alcott's Fruit-lands*, 163.

20. Ibid., 162–63.

21. Ibid., 163.

22. Abigail May Alcott, Journal Entry for August 1843, in A. B. Alcott, *Journals*, 154.

23. Abigail May Alcott, Journal Entry for 26 August 1843, in A. B. Alcott, *Journals*, 155.

24. Emerson, "New England Reformers," in *Essays and Lectures*, 591–92.

25. Ibid., 591.

26. Charles Lane to William Oldham, 29 September 1843, in Sears, comp., *Bronson Alcott's Fruitlands*, 94.

27. Sears, comp., *Bronson Alcott's Fruitlands*, 39.

28. Ibid., 121; Stern, *Louisa May Alcott*, 38.

29. Journal of Isaac Hecker, in Sears, comp., *Bronson Alcott's Fruitlands*, 76–77.

30. Ibid., 77.

31. Ibid., 76.

32. Ibid., 78.

33. Ibid., 84.

34. Sears, comp., *Bronson Alcott's Fruitlands*, 85.

35. Ibid., 79.

36. Ibid., 81.

37. Ibid., 82.

38. Ibid., 85.

39. Journal of Isaac Hecker, in Sears, comp., *Bronson Alcott's Fruitlands*, 84.

40. L. M. Alcott, 8 October 1843, *Journals*, 46.

41. L. M. Alcott, 12 October 1843, *Journals*, 46.

42. L. M. Alcott, 2 November 1843, *Journals*, 47.

43. Abigail May Alcott to Samuel J. May, Fruitlands, n.d., MS Am 1130.9(25).

44. Ralph Waldo Emerson to Margaret Fuller, Concord, 7 August 1843, in *Letters*, III, 196.

CHAPTER SEVEN: LOST ILLUSIONS

1. Charles Lane, "A Day with the Shakers," in Fogarty, comp., *American Utopianism*, 22. Although Lane reported the use of coffee and tea among the Harvard Shakers, these substances were strongly discouraged in the typical Shaker community. Either there was some unusual laxity in the Harvard colony, or Lane was mistaken about these iniquities.

2. Ibid., 23.

3. Holloway, *Heavens*, 67.

4. Ibid., 69.

5. Abigail May Alcott, Journal Entry for 26 August 1843, in A. B. Alcott, *Journals*, 154.

6. Sears, comp., *Bronson Alcott's Fruitlands*, 121.

7. Anna Alcott to Abigail May Alcott, Fruitlands, n.d., Fruitlands Museum, Harvard, Mass.

8. L. M. Alcott, 12 October 1843, *Journals*, 46.

9. L. M. Alcott, 2 November 1843, *Journals*, 46–47.

10. L. M. Alcott, 14 September 1843, *Journals*, 45.

11. L. M. Alcott, 8 October 1843, *Journals*, 46.

12. Dahlstrand, *Amos Bronson Alcott*, 198.

13. L. M. Alcott, "Transcendental Wild Oats," in Sears, comp., *Bronson Alcott's Fruitlands*, 165.

14. Sears, comp., *Bronson Alcott's Fruitlands*, 114–15.

15. Abigail May Alcott to Samuel J. May, Fruitlands, n.d., MS Am 1130.9(25), Houghton Library, Harvard University.

16. Bedell, *Alcotts*, 226.

17. Sears, comp., *Bronson Alcott's Fruitlands*, 120.

18. Ralph Waldo Emerson to Margaret Fuller, Concord, 17 December 1843, in *Selected Letters*, 297.

19. Elbert, *Hunger for Home*, 60.

20. Bunyan, *Pilgrim's Progress*, 13.

21. Abigail May Alcott to Samuel J. May, 11 November 1843, MS Am 1130.9(25).

22. Abigail May Alcott to Charles May, 6 November 1843, MS Am 1130.9(25).

23. Alcott biographer Madelon Bedell has even surmised a budding homosexual liaison between Alcott and Lane, though this supposition appears to rest more on imagination than on evidence. Bedell, *Alcotts*, 228.

24. Sears, comp., *Bronson Alcott's Fruitlands*, 122–23.

25. L. M. Alcott, 20 November 1843, *Journals*, 47.

26. Sears, comp., *Bronson Alcott's Fruitlands*, 110–11.

27. Charles Lane to William Oldham, quoted in William Harry Harland, "Bronson Alcott's English Friends," Fruitlands Museum, Harvard, Mass.

28. Ralph Waldo Emerson to Margaret Fuller, Concord, 17 December 1843, in *Selected Letters*, 297.

29. L. M. Alcott, 10 December 1843, *Journals*, 47.

30. L. M. Alcott, October 1856, *Journals*, 79.

31. Abigail May Alcott, Journal Entry for 1 January 1844, in A. B. Alcott, *Journals*, 156.

32. Abigail May Alcott to Samuel J. May, 11 January 1844, in Bedell, *Alcotts*, 231.

33. L. M. Alcott, "Transcendental Wild Oats," 170–72.

34. Sears, comp., *Bronson Alcott's Fruitlands*, 127.

35. A. B. Alcott to Junius S. Alcott, Concord, 28 October 1844, in *Letters*, 115.

CHAPTER EIGHT: FATHER AND DAUGHTER

1. Elizabeth Palmer Peabody to Sophia Hawthorne, in Mellow, *Nathaniel Hawthorne*, 405.

2. Abigail May Alcott, Journal Entry for 3 February 1844, in A. B. Alcott, *Journals*, 157.

3. A. B. Alcott to Junius S. Alcott, Still River, Mass., 15 June 1844, in *Letters*, 111.

4. Mike Volmar, Curator, Fruitlands Museum, e-mail message to author, 30 November 2006.

5. Bedell, *Alcotts*, 292.

6. Sears, comp., *Bronson Alcott's Fruitlands*, 122.

7. Bedell, *Alcotts*, 233.

8. Swayne, *Story of Concord*, 135.

9. A. B. Alcott, 9 February 1851, *Journals*, 241.

10. Abigail May Alcott, Journal Entry for 28 January 1844, in A. B. Alcott, *Journals*, 157.

11. Bedell, *Alcotts*, 300.

12. N. Hawthorne, "The Artist of the Beautiful," in *Tales and Sketches*, 920.

13. A. B. Alcott, 6 October 1851, *Journals*, 254.

14. N. Hawthorne, "The Hall of Fantasy," in *Tales and Sketches*, 1492.

15. N. Hawthorne, "The Custom-House," in *Collected Novels*, 133, 140.

16. Emerson, *Journals and Miscellaneous Notebooks*, IX, 86.

17. Emerson, "New England Reformers," in *Essays and Lectures*, 598.

18. As literary critic Jeffrey S. Cramer has observed, one of the principles that Thoreau gleaned from Fruitlands was a philosophical rejection of animal labor. Thoreau expressed Alcott's thoughts on the subject in a well-turned chiasmus: "I am wont to think that men are not so much the keepers of herds as herds are the keepers of men." Thoreau added that no nation of philosophers would consent to the use of animal labor. However, he noted with a glint of Yankee practicality, "There never was and is not likely soon to be a nation of philosophers." Thoreau, *Walden*, 54.

19. A. B. Alcott to Junius S. Alcott, Boston, 7 December 1850, in *Letters*, 160.

20. Abigail May Alcott, Journal Entry for 22 March 1844, in A. B. Alcott, *Journals*, 158.

21. Abigail May Alcott, Journal Entry for 23 May 1844, in A. B. Alcott, *Journals*, 158.

22. Annie M. L. Clark, *The Alcotts in Harvard*, in Shealy, ed., *Alcott*, 120.

23. Frederick L. H. Willis, *Alcott Memoirs*, in Shealy, ed., *Alcott*, 177.

24. Ibid., 177–78.

25. Ibid., 171.

26. Clark, *The Alcotts in Harvard*, 121.

27. L. M. Alcott, n.d. 1845, *Journals*, 56.

28. A. B. Alcott to Junius S. Alcott, Concord, 28 January 1845, in *Letters*, 119.

29. Nathaniel Hawthorne to G. W. Curtis, Concord, 14 July 1852, in *Letters, 1843–1853*, 567.

30. Ibid.

31. Ibid.

32. A. B. Alcott, 9 February 1847, *Journals*, 190.

33. L. M. Alcott, "Recollections of My Childhood," in Shealy, ed., *Alcott*, 36.

34. L. M. Alcott, March 1846, *Journals*, 59.

35. A. B. Alcott, 3 January 1846, *Journals*, 170.

36. Stern, *Louisa May Alcott*, 46.

37. Willis, *Alcott Memoirs*, 172.

38. Edward W. Emerson, "When Louisa Alcott Was a Girl," in Shealy, ed., *Alcott*, 95.

39. Stern, *Louisa May Alcott*, 58.

40. Edward W. Emerson, "When Louisa Alcott Was a Girl," 94.

41. A. B. Alcott, April 1846, *Journals*, 176.

42. Thoreau, *Walden*, 43.

43. Ibid., 259.

44. Ibid., 260.

45. Emerson, "Friendship," in *Essays and Lectures*, 352.

46. A. B. Alcott, 28 June 1846, *Journals*, 182.

47. A. B. Alcott, 12 August and 18 October 1847, *Journals*, 196.

48. Bedell, *Alcotts*, 251.

49. L. M. Alcott, "Recollections of My Childhood," 36.

50. Ibid.

51. Clara Gowing, *The Alcotts As I Knew Them*, in Shealy, ed., *Alcott*, 137.

52. L. M. Alcott, n.d. 1845, *Journals*, 55–56.

53. L. M. Alcott to Sophia Gardner, Concord, 23 September 1845, in *Selected Letters*, 4.

54. Barton, *Transcendental Wife*, 126; L. M. Alcott to Sophia Gardner, Concord, 23 September 1845, in *Selected Letters*, 4.

55. Barton, *Transcendental Wife*, 126–27; Saxton, *Louisa May*, 180.

56. Bedell, *Alcotts*, 256.

57. Thoreau to Ralph Waldo Emerson, in Saxton, *Louisa May*, 176.

58. L. M. Alcott to Sophia Gardner, Concord, 23 September 1845, in *Selected Letters*, 4.

59. Lydia Hosmer Wood, "Beth Alcott's Playmate: A Glimpse of Concord Town in the Days of *Little Women*," in Shealy, ed., *Alcott*, 165.

60. L. M. Alcott, n.d. 1845, *Journals*, 57.

61. L. M. Alcott to Maggie Lukens, 5 February 1884, in *Selected Letters*, 276.

62. L. M. Alcott, n.d. 1845, *Journals*, 57.

63. A. B. Alcott, *Sonnets*, 79.

64. L. M. Alcott, "Recollections of My Childhood," 35.

65. Clark, *The Alcotts in Harvard*, 122.

66. Willis, *Alcott Memoirs*, 181; Edward W. Emerson, "When Louisa Alcott Was a Girl," 95; Cheney, ed., *Louisa May Alcott*, 328.

67. Cheney, ed., *Louisa May Alcott*, 328.

68. Anna Alcott, Journal, 1 September 1845, 3 September 1846, in Bonstelle, ed., *Little Women Letters*, 131, 133; L. M. Alcott, August 1850, *Journals*, 63.

69. Wood, "Beth Alcott's Playmate," 167.

70. Bedell, *Alcotts*, 245.

71. L. M. Alcott, *Little Women, Little Men, Jo's Boys*, 10.

72. Anna Alcott Pratt, "A Foreword by Meg," in Shealy, ed., *Alcott*, 75; Wood, "Beth Alcott's Playmate," 165.

73. Edward W. Emerson, "When Louisa Alcott Was a Girl," 92.

74. A. B. Alcott to Anna, Louisa, Elizabeth, and May Alcott, Ham Common, 15 July 1842, in *Letters*, 83.

75. A. B. Alcott, 6 October 1851, *Journals*, 254.

76. A. B. Alcott, April 1846, *Journals*, 175.

77. A. B. Alcott, March 1846, *Journals*, 173.

78. L. M. Alcott, March 1846, *Journals*, 59.

79. Stern, *Louisa May Alcott*, 57.

80. Abigail May Alcott to Samuel J. May, 17 April 1845, in Bedell, *Alcotts*, 239.

81. Abigail May Alcott, Diary, 24 November 1846, in Bedell, *Alcotts*, 239.

82. A. B. Alcott, 16 March 1846, *Journals*, 173.

83. L. M. Alcott, *Little Women, Little Men, Jo's Boys*, 89.

84. A. B. Alcott, 16 March 1846, *Journals*, 173.

85. Abigail May Alcott to Samuel J. May, 17 April 1845, in Barton, *Transcendental Wife*, 123.

86. A. B. Alcott, *Concord Days*, 46.

87. Dahlstrand, *Amos Bronson Alcott*, 232.

88. Ibid.

89. Wood, "Beth Alcott's Playmate," 167.

90. Heilbrun, *Writing*, 64.

91. A. B. Alcott, 13 May 1839, *Journals*, 128.

92. Emerson, *Journals and Miscellaneous Notebooks*, VII, 539.

93. L. M. Alcott, "Recollections of My Childhood," 36.

94. A. B. Alcott, Journal for 1848, 7 April, MS Am 1130.12(17), Houghton Library, Harvard University.

95. Bedell, *Alcotts*, 272.

96. L. M. Alcott, "Recollections of My Childhood," 37.

97. Ibid.

CHAPTER NINE: DESTITUTION

1. A. B. Alcott to Louisa and May Alcott, Boston, 17 June 1849, *Letters*, 151.

2. L. M. Alcott, May 1850, *Journals*, 61.

3. Bedell, *Alcotts*, 282.

4. L. M. Alcott, n.d. 1851, *Journals*, 65.

5. A. B. Alcott, *Journals*, 198; Bedell, *Alcotts*, 272.

6. L. M. Alcott, "Recollections of My Childhood," in Shealy, ed., *Alcott*, 37.

7. L. M. Alcott, August 1850, *Journals*, 63.

8. With gleaming sarcasm, Ellery Channing referred to Bronson's ever-increasing compendium of journals as the "*Encyclopédie de Moi-Même en Cent Volumes.*" Saxton, *Louisa May*, 189.

9. L. M. Alcott, May 1850, *Journals*, 61, 62.

10. Dahlstrand, *Amos Bronson Alcott*, 221.

11. L. M. Alcott, "Recollections of My Childhood," 38.

12. Ibid., 37.

13. L. M. Alcott, July 1850, *Journals*, 63. Emphasis in original.

14. L. M. Alcott, "Recollections of My Childhood," 38.

15. L. M. Alcott, *Little Women, Little Men, Jo's Boys*, 251–52.

16. Dahlstrand, *Amos Bronson Alcott*, 228.

17. Shepard, *Pedlar's Progress*, 438.

18. A. B. Alcott, Diary for 1850, 2 February, MS Am 1130.12(19), pp. 166–67, Houghton Library, Harvard University.

19. Saxton, *Louisa May*, 178; Dahlstrand, *Amos Bronson Alcott*, 229.

20. Taking the content of the poem at its word, Madelon Bedell has speculated that Alcott's demons indeed pursued him out of his home and that he spent some undetermined time wandering about Boston in a state of temporary derangement. Bedell, *Alcotts*, 299. Although other Alcott biographers have responded less literally to "The Return," all agree that his work on "Tablets" brought on an almost total mental breakdown. Odell Shepard writes that Alcott's visions were so potent that they "nearly snatched him out of life as this world knows it." Shepard, *Pedlar's Progress*, 442.

21. A. B. Alcott, 30 June 1850, *Journals*, 231–32.

22. A. B. Alcott, 13 July 1850, *Journals*, 232.

23. A. B. Alcott to Abigail May Alcott, Concord, 17 September 1849, in *Letters*, 152.

24. Ibid.

25. Anonymous, "An Evening with Alcott," in A. B. Alcott, Autobiographical Collections, 1868–71, MS Am 1130.11(7), p. 68, Houghton Library, Harvard University.

26. Ibid.

27. A. B. Alcott, Journal for 1837, Week VIII (February), MS Am 1130.12(10), p. 125, Houghton Library, Harvard University.

28. Anonymous, "An Evening with Alcott," 68.

29. Ibid.

30. Dahlstrand, *Amos Bronson Alcott*, 222.

31. L. M. Alcott, n.d. 1850, *Journals*, 62.

32. L. M. Alcott, "How I Went Out to Service," in *Alternative Alcott*, 350.

33. Ibid., 354.

34. Ibid, 358.

35. Richardson, *Emerson*, 112; Reynolds, *John Brown*, 208.

36. A. B. Alcott, 4 April 1851, *Journals*, 244.

37. L. M. Alcott, n.d. 1851, *Journals*, 65.

38. Von Frank, *Trials*, 29.

39. A. B. Alcott, 15 April 1851, *Journals*, 246.

40. A. B. Alcott, 25 April 1851, *Journals*, 248.

41. A. B. Alcott, 31 May 1851, *Journals*, 249.

42. Abigail May Alcott to Samuel J. May, 28 April 1851 and 14 December 1852, in Bedell, *Alcotts*, 283.

43. Abigail May Alcott, Diary, 4 April 1850, in Bedell, *Alcotts*, 276.

44. L. M. Alcott, n.d. 1852, *Journals*, 67.

45. Ibid.

46. A. B. Alcott, Diary for 1850, 197.

47. Anna Alcox, Diary, 26 April 1852, in Bedell, *Alcotts*, 315.

48. A. B. Alcott, Journal, 8 May 1852, in Shepard, *Pedlar's Progress*, 445.

49. Anonymous, *Semi-Weekly Eagle* (Brattleboro, Vt.), 18 March 1852.

50. A. B. Alcott, 6 January 1850, *Journal*, 220.

51. A. B. Alcott to Anna Bronson Alcott, Cincinnati, 22 November 1853, in *Letters*, 171.

52. A. B. Alcott to Mrs. A. Bronson Alcott, Cleveland, 11 December 1853, in *Letters*, 177.

53. A. B. Alcott to Mrs. A. Bronson Alcott, Medina, Ohio, 4 December 1853, in *Letters*, 177.

54. L. M. Alcott, n.d. 1854, *Journals*, 71.

55. A. B. Alcott to Anna Bronson Alcott, Cincinnati, 16 November 1853, in *Letters*, 171; A. B. Alcott to Mrs. A. Bronson Alcott, Medina, Ohio, 4 December 1853, in *Letters*, 176; A. B. Alcott to Mrs. A. Bronson Alcott, Syracuse, 18 December 1853, in *Letters*, 180.

56. A. B. Alcott to Mrs. A. Bronson Alcott, Syracuse, 15 January 1854, in *Letters*, 182, 183.

57. A. B. Alcott, 9 February 1874, *Journals*, 446.

58. Bedell, *Alcotts*, 332; Von Frank, *Trials*, 62–70.

59. Wendell Phillips himself was not present; he was hard at work still trying to find some means of securing Burns's release.

60. Among the most odious provisions of the 1850 Fugitive Slave Law was that it authorized the payment of ten dollars to the commissioner who determined that a person brought before him was a fugitive, but only five dollars in a case where the detained person was set free.

61. Stern, ed., *L. M. Alcott*, 11.

62. A. B. Alcott, 2 June 1854, *Journals*, 273.

63. A. B. Alcott, 11–13 August 1854, *Journals*, 274.

64. Thoreau, *Walden*, 261, 260.

65. L. M. Alcott, n.d. 1854, *Journals*, 72; L. M. Alcott, 1 January 1855, *Journals*, 73. Louisa's journals report the earnings of *Flower Fables* in one place as thirty-two dollars, and thirty-five in another.

66. L. M. Alcott to Abigail May Alcott, 25 December 1854, in *Selected Letters*, 11.

67. L. M. Alcott to Amos Bronson Alcott, 25 December 1854, in *Selected Letters*, 12–13.

68. L. M. Alcott, June 1855, *Journals*, 75.

69. A. B. Alcott, 3–8 September 1855, *Journals*, 276.

70. The stories included "The Sisters' Trial," "Bertha," and "Genevieve."

71. L. M. Alcott, November 1855, *Journals*, 75.

72. A. B. Alcott, 9 November 1855, *Journals*, 277.

73. L. M. Alcott to Amos Bronson Alcott, 28 November 1855, in *Selected Letters*, 13–14.

74. A. B. Alcott, 9 February 1866, *Journals*, 379.

75. A. B. Alcott to Louisa May Alcott, Walpole, N.H., 27 November 1855, in *Letters*, 190.

76. Ibid.

77. L. M. Alcott to Miss Seymour, 21 September 1856, in *Selected Letters*, 16.

78. L. M. Alcott, *Moods*, 227.

79. A. B. Alcott to Louisa May Alcott, 31 March 1856, in *Letters*, 191.

80. A. B. Alcott to Mrs. Anna Alcott, 5 August 1856, in *Letters*, 193.

81. A. B. Alcott to Mrs. A. Bronson Alcott, 4 October 1856, in *Letters*, 198–99.

82. Ibid., 198.

83. L. M. Alcott to Amos Bronson Alcott, Boston, 29 November 1856, in *Selected Letters*, 26.

84. Ibid.

85. Shepard, *Pedlar's Progress*, 446.

86. A. B. Alcott, 4 October 1856, *Journals*, 286–87.

87. A. B. Alcott, 9 November 1856, *Journals*, 288.

88. A. B. Alcott, 10 November 1856, *Journals*, 290–91.

89. Richardson, *Henry Thoreau*, 348–49.

90. Euripides, *Medea*, 16.

91. A. B. Alcott to Mrs. A. Bronson Alcott, 2 March 1857, in *Letters*, 234.

92. A. B. Alcott to Abigail May Alcott, New Haven, 13 March 1857, in *Letters*, 239.

93. L. M. Alcott, June 1857, *Journals*, 85

94. L. M. Alcott, July 1857, *Journals*, 85.

95. Ibid.

96. Ibid.

97. A. B. Alcott to Mrs. A. Bronson Alcott, Walpole, N.H., 3 August 1857, in *Letters*, 246.

98. A. B. Alcott to Anna Alcott, Walpole, N.H., 28 August 1857, in *Letters*, 251.

99. A. B. Alcott to Anna, Louisa, and May Alcott, Boston, 9 September 1857, in *Letters*, 252–53.

CHAPTER TEN: ORCHARD HOUSE

1. Nathaniel Hawthorne to William D. Ticknor, Leamington, England, 5 November 1857, in *Letters, 1857–1864*, 127–28.

2. A. B. Alcott to Abigail May Alcott, Buffalo, 14 December 1857, in *Letters*, 269.

3. Alfred Whitman, "Meg, Jo, Beth and Amy, Told by Laurie," in Shealy, ed., *Alcott*, 106.

4. Stern, *Louisa May Alcott*, 81–82.

5. Whitman, "Meg, Jo, Beth and Amy," 106.

6. A. B. Alcott, 23 January 1858, *Journals*, 303.

7. Ibid., 304.

8. L. M. Alcott, 14 March 1858, *Journals*, 88.

9. Ibid., 89.

10. Ibid.

11. Ibid.

12. A. B. Alcott, 14 March 1858, *Journals*, 307.

13. L. M. Alcott to Eliza Wells, Concord, 19 March 1858, in *Selected Letters*, 32.

14. Ibid., 33.

15. Ibid.

16. L. M. Alcott, 14 March 1858, *Journals*, 89.

17. L. M. Alcott, MS Am 1130.13(16), Houghton Library, Harvard University.

18. A. B. Alcott, Diary for 1858, 14 March, MS Am 1130.12(28), p. 127, Houghton Library, Harvard University.

19. A. B. Alcott, 16 March 1858, *Journals*, 307.

20. L. M. Alcott, 14 March 1858, *Journals*, 88.

21. A. B. Alcott, 4 April 1858, *Journals*, 307–8.

22. A. B. Alcott, 18 September 1858, *Journals*, 309.

23. L. M. Alcott, May 1858, *Journals*, 89.

24. A. B. Alcott, 7 April 1858, *Journals*, 308.

25. L. M. Alcott, May 1858, *Journals*, 89.

26. L. M. Alcott, *Little Women, Little Men, Jo's Boys*, 236.

27. L. M. Alcott, May 1858, *Journals*, 89.

28. L. M. Alcott, July 1858, *Journals*, 90.

29. L. M. Alcott, *Work*, 123.

30. Ibid., 124.

31. L. M. Alcott, October 1858, *Journals*, 90.

32. Ibid., 90–91.

33. L. M. Alcott to the Alcott Family, October 1858, in *Selected Letters*, 34–36.

34. A. B. Alcott, 16 February 1858, *Journals*, 306.

35. A. B. Alcott, Diary for 1858, 13 October, 346.

36. A. B. Alcott to Abigail May Alcott, Syracuse, 4 December 1858, in *Letters*, 282.

37. A. B. Alcott, Diary for 1858, 1 November, 381. The entry reads, "Write to Louisa concerning her story for the Atlantic Monthly." At that time, Louisa had not yet sent any of her work to *The Atlantic*, so Bronson's letter must have concerned the prospect of a future submission. In her journal for the month of November 1858, Louisa wrote, "I even think of trying the 'Atlantic.' There's ambition for you." *Journals*, 92.

38. L. M. Alcott, November 1858, *Journals*, 92.

39. Ibid.

40. Anna Bronson Alcott to Amos Bronson Alcott, Apple-Slump, 7 December 1858, MS Am 1130.9(27), Houghton Library, Harvard University.

41. A. B. Alcott to May Alcott, St. Louis, 2 January 1859, in *Letters*, 291.

42. L. M. Alcott, November 1858, *Journals*, 91–92.

43. Ibid., 91.

44. L. M. Alcott, "Love and Self-Love," in *Selected Fiction*, 56–75.

45. Ibid., 68.

46. Anna Bronson Alcott to Amos Bronson Alcott, Apple-Slump, 7 December 1858.

47. L. M. Alcott, November 1858, *Journals*, 92.

48. A. B. Alcott to Abigail May Alcott, Syracuse, 4 December 1858, in *Letters*, 283.

49. Anna Bronson Alcott to Amos Bronson Alcott, Apple-Slump, 7 December 1858.

50. A. B. Alcott to Abigail May Alcott, Chicago, 27 December 1858, in *Letters*, 288.

51. A. B. Alcott to Louisa May Alcott, Chicago, 23 December 1858, in *Letters*, 286.

52. Abigail May Alcott to A. Bronson Alcott, (Concord), 25 December 1858, MS Am 1130.9(27).

53. Anna Bronson Alcott to Amos Bronson Alcott, (Concord), 26 December 1858, MS Am 1130.9(27).

54. Ibid.

55. A. B. Alcott to Louisa May Alcott, Cleveland, 7 February 1859, in *Letters*, 298.

56. A. B. Alcott to Mrs. A. Bronson Alcott, St. Louis, 17 January 1859, in *Letters*, 294.

57. A. B. Alcott to Mrs. A. Bronson Alcott, Cincinnati, 30 January 1859, in *Letters*, 296.

58. Ibid.

59. A. B. Alcott to Mrs. A. Bronson Alcott, Cleveland, 13 February 1859, in *Letters*, 299.

60. A. B. Alcott to Mrs. A. Bronson Alcott, Cincinnati, 21 January 1859, in *Letters*, 295.

61. A. B. Alcott, 4 March 1859, *Journals*, 314.

62. Ibid., 313.

63. L. M. Alcott, March 1859, *Journals*, 94.

64. Walther, *Shattering*, 63.

65. Reynolds, *John Brown*, 144.

66. A. B. Alcott, 8 May 1859, *Journals*, 315–16.

67. Horace Traubel, *With Walt Whitman*, IV, 293.

68. L. M. Alcott, September 1859, *Journals*, 95.

69. A. Bronson Alcott, Diary for 1859, 23 October, MS Am 1130.12(29), p. 583, Houghton Library, Harvard University.

70. A. Bronson Alcott, Diary for 1859, 8 May, 314.

71. A. Bronson Alcott, Diary for 1859, 23 October, 583.

72. L. M. Alcott to Alfred Whitman, Concord, 8 November 1859, in *Selected Letters*, 49.

73. Ibid.

74. A. Bronson Alcott, Diary for 1859, 23 October, 584.

75. A. Bronson Alcott, Diary for 1859, 26 October, 591.

76. A. Bronson Alcott, Diary for 1859, 19 November, 632–33.

77. A. B. Alcott, 17 February 1860, *Journals*, 326.

78. A. B. Alcott, 23 May 1860, *Journals*, 326.

79. L. M. Alcott, May 1860, *Journals*, 99.

80. Ibid.

81. Ibid.

82. Ibid.

83. A. B. Alcott, 23 May 1860, *Journals*, 326.

84. Julian Hawthorne, "By One Who Knew Her," in Shealy, ed., *Alcott*, 206.

85. L. M. Alcott to Adeline May, July 1860 (?), in *Selected Letters*, 57.

86. Julian Hawthorne, "By One Who Knew Her," 205.

87. Julian Hawthorne, "The Woman Who Wrote *Little Women*," in Shealy, ed., *Alcott*, 193.

88. Louisa May Alcott, *Little Women, Little Men, Jo's Boys*, 281.

89. A. B. Alcott to Mrs. Anna Alcox, Concord, 30 December 1860, in *Letters*, 318.

CHAPTER ELEVEN: WAR

1. A. B. Alcott, Diary for 1861, 1 January, MS Am 1130.12(31), p. 16, Houghton Library, Harvard University.

2. L. M. Alcott, January 1861, *Journals*, 103.

3. Ibid.

4. L. M. Alcott, February 1861, *Journals*, 103.

5. A. B. Alcott to May Alcott, Concord, 10 or 11 February 1861, in *Letters*, 320.

6. Ibid.

7. L. M. Alcott, February 1861, *Journals*, 104.

8. Ibid.

9. L. M. Alcott to Anna Alcott Pratt, Concord, 18 (?) March 1861, in *Letters*, 63.

10. Thoreau to Daniel Ricketson, Concord, 22 March 1861, in *Correspondence*, 609.

11. L. M. Alcott to Anna Alcott Pratt, Concord, 18 (?) March 1861, in *Letters*, 64n.

12. Thoreau to Parker Pillsbury, Concord, 10 April 1861, in *Correspondence*, 611.

13. Ralph Waldo Emerson to Arthur Hugh Clough, Concord, 16 April 1861, in *Letters*, IX, 45.

14. Emerson, *Journals and Miscellaneous Notebooks*, XV, 172, 180.

15. A. B. Alcott, Diary for 1861, 20–21 May, 440.

16. A. B. Alcott, Diary for 1861, 26–30 April, 386.

17. A. B. Alcott, Diary for 1861, 2 April, 357.

18. L. M. Alcott to Alfred Whitman, Concord, 19 May 1861, in *Selected Letters*, 64.

19. Saxton, *Louisa May*, 244.

20. L. M. Alcott to Alfred Whitman, Concord, 19 May 1861, in *Selected Letters*, 64.

21. Ibid., 65.

22. A. B. Alcott, Diary for 1862, 6 January, MS Am 1130.12(32), p. 42, Houghton Library, Harvard University.

23. L. M. Alcott, April 1862, *Journals*, 109.

24. L. M. Alcott, April/May 1862, *Journals*, 109.

25. L. M. Alcott to Alfred Whitman, 6 April 1862, in *Selected Letters*, 73.

26. Anne Brown Adams, [Louisa May Alcott in the Early 1860s], in Shealy, ed., *Alcott*, 10.

27. Gowing, *Alcotts*, 68.

28. A. B. Alcott, Diary for 1862, 39.

29. A. B. Alcott, Diary for 1861, 2–3 May, 396.

30. A. B. Alcott, Diary for 1862, 1 January, 6.

31. Ibid.

32. A. B. Alcott, 7 May 1862, *Journals*, 347.

33. L. M. Alcott to Sophia Foord, Concord, 11 May 1862, in *Selected Letters*, 75.

34. Ibid.

35. Davis, *Rebecca Harding Davis,* 38–40. Davis's antipathy to Bronson Alcott was so powerful that one hesitates to credit all the details of her account of him, some of which either run counter to the impression created by all other accounts or flatly contradict established evidence. For instance, describing the party mentioned in the text, she reports that Alcott dined heartily on a sirloin of beef—an alleged lapse in his vegetarian principles such as was never recorded elsewhere. Davis also maintains that, in building Emerson's summer cottage, Alcott neglected to include a door, an assertion that fails to account for the portal clearly represented in the one sketch of the structure.

36. A. B. Alcott to Mrs. A. Bronson Alcott, 21 September 1862, in *Letters,* 330.

37. L. M. Alcott, *Little Women, Little Men, Jo's Boys,* 466.

38. L. M. Alcott, *Hospital Sketches,* 55.

39. Saxton, *Louisa May,* 251; Stern, *Louisa May Alcott,* 112.

40. L. M. Alcott, December 1862, *Journals,* 110.

41. Ibid.

42. L. M. Alcott, *Hospital Sketches,* 56–61.

43. Ibid., 62.

44. Ibid., 66.

45. Ropes, *Civil War Nurse,* 112.

46. Rable, *Fredericksburg!,* 177–84.

47. Ibid., 238.

48. Gowing, *Alcotts,* 21.

49. Whitman, *Walt Whitman's Civil War,* 91.

50. Morris, *Better Angel,* 143–44.

51. L. M. Alcott, *Hospital Sketches,* 69.

52. L. M. Alcott, December 1862, *Journals,* 111.

53. L. M. Alcott, *Hospital Sketches,* 70.

54. Ibid., 78.

55. L. M. Alcott, 4 January 1863, *Journals,* 113–14.

56. Ibid., 114.

57. L. M. Alcott, *Hospital Sketches,* 97.

58. L. M. Alcott, 4 January 1863, *Journals,* 115.

59. L. M. Alcott, *Hospital Sketches,* 87.

60. Ibid., 88.

61. Ibid., 94.

62. Ibid., 80, 77.

63. Stern, *Louisa May Alcott,* 121.

64. Hannah Ropes to Alice Shephard Ropes, Georgetown, 11 January 1863, in Ropes, *Civil War Nurse,* 121.

65. L. M. Alcott, *Hospital Sketches,* 99.

66. Ibid., 106.

67. A. B. Alcott, Diary for 1863, 1 January, MS Am 1130.12(33), pp. 3–4, Houghton Library, Harvard University.

68. A. B. Alcott, 8 January 1863, *Journals*, 352.

69. Julian Hawthorne, "The Woman Who Wrote *Little Women*," in Shealy, ed., *Alcott*, 195.

70. Hannah Ropes to Edward Elson Ropes, Georgetown, 9 January 1863, in Ropes, *Civil War Nurse*, 121.

71. L. M. Alcott, *Hospital Sketches*, 94.

72. L. M. Alcott, January 1863, *Journals*, 116.

73. L. M. Alcott, *Hospital Sketches*, 101.

74. Ibid., 106–07.

75. Ibid., 107.

76. Ibid.

77. Martha Saxton has written that there remained some hope that Louisa might still be able to continue her work. Saxton, *Louisa May*, 256.

78. A. B. Alcott, 18 January 1863, *Journals*, 353.

79. A. B. Alcott, 19 January 1863, *Journals*, 353.

80. A. B. Alcott, 21 January 1863, *Journals*, 353.

81. L. M. Alcott, December 1862, *Journals*, 110.

CHAPTER TWELVE: SHADOWS AND SUNLIGHT

1. Abigail May Alcott to Samuel J. May, Concord, n.d. (1863), MS Am 1130.9(28), Houghton Library, Harvard University.

2. Sophia Hawthorne to Annie Fields, in Mellow, *Nathaniel Hawthorne*, 562.

3. Abigail May Alcott to Samuel J. May, Concord, n.d. (1863), MS Am 1130.9(28).

4. A. B. Alcott to Anna Alcott Pratt, Concord, 27 January 1863, in *Letters*, 333.

5. A. B. Alcott, 1 February 1863, *Journals*, 354; A. B. Alcott, Diary for 1863, 11 February, MS Am 1130.12(33), p. 46, Houghton Library, Harvard University.

6. Abigail May Alcott to Samuel J. May, Concord, n.d. (1863), MS Am 1130.9(28).

7. L. M. Alcott, January 1863, *Journals*, 116–17.

8. Ibid., 117.

9. Ibid.

10. A. Bronson Alcott to Anna Alcott Pratt, (Concord), 29 January 1863, in *Letters*, 334; L. M. Alcott, *Journals*, 112n.

11. Abigail May Alcott to Samuel J. May, (?) February 1863, MS Am 1130.9(28).

12. J. Hawthorne, *Memoirs*, 63.

13. L. M. Alcott, February 1863, *Journals*, 117.

14. Ibid.

15. L. M. Alcott, March 1863, *Journals*, 118.

16. Unidentified clipping in A. B. Alcott, Diary for 1863, 97.

17. Unidentified clipping in A. B. Alcott, Diary for 1863, 67.

18. A. B. Alcott, "The Transcendental Club and The Dial: A Conversation by A. Bronson Alcott," 23 March 1863, Autobiographical Collections, 1856–67, MS Am 1130.11(6), p. 153, Houghton Library, Harvard University.

19. L. M. Alcott to Anna Alcott Pratt, 30 March 1863, in *Selected Letters*, 83.

20. A. B. Alcott to Anna Alcott Pratt, Concord, 30 March 1863, in *Letters*, 337.

21. L. M. Alcott, February 1863, *Journals*, 117.

22. Abigail May Alcott to Samuel J. May, Concord, n.d. (1863), MS Am 1130.9(28).

23. Elbert, *Hunger for Home*, 231.

24. J. Hawthorne, *Memoirs*, 63.

25. Ibid.

26. L. M. Alcott, April 1863, *Journals,* 118.

27. A. B. Alcott to Mrs. Anna Alcox, 25 March 1863, in *Letters,* 336.

28. J. Hawthorne, *Memoirs,* 63.

29. L. M. Alcott, "Notes and Memoranda," 1863, *Journals,* 122.

30. L. M. Alcott, *Journals,* 123n.

31. A. B. Alcott to James Redpath, Concord, 19 November 1860, in *Letters,* 317.

32. A. B. Alcott to James Redpath, Concord, 27 July 1863, in *Letters,* 345.

33. L. M. Alcott to James Redpath, July (?) 1863, in *Selected Letters,* 87.

34. L. M. Alcott, *Journals,* 124n.

35. L. M. Alcott to Alfred Whitman, September 1863, in *Selected Letters,* 91.

36. J. Hawthorne, "The Woman Who Wrote *Little Women,*" in Shealy, ed., *Alcott,* 195–96.

37. L. M. Alcott, May 1863, *Journals,* 119.

38. A. B. Alcott, 26 August 1863, *Journals,* 357.

39. L. M. Alcott, "My Contraband," in *Alternative Alcott,* 93.

40. Ibid., 86.

41. L. M. Alcott to Miss Russel, 13 July 1863 (?), in *Selected Letters,* 85.

42. L. M. Alcott, October 1863, *Journals,* 121.

43. L. M. Alcott to James Redpath, February 1864 (?), in *Selected Letters,* 103.

44. A. B. Alcott, 28 February 1864, *Journals,* 362.

45. L. M. Alcott, May 1864, *Journals,* 130.

46. A. B. Alcott, 23 May 1864, *Journals,* 364.

47. Ibid.

48. Saxton, *Louisa May,* 233–34, 272.

49. L. M. Alcott, September 1864, *Journals,* 131.

50. A. K. Loring to Louisa May Alcott, n.d., MSS 6255, Papers of Louisa May Alcott, University of Virginia Special Collections.

51. L. M. Alcott, October 1864, *Journals,* 132.

52. L. M. Alcott to Abigail May Alcott, 25 December 1864, in *Selected Letters,* 106.

53. For instance, she had written in her journal in April 1864, "Don't despair, 'Moods,' we'll try again by & by." She later added, "Alas, we did try again." *Journals,* 129, 135n.

54. L. M. Alcott, December 1864, *Journals,* 133.

55. Emerson, "Experience," in *Essays and Lectures*, 473; L. M. Alcott, *Moods*, 1.

56. L. M. Alcott, *Moods*, 84.

57. Ibid., 190.

58. Ibid., 237, 37.

59. Ibid., 146.

60. Ibid., 25.

61. Ibid., 24.

62. Ibid., 24, 22.

63. Ibid., 179.

64. Jamison, *Touched with Fire*, 5, 88.

65. Madeleine Stern, telephone conversation with author, 27 August 2006.

66. Kay Redfield Jamison, e-mail message to author, 26 August 2006.

67. Emerson, "History," in *Essays and Lectures*, 237.

68. Emerson, "Self-Reliance," in *Essays and Lectures*, 259.

69. Alice James, *Diary*, 71.

70. A. B. Alcott, 26 December 1864, *Journals*, 367–68.

CHAPTER THIRTEEN: JOURNEYS EAST AND WEST

1. A. B. Alcott, 15 April 1865, *Journals*, 371.

2. L. M. Alcott, April 1865, *Journals*, 140.

3. Ibid.

4. Stern, *Louisa May Alcott*, 142.

5. A. B. Alcott, 29 July 1865, *Journals*, 374.

6. A. B. Alcott, 4 July 1865, *Journals*, 372.

7. Whitman, "The United States to Old World Critics," in *Complete Poetry*, 628.

8. A. B. Alcott, 13 April 1865, *Journals*, 371.

9. L. M. Alcott, *Work*, 75.

10. L. M. Alcott, July 1865, *Journals*, 141.

11. A. B. Alcott, 18 July 1865, *Journals*, 373.

12. Ibid.

13. L. M. Alcott, *Journals*, 147n.

14. L. M. Alcott to Amos Bronson Alcott, 31 July 1865, in *Selected Letters*, 111.

15. L. M. Alcott, August 1865, *Journals*, 141.

16. Henry James Jr., "Miss Alcott's *Moods*," 280–81.

17. A. B. Alcott, 30 September 1865, *Journals*, 375.

18. Ruskin fully elaborates his theory of the grotesque in the essay "Grotesque Renaissance," in *Stones of Venice, Complete Works*, XI, 135–95.

19. A. B. Alcott, 19–21 October 1865, *Journals*, 375.

20. L. M. Alcott, "Up the Rhine," "Life in a Pension," "A Dickens Day."

21. Henry James Jr., "Swiss Notes," in *Collected Travel Writings*, 630–31.

22. Louisa May Alcott, "Life in a Pension," 2.

23. Ibid.

24. Ibid.

25. Ibid.

26. Ibid.; L. M. Alcott, *Aunt Jo's Scrap-Bag*, 16.

27. L. M. Alcott, *Aunt Jo's Scrap-Bag*, 17.

28. Ibid., 18.

29. Ibid., 21; L. M. Alcott, "Life in a Pension," 2.

30. L. M. Alcott, *Aunt Jo's Scrap-Bag*, 19–20; L. M. Alcott, "Life in a Pension," 2.

31. L. M. Alcott, November 1865, *Journals*, 145.

32. Ibid.

33. L. M. Alcott, *Journals*, 148n.

34. L. M. Alcott, December 1865, *Journals*, 145.

35. L. M. Alcott, *Journals*, 148n.

36. L. M. Alcott, *Aunt Jo's Scrap-Bag*, 27.

37. Ibid.

38. Ibid., 16, 18, 34.

39. L. M. Alcott, December 1865, *Journals*, 145.

40. Heilbrun, "Alcott's *Little Women*," in *Hamlet's Mother*, 141–43.

41. L. M. Alcott to Alfred Whitman, 6 January 1869, in *Selected Letters*, 120.

42. Louisa May Alcott, (Untitled), *Boston Commonwealth*, 21 September 1867.

43. A. B. Alcott to Mrs. A. Bronson Alcott, St. Louis, 20 February 1866, in *Letters*, 385.

44. A. B. Alcott to Mrs. A. Bronson Alcott, St. Louis, 26 February 1866, in *Letters*, 386.

45. Dahlstrand, *Amos Bronson Alcott*, 282.

46. Ibid., 282–83.

47. A. B. Alcott to Louisa May Alcott, Concord, 18 March 1866, in *Letters*, 389–90.

48. L. M. Alcott, July 1866, *Journals*, 152.

49. L. M. Alcott, November 1866, *Journals*, 153.

50. L. M. Alcott, quoting Abigail May Alcott, August 1866, *Journals*, 153.

51. Bedell, *Alcotts*, 258n.

52. A. B. Alcott to Mrs. A. Bronson Alcott, St. Louis, 30 November 1866, in *Letters*, 397.

53. A. B. Alcott to Mrs. A. Bronson Alcott, St. Louis, 3 December 1866, in *Letters*, 398.

54. L. M. Alcott, January 1867, *Journals*, 157.

55. Franklin Benjamin Sanborn to Benjamin Lyman, 23 February 1867, in Cameron, *Young Reporter*, 45.

56. A. B. Alcott to Mrs. Frances D. Gage, Concord, 14 April 1867, in *Letters*, 406.

57. A. B. Alcott to Charles D. B. Mills, Concord, 20 February 1867, in *Letters*, 403.

58. A. B. Alcott to Mary E. Stearns, Concord, 13 April 1867, in *Letters*, 405.

59. L. M. Alcott, August 1867, *Journals*, 158.

60. L. M. Alcott, September 1867, *Journals*, 158.

61. L. M. Alcott, January 1868, *Journals*, 162.

62. Ibid.

63. L. M. Alcott, 7 January 1868, *Journals*, 162.

64. L. M. Alcott, "Happy Women," in Stern, ed., *L. M. Alcott*, 149.

65. L. M. Alcott, 18 January 1868, *Journals*, 163.

66. L. M. Alcott, 14 February 1868, *Journals*, 164.

67. Ibid., 165.

68. L. M. Alcott, "Happy Women," in Stern, ed., *L. M. Alcott*, 146.

69. Ibid., 147.

70. Ibid., 148.

71. Ibid.

72. L. M. Alcott to Richard Rogers Bowker, 4 October 1877, in *Selected Letters*, 224.

73. L. M. Alcott, 17 February 1868, *Journals*, 165.

74. A. B. Alcott to Louisa May Alcott, Concord, 19 February 1868, in *Letters*, 427.

75. L. M. Alcott, May 1868, *Journals*, 165–66.

76. Ibid., 165.

CHAPTER FOURTEEN: MIRACLES

1. Alcott to Miss Churchill, 25 December 1878 (?), in *Selected Letters*, 232.

2. L. M. Alcott, June 1868, *Journals*, 166.

3. Stern, *Louisa May Alcott*, 175.

4. L. M. Alcott, 15 July 1868, *Journals*, 166.

5. Ibid.

6. Ibid.

7. L. M. Alcott, 26 August 1868, *Journals*, 166.

8. L. M. Alcott, *Little Women, Little Men, Jo's Boys*, 246.

9. L. M. Alcott, 26 August 1868, *Journals*, 166.

10. Ibid.

11. Bunyan, *Pilgrim's Progress*, 163–64.

12. L. M. Alcott, *Little Women, Little Men, Jo's Boys*, 5.

13. Bunyan, *Pilgrim's Progress*, 169.

14. L. M. Alcott, *Little Women, Little Men, Jo's Boys*, 510.

15. Thomas Niles to Louisa May Alcott, Boston, 20 July 1869, in L. M. Alcott, *Little Women*, 423.

16. L. M. Alcott, *Little Women, Little Men, Jo's Boys*, 164.

17. Ibid., 214.

18. Ibid., 398.

19. Ibid., 234.

20. Ibid.

21. Ibid., 229.

22. L. M. Alcott, September 1872, *Journals*, 183.

23. Madeleine Stern, conversation with author, 1 September 2006.

24. Paludan, *A People's Contest*, 306–7n.

25. Julian Hawthorne, "The Woman who Wrote *Little Women*," in Shealy, ed., *Alcott*, 200–01.

26. L. M. Alcott, *Journals*, 169n.

27. Elbert, *Hunger for Home*, 169.

28. L. M. Alcott, 1 November 1868, *Journals*, 167.

29. L. M. Alcott, 16 November 1868, *Journals*, 167.

30. L. M. Alcott, 29 November 1868, *Journals*, 167.

31. L. M. Alcott, 1 November 1868, *Journals*, 167.

32. L. M. Alcott to Elizabeth Powell, Concord, 20 March 1869, in *Selected Letters*, 125.

33. L. M. Alcott, 1 November 1868, *Journals*, 167.

34. L. M. Alcott to Elizabeth Powell, Concord, 20 March 1869, in *Selected Letters*, 124–25.

35. L. M. Alcott to Samuel J. May, Boston, 22 January 1869, in *Selected Letters*, 122.

36. L. M. Alcott to Thomas Niles, early 1869, in *Selected Letters*, 119.

37. L. M. Alcott, 1 November 1868, *Journals*, 167; L. M. Alcott to Elizabeth Powell, Concord, 20 March 1869, in *Selected Letters*, 125.

38. L. M. Alcott, *Little Women, Little Men, Jo's Boys*, 154.

39. Ibid., 510.

40. Ibid., 515.

41. Ibid., 491.

42. Ibid., 7.

43. Some of the foregoing analysis appeared in Matteson, "An Idea of Order at Concord," 451–67.

44. L. M. Alcott, January 1869, *Journals*, 171.

45. Dahlstrand, *Amos Bronson Alcott*, 290.

46. A. B. Alcott, 26 July 1871, *Journals*, 422.

47. A. B. Alcott, *Tablets*, 99.

48. Ibid.

49. Ibid., 45.

50. L. M. Alcott, September 1868, *Journals*, 166.

51. A. B. Alcott, *Tablets*, 33.

52. Ibid., 50.

53. Ibid., 46.

54. Ibid.

55. Ibid., 89.

56. Ibid., 90.

57. Emerson, *Nature,* in *Essays and Lectures*, 7.

58. A. B. Alcott, *Tablets*, 159.

59. A. B. Alcott, 26–27 December 1876, *Journals*, 393.

60. Shepard, *Pedlar's Progress*, 501.

61. A. B. Alcott, *Journals*, 472.

CHAPTER FIFTEEN: "THE WISE AND BEAUTIFUL TRUTHS
OF THE FATHER"

1. A summary of Bronson's tabulations of Louisa's sales may be found in Myerson, "'Our Children Are Our Best Works,'" 262.

2. A. B. Alcott, 4 September 1869, *Journals*, 400.

3. Ibid.

4. L. M. Alcott, April 1869, *Journals*, 171.

5. L. M. Alcott to Samuel J. May, Boston, 22 January 1869, in *Selected Letters*, 121.

6. L. M. Alcott, April 1869, *Journals*, 171.

7. L. M. Alcott to the *Springfield Republican*, Concord, 4 May 1869, in *Selected Letters*, 128.

8. Ibid., 127.

9. L. M. Alcott, April 1869, *Journals*, 171.

10. A. B. Alcott, 30 April 1869, *Journals*, 396.

11. Ibid.

12. A. B. Alcott to Mrs. Ednah D. Cheney, Concord, 12 October 1869, in *Letters*, 496.

13. L. M. Alcott to the Alcott Family, 13 (–14) May 1870, in *Letters*, 135.

14. Alcott, *An Old-Fashioned Girl*, 283.

15. Ibid., 196.

16. A. B. Alcott to William Torrey Harris, 12 May 1867 and 15 January 1869, in *Letters*, 406, 458.

17. A. Bronson Alcott to William Torrey Harris, 22 December 1857, in *Letters*, 272.

18. A. B. Alcott, 1 December 1869, *Journals*, 403.

19. Ibid., 403.

20. Ibid., 403–4.

21. L. M. Alcott to the Alcott Family, Vevey, 20 September 1870, in *Selected Letters*, 151.

22. L. M. Alcott to the Alcott Family, Dinan, 30 May 1870, in *Selected Letters*, 137.

23. L. M. Alcott to Abigail May Alcott, 24 June (–2 July) 1870, in *Selected Letters*, 139.

24. L. M. Alcott, April 1870, *Journals*, 174.

25. L. M. Alcott to Abigail May Alcott, Vevey, 21 August 1870, in *Selected Letters*, 148.

26. Ibid.

27. L. M. Alcott, (Poems, 1859–1878), MS Am 1130.13(16), Houghton Library, Harvard University.

28. Ibid.

29. L. M. Alcott to Thomas Niles, Bex, 7 August 1870, in *Selected Letters*, 145.

30. L. M. Alcott to the Alcott Family, Vevey, 20 September 1870, in *Selected Letters*, 152.

31. L. M. Alcott, 10 November 1870, *Journals*, 175.

32. Ibid.

33. L. M. Alcott to Anna Alcott Pratt, (?) December 1870, in *Selected Letters*, 153.

34. One of Louisa's letters suggests that she had already made a good start on her next novel, *Little Men,* when news of John's death reached Rome. L. M. Alcott to (unknown), Rome, 29 December 1870, in *Selected Letters*, 158. Her journals create the contrary impression that she began the book after receiving word of Anna's loss. L. M. Alcott, n.d. 1871, *Journals*, 177.

35. Clark, *Louisa May Alcott*, 152.

36. Ibid.

37. Peabody, "Preface to the Third Edition," in *Record of Mr. Alcott's School*, 3–4.

38. L. M Alcott, June 1871, *Journals*, 178.

39. Ibid.

40. Ibid.

41. A. B. Alcott to Ellen A. Chandler, Concord, 28 August 1871, in *Letters*, 537.

42. L. M. Alcott to James T. Fields, 3 July 1871, in *Selected Letters*, 160.

43. L. M. Alcott, July 1871, *Journals*, 179.

44. L. M. Alcott to Florence Hilton, 13 March 1874, in *Selected Letters*, 182.

45. L. M. Alcott to Mrs. H. Koorders-Boeke, 7 August 1875, in *Selected Letters*, 194.

46. L. M. Alcott to the Lukens Sisters, Boston, 2 October 1874, in *Selected Letters*, 185.

47. Ibid., 185–86.

48. Dahlstrand, *Amos Bronson Alcott*, 315.

49. Anonymous, "The 'Concord Authors,'" in A. B. Alcott, Autobiographical Collections, 1878–79, MS Am 1130.11(9), Houghton Library, Harvard University.

50. L. M. Alcott, "Reminiscences of Ralph Waldo Emerson," in Bosco and Myerson, eds., *Emerson*, 90.

51. A. B. Alcott to Ellen A. Chandler, 27 July 1872, in *Letters*, 561.

52. A. B. Alcott, *Concord Days*, 3.

53. Ibid., 4.

54. Whitman, "A Backward Glance o'er Travel'd Roads," in *Complete Poetry*, 671.

55. A. B. Alcott, *Concord Days*, 42.

56. Whitman, "So Long!" in *Complete Poetry*, 611.

57. A. B. Alcott, *Concord Days*, 83, 84, 86, 51.

58. Ibid., 271.

59. L. M. Alcott, November 1872, *Journals*, 183–84.

60. L. M. Alcott to Edwin Munroe Bacon, Concord, 14 July 1874, in *Letters*, 183.

61. L. M. Alcott, *Work*, 117.

62. Ibid., 21.

63. Ibid., 149.

64. Ibid., 101.

65. Ibid., 343.

66. L. M. Alcott to the Lukens Sisters, Concord, 4 September 1873, in *Selected Letters*, 176.

67. L. M. Alcott, *Work*, 86.

68. Ibid., 87.

69. L. M. Alcott, January 1874, *Journals*, 191.

70. L. M. Alcott, June, July, August 1875, *Journals*, 196.

71. L. M. Alcott, September and October 1875, *Journals*, 191.

72. L. M. Alcott to Samuel E. Sewall, 28 September 1875, in *Selected Letters*, 196.

73. L. M. Alcott, January 1874, *Journals*, 191.

74. Ibid.

75. A. B. Alcott, 9 April 1874, *Journals*, 448.

76. Ibid.

77. A. B. Alcott to F. E. Anderson, Concord, 8 April 1875, in *Letters*, 648. Alcott wrote "honory" for "honorary" and "suprising" for "surprising."

78. L. M. Alcott. April 1873, *Journals*, 187.

79. L. M. Alcott, March 1874, *Journals*, 192.

80. Swayne, *Story of Concord*, 161.

81. L. M. Alcott, September 1876, *Journals*, 201.

82. L. M. Alcott, "Notes and Memoranda" 1876, *Journals*, 202.

83. L. M. Alcott, January 1877, *Journals*, 204.

84. Ibid.

85. Abigail May Alcott, Journal, 15 July 1877, bMS Am 1817.2(15), Houghton Library, Harvard University.

86. Ibid.; L. M. Alcott, September 1877, *Journals*, 205.

87. L. M. Alcott, October 1877, *Journals*, 205.

88. Ibid.

89. A. B. Alcott to Abigail May Alcott, 8 October 1877, bMS Am 1817.2(15).

90. L. M. Alcott, October 1877, *Journals*, 206.

91. Stern, *Louisa May Alcott*, 263.

92. L. M. Alcott to Mrs. A. D. Moshier, 16 December 1877, in *Selected Letters*, 226.

93. L. M. Alcott, January 1878, *Journals*, 209.

94. A. B. Alcott, 10–14 June 1878, *Journals*, 490.

95. A. B. Alcott, 30 May 1878, *Journals*, 489.

96. A. B. Alcott, 29 May 1878, *Journals*, 488–89.

97. L. M. Alcott, November 1877, *Journals*, 206.

98. L. M. Alcott, April 1878, *Journals*, 209.

99. A. B. Alcott, 24 November 1877, *Journals*, 480.

100. Anonymous, "The Concord Summer School of Philosophy," in A. B. Alcott, Autobiographical Collections, 1878–79.

101. Anonymous, "Concord and its People," in A. B. Alcott, Autobiographical Collections, 1878–79.

102. Anonymous, "The Science of Things," in A. B. Alcott, Autobiographical Collections, 1878–79.

103. Ibid.

104. Ibid.

105. Anonymous, "Thoreau's Thoughts," in A. B. Alcott, Autobiographical Collections, 1878–79.

106. L. M. Alcott, August 1879, *Journals*, 216.

107. Ibid.

108. A. B. Alcott, 22 August 1879, *Journals*, 511.

109. A. B. Alcott, 29 November 1879, *Journals*, 514.

110. A. B. Alcott to May Alcott Nieriker, Concord, 27 November 1879, in *Letters*, 786.

111. L. M. Alcott, November 1879, *Journals*, 217.

112. L. M. Alcott, 31 December 1879, *Journals*, 218.

113. Ibid., 219.

114. A. Bronson Alcott, 31 January 1880, *Journals*, 515–16.

115. A. Bronson Alcott, "Love's Morrow," in *Letters*, 798.

116. Louisa May Alcott, "Our Madonna," in *Poetry*, 37–38.

117. Bedell, *Alcotts*, 283.

118. L. M. Alcott to Lucy Stone, 1 October 1873, in *Selected Letters*, 178.

119. L. M. Alcott to *The Woman's Journal*, 30 March 1880, in *Selected Letters*, 245–47.

120. L. M. Alcott, September 1880, *Journals*, 227.

121. A. B. Alcott, 15 May 1881, *Journals*, 523.

122. A. B. Alcott, 9 December 1881, *Journals*, 529.

123. A. B. Alcott, 17 September 1880, *Journals*, 527.

124. Ibid., 528.

125. L. M. Alcott, December 1881, *Journals*, 231.

CHAPTER SIXTEEN: "COME UP WITH ME"

1. L. M. Alcott, *Moods*, 225.

2. Ibid.

3. A. B. Alcott, "Observations on the Spiritual Nurture," 204.

4. L. M. Alcott, *Moods*, 227.

5. Ibid., 257.

6. Ibid., 244.

7. Ibid., 272.

8. Ibid., 209.

9. L. M Alcott to Maria S. Porter, after 24 October 1882, in *Selected Letters*, 261.

10. A. B. Alcott, *Sonnets*, 131, 119, 113.

11. Ibid., 75.

12. Ibid., 77.

13. Ibid., 73.

14. Ibid., 39.

15. A. B. Alcott to William T. Harris, Concord, 20 May 1870, in *Letters*, 513.

16. A. B. Alcott, 25 January 1876, *Journals*, 465.

17. Stern, *Louisa May Alcott*, 288–89.

18. A. B. Alcott, 8 March 1882, *Journals*, 532.

19. A. B. Alcott, *Sonnets*, 39.

20. Ibid., 109; see also A. B. Alcott, 3–4 February 1882, *Journals*, 532.

21. A. B. Alcott, 13 April 1882, *Journals*, 533.

22. Emerson, "Spiritual Laws," *Essays, First Series,* in *Essays and Lectures,* 321.

23. A. B. Alcott, 26 April 1882, *Journals*, 533.

24. L. M. Alcott, April 1882, *Journals*, 233–34.

25. A. B. Alcott, 26 April 1882, *Journals*, 533.

26. L. M. Alcott, 27 April 1882, *Journals*, 234.

27. L. M. Alcott, "Reminiscences of Ralph Waldo Emerson," in Bosco and Myerson, eds., *Emerson*, 90.

28. L. M. Alcott, November 1882, *Journals*, 236.

29. L. M. Alcott to Laura Hosmer, 25 July 1882, in *Selected Letters*, 259.

30. L. M. Alcott, July 1882, *Journals*, 235.

31. A. B. Alcott, 29 July 1882, *Journals*, 535.

32. A. B. Alcott, 30 September 1882, *Journals*, 536.

33. A. B. Alcott, 17 September 1882, *Journals*, 536.

34. A. B. Alcott, 22 October 1882, *Journals*, 537.

35. L. M. Alcott, October 1882, *Journals*, 235.

36. L. M. Alcott to Maria S. Porter, after 24 October 1882, in *Selected Letters*, 261.

37. L. M. Alcott to Mary Preston Stearns, 4 November 1882, in *Selected Letters*, 262.

38. L. M. Alcott to Mary Preston Stearns, (fall 1883?), in *Selected Letters*, 273.

39. L. M. Alcott to Ednah Dow Cheney, 18 November 1882, in *Selected Letters*, 263.

40. L. M. Alcott, December 1882, *Journals*, 236.

41. Stern, *Louisa May Alcott*, 295.

42. L. M. Alcott to Mary Preston Stearns, 30 December 1882, in *Selected Letters*, 266.

43. L. M. Alcott to Mary Preston Stearns, 31 May (1883?), in *Selected Letters*, 270.

44. L. M. Alcott to Amos Bronson Alcott, 29 November 1885, in *Selected Letters*, 294–95.

45. L. M. Alcott to Maria S. Porter, October (?) 1882, in *Selected Letters*, 261.

46. L. M. Alcott, June 1883, *Journals*, 239.

47. L. M. Alcott to Elizabeth Wells, 9 October 1883, in *Selected Letters*, 273.

48. L. M. Alcott, September 1883, *Journals*, 240.

49. L. M. Alcott to Elizabeth Wells, 9 October 1883, in *Selected Letters*, 273.

50. L. M. Alcott, December 1884, *Journals*, 245.

51. L. M. Alcott, February 1885, *Journals*, 250.

52. L. M. Alcott, "To My Brain," in *Poetry*, 44.

53. L. M. Alcott to Frank Carpenter, 1 April 1887, in *Selected Letters*, 307–8.

54. L. M. Alcott, *Little Women, Little Men, Jo's Boys*, 803.

55. Ibid., 856.

56. William James, "Address at the Centenary of Ralph Waldo Emerson, May 25, 1903," in *Writings*, 1123.

57. L. M. Alcott, *Little Women, Little Men, Jo's Boys*, 829.

58. Ibid., 834.

59. L. M. Alcott to Thomas Niles, June (?) 1886, in *Selected Letters*, 299.

60. L. M. Alcott to Thomas Niles, 3 October 1886, in *Selected Letters*, 300.

61. L. M. Alcott, *Little Women, Little Men, Jo's Boys*, 1063.

62. L. M. Alcott, 12 September 1886, *Journals*, 280.

63. L. M. Alcott to Florence Phillips, 20 October 1886, in *Selected Letters*, 302.

64. L. M. Alcott to Edward Bok, 16 June 1887, in *Selected Letters*, 313. Louisa's count included a number of works that require some indulgence to be thought of as books, including reports of the Concord School Committee, and early writings for which Elizabeth Palmer Peabody deserved the lion's share of the credit.

65. L. M. Alcott to Anna Alcott Pratt, 27 November 1887, in *Selected Letters*, 324n.

66. L. M. Alcott, 27 February 1888, *Journals*, 333.

67. Anna Alcott Pratt to Alfred Whitman, 17 February 1889 (?), cited in Stern, *Louisa May Alcott*, 330–31.

68. L. M. Alcott to Maria S. Porter, 4 March 1888, in *Selected Letters*, 337.

69. Ibid.

70. L. M. Alcott, "Free" ("Poems"), MS Am 1130.13(17), Houghton Library, Harvard University.

71. Ralph Waldo Emerson, "Address to the Inhabitants of Concord at the Consecration of Sleepy Hollow, September 29, 1855," in *Miscellanies*, 436.

72. Swayne, *Story of Concord*, 166; Anderson, *World of Louisa May Alcott*, 112.

73. L. M. Alcott to Maggie Lukens, 5 February 1884, in *Selected Letters*, 276.

74. Bedell, *Alcotts*, xv.

BIBLIOGRAPHY

Alcott, A. Bronson. Autobiographical Collections. MS Am 1130.11, Houghton Library, Harvard University.

———. *Concord Days.* Boston: Roberts Brothers, 1872.

———. *Conversations with Children on the Gospels.* 2 vol. Boston: James Munroe, 1836.

———. *The Journals of Amos Bronson Alcott.* Edited by Odell Shepard. Boston: Little, Brown, 1938.

———. Journals and Diaries of Amos Bronson Alcott. MS Am 1130.12, Houghton Library, Harvard University.

———. Letterbooks of Amos Bronson Alcott. MS Am 1130.9, Houghton Library, Harvard University.

———. *The Letters of A. Bronson Alcott.* Edited by Richard L. Herrnstadt. Ames: Iowa State University Press, 1969.

———. *New Connecticut: An Autobiographical Poem.* Boston: [privately printed], 1887.

———. "Observations on the Life of My First Child [Anna Bronson Alcott] During Her First Year." bMS Am 1130.10(1), Houghton Library, Harvard University.

———. *Observations on the Principles and Methods of Infant Instruction.* Boston: Carter and Hendee, 1830.

———. "Observations on the Spiritual Nurture of My Children." bMS Am 1130.10(6), Houghton Library, Harvard University.

———. "Psyche: An Evangele; in Four Books." bMS Am 1130.10(9), Houghton Library, Harvard University.

———. "Researches on Childhood." bMS Am 1130.10(6), Houghton Library, Harvard University.

———. *Sonnets and Canzonets.* Boston: Roberts Brothers, 1882.

465

———. *Tablets.* Boston: Roberts Brothers, 1868.

———. Works of Amos Bronson Alcott. bMS Am 1130.10, Houghton Library, Harvard University.

Alcott, Louisa May. Additional Papers of Louisa May Alcott. bMS Am 1130.13, Houghton Library, Harvard University.

———. *Alternative Alcott.* Edited and with an introduction by Elaine Showalter. New Brunswick, N.J.: Rutgers University Press, 1988.

———. *Aunt Jo's Scrap-Bag: My Boys, Etc.* Boston: Roberts Brothers, 1872.

———. "A Dickens Day." *The Independent* 19, no. 995 (December 26, 1867).

———. *Hospital Sketches.* Edited by Alice Fahs. New York: Bedford/St. Martin's, 2004.

———. *The Inheritance.* New York: Penguin Putnam, 1998.

———. *The Journals of Louisa May Alcott.* Edited by Joel Myerson and Daniel Shealy, with an introduction by Madeleine B. Stern. Boston: Little, Brown, 1989.

———. "Life in a Pension." *The Independent* 19, no. 988 (November 7, 1867).

———. *Little Women.* Norton Critical Edition. Edited by Anne K. Phillips and Gregory Eiselein. New York: W. W. Norton, 2004.

———. *Little Women, Little Men, Jo's Boys.* Edited by Elaine Showalter. New York: Library of America, 2005.

———. *Moods.* Edited and with an introduction by Sarah Elbert. New Brunswick, N.J.: Rutgers University Press, 1991.

———. *An Old-Fashioned Girl.* Boston: Little, Brown, 1997.

———. Papers of Louisa May Alcott. Charlottesville: University of Virginia Special Collections.

———. *The Poetry of Louisa May Alcott.* Edited by Maria Powers. Concord, Mass.: Louisa May Alcott Memorial Association, 1997.

———. *Selected Fiction.* Edited by Daniel Shealy, Madeleine B. Stern, and Joel Myerson. Boston: Little, Brown, 1990.

———. *The Selected Letters of Louisa May Alcott.* Edited by Joel Myerson and Daniel Shealy, with an introduction by Madeleine B. Stern. Athens: University of Georgia Press, 1995.

———. *Spinning-Wheel Stories.* Boston: Little, Brown, 1900.

———. [Untitled.] *Boston Commonwealth* 6, no. 3 (September 21, 1867).

———. "Up the Rhine." *The Independent* 19, no. 972 (July 18, 1867).

———. *Work: A Story of Experience.* Edited and with an introduction by Joy S. Kasson. New York: Penguin, 1994.

Alcott Family. Additional Papers. MS Am 1817.2, Houghton Library, Harvard University.

Anderson, William. *The World of Louisa May Alcott.* New York: Harper Perennial, 1995.

Anonymous. *Hints to Parents on the Civilization of Children in the Spirit of Pestalozzi's Method.* 6 pamphlets. 5th ed. London: Harvey and Darton, 1827.

Barton, Cynthia H. *Transcendental Wife: The Life of Abigail May Alcott.* Lanham, Md.: University Press of America, 1996.

Bedell, Madelon. *The Alcotts: Biography of a Family.* New York: Clarkson N. Potter, 1980.

Bonstelle, Jessie, ed. *Little Women Letters from the House of Alcott.* Boston: Little Brown, 1914.

Bosco, Ronald A., and Joel Myerson, eds. *Emerson in His Own Time.* Iowa City: University of Iowa Press, 2003.

Brooks, Van Wyck. *The Flowering of New England, 1815–1865.* New York: E. P. Dutton, 1936.

Bunyan, John. *The Pilgrim's Progress.* Edited with an introduction and notes by W. R. Owens. New York: Oxford University Press, 2003.

Cameron, Kenneth Walter. *Young Reporter of Concord.* Hartford, Conn.: Transcendental Books, 1978.

Capper, Charles. *Margaret Fuller: An American Romantic Life, The Private Years.* New York: Oxford University Press, 1992.

Cheney, Ednah Dow, ed. *Louisa May Alcott, Her Life, Letters, and Journals.* Boston: Little, Brown, 1928.

Clark, Beverly Lyon, ed. *Louisa May Alcott: The Contemporary Reviews.* Cambridge, U.K.: Cambridge University Press, 2004.

Coleridge, Samuel Taylor. *Aids to Reflection.* Eugene, Oreg.: Wipf and Stock, 2006.

Dahlstrand, Frederick C. *Amos Bronson Alcott: An Intellectual Biography.* Rutherford, N.J.: Fairleigh Dickinson University Press, 1982.

Davis, Rebecca Harding. *Rebecca Harding Davis: Writing Cultural Autobiography.* Edited by Janice Milner Lasseter and Sharon M. Harris. Nashville, Tenn.: Vanderbilt University Press, 2001.

The Dial: A Magazine for Literature, Philosophy and Religion. Boston: Weeks, Jordan and Company, 1841.

Douglas, Thomas. *Autobiography of Thomas Douglas, Late Judge of the Supreme Court of Florida.* New York: Calkins and Stiles, 1856.

Dwight, Timothy. *Travels in New-England and New-York.* 4 vol. London: W. Baynes and Son, 1823.

Elbert, Sarah. *A Hunger for Home: Louisa May Alcott and* Little Women. Philadelphia: Temple University Press, 1984.

Emerson, Ralph Waldo. *The Complete Sermons of Ralph Waldo Emerson.* Edited by Albert J. von Frank. 4 vol. Columbia: University of Missouri Press, 1989.

————. *The Early Lectures of Ralph Waldo Emerson.* 3 vol. Cambridge, Mass.: Harvard University Press, 1959–72.

————. *Essays and Lectures.* New York: Library of America, 1983.

————. *Journals and Miscellaneous Notebooks.* Edited by William H. Gilman et al. 16 vol. Cambridge, Mass.: Belknap Press of Harvard University Press, 1960–82.

————. *Journals of Ralph Waldo Emerson.* Edited by Edward Waldo Emerson and Waldo Emerson Forbes. 10 vol. Boston: Houghton Mifflin, and Cambridge, Mass.: Riverside Press, 1906–14.

————. *The Letters of Ralph Waldo Emerson.* Edited by Ralph L. Rusk. 10 vol. New York: Columbia University Press, 1939.

————. *Miscellanies.* Boston: Houghton Mifflin, 1904.

————. *The Selected Letters of Ralph Waldo Emerson.* Edited by Joel Myerson. New York: Columbia University Press, 1997.

Emerson, Ralph Waldo, and Thomas Carlyle. *The Correspondence of Emerson and Carlyle.* Edited by Joseph Slater. New York: Columbia University Press, 1964.

Euripides. *Medea, Hippolytus, Electra, Helen.* Translated by James Morwood. Oxford: Clarendon Press, 1997.

Fogarty, Robert S., comp. *American Utopianism.* Itasca, Ill.: F. E. Peacock, 1972.

Franklin, Benjamin. *The Autobiography and Other Writings.* Edited with an introduction by L. Jesse Lemisch. New York: New American Library, 1961.

Fuller, Margaret. *The Letters of Margaret Fuller.* Edited by Robert N. Hudspeth. 6 vol. Ithaca, N.Y.: Cornell University Press, 1983–94.

Goethe, Johann Wolfgang von. *Faust I & II.* Translated and edited by Stuart Atkins. Princeton, N.J.: Princeton University Press, 1994.

Gowing, Clara. *The Alcotts As I Knew Them.* C. M. Clark, 1909.

Hawthorne, Julian. *The Memoirs of Julian Hawthorne.* Edited by Edith Garrigues Hawthorne. New York: Macmillan, 1938.

Hawthorne, Nathaniel. *Collected Novels.* New York: Library of America, 1983.

————. *The Letters, 1843–1853.* Edited by Thomas Woodson et al. Vol. 16 of *The Centenary Edition of the Works of Nathaniel Hawthorne.* Columbus: Ohio State University Press, 1985.

————. *The Letters, 1857–1864.* Edited by Thomas Woodson et al. Vol. 18 of *The Centenary Edition of the Works of Nathaniel Hawthorne.* Columbus: Ohio State University Press, 1987.

————. *Tales and Sketches.* New York: Library of America, 1982.

Heilbrun, Carolyn G. *Hamlet's Mother and Other Women.* New York: Columbia University Press, 1990.

————. *Writing a Woman's Life.* New York: Ballantine Books, 1989.

Hochfield, George, ed. *Selected Writings of the American Transcendentalists.* New Haven, Conn.: Yale University Press, 2004.

Holloway, Mark. *Heavens on Earth: Utopian Communities in America, 1680–1880.* 2d ed., rev. New York: Dover, 1966.

James, Alice. *The Diary of Alice James.* Edited by Leon Edel with an introduction by Linda Simon. Boston: Northeastern University Press, 1999.

James, Henry, Jr. *Collected Travel Writings: The Continent.* New York: Library of America, 1993.

————. "Miss Alcott's *Moods.*" *North American Review* 101 (July 1865): 276–81.

James, William. *Writings, 1902–1910.* New York: Library of America, 1987.

Jamison, Kay Redfield. *Touched with Fire: Manic-Depressive Illness and the Artistic Temperament.* New York: Free Press, 1996.

Marshall, Megan. *The Peabody Sisters: Three Women Who Ignited American Romanticism.* Boston: Houghton Mifflin, 2005.

Martineau, Harriet. *Society in America.* 3 vol. London: Saunders and Otley, 1837.

Matteson, John. "An Idea of Order at Concord: Soul and Society in the Mind of Louisa May Alcott." In *A Companion to American Fiction, 1865–1914,* edited by Robert Paul Lamb and G. R. Thompson. New York: Blackwell, 2005.

McCuskey, Dorothy. *Bronson Alcott, Teacher.* New York: Macmillan, 1940.

McPherson, James M. *Battle Cry of Freedom: The Civil War Era.* New York: Oxford University Press, 1988.

Mellow, James R. *Nathaniel Hawthorne in His Times.* Boston: Houghton Mifflin, 1980.

Milton, John. *Complete Poems and Major Prose.* Edited by Merritt Y. Hughes. New York: Macmillan, 1957.

Morris, Roy, Jr. *The Better Angel: Walt Whitman in the Civil War.* Oxford: Oxford University Press, 2000.

Myerson, Joel. " 'Our Children Are Our Best Works': Bronson and Louisa May Alcott." In *Critical Essays on Louisa May Alcott,* edited by Madeleine B. Stern. Boston: G. K. Hall, 1984.

Orcutt, Samuel. *History of the Town of Wolcott (Connecticut) from 1731 to 1874.* Waterbury, Conn.: Press of the American Printing Co., 1874.

Paludan, Phillip Shaw. *A People's Contest: The Union and the Civil War, 1861–1865.* New York: Harper and Row, 1988.

Peabody, Elizabeth Palmer. *Record of Mr. Alcott's School: Exemplifying the Principles and Methods of Moral Culture.* 3d ed. Boston: Roberts Brothers, 1874.

———. *Record of a School: Exemplifying the General Principles of Spiritual Culture.* Boston: James Munroe, 1835.

Rable, George C. *Fredericksburg! Fredericksburg!* Chapel Hill: University of North Carolina Press, 2002.

Rainer, Joseph T. "The 'Sharper' Image: Yankee Peddlers, Southern Consumers, and the Market Revolution." *Business and Economic History* 26, no. 1 (fall 1997), 27–44.

Reynolds, David S. *John Brown, Abolitionist.* New York: Albert A. Knopf, 2005.

Richardson, Robert D., Jr. *Emerson: The Mind on Fire.* Berkeley: University of California Press, 1995.

——— *Henry Thoreau: A Life of the Mind.* Berkeley: University of California Press, 1986.

Ropes, Hannah Anderson. *Civil War Nurse: The Diary and Letters of Hannah Ropes.* Edited with introduction and commentary by John R. Brumgardt. Knoxville: University of Tennessee Press, 1980.

Ruskin, John. *The Stones of Venice* in *The Complete Works of John Ruskin.* 39 vol. Edited by E. T. Cook et al. London: George Allen, 1904.

Sanborn, Franklin B. *Bronson Alcott at Alcott House, England, and Fruitlands, New England, 1842–1844.* Cedar Rapids, Iowa: Torch Press, 1908.

———. *Recollections of Seventy Years.* 2 vol. Boston: Gorham Press, 1909.

Saxton, Martha. *Louisa May: A Modern Biography of Louisa May Alcott.* Boston: Houghton Mifflin, 1977.

Sears, Clara Endicott, comp. *Bronson Alcott's Fruitlands; with Transcendental Wild Oats, by Louisa May Alcott.* Boston: Houghton Mifflin, 1915.

Shealy, Daniel, ed. *Alcott in Her Own Time.* Iowa City: University of Iowa Press, 2005.

Shepard, Odell. *Pedlar's Progress: The Life of Bronson Alcott.* Boston: Little, Brown, 1937.

Stern, Madeleine B. *Louisa May Alcott: A Biography.* Boston: Northeastern University Press, 1996.

Stern, Madeleine B., ed. *L. M. Alcott: Signature of Reform.* Boston: Northeastern University Press, 2002.

Strickland, Charles. "A Transcendentalist Father: The Child-Rearing Practices of Bronson Alcott." *Perspectives in American History* 3 (1969): 5–73.

Strouse, Jean. *Alice James: A Biography.* Boston: Houghton Mifflin, 1980.

Swayne, Josephine Latham. *The Story of Concord Told by Concord Writers.* Boston: Meador, 1939.

Thoreau, Henry David. *The Correspondence of Henry David Thoreau.* Edited by Walter Harding and Carl Bode. New York: New York University Press, 1958.

———. *Journal, Volume I, 1837–1844.* Edited by Elizabeth Witherell et al. Princeton, N.J.: Princeton University Press, 1981.

———. *Journal, Volume II, 1842–1848.* Edited by Elizabeth Witherell et al. Princeton, N.J.: Princeton University Press, 1984.

———. *Journal, Volume VI, 1853.* Edited by Elizabeth Witherell et al. Princeton, N.J.: Princeton University Press, 2000.

———. *Walden: A Fully Annotated Edition.* Edited by Jeffrey S. Cramer. New Haven, Conn.: Yale University Press, 2004.

———. *A Week on the Concord and Merrimack Rivers; Walden, or, Life in the Woods; The Maine Woods; Cape Cod.* New York: Library of America, 1985.

Traubel, Horace. *With Walt Whitman in Camden.* 7 vol. Philadelphia: University of Pennsylvania Press, 1953.

Von Frank, Albert J. *The Trials of Anthony Burns: Freedom and Slavery in Emerson's Boston.* Cambridge, Mass.: Harvard University Press, 1998.

Walther, Eric H., *The Shattering of the Union: America in the 1850s.* Wilmington, Del.: Scholarly Resources, 2004.

Warner, Michael, ed. *American Sermons: The Pilgrims to Martin Luther King Jr.* New York: Library of America, 1999.

Whitman, Walt. *Complete Poetry and Collected Prose.* New York: Library of America, 1982.

———. *Walt Whitman's Civil War.* Compiled and edited by Walter Lowenfels. New York: Knopf, 1960.

INDEX

Page numbers in *italics* refer to illustrations.
Page numbers beginning with 429 refer to endnotes.